Th.

Medieval Rural Settlement
Britain and Ireland, AD 800–1600

edited by

Neil Christie and Paul Stamper

WIND*gather*
PRESS

To all those
who since the formation of the deserted medieval village research group in 1952
have walked, surveyed and dug,
talked, thought, and written
to advance the study of medieval settlement

Windgather Press
is an imprint of
Oxbow Books, Oxford

ISBN 978-1-905119-42-4

A CIP record for this book is available from the British Library

This book is available direct from

Oxbow Books, Oxford, UK
(Phone: 01865-241249; Fax: 01865-794449)

and

The David Brown Book Company
PO Box 511, Oakville, CT 06779, USA
(Phone: 860-945-9329; Fax: 860-945-9468)

or from our website

www.oxbowbooks.com

*Front cover: Plan of Alnham village from an estate map of 1619
(courtesy of the Estate and Collection of the Duke of Northumberland)*
*Back cover (top to bottom): Moelfre City, Radnorshire (© Clwyd-Powys Archaeological Trust: 05-c-229)
The north-west block of tofts at West Whelpington (© Stuart Wrathmell)
Conjectural reconstruction of the Middle Saxon tribute collection centre at Higham Ferrers (© Oxford Archaeology)
Potters Lyveden, Northamptonshire, 1973 (© John Steane)
Aerial photograph of the multi-period settlement of Jarlshof, Shetland (© RCAHMS)*

Printed by
Short Run Press, Exeter

Contents

Foreword

Chris Taylor
Vice-President, MSRG

It is more than 50 years since I began to study rural settlement in Britain, and well over 60 if you include my gradual but haphazard realisation that settlements had settings and shapes that related to their past. I have thus lived through, seen and, indeed, sporadically contributed to much of the development of the subject that is brought up to date by this book.

Through that time we have gone from belief in austere determinism to accepting the importance of human intervention and then back to more complex determinism; from the alleged impact of democratic Saxon settlers on the landscape, via authoritarian control, and thence to the influence of a peasant society, albeit with a somewhat more intricate social structure than that of the settlers. We have seen the examination of simple unchanging settlements replaced by the study of complex villages and hamlets that resulted from continuous change arising from expansion, contraction, desertion or movement. And we have wrestled with the differences between deliberate planning and accidental regularity at all periods. We have studied rural settlements both singly and collectively, have mapped them, excavated them, investigated their standing buildings and researched their documentary history. We have looked at their inhabitants, their actions, failures and successes as both individuals and communities. Their possessions, constructed, collected or manufactured, of every type and place of origin, have been studied, often with the assistance of modern scientific techniques. The settings of settlements at all levels, physical, economic, social and even symbolic, have been subjected to minute examination, while their beginnings, ends and futures have been scrutinised.

The result of all this varied research has been the spectacular growth of what started as a somewhat limited subject. Originally it was almost entirely the preserve of geographers and local historians; now it is a multi-disciplinary enquiry involving archaeologists, social, economic, landscape, architectural and art historians as well as environmental scientists and others, and its influence has spread far beyond mere settlement studies.

Thus, perhaps, it would seem timely to see this book as illustrating the collective achievement of all the scholars involved and to recognise it as a landmark in the development of the subject. Alas, I do not believe that this is so. For, although the book is undoubtedly important and, hopefully, will have some impact, it is only a summary of the state of rural settlement studies in Britain in 2010. Further, it is likely that, as with all good academic works, it will be out-of-date before it reaches the bookshops. But of course this is precisely what should happen. Indeed, I have always taken the view that if any of our writing is not immediately severely criticised, rejected as inadequate, wrong-headed in conception and in need of total revision, we have failed. Success in historical studies should be measured only by the extent to which ideas and interpretations are taken forward, written off and replaced by new ones – or, in some cases, by old ones.

None of us ever produces 'the last word'. I too have published what is now regarded as rubbish. My first major work on settlement history (on Whiteparish in Wiltshire) in 1967, was largely misconceived, although the excuse is that it was, inevitably, written in its time and of its time. I could do no more.

Curiously I have never been taken to task over it, as I should have been – either no one has noticed its inadequacies, or they have been too polite to tell me! Personally I have been less well behaved, and over the years have disagreed with various methodologies and interpretations, most recently with landscape characterisation which I regard as merely a more complicated and polished return to ideas rejected 40 odd years ago. However, if nothing else, with age sometimes comes wisdom, and I now see that even the cyclical nature of some of our work has its advantages.

As individual scholars we can do little to add much to the understanding of our chosen subject. We are not involved in the completion of the roof of the great structure that is rural settlement studies, only adding the odd, and often ill-fired, brick to the lower courses. The building will not be completed in our lifetimes – it probably never will be. Every generation rewrites its own history. That is all that is possible. What we produce usually says more about our world today than about the world gone by.

This is not to deny that the work we have done and will continue to do is of value. The slow development of settlement studies in Britain, as well as abroad, with its cyclical, and often repetitive, appearance of 'new ideas', as it seems to some of its more ancient participants, *is* important. It seems to me that we are not just gradually bettering our understanding of the homes, settlements and landscapes of our predecessors but learning of their hopes, aims, achievements and beliefs. And seeing them as real *people*, very close to us in many respects, and only lacking our technology, and perhaps our cynicism.

While others will undoubtedly want more from settlement studies and from this book in particular, and may even get it, this is the modest philosophy that has kept me involved in the subject over the years. I believe that the following pages are a first-class example of the way our discipline has progressed and will continue to progress. It certainly demonstrates the splendid results of both the scholarship and the almost boundless enthusiasm of my friends and colleagues in the Medieval Settlement Research Group.

Contributors

Dr Terry Barry
Associate Professor, Department of History,
Trinity College, Dublin

Dr Neil Christie
Reader in Archaeology, School of Archaeology
and Ancient History, University of Leicester

Dr Oliver Creighton
Associate Professor in Archaeology, Department
of Archaeology, University of Exeter

Dr Chris Dalglish
Lecturer in Archaeology, School of Humanities,
University of Glasgow

Prof. Christopher Dyer
Formerly Professor in English Local History,
Centre for English Local History,
University of Leicester

Paul Everson
Formerly Head of Field Survey, English Heritage

Dr Mark Gardiner
Senior Lecturer in Medieval Archaeology, School
of Geography, Archaeology and Palaeoecology,
Queen's University, Belfast

Prof. David A. Hinton
Professor of Archaeology, School of Humanities,
University of Southampton

Dr Della Hooke
Honorary Fellow, Department of Arts and Social
Sciences, University of Birmingham

Prof. Audrey Horning
Professor of Archaeology, School of Geography,
Archaeology and Palaeoecology, Queen's University,
Belfast

Dr Richard Jones
Lecturer in Landscape History, Centre for English
Local History, University of Leicester

Dr Jonathan Kissock
Senior Lecturer in History, School of Education,
University of Wales, Newport

Dr Carenza Lewis
Director, Access Cambridge Archaeology,
University of Cambridge

Dr Keith Lilley
Reader in Historical Geography, School
of Geography, Archaeology and Palaeoecology,
Queen's University, Belfast

Edward Martin
Archaeological Officer, Suffolk County Council
Archaeological Service

Dr Susan Oosthuizen
Academic Director, Institute of Continuing
Education, University of Cambridge

Bob Silvester
Deputy Director, Clwyd-Powys Archaeological
Trust

Paul Stamper
Senior Adviser, Designation Department,
English Heritage

Dr Chris Taylor
Formerly Head of Archaeological Survey,
Royal Commission on Historical Monuments
England

Dr Gabor Thomas
Lecturer in Archaeology, Department of
Archaeology, University of Reading

Dr Sam Turner
Senior Lecturer in Archaeology, School of
Historical Studies, University of Newcastle

Robert Wilson-North
Historic Environment Manager, Exmoor National
Park Authority

Dr Stuart Wrathmell
West Yorkshire Archaeology, Archives and Ecology

Dr Rob Young
Historic Environment Adviser, North-East Region,
English Heritage

List of Figures

PART I
CONTEXTS, CHRONOLOGIES AND FORMS

CHAPTER 1

Introduction: Medieval Rural Settlement Research. Emergence, Examination and Engagement

Mark Gardiner, Neil Christie and Paul Stamper

A cross-country scramble across darkening fields brought us at last to consolidation. The earthworks, accentuated by the long shadows of the disappearing sun, seemed tremendous. Ploughmarks, fishponds, boundary-mounds… all were on a gargantuan scale.[1]

The past: ways of looking and thinking

The study of rural settlement and landscape has been a prominent part of archaeological research on the Middle Ages ever since the 1950s. It has attracted an extraordinary level of interest from both professionals and amateurs. This is particularly apparent if we compare it with the study of medieval towns which remains by comparison a minority pursuit. The study of churches or monastic sites, even though these are widely visited, also do not have a similar following. The countryside has been the subject of countless television programmes, and conferences on the subject attract substantial audiences. What is it about the rural landscape of the Middle Ages which has such a pull for many who might have little fascination with history and only a passing interest in being in the countryside? There is a perception that the countryside still retains evidence of a past world. Unlike towns, which have been reworked by commercial and industrial development, the countryside is imagined to have remained largely immune from such developments; it preserves an earlier world hidden away in villages, churchyards and woodlands. Indeed, the impression is that traces of the past remain barely concealed and awaiting discovery.

Such a view of the countryside could only arise when the majority of the population lived in towns and was separated from its rural roots by a generation and more. By the last decades of the nineteenth century it was possible for the urban middle class to regard the countryside as place of renewal and escape from the dirt of the town. Such ideas found their literary expression in William Morris's *News from Nowhere* (1888), and it was natural that followers of Morris, inspired by his vision of guilds of workers, should look to the countryside as the place where communities of artisans could be established. The best known of these was C. R. Ashbee's community of craft-workers at Chipping Camden which moved there from London in 1902, but this was far from the only one. Similar groups were established in 1896 at Haslemere (Surrey) by Godfrey Blount, a friend of Ashbee, and at Ditchling (East Sussex) in 1907 by Eric Gill.[2] The Haslemere community, named the Peasant Arts Society, sought to re-establish a connection between production and vernacular traditions. But it also had a wider aim, namely 'to make a Country Movement… effect the re-population of England and the restoration to our people of their Hands, their Faith and their Country-side'.[3]

There was an obvious affinity between the Arts and

Crafts movement inspired by Ruskin's rejection of industrial production, Morris's idealisation of medieval society and the emerging conservation movement of the late nineteenth century. In 1878 Morris had founded the Society for the Protection of Ancient Buildings which was particularly concerned with the standards and manner of restoration of churches. Ashbee took this concern in another direction and in 1894 played a formative role in establishing the Watch Committee to record and protect London's architectural heritage. From this small organisation emerged The Survey of London, which from 1910 received official support from London County Council to record the history and architecture of the metropolis. Ashbee was also associated with the other emerging conservation body of that period, the National Trust. This was established in 1895 both to preserve places of natural beauty and historic interest, and Ashbee joined its committee the following year.[4] The founders of the National Trust held many of the views associated with Ruskin. Indeed, two of them, Hardwicke Rawnsley and Octavia Hill, owed their acquaintance to an introduction made by him. Even before the foundation of the Trust, both had also been involved in the fight to preserve public access to open spaces, as had the third founder, Robert Hunter, who had presented the legal arguments for saving Epping Forest from enclosure.[5] The mutual interests of the National Trust in preserving places of historic interest and those of local archaeological societies were signalled when the latter were invited to become affiliates, and by 1903 a full 18 had done so.[6]

A key figure linking the Arts and Crafts movement with an interest in the historic landscape was Heywood Sumner. Sumner combined the developing interest in earthworks fostered by the Congress of Archaeological Societies through its Ancient Earthworks Committee with an artistic style which was derived from Arts and Crafts illustration. He demonstrated that it was possible to undertake both scientific survey and sensitive draughtsmanship, neither of which was particularly notable in, for example, Hadrian Allcroft's *Earthwork of England* of 1908,[7] or the early volumes of the *Victoria County History*, which catalogued earthworks on a county-by-county basis. In the hands of a skilled illustrator the hachure survey was developed into an extremely

subtle means of depicting changes in slope and a key tool in the emergence of analytic survey. This is seen, for instance, in the first of the volumes, *An Inventory of the Historical Monuments in Hertfordshire* (published in 1911), of the Royal Commission on Ancient and Historical Monuments for England, set up in 1908 to record by inventory monuments which predated 1700, and to make recommendations for their preservation. The hachure technique was developed particularly by H. S. Toms. Toms was an exceptionally good observer and surveyor of earthworks and a fine illustrator, able to produce not only clear plans, but also passable illustrations in Sumner's style.[8] In spite of his own skill, from 1913 a number of his surveys were drawn up for publication by Robert Gurd, a professional draughtsman and, according to a recent appraisal, 'a man whose style and achievement have rarely been bettered'. Gurd retained some elements of the whimsy of Arts and Crafts style in, for example, the Roman legionary whose serves as the north point of a map of a Roman station drawn in 1923, or the depiction of a folded corner of a map in a plan the previous year, though on the whole his work was functional rather than ornamental.[9]

The transition from an appreciation and recording of individual sites to a realisation that they were part of wider archaeological landscapes was only possible with the development of aerial photography which revealed the extent of remains, both upstanding and those that survived as soil marks. The publication by O. G. S. Crawford of a paper on aerial photography, together with the accompanying map, established simultaneously both the ubiquity of remains and the potential for archaeology to place them in some sort of chronological order. Crawford introduced the term 'Celtic fields' to described the remains of Iron Age and Roman agriculture and distinguished them from 'Saxon' agriculture marked by strip lynchets. He recalled an early June morning when, flying over Salisbury Plain, he realised that the greater part of the zone was covered with traces of 'Celtic fields'.[10] The implications of Crawford's discovery were immense. It suggested not only that the landscape had occasional and often large fragments of the past on show, such as henges and cairns or larger monuments such as hill-forts, but it also indicated that much more had survived into the present, inscribed on the ground.

Figure 1.1. Maurice Beresford at Wharram Percy, 1962. (Photo: Brenda Rose, reproduced by kind permission of Paul Stamper)

Indeed, he saw that it was possible to reconstruct entire landscapes of the past from aerial photography and ground survey.

Yet, in spite of these insights, Crawford was able to dismiss the medieval or later animal enclosure recorded on an aerial photograph of Cherhill Down (Wiltshire) with the comment that 'The earthworks on this plate are none of them of any particular interest'.[11] The recognition of the significance of medieval remains and the contribution of that period to the present landscape in fact had to wait until the period after the Second World War. It was not that earlier fieldworkers had ignored the copious medieval remains – after all, under Crawford's supervision as Archaeological Officer, they had been carefully noted in the Ordnance Survey records[12] – but they had either not been recognised for what they were, or had been regarded as less significant when considered alongside prehistoric and Roman earthworks.

The revelation which had to wait until the 1950s was that the medieval remains on aerial photographs were just one element of a broader historic landscape. Hedges, road, villages, standing buildings and churches could be considered alongside the humps and bumps of ridge and furrow, and of tofts and crofts, to allow a broad view of the landscape of the Middle Ages. That resource opened up by W. G. Hoskins and Maurice Beresford was a natural extension of Crawford's discovery from the air. He had established the concept of the ancient landscape which could be viewed from the air and mapped from photographs and on the ground. Beresford (Figure 1.1) appreciated that aerial photographs provided a unique and informative resource and duly included them in *The Lost Villages of England*. He took this further in 1958 when he published, in co-operation with J.K.S. St Joseph, a volume of aerial photographs of the medieval remains of Britain, which was almost as influential, at least among those studying the period, as Crawford's photographs of the earthworks of the chalk downland had been 30 years earlier.[13]

The implications of a wider perspective apparent from the air and from the ground took a long time to absorb, for it required moving from the concept of the archaeological site to an appreciation of the ubiquity of remains of the past. The particular genius of Hoskins and Beresford was to take the further leap and realise that archaeology did not remain merely in the ground, but also in numerous features in the countryside. That idea was so radical that the ramifications of it were still being worked out some decades later. Indeed, it took until the late 1980s for Stuart Wrathmell finally to make the connection between the 'ephemeral' buildings excavated by archaeologists and standing structures. He argued that the sole difference was that those which were excavated had been abandoned and standing buildings had been continued to be maintained.[14] Rackham's discussion of trees and woodland was no less important, for it showed that the living vegetation also reflected the medieval countryside. Indeed, some coppice trees were of medieval origin and had survived over many centuries through a continuous cycle of cutting and re-growth.[15]

It is not necessary to discuss in detail the history of the study of medieval settlement here. That is considered in Chapter 2 by Paul Everson and Chris Dyer below. Instead, it is useful to set the emergence of the study into the broader intellectual context. The end of the Second World War marked a new interest in planning the environment, a process of constructing new buildings while preserving the remains of the past. The National Buildings Record had been set up during the course of the war to take stock of the number of historic buildings and to save them from unthinking destruction; the Town and Country Planning Acts of 1944 and 1947 allowed for the listing and recording of these before they were demolished.[16] The study of vernacular buildings was gradually developing under the direction of R. A. Cordingley who became Professor of Architecture in 1946 at Manchester University. His interest had developed during his time as architect to the National Coal Board and a wish to ensure that new houses adopted the local vernacular.[17] Such an approach was itself derived from the Arts and Crafts concern to follow the style established by the local vernacular.[18]

The influence of the Arts and Crafts aesthetic also continued to be felt in the study of earthworks. The carefully surveyed earthworks recorded in the volumes prepared by the Royal Commission on Historical Monuments of England in the 1960s and 1970s continued to be depicted with hand-drawn hachures, and even the most recent advice note includes a plan drawn in that manner. Matthew Johnson sees such surveys as potentially seductive, noting that, in contrast with a standard line plan, 'a well-executed hachured plan is far more aesthetically pleasing, an object of beauty'.[19]

This brief summary of the intellectual genealogy of the study of medieval rural settlement studies has, we hope, emphasised the way in which it grew out the Ruskinite vision of the past, as developed by William Morris and his followers. The emerging interest in the Middle Ages was not a dry historicism, but sprang from a sense of the relevance of the past to the present. This was expressed not only in a passion to preserve and record what remained, but in a view that the virtues of the past, particularly of the countryside, had been lost. There was a further element. Running through the thought of Morris, Ashbee and Crawford, as well as more recent workers, including the historian Rodney Hilton and the authority on vernacular

buildings, Eric Mercer, was a left-wing streak. Maurice Beresford certainly had this, although it was expressed less in dogma (Robin Glasscock's *Independent* obituary of 14.1.2006 classified him politically as 'old Labour') than in practical concern and help for the educationally or socially underprivileged. After spells of wartime social work in London and Birmingham (while registered as a Conscientious Objector), he was appointed warden of an adult education centre in Rugby; here it was, in 1945 (aged 25), that he made the seminal identification of the remains of the lost village of Bittesby village in Leicestershire. Those who had fallen into criminality were a particular and lifelong concern of his; in the 1950s and 1960s approved school (borstal) boys were given the opportunity to do 'hearty' work like trench-opening and backfilling at Wharram, and for much of his life he was a prison visitor: among the interests noted in his 2005 *Who's Who* entry was 'delinquency'.[20] The radicalism of other scholars of the medieval countryside was similarly expressed less politically but rather in religious non-conformity, in a sense of social inclusivity and in a belief in the rejuvenating possibilities of countryside and the right of public access. These various ideas recurred throughout the twentieth century in many organisations with different emphases and in new combinations, like the transparent objects viewed through the eyepiece of a kaleidoscope.

The purpose of trying, above, to identify the context of medieval landscape studies has not been merely to claim an intellectual ancestry for it, but to argue that it offers a very distinct vision of the past and that it arose out of a sense of political and social engagement. Matthew Johnson, writing about the landscape tradition in British archaeology, sought, as others have, to place Hoskins at the centre of the study. From the perspective offered here, Hoskins's lack of a radical and socially inclusive perspective, and the expressions of a conservative, lapsarian regret which permeate *The Making of the English Landscape*, place him somewhat apart from the tradition.[21] However, the argument is fundamentally not about whether Hoskins was or was not aligned with the tradition of landscape study, but rather about the approach of the study to the landscape.

The case presented here is that implicit in much of

the writing about medieval settlement and landscape has been an engagement with the past driven more strongly than is normal in historical studies by a wish to help understand and to inform contemporary society. It is argued that medieval settlement and landscape studies have not lacked a theoretical position, though it has not as much to the fore as in prehistoric archaeology. Instead, the relationship of the past to the present runs like an under-current through many works on the medieval rural landscape. The arguments presented in Alan MacFarlane's *The Origins of English Individualism* and Hilton's response to it were all about contemporary politics.[22] *The Origins* may not have been a book about the landscape specifically, but it was about the character of medieval rural society. Once we appreciate an implicit social engagement is a feature in a number of studies on the medieval countryside, then it is possible to understand some of its preoccupations. It is arguable that one of the aspects behind the continuing fascination with the emergence of the village is not merely an historical problem about a certain geographical form of settlement, but an interest in the appearance of a social formation, the village community.

This brings us to the final point which is to affirm that prehistoric and medieval landscape archaeology have taken separate paths. Johnson has noted that late medieval archaeologists, with access also to a rich documentary record, avoid using the abstract and generalising terms of their prehistoric or even their early medieval counterparts, preferring to use historically specific language: feudalism is chosen instead of the less specific notion of social power.[23] The reasons for this should now be clear. It is not just that instead of using abstractions, late medievalists happen to use context-specific terminology; it is that the late Middle Ages, in particular, matter. They are far enough away to be apart from us, but sufficiently similar to us to be imaginable and relevant. The medieval rural landscape is the place at which the past and the present meet, and the context in which ideas of what we are and how we view ourselves are being worked out.

The present: new thoughts and questions

This book does not adopt a single or fixed position on the character of the medieval countryside, and there is

certainly no party line. The views here are as diverse as the authors. The book overall takes its origins from discussions within the committee gatherings of the Medieval Settlement Research Group (MSRG). Here it was recognised that, despite the valuable outputs of the Group in terms of Spring and Winter seminars and day conferences, along with its well-respected journal (now *Medieval Settlement Research*, formerly the *Annual Report of the Medieval Settlement Research Group*) and Policy Statements distributed and accessible via the website, there was no monograph published by the Group that embodied and flagged the scale, variety and depth of research on medieval rural settlement undertaken by its members across so many years. This new volume is, put simply, designed to fill that gap and to act as a flagship publication, highlighting the very active field of rural settlement studies in Britain and the input of MSRG members into that field. As readers of the journal will know, a rich range of work, whether derived from field-work, documentary history or even laboratory studies, is frequently reported, each year adding new insights into the sequences and forms of settlement, land use and human presences in different counties and regions, while also showing the ways that theory can be applied or old studies and data re-interpreted. The journal also draws on MA and PhD studies and casts its net into Europe too.

There is no need here to identify in detail the roots of the MSRG (see instead the valuable introduction by Chris Taylor in *Deserted Villages Revisited*),[24] but it is pertinent to observe how the first incarnation, the Deserted Medieval Village Research Group, coincided with the start of the major, widely recognised village excavations led by the late John Hurst and Maurice Beresford at Wharram Percy in North Yorkshire from 1950: while the detailed publications attached to this long-term project of excavation, survey, finds analysis, etc. only began to appear from the late 1970s (see Chapter 15, this volume), and with the final volume (XIII) due in 2012, the MSRG, active as a formal body from 1986, has not had a single attached project (with related monographs) as its own flagship. Nonetheless, its name has been attached to a number of surveys and projects, most notably the AHRC-funded Whittlewood project from 2002–04,[25] and to a significant AHRC-funded programme of workshops and seminars held across Britain and Northern Ireland in 2007 entitled 'Perceptions of Medieval Landscape and Settlement':[26] the first was influential in providing new data and methodologies for assessing village origins, growth and economic interactions in the Midlands; the second consisted of highly stimulating sessions on a variety of theoretical and related themes such as 'Planning and Meaning', 'Working and Sharing' and 'Belonging, Communication and Interaction', which have seen an impact in subsequent projects and publications.

The MSRG recently produced two essential documents which are of high relevance to this new publication on rural settlement in medieval Britain. Our *Revised Policy Statement*, naturally drawing upon various published or online Regional Research Agendas and Resource Assessments,[27] offered both an agenda of study and a strategy of research and related priorities, observing how studies have evolved or, in some instances, not evolved.[28] The Statement pointed to a continuing emphasis on deserted sites and a neglect of smaller rural units such as hamlets and individual farms and of active rural seats, and to failures to draw adequately on developer-led field results. It identified also how many Historic Environment Records (HERs) offer a sometimes sketchy record of medieval rural settlement and their variations, which makes the research task problematic; at the same time, it recognised that related work on medieval rural landscapes is still uneven between counties.

The second key report was a Research Review,[29] covering the decade between 1996 and 2006: drawing together the main strands of a vast array of research in archaeological, historical, environmental and other science-based fields, the Review could identify a much enhanced image of rural Britain across the mid-first to mid-second millennium AD, one benefiting from closer interrogation and interpretation of the structural and material data, and also from increased co-operation between disciplines – witnessed, for example, in the Whittlewood project, integrating archaeology survey, excavation (including test-pitting in existing villages), standing building survey, geomorphological study, pollen studies, and toponymic analysis, with data gathered, mapped and analysed via a GIS (Figure 1.2).

But although this Review identified extensive

academic contributions, with papers, projects and some regional overviews – key publications among these being Lewis *et al.* (1997), Hooke ed. (2000), Roberts and Wrathmell (2002), Govan ed. (2003) for Scottish medieval and later rural sites, Roberts ed. (2006a) on deserted sites in Wales, and Turner ed. (2006c) on Devon and Cornwall, and bolstered since by the 'Landscape History after Hoskins' volumes (Gardiner and Rippon (eds) 2007), centred on medieval landscapes, and Barnwell and Palmer eds (2007) for the post-medieval period) and Rippon (2008) – it remains the case that an up-to-date academic volume bringing together surveys (oriented by period and region) for all of medieval Britain is lacking and long overdue. Beresford and Hurst's *Deserted Medieval Villages* (1971) was the first major overview of the subject, and especially of the contribution of archaeology, since Beresford's *Lost Villages* of 1954. Studies since then, such as Aston *et al.*, *The Rural Settlements of Medieval England* (1989), while often reporting important work (which has, of course, regularly appeared as site-specific studies in journals such as *Landscape History*, county journals and the *Annual Reports* of the MSRG), have not attempted comprehensive coverage. This fuller MSRG publication is thus timely, enabling scholars to reflect on work generated in regions across Britain and to provide an essential guide for new scholars wanting to start or to expand their studies in medieval rural settlement. The volume is also, on many levels, responding to Chris Taylor's view nearly 20 years ago, that 'The last thirty years' work in medieval rural settlement in England has not produced any clear pattern. Indeed, matters have become increasingly complex and confused.'[30]

This present volume thus has four main objectives: (i) to identify and characterise the range of medieval expressions in the landscape of Britain; (ii) to highlight the value and significance of exploring the variety of medieval rural settlement forms; (iii) to consider connections and differences between regions; and (iv) to flag current research targets and methods, gaps in knowledge, and routes for future study. The book is organised into two main parts: the first comprises papers introducing the roots of investigation into medieval rural settlement, the evolution of the methods of study of sites

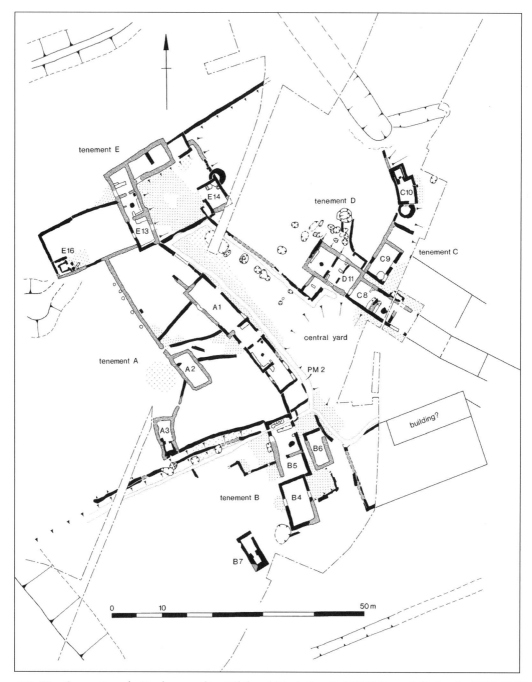

Figure 1.2. West Cotton, Raunds, Northamptonshire. While published after the MSRG Research Review for 1996–2006, this major excavation, undertaken in the later 1980s, successfully integrates an array of techniques and approaches to interpreting early medieval and medieval settlement sites. The plan here relates to c. _AD 1300 when an earlier, small manorial complex was abandoned and the site redeveloped as a hamlet of up to seven tenements. Several of these, with three-roomed houses (kitchen cross-passage chamber and open hall), were arranged either side of a funnel-shaped central yard. But by 1350 the hamlet was shrinking, that process continuing until by around 1450 West Cotton was no more. (Plan reproduced by kind permission of Northamptonshire Archaeology)_

and landscapes, and the principal chronological developments and structural types. Part II consists of a number of regional surveys, some based on individual counties, or groups of counties and regions, or on country, but each providing up-to-date statements on research in those spaces regarding settlement forms and landscape impacts across the full early medieval to late medieval periods. We should point out that the regional survey chapters were not designed to provide full or in any way comprehensive coverage of all areas of Britain, but they explore a sizeable and, we hope, representative sample. Distinctive to these papers is the inclusion of 'feature boxes', presented to highlight a theme or aspect of particular relevance or visibility for that zone and to summarise specific key sites, one of which readers can visit on the ground. For example, in the chapter by Sam Turner and Rob Wilson-North (Chapter 9), the selected topic is 'Dispersed settlement' and the featured sites are Mawgan Porth (Cornwall) and Badgworthy on Exmoor. Finally, an Appendix offers a practical guide to how (and where) to initiate and undertake study (in archive and on foot) on medieval rural settlement in the UK and Ireland.

What key themes and arguments stand out in this body of research? To a degree it is not the task of the editors to highlight specific elements since these may simply appeal most to our own research leanings, and each reader will hopefully draw their own conclusions and points of debate as they read through the papers. But there are evident foci of debate which will naturally emerge and which we simply list here:

(a) village origins and early medieval land patterns
(b) the extension of village forms and questions of planning
(c) variabilities of settlement forms, identifying persistences of dispersed forms
(d) structural forms and developments
(e) field systems and land use
(f) economics and markets
(g) landscape manipulation and conflicts with the environment
(h) parks and woodlands
(i) populations in villages and on the land
(j) status and the land: authorities and patrons – landlords, Church, monasteries as agents of change
(k) interconnections between farms and village and between villages and towns

(l) chronological and economic peaks and troughs
(m) depths and coverage of research, from site to landscape. What new techniques are being or should be deployed? Where should the next stages of research lead us? How well are the varied data sources being integrated?

We need also to stress how the papers here are not meant to be identikit texts, with the same issues raised and debated; each author or pair of authors draws on their own experiences and necessarily draws on the often diverse types of evidence to hand to provide a current image. For some the balance may be more to the later medieval period; for others the emphasis lies in the pre- and immediate post-Conquest centuries; for others still the nature of the land and of the population dictates the themes discussed; and in some cases the manipulation of the land and its resources provides the key angle of debate.

This is, therefore, the work of many scholars, themselves variously drawn from universities, national heritage bodies, national parks, commercial archaeological units, county councils and museums. Thus, finally, the editors would like to acknowledge the numerous contributing authors: the line-up has undergone some transformations since the project was first planned, but we thank all those who have responded to requests to fill in a variety of gaps that emerged *en route* to the end product. All contributors are to be thanked for following guidelines closely, thereby saving the editors much time, and for speedy responses to referee and editorial comments and suggestions. We are very grateful for Chris Taylor for contributing a typically brisk Foreword and for his advice during the compilation of the book. The editors acknowledge a publication subvention from the MSRG itself to help in the production costs of the volume. We thank Oxbow Books for agreeing to take on the publication within the Windgather series, and are grateful to Clare Litt and Tara Evans for seeing things through in Oxford for us; we also pass thanks to Jane Olorenshaw for her highly efficient and accurate indexing and copy-editing work. Lastly we would like to recognise all members, past and present, of the MSRG for their input across seminars, fieldtrips, projects, articles in the journal, ideas at conferences, wider fieldwork and research, and from correspondence, who have thereby provided much of the meat which has found its way into this volume. We hope that, like the MSRG Policy Statement, this volume will do much to inform and guide current and future researchers into medieval rural settlements, landscapes and populations across Britain and elsewhere.

Notes

1. Beresford 1954, 273. The impressive site in question was Thorpe le Glebe, Nottinghamshire.
2. Cumming and Kaplan 1991, 71.
3. Myzelev 2009, 601.
4. Crawford 1985, 57–66, 94; Hobhouse 1987, 25–30.
5. Fedden 1968, 4–7.
6. Fedden 1968, 12
7. Allcroft 1908.
8. Bradley 1989. For an illustration by Toms in Sumner's style, see Toms 1922, fig. 5. See also Bowden (ed.) 1999, 19–22.
9. Curwen and Curwen 1922, 33; Goddard 2000, 7; Winbolt 1923, 82.
10. Crawford 1923, 349, 352; Crawford and Keiller 1928, 7.
11. Crawford and Keiller 1928, 234.
12. Hauser 2008, 60–64.
13. Beresford 1954; Beresford and St Joseph 1958. See also Gerrard and Rippon 2007, 531–532.
14. Wrathmell 1989.
15. Rackham 1976.
16. Croad 1989, 24–25; O'Neil 1948, 34–35.
17. Quiney 1994, 229.
18. For a recent discussion in the context of the Lake District, see Whittaker 2011, 100–102.
19. English Heritage 2007; Johnson 2007, 95. See also Brown 1987, chapters 3 and 4; Bowden (ed.) 1999, 52–67 on drawn surveys.
20. Glasscock 2009.
21. Matless 1998, 274–277; Matless 2002, 87–94.
22. Hilton 1980; Macfarlane 1978; White and Vann 1983.
23. Gardiner and Rippon 2009, 70, citing Johnson 2007, 59–60.
24. Taylor 2010.
25. Jones and Page 2006.
26. Dyer 2007.
27. E.g. Petts and Gerrard (eds) 2006; Cooper (ed.) 2006.
28. MSRG 2007.
29. Gardiner 2006a. See also MSRG website: http://www.britarch.ac.uk/msrg/
30. Taylor 1992, 9. This key paper in fact is one where Taylor revisits his own earlier views of patterns and sites, including Whiteparish, noted in his Foreword to this book.

CHAPTER 2

The Development of the Study of Medieval Settlements, 1880–2010

Christopher Dyer and Paul Everson

Beginnings, 1880–1915

British intellectuals before 1880 took remarkably little academic interest in the history of villages, peasants or fields, although many of them were employed by institutions with rural estates. Victorian historians' interest in the medieval countryside developed as an offshoot of their central preoccupation with constitutional history. Even as they explored the government of the manor and village, they were broad-minded enough to see that an understanding of village plans and the layout of fields might help to elucidate the hides, ploughlands and tenures which were their main focus of interest. Accordingly, an excellent plan of the settlement and fields of Hitchin (Hertfordshire) was used to illustrate Seebohm's discussion of the English village community published in 1883.[1] In a response designed to demonstrate the Germanic rather than the Roman antecedents of English rural society, F. W. Maitland in 1897 illustrated the point that the vill in Domesday Book could have been either a nucleated village or a group of dispersed settlements, by reproducing two sections of Ordnance Survey maps, contrasting 'A land of villages' (in the Thames valley) with 'A land of hamlets' in Devon.[2] Both scholars were familiar with the geographical advances made by Meitzen, who classified the plan forms of the villages of Germany, and made historical deductions about their origin and function. No British geographer or historian attempted to imitate this German research on a large scale, though H. L. Gray published in 1915 a gazetteer of field systems,

and drew a map which is still reproduced.[3] He identified the 'midland system', characterised by the division of the village territory into two or three open fields, which predominated in a broad belt running through the country from Co. Durham in the North-East down to Dorset.

The thinking of all these scholars was influenced by an ethnic approach – that is, identifying the Germanic, Celtic and Roman influences on fields, settlements and manors – which was rejected during the twentieth century.

Archaeology in 1883–1915 was still emerging as an academic subject, being mainly practised at universities by classicists and a growing number of prehistorians. The study of medieval settlements, however, was left to antiquarians. The early county historians such as Dugdale (for Warwickshire, in 1656) and Bridges, whose history of Northamptonshire was published in 1791, commented on deserted village sites.[4] The earliest excavations were of course carried out by amateurs, or by scholars without any special expertise. The excavations at Woodperry (Oxfordshire) have a claim to have been first in the field as they were published in 1846, and trenches had been dug into a number of deserted villages by the time that St Clair Baddeley produced useful plans of buildings from his work at Hullasey (Gloucestershire) in 1910. A hamlet site in Cornwall, Trewortha, was excavated by Baring-Gould with worthwhile results in the 1890s.[5]

Scientific approaches, 1915–1945

Between the wars the historical study of medieval rural society and agriculture was making great advances, in which broad questions about social structure, estate management and money rents were answered critically by analysis of written sources.[6] Much of the writing was at too high a level of generality to deal at length with particular places, though N. S. B. and E. C. Gras devoted a book to Crawley (Hampshire), and the Orwins' work on the open fields used Laxton (Nottinghamshire) as its principal example.[7] The quality of the work reflected the advance of economic history as a discipline under the strong influence of the social sciences. Historical geography, also emerging as a highly professional sub-discipline, was applied to the systematic mapping of historical data, which is best displayed in the first edition (1936) of H. C. Darby's *An Historical Geography of England before AD 1800*, in which authors such as Darby himself and R. A. Pelham illustrated their chapters with maps of counties, regions and the whole country showing such features as cloth-making centres. Noticeably, the section on the English village has maps of population densities derived from Domesday, but no plan of a village.[8]

Archaeology began to engage seriously with medieval rural settlements in the 1930s, thanks to the efforts of pioneering scholars who realised the potential value of excavated material evidence. Christopher Hawkes, a prehistorian with a broad imaginative approach, noted in 1937 the many deserted village sites available for excavation, and saw their potential: 'an archaeologist's picture of a fourteenth-century English peasant community would be a unique contribution…'[9] Notable projects of the 1930s included the identification and excavation by Aileen Fox of thirteenth-century houses on Gelligaer Common (Glamorgan), which could have belonged either to permanently inhabited farmsteads or to shielings occupied only during the summer grazing season.[10] Meanwhile, Martin Jope excavated a farmstead on Dartmoor and R. L. S. Bruce-Mitford began work on the deserted village of Seacourt on the outskirts of Oxford.[11] Excavators were thus successfully engaging with key problems for advancing the subject: that is the recognition of the remains of medieval peasant buildings, and the dating of occupation by means of locally made pottery.

The subject takes off, 1945–1979

The great expansion in medieval settlement studies came about in the 1940s because of the systematic investigation of deserted medieval villages (DMVs). The new energy in academic life after the end of World War II, with its democratic and progressive inspiration, promoted subjects which shed light on the lives of ordinary people in the past. Students in adult education classes, which both W. G. Hoskins and Maurice Beresford taught, were enthusiastic for archaeology and local history.[12] Hoskins's research contribution was to identify sites in Leicestershire, and Beresford did the same in Warwickshire; their findings received wider recognition in June 1948 when a gathering of academics from a seminar in Cambridge, led by M. M. Postan, visited sites in Leicestershire.[13] Both Beresford and Hoskins combined documentary research with analysis of maps and fieldwork – something which would now be called interdisciplinary – and would eventually lay the foundations of landscape history. Hoskins regarded deserted villages as an important dimension of economic history, but they were not for him an all-consuming passion; Beresford, however, building on his Warwickshire research, devoted himself single-mindedly to the subject for some years, and this enabled him to write the *Lost Villages of England*, published in 1954.[14] The scope of the work was further extended in 1952 when John Hurst from Cambridge took over the direction of excavations which Beresford had begun in perhaps rather amateurish fashion at Wharram Percy, though Beresford remained as a collaborator (Figure 2.1). In the same year the Deserted Medieval Village Research Group was founded, which brought together a combination of archaeologists, geographers and historians, and included both professionals and local enthusiasts.[15] One of the Group's objectives was to compile and circulate county lists of DMVs, selected according to a rigorous and consistent set of criteria. Some of these were published separately, notably for Northamptonshire and Oxfordshire,[16] but all of the lists were assembled into a national gazetteer and distribution map which were published in 1971 as part of a volume of 'studies' of deserted medieval villages. The lists continued to be refined and extended through the 1970s.[17] The majority of the DMVs lay in a belt of counties, from Northumberland down through the East Midlands to Dorset and Hampshire. It was initially believed that more could be found in such counties as Shropshire, Lancashire or Essex, but it was realised eventually that they were largely absent from both western and south-eastern counties because the settlement pattern there was dominated by hamlets and isolated farms – there were few deserted villages because there had been few villages.

Among tens of thousands of medieval rural settlements in Britain, why were the 2,263 deserted villages (revised upwards to 2,813 in 1977) the principal interest of researchers for so long? They represented a minority of the larger settlements which we have agreed to call villages, and an even smaller percentage of settlements as a whole. Noticeably, no other type of archaeological site is described by reference to its present inhabited or uninhabited state – for example, there are no 'deserted Roman villas' or 'deserted castles'. Alongside the deserted medieval sites were a larger number of villages that were much reduced in size, and many hamlets and farmsteads have also been abandoned or have shrunk. A very high proportion of medieval settlements, however, are still inhabited, so survival should be regarded as a normal experience of villages, hamlets and farmsteads. Perhaps part of the explanation for the high profile of the deserted villages lies in the romantic sense of loss associated with abandonment, and a further note of drama was added by Beresford's explanation of desertions, which he believed were caused by the expulsion of the peasantry by a greedy upper class attracted by the profits of the sheep pasture that replaced the village and its fields. *Lost Villages*, which conveys the excitement of discovery, as well as regret for the destruction of communities and some indignation at past injustices, was written attractively for a wide readership.

The advantage of extending research beyond deserted villages became widely accepted, and in 1971 it was decided that the word 'Deserted' should be dropped and that the title 'Medieval Village Research Group' better described the research interests of the Group's members.

Archaeologists were drawn to the deserted villages for very practical reasons. First, they provided an opportunity to study village plans as surviving earthworks. Much of the thinking about plan forms

was after all based on maps of existing villages, which may have recently changed their shape. The well-preserved deserted village, with its streets, boundaries, houses and other features fossilised in the modern landscape since the last inhabitants left in, say, AD 1400 or 1500, tells us about the last phase of the medieval settlement. Secondly, the deserted village site also provided an opportunity for excavation: in surviving villages, much of the earlier evidence is inaccessible or has been destroyed, whereas excavation in a deserted village has a better chance of recovering information about houses, artefacts, layout and origin.

In the three decades after scientific excavation began at Wharram Percy, single houses in deserted village sites were dug in different parts of the country (though in no way in a co-ordinated fashion), and these samples, such as Holworth (Dorset) and Martinsthorpe (Rutland), contributed usefully to building up knowledge of local styles of building and house plans.[18] At least a dozen village sites were excavated much more extensively, although reports were published sometimes 20 or more years after the work was completed, and, sadly, some are still awaited. On three sites, West Whelpington (Northumberland), Great Linford (Buckinghamshire) (Figure 2.2) and Caldecote (Hertfordshire), the excavated area extended over a high proportion of the whole village.[19] A number of hamlets and farmsteads were excavated, many of them in the South-West (Devon and Cornwall) but also in Wales, Shropshire and North Yorkshire.[20] Although all of the sites were occupied in the Middle Ages, Cowlam (East Yorkshire), Great Linford, Riplingham (East Yorkshire) and West Whelpington were not abandoned until the late seventeenth and eighteenth centuries.[21]

Much of this digging involved little or no public expense, as labour was provided by volunteers or unpaid students. Many of the directors had 'taught themselves' about medieval archaeology, having come into the profession from many walks of life; if they had archaeology degrees, they had not necessarily taken courses on the medieval period.[22] They did not in those days have to justify their choice of site, or define their aims by providing a 'research design'. Beresford's initial objective was to establish that there was a settlement under the visible earthworks, and this was readily proved by finding building materials,

Figure 2.1. Maurice Beresford (left) and John Hurst at Wharram Percy in 1979 (Photo: Paul Stamper).

Figure 2.2. Great Linford, Buckinghamshire: area excavation in 1975 in advance of development for Milton Keynes new town, showing Building 10. Despite superficially good preservation, extrapolating details of the above-ground form of medieval houses can be problematic. This example may have had a long and complex structural history before abandonment in the fifteenth century. A broad cross passage (beyond the circular oven) bounds the far-side hall, suggesting longhouse origins. Yet rather than a byre, the middle room apparently served as a kitchen or second living room, and that nearest the camera a dairy or buttery. (Photo: Paul Stamper)

pottery and artefacts, which were often only thinly covered by turf. It was some time, however, before the earthworks were fully explained – the large depressions which puzzled many visitors to deserted village sites were identified in the 1970s as farmyards which had become depressed by the wear and tear to their surface, and through constant removal of earth and dung.[23] One of the other main aims of the Wharram excavations was to provide archaeological evidence for the date of desertion, which was not precisely recorded in the documents. (The excavation reports are listed chronologically after the Notes at the end of this chapter.) It could eventually be said that a few pieces of pottery and artefacts found on the main village site could be dated to the early sixteenth century.[24] On the other excavated sites the last phase of occupation varied between the eleventh and the nineteenth centuries, with a considerable number coming between 1380 and 1600. Hurst's more ambitious agenda was rather similar to that expressed by Hawkes in 1937: namely to explore the material culture of the peasants. At the back of the minds of excavators of many sites was the hope that the history of the village could be pushed back to the Anglo-Saxon period. It was not known with any certainty if settlement plans had changed, or had remained much the same for centuries. As Roman and prehistoric artefacts and pottery often figured among the finds, the possibility even arose of long-term continuity of occupation.

The recovery of house plans was the primary objective of many excavations. This could be pursued as a realistic aim because, unlike many Roman or prehistoric sites, the outlines of the walls were visible as earthworks in the turf, and the mode of open-area excavation, which became universal following the success of the Wharram model, could be designed to include the whole building with as much of the surroundings as possible. Exposing the building foundation often posed no problems, because many of the excavations selected sites in regions with easily obtained building stone – such as the moorlands of the South-West, chalk country in the southern downlands or the Yorkshire wolds, and the Cotswolds. As excavation skills developed, it became possible to recover house plans from sites such as Barton Blount (Derbyshire) and 'Goltho' (Lincolnshire) on the midland clays where stone was very scarce, and walls were marked by lines of pad stones or even

Figure 2.3. Caldecote, Hertfordshire, July 1976. Guy Beresford drives the digger, while a volunteer uses an onion hoe to clean the surface. (Photo: Jonathan Hunn)

more subtle signs. The pioneer of these sensitive techniques, Guy Beresford, also applied them at Caldecote (Hertfordshire) (Figure 2.3).[25]

In buildings in the regions with stone walls standing as high as a metre, such details as built-in seats or ovens were preserved. It was sometimes supposed that the walls were built high, up to the eaves, but often low foundations supported walls of timber and wattle and daub, or sometimes of cob or clay. Most buildings were between 8 m and 15 m long and 4–5 m wide, and were divided into two or three spaces or rooms.[26] Doors tended to be placed in the long walls. Floors were of earth or chalk, or sometimes attempts had been made to give them a stony or pebbly surface. Roofs were seen to be usually of thatch, though there might be a small number of stone slates or ceramic tiles, perhaps placed around the smoke hole. Hearths were sited either in the middle of the floor or against a wall, the former implying an open hearth below a smoke hole, with no chimney or smoke hood.

Houses provoked controversy, focusing on their construction, durability and functions. Timber-framed buildings survived in large numbers, and were being studied by members of the Vernacular Architecture Group. The standing buildings were not closely datable, however, and no-one was sure about which social group built and occupied them. It was widely believed that excavations would reveal the structure of the 'authentic' peasant house, which was likely to be inferior to the Wealden houses of the

South-East or the cruck houses of western England and Wales. It was suggested that the walls and roofs of the excavated houses would have been made of rough branches rather than solid timbers. In general it was argued that houses were so insubstantial that they were rebuilt at regular intervals, but by 1979 in the case of Wharram this idea had been quietly discarded.[27]

The function and layout of buildings provoked more debate. The typical peasant house, it was argued, was the long house, in which animals occupied one end. A building type well known from modern survivals in the highland zone was therefore thought to have been prevalent everywhere, and it was also doubted that there were many specialist agricultural buildings. On sites over much of southern and midland England, however, houses seemed to have been used solely as human dwellings, and barns were identified, at Barton Blount for example.[28] Were buildings with kilns and ovens to be interpreted as barns with facilities for drying and processing grain, or as dwellings with developed food-processing facilities, or as bakehouses or kitchens? Such puzzles were presented at Hangleton (Sussex) and Hound Tor (Devon) (Figure 2.4).[29] Perhaps there were changes over time, and peasant 'farms', with dwellings and agricultural buildings grouped around a yard, emerged at the end of the Middle Ages? At some sites, however, this arrangement was certainly in use in the thirteenth century. But there were real problems in identifying the uses to which rooms and buildings were put, as hearths were not always easily identified, and rooms of all kinds, not just byres, seem to have been provided with drains. Buildings could be changed from one use to another, like the house at Hangleton which was converted into accommodation for animals as pastoral farming expanded at the end of the Middle Ages.[30]

The sample of buildings which was being discussed belonged to the later phases of abandoned settlements, and so much of the debate about construction and function related to houses built and occupied in the thirteenth, fourteenth and fifteenth centuries. This was the period when houses were being founded on stone foundation walls, or on pad stones if stone was scarce. Previously, from the ninth to the twelfth centuries, houses, sometimes similar in plan to those of the later Middle Ages, were constructed using vertical timbers set in post holes, or on horizontal beams. Those which rested on the ground surface, sometimes using clay or

cob as their main wall material, left few traces for the excavators except for the edge of floors, or eaves drip-trenches, which defined the outline of the house.[31] Few complete building plans of this period could be obtained from villages deserted in the later medieval period because the later occupation damaged the vestiges of timber buildings, and more useful evidence came from sites abandoned in the early Middle Ages, such as Eaton Socon (Bedfordshire).[32] The transition to stone foundations did not happen in all cases, so buildings constructed entirely of timber and earth persisted in the fourteenth and fifteenth centuries, and beyond. Excavators who may have hoped to find settlements of the fifth and sixth centuries stratified below villages deserted up to a thousand years later were disappointed. Often the earliest phases that could be found were dated to the eleventh or twelfth centuries. A continuous sequence of buildings from the ninth century onwards, which were claimed for some settlements in the South-West, is now thought to be based on a misinterpretation.[33]

The best way of understanding villages in a longer time dimension, however, was not to dig deeper beneath their houses, but to step back and see the village as a whole, and to consider its place in a wider landscape. A complete village consisted of a range of structures, not just the roads, boundaries, ponds and parks, but also the manor houses and churches. These latter buildings were obviously important, but some archaeologists felt uncomfortable with them, and not many were excavated. It was realised that the layout of villages could go through radical changes: at Wharram, the manor house site of the twelfth century was abandoned and used for peasant houses in the thirteenth, while the moated site at Milton (Hampshire) was built on a site previously part of the village.[34] Evidence for replanning of a village on new alignments came from excavations at Wythemail (Northamptonshire) and from analysis of earthworks at Bardolfeston in Dorset.[35] West Whelpington was replanned after a Scottish raid, and tenements at Caldecote were reduced in number and increased in size after the Black Death, and there was also a reorganisation into larger holdings at Hangleton.[36]

The great discovery (or rather rediscovery) was of village planning. Excavations of boundary banks could establish, at Upton in Gloucestershire, for example, that the regular plan of toft boundaries surrounded by a boundary bank was probably of pre-Conquest origin.[37] In the early and mid-1970s historical geographers argued from analysis of maps and documents that a master plan of almost geometric regularity had been imposed on some northern villages by their lords in the twelfth century or earlier.[38] Colin Platt, who thought about such problems in general terms, pointed out that the community showed signs of a collective orderly mind, and thus argued that not all plans should be attributed to the lords.[39] Villages like Barton Blount grew piecemeal in five phases, as if groups of tofts were added to the settlement as population grew; other villages which merged when separate nuclei expanded could be called polyfocal.[40]

The village lived on the produce of the land in its territory, and it became increasingly common for the research to extend to the fields, woods and pastures surrounding settlements. In this way Lyveden (Northamptonshire) (Figure 2.5) was recognised as one of a number of dispersed settlements that belonged in a woodland landscape, with patches of cultivation and extensive woods which provided its potters and iron workers with fuel.[41] Wade-Martins showed through fieldwalking in Norfolk evidence for the complex movements of settlements from the vicinity of the church to larger nucleations and then to the edges of greens by the twelfth century.[42] The tendencies for villages to increase in size and spread over the landscape in the twelfth and thirteenth centuries fitted the characterisation of these centuries as an age of colonisation and agricultural expansion. Village territories belonged to large ancient estates, for which the term 'multiple estate' was devised by the historical geographer Glanville Jones.[43] Excavated village sites like that at Upton (Gloucestershire) could be assigned a role as a subsidiary settlement on the upland pasture of a great estate based at Blockley, which fitted the model proposed by Jones as it had a pre-Conquest history and may have been a significant land unit in the Roman and prehistoric periods.[44]

Importantly, the tendency to take into account the wider landscape context drew attention to the full range of settlements, including hamlets and farmsteads. Taylor showed that a parish in the woodlands of Wiltshire, Whiteparish, contained a complex array of settlements, large and small.[45] Hamlets were already being excavated, notably in the South-West, but only gradually did researchers adopt an agenda of mapping and listing dispersed settlements, as was done in the case of Dartmoor by Linehan in the mid-1960s.[46] Moated sites were the great exception, because they were the subject of regional studies, leading to a co-ordinated nationwide collection of data in the 1970s, which enabled them to be counted (5,307) and mapped.[47] Some moats were part of the fabric of nucleated villages, but most had a place in patterns of dispersed settlements, especially in low-lying woodland landscapes. They were seen to be concentrated in very large numbers in Essex and Suffolk, and with a significant cluster in the West Midlands. Not just lords of manors and parish clergy, but better-off peasants too could have aspired to live in a house surrounded by a moat. To these could be added a category of dispersed settlement which was definitely imposed from above, namely the monastic grange, which might be found in areas of nucleated settlements, but were often located in wooded country, or on uplands, where lords, both religious and secular, also built establishments for managing stock, namely vaccaries and bercaries.[48]

The various developments sketched above were the results of combinations of disciplines, and especially archaeology and geography. A reference is needed to the achievements of historical geography, which reached its high point in the 1970s. Darby pursued his agenda, already apparent in the 1930s, of mapping Domesday data county-by-county according to a consistent formula, and this was triumphantly completed and celebrated in a general survey of the whole country in 1977.[49] Not only did the series map the population, ploughs, woodland, mills and fisheries of the 1086 survey, but in each county geographical subdivisions were identified in an anticipation of later landscape characterisation. Again by enlisting the contributions of colleagues and coordinating their efforts, he also published in 1973 a historical geography which gave a picture of spatial change over time by analysing slices of evidence for 1086, 1334, 1377 and 1524.[50] These generalised maps gave a background for rural settlements, but lacked local detail. Another group of geographers, led by Darby's students Baker and Butlin, compiled a regional survey of field systems published in 1973, which Trevor Rowley followed by holding a conference in 1978 (later published), which explored the interpretation of

Figure 2.4. Hound Tor, Devon: a longhouse complex, looking outward to more cultivable lands below. (Photo: Paul Stamper)

Figure 2.5. Potters Lyveden, Northamptonshire, 1973: a longhouse (left) stands on one side of a cobbled yard, with a late fifteenth-century tile kiln to the right. Rockingham Forest's ample supplies of clay and wood meant that many of the local villages made pottery and tiles. (Photo: John Steane)

open fields and their origins.[51] The school of historical geography led by Thorpe at Birmingham kept its nose (and eyes) nearer to the ground. Thorpe himself (after pursuing an old-fashioned ethnic approach to the green village) produced a full account of a single settlement, Wormleighton (Warwickshire), while among his students Roberts worked on dispersed settlement in the Forest of Arden and then on planned villages in the North-East, and Aston and Bond went on to drive landscape studies forward in a variety of directions.[52]

After the original impetus by two economic historians in the 1940s, historians did not make as important a contribution as they could have done. Hoskins's successors at Leicester achieved notable advances in landscape and village studies, including Finberg's very influential revival of the idea that the manor and village could be traced back to the Roman villa, based on the example of Withington (Gloucestershire).[53] Thirsk and Everitt worried at the problem of defining regional variety, and came up with a map of farming regions, and the very influential idea of *pays*, which enabled the countryside to be divided into meaningful categories, such as champion, woodland and wold.[54]

Some interest was provoked by Beresford's depopulation hypothesis, which attracted criticisms from both right (by Kerridge) and left (by Hilton).[55] But the big idea which dominated historical thinking was Postan's hypothesis of population growth followed by crisis. Deserted villages, Postan hoped, would support his theories, but when he found that they were not located on marginal land, and were abandoned long after the demographic collapse of the fourteenth century, he lost interest.[56] The theory that climatic deterioration had some bearing on the late medieval crisis was suggested by the ditch-digging on settlement sites, but was not favoured by historians. They investigated peasant poverty, and seemed unaware that the houses and finds from village sites, as Platt pointed out, revealed how some peasants were not so poor and cut off from trade.[57] Some historians saw the value of the excavated evidence for the study of living standards and styles of life.[58] Otherwise historians were working on population, families and other dimensions of peasant society, and regrettably they rarely saw connections with the material evidence.

The concentration on the nucleated village encouraged research within England on the central belt of countryside where villages and open fields were most plentiful. It was difficult to extend this interest to Wales, Scotland and Ireland, because of the scarcity of large nucleated settlements. Each country had its own traditions of rural settlement research, but a common theme was the distinction between areas of Anglo-Norman domination and the larger areas in which native populations had most influence. In Wales an interest in the hafod settlements on summer pastures resulted in excavations in the 1930s, and in Ireland distinctive sites, small ring forts or raths, were counted, surveyed, excavated and listed. In Scotland the hamlet settlement, the ferm toun, attracted attention from geographers and the Scottish Royal Commission. Reports on all three countries were made to the 1971 *Deserted Medieval Villages* book.

Widening perspectives: 'landscape'

As the 1980s unfolded, two trends were to the fore. Final publications resulting from numbers of substantial excavation projects on deserted village nucleations appeared, following on the heels of the first of the diverse series of Wharram studies, published in 1979.[59] Secondly, and drawing strongly on traditions in adult education teaching, attention to the context of settlements developed strength, in what were widely termed 'landscape approaches'.[60] Occasionally, there was an immediate interplay between the two. Guy Beresford's study of 'Goltho' manor (Lincolnshire), companion to his village report of a decade earlier, caught the attention of students of castles for its controversially early dating of the manor's ringwork and motte and the attention of those interested in vernacular architecture for its stimulating reconstructions of simply framed timber buildings from the excavated evidence. The revisionist perception was made that the settlement investigated had actually been the village of Bullington (which boasted a full range of documentation for village, manor and church) rather than the woodland hamlet or farm of Goltho (which was scarcely documented). The idea's origin lay not in the direct evidence about the settlement, however, but rather from just that wider contrast between village and hamlet and between open common-field arable and woodland zones with different patterns of resource and exploitation, and was probably more characteristic of contemporary researchers' interests.[61] Such landscape approaches to what had previously been thought of – at least in simple listings – as regional variations of deserted medieval villages began to offer radically changed perspectives. A series of studies by David Austin and his co-workers in south-west England, for example, brought new understanding to the long-studied hamlets and farmsteads in that region.[62]

The Society for Landscape Studies had been founded in 1979 'with the aim of promoting the study of the landscape in all its aspects', principally through its annual journal *Landscape History* but it was very much given impetus by the group of young scholars who had produced the monumental study of the medieval and pre-medieval archaeology of West Yorkshire.[63] While never much exercised with theoretical issues about what might be meant by 'landscape' or 'landscape history', as explored for example by cultural geographers and others, the subject was located rather within an empirical tradition of medieval and later studies in the manner of Hoskins.[64] The new Society reflected a contemporary trend in thinking and duly attracted the active support of many people also engaged in settlement studies. What became increasingly clearly articulated was that simply listing 'deserted medieval settlements' – and even extending the categorisation to 'shrunken settlements', or even to 'living settlements' – was not adequate. It represented the continued tyranny of the pigeon-holing of archaeology, by which remains were slotted into limited and discrete and easily recognised types. This did not reflect actual experience of the complexity of settlement forms and it left large zones of Britain apparently without archaeological evidence of medieval settlements. In some areas, the National Monuments Record (NMR) and the newly created county-based Sites and Monuments Records (SMRs) promoted the drawing of lines around sites and their treatment as monuments. This led, unhelpfully, to the presumption that a place-name and other documentation must represent a former nucleated settlement – even where no plausible trace was detectable. Some scholars (perhaps especially those whose professional activity limited their focus to classifiable 'monuments') saw that desertion or shrinkage might, wholly or partly, be a matter

of redistribution of population within a territory – typically a parish or township – and that the organisation of settlement could be dynamic and cyclical, requiring suitable approaches to understand it. Taylor invoked the image of balls on a billiard table, and both his own writing and work by Royal Commission for Historical Monuments of England (RCHME) that he guided persistently strained against the strait-jacket of merely recording monuments.[65]

Alongside landscape approaches, then, a high-level distinction between nucleated and dispersed settlement patterns came to be fundamental to thinking in settlement studies. People came to these interlinked issues in a variety of ways.

Excavators such as David Austin at Thrislington (Durham) had taken the bold step, in the context of rescue excavation with limited time and resource, to investigate the boundaries and outer limits of the settlement layout, away from a narrow focus on building plans and artefacts (Figure 2.6); he had also carried out extensive fieldwalking surveys as background to work at Hart, also in County Durham, in a way that two decades later would be a voluntary group or community activity.[66] At Wharram, ever the test-bed, trenching of boundaries on the pattern of Rahtz's approach at Upton (see above) produced remarkable and unexpected evidence of both Roman and early medieval occupation. For a moment it seemed that such trenching might become a major tool of investigation of abandoned settlements, but it was difficult to give an explanatory context to this evidence alone, given the limited scale of the work. Fieldwalking investigation of the whole parish followed.[67]

Historians with a topographical bent, such as the editors of Victoria County History volumes, often came directly and without fuss to a clear appreciation of the settlement pattern they were dealing with – Shropshire with a pattern of multiple hamlets and farmsteads per parish being a good example – whereas archaeologists, still keen on listing and monumentalising, were slow to articulate an account of field evidence in such clear terms.[68] For aerial prospection, with its established focus on discrete sites, dispersed settlement and landscape approaches proved surprisingly difficult, this despite the fact that the early post-war near-vertical aerial photographs (now publicly accessible in the NMR), capturing a view of the countryside before large-scale

Figure 2.6. Thrislington, Co. Durham: excavations in 1973–74 in advance of quarrying revealed large parts of the stone-built medieval village. Seen here is Toft C, with Tofts B and A beyond. (Photo: Richard Daggett and David Austin)

mechanised farming, proved in some areas helpful in giving access to now-lost patterns of settlement. The comprehensive character of the National Mapping Programme, initiated in England in 1988 and aiming at country-wide transcription of archaeological evidence captured in aerial photographs systematically and to a common standard, in principle afforded just the sort of material to make a major contribution to these shifts in settlement studies. But, slightly puzzlingly – and in part because of the Programme's focus on creating records of monuments by plotting and categorising according to shape and site type, rather than interpreting settlement patterns and relationships – it scarcely did.[69]

By contrast, non-excavating field surveyors such as Christopher Taylor, who certainly had encountered the field remains of dispersed settlement, were clear in their own minds that it differed from traditional deserted nucleations, and made attempts to articulate that, notably on the basis of work in Bedfordshire.[70] Taylor had earlier encountered medieval settlements of various forms in Dorset, including his first planned village at Holworth, a settlement at Bardolfeston whose earthworks showed that it had been replanned on a different alignment, and the remarkable run of physically contiguous but administratively separate settlements that lined the chalk valleys of southern Dorset.[71] Grounded in fieldwork skills of inquisitive observation developed within the RCHME by Collin Bowen, whose simple practice he himself set out for others to imitate,[72] Taylor's distinctive enthusiasm was to interpret and explain. Through a vigorous campaign of original fieldwork in Cambridgeshire and Northamptonshire, he developed a series of ideas about medieval settlements including the so-called polyfocal form of many large nucleations, the occurrence of internal change in village plans (sometimes amounting to a complete re-casting), of planned additions and of mobility of settlement.[73] All of these spoke of continuous change in settlements through time, and the temporary – almost aberrant – nature of nucleation on the long view. Most of all, Taylor was impressed with the evidence of scattered early medieval settlements in Northamptonshire parishes such as Great Doddington, Brixworth and Maidwell – known from fieldwalking surveys by Foard, Hall and others and evidently pre-dating the villages – and he took that as an indication that the villages, far from being the foundations of Anglo-Saxon settlers as traditionally thought, were late, replacing a dispersed pattern that had formerly been universal.[74] In the same county, excavations from

1985–89 at West Cotton near Raunds, revealed just such an emergence as well as later, radical, re-ordering (Figure 2.7).

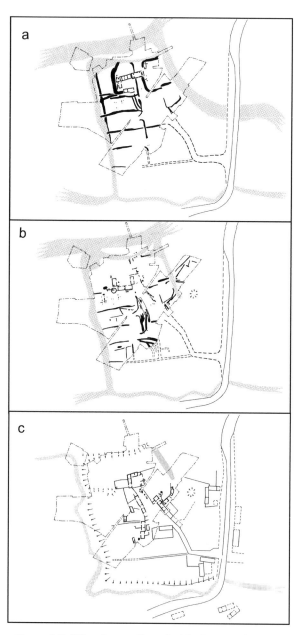

Figure 2.7. West Cotton, Raunds, Northamptonshire: the chronological sequence (a) late Saxon settlement (AD 950–1150); (b) the medieval manor (1150–1250); and (c) the medieval manor and hamlet (1250–1450). (Plan reproduced by kind permission of Northamptonshire Archaeology)

Though Brian Roberts was to provide a reminder that this was only one conceivable pattern of development that might fit our stock of information, Taylor's formulation became the dominant model of village origins. It formed the basis for an ambitious, large-scale project – one of several in the following two decades – to look at the origin and development of the medieval nucleated village in Northamptonshire. This, the Raunds Area Project, examined a group of parishes/townships in central Northamptonshire, encompassing a pre-Conquest administrative unit and covering topographical zones from river flood plain to clay-land watershed.[75] The concept of a 'village moment' was also persuasively articulated in the conclusions to a research study aimed, in part, at identifying a locale in the English midlands for a next-generation field project to succeed that at Wharram Percy.[76] With the re-casting of settlement, it seemed likely that creation of open communal field systems and local church foundation were intimately bound up. In addition to efforts to investigate this directly, as at Raunds and through David Hall's remarkably comprehensive studies of ridge-and-furrow field systems that have made Northamptonshire the epitome of that topic,[77] evidence for this process and its dating came from two unlooked-for directions. One was the ambitious, long-term project at West Heslerton in the Vale of Pickering, where a key feature was geophysical prospection to produce a detailed mapping of buried features for a 10 km strip of the settlement zone along the side of the valley. Remarkable for its revelation of a richness of pre-medieval features, in its overall sweep it, at the same time, but less obviously, documented the moment of the landscape's comprehensive re-casting, setting the date for that occurrence to the later tenth century.[78] Paralleling that, a study in Lincolnshire of the Anglo-Saxon stone funerary sculpture identified the moment of parish formation and creation of local church graveyards there as also lying in the late tenth century.[79] This was a later date for nucleation than had appeared to be the case on the basis of the pottery from the superseded early medieval scatters in Northamptonshire, with the eighth or ninth century more generally suggested.[80]

But the most substantial and effective new attempt to investigate this issue of origins occurred within the Whittlewood Project (piloted between 2000 and 2002 and extended to a full five-year span to 2005), based in the woodland zone spanning the border between southern Northamptonshire and northern Buckinghamshire. Here, quite similar fieldwork information to that recovered in central Northamptonshire was persuasively interpreted as indicating the later date. At the same time, the Whittlewood results argued that the process was a long, drawn-out one, in contrast to the immediate, comprehensive re-casting presumed in Lincolnshire or Yorkshire, and that the outcome of 'the moment' might equally be a dispersed or nucleated pattern.[81]

Settlement character: bottom-up and top-down

Taylor and others, then, were articulating very clearly the fundamental distinction between nucleated and dispersed settlement by the early 1980s, and when the (D)MVRG discussed dispersed settlement Harold Fox wrote strikingly of 'countrysides where villages never appeared'.[82] In 1986 the Group transformed itself, most obviously by formally merging with the formerly separate Moated Sites Research Group.[83] But moated sites in many parts of the country were simply one part of a variety of dispersed settlement patterns and the more far-reaching aims of the new Medieval Settlement Research Group became medieval rural settlement in any and all of its forms – and, for some, medieval settlement *tout court*, thereby including towns and castles and monastic institutions for example.

Before the end of the 1980s, research projects had been planned specifically in the zones of dispersed settlement and their results duly delivered. Quite outstanding in their clarity of purpose and notably informative in their results was a series of projects in the West Midlands undertaken and reported by Chris Dyer.[84] These illustrated two things pre-eminently: firstly, how dynamic and adaptable dispersed settlement might characteristically be, its elements changing location within a given topographical framework; secondly, by what means, combining many forms of fieldwork but especially requiring good contemporary documentation, one might successfully approach this character of settlement. An ambitious project in advance of the new Roadford reservoir in Devon saw these new agendas invoked

in a rescue situation, but outcomes did not match ambition. More traditional approaches on Bodmin Moor yielded more significant results.[85]

A very interesting phenomenon that began to attract useful attention was seasonal settlement of various forms. These related in their origin to transhumance exploiting specialist resources of various sorts – of woodland, downland, moor, fen, marsh and coast.[86] Most simply viewed as a contributory factor to the diverse forms of dispersed settlement, the significance of these seasonal sites is potentially more complex. Many were abandoned, to become archaeologically identifiable as sheep-cotes, shielings and the like; but others among these temporary 'non-settlements' could themselves became permanently occupied, sometimes as quite large villages (which, as with the coastal fishing bases studied by Harold Fox, appear alien within a traditional settlement pattern), on or near the earlier location. This is readily understood in a later medieval sequence as a significant change of character and function, where it would be a category mistake to equate the two, as if one was just a bigger and better-organised form of the other. It has yet to be explored, however, whether there is something to be learned here about the relationship, in some cases, between our early medieval settlement evidence, identified by fieldwalking and remote sensing, and later medieval village nucleations: namely a change between specialist temporary and permanent occupation.[87]

Despite excellent specific initiatives such as Dyer's, there was no overall grasp of the locales and varieties of dispersed settlement in the UK as a whole, and very little catalogued information in the public domain on which to plan conservation or protection agendas. The absence of such a framework even affected exceptional investigative opportunities such as that afforded by the development of the new city of Milton Keynes in rural Buckinghamshire; at worst, it caused misunderstanding about the various forms of dispersed settlement affected and its misconstruing as nucleated.[88]

A remedy, sponsored by English Heritage, was sought by an achievable top-down approach of characterising historic settlement forms countrywide, using the earliest reliable and consistent mapping available, namely the early to mid-nineteenth-century Ordnance Survey coverage, rather than the alternative option of waiting on the accumulation of specific studies to create any sort of overall picture. The result was the Roberts and Wrathmell *Atlas of Rural Settlement in England*, and an associated volume of discussion.[89] Alternative bottom-up approaches were subsequently implemented in Scotland (the Medieval or Later Rural Settlement (MoLRS) initiative) and Wales, in both cases conceived principally as exercises in cataloguing abandoned and predominantly dispersed rural settlement for the first time.[90] The Irish Discovery Programme tackled medieval settlement in the Republic in a more traditional, problem-oriented manner by looking thematically at English peasant settlement in Anglo-Norman manors of the Pale and contrasting the forms of Gaelic settlement in other areas.[91] The short-term effect of the English *Atlas* might have been to grapple with the lack of conventional medieval settlement data in many areas, in contrast to the plethora in what became identified as England's Central Province of settlement, and to encourage other conservation strategies than the protection of identifiable earthworks. But its usefulness was far wider and research-oriented – in explanation, in framing questions and in the stimulation of ideas.[92] Perhaps most importantly it promoted the proposition – inviting investigation and explanation – that observed patterning of settlement forms in identifiable regions, sub-regions and local zones has a cultural basis, sometimes of great antiquity. This contrasted with a basis in soil type and aspect, together determining farming practices, as has alternatively been advocated by Tom Williamson.[93]

A complementary initiative by English Heritage during the last decade of the twentieth and first of the twenty-first century was 'Historic Landscape Characterisation', designed to identify patterning of historic land-use county-by-county and region-by-region.[94] Principally developed as a tool to support practical planning and conservation initiatives, its relevance to traditional settlement studies was perhaps not obvious; but in capable hands there were strong signs of its research potential.[95] Used intelligently, the methodology was employed in East Anglia, away from the open, communal field systems of the Central Province and their fossilised ridge-and-furrow furlongs, to identify locally characteristic field systems, and alongside them bundles of other characteristics – greens, commons and woodlands, road patterns, resource exploitation and rural industry – that sat

not only with distinctive settlement forms but also distinctive building types.[96] Perhaps other factors will prove to correlate: even the incidence of ecclesiastical provision and its scale and formal development.

This (in 2010) is as yet scantly explored territory, but offers the prospect of identifying interdependencies of settlement, land use and resource exploitation approaching Taylor's call, long ago, for 'total archaeology', rich in significant connections rather than mere accumulation of data.[97]

New values and changing perspectives: 'a normal component of all settlement history'

The study of rural settlement has indeed always been interdisciplinary. There was plenty of evidence for that continuing multi-facetted nature through this recent period. The study remained a meeting point for history, geography and archaeology, of course, and benefited from the active commitment and lively contribution of eminent scholars in those disciplines, transforming recorded detail into an accessible wider picture and significance.[98] The morphology of settlements – M. R. G. Conzen's proposition that settlement is the 'geographical record of its own evolution' – continued to attract study, and to suggest, notably through Brian Roberts's investigations, that deliberate planning of settlements was commonplace and might have common origins and European ramifications.[99] Pottery studies, long relied on for dating excavated occupation sequences, with secure local and regional type series coming to be established in all parts of the country – typically on the basis of complex, well-stratified urban contexts – have come to pay more attention to the actual uses of the vessels represented and the information they may give about everyday peasant life and trade networks.[100] The same shift of emphasis applied, too, to metalwork and other finds, with the successful Portable Antiquities Scheme bringing to light significant quantities of medieval rural material after its inception in 1997.[101]

Our understanding of the quality of peasant buildings on the basis of excavated evidence and associated finds was strikingly revised by Stuart Wrathmell's reassessment of the structures at Wharram Percy, which he demonstrated were substantial cruck buildings – long-lived and carefully repaired, rather than flimsy and frequently replaced (Figures 2.8

Figure 2.8. Wharram Percy, North Yorkshire: House 6 under excavation 1962. The group stands within the longhouse whose side wall (running down the centre), flimsy and irregular, misled a generation of archaeologists into believing these were short-lived buildings. (Photo: Brenda Rose, reproduced by kind permission of Paul Stamper)

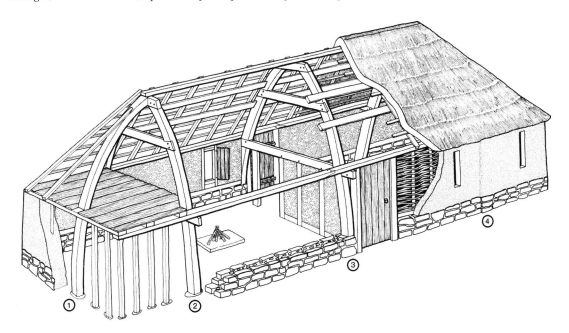

Figure 2.9. Wharram Percy, North Yorkshire. Stuart Wrathmell's 1989 reinterpretation of Wharram-type longhouses as substantial and long-lived cruck buildings. The chalk walls, spanning bay to bay, have no structural function and can easily be rebuilt on a piecemeal basis. (Drawing by Chris Philo, reproduced courtesy of Wharram Research Project)

and 2.9).[102] Significantly, this revision brought the excavated evidence much closer to the building traditions of surviving vernacular structures, whose study has continued vigorously in its own right.[103] There has also been a growing interest in assessing this material evidence in nuanced and theoretical ways in order better to understand the quality and experience of peasant culture.[104] Still perhaps underdeveloped, this approach points to a further direction in which studies may be expected to grow and to draw fresh insights from what are now quite large archaeological data-sets, and to link up with themes of power and community and individualism that have long interested historians.[105] The POMLAS ('Perceptions of Medieval Landscape and Settlement') seminar series in 2008, promoted by the MSRG, sought similar new avenues of thought about the mentality and culture that lay behind the forms and histories of medieval settlements.[106] In an approach with wider applicability, Roberta Gilchrist's subtle discussion of popular beliefs as revealed in medieval burial practices pursued another aspect of these issues through a large body of data, much of it from excavation of monastic cemeteries, that had not been exploited in this way, identifying meaning in objects and their specific deposition.[107] Similarly, original work came forward on the minor features of the medieval landscape – such as wayside crosses, points of transition from one cultivation zone to another, and pre-medieval remains – which were the everyday experience of peasants' lives and the reference points for communal memory.[108]

Direct contact with the population of rural settlement through excavation of graveyard populations on any significant scale has generally been rare – except at Wharram Percy. Publication of the results of studying that large group, numbering nearly 700 individuals and amounting (as is estimated) to somewhere between a third and a half of the total buried at Wharram, has been a major landmark, therefore, not only allowing a direct appreciation of the health and diet of a remote rural community but also enabling comparisons with better-studied medieval urban communities.[109] Some effective insights from environmental evidence have resulted from more systematic and informed sampling, better correlations of different sources – soils, animal bone, pollen/seeds/macro- and micro-flora, etc. – and a

sharper focus on the objective of understanding a distinctive local economy and environment, often through periods of change. Favourable conditions at West Cotton within the Raunds study area enabled especially informative results of the consequences of flooding and alluviation.[110] A feature of fieldwalking studies was a renewed evaluation of manuring scatters, often reckoned mere 'background', and their value in understanding arable farming practices.[111]

There has also been a notable revival of interest in the relevance of place-names to settlement history, after a protracted period when that technical and specialist branch of scholarship rather followed its own agendas and, despite many efforts, deployed modes of thinking that seemed to run in parallel with archaeological and historical work, as opposed to connecting with them.[112] Notably, the large areas covered by the Whittlewood Project allowed specialist study of place- and field-names to form an integral component of the enterprise; and a further AHRC-funded seminar series in 2009 – 'Sense of Place in Anglo-Saxon England' (SPASE) – built productively on that experience.[113] Study of the church as a key focus of rural communities has been an early and persistent feature of settlement studies, led by excavation and recording of St Martin's church at Wharram. Publication of the results of this in 1987 produced a complex sequence of growth and decline that has stood, despite some puzzling aspects, as a paradigm for church and settlement studies.[114] Excavation of the lost church at Raunds Furnell in the context of the creation of a manorial curia and peasant properties in that sector of the larger medieval village provided an equally important exemplar of the link between settlement and church.[115] Much influenced by that, and wishing to test easy assumptions about the ubiquitous link of lordship with church foundation and patronage, a study of eleventh-century building in Lincolnshire used simple morphological analysis of village forms to categorise church locations. By revealing several alternatives to an intimate proximity of church and seat of lordship, including foundation on public space, the study opened up for settlement studies a wider range of different characteristic relationships between church and settlement (and, by inference, its community) than had perhaps been envisaged hitherto.[116]

This was a period of large-scale projects. Just as

Wharram had developed in variety and complexity of activity and aspiration over a period of 40 years until fieldwork finished in 1990, and had brought maturity to settlement studies thereby,[117] new projects sought to deploy multi-disciplinary approaches and to engage not only large numbers of students but (more importantly) local communities in the study of their own locale. The simple technique of test-pitting within living settlements, deployed within the Shapwick and Whittlewood projects, and the organisation of so-called 'Big Digs' combined an effective methodology with direct public participation in the process and experience of its results. As an approach it was further developed for educational and community involvement by Carenza Lewis.[118] Millennium (and later) study projects by rural communities, often supported by Heritage Lottery Fund grants which required professional guidance and published results, reinvigorated an old tradition of local history that had rather faltered with the widespread retreat, since the later 1980s, from adult education teaching.

In what was commonly characterised as 'a landscape approach', most research projects extended their scope to at least a whole parish, thereby ensuring a proper attention to a settlement's context and interrelationship with its neighbours. The Whittlewood Project encompassed 12 parishes, explicitly seeking a scale lying between local and national that might purposefully address the questions it set itself; and it was notably successful in that objective. A recent study of the Rockingham Forest area of Northamptonshire, extending to over 570 km², offers a similarly ambitious and stimulating approach, combining archive research and field survey to great effect through the medium of Geographical Information Systems (GIS).[119] It reflected, too, a nationwide development of local databases from Sites and Monuments Records (SMRs) to Historic Environment Records (HERs), where information on archaeological sites and historic buildings was typically integrated with other spatial information about land-use. Held in a common GIS, data became susceptible to sophisticated manipulation and interpretation.

All these large projects have produced very sizeable quantities of data, these of especial value since the studies addressed parts of the country or topographical zones – like Somerset and the Severn marshes – where limited detailed work had taken place previously.[120] Typically of the way such projects engage with the *longue durée* of settlement, reported results of the Raunds Project have included substantial accounts of a Roman villa and of major prehistoric as well as earlier medieval monuments.[121]

The question of project scale in providing an effective link between bottom-up investigative studies and the national or regional landscape and settlement characterisation work described above is one that no doubt merits more attention and experiment. Useful potential probably lies in the final publication of even long-delayed results, where the original fieldwork was conceived in a wholly earlier mind-set, as well as in new work. Publication of Guy Beresford's 1973 excavations at Caldecote in Hertfordshire hints at this.[122] Yet to exploit that potential would have required not only attention to quite traditional opportunities to integrate important excavated results with excellent historical documentation, which were missed,[123] but also an awareness of modern thinking about settlement patterning and landscape characterisation. Indeed, part of this site's special potential lay in its situation within what the Roberts and Wrathmell *Atlas* identifies as the boundary zone between the Central and South-Eastern provinces and in an area of settlement 'anomalies'.[124] Such boundary locations, as Roberts has asserted, offer special opportunities for enhancing understanding of historic change in settlement patterns.

Opportunities, taken or lost, nevertheless illustrate the vigour and continuing development of medieval settlement studies. A number of reviews, such as that undertaken by the MSRG, underscored the point, indicating both an impressive range and diversity of work done in the last decade,[125] and outlining many challenges and opportunities to pursue issues of wide relevance that can only be addressed through the combination of approaches that medieval settlement studies in Britain have nurtured.[126] The deserted medieval village that was once, rather narrowly, the principal focus of research has become, in Chris Taylor's telling phrase, 'a normal component of all settlement history'.[127]

With the direction taken by settlement studies in the last 30 years, it is now perhaps difficult to believe that any substantial study project on medieval settlement would not seek to embrace a landscape approach or display a lively awareness of the varieties of patterns of settlement to be encountered and the possibility that their form results from dynamic change. Size of undertaking, however, does not offer the only way forward. Much of interest and value has been achieved by community involvement, and the challenge here is always perhaps to demonstrate the significance of data gathered. Since it is a meeting-place of disciplines, too, the range of specialist work – often by individuals – that may afford contributions relevant to settlement research is large. Many large-scale projects themselves, though producing admirable bodies of information and richly textured results, do not simply by virtue of their size amount to landscape studies. A few have plausibly made that leap to explore the character of their chosen landscape, to view local settlements as an integral part of that, and to encompass contemporary perception

and activity there. We may recall that the European Landscape Convention – commonly known as the Florence Convention, to which the UK became a signatory in 2007 – adopts a formal definition of 'landscape' that sees it as an entity that is *perceived by people*, as opposed to 'land', which is about physical form and material objects.[128] Settlement studies still too often stop at describing the latter. Addressing the issues implied by approaches where perception and performance or practice are key concepts in how we gain understanding from our evidence is a prospect that still lies largely ahead, though David Austin, writing about Barnard Castle (Durham) and its estate, has provided an example that may prove very influential.[129] Success in this will mark a further stage of maturity for a subject that has already developed out of all recognition in the course of two scholarly generations since the 1950s.

Notes

1. Seebohm 1883, maps 1–5.
2. Maitland 1897, 32–47.
3. Gray 1915.
4. Beresford and Hurst 1971, 49–50.
5. Beresford and Hurst 1971, 80–82; St Clair Baddeley 1910.
6. Douglas 1927; Smith 1943; Postan 1937.
7. Gras and Gras 1930; Orwin and Orwin 1938.
8. Darby 1936, 189–213, 230–256.
9. Bruce-Mitford 1940.
10. Fox 1939.
11. Jope and Threlfall 1958; Bruce-Mitford 1940.
12. Taylor 2005, recalling the powerful influence of adult education.
13. Dyer and Jones 2010, xvii.
14. Beresford 1954a and 1986.
15. Hurst 1986.
16. Allison *et al.* 1965; 1966.
17. Beresford and Hurst 1971; Beresford *et al.* 1980.
18. Rahtz 1959; Wacher 1963–64.
19. Jarrett and Wrathmell 1977; Mynard and Zeepvat 1991; Beresford 2009.
20. E.g. Dudley and Minter 1962–63; Thomas and Davies 1970–72; Barker 1966; Addyman *et al.* 1966.
21. Brewster and Hayfield 1988; Wacher 1966.
22. Rahtz 2001, 68.
23. Beresford 1975, 13–18.
24. Andrews and Milne 1979, 139.
25. Beresford 1975, 19–31; 2009: 48–50, 81–89.
26. Beresford and Hurst 1971, 83–115.
27. Andrews and Milne 1979, 26–73.
28. Beresford 1975.
29. Holden 1963, 85–94; Beresford 1979.
30. Holden 1963, 81.
31. Rahtz 1976.
32. Addyman 1965.
33. Austin 1985a.
34. Hurst and Hurst 1967.
35. Hurst and Hurst 1969; Taylor 1974b, 63.
36. Jarrett and Wrathmell 1977; Hurst and Hurst 1964, 94–95.
37. Rahtz 1969b, 98–103.
38. Allerston 1970; Roberts 1972; Sheppard 1974.
39. Platt 1978, 37–38.
40. Beresford 1975, 9; Taylor 1977.
41. Steane and Bryant 1975, 44–48.
42. Wade-Martins 1980.
43. Jones 1976.
44. Hilton and Rahtz 1966, 74–82.
45. Taylor 1967.
46. Linehan 1966.
47. Le Patourel 1973; Aberg 1978b.
48. Platt 1969; Moorhouse 1989.
49. Darby 1977.

50. Darby 1973.
51. Baker and Butlin 1973; Rowley 1981.
52. Thorpe 1962; 1965; Roberts 1968; Aston and Rowley 1974; Bond 1974.
53. Finberg 1955.
54. Everitt 1977.
55. Kerridge 1955; Hilton 1957.
56. Postan 1972, 115–116.
57. Platt 1978.
58. Hilton 1966.
59. Wharram I: see Hurst 1979. E.g. Raunds (Northants.), Cadman 1983; Goltho (Lincs.), Beresford 1987 completing the account of 1975; West Whelpington (Northumberland), Evans and Jarrett 1987, Evans *et al.* 1988; Thrislington (Durham), Austin 1989a.
60. Aston 1985.
61. Everson 1988.
62. Austin *et al.* 1980; 1985a; Austin 1989a; Austin and Walker 1985.
63. www.landscapestudies.com; Faull and Moorhouse 1981.
64. E.g. Cosgrove and Daniels 1988; Wylie 2007; Johnson 2007. But see, exceptionally, Austin 1985b.
65. E.g. Taylor 1983; Everson 1986; Everson *et al.* 1991.
66. Austin 1976; 1989a; compare Liddle 1994.
67. Beresford and Hurst 1990, 68–84; Wharram V: see Hayfield 1987.
68. Baugh 1998; Everson and Wilson-North 1993.
69. Bewley 1995; Everson 2000.
70. Brown and Taylor 1989. See also Brown and Taylor 1991; Taylor 1995a.
71. Taylor 1970, 108, Figs 6 and 15, Plate 17.
72. Bowen 1961; Taylor 1974b.
73. Taylor 1977; 1978; 1981; 1982.
74. Foard 1978; RCHME 1981, xxxviii–xlvi. See also Brown and Foard 1998.
75. Roberts and Wrathmell 2002, figs 1.6, 3.12, 7.4; Parry 2006.
76. Lewis *et al.* 1997.
77. Hall 1995; Hall 2001b.
78. Powlesland 2003.
79. Everson and Stocker 1999.
80. Brown and Foard 1998; Hamerow 1991; 2002.
81. Jones and Page 2006, 222–243.
82. Taylor 1981; Fox 1983b.
83. Le Patourel 1986.
84. Dyer 1990; 1991.
85. See Griffith 1988, 124–127 (Roadford); Johnson and Rose 1994 (Bodmin).
86. Fox 1989b; Dyer 1995; Fox 1996.
87. Everson and Stocker in Wharram XIII: see Wrathmell (ed.) forthcoming.
88. Croft and Mynard 1993; Everson 1995.
89. Roberts, Stocker and Wrathmell 1993; Roberts and Wrathmell 1995; 2000; 2002.
90. Scotland – Hingley 1993; Govan 2003. Wales – Roberts 2006a.
91. O'Connor 1998.
92. Lewis 2006.
93. Williamson 1998a.
94. Fairclough 1999.
95. Turner 2006a; 2006b. See the group of articles in *Landscapes* 8.2 (2007).
96. Hall 1995; 2001b; Martin and Satchell 2008.
97. Taylor 1974c.
98. E.g. Dyer 1989; Faith 1997; Roberts 1987; 1996; Taylor 1983; Williamson. 2003.
99. Roberts 1982; 1990; 2008.
100. Mellor 1994; Moorhouse 1986.
101. Hinton 2010 for a recent review; http://finds.org.uk/.
102. Wharram VI: see Wrathmell 1989, and contrast Hurst 1965.
103. See the activities and publications of the Vernacular Architecture Group, http://wwww.vag.org.uk, and its long-established journal, *Vernacular Architecture*; Gardiner 2000.
104. Johnson 1993; 2010; Smith 2009; 2010.
105. Dyer 1985; Harvey 1989.
106. Dyer 2007b; http://www.britarch.ac.uk/msrg/pomlashome.htm.
107. Gilchrist 2008; see Gilchrist and Sloane 2005.
108. Whyte 2009. See also Reynolds 2009 for other approaches to these issues.
109. Wharram XI: see Mays *et al.* 2007.
110. Chapman 2010.
111. Jones 2004.
112. Gelling 1978; 1984; Gelling and Cole 2000 give access to much of that work. See Chapter 3.
113. Jones and Page 2006; www.spase.org.uk.
114. Wharram III: see Bell and Beresford 1987; but see the revised understanding of phasing and details by Stocker in Wharram XIII: Wrathmell (ed.) forthcoming, Chapter 19.
115. Boddington 1996.
116. Stocker and Everson 2006.
117. Beresford and Hurst 1991 is good on the evolution of that project; Wharram I–XIII: see list following the Notes, below.
118. Jones and Page 2006: especially figures 60, 62, 74, 75; Gerrard with Aston 2007; Lewis 2007. See Chapter 3.
119. Foard *et al.* 2009.
120. Gerrard with Aston 2007; Rippon 2006.
121. Neal 1989; Parry 2006; Hardy and Healy 2007;

Audouy and Chapman 2008; Chapman 2010.

122. Beresford 2009.
123. Dyer 2009.
124. Roberts and Wrathmell 2000; Roberts and Wrathmell 2003, 86–89.
125. Gardiner 2006a; see also Gerrard 2003, 138–142.
126. Gerrard 2009; Gilchrist and Reynolds 2009. MSRG itself has defined and periodically redefined agendas for future work in the field. MSRG 1996, most

recently revised October 2007; MSRG website at http://www.britarch.ac.uk/msrg. For an external view on the history and preoccupations of British settlement studies, see Watteaux 2009.
127. Taylor 2010, 6.
128. Fairclough 2006; http://www.coe.int/t/dg4/cultureheritage/heritage/landscape/; ESF-COST 2010.
129. Austin 2007.

Wharram: A Study of the Settlement on the Yorkshire Wolds
Major publications listing

Wharram I
Hurst, J. 1979. *Domestic Settlement I: Areas 10 and 6*, Society for Medieval Archaeology Monograph 8.

Wharram II
Rahtz, P. and Watts, L. 1983. *Wharram Percy: The Memorial Stones of the Churchyard*, York University Archaeological Publications 1.

Wharram III
Bell, R. D. and Beresford, M. 1987. *Wharram Percy: The Church of St Martin*, Society for Medieval Archaeology Monograph 11.

Wharram IV
Rahtz, P., Hayfield, C. and Bateman, J. 1986. *Two Roman Villas at Wharram Percy*, York University Archaeological Publications 2.

Wharram V
Hayfield, C. 1987. *An Archaeological Survey of the Parish of Wharram Percy, East Yorkshire. 1. The Evolution of the Roman Landscape*, BAR British Series 172.

Wharram VI
Wrathmell, S. 1989. *Domestic Settlement 2: Medieval Peasant Farmsteads*, York University Archaeological Publications 8.

Wharram VII
Milne, G. and Richards, J. 1992. *Two Anglo-Saxon Buildings and Associated Finds*, York University Archaeological Publications 9.

Wharram VIII
Stamper, P. and Croft, R. A. 2000. *The South Manor Area*, York University Archaeological Publications 10.

Wharram IX
Rahtz, P. and Watts, L. 2004. *The North Manor and North-west Enclosure*, York University Archaeological Publications 11.

Wharram X
Treen, C. and Atkin, M. 2005. *Water Resources and their Management*, York University Archaeological Publications 12.

Wharram XI
Mays, S., Harding, C. and Heighway, C. 2007. *The Churchyard*, York University Archaeological Publications 13.

Wharram XII
Harding, C., Marlow-Mann, E. and Wrathmell, S. 2010. *The Late- and Post-medieval Vicarage and Post-medieval Farmstead*, York University Archaeological Publications 14.

Wharram XIII
Wrathmell, S. (ed.) forthcoming. *A History of Wharram Percy and its Neighbours*, York University Archaeological Publications, 15.

CHAPTER 3

Methodological Approaches to Medieval Rural Settlements and Landscapes

Richard Jones and Della Hooke

Introduction

The study of rural settlements and landscapes has always lain at the heart of medieval archaeology in Britain. Indeed, from the very inception of the sub-discipline, and especially from the post-war period forwards, it has been the complex and still not fully resolved issues of village nucleation and open-field farming that have served in large part to frame the medieval archaeologist's research agenda.[1] If the recent charge that medieval archaeology has been slow to embrace archaeological theory is accepted, as it probably should be, then such perceived failures must be set against the major contribution that practitioners in this scholarly field have made to the advancement of methodology.[2] For as the focus of rural settlement and landscape research has shifted over the last 60 years, so those interested in developments within the English countryside during the Middle Ages have been forced to find new ways of retrieving reliable, robust and sufficient data upon which their analyses depend. The methods that they have championed and perfected now find much broader application in other temporal and geographical contexts. In respect to archaeological methodology, then, the contribution of medieval settlement and landscape study extends far beyond its immediate concerns.

To understand methodological innovation, we must begin by recognising how medieval settlement and landscape research has changed. This is outlined in more detail elsewhere in this volume, but here it may suffice to identify what might be considered the six principal shifts that have acted as the stimuli for changes in field and, one might add, archival practice. First is the transfer of interest away from the study of village failure, and the phenomenon of village desertion in particular, to that of village origins. Secondly, the rejection of the narrow study of nucleated villages to a more inclusive exploration of the full range of rural settlement types – villages, hamlets, farmsteads, castles, moated sites, hunting lodges and so on. This has led, thirdly, to an increased awareness of the need to understand medieval settlement beyond the champion arable zones of lowland England, in areas of woodland and marsh, for instance, or on the coast or in the uplands. Fourthly, as the regional loci for study have broadened out, so has interest in the wider landscape. Now settlements are rarely studied in isolation; rather they are viewed as integral to, but only part of, much larger landscapes, to be explored in tandem with their surrounding countryside. Fifthly, in recognition of the fact that failed villages may in some ways be an atypical settlement experience, the last two decades have witnessed a growing interest in the archaeology of surviving or living villages. Finally, there has been a general rejection of single-unit studies, whether centred on a village, a parish, a manor or an estate, in favour of studies of larger areas that have allowed individual settlement and landscape histories to be compared and contrasted.

Such changes, of course, have had important operational repercussions. The two key problems that they have posed to students of the medieval landscape are those of scale and access. As the areas of investigation have increased in size, so new methods have had to be sought that provide a means by which larger areas can be explored in both an intellectually and statistically valid manner. A balance has had to be found between sampling the wider landscape without losing the resolution and wealth of detail that small-scale studies offer. Related in many ways to scale is the issue of access: as the study of medieval rural settlements has moved into inhabited villages, so the opportunities to get at archaeological deposits have become more limited, buried as they are under occupied houses and gardens. Likewise, as the focus of research has moved from its core areas of central and south-eastern England, so investigators have had to face the problems of working in locales lacking pottery and, thus, crucial dating evidence for the early medieval period, as well as working in more pastoral areas in which recourse to techniques such as fieldwalking are denied. Such then have been the challenges set by the modern research agenda which have prompted the review of the methodologies deployed. How these challenges have been met is no better exemplified than by the different approaches that have been taken to the excavation of rural settlements.

Medieval rural settlement: archaeological approaches

In the early 1950s, all large-scale archaeological excavations in Britain used the grid or box system as developed by Pitt-Rivers and popularised by Sir Mortimer Wheeler. This method sacrificed the recovery of evidence in plan for the preservation of wide baulks in which the vertical record was preserved. It was rare, then, that full building footprints were ever fully exposed. This was the technique initially used at Wharram Percy (North Yorkshire). Earlier village excavations, such as those undertaken as far afield as Bineham (Somerset), Balsdean (Sussex), Markshall (Norfolk), Olney (Northamptonshire), Flixton, Staxton (both North Yorks.) and Wauldby (Yorkshire East Riding), and Garmondsway (Durham), tended to be restricted to small trenches, which often meant that those archaeological deposits that were encountered were extremely difficult to interpret.[3] In 1953, however, following the example set by Axel Steenberg on the

site of Store Valby in Denmark, the excavators at Wharram Percy trialled open-area excavation for the first time in England. In lieu of baulks, all finds were given three-dimensional coordinates to preserve their stratigraphic relationships, enabling complete floor plans of peasant buildings to be exposed.[4] Although the method proved successful, it took time for it to be universally accepted and it was not until the mid-1960s that it became customary for other rural settlements, such as Grenstein (Norfolk) and South Witham (Lincolnshire), to be treated in the same way.[5]

Open-area excavation lends itself particularly to deserted village sites, where access to the archaeology is unencumbered by modern development and where the lack of subsequent activity ensures that the relevant medieval deposits tend to lie not far below the modern ground surface. In some cases, such as at West Stow (Suffolk),[6] West Heslerton (North Yorks.),[7] Goltho (Lincolnshire)[8] and Great Linford (Buckinghamshire),[9] the areas that have been opened are impressive. But, to date, no British deserted village has been subject to total excavation, or indeed to investigation on the scale of continental sites such as Vorbasse (Jutland) or Feddersen Wierde (Lower Saxony).[10] Thus, despite 40 years of excavation at Wharram Percy, only a tiny proportion of the village has been excavated.

Within living villages, the opportunities for open-excavation are far more limited. But, where they have presented themselves, these have occasionally been taken. Excavations in north Raunds (Northamptonshire) is one case in point, the results demonstrating just how vital the investigation of large spaces is in tracing settlement development over the long term.[11] And excavations just beyond them, such as those at Yarnton and Cassington (Oxfordshire), have been equally informative.[12] But in the last two decades, with changing economic and academic priorities, the sampling of the medieval deposits that lie under these places has largely consisted of small-scale intervention often undertaken in advance of building development. The introduction of planning policy guidance in 1990 (PPG 16), which established the framework for developer funding of archaeology, has unquestionably led to the recording of evidence vital to understanding medieval rural settlement growth and decline. Unfortunately, reports of findings often lie unpublished, remaining as so-called 'grey literature' lodged in county Historic Environment Records or HERs (previously Sites and Monuments Records – SMRs). Short notices appear in the annual round-up included in *Medieval Settlement Research*, the journal and annual report of the Medieval Settlement Research Group, or in online resources of major journals such as *Medieval Archaeology*. But little effort has been devoted to developing fuller accounts of particular settlement histories through the combination of these small investigations.

This depressing picture of the fragmentation of archaeological enquiry within rural settlement cores over recent years has been balanced by the development of the technique of test pitting. First used to effect in the study of Somerset village of Shapwick,[13] the method was extensively used during the Whittlewood Project (Buckinghamshire/Northamptonshire) where fourteen medieval rural settlements were investigated in this way.[14] Test pitting is also the principal research method currently being used in the Currently Occupied Rural Settlements (CORS) project (Norfolk/Cambridgeshire) (see Lewis, Appendix to this volume).[15] In essence, test pitting seeks to solve the problem of accessing below-ground archaeology where space and opportunities are limited. By sinking small 1 × 1 m holes across the occupied modern village the main aim is to recover datable material culture, particularly pottery, rather than expose *in situ* features. Such keyhole surgery permits the investigation of areas that would otherwise be inaccessible, particularly private gardens. When pottery finds of different periods are plotted and their relative densities within individual test pits considered, a dynamic model can be created of the history of the settlement: the location and extent of the earliest phases of the settlement can be mapped, particularly in regions where the early medieval pottery sequence is complete (the technique has obvious limitations in those that were largely aceramic in the early medieval period); later finds potentially show the direction and pace of settlement growth. Similarly, the absence of evidence for habitation in peripheral test pits allows the full extent of occupation to be defined at any given period. Drop-off of material culture might equally be taken as a sign of settlement

contraction or desertion. There are two requirements that are essential to the success of this method: the first is the number of test pits excavated, with a minimum of *c.* 20 probably required for a small village, although the greater the number the greater the certainty that the patterns that are being detected are representative of the settlement as a whole. For instance, at Shapwick, a regular nucleated village, 81 test pits were sunk, while at Silverstone (Northamptonshire), a polyfocal settlement extending over a much larger area than Shapwick, 119 test pits were excavated.[16] The second requirement is their distribution: test pits should be spread evenly across the settlement rather than concentrated in areas that carry the highest archaeological potential, since in the analysis it is the unproductive test pits as well as the productive ones that help to define the spatial and chronological parameters of medieval occupation.

Suffice to say, profound understanding of a particular settlement's history is best sought when these three scales of investigation can be brought together, for all have their utility and limitations. Test pitting offers a means of producing general spatial and temporal models, effectively a background framework across the whole of any given village. Areas that can be investigated in this way are not dictated by access (where there is open space) or where modern development is to take place, but rather can be chosen to address particular research questions. But detail is rarely forthcoming; it is often very difficult to be precise about the character of occupation in any given area in terms of form, function, and status based on the limited recovery of material culture or exposure of occupation levels. Here we remain reliant upon open-area excavation, but of course this is only possible where gaps remain within the modern settlement plan. What test pits do allow, however, is a means by which the information from open-area excavations and developer-led interventions can be assessed within the wider context of the settlement as a whole. Value judgements can therefore be made about the typical or atypical nature of the evidence recovered in all three contexts.

Excavation may offer the only means by which chronology can be established, but is only one of a suite of techniques now deployed to reconstruct settlement plans themselves. In terms of the below-ground evidence, geophysical survey clearly plays an important part, although in its application on medieval rural sites few methodological innovations have been made. Resistivity, magnetometry, magnetic susceptibility and ground-penetrating radar have all proved useful in identifying buried features or signs of medieval activity.[17] It is impossible to generalise on which techniques to apply, when and where, for their efficacy is wholly dependent upon the nature of the archaeology itself, the depth to which it is buried, local geologies, ground conditions (wet or dry), modern land use, and so forth. As with excavation, it has often been where a range of surveys have been undertaken that the results have been most revealing. Far more exciting for medieval settlement study, however, are advances made in soil analysis: the association of high levels of phosphorus with human and livestock activity has long been recognised, but soil analysis is now commonly extended to look at the levels of heavy metals such as lead, copper, zinc, cadmium, nickel, cobalt and chromium which might be deposited through everyday living, industrial activities, waste disposal or manuring. Those carrying out research on rural sites have been quick to identify the potential of wider soil analysis, having been employed to great effect within the fields of Shapwick,[18] where it helped locate the extent of abandoned outlying elements of the medieval settlement pattern, and at Puxton (Somerset), where it helped establish the former area occupied by the village.[19]

Above ground, the evidence for medieval settlement can take multiple forms, of which we might identify the perpetuation of plot boundaries, settlement earthworks and standing buildings. The characterisation of medieval settlement morphology often begins with a map. Where early maps do not exist, the basic starting points for analysis are often first edition Ordnance Survey (OS) maps of the late nineteenth century. Standardised in their conventions and covering the whole of the country, they offer the opportunity to compare and contrast village and hamlet layouts across regions. Such maps certainly offer a means of assessing relative levels of nucleation and dispersion in any given locality.[20] And they also provide the necessary detail for the analysis of individual places and their categorisation into larger groups based on plan. Regularly encountered terms such as 'regular grid plans', 'regular radial plans',

'rows', 'agglomerations' and 'polyfocal settlement' have been used by historical geographers from the late 1970s,[21] to be joined more recently by descriptors such as 'large nucleated cluster', 'regular row nucleated cluster', 'common-edge dispersed settlement', and 'interrupted row dispersed settlement'[22], or 'complex multiple row' and 'irregular agglomerated plan with(out) green'.[23] What is meant by these terms with regard to the type of settlement that might be found on the ground is often difficult to establish, since all contain a degree of subjectivity. Nevertheless, they are a vital part of unpicking the complexities of rural settlement morphology.

How useful this terminology really is as a means of describing the original layout of these places can be questioned; for in some places it can be demonstrated that villages underwent episodes of extensive replanning which, in the most extreme instances, could result in the wholesale realignment of roads, trackways and messuage boundaries, or the shifting of church and manor house.[24] The issue of pre-nineteenth-century settlement shift is particularly acute, for instance, in East Anglia. Elsewhere, however, stability of form can be demonstrated from the OS maps. Metrical analysis of plot frontages as they appear at this late date often reveal that they were based on multiples or fractions of the earlier medieval perch, generally measured at 16 ½ feet but with local variations (a fact often obscured from students who have grown up with metric measurements). The identification of variations in plot size can potentially lead to the identification of particular blocks or settlement units that help to unravel the complexities of its development.[25] Confidence in the interpretation is raised, of course, wherever earlier maps can be compared to the OS map and be shown to support the findings. Indeed, retrospective cartographic analysis, now greatly aided by Geographic Information Systems (GIS) which allow maps of different ages to be overlain, has become a standard tool in the analysis of medieval rural settlement.[26]

The surveying of village earthworks has clearly benefited from technological improvements over the decades. Tape measurements using offsets and trilateration, as well as plane tables, have been superseded first by theodolites and dumpy levels, and more recently by Electronic Distance Measurers (EDMs) and Total Stations.[27] Potentially these offer greater precision (± 5 mm accuracy) in three dimensions but, in reality, establishing precise breaks of slope, on often 'soft' and degraded earthworks is a matter than only an experienced eye can decide. Computer Aided Design (CAD) software and other graphics packages can aid the plotting of survey results, but many would argue that traditional Royal Commission hachure plans (now computer generated, then hand-finished) remain peerless in their accuracy and aesthetic qualities.[28] Earthwork survey is not simply a process of recording, rather it should be thought of more as a process of interrogation and interpretation. The surveyor's art is to remove the extraneous to reveal the significant; for it is by so doing that the critical relationships between features are brought to light, allowing the phases of development on a particular site to be disaggregated. Absolute dating, of course, still requires excavation. Total surface plotting, as can be achieved using Global Plotting Systems (GPS), and high-resolution elevation data collected by Light Detection and Ranging survey (LiDAR) are beginning to find their application in the study of medieval settlements and landscapes. However, these also fail to differentiate between archaeological and 'natural' features and do not necessarily lead directly to greater comprehension of the earthworks identified (but see below for the use of LiDAR in plotting earthworks within woodland).

Of the standing buildings of the medieval period, it is often only the church that survives in many places. Close examination of these structures continues to pay dividends, revealing subtleties and complexities in their development that have previously gone unnoticed. They remain extremely useful socio-economic and demographic indicators that *potentially* help to chart settlement growth (the size of the nave increasing to accommodate greater numbers of people, the addition of aisles and so forth), the relative wealth of communities at different periods (e.g. new fenestration, show fronts, roof heightening and the addition of clerestories), and the levels of patronage and lordly investment (e.g. the flamboyance of chancels, sepulchral monuments). However, in recent years (perhaps beginning with criticism of the lack of emphasis on changing religious practice in the interpretation of the expansion and contraction of the church at Wharram Percy), this emphasis has shifted towards an appreciation of these spaces in terms of their liturgical use:[29] for instance the movement of the high altar or the use of the West Tower within funereal rites.[30] Furthermore, how the church sits within the broader settlement plan, whether central or peripheral, coupled with the manorial curia or separate from it, has also received greater attention.

In terms of domestic buildings, the limitations of listing and classification based on exterior examination alone have been exposed through more thorough investigation of house interiors. This has revealed a level of medieval fabric survival that was previously unappreciated. The result has been that distribution maps of particular vernacular architectural styles have been in constant need of redrawing.[31] Cruck-framing, for instance, seen a decade ago as a predominantly western tradition, has now been extended across the Midlands and into the eastern counties. In addition to this, continued dendrochronological dating has demonstrated the survival of previously unknown twelfth- and thirteenth-century structures in both town and country, one of the finest examples of which is Fyfield Hall (Essex), dated to the late twelfth century. Perhaps the most fascinating insights to emerge in recent years from the study of these buildings has been the identification of surviving late-medieval smoked-blackened thatch, which not only points towards the open interior of these particular homes, but preserves evidence of the kinds of crops and weeds that were growing in the surrounding countryside.[32] It is here that the study of individual buildings grades into the wider appreciation of the medieval landscape and its reconstruction.

Medieval rural settlements and landscapes: place-name, charters and field-name evidence

Historical evidence for settlement studies begins in the early medieval period through the medium of place-names and charters. Since such names only begin to be recorded in the seventh century at the earliest and most are recorded much later,[33] we have little way of knowing the names given to settlements before this date, although a relatively small number of names appear to have had a British origin.

At present, there is only limited understanding of what specific place-name terms may indicate about the actual nature and form of settlement and in the documents names often refer to estates rather than to individual settlements. Even when certain habitative terms clearly referred to the settlements themselves, it has yet to be clarified what these may have implied in terms of size and morphology. Some habitative terms clearly indicate groups of houses, among them *tūn* and *cot* – the latter probably little more than a cluster of cottages – and many *worth*s must have been single farms,[34] while others terms appear to have been more closely related to function – such as the *wīc*s (one sense being a dairying establishment). Others reveal more about the nature of the surrounding countryside – names with *lēah*, *holt*, *graf*, etc., from various kinds of 'wood' – or related to the local topography, such as estates or settlements named after rivers or hills. It is believed that the latter form of name giving was one of the earliest styles practised, even continuing an earlier Roman method of naming places.[35] Neither were settlement names necessarily fixed for all time – a minority being perhaps indicative of a settlement type and function at a specific moment of time, with names changing for as yet unexplained reasons.

The mapping of place-names nevertheless helps to provide a framework for understanding the nature of the early medieval countryside. Concentrations of particular kinds of names may indicate regions that by then were largely cleared and probably intensively cultivated. These include the *tūn* names which often appear to have indicated the newly emerging villages as nucleation progressed. Topographical names also abound in such regions, especially for the centres of multiple estates. In contrast, names indicative of woodland are spread – if rather more thinly – over what were more heavily wooded marginal regions; here, too, might be found many of the isolated *worth* farmsteads. The mapping of names in this way, related to the local topography, rarely fails to give a relatively clear indication of early medieval land use.

By the later seventh century, many land transactions were beginning to be recorded in charters, especially when this involved ownership by the Church. Although these documents were specifically conveying rights over land they usually name the estate involved and, as time progresses, more and more are accompanied by clauses describing the landmarks to be found along the boundaries of the estate. Unfortunately this kind of evidence is not found for the whole of the country

but mainly survives for parts of the midlands and south. The majority of boundary clauses are roughly contemporary with the main document, although occasionally a boundary clause might be added at a later date, such as with the large estate of *Wican* in west Worcestershire, granted to the Church of Worcester in the mid-eighth century, which acquired a boundary clause that was probably added in the eleventh century.[36] A very few are forgeries but, as most of these were in fact drawn up within the early medieval period, they are still of use for understanding the landscape features then present.

Many of the landmarks noted in such clauses tend to be obvious natural features, such as a ridge or the end of a hill, a stream or a spring, or references to the vegetation of the locality, such as woods or even single trees;[37] others are man-made features considered suitable for marking the line of the boundary – roads, for instance, or more precisely located single objects such as stones. In general, the more precise a landmark was the better; the boundaries were probably described by local surveyors and could be examined in the field should disputes arise.[38] Most settlements of the period probably fell well within the boundaries of the estates and therefore find no mention in the clauses, but there are regions where settlements do appear rather more frequently than usual. These must surely indicate that at least some dispersed settlements were present in these regions in this period.

Perhaps surprisingly, such settlements appear in the charter boundaries for the Vale of Evesham in Worcestershire, which by medieval times was a region of nucleated settlements set within their fully fledged open fields.[39] Although the charters that refer to these landmarks are often late, and some are of dubious authenticity, they clearly indicate that minor settlements were still to be found here at the end of the early medieval period and that nucleation in this region was an on-going affair which was by then far from complete (Figure 3.1a). The settlements themselves are described in this area by the terms *cot*, *wīc* or *worth* (including *byrdingcwican* at Elmley Castle, *bunewyrþe* at Littleton, and *potintun* or *poticot* at Bengeworth).[40] Such settlements appear, however, more frequently in the charter bounds in the centre and north-east of the county, regions where nucleation was probably even more delayed and never so rigidly carried out (Figure 3.1b). These were regions with areas of heathland,

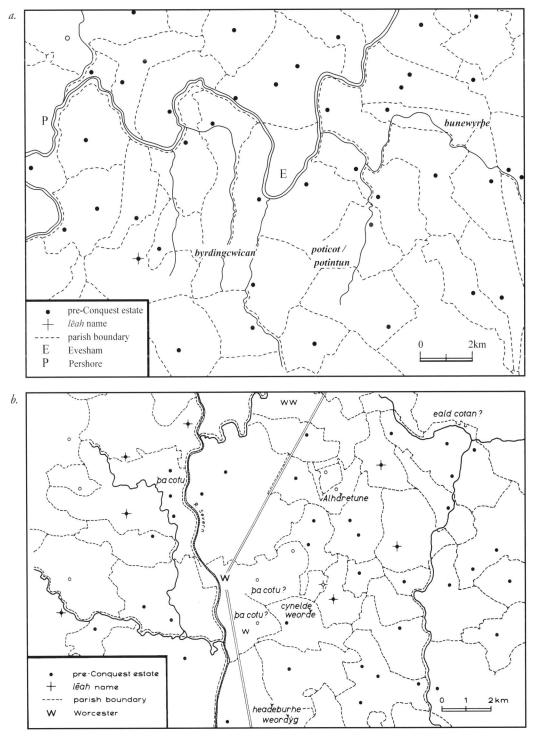

Figure 3.1. Boundary settlements recorded in Worcestershire charters. Pre-Conquest estates are also noted (with open circles indicating later recorded estate centres). a: the Evesham region; b: the Worcester region.

woodland and marshland still surviving in medieval times, characterised often by long-established single farms set within their own fields (here *worth* is more frequent). In Devon, occasional references to *worth* settlements (such as *burhgeardes worðig*, probably 'Burgheard's farmstead', below Hackpen Hill in Culmstock, or *ellewörðie* on the downs above Budleigh Salterton) again provide a clue to the dispersed nature of settlement that characterised much of the south-west. [41] Only the systematic plotting of landscape features across an entire county area can reveal such variations in landscape patterns. Another way in which charters might provide some indication of settlement distribution is through the size of the estates themselves: for instance, in Worcestershire they reveal the frequency of small townships that were recognised communities within the parishes around Worcester and elsewhere, while in Cornwall they indicate the small *tre, *tref* holdings, [42] often unrecorded in any other way at this date, that were being incorporated into the English-style administrative system in the later part of the period. [43]

Habitative names suggesting lost settlements occasionally survive as field-names on historical maps. Indeed, at Shapwick, in spite of extensive archaeological survey, such names remain the main source of evidence for several minor early medieval or medieval settlement sites. Across the country, many such names, especially where they are referred to by Old English habitative terms such a *cot, tūn, wīc, worth* or *bold*, are likely to indicate the location of 'lost' settlements; in areas that were virtually aceramic in the early medieval period this might be the only readily detectable source of evidence (in fact follow-up excavation confirmed occupation at two sites indicated by *cot* and *worth* field-names in southern Warwickshire), for the period prior to full nucleation. [44]

The utility of place-names and field-names as a tool for settlement and landscape reconstruction does not end with the Norman Conquest, since throughout the Middle Ages the named landscape of England was in perpetual evolution. The Anglo-Norman contribution to the place-name corpus may not have been great but it was nevertheless significant: terms such as *Laund,* 'a lawn', and *Park* point towards changes in the arrangement of the landscape to facilitate the hunting and management of deer and other animals

of the chase; names such as *Beaulieu* (Bewdley, Worcestershire), *Beauvoir* (Leicestershire) and *Malpas* (Cornwall) reflect contemporary qualitative appreciation (the two former) or detestation of particular places (the last); and manorial affixes, such as those of Kingston Bagpuize (Oxfordshire), Golborne Bellow (Cheshire) and Abington Pigotts (Cambridgeshire) – the majority of which were coined in the thirteenth and fourteenth centuries – reflect changing relationships between landowners and their manors, as well as acting as useful signposts for distant bureaucrats who sought to differentiate between places with similar names. And, as seen, field-names remained more conservative, often preserving distant memories of earlier land clearance as well as lost settlement.

Reconstructing the medieval landscape: the field evidence

Various techniques are now regularly used to provide a much broader vision of the medieval countryside beyond the villages, hamlets and farmsteads themselves. Of these, systematic fieldwalking has arguably been the most effective in producing new ideas. Modern fieldwalking methods owe much to those interested in the process of village formation and their desire to add greater precision to the chronology of open-field introduction. Foard's seminal paper published in 1978, which explored the usefulness of the technique for the identification of pre-nucleated village settlement and the problems of interpretation associated with this type of survey, set the methodological agenda. [45] Thirty years on, many thousands of hectares of modern ploughland surface have now been scanned for artefactual material across the country, with counties such as Norfolk and Northamptonshire leading the way. But no county can match the coverage now enjoyed by Leicestershire, where the establishment of a network of local groups working to a common system has resulted in the production of a vast quantity of data relevant to the medieval period.

Initial interest in the identification of 'sites' and the reconstruction of settlement patterns and densities has now given way to a more holistic approach to the evidence, with 'off-site' evidence now placed on a par with the 'on-site'. Likewise, many of the simple principles upon which interpretation were formerly based are now being questioned, some even going so far as to question fundamentally the validity of the technique.[46] The location of dense concentrations of pottery, presumably discarded at source, still tends to be viewed as the best evidence for lost settlement.[47] Confidence in such an interpretation rises when the assemblage can be shown to contain a greater range of pottery fabrics than the surrounding field scatters, and when this material is found in association with stone and ceramic building material and other cultural artefacts. Low levels of abrasion and fragmentation of sherds also point to deposition outside the plough zone. But it is often difficult to establish settlement edges with precision, as the high densities of pottery associated with settlement often grade into the highly manured fields (manure containing discarded pottery) that immediately surround them.[48] Further blurring of this division can also result from the practice of dumping domestic material beyond the settlement itself; in some instances, the removal of almost all material valued as manure and its spreading on to the fields leaves the settlement itself clean, and in these instances the identification of their location relies on seeing the gaps in the field scatters rather than concentrations.

In terms of land use, the presence or absence of pottery derivative of manuring with domestic waste and animal dung still remains useful. By mapping low-density ceramic scatters it is possible to suggest the area of cultivation at particular periods (the pottery is datable) and to chart the increase of ploughlands over the medieval centuries. Likewise, areas that fail to produce this evidence might be suggested as having remained beyond the arable zone, and here topographical and historical evidence might be brought to bear to establish whether such areas were used as pasture, woodland, meadow and the like. However, recent surveys have warned us to use this formula cautiously.[49] Peripheral fields and furlongs, despite being ploughed, might receive a fraction of the manure compared with those areas immediately outside the settlement; thus the related pottery evidence remains limited. Furthermore, many archaeologically invisible soil restoratives were used in addition to domestic detritus containing visible pottery, of which green manure (the ploughing back in of stubble, etc.), marling, sanding and burning

might be cited. The field evidence only points, then, to a minimum acreage under the plough, rather than a maximum, and this should be borne in mind when analysing such data.

Collected fieldwalking data represent the single largest national archaeological resource available for the study of medieval settlements and landscapes. Unfortunately, only a minute fraction has been fully published or properly archived and, consequently, its true potential remains untapped. The lack of a standardised field methodology and statistical presentation adds to this problem. Cross interrogating data from different surveys which have variously used grid or line walking, different transect intervals or stint lengths, is near impossible. Some data are recorded to broad periods ('early medieval', 'medieval', 'late medieval') whose chronological parameters are rarely defined; other material is recorded by fabric type. Furthermore, the interpretation of what was happening in the fields is often hindered by a lack of understanding of what was happening in the settlements (how much pottery was in circulation, how much remained in the village, how much was taken out to the fields, etc.).[50] Looking to the future, these issues demand attention, and their resolution will almost certainly generate much that will help to push medieval settlement and landscape studies forward.

The study of the medieval landscape has clearly benefited from continuing environmental sampling. While the number of period-specific pollen cores that have been collected remains small, particularly in central lowland England where appropriate deposits are more difficult to identify than in the uplands to the north and west, or on the fenlands in the south and east, the results have nevertheless been important.[51] They have offered a mixed picture, for instance, of woodland clearance and regeneration during the post-Roman centuries, and have pointed towards continuities and discontinuities within arable and pastoral economies over the *longue durée*. Hedgerow studies continue to be informative, despite fundamental concerns about Hooper's Rule (number of woody species per 30 m section = number of centuries), and help to reconstruct the story of enclosure particularly in the later medieval period.[52] Perhaps more important now is the study of hedgerow flora, and in particular indicator plants such as Dogs Mercury, which serve to identify whether hedgerows were newly formed or represent remnants of former large blocks of woodland. Hedgerow fauna have been equally informative. Snails and insects are often adapted to very particular ecological niches: woodland or open grassland, for example, and over very long periods can be shown to migrate very slowly. Collected through hedge beating (and even hoovering as used during the Shapwick Project), their presence or absence can aid the characterisation of the earlier pre-enclosure landscapes.[53]

Earthworks, too, are vital to any understanding of broader landscapes. The mapping of the evidence for medieval field systems, whether it be surviving ridge and furrow under pasture in the Midlands, or the last echoes of headlands within the modern ploughlands of East Anglia, or the perpetuation of ancient walled or hedged fields – all tell a story. The precise mapping of ridge and furrow across Northamptonshire, for example, provides a vivid picture of common-field landscapes, and has led to a reappraisal of their development (notably the transition from long furlongs to short furlongs),[54] and is beginning to be used to question just how open and lacking in woodland and woodland pasture these areas really were.[55] Where upstanding earthworks are not visible on the ground surface, traces can often be detected under the right circumstances through aerial photography or extensive geophysical survey. One of the most problematic environments for study remains woodland, although transect walking can sometimes be used to plot the banks and ditches associated with medieval coppice management, and other internal features such as drainage and quarrying.[56] The method has also proved successful in identifying ridge and furrow in places where post-medieval woodland regeneration and planting has taken place. The potential of LiDAR, which enables subtle earthworks to be recorded from the air even through tree cover, while yet to be fully realised given its recent introduction, will certainly lead to new discoveries and a reassessment of medieval land use more generally.

The recognition of countryside character

Behind all successful studies of individual settlements and landscapes lies an appreciation of how the particular fits, or else sits uncomfortably, within more general regional and national frameworks. The patterns revealed by place-names and charters, cartographic analysis, archaeological fieldwork, and the study of topography and the natural environment, have been incorporated into many of the landscape characterisation programmes that have been carried out in recent years. One of the most recent, by Roberts and Wrathmell, using mapping as the major tool of presentation, divides England up into a series of provinces and sub-regions based primarily upon the pattern of settlement identified on mid-nineteenth century maps, distinguishing between varying settlement densities.[57] Nucleated villages dominate across the spine of England, to the north and west the pattern remains predominantly dispersed, while to the south-east the picture is more mixed. Furthermore, Roberts and Wrathmell have shown how far such patterns can be related to the earlier evidence of place-names, archaeological data and field systems, etc.[58] A weakness of the 'straight mapping' of the settlement density approach of Roberts and Wrathmell, however, is the occasional failure to relate settlement patterns to the wider economic regions in which both 'village' and dispersed settlements played a contributory part – with artificial boundaries dividing, for instance, the less intensively developed Warwickshire Arden, with its surviving woodland, heathland and pasture, from the more intensively cultivated Feldon, despite the fact that these regions were clearly linked and interdependent for the utilisation of resources throughout the prehistoric and historic periods. More detailed regional studies have been able to penetrate these associations in greater depth and the recognition of 'countryside character' has become a driving force in planning.

The idea itself is not new, since, of course, sixteenth-century writers like John Leland (1535–43) and William Harrison had clearly noticed the changing character of the countryside as they travelled.[59] On a wider scale, Sir Cyril Fox had published *The Personality of Britain* in 1932, which not only looked at the differences in the archaeological evidence from the Highland and Lowland zones of Britain, but also commented upon the kinds of society that might have existed in these regions in the past, influenced by their individual character.[60] Others continued to comment upon particular aspects which differed regionally across the country, such as Gray on field systems[61] (some writers then attempting to explain these in the light of perceived ethnicity),[62] or Thirsk on medieval field systems and early modern farming regions.[63] The work of Clifford Darby and his colleagues (1952–67) in identifying regions based upon the statistics of Domesday Book has remained fundamental to the present day.[64] Oliver Rackham's division of the rural landscape of lowland England into regions, comparing 'Planned Countryside', largely distinguished by villages but with outlying farms established largely after enclosure, with 'Ancient Countryside', characterised by ancient isolated farms, hamlets and small towns, has proved a useful scheme that incorporates the historical evidence.[65] The uplands of England he terms the 'Highland Zone', including Cornwall, parts of the Welsh border land and the Pennines, differentiated upon topographical and ecological grounds, although much of this zone is also one of dispersed settlement.

The landscape is, however, never static and regional distinctiveness has been more pronounced in some periods than in others. In general, contrasts must have been more obvious when the medieval open fields were at their most extensive, as in the period prior to the Black Death, and when assarting was still taking place in more marginal regions, especially in wooded areas. At a later stage, village desertion and retraction of the common fields might blur the differences as extensive areas of sheep or cattle pasture became a feature in what had been primarily arable zones. Development in modern times, especially the break-up of pasture for arable or the growth and spread of settlement, has further weakened the distinctiveness of historic character regions.

Rackham's work may have helped to encourage administrators involved in countryside planning to consider the conservation of countryside character more effectively. In the early 1990s, at the instigation of the then Countryside Commission, Warwickshire County Council (1993) carried out a survey of that county which incorporated an historic appraisal in defining the recognition of regional characteristics as a guide to countryside management[66]; subsequently, English Heritage addressed the archaeological and historical component of characterisation by funding studies in many parts of the country, beginning in Cornwall in 1994 (published by Cornwall County Council in 1996).[67] Although the emphasis is upon understanding the present-day landscape, the factors that have contributed to present diversity must inevitably include landscape evolution as a primary force. These studies have been largely desk-based but have made full use of archaeological data contained in county HERs – covering archaeological sites, historic parklands, information on standing buildings, and historical maps. Recently, Rippon has introduced many of the techniques available which can help to unravel the history of the countryside – techniques that were instrumental in the detailed study of the landscape of Shapwick.[68] And where these have been used for scholarly enquiry, rather than simply as management tools, the ideas that Historical Landscape Characterisation carries the potential to generate are clear to all.[69] Rippon has also discussed the diversification of landscape character in southern Britain, tracing much of this back to the years either side of the Norman Conquest.[70]

A consistent outcome of all these studies is definition of the deeply entrenched division between former open-field landscapes with their predominantly nucleated villages, running in a broad strip across England from Somerset and Dorset in the south to Northumberland and County Durham in the north, and the more dispersed nature of settlement in former marginal or woodland regions both to the north and west of the village belt, and in south-eastern England and parts of East Anglia. These patterns can clearly be traced back into the medieval period and beyond, and are obviously closely related to historical land use but have, remarkably, survived the vicissitudes of historical change and even the proliferation of settlement in recent decades.

Conclusion

The very nature of the evidence for medieval settlements and landscapes demands that disciplinary boundaries are crossed if they are to be fully understood. Undoubtedly, archaeology has taken the lead, particularly following the development of landscape archaeology in the 1970s and 1980s. The revision of long-standing assumptions has tended to be driven by new archaeological discoveries emanating from new field methodologies, rather than from history or historical geography. But these two still command considerable attention: the historical geographers have provided important frameworks within which local studies can be placed, while social, economic, and agrarian histories continue to add to our understanding of how rural communities functioned and why their settlements and landscapes should look like they did. Looking to the future, if progress is to be made in resolving some of the outstanding issues surrounding medieval settlements and landscapes, multidisciplinary approaches offer one way forward. Equally vital will be to continue to work at a variety of nested scales, thus articulating the local and the particular with the regional, national,

and indeed international. The holy grail remains true interdisciplinarity, where the separate scholarly agenda of historians, geographers, archaeologists, onomasts and others can be combined together on an equal footing, where methodologies from one area of study can be borrowed by another, and where the questions to be addressed must remain flexible so that they can react to the fast-moving and ever-changing research environment created. The complexities of achieving this end should not be underestimated, but it is surely worth striving for, since the rewards are potentially high.

Notes

1. Gerrard 2003, 99–107.
2. Johnson 2007.
3. Hurst 1971, 83, 85–89.
4. Andrews and Milne 1979.
5. Wade-Martins 1980b, 93–161; Gerrard 2003, 117.
6. West 1985.
7. Powlesland 1995.
8. Beresford 1987.
9. Mynard *et al.* 1992.
10. Hamerow 2002, 52–99.
11. Audouy and Chapman 2008, 51.
12. Hey 2004.
13. Gerrard and Aston 2007, 244–260.
14. Jones and Page 2006.
15. Lewis 2007.
16. Jones and Page 2006, 170–173.
17. Hey 2004, 229–251.
18. Gerrard and Aston 2007, 183–199.
19. Rippon *et al.* 2001.
20. Roberts and Wrathmell 2000.
21. Roberts 1977, 127; Taylor 1977.
22. Lewis *et al.* 2001, 52.
23. Roberts 2008.
24. Page and Jones 2007.
25. Roberts 2008.
26. Gerrard and Aston 2007, 44–101.
27. Bowden 1999.
28. E.g. RCHME 1982.
29. Barnwell 2004.
30. Everson and Stocker 2006, 111–115.
31. See Vernacular Architecture.
32. Letts *et al.* 2000.
33. Cox 1975–76.
34. Hooke 1985c, 135–138.
35. Gelling 1984, 5–7; Cox 1975–76.
36. Sawyer 1968, S 142; Hooke 1990, 69–78.
37. Hooke 2010; Hooke 1990.
38. Hooke 1998, 90–91.
39. Hooke 1985a.
40. Hooke 1990, 362–365, 408–417, 344–347.
41. Hooke 1994b, 13–41, 200–203.
42. Hooke 1985b, 108–113.
43. Hooke 1999, 101.
44. Ford 1976, 287.
45. Foard 1978.
46. Gerrard 1997.
47. Shennan 1985.
48. Shaw 1993.
49. Jones 2004.
50. Jones 2004.
51. Dark 2000.
52. Barnes and Williamson 2006.
53. Gerrard and Aston 2007, 332–341.
54. Hall 1995.
55. Pers. comm. R. Liddiard and T. Williamson; Foard *et al.* 2009.
56. Hall 2001a.
57. Roberts and Wrathmell 2000.
58. Roberts and Wrathmell 2002.
59. Toulmin Smith 1964; Edelen 1994.
60. Fox 1932.
61. Gray 1915.
62. Joliffe 1933; Homans 1941.
63. Thirsk 1987.
64. Darby 1952–67.
65. Rackham 1986.
66. Warwickshire County Council 1993.
67. Cornwall County Council 1996.
68. Rippon 2004.
69. Martin and Satchell 2008.
70. Rippon 2008.

CHAPTER 4

The Prehistory of Medieval Farms and Villages: From Saxons to Scandinavians

Gabor Thomas

Introduction: sources and approaches

The vast majority of rural settlements occupied in the British Isles during the later Middle Ages first appeared in the landscape long before their earliest recorded documentation: for England the first significant historical horizon is Domesday Book at the end of the eleventh century; but for many other regions – Ireland, Wales and Scotland included – sites of habitation went unrecorded for significantly longer. Consequently, those seeking to unravel the biographies of settlements, communities and landscapes back into the Early Middle Ages must chiefly rely upon material evidence locked up in the landscape, to be extracted and interpreted using approaches drawn from archaeology and related disciplines. What distinguishes these studies from those undertaken in the depths of prehistory, however, is that the early medieval landscape *can* be glimpsed from non-material perspectives including place-names and historical sources. The process of integrating these comparative strands of evidence poses particular challenges in the pre-Norman era, when historical sources are thin on the ground and generally bereft of the rich topographic detail characterising manorial records and other later medieval documents. Yet, if such endeavour often exposes the tensions existing between different disciplinary perspectives, it also creates a dialogue from which modern researchers stand to gain a more sophisticated understanding of how the landscape was experienced and imagined by early medieval people in their daily lives.

The past 30 years, and the past decade in particular, have witnessed revolutionary developments in our understanding of rural life in the British Isles over the closing centuries of the first millennium AD. The key impetus has been a surge in new archaeological data, particularly in the form of excavated early medieval settlements, though, in the case of England, any assessment also needs to acknowledge the important contribution made by field-walking and metal-detecting in locating settlements and defining broader trends in settlement patterns. The past decade has also seen the completion of a series of innovative research projects harnessing new fieldwork methodologies and inter-disciplinary approaches specifically aimed at unlocking the origins of regional diversity in the medieval countryside, from classic nucleated landscapes of the English Midlands to dispersed settlement patterns characterising such regions as south-west England and Northern Ireland. As a result of these and other recent achievements, archaeological approaches are becoming increasingly central to studies of the early medieval landscape, helping to revitalise long-running debates and set new research agendas.

This overview takes the opportunity to highlight how these developments are transforming archaeologists' perceptions of the 'prehistory' of medieval farms and villages in Britain and Ireland. But it is first necessary to note some words of caution. Any study which attempts (as here) to cast the net over the entirety of the British Isles must confront strong regional contrasts in the character, quality and quantity of archaeological evidence which complicate comparisons. Ephemeral in character and notoriously difficult to find using standard forms of archaeological prospection – field-walking, geophysics, aerial photography – early medieval settlements remain an elusive category for many parts of Britain and Ireland. As we shall see, commercial archaeology has played a crucial role in populating the landscape with more sites and data, but only in those regions where relatively large windows of landscape have been opened up as a result of road and rail schemes, quarrying and housing developments.[1] Added to this imbalance are major differences in the physical preservation of excavated settlements. At one end of the spectrum one can highlight sites which rank as some of the best-preserved settlements in the whole of early medieval Europe – for example, the platform rath of Deer Park Farms, Co. Antrim, Ireland, enjoying unrivalled organic preservation of house structures and artefacts, through to the remarkable sequence of stone-walled longhouses at Cille Pheadair, on the Hebridean island of South Uist, cocooned under a protective coating of windblown sand.[2] Yet such cases are in the minority: typically, as in the case of most Anglo-Saxon rural settlements, the evidence presents itself in a characteristically fugitive form – shadowy impressions of *groundfast* timber buildings, often with only partially preserved ground-plans, which are hard to phase and to interpret in either structural or functional terms. Further constraining interpretation is the overarching problem of imprecise chronological frameworks for dating rural settlements. In the period under review many regions of the British Isles were aceramic (indeed, Eastern England remains the only region where pottery can be used as a precise dating tool prior to the tenth century) and the problem is exacerbated by the wide error margins in radiocarbon calibration for the later first millennium AD.

In order to counteract these imbalances and to negotiate the bewildering regional diversity characterising early medieval settlement archaeology in the British Isles, this survey takes a broad comparative approach. More particularly, it will examine three themes designed to showcase how archaeologists have brought deeper meaning to the early medieval countryside: transitions and trajectories, interconnections and hierarchy and cultural diversity. It will conclude by considering future research themes and directions.

Rural transitions and trajectories: the creation of medieval landscapes

The final three centuries of the first millennium AD constitute a period of radical socio-economic transformation in North-West Europe and the British Isles were swept up by these changes. By the end of the tenth century, England had emerged onto the European stage as a unified feudal state, underpinned by a heavily exploited countryside and an expanding population. While Wales, Scotland and Ireland followed independent trajectories, they too experienced many of the transformations seen in England: political centralisation, increasing social stratification and the rise of new elites, intensified rural production and new forms of exchange and economic consumption.[3]

Understanding how these meta-narratives played themselves out in the countryside represents a considerable challenge, one which can only be met by charting localised rural transitions through the archaeological record and other sources such as place-names. This section reviews relevant progress in this area, commencing with data-rich regions of British Isles, following with, by way of contrast, the Highland zone and especially the south-west of England where off-site environmental sequences have been used to enhance the more limited repertoire of excavated settlements.

(i) Anglo-Saxon England

It is now well established that settlement patterns in most parts of England were redefined during the later first millennium AD. This redefinition accounts for the fact that the overwhelming majority of medieval farms and villages have origins which, when investigated, can rarely be pushed back beyond the eighth century at the earliest (and many came into existence considerably later); and for the fact that Early Anglo-Saxon occupation is frequently confined to sites which were either abandoned or relocated over the seventh and eighth centuries AD. Early conceptualisations of this process, enshrined in the model known as the 'Middle Saxon Shift', placed emphasis on environmental triggers – a settlement drift from light, easily worked soils confined to plateaus and hilltops, to heavier, more fertile soils in surrounding valleys.[4] Over the past 30 years, an accumulating body of archaeological information derived from an expanded geographic base has allowed archaeologists to critique and refine this model, leading to a more sophisticated appreciation of chronological and regional variations in the transition to a more stable, and recognisably medieval, settlement pattern.[5]

Field-walking surveys and, more recently, test-pitting in village cores have provided crucial evidence for examining the chronology and mechanisms associated with the emergence of medieval settlement patterns, but excavation has also made a vital contribution by demonstrating that the socio-economic changes seen at broad landscape scale also had direct impacts on the internal fabric of Anglo-Saxon settlements and communities. Although the two scales provide complementary perspectives on rural change over the later Anglo-Saxon period, it is convenient to consider them in turn when reviewing recent developments in understanding.

Research examining the emergence of regional variability in settlement patterns has been dominated by a long-running debate on the origins of nucleated villages and common fields in the English Midlands, although it should be remembered that so-called 'Champion countryside' is an aberrant and relatively late development. Causal factors, chronology and process have all been placed under critical scrutiny as the debate has evolved and the issue of causation, in particular, continues to polarise academic opinion.[6] The one point on which there is general agreement is that the creation of nucleated villages proceeded over a drawn-out period, extending from the Middle Saxon period until well beyond the Norman Conquest. Many scholars would also accept that there were regional and localised variations in the timing and intensity of the process as experienced in different parts of England's 'Central Province'[7] and, accordingly, that grandiose theories on village origins are becoming increasingly untenable. In this sense, contrasting views on whether village formation proceeded as a gradual process commencing before AD 850, or instead within a compressed 'village moment', confined to the period after AD 850, arguably run the risk of drawing too sharp a distinction in the archaeological record.[8]

One micro-region which appears to subscribe to the later of the two chronological models is the block of parishes straddling the Buckinghamshire/ Northamptonshire border examined by the Whittle-wood project.[9] Here it has been argued that villages aggregated at pre-existing foci ('pre-village nuclei', forming part of a wider pool of dispersed farmsteads populating the Middle Saxon landscape), rather than in at *de novo* plantations, a hypothesis which breaks new ground in explaining the origins of the mosaic settlement pattern of dispersed hamlets and nucleated villages characterising the medieval landscape of Whittlewood, and indeed, many other parts of England's Central Province (Figure 4.1). On the other hand, studies undertaken in other parts of the Midlands and eastern England, indicate that nucleation could occur up to a century or more earlier.[10] This long chronology takes on additional significance when viewed against evidence for broader-scale landscape change linked to rural and economic intensification over the 'Long Eighth Century': the exploitation of new environmental niches such as wetlands and woodlands, the adoption of new forms of land management/field systems, and increased levels of alluviation in river catchments such as the Upper Thames.[11] Situated thus, the emergence of nucleated villages in the English Midlands can be seen as a distinct regional response to widespread socio-economic change which triggered rural developments across many parts of Middle Saxon England.

Although recent research has placed increased emphasis on Middle Saxon developments as a context for the origins of nucleated villages, the Late Saxon period is still acknowledged by many scholars as critical phase in the emergence of medieval countryside. A study of Northamptonshire has proposed that, in a 'Great Replanning' of the tenth century, existing nucleated settlements were substantially reconfigured in association with the laying out of common fields.[12] Late Saxon settlement replanning has been advanced for other regions of champion countryside, including that examined by a major scheme of research at Shapwick, Somerset; an ambitious programme of test-pitting targeting village cores across eastern England is yielding yet further evidence for the same process, although preliminary results serve as a reminder that dispersed farmsteads also came into existence at this time.[13]

These studies introduce a further intricacy in the debate on the origins of the medieval countryside: whether nucleated villages and common fields came into being at the same time? While some have argued that

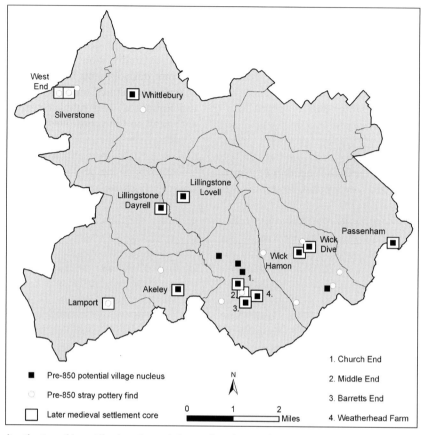

Figure 4.1. The distribution of 'pre-village' nuclei and dispersed settlements before AD 850 in the Whittlewood area. (Source: Jones and Page 2006, Figure 30).

the two form an umbilical relationship, others scholars have exercised more caution, perhaps unsurprisingly given the difficulties of proving contemporaneity between field systems and adjacent settlements on archaeological grounds.[14] A complicating factor, even in the few cases where the relationship between Late Saxon settlements and surrounding fieldscapes can be placed under direct examination, is whether pre-Conquest open fields of the type identified at Raunds (Northamptonshire) were cultivated in the same way as medieval fields.[15] One of the most recent contributions to grapple with this question argues that settlement nucleation and field systems followed independent lines of chronological development, concluding that 'the concentration of nucleated settlement and common fields within the "central province" indicates that a connection between the

two is likely, even though they do not appear at this stage to have been contemporary, but we still do not know what the relationship was'.[16]

Turning attention to excavated sites, one of the key insights gained by rural settlements being examined on a large scale is that the Middle Saxon repertoire evidently includes sizeable agglomerations with planned layouts, as recognised at West Fen Road, Ely (Cambridgeshire), Catholme (Staffordshire) and Cottenham (Cambridgeshire).[17] These sites and others of related character lend support to the contention (as also supported by studies of settlement patterns) that some previous studies on the subject of village origins have placed undue attention on Late Saxon 'manorialisation' as an historical context for settlement nucleation.[18] A further aspect of the diversity displayed by a proliferating range of Middle

Saxon rural settlements is the evidence for regional variation in settlement form, as expressed in a series of settlements located on the Thames and Trent gravels sharing combinations of large enclosures with integrated trackways, as excavated at Little Paxton (Cambridgeshire) and Yarnton (Oxfordshire).[19]

Most Middle Saxon settlements excavated on a large-scale exhibit subsequent phases of development over the Late Saxon period; and those which can be tightly phased (e.g. Flixborough) demonstrate marked transitions in lifestyle over the occupation sequence (see below). In some cases, as at Cottam on the Yorkshire Wolds, this could involve multiple spatial shifts suggesting that the theme of settlement mobility, while perhaps more familiar in an Early-to-Middle-Saxon context, persisted into the later first millennium landscape.[20] Other settlements evolved within a more stable spatial framework, although the sequence might sometimes involve quite radical change.

Excavations at Raunds (Northamptonshire), for example, have provided a striking archaeological visualisation of Late Saxon settlement replanning in action: within a short period spanning as little as a single human generation (*c.* AD 900–950), an existing 'Anglo-Scandinavian' farm with Middle Saxon antecedents was reconstituted to form an imposing manorial compound keyed into (along with an adjacent low-status settlement and also open fields) a regulated framework of rectilinear plot boundaries based on a standard unit of one acre (Figure 4.2); excavations at nearby West Cotton in fact reveal that the same transformation swept up whole tracts of the Northamptonshire countryside.[21]

Synthesis of settlement biographies of the type excavated at Raunds has allowed chronological trends to be recognised in the morphology and internal anatomy of later Anglo-Saxon settlements reflecting broader socio-economic change. One of the clearest is the appearance (from the seventh century onwards) of rigidly defined settlement layouts employing ditched enclosure systems, often displaying evidence for repeated recutting and, in more dramatic cases, extensive reconfiguration and remodelling.[22] This tendency points in the direction of a more closely bounded landscape associated, on the one hand, with more intensive forms of animal husbandry and, on the other, with growing social constraints imposed by legally proscribed definitions of property.

One of the corollaries of a more closely bounded landscape is increased settlement stability, and this is a theme which finds clear expression in the excavated fabric of many later Anglo-Saxon settlements. Relevant developments include a proliferating range of 'service structures' including latrines (both housed and unhoused) and rubbish pits, denoting spatial restriction and the controlled discard of human and domestic waste.[23] Settlement stability also registers in a variety of measures designed to prolong the life of *earthfast* timber houses: innovations such as stone footings and narrow-aisled construction, and evidence for the periodic repair, and sometimes total reconstruction, of buildings.[24] The desire to extend the life of dwellings to encompass several generations may again be taken as evidence for the emerging importance of legally defined property in relation to landholding and inheritance.

(ii) Ireland

An unprecedented surge in commercial archaeology over the past decade, fuelled by a major programme of state-funded road-building, has been a catalyst for a fundamental reappraisal of rural life in early medieval Ireland.[25] The archaeology revealed by these excavations indicates that archetypal forms of 'early Christian' settlement enshrined in the ringforts, cashels and crannogs which pepper the Irish landscape, form part of a much broader continuum of enclosed settlement embodying considerable regional and chronological diversity. The variability is now so great that there have been calls to dispense with the term 'ringfort', long the defining label applied to the study of early Irish settlements, in favour of the more flexible substitute 'enclosed settlement'.[26]

This influx of new archaeological data, augmented by zooarchaeological research and radiocarbon dating, is promoting a more dynamic view of the early medieval Irish countryside. Whereas previous scholarship tended to emphasise continuity across the second half of the first millennium, recent studies demonstrate that the period embraces key transitions in the physical character, lifestyle and economy of Irish settlements, according with the statement that 'the ninth and tenth centuries marked a watershed in economic, social and political terms and thus should signal the start of a different period of study for Irish archaeology and history'.[27]

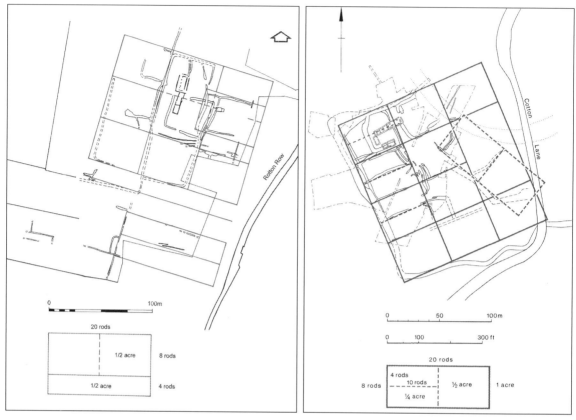

Figure 4.2. Reconstruction of plot divisions associated with the Late Saxon replanning of Raunds, Northamptonshire. (Source: Audouy and Chapman 2009, fig. 4.1)

Underpinning this new paradigm is mounting evidence for a pronounced shift in the agricultural economy of early medieval Ireland over the ninth and tenth centuries: a fragmentation of the former cattle-dominated regime and a turn to cereal cultivation as an alternative strategy for amassing rural surplus. The evidence for this comes from the convergence of two archaeological tendencies: firstly, a decline in the representation of cattle in zooarchaeological assemblages of the ninth to tenth centuries (mirrored by increases in sheep and pig), a trend consistent with the view that dairying was at this time joined by new specialised forms of animal husbandry,[28] and secondly, changes in settlement form suggesting that the desire to contain and protect stock (arguably the most likely function of the enclosures defining ringforts and cashels) ceased to be a primary consideration in the construction of farms and homesteads. Reflecting

this shift is the occupation of so-called 'platform raths', characterised by an artificially raised interior, sometimes completed as a secondary modification to a pre-existing enclosures, which (unlike earlier single and multivallate ringforts) display a strong preference for arable soils. At the same time there is a proliferation of unenclosed sites of the type represented at Knowth (Co. Meath) in the ninth to eleventh centuries, typically, as here, occurring in combination with souterrains and rectangular houses.[29]

Another recent development associated with large-scale excavations in Ireland is the identification of 'cemetery settlements' in the category of Raystown (Co. Meath), which display certain affinities with the settlement archaeology of later Anglo-Saxon England, including palimpsests of re-cut enclosure systems and the phenomenon of unaccompanied

Figure 4.3. Conjectural reconstruction of Raystown, Co. Meath, c. AD 900. (Source: Seaver 2006, Illustration 11)

burial within or adjacent to settlement enclosures (Figure 4.3).[30] The extent to which these complex multi-functional sites might represent undocumented monastic establishments is a question which will no doubt come under close scrutiny in future syntheses; whatever the case, their existence hints at a much more complex settlement hierarchy in early medieval Ireland that could have been predicted purely on the basis of contemporary historical sources.

(iii) Britain's Highland zone
How has an appreciation of early medieval rural transitions moved forward in areas which have not benefited from a surplus of excavated settlements? It must be admitted that our understanding of such processes in regions such as south-west England, Wales and northern Britain – areas characterised by relatively low population densities, dispersed settlement patterns

and pastoral-oriented farming economies – has not moved forward in the same way as it has for Ireland and lowland England. Notable exceptions include maritime zones such as Atlantic and Northern Scotland where active coastal erosion has brought to light early medieval occupation, typically, as on the Hebridean island of South Uist, as part of multi-period sequences demonstrating long-term settlement continuity (albeit with changing architectural forms and economic regimes) stretching back into the Iron Age and forwards into the later Middle Ages.[30]

While some regions of Britain do indeed display clear signs of long-term stability in settlement patterns, recent work in the counties of Devon and Cornwall has critiqued the generalisation that all thinly populated areas of Britain's Highland zone represent fossilised relics of 'ancient countryside'. To appreciate fully the dynamic character of these

English landscapes, it has been necessary to augment a limited number of excavated settlements with evidence for large-scale landscape change reflected in palaeoenvironmental sequences, field-systems, territorial boundaries and place-names. These complementary sources converge on a widespread intensification in land-use over the seventh to the ninth centuries AD connected to the introduction of a regionally distinctive form of rotational agriculture known as 'convertible husbandry'.[31] According to current theories, this development was accompanied by the creation of settlements bearing *tre* place-names and associated strip-cultivated fields which set the framework for the medieval countryside.[32]

One would very much like to know how these proposed changes influenced the internal fabric of settlements themselves, but the evidence in this region of England is very limited. Clear signs of a disruption in settlement patterns during the sixth and seventh centuries is embodied in the abandonment of hillforts and promontories at the apex of the settlement hierarchy (e.g. Tintagel, Cornwall), sites which may have declined in response to a disruption in the long-distance trading networks which formerly fuelled a gift-exchange economy based upon luxury imports.[33] A rupture lower down the social spectrum can also be seen in the abandonment of lowland enclosures known as 'rounds' of which Trethurgy provides the classic excavated paradigm.[34] Broad-scale modelling of the historic landscape further suggests that the foundation of local churches provided a key mechanism for the spatial redefinition of settlement patterns between the seventh and ninth centuries, a template that certainly appears to fit the post-abandonment sequence of Tintagel.[35] Yet, with the exception of the Cornish site of Mawgan Porth and upland farms on Dartmoor, which provide a glimpse of the rural scene at the very end of the millennium, the character of rural settlement during and in the immediate aftermath of the phase of landscape intensification remains elusive in the extreme.[36]

Settlement hierarchy: producers, consumers and specialists

Early medieval society was stratified and hierarchical – a pyramid with kings at the apex, the unfree at the base and a broad spectrum of peasantry, specialists

and aristocracy in the middle, bound together by a system of reciprocal obligations and services. Political centralisation over the latter centuries of the first millennium AD served to redefine the relationships between these different ranks, leading to greater social differentiation and inequalities of wealth. Rural settlement archaeology offers a variety of perspectives on the theme of increasing social stratification and its physical expression in the early medieval countryside. Yet there remain strong imbalances in the character of the evidence. Across the British Isles, understanding is dominated by the upper echelons of the settlement hierarchy – sites sharing relatively good documentary coverage, prominence in the landscape (by virtue of being sited next to churches or in striking topographic locales), and strong archaeological signatures, i.e. comparatively rich finds assemblages, complex structural remains, etc. Conversely, archaeologists are poorly informed about the character and frequency of lower status settlements inhabited by bond peasants and the unfree, otherwise infrequently glimpsed in place-names and historical sources.

Redressing this imbalance remains a pressing research priority, but we also need to consider whether this gap is partly a modern construct arising from archaeologists' tendency to polarise early medieval settlements into discrete social categories, when in reality the situation may have been rather different given that the social composition of most high-status residences is likely to have included a servile element. Below, some of the approaches to and problems of interpreting settlement hierarchy are placed under the spotlight, again under broad regional headings.

(i) Ireland, Western and Northern Britain

In Celtic-speaking regions of the British Isles, the main thrust of work has involved attempts to define social gradations existing at the upper and more visible end of the settlement hierarchy, expressed in various forms of enclosed site – hillforts, coastal promontories, ringforts, duns, rounds and crannogs. Here it may be noted that bond and peasant communities, insofar as they formed discrete social enclaves in the landscape, appear to have occupied a broad and poorly defined repertoire of unenclosed sites, manifested variously in materially poor houses and souterrain complexes in Ireland, hut-groups in Wales and Pitcarmick-type settlements in Pictish Scotland.[37]

Hillforts and other residences of power occupied in post-Roman Britain betray their status in a consistent range of attributes: elaborate defences/enclosure systems and gateways, imported luxuries, fine metalworking, the consumption and redistribution of food-renders; sites such as Dunadd, Argyll, Scotland, also attest to a role in royal inauguration rituals and public assembly.[38] Yet, as we have seen, this visibility recedes in the transition from the post-Roman to the medieval settlement pattern, when the majority of hillforts and coastal promontories were abandoned in favour of unenclosed sites. The nature of elite settlement in the period after AD 800 becomes more difficult to characterise, reliant as we are on glimpses obtained from a small, geographically and culturally disparate sample including the Scottish sites of Forteviot (Perthshire), the Brough of Birsay (Orkney) and the Welsh crannog of Llangorse (Powys).[39] On the other hand, any appraisal of this issue needs to take into account the agency of monastic establishments in redefining how aristocratic culture was articulated in the landscape; the recent publication of excavations at the Pictish monastery of Portmahomack and other comparable institutions in northern Britain has created a new threshold for examining this issue.[40]

In Ireland, discussions of site hierarchy have been framed in relation to early laws, providing as they do a detailed, if idealised, view of contemporary social stratification spanning a multitude of subtle gradations.[41] Traditionally, simple morphological criteria (the number of enclosures and the size of the area enclosed) have been used as a basis for ranking ringforts, large trivallate examples being attributed to the upper – royal – end of the social spectrum and small univallate examples to low- to middle-ranking farmers. Simplistic assumptions of this kind have been called into question by recent scholarship emphasising the need to view sites within their landscape and territorial context. For example, in a critical examination seeking to identify royal sites in Irish landscape, Warner has shown that it is imperative to combine an appreciation of morphological characteristics (the number and scale of enclosures versus the size of the enclosed interior) with spatial relationships existing between ringforts and ritual mounds, early church sites, roadways and lesser enclosures.[42] Other studies have attempted to interpret hierarchical interrelationships on the

evidence of distributional patterns, as, for example, the tendency of high- and low-status ringforts to co-occur at the edge of territories, but these theories have yet to be tested rigorously through fieldwork and excavation.[43]

The excavation of Irish ringforts and crannogs since the 1940s has provided a series of alternative material criteria for examining the theme of settlement hierarchy, with sites such as Lagore, Garranes and Ballinderry producing an array of elite lifestyle signatures – fine metalworking, imported luxuries, prestige jewellery – echoing the range seen on excavated hillforts in post-Roman Britain.[44] Recently, there has been an attempt to extend comparisons across the social spectrum using a ranking system (loosely correlated to social scales given in the early Irish laws) employing intensity scores measured across a series of economic activities, including crop cultivation, animal husbandry and various forms of craft production.[45] One of the important insights to emerge from this study is that crannogs, hitherto conceptualised as an archetypal form of elite settlement, may in fact relate to a broad range of social scales – a conclusion which echoes new interpretations of island lakeside occupation based upon excavation and archaeological survey.[46]

(ii) Anglo-Saxon England

The recent explosion of archaeological data has opened up several new avenues for investigating manifestations of settlement hierarchy in the Anglo-Saxon countryside. Yet, with this increasing diversity of sites come in-built ambiguities and problems of interpretation: what categories of archaeological evidence (buildings, portable material culture, economic resources, etc.) should we use to attribute settlement status? And to what extent can the status and character of excavated sites be interpreted through the lens of contemporary literary sources?[47]

These problems are felt most acutely in the poorly documented Middle Saxon period when the diversity of excavated settlements expands to encapsulate a range of consumer sites: emporia/wics, monasteries, royal vills and other aristocratic estate-centre complexes. Beyond the relative certainty of wics and well-documented Northumbrian monasteries such as Whitby, Wearmouth and Hartlepool, it is hard to characterise excavated settlements using established

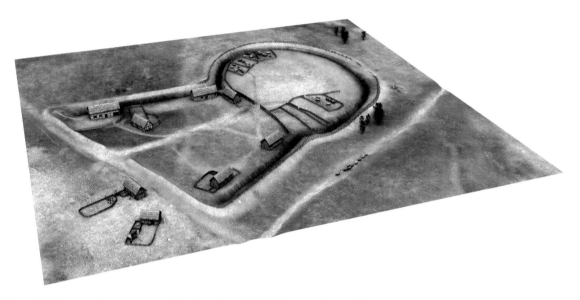

Figure 4.4. Conjectural reconstruction of the hypothesised Middle Saxon tribute collection centre at Higham Ferrers, Northampton-shire. (Source: Hardy, Charles, and Williams 2007, pl. 5.3. Drawn by Pete Lorimer, © Oxford Archaeology)

historical labels (minster, royal vill, etc.) as there is a strong degree of overlap in their archaeological signatures. This issue has now been examined in exhaustive detail in relation to Flixborough, Brandon and Northampton, Middle Saxon sites of high-status character which, depending upon viewpoint, might be interpreted alternatively as secular and/or royal estate-centres with an ecclesiastical component, pre-Viking monastic communities following a 'secularised' lifestyle of excess and conspicuous consumption, or mutable entities which progressed through both of these states.[48] So-called 'Productive sites' identified through metal-detecting complicate the picture still further, for although it is possible to rank them internally according to the size of their metalwork and coinage assemblages, without excavation it is very difficult to interpret their social character and role.[49]

While the broad pool of settlements dating from the seventh to the ninth centuries AD ultimately defies rigid social/functional categorisation, headway can be made by thinking about how sites functioned in relation to territorial infrastructure and systems governing the exaction and circulation of royal tribute. A good case in point is the Northamptonshire site of Higham Ferrers, whose Middle Saxon phase

features a large stock enclosure, a series of timber storehouses and barns and a malting oven used for converting agrarian surplus into ale/beer (Figure 4.4).[50] On the basis of these attributes (in their different ways all concerned with the controlled conversion of food-rent), there is a compelling case for viewing the excavated complex as tribute-collection centre of a royal vill, the domestic component of which has been tentatively identified at the nearby site Irthlingborough. Moreover, it should be noted that the expanded corpus of Middle Saxon settlements also includes a broad base of producer sites which we might expect to find embedded within the territorial fabric of multiple estates.[51] Under this category we can include such sites as Pennyland (Buckinghamshire) engaged in specialised forms of stock-rearing, and seasonally occupied coastal settlements such as 'Sandtun' (Kent), a tenurial outpost of the monastic community of Lyminge which provisioned the latter with imported commodities, seafood and salt.[52]

As one progresses into the later ninth century and beyond, distinctions between high-status settlements, on the one hand, and those occupied by the rural peasantry, on the other, become more sharply defined in certain areas of the archaeological record. One of the key social drivers behind this trend was the burgeoning ranks of a lower aristocracy who developed a common 'seigneurial' identity expressed in distinct codes of behaviour, material culture and visual display.[53] It is at precisely this time that rural settlements become increasingly differentiated in terms of their zooarchaeological assemblages, a pattern which accords with the view that certain foods (particularly those procured through hunting and fishing) attained connotations of luxury and status.[54] On the other hand, as borne out by the relatively undifferentiated range of portable metalwork found in association with tenth-to-eleventh-century rural settlements, prestige jewellery and personal ornaments of the type found in impressive quantities at Middle Saxon sites such as Flixborough and Brandon, appear to have largely fallen out of favour as a means of expressing rank and social status amongst the Late Saxon 'thegnly' classes.[55]

A possible explanation for the latter trend is that estate surplus was increasingly being diverted into the aggrandisement of manorial residences as an arena for displaying rank and social exclusivity, a contention

supported by a rapidly expanding number of Late Saxon thegnly complexes. The identification of such sites with reference to an eleventh-century text, *GeÞyncðo*, with its oft-quoted list of thegnly attributes – a church, kitchen, bell-house and enclosure gate – is now well-rehearsed in relevant literature with a familiar line-up of protagonists: Goltho (Lincolnshire), Portchester and Faccombe Netherton (Hampshire) and Sulgrave (Northamptonshire).[56] Here the opportunity is taken to showcase a recently excavated case-study at Bishopstone (East Sussex) which provides new insights into elite accommodation and lifestyles of the later Saxon era.[57] Occupying the slopes of a prominent chalk spur capped by St Andrew's, one of the county's best preserved pre-Conquest churches, the excavated complex first comes into coherent view during the ninth century as a formally planned suite of timber buildings organised around an open courtyard, an arrangement shared by several contemporary thegnly residences, including Portchester (Hampshire) (Figure 4.5).[58] Individually, the buildings excavated at Bishopstone also conform

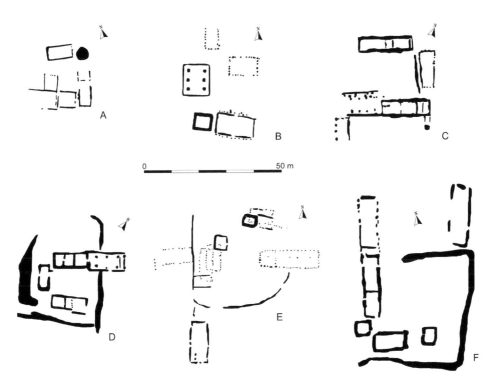

Figure 4.5. Late Saxon manorial complexes displaying courtyard ranges: (A) Bishopstone; (B) Portchester; (C) Goltho; (D) West Cotton; (E) Springfield Lyons; (F) Raunds. (Source: Thomas 2010, fig. 8.5)

Figure 4.6. Aerial view of excavations on Bishopstone village green, 2005, showing part of a later Anglo-Saxon high-status complex. A large timber hall can be seen to the right of the trench with a dense concentration of rock-cut pits below, some of which cut earlier structures. (Photograph © Gabor Thomas)

to expectations of high-status accommodation: spacious halls, some with detached latrine structures, and most exuberant of all, a free-standing timber tower provided with an internally accessed cellar possibly used as a strong-room. On the eastern edge of this domestic compound was a dense concentration of rock-cut pits associated with the discard of domestic waste and human cess (Figure 4.6). While pit clusters are less typical of contemporary manorial compounds (and later Saxon settlements in general) this clear evidence for functional zoning should be taken as a further expression of the spatial formality characterising the upper echelons of the settlement hierarchy. Indications of Bishopstone's privileged social status were also reflected in the zooarchaeological record (most notably in respect to the consumption of pig and marine fish at levels well above the national average), and items of portable material culture, including a delicate casket with decorative iron strapping and an elaborate set of door hinges contained in an iron hoard.

At the other end of the social spectrum, rectilinear plots housing peasants and slaves are sometimes found on the periphery of manorial compounds, as revealed by large-scale excavations at Goltho and Raunds.[59] Peasant settlements also appear in isolation. As one might expect, farms and hamlets occupying this social level, represented by the later tenth- to eleventh-century occupation excavated at North Elmham (Norfolk) and the site of Chestfield near Whitstable (Kent), lack the formality and structural range of contemporary thegnly residences, as reflected in their unstructured layouts and weakly defined enclosure systems.[60]

Peopling settlements: tracking cultural diversity in the early medieval countryside

From the later ninth and in the tenth centuries the British Isles absorbed the full impact of a Scandinavian cultural diaspora which swept across the north-west of Europe and beyond into the North Atlantic. The result was the establishment of Norse colonies in the Northern and Western Isles of Scotland, on the Isle of Man, in coastal zones of north-west England and within urban enclaves on the east coast of Ireland; in England the Anglo-Saxon kingdoms of Mercia, East Anglia and Northumbria were colonised by Scandinavians of predominantly Danish stock who rapidly became assimilated within the countryside and in the expanding populations of nascent towns such as York and Lincoln. The investigation of these epoch-defining events has traditionally been guided by historical, art-historical and place-name scholarship. But archaeology, with its rapidly expanding material datasets, now increasingly interpreted with reference to theoretically informed perspectives on ethnic identity and cultural interaction, has shifted the emphasis away from simplistic questions of scale towards an understanding of the complex social processes which lie behind Scandinavian acculturation in the British Isles.[61] This section will examine how different sources of material evidence have been used to inform relevant debates, paying particular attention to the challenges and complexities of determining the ethnic composition of early medieval rural communities archaeologically.

(i) Scotland and the Irish Sea zone

The most powerful and enduring legacy of Scandinavian settlement in the British Isles is to be found in the Northern and Western Isles of Scotland and the Isle of Man where stable Norse colonies survived for hundreds of years after the initial influx of Viking immigrants. Place-name and linguistic evidence clearly points to the emergence of a Norse-dominated cultural milieu within these regions, although these sources of evidence cannot be calibrated closely enough to determine whether this rise to dominance was a drawn-out process or alternatively a swift, directly imposed, cultural transition during the Viking Age. The same regions have yielded some of the most spectacular testimony to Scandinavian settlement seen anywhere in the Viking world, including a corpus of richly furnished pagan Norse burials and a concentration of silver hoards embracing such unprecedented collections of wealth as at Skaill, Orkney.[62]

The settlement archaeology of these regions, much of it well preserved, by early medieval standards, has been used to support radically divergent models of Scandinavian acculturation, from ethnic genocide on

the one hand, to peaceful co-existence on the other.[63] It is easy to appreciate the centrality of settlement archaeology to these debates. Unlike the English Danelaw, many Scottish settlements have produced alien longhouse architecture of a type distinguishable from the mainstream repertoire of native dwellings characterised by cellular forms. Furthermore, houses of this form are frequently accompanied by portable objects either made in Norway or else influenced by Viking styles.

Impressive as such evidence might first appear, there are manifold problems involved in attempting to interpret these sites with specific reference to ethnic interactions between native and Norse communities during the Viking Age.[64] To take an example, the commingling of portable artefacts of both native and Norse manufacture derived from contemporary stratigraphic contexts at sites such as Buckquoy, Orkney (where longhouses are directly superimposed on native cellular structures) has proved highly influential in promoting the idea that native and immigrant communities lived side by side harmoniously. Yet, given continuity of occupation, the indigenous Pictish element to these assemblages is just as likely to represent stratigraphic contamination from pre-Norse horizons.[65] Due attention also needs to be given to issues of chronology. Several of the sites to have produced classic longhouse architecture – Jarlshof, Shetland, Quoygrew, Orkney – date to the Late Norse period (AD 950 and later) and thus do not bear direct witness to cultural interaction during the Viking Age, but rather (like linguistic change) an extended period of Scandinavian acculturation. Moreover, due to poor chronological resolution, it is impossible to determine whether indigenous and Norse settlements co-existed at the same time, and by implication, whether the transition in architectural traditions was a gradual or a swift process.[66]

The results of a recent programme of excavations on the Hebridean island of South Uist serve as a reminder that there is a strong regional dimension to the relationship between immigrant and indigenous communities, further emphasising the fact that Scandinavian acculturation in Scotland, and the British Isles more generally, cannot be reduced to a single, all-encompassing model.[67] Although classic longhouse architecture (alongside Scandinavian material culture) is represented amongst the earliest

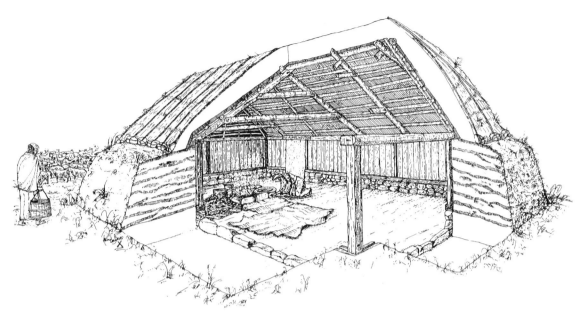

Figure 4.7. Conjectural reconstruction of a semi-subterranean house at Bornais, South Uist. (Source: Sharples 2005, fig. 107. Drawn by Ian Dennis, © Niall Sharples)

phases of the site of Bornais, later occupational phases here and at the neighbouring site of Cille Pheadair exhibit examples of semi-subterranean houses revetted into sand redolent of a blending of Hebridean and Norse constructional traditions (Figure 4.7). The regional flavour of these Hebridean sites is further underscored by the direction of change taken by the rural economy in association with Norse acculturation. In accordance with Late Norse farmsteads excavated in Caithness and the Northern Isles, changes to animal husbandry practices can be detected alongside a marked intensification in marine fishing, but on Hebridean sites the emphasis shifted to beef-rearing instead of dairying, and the principal catch was herring, as opposed to cod, saithe and ling.[68]

The problems of understanding the ethnic connotations of rural settlements are no less acute when one moves south into the Irish Sea. The frontiers of the alien longhouse tradition may, on the evidence of such Manx sites as Braaid, Marrown, and Cronk ny Merriu, have penetrated into this sphere of Viking activity, but, unlike more closely datable hoards and burials, the longhouse phase of these settlements cannot be directly associated with establishment of a Hiberno-Norse colony on the Isle of Man triggered by the expulsion of the Vikings from Dublin in AD 902.[69] The basis for such a link is in any case rendered questionable by the fact that the archetypal urban dwelling found in Hiberno-Norse towns in Ireland more likely represents a native constructional adaptation to the urban environment than an alien prototype.[70]

As far as Ireland is concerned more generally, the distinct lack of rural sites displaying clear evidence of Scandinavian influence is partly to be explained by the fact that Hiberno-Norse assimilation was largely (as place-names and historical sources suggest) confined to urban centres such as Dublin, Waterford, Wexford and Limerick and their immediate hinterlands.[71] Recent commercial archaeology in Ireland, while confirming this general impression, has brought to light a site at Cherrywood (Co. Dublin), which provides hints in its structures (including a Dublin 'Type 1' house) and material assemblages (a fragment of a Norwegian whalebone plaque) that the culture of Hiberno-Norse towns did indeed radiate out into the rural hinterland.[72] The other significant development of recent years is an expansion of archaeological information on fortified Viking encampments known as *longphorts*, including the spectacular discoveries made at Woodstown (Co. Waterford) and a series of excavations in Dublin shedding light on an early Scandinavian enclave – possibly relating to the historically attested *longphort* established in AD 841 – focused on the 'Black Pool', from which the town takes its name.[73] The ethnic affiliations of the Irish *longphort* can be examined in a way simply not possible for the general run of rural settlements in Viking-age Britain, for they include male warrior burials yielding isotopic signatures consistent with an origin in Scandinavia or else in Norse colonies in Western Scotland.

The sites of Meols on the Wirral peninsula (Merseyside) and Llanbedrgoch, Anglesey, provide an impression of the direction taken by settlements in areas of Viking acculturation on the eastern (British) seaboard of the Irish Sea, although the basis for making generalisations is mitigated by a dearth of early medieval settlement archaeology in these regions.[74] Both sites demonstrate long sequences of activity and occupation, confirming the impression that Vikings here (as in many parts of the British Isles) implanted themselves within existing settlements and territorial structures. Of the two sites, Llanbedrgoch, that subject to modern scientific excavation, provides by far the best structural archaeology, including a semi-subterranean house with central hearth and side benches providing a Welsh equivalent to the hybrid constructional traditions recognised on Late Norse sites in South Uist.[75] In their cultural assemblages, both sites demonstrate a strong maritime trade dimension, with finds of ingots, weights and hack-silver, combined imported objects from Dublin and other centres of production demonstrating that these communities were keyed into Viking networks extending across the Irish Sea and further afield. They also share examples of so-called 'Irish Sea' metalwork – roundel-decorated buckles and strap-ends, hexagonal bronze bells and lobe-headed pins – reflecting the emergence of a distinct regional culture spread within the ambit of Norse acculturation.[76]

(ii) England

The settlement archaeology of the English Danelaw has proved remarkably resistant to the identification of Scandinavian immigrant populations, at least under traditional approaches to recognising ethnic identity in the archaeological record. Previous assertions that the stone-walled building complexes excavated on upland sites such as Ribblehead (N. Yorkshire) and Simy Folds (Co. Durham) represent English expressions of Norse longhouse architecture have not stood up to critical scrutiny; these structures (along with bow-shaped timber halls found on other sites) are more correctly attributed to the regional diversity indigenous to the later Anglo-Saxon England, on which we are now much better informed thanks to an expanded number of excavated sites.[77]

In the past, the absence of 'alien' forms of architecture in the Danelaw has been explained in various ways: that the farms and residences of Viking immigrants lie unexcavated beneath modern villages; that in contrast to Scandinavian Scotland, there was a much greater degree of overlap between building traditions in Anglo-Saxon England and the homelands of the immigrant community, in this case, southern Scandinavia; and that incoming Danes exerted their political dominance by coercing subjugated Anglo-Saxon communities to construct buildings for them. None of these theories provides a convincing explanation when scrutinised against the greatly expanded number of excavated sites and an understanding of the social mechanisms characterising Scandinavian acculturation in other parts of the British Isles. As recent studies have argued, the real answer to this conundrum lies in the evidently rapid assimilation of Scandinavian immigrants to Anglo-Saxon cultural norms (as also seen in religious affiliation), resulting in the emergence of a hybrid 'Anglo-Scandinavian' identity.[78]

The discovery of Viking-inspired ornamental metalwork on excavated settlements and by metal-detector enthusiasts has played a crucial role in helping to map the spread of this identity across the countryside, augmenting the evidence provided by place-names with which the metalwork corpus shares a broadly complementary Danelaw distribution (Figure 4.8). While material of Scandinavian manufacture is rare from excavated settlements, the rapidly expanding corpus of metal-detector finds recorded through the Portable Antiquities Scheme does include a growing contingent of Viking brooches almost certainly transported across the North Sea by

Gabor Thomas

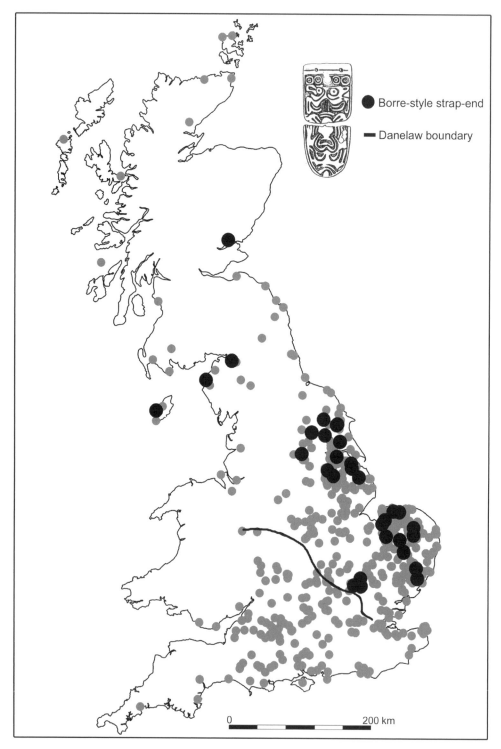

Figure 4.8. Find locations of late ninth- to tenth-century Anglo-Scandinavian strap-ends shown against the background distribution of all contemporary strap-ends from Britain. (Source Thomas 2000, with additions)

female immigrants covering the social spectrum.[79] Scandinavian acculturation is otherwise evidenced by styles of brooch and belt-fitting fusing Viking and native Anglo-Saxon elements, a hybrid fashion popularised across the Danelaw in both urban and rural environments.[80] At Cottam, a rare example of a metal-detected site sampled by excavation, it has even been possible to link the emergence of Scandinavian-influenced metalwork styles with a localised settlement shift, suggesting that 'Anglo-Scandinavian' identity was closely bound with new patterns of lordship.[81]

The latter site joins a growing corpus of excavated settlements in the Danelaw offering opportunities for investigating Scandinavian influence on expressions of status within settlements – arguably a more profitable line of enquiry than attempting to assign ethnic labels to their inhabitants. As long appreciated by historians and place-name scholars, one of the primary mechanisms underpinning Viking land-taking in the Danelaw was the takeover of existing estates by Scandinavian elites, a process which disrupted prevailing patterns of lordship and accelerated the fragmentation of landholdings.[82] The initiation of settlement nucleation at Raunds, reflected *inter alia* in the establishment of an 'Anglo-Scandinavian' farm with a high-status focus (subsequently revamped into the Late Saxon manorial compound with its long-range complex), is sufficiently closely dated by ceramics to speculate that the lord responsible for these aggrandisements, if not necessarily Scandinavian by descent, belonged to a landowning elite who must have directly profited from the changed political circumstances triggered by Viking settlement in the Danelaw.[83]

Conclusions and future research directions

In summary, the archaeological resource for early medieval settlement in Britain and Ireland is unevenly distributed in the extreme. One of the imperatives of future research must be to generate more high-quality data for the black holes – the south-east lowlands of Scotland, Wales and north-west England, to name some of the most obvious candidates. Future discoveries will doubtless come to light through commercial archaeology, but this mechanism will never yield for these zones what it has for more

densely populated regions of England and Ireland. Clearly, we need to harness alternative strategies. One potential model is the targeting of currently occupied village cores, as successfully deployed by a growing number of university-led research projects in lowland England. Although test-pitting faces limitations in aceramic zones, allied with geophysics it nevertheless constitutes a useful methodology for pinpointing archaeological features – structural footprints, boundary ditches, rubbish pits and graves – which can provide crucial evidence for the embryonic history of rural settlements

Another part of the solution, addressing the difficulty of locating early medieval sites using standard forms of prospection, lies with predictive modelling drawing upon historic landscape characterisation and place-names. Studies of this kind have proliferated in recent years in response to the current vogue for landscape archaeology, but in most cases the models generated remain to be tested by archaeological fieldwork. To take just one example, analysis of the historical landscape of the western Sussex Weald and neighbouring Surrey has identified a distinctive class of arc-shaped boundary (defined by roads and streams) conjectured to represent pre-Conquest settlement and land-use: targeting these features could bring much-needed evidence to bear on the character of Anglo-Saxon settlement within the *Andredeswald*.[84]

Metal-detector finds recorded through the Portable Antiquities Scheme hold enormous potential for locating sites and reconstructing early medieval settlement patterns in England and Wales, yet the resource remains under-utilised. The Viking and Anglo-Saxon Landscape and Economy project hosted by the University of York has drawn attention to this potential and begun to address a series of methodological issues involved with interpreting metal-detector sites against other sources of archaeological data.[85] Considerable uncertainty surrounds the characterisation of sites identified through ploughsoil signatures (including those falling within the so-called 'Productive site' category) and how to relate them to conceptions of settlement hierarchy and site function derived from excavated data.[86] For this reason it is encouraging to see a new generation of scholars confront this issue head on by targeting Productive sites in eastern England with an integrated survey methodology – combining field-walking, metal-detecting, geochemical survey and trial-trenching – previously applied to early medieval rural settlements in Denmark.[87]

Moving on to issues of interpretation, the settlement archaeology of the early medieval period remains considerably under-theorised, especially in comparison to contemporary cemeteries and landscapes studied from a Christian/ideological perspective. As seen, this imbalance is starting to be redressed by studies examining trends in settlement morphology and timber building construction as a reflection of broader socio-economic change.[88] Yet, with the exception of a thought-provoking examination of the origins of the English village viewed from the perspective of feudal power relations,[89] little attempt has been made to interrogate early medieval settlements as 'dynamic social arenas'.[90] This situation could be remedied by harnessing spatial analysis and phenomenological approaches focusing on inter-relationships between buildings, viewsheds, access points and movement through settlements. But if we are to gain a more nuanced appreciation of the social life of early medieval rural settlements it is important that analysis is extended beyond the conceptual frame of structures and the built environment to a consideration of who did what where – namely, the spatial context of daily activities.

Of course, rural settlements and the daily travails of an agricultural existence were themselves ritualised domains within early medieval society. It should be remembered that during the period under review, the 'Christianisation' of early medieval Britain and Ireland was a long way from being fully actualised: long-standing expressions of 'folk magic' and superstitious practice endemic to rural communities attuned to the natural world were evidently tolerated by the fledgling church or else reassigned new meaning within a Christianised milieu.[91] Relevant here is a growing repertoire of isolated graves and unaccompanied cemeteries recovered from rural settlements of the seventh to ninth centuries in both England and Ireland, evidence that, in the period before churchyard burial was established as the norm, houses, property and the domestic sphere exerted a powerful influence over the burial of certain individuals.[92] These human burials belong to a wider spectrum of ritual deposits – in an Anglo-Saxon context, dubbed 'special deposits' – now being recognised on rural settlements across early medieval Britain and Ireland.[93] The pulling

together of such evidence from grey literature and unpublished excavation archives would provide the basis for a much richer appreciation of the ritual and symbolic life of the rural peasantry during an age of religious transition.

In addition to looking inwards, the landscape context of early medieval settlements – how they articulated with routeways, boundaries and topographic settings – also deserves closer attention, harnessing the power of interdisciplinary perspectives informed by place-names, historical and cartographic sources.[94] More regional studies are also needed to investigate the interplay between settlements and rural intensification, particularly in relation to the exploitation of specialised ecological niches such as wetlands and woodlands, an aim calling for a tighter integration of zooarchaeological and environmental assemblages in the process of site interpretation. A preliminary study based on data gathered from extensive coastal surveys in eastern England certainly highlights the potential of this approach, showing that, contrary to existing models of early medieval wetland colonisation, viable settlement could be achieved *before* the construction of permanent sea defences by weighting cereal production towards salt-tolerant barley.[95]

Ultimately, the construction of more sophisticated interpretative models for early medieval farms and villages will depend upon situating the British Isles in their European context; after all, the rural transitions examined in this chapter were responses to socio-economic trends of continental scale and magnitude. Beyond the arena of Scandinavian settlement where issues of migration and ethnicity form a central focus of study, native archaeologists working in the later centuries of the first millennium AD all too rarely stray beyond national boundaries in seeking broader comparisons and frameworks for interpreting rural settlements and landscapes. Such isolationism stands at odds with a period which is otherwise celebrated for expanding trade networks, the forging of dynastic alliances between emergent European states, and the unifying influence of Christianity and monasticism. Studies which have attempted to bridge national fault-lines[96] serve as a reminder that we have much still to learn about how early medieval communities native to the British Isles emulated, adapted and resisted continental influences, whether in relation to the organisation of farms, the construction of houses, and the logistics of rural production.

An overall assessment of developments in the field over the past ten years indicates that the study of early medieval rural settlements in the British Isles has reached a turning-point. One senses a growing mood of self-reflection amongst period specialists as they cast a critical eye over the past and turn attention to the future. Type-sites, models and paradigms inherited from the pioneering generations of the discipline of medieval archaeology – from the origins of the English village to the economy of the Irish rath – are in the process of being overturned and re-evaluated in the wake of new data and new approaches to interpretation. The next decade promises to be defining era in early medieval settlement studies as archaeologists apply themselves to understanding and interpreting the complexity and diversity which we now know to characterise the prehistory of medieval farms and villages.

Further reading

An overview of early medieval settlements in Celtic-speaking regions of Britain and Ireland can be found in L. Laing's *The Archaeology of Celtic Britain and Ireland c. AD 400–1200* (Cambridge, 2006) and in contributions to P. Stafford (ed.), *A Companion to the Early Middle Ages: Britain and Ireland c. 500–1100* (London, 2009) (nb. S. Crawford, 'Settlement and social differentiation', pp. 432–445). A further key source examining the rural landscape of mainland Britain is P. Fowler's *Farming in the First Millennium: British Farming between Julius Caesar and William the Conqueror* (Cambridge, 2002). For more detailed examinations of Scotland, Wales and Ireland respectively, see S. Foster's *Picts, Gaels and Scots* (Edinburgh, 2004), N. Edwards and A. Lane's edited volume *Early Medieval Settlements in Wales AD 400–1100* (Bangor, 1988) and N. Edwards'

The Archaeology of Early Christian Ireland (London, 1996). Recent Irish case-studies appear in a series of publications by the National Roads Authority, e.g. J. O'Sullivan and M. Stanley (ed.), *Settlement, Industry and Ritual* (2006). Works specifically dealing with Scandinavian settlement in these regions include: J. Graham-Campbell and C. Batey's *Vikings in Scotland* (Edinburgh, 1997), M. Redknap's *The Vikings in Wales* (Cardiff, 2000), and the following edited volumes: T. Larsen's, *The Vikings in Ireland* (Roskilde, 2001) and H. B. Clarke, R. O'Floinn and M. Mhaonaigh's *Ireland and Scandinavia in the Early Viking Age* (Dublin, 1998).

For Anglo-Saxon England, A. Reynolds' *Later Anglo-Saxon England* (Stroud, 1999) remains a fundamental source, while various aspects of the rural scene will receive updated treatment in the *Oxford Handbook in Anglo-Saxon Archaeology* (edited by H. Hamerow, S. Crawford and D. Hinton, Oxford 2011). N. J. Higham and M. J. Ryan (eds), *The Landscape Archaeology of Anglo-Saxon England* (Woodbridge, 2010) contains several valuable papers on settlements, fields, farming and the environment. S. Rippon's *Beyond the Medieval Village* (Oxford, 2008), the latest in a long line of books to discuss the origins of the English village, provides an engaging synthesis with an extensive bibliography covering a wide range of regional case-studies. For an overview of metal-detected rural settlements see T. Pestell and K. Ulmschneider's edited work *Markets in Early Medieval Europe: Trading and 'Productive Sites' 650–850* (Macclesfield, 2003). Scandinavian settlement in England is covered by the following edited volumes: D. M. Hadley, and J. D. Richards's *Cultures in Contact: Scandinavian Settlement in England in the Ninth and Tenth Centuries* (Turnhout, 2000) and J. Graham-Campbell, R. Hall, J. Jesch and D. Parsons' *Vikings and the Danelaw* (Oxford, 2001).

Notes

1. For Ireland, see Kinsella 2010.
2. Lynn 1991; Parker Pearson *et al.* 2004a.
3. Wickham 2005.
4. Arnold and Wardle 1981.
5. Hamerow 1991.
6. Rippon 2008, 12–26.
7. Roberts and Wrathmell 2002, 124 and 144, fig. 1.1.
8. Rippon 2008, 13.
9. Jones and Page 2004.
10. Brown and Foard 1998.

11. The evidence is pulled together in Rippon 2007 and Rippon 2010.
12. Brown and Foard 1998.
13. Gerrard with Aston 2007; Lewis 2007; Lewis 2010.
14. Jones and Page 2006, 104.
15. Parry 2006.
16. Oosthuizen 2010, 130.
17. Mortimer, Regan and Lucy 2005; Mortimer 2000; Losco-Bradley and Kinsley 2002.
18. Reynolds 2003, 2005.
19. Addyman 1969; Hey 2004.
20. Richards 2002.
21. Audouy and Chapman 2009.
22. Reynolds 2003; Hamerow 2010.
23. Reynolds 2003, 130.
24. Gardiner 2004; Thomas 2010b, 189–193.
25. O'Rourke 2006.
26. Fitzpatrick 2009; Kinsella 2010.
27. Kerr 2007, 116.
28. McCormick 2008; McCormick and Murray 2007.
29. Kerr 2007; McCormick and Murray 2007.
30. Seaver 2006.
30 Sharples and Parker Pearson 1999.
31 Rippon 2006; Rippon 2008, 122–137.
32 Turner 2006e; Herring 2006.
33 Campbell and Lane 1994.
34. Quinnell 2004.
35. Turner 2006d, 30.
36. Bruce-Mitford 1997.
37. For an overview see Laing 2006, 31–63; Crawford 2006.
38. Alcock 1988; Alcock 2003.
39. Aitchison 2006; Morris 1996; Redknap and Lane 1994.
40. Carver 2008; Lowe 2008.
41. Patterson 1994.
42. Warner 1988.
43. Stout 1991; Kerr 2007.
44. For overview see Edwards 1990.
45. Comber 2008.
46. E.g. O'Sullivan *et al.* 2007.
47. Crawford 2006
48. Loveluck 2001; Blair 1996; Blair 2005, 204–211.
49. Ulmschneider 2000; Pestell and Ulmschneider 2003.
50. Hardy, Charles and Williams 2007.
51. Faith 1997.
52. Williams 1993; Gardiner *et al.* 1991; Thomas 2010a.
53. Senecal 2001.
54. Sykes 2004, 2007.
55. Hinton 2005.
56. Williams 1992; Morris 1989: 227–274; Reynolds 1999, 112–134.
57. Thomas 2010b.
58. Cunliffe 1976.
59. Audouy and Chapman 2009, 28–31; Beresford 1975.
60. Wade-Martins 1980; Allen 2004; Gardiner forthcoming.
61. Hadley and Richards 2000.
62. For a recent overview see Hall 2007.
63. Barrett 2004.
64. Discussed in Barrett 2008.
65. Graham-Campbell and Batey 1997, 160–164.
66. Barrett 2008, 415–418.
67. Sharples and Parker Pearson 1999.
68. Parker Pearson *et al.* 2004a, 125–144.
69. For relevant sites see Wilson 2008, 87–104.
70. Wallace 1992.
71. Clarke 1998.
72. Ó'Néill 2006; Johnson 2004, 66–70.
73. Sheehan 2008; Simpson 2005; O'Donovan 2008.
74. Redknap 2000: 69–87; Griffiths, Philpott and Egan 2007, 58–76.
75. Sharples and Parker Pearson 1999.
76. Griffiths 2004.
77. Coggins 2004; King 2004.
78. Richards 2000.
79. Leahy and Patterson 2001; Kershaw 2009.
80. Thomas 2000.
81. Richards 2002.
82. Hadley 2006, 84–89.
83. Audouy and Chapman 2009, 51.
84. Chatwin and Gardiner 2006.
85. Naylor and Richards 2006.
86. Pestell and Ulmschneider 2003.
87. Davies 2010.
88. Reynolds 2003; Hamerow 2010; Gardiner 2004.
89. Saunders 2000.
90. Hamerow 2010.
91. Pluskowski and Patrick 2003.
92. Zadora-Rio 2003; Hadley 2007; Astill 2009.
93. Hamerow 2005; O'Sullivan 2008; Thomas 2008; Parker Pearson 2006.
94. Reynolds 2009.
95. Murphy 2010.
96. See published proceedings of themed conferences organised under the auspices of *Ruralia*, e.g. Klápště 2002.

CHAPTER 5

Seigneurial and Elite Sites in the Medieval Landscape

Oliver Creighton and Terry Barry

Introduction

Any study of medieval settlements or landscapes will be incomplete without considering the residences of the contemporary social elite and the ways that these sites were set within and impacted upon the countryside. Research into castles, manor houses and other characteristically 'elite' sites is crucial, of course, for furthering our understanding of the structures of authority through which the rural landscape was managed and organised. The architecture of these buildings had purposes and meanings beyond the strictly functional: lordly residences were all, in some senses, icons of authority that would have loomed large in the 'peasant's eye view' of the medieval countryside. So too would the conspicuous trappings of seigneurial authority with which these sites were associated, including mills, moats, fishponds, dovecotes and deer parks. This was reinforced in contexts such as Anglo-Norman Ireland, where lordly sites were often regarded as the symbols of domination by a foreign power. Moreover, the owners and builders of seigneurial sites were also clearly active agents in the transformation of the countryside, in some cases creating planned villages, laying out field systems and creating 'designed' settings for their residences that showcased wealth and social status.

Nevertheless, we should be careful not to adopt a 'top down' view of the medieval rural scene, whereby lords somehow moulded the rural landscape with impunity in pursuit of their own interests, irrespective of the wishes of wider populations and the operation of customary law. At one level the medieval countryside was indeed ordered from above by the elite power-holders within society; but it was also structured from within by the performances and actions of those inhabiting the everyday workaday world. And it is the shifting dynamic – between lordship and community – that is critical to any sophisticated understanding of the place of seigneurial and elite sites within the medieval rural scene. Using examples and case studies from Britain and Ireland, this chapter will show how archaeologists and landscape historians are transforming our understanding of lordly sites within their rural landscapes. The first section deals primarily with evidence for residences themselves, before considering some aspects of the impact of lordship on wider settlement patterns. The second section examines how lordly sites were keyed into their local contexts through the ordering of surrounding demesne lands. The chapter concludes with a brief discussion of how related research might advance in the future; it identifies some important lacunae in our understanding of the subject as well as highlighting possible avenues for future work.

Introducing elite sites: types, regions, contrasts

As physical entities, the structures of manor houses, castles and other noble residences would have stood out from the countryside, their distinctive architectural forms signalling the elevation of their residents above the vernacular world. This conspicuous display of social separateness was often further accentuated by

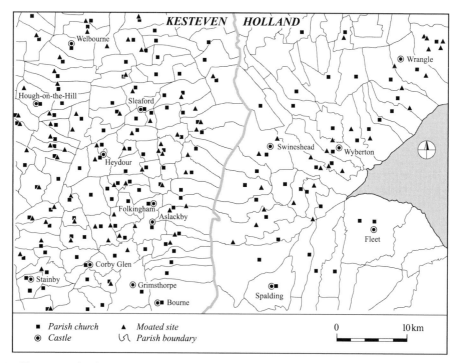

Figure 5.1. Lordship sites and settlement patterns in part of south Lincolnshire. Note how in the district of Kesteven manor, church and village are conjoined, while in Holland the three elements are found separately. (Source: Creighton 2005b. Illustration by Mike Rouillard, based on Healey 1977, with additions)

the demarcation of the residential complex within an enclosure of some sort, embracing the appurtenances of lordship and privatising a visibly seigneurial zone. Yet such sites were simultaneously manorial centres that were integrated into the everyday workings and rhythms of the countryside. Lordship sites of all sorts were not separate from the settlement pattern but embedded within it and part and parcel of its regionally varied character (Figure 5.1). For instance, across large tracts of Yorkshire, manorial centres are frequently found integrated into the plans of regular villages; in Devon and Cornwall they are usually isolated features within a rural settlement pattern that generally lacked large nucleations, as was also the case across much of Ireland; and in Norfolk, they were often elements within the characteristically fluid and shifting settlements that developed around the edges of commons and greens. Equally important regional variations of this sort can be identified in Wales and Scotland.

Behind the outward proclamation of elevation

above the community, lordly power bases usually acted as a social and economic nexus within their localities. Hence, most castles and lordly residences would have housed the manorial court in their immediate vicinity; they were places where justice was administered and where rents were paid. Countless seigneurial sites stood next to parish churches, many of these foundations of the local aristocratic family. Frequently the church was physically embraced within the manorial enclosure; sometimes, common patronage was actively advertised by architectural parallels between church and manor (Figure 5.2). Another relationship that can be observed several thousand times across the British and Irish landscapes is the physical link between sites of lordship and mills (most often a watermill), these places being designated locations for the processing, storage and redistribution of an agricultural surplus. All these relationships provide different but clear types of evidence for interaction between rural populations and a seigneurial zone that was not hermetically sealed but operated as a living and working part of the rural economy on an everyday basis.

Defining elite sites

Academic scholarship has tended to subdivide the buildings and archaeological sites related to medieval lordly residences into watertight categories. Prominent among these are labels such as 'moated site', 'manor house', 'castle', 'palace' and 'tower house'. Studies of these different site-types have, to a large extent, developed along quite separate trajectories, generating their own proud traditions of scholarship; and most of them even have their own dedicated research groups, literatures, terminologies, methods, approaches and classic case-studies. We should remember, however, that these distinctions between different types of lordship sites are often a reflection of how scholarship around the subject has developed rather than reflecting genuine distinctions that medieval people would have been aware of. For example, the distinction between lordly sites with and without defences, serious or not, is in some sense rather artificial. In medieval England, royal administrative officials often did always differentiate between castles and non-defended palaces, referring in the documents that relate to their construction and upkeep to all manner of grand buildings as, simply, the 'king's houses'.[1] Some of the terms used to describe elite sites have medieval origins, but many do not: thus the term 'tower house' dates to the nineteenth century, while familiar terms in the archaeological fieldworker's lexicon such as 'ringwork' and 'moated site' represent modern archaeological jargon rather than concepts rooted in the Middle Ages. The notion of what, for instance, constituted a 'castle' changed through the medieval centuries, while different members of medieval society saw these buildings in varying ways, with contemporary perceptions of such places depending upon class, gender and personal circumstances.

These different terms for medieval lordly sites are also not mutually exclusive. Indeed, it is argued here that the vast majority of castles and tower houses functioned as manorial centres and hence 'manor houses' of sorts; many such minor lords held single manors only; and in other cases the individual manor was a component part of a much wider lordship. Medieval noble families often possessed more than one residence, and different lordship sites within such a network often served different functions – *capita* (or head manors), occasional hunting lodges, favoured summer and winter residences, and so on. Many elite residences saw re-building and transformation through the centuries, in some cases gaining and shedding defences as tastes changed and the place of their owners rose and fell in the social order. A key challenge for the future is, of course, to address the fact that our understanding of the medieval rural scene has been compartmentalised into these different categories, effectively retarding any ambition we might have towards the appreciation of the countryside *in toto*.

These issues and caveats aside, it is still helpful to consider briefly the principal types of elite site with which this chapter is concerned, before going on to assess their wider impacts and landscape settings. It necessarily deals with sites reflecting a very diverse range of builders and owners, with widely varying levels of wealth and different motivations, from royal palaces to the residences of minor mesne lords.

Moats and manors

Certain types of lordship site have always been more central to the concerns of medieval settlement historians than others. In particular the study of moated sites has somehow seemed a 'natural' branch of settlement history; indeed, the Medieval Settlement Research Group was formed in 1986 following the merger of the Moated Sites Research Group with the Deserted Medieval Village Research Group, recognising that moated sites clearly formed a component part of the total settlement pattern. In the period of its existence (1971–86), meticulous regional recording by the Moated Sites Research Group's members more than doubled the known number of moated sites in England, with well over 5,000 identified.[2] The heyday for studies of moated sites was the late 1970s and early 1980s, however, with little dedicated literature on the phenomenon emerging since.[3]

The term 'moated site' is widely applied across British and Irish landscapes, defined loosely by the enclosure of a site within a water-filled moat. Explanation of the moat-building phenomenon, which originated in the thirteenth century, has usually involved balancing perceived 'functional'

Figure 5.2. Manor and church, East Quantoxhead, Somerset. This manorial complex lay within a curia containing a mill, fishponds, dovecote, gardens and agricultural buildings. (Photograph © Oliver Creighton)

incentives for moat construction (drainage; provision of fishponds and water supply; serious military defence/security against lawlessness) with 'social' motivations (emulation of social superiors; status of moat possession; symbolic division from the peasantry). We should recognise, however, that the distinction between moated and unmoated manorial sites is to some degree rather meaningless – being more a product of the archaeologist's desire to classify rather than reflecting the realities of the medieval world. Long recognised to cluster in low-lying as also in wooded regions, they are classically interpreted as evidence of high-medieval expansion, especially in 'village England'. Particularly closely researched, for example, has been the link between moated sites and the expansion of settlement through assarting in densely wooded districts and the colonisation of new zones seen (rightly or wrongly) as 'marginal'.

Many (but by no means all) moated sites represent the residences of quite petty medieval lords. In Suffolk, one of the most densely moated counties in England, with over 700 examples and a density of 40–50 moats per 100 km[2], an 'island' size in excess of 0.4 hectares tends to indicate a site of manorial status rather than the residence of a free tenant.[4] Survey of moated sites in north-east Shropshire has similarly highlighted a broad correlation between the size of the moated island and the social status of the site.[5] Archaeological survey has also shown that single, simple moats in isolation are not always the most common type of field monument; many were closely associated with other appurtenances of lordship, most commonly paddocks and enclosures, but also fishponds, settlement remains and subsidiary moats, as well attested in north-east Lincolnshire.[6]

Fieldwork and excavation have revealed the origins and functions of these sites to be especially varied, and we should certainly not assume that all at some stage contained residences. Some moated sites functioned as gardens, pleasure grounds, vineyards and orchards (especially where one smaller moat is subsidiary to another); others were granges linked

Figure 5.3. Cloonfree moated site, Co. Roscommon: digital terrain model of a Gaelic lordship site. (Image reproduced with the permission of Dr Niall Brady and the Discovery Programme)

to religious houses or park lodges.[7] Field survey and related documentary research focused on medieval moated sites near Arlington in the Rape of Pevensey (East Sussex), have identified a pattern of paired moats, lying 0.5 km apart, with the water exiting from one moat and flowing into a second that often took a 'figure of eight' form. Such a relationship shows co-operation and probably a tenurial connection between sites.[8]

In Ireland, some of the smallest moated sites were probably used solely as cattle enclosures in the lawless environment that often prevailed in the Anglo-Norman colony.[9] The distribution pattern of moated sites indicates a concentration on the peripheries of the zone of Anglo-Norman lordship, where the settlers needed the defences provided by the moat, bank and palisade.[10] Yet in the last 20 years or so it has become apparent that moated sites were also being constructed by the Gaelic-Irish nobility, such as the O'Conors of Roscommon. One good example is located at Cloonfree (Co. Roscommon) (Figure 5.3),

attested stronghold of Aodh O'Conor at the start of the fourteenth century.[11] In Scotland, moated sites have received comparatively little attention, certainly compared to Norman castles, although sufficient is known from sites such as Dunrod (Kirkcudbright) to confirm that moats served to express the status of lordly dynasties, often in dispersed settlement landscapes.[12]

There is likewise a long tradition of other medieval manorial sites being studied as component parts of the wider settlement pattern. The long-term archaeological investigations at Wharram Percy (North Yorks.) famously revealed evidence for two manor sites. The conventionally accepted sequence is that one of these (the South Manor) was a construction of the twelfth century and was replaced by another (the North Manor) in the thirteenth century;[13] but key questions remain unanswered, highlighting once again the considerable methodological challenges of unravelling settlement development through archaeology. Extensive excavations of the South Manor did not in fact reveal any evidence for a hall, nor a kitchen, while the material assemblage shows remarkably little twelfth- and thirteenth-century material and, indeed, no compelling evidence for the presence of a seigneurial household at all.[14] In contrast, the North Manor comprised a more extensive and diverse range of buildings around a courtyard complex: while documentary evidence shows its main *floruit* to have been in the early fourteenth century, the ceramic evidence indicates much longer-lived occupation, with Iron Age and Romano-British features on the site providing tantalising glimpses of high-status antecedents.[15]

The example of Barentin's manor in Chalgrove, a thirteenth- to fifteenth-century manorial complex in Oxfordshire, showcases how archaeology can reveal the emergence of a knightly family through material evidence for building plans, portable artefacts and environmental remains (here, for example, the occupants either grew or imported walnuts, plums and grapes).[16] Even so, this project was carried out in the late 1970s and focused overwhelmingly on the principal structures in a way that might now seem quite limiting; today, the research design would incorporate geophysical survey, more sophisticated environmental approaches, and pay more attention to the area beyond the moat.

Castles, tower houses and other defensive sites
In contrast, studies of castles for long lay beyond the horizons of landscape history, and it is only much more recently that their important roles within the evolution of the rural landscape have come to be more fully appreciated. The field of castle studies ('castellology') was long dominated by militaristic and 'site-centric' approaches that often served to sever these structures from their wider landscape settings, although this is changing fast.[17] Castles represented some of the largest, highest-status and most visually imposing elite sites in the medieval landscape, yet equally important from the perspective of settlement history are the manorial functions of castles. We are increasingly realising that the distribution map of castles does not represent a coherent system of defence; rather, at a local scale, castles occur in much the same sorts of locations as other manorial sites. The number of castles is unknowable, but they were overwhelmingly rural seats: at least 1,125 sites are

known across the counties of England alone, with over 82 per cent located in the countryside.[18]

Behind the defences, most castles worked as farms and estate centres that were intimately tied to the exploitation of the land. Excavation is revealing more and more of the workaday lives of castles, with environmental evidence providing particularly valuable insight into their roles as points of interface between the seigneurial sphere and territories beyond. At Sandal Castle (West Yorks.), for instance, integrated environmental analysis has charted the progressive clearance of the surrounding estate between the twelfth and fifteenth centuries; and at Okehampton (Devon), it has shown how the management of an associated deer park changed in the fourteenth century with a mass introduction of fallow deer that transformed the local ecology.[19]

In Ireland, studies of castles have often been integrated within the framework of later medieval rural archaeology and Norman fortified sites seen as components within evolving settlement patterns.[20] One reason for this is the relative youth of these fields of scholarship compared to England (medieval studies in Ireland being long dominated by the early Christian period). Another is that enclosed sites formed such an important part of the Irish settlement map in the pre-Norman period, so that in this part of Europe castles were always 'at home' in settlement study, with the earthworks of timber castles in particular perpetuating a long-established tradition of ringforts in the Irish landscape. These ringforts were the defended settlements of the 'free' element in pre-Norman Irish society and mainly functioned as defended farmsteads. However, only a small number of the morphologically more complex examples probably enjoyed any kind of military or offensive function.[21] In fact, in a recent paper, Fitzpatrick has cogently argued, based partly on her pioneering work in the Burren area of Co. Clare, that we should perhaps not use the term 'ringfort' term any longer as it is misleading; a better term to employ for the 'wide range of native enclosures' that were to be found in Ireland from the seventh to the seventeenth centuries might be 'native enclosed settlements'.[22]

O'Conor has also suggested that we need also to examine the term *longphort* (a stronghold, or fortress) as employed by the Gaelic Irish annalists in the thirteenth and fourteenth centuries to describe high-status sites not seen as castles but which were probably defensive in aspect.[23] One of the problems with this particular term is that it covers a wide range of meanings, including that of a temporary fortified camp of Viking date.[24] However, O'Conor has found several examples of *cashels,* drystone-enclosed settlement sites, again in the western half of Ireland, that in the period before AD 1400 were called *longphorts* in the Gaelic Irish sources.[25] These, along with some of the 1,000 or so *crannógs* (artificially built islands in a lake) found concentrated in the north-western corner of Ireland, were the characteristic elite sites of the Gaelic Irish nobility in the Middle Ages.[26]

There has also been an important excavation, from 2004 to the present, of a Gaelic Irish high-status site at Tulsk, Co. Roscommon, directed by Dr Niall Brady of the Discovery Programme. The site originally presented itself as a possible raised ringfort with no clue as to the sheer amount of masonry structures that have since come to light. It still retains a dominant position in the wider topography and suggests that this was a location of primary importance throughout the medieval period. The excavations have now revealed a sequence of five main horizons of activity, two of which are early medieval in date, and two (when the site was re-fortified in stone) later medieval and early modern/Elizabethan. The excavator speculates that these phases may mark the site of a late medieval castle. Historically it is attested that a castle was founded in Tulsk in 1406, and must be associated with the emergence of the O'Conor Roe as a separate and distinct line of the O'Conors, in 1385.[27] Although there are contemporary written references to the possibility of castles being constructed by the most powerful Gaelic Irish families, and especially the O'Conors, in the first half of the twelfth century, there is still no archaeological evidence for their existence. Certainly there would have been no overlap of site location between these few examples and the considerably greater number of Anglo-Norman castles that were built after 1169. At the present time there is only one example of even an approximate location, that at the important town of Athlone, Co. Westmeath; but even here the earlier O'Conor fortification is located on the eastern bank of the River Shannon, probably under the modern town, while the Anglo-Norman

castle is to be found on the western bank guarding the important nucleated settlement against the Gaelic Irish of Connacht.[28]

Tower houses represent a category of high-status medieval residence distinct in terms of their geographical distribution and interrelationship with the landscape as well as the social status of their lords. Distributed particularly widely in Ireland (especially in the west), as well as Scotland and northern parts of England, they primarily represent a late medieval development. The many thousands of known examples in Ireland made this the most densely castellated region of medieval Europe.[29] Archaeologists there are increasingly realising that standing towers often represent vestiges of more extensive settlement complexes, and future attention is likely to be focused on the 'bawns' (or walled outer courtyards) that were integral to the working lives of these places (Figure 5.4). Most tower houses will have functioned as the defended houses and estate centres of the middle range of the aristocracy in Ireland, and the same holds broadly true of northern England and Scotland. Therefore, they would have needed other subsidiary structures, such as a hall and chapel, as well as an array of agricultural facilities, if only to ensure that the diverse socio-economic workings of the manor were adequately catered for in the building stock.[30] In Ireland there is also increasing evidence, both archaeological and historical, to confirm that many tower houses were the centres of settlement nucleation.[31]

Palaces and mansions

In status terms a very clear difference usually exists between 'magnate houses' (the greater houses of the medieval nobility) and the manor houses of more petty lords. The greater houses of England and Wales have been the subject of a magisterial new survey.[32] As well as exhibiting high-quality living through the full range of domestic buildings, magnate houses were defined by ostentatious architecture, emphasising the roles of these places as forms of social expression. The need to impress was frequently extended to their landscape settings: exquisite gardens, seclusion from the working landscape and grand routes of approach – which can all be revealed by survey, fieldwork and historical research, as achieved at Dartington (Devon), for example.[33]

Figure 5.4. Aughnanure, Co. Galway: an Irish tower house within a walled bawn. The structure in the foreground is a tower adapted as a manorial dovecote. (Photograph © Oliver Creighton)

At the very summit of the spectrum of elite sites were royal palatial residences, although other palaces were owned by episcopal lords (such as bishops and archbishops). The landscape settings of these sites could vary tremendously, especially as the higher ranks of the medieval elite tended to maintain networks of residences, each serving subtly different purposes. In the countryside, however, palaces tended to be more secluded than other forms of high-status building. Detailed archaeological and historical surveys of the royal palaces of Clarendon (Wiltshire) and Woodstock (Oxfordshire) in particular demonstrate how these complexes were buried deep within enormous deer parks and surrounded by lavish gardens.[34]

Lords and settlements

In their classic study of the medieval rural landscape of Europe, *The Village and House in the Middle Ages*, Chapelot and Fossier saw the 'seigneurial cell' as providing a framework for rural life and natural point for the nucleation of settlements across *c.* AD 950–1100. In the *longue durée* of European settlement history, high-status sites in general became increasingly differentiated within more ordered rural settlements between the eighth and eleventh centuries, although with antecedents in the *Herrenhöfe* (large chiefly farmsteads, often enclosed) of the fourth and fifth centuries. The increasing visibility of lordship in the rural landscape was manifested most commonly through their clear physical demarcation within enclosures; through their zoning into distinct areas within settlement plans; and through the association of elite sites with churches and chapels, which became such a characteristic feature of the medieval rural scene.

Archaeological excavation and field survey have furnished us with several classic case studies of the impact of lordship on rural settlements. At Raunds (Northamptonshire) the sequence of village formation revealed by detailed excavations in the late 1970s and early 1980s has been interpreted as providing unambiguous evidence for a single act of plantation by a manorial lord.[35] Here, the regulated settlement formed around a high-status focus that began in the late ninth century and grew to become the Furnells manor site with its associated church; the result was a clearly structured and hierarchical village arrangement. Some of the best-known and best-studied English medieval villages of all bear the hallmark of seigneurial planning and regulation. Laxton (Nottinghamshire), famous for its substantially surviving open field system, probably gained its planned form in the twelfth century, when a large and impressive motte and bailey castle on the northern edge of the settlement was the administrative centre of Sherwood Forest.[36]

The Oxfordshire village of Middleton Stoney, the subject of an important interdisciplinary research project in the late 1970s and early 1980s, provides another very clear case in point. While the seigneurial tower here was a relatively short-lived presence, being established by the de Camville family in the mid-twelfth century but pulled down by the orders of King John in 1216, in this time the lords re-planned the village, established a park, re-routed the road network and founded a church.[37] A major case study of a seigneurial settlement development in Scotland is Rattray (Aberdeenshire), where the process of nucleation between the thirteenth and fifteenth centuries came under the shadow of a manorial centre that developed from a motte beside a harbour.[38] Although legally defined as a burgh (town), excavation has shown the settlement to have had an essentially rural economy, so that the label 'rural borough' is appropriate. Rural boroughs attached to manorial centres also existed in Anglo-Norman Ireland, including the important deserted example at Bunratty (Co. Clare).[39]

Debating the role of lordship in settlement change
The link between a seigneurial presence and settlement planning is not always straightforward, however, as demonstrated most clearly at Wharram Percy, the quintessential deserted medieval village, subject to seasons of painstaking excavation over four decades:

while generally accepted that the settlement has planned origins, it is fundamentally unclear when the regular two-row village actually came into being. The Middle Saxon, Scandinavian and Norman periods have all been suggested as possibilities, but the answer remains uncertain, despite the extensive archaeological scrutiny.[40] Likewise, at Shapwick, in Somerset, a ten-year research project has highlighted the remarkable potential of interdisciplinary landscape investigation to unravel long-term patterns of settlement evolution, but questions remain over the precise origins of the medieval village. Archaeological evidence confirms a regular village with a ladder-type plan to have been in existence by the tenth century, but it is uncertain whether this was the result or one, two or more phases of growth, although re-organisation of the estates of Glastonbury Abbey provides a likely context for the settlement's planning.[41] Another key example is perhaps the most fully archaeologically studied Norman earth and timber castle anywhere in Europe, namely the borderland motte and bailey castle of Hen Domen (Powys), where, despite many seasons of minutely detailed excavation between 1960 and 1992, much about the site's context within the settlement landscape remains obscure (Figure 5.5), in particular whether the castle was always an isolated landscape feature in a dispersed settlement landscape or whether it was associated with a dependent community. While there are suggestions in the documentary record that a borough was being encouraged by the de Bouler lords in the late twelfth century, and while this may lie under the hamlet east of the castle, its size, date and physical character remain entirely unknown.[42]

Another key problem is that many archaeological studies have tended to examine and interpret lordship sites separately from surrounding settlements. The important and controversial site of 'Goltho' on the flat claylands of Lincolnshire exemplifies this issue (Figure 5.6): the deserted village here, comprising a regular double row of crofts attached to a less regular settlement core, was extensively excavated in the 1960s and remains a frequently cited case study of late medieval rural depopulation.[43] A manorial site on the southern edge of the village was also thoroughly excavated, providing remarkable (and unanticipated) evidence of long-term aristocratic continuity running from the early medieval period until the site's desertion in the thirteenth century in favour of a new

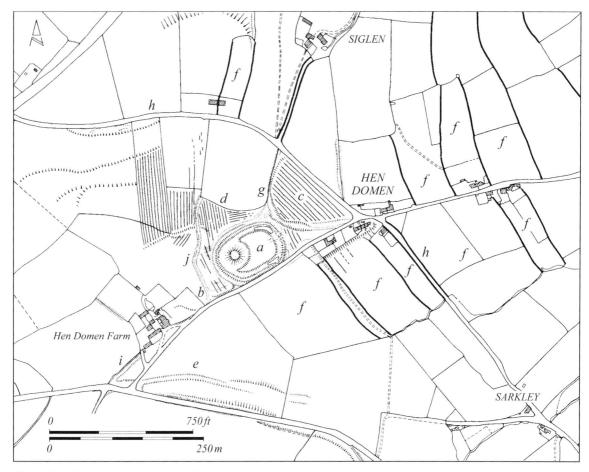

Figure 5.5. Hen Domen, Powys: plan of the Norman earth and timber castle and its landscape setting. (Source: Higham and Barker 2000. Illustration by Mike Rouillard, reproduced with the permission of Dr Bob Higham)

and more isolated residence.[44] Yet neither of the two published excavation reports adequately relate the aristocratic site to the development of the village (nor *vice versa*). Moreover, fundamental questions remain not only concerning the dating of the manorial site, but the administrative context of the manor within which it lay; a compelling case can be made that the identification of the excavated site as 'Goltho' is incorrect, this perhaps being Bullington.[45] The complexities of tenurial geography in this area create extraordinary complex challenges of relating the physical realities of excavated sites to the framework of medieval lordship. These issues aside, the site does provide us with more insight into the role of aristocratic agency in re-organising a rural parish.

The site of lordship comprised a magnate core along with its proprietary church/chapel, and its owners were responsible for founding a new Gilbertine priory, creating a deer park and, in all probability, adding a planned extension to the village.[46] It was not until the thirteenth century that this long-lived aristocratic presence came to a halt, with the centre of lordship shifting to a new residence, set in splendid isolation within a new park suitably uncluttered by the peasantry.

The example of Goltho reminds us that the sites of manorial centres were not necessarily fixed; rather, lords often found it in their interests to relocate their residences. Manorial *curiae* were frequently mobile over the centuries, being upgraded, downgraded and

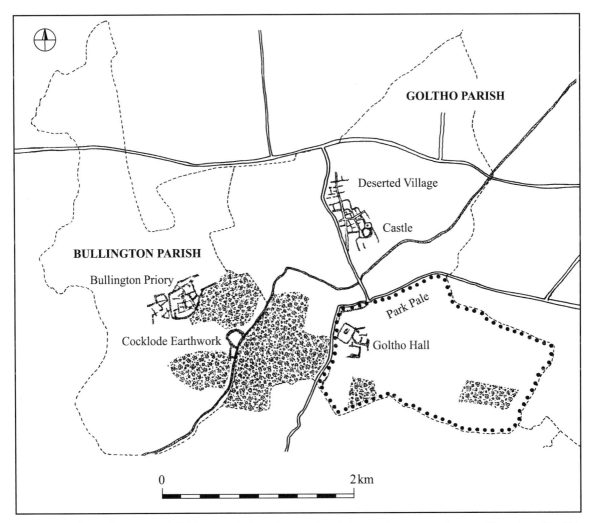

Figure 5.6. The landscape around Goltho, Lincolnshire, showing the relationship between the deserted village, sites of lordship and the priory of Bullington. (Source: Creighton 2005b, based on Everson 1990, with additions)

relocated as circumstances changed, their numbers increasing and decreasing through time.[47] Indeed, fieldwork and historical research mapping the pattern of medieval settlement in the Forest of Rockingham in north-east Northamptonshire have shown the subdivision of manors during the Middle Ages and consequent desertion and movement of manorial residences to be a common theme in settlement evolution, although in this district at least churches prove to be more stable elements through the high medieval centuries.[48]

On occasion the movement of a manorial centre to

a fresh location could cause disruption to the fabric of a settlement. At Lillingstone Lovell (Buckinghamshire), for example, archaeological investigation forming part of the ground-breaking Whittlewood Project showed that an enclosed manorial complex of the late thirteenth century was inserted into the heart of an extant settlement; its construction coincided with the re-planning of the street network and a linear expansion of the village, implying the relocation of displaced tenants.[49] By way of contrast, excavations at West Cotton (Northamptonshire) forming part of the Raunds Area Survey, uncovered a sequence of manorial mobility representing almost the reverse process: between the mid-thirteenth and early fourteenth centuries the manorial complex was relocated to a new area east of the village, its former site being replaced by peasant houses; however, the new manor site was itself short-lived, coming to be replaced by a further two or three tenements.[50]

Many of these examples tell us about the impact of locally based seigneurial families at the scale of individual parishes. We should certainly not assume that the most powerful lords exerted the most profound impact on the rural landscape; in fact, there are powerful arguments that the lesser aristocracy were key agents of change, being a permanent presence in their immediate localities, being closer to the everyday running of estates, and having a direct motivation for re-ordering settlements.[51] The agency of lordship in village planning more generally has been the subject of intense debate.[52] New evidence currently shows no sign of resolving the issue, but what is perhaps becoming clearer is the way in which the impact of lordship took forms that were regionally (and sub-regionally) distinctive, depending not only on the nature of the environment and settlement pattern, but also influenced by variations in the manorial system and by whether lordship was or was not divided in different zones. The impact of lordship on non-nucleated landscapes remains far more difficult to come to grips with, as these zones lack the regular settlement forms that are the hallmarks of planning. Nonetheless, in four counties of the English East Midlands that were the focus of systematic medieval settlement mapping and research in the early 1990s, the impact of seigneurial authority was still clearly tangible in many zones of dispersed settlement, with the lords of moated manorial sites playing an active role in re-ordering landscapes, parcelling out land and establishing peasant farms in new areas.[53] That landlords were quite capable of re-organising dispersed settlement landscapes is also well illustrated for Ireland where both Anglo-Norman and Gaelic Irish lords often controlled areas that were characterised by dispersed settlements.[54]

The inner core: elite sites as estate centres

Most lordship sites had enclosed units of some sort attached to them: castles were invariably accompanied by baileys or wards; tower houses by bawns; palaces and magnate houses by courtyards; and manor houses by *curiae*. The technologies used to enclose the manorial compound could vary: earthworks, moats, palisades, walls and hedges were all used in different contexts to define the core. This zone might embrace semi-public buildings such as halls and churches as well as seigneurial appurtenances including gardens, and most would also have housed agricultural activities of some sort, including granaries, mills and barns. Yet the appearance of medieval lordly sites as field monuments in the present-day landscape may give little indication that they were bustling centres of farming activity. The Irish tower house presents a case in point. From the time of their first serious study, by Leask in 1941,[55] tower houses have traditionally been viewed as isolated and self-contained monuments, and yet documentary evidence, most notably the *Civil Survey* of the 1650s, reveals that freestanding masonry towers often represented but a single vestige of a more extensive settlement complex, with structures such as mills, halls, subsidiary lodgings and churches formerly adjoining, sometimes in an enclosed 'bawn'. Indeed, some of them were even the centres of significant nucleated rural settlements.[56]

Most lordship sites had ready access to gardens of some sort, ranging from modest enclosed vegetable plots through to exquisite landscaped pleasure grounds intended to impress and even overawe contemporaries. Only now are we beginning to appreciate the ubiquity as well as sometimes the scale and sophistication of these features. For example, Clarendon Palace (Wiltshire) possessed some of the most elaborate gardens of any medieval site in Britain and Ireland so far explored. Ignored or misunderstood by early excavators, new archaeological and historical analysis has shown that the palace was flanked by an elaborate arrangement of terraced gardens, aligned below the domestic lodgings that overlooked the site's semi-ornamental 'inner park', itself set within Britain's largest medieval deer park, surrounded by a pale over 16 km long.[57] In Ireland, just outside the walls of Trim Castle in Co. Meath (Figure 5.7), one of the largest Anglo-Norman castles, archaeologists have retrieved plant samples from a possible herb garden on the fertile soil of the River Boyne's flood plain.[58] Further west, at Athenry Castle in Co. Galway, excavation of a cess pit beside a latrine produced macrofossils as well

Figure 5.7. Trim Castle, Co. Meath: the Anglo-Norman donjon (or keep). (Photograph © Terry Barry)

as faunal remains which give insights into the diet and the general economic wellbeing of its inhabitants. The most important source of meat here in the thirteenth and fourteenth centuries was beef, with significant but lower quantities of mutton and pork but very little venison consumed, showing that the diet of the castle's occupants was broadly comparable to contemporary town dwellers in Dublin and Cork.[59]

It is now quite widely recognised that many appurtenances of lordship were articulated in a manner suggesting quite deliberate intentions to impress contemporaries and advertise social status.[60] Features of the medieval landscape once interpreted in purely functional terms are now seen as imbued with symbolic status. For instance, so frequently are church and mill found in close physical proximity to the manorial centre that the three institutions can be characterised as a seigneurial 'triad', arguably representing a means of social control as much as a collection of economic and other resources.[61] The

juxtaposition of sites of lordship with ecclesiastical foundations is especially commonplace; together, church and manor formed a 'magnate core' that, in nucleated landscapes, often formed a point for early settlement growth.[62] Many parish churches grew from proprietary foundations and were not uncommonly situated within or on the edge of the manorial enclosures, so that surrounding populations would have had to enter the seigneurial sphere to worship. In the southern and eastern Yorkshire Wolds, for example, mapping of settlement morphology revealed 64 per cent of churches were located either within manorial enclosures or directly opposite manor houses.[63]

The obligation of tenants to use the lord's mill was another reason for the manorial site's role as a central place within the landscape. Demesne watermills were similarly typically situated on the edges of manorial *curiae*, their feeder systems and millponds sometimes component parts of water control systems including

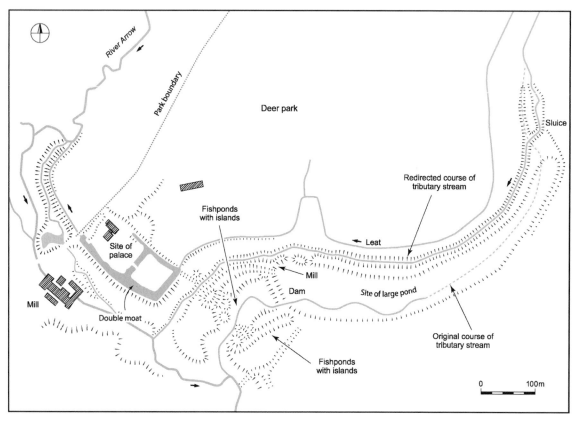

Figure 5.8. Alvechurch, Worcestershire: a medieval bishop's palace associated with a suite of water features and ponds that might now be characterised as a 'designed landscape'. (Source: Creighton 2009, based on Aston 1970–72, with additions)

moats or fishponds. A startling discovery of a moated milling complex came at Boreham airfield (Essex), where the site was excavated in advance of gravel extraction: occupied only from the twelfth to the mid-thirteenth century, the site comprised a house, outbuildings, granary and a large 'sunken-post' windmill, all embraced within a large moat up to 6 m wide.[64] The tenurial context remains obscure, however, and it is not entirely certain that it represents a manorial centre as opposed to the residence of a free tenant.

The 'lordly landscape' was further characterised by the management and conspicuous exploitation of certain types of animal. In approaching lordly sites from an archaeological viewpoint, examining and measuring present-day field monuments, we should not neglect the importance of animals in contemporary medieval experiences of these elite

settings: a flock of doves circling the lordly residence (and eating the crops of peasants!) might create a profound impression, for instance. The introduction of new and alien species such as fallow deer, rabbits and peacocks was closely tied to lordly exploitation, and the display and management as well as the hunting and consumption of these animals made explicit statements of social status.

Possession of a dovecote was another widely recognised symbol, the appearance of the dove having a special emblematic role in aristocratic culture.[65] Dovecotes (*columbaria*) often stood near gateways, in gardens or prominently elsewhere on the demesne, their architecture becoming more ostentatious through the centuries. In contrast to fishponds (see below), which were rare in Ireland, the idea of the dovecote was exported to manorialised Anglo-Norman districts of Ireland, and several examples are documented, sometimes in deer parks.[66] Rabbit farming might seem a somewhat peripheral activity in the medieval countryside, but again it is a form of exploitation closely tied to elite sites. Rabbit-keeping was established in England from the mid-twelfth century and exported to Ireland and Wales in the thirteenth century, although it remained rare in Scotland.[67] In certain cases the location of warrens was quite deliberately chosen with social messages in mind, characteristically occupying the edges of scarps or hilltops and in some cases marking physically the privatisation of tracts of landscape.

Fishponds were important elements in and around manorial complexes: these features were jealously guarded symbols of lordship and the bream, pike and roach they were stocked with were prized elements of high-status diet.[68] The largest ponds could transform the appearance of huge tracts of landscape and enhance the architectural qualities of noble buildings (Figure 5.8). More typically, demesne ponds formed the barrier of the manorial *curia*, in many cases influencing how a site was accessed and experienced; not uncommonly the manorial compound was accessed by passing lines of fishponds on either side.[69] The *vivarium* was a larger pond for breeding fish, while the *servatorium* was a smaller unit where stock was held prior to delivery to the table, and hence close to the residence. Swanneries and heronries were additional hallmarks of elite exploitation incorporated into these watery seigneurial settings.

The quintessential elite landscape was, however, the deer park. Sometimes caricatured as live larders and/or hunting reserves, deer parks were long under-studied elements of the medieval elite landscape, but a recent upsurge in research is setting medieval parks in their social, economic and landscape contexts and revealing important geographical variations in the phenomenon of emparkment.[70] Detailed analysis of the Hertfordshire evidence, for example, confirms that this county had an unusually high density of parks; high and wooded areas were favoured, with a tendency for early parks to lie adjacent to manorial sites; and from the fourteenth century it was increasingly the case that residences stood within parks.[71] However, the label 'deer park' is often misleading, as these units framed a much wider variety of elite activities:[72] parks formed backcloths for elite residences, privatising their settings from settlements and communities and

providing secluded contexts for other diagnostically elite forms of land management such as fishponds and rabbit warrens. The idea of the deer park as a designed landscape developed dramatically in the thirteenth and fourteenth centuries, especially through the creation of 'little parks' that had visual relationships with domestic apartments, dominating views and having garden-like qualities, as apparent in royal contexts at Ludgershall (Wiltshire) and Windsor (Berkshire). Deer parks have until recently similarly been under-studied in Ireland, in part a reflection of the fact that no formal system of licensing existed (as in Wales). Research on this subject is now showing the close relationships that often existed between Anglo-Norman castles and deer parks at places such as Carlow; Murphy and O'Conor have managed to identify at least 11 examples from the surviving historical sources.[73]

Further research horizons and conclusions

This chapter may have created the impression of a wealth of examples and case studies providing insights into all aspects of elite sites and their impact on the rural scene, and in many ways our understanding of the subject has indeed been transformed. Yet serious lacunae exist and future research in the area must confront considerable challenges. In England, particularly alarming is the decline of the sort of long-term research-led excavations exemplified by Wharram Percy and Hen Domen – among Europe's foremost case studies of deserted villages and earth and timber castles respectively. In the Republic of Ireland only one motte castle has been fully excavated (but not properly published), at Lurgankeel in Co. Louth. Funding is, it must be acknowledged, a major issue and scope for research projects of the Hen Domen type is in reality currently problematic. In some senses, fresh high-quality data are in short supply, yet other opportunities exist – especially via the enormous growth in 'grey literature' (reports with limited distribution, usually produced for the commercial sector, yet often containing invaluable fieldwork results if at very variable scale and too rarely flagged for wider consumption). Sifting and synthesis of this body of research and re-analysis of previous work hold great promise. There are also some disquieting geographical imbalances in our data set: a midland-centric view of the subject remains dominant, and detailed case studies and projects are needed from elsewhere in the British Isles. Another crucial priority is that future scholarship should not be as rigidly compartmentalised as it has been in the past, with castles, moated sites, manor houses and so on forming cosy and self-contained areas of study.

There are multiple theoretical issues associated with the recognition of elite settings as 'lordly landscapes' that have designed and even aesthetic qualities. We should be careful about automatically attributing symbolic characteristics to manorial facilities and landscapes; ordered estate management should not be confused with conscious 'design' of the medieval countryside in the same manner of post-medieval 'polite' estate landscapes. But caution is needed: 'design' was not an authentically medieval concept; many of the features of the lordly landscape are difficult to date; and we may be seeking relationships where none existed. Nonetheless, symbolism has been under-researched in the medieval landscape, where interpretation has too often dominated by functionalist approaches.

This important aspect of medieval rural settlement archaeology remains under-developed in Ireland, although there are signs that this is changing.[74] After all, the question of symbolism in the elite landscape has another important dimension in medieval Ireland, where much of the native population would have been opposed, to different degrees, to the Anglo-Normans constructing castles and moated sites within the lordship that encompassed roughly two-thirds of the island. The other third, mainly in the north-west and west, remained outside the remit of the Anglo-Normans throughout the Middle Ages. O'Conor has written about how the Gaelic Irish had to adapt their military tactics in battle against the heavily armoured, mounted, knights that were central to the battle line of the Anglo-Norman invaders in 1169.[75] They could not hope to match them in open warfare, but they employed the techniques of 'asymmetric warfare' that we are familiar with today in the twenty-first century, in places such as Iraq and Afghanistan. According to O'Conor, the Gaelic-Irish warriors employed the natural landscape, that they knew so well, to conceal themselves from the invaders. Thus, their high-status

defensive settlements would have probably blended into the landscape more completely, and, in lacking the permanence of Anglo-Norman castles, are thus harder for archaeologists to locate.

The need to overcome an inherently 'top down' view of the medieval rural scene is also pressing. The working vernacular world and the elite sphere were not separate, but interacted with each other in complex ways, and it has been shown that there are dangers in assuming that physical changes to the landscape necessarily resulted from 'top down' lordly planning and re-organisation. Peasants might plan villages and even found churches, for example. Negotiation and compromise may lie behind what outwardly appear to be 'planned' landscapes and settlements. There were also limits to the powers of lords; they did not plan, transform and manipulate the landscape according to pre-conceived grand plans. Designed settings for medieval noble residences formed the 'public face' of lordship, but we might question whether they disguise inherent limitations in the effectiveness of authority.[76] How often did the sort of seigneurial showmanship expressed through ponds, parks and noble architecture represent the pretensions of more minor families than these schemes of re-organisations outwardly proclaimed? How often did these outward trappings of lordly rank mask aristocratic families under pressure, notably in the context of the post-1300 'crisis of feudalism'? In what sense were landscapes of power, status and authority also landscapes of resistance?

Crucially, there was no blueprint for a lordly landscape: all were tailored to particular settlement landscapes and their creation mediated by variations in the manorial system; and in some parts of Britain and Ireland radically different traditions are apparent. We should certainly not export models from one region to another uncritically. In particular, we should not impose Anglo-French models of manorial organisation on other regions of Britain and Ireland without careful consideration. For example, on the western Isles of Scotland it was control of the seascape rather than the landscape which is key for understanding the contexts of many medieval lordship sites.[77] Similarly, in parts of western Ireland with a strong Gaelic influence, building permanent sites of lordship was not so integral, since here lordly authority was expressed through commanding men and cattle, through genealogy and through poetry rather than 'English' notions of lordship.

Perhaps most important of all, the study of designed aspects of medieval landscape has great potential to open up lines of study relevant to European archaeology as a whole. It is important that we look at the broader European perspective outside Britain and Ireland, and in this regard the recent publication of the first volume of *The Archaeology of Medieval Europe* (edited by J. Graham-Campbell, Aarhus, 2007) is important in a subject which has so often shirked wider comparison and contrast. We in Britain and Ireland arguably have much to learn from developments in, say, Italy, where longer-term research projects exploring castle and landscape are more commonplace. In this sense research by the Department of Medieval Archaeology at the University of Siena in many ways points the way forward: Tuscan archaeology has produced new data on early medieval settlement patterns of sufficient quality and over sufficiently wide areas to challenge old paradigms and enable new models for the transformation of villages in the period to be developed.[78]

Across Western Europe it has been convincingly argued that all levels of the aristocracy arguably shared a common 'spatial ideology' underlain by an hierarchical Christian worldview and spread through social networks.[79] If such an aristocratic code is a valid concept then it is also clear that it was mediated through different landscapes and realised through the actions of lords of varying status with access to different resources. Our understanding of lordly sites and landscapes will only advance if future studies take greater account of this wider, pan-European context.

Further reading

The key source on noble buildings in England generally, including palaces, manor houses and castles, is A. Emery's three-volume work *Greater Medieval Houses of England and Wales* (Cambridge, 1996–2006). The rural archaeology of elite sites in Ireland is dealt with in K. D. O'Conor's *The Archaeology of Medieval Rural Settlement in Ireland* (Dublin, 1998) and more recently in C. Corlett and M. Potterton's *Rural Settlement in Medieval Ireland* (Bray, 2009). For the researcher interested in tackling the history or archaeology of any specific castle in England and Wales, the key work of reference remains D. J. Cathcart King's magisterial two volume *Castellarium Anglicanum* (New York, 1983), which comprises an extensive index of known sites, along with an invaluable annotated bibliography. A more up-to-date bibliography covering fortifications from the Norman Conquest up to the twentieth century is J. R. Kenyon's *Castles, Town Defences and Artillery Fortifications. A Bibliography 1945–2006* (Donington, 2008). For a synthesis of research on castles in their landscape settings see O. H. Creighton's *Castles and Landscapes: Power, Community and Fortification in Medieval England* (London, 2005). The *Castle Studies Group Journal* contains many relevant articles, while for the wider European scene the proceedings of the *Château Gaillard* colloquium is the best starting point.

For medieval parks, two important recent volumes are available: R. Liddiard's edited work *The Medieval Park: New Perspectives* (Bollington, 2007), which contains several valuable papers on all aspects of parks in different regions, and S. A. Mileson's *Parks in Medieval England* (Oxford, 2009). For an overview of elite landscapes in Britain and Ireland, see O. H. Creighton's *Designs Upon the Land: Elite Landscapes of the Middle Ages* (Woodbridge, 2009).

Notes
1. Brown *et al.* 1963.
2. Le Patourel 1986, 17.
3. Aberg 1978b; Aberg and Brown 1981; Wilson 1985.
4. Martin 1989, 14.
5. Fradley 2005, 18.
6. Everson *et al.* 1991.
7. Creighton 2009, 88–99.
8. Hollobone 2002, 38.
9. Barry 1977.
10. Barry 1987, 84–93.
11. O'Conor 1998; Brady 2003, 23.

12. Dransart 2008; see also Yeoman 1995, 86–107 on earthwork castles in Scotland more generally.
13. Beresford and Hurst 1990, 69–84.
14. Stamper and Croft 2000, 201–203.
15. Rahtz and Watts 2004, 293–296.
16. Page *et al.* 2005.
17. Johnson 2002; Creighton 2005b; Liddiard 2005.
18. Creighton 2005a, 281.
19. Creighton 2005b, 9–34.
20. O'Conor 1998, 25–26.
21. Stout 1997.
22. Fitzpatrick 2009, 303.
23. O'Conor 1998.
24. Graham 1988, 125.
25. O'Conor 1998, 85–87.
26. O'Conor 1998.
27. Barry 2008b, 130–131.
28. Barry 2008a.
29. Barry 1987; 2008b, 129.
30. Barry 2006.
31. O'Connor 1987, 21–35.
32. Emery 1996–2006.
33. Emery 2007.
34. Bond and Tiller 1997; James and Gerrard 2007.
35. Audouy and Chapman 2008, 52–53, 28–31.
36. Creighton 2005b, 207–210.
37. Rahtz and Rowley 1984.
38. Murray and Murray 1993.
39. O'Conor 1998, 43–46.
40. Stamper and Croft 2000, 197–198.
41. Gerrard 2007, 974–981.
42. Higham and Barker 2000, 11–12, 149.
43. Beresford 1975.
44. Beresford 1987.
45. Everson 1995.
46. Creighton 2005b, 21–27.
47. Gardiner 2007b, 180–181.
48. Foard *et al.* 2009, 64.
49. Jones and Page 2006, 162.
50. Parry 2006, 276.
51. Lewis *et al.* 1997, 207.
52. Dyer 1985; Harvey 1989.
53. Lewis *et al.* 1997, 204–205.
54. O'Conor 1998.
55. Leask 1941.
56. Barry 2006.
57. James and Gerrard 2007.
58. M. Potterton pers. comm. 2005.
59. Papazian 1991.
60. For an overview, see Creighton 2009.
61. Langdon 2004, 108.
62. Morris 1989, 248–255.
63. McDonagh 2003, 17.
64. Clarke 2003, 69–78; Ingle and Saunders 2011, 97–101 on other moated sites in Essex.
65. Landsberg 1996, 72–73.
66. Murphy and O'Conor 2006.
67. Williamson 2007, 11–30.
68. Aston 1988a.
69. Creighton 2009, 114–119.
70. Liddiard 2007; Mileson 2009.
71. Rowe 2009.
72. Creighton 2009, 122–166.
73. Murphy and O'Conor 2006, 56. See also Liddiard and Williamson 2008.
74. O'Keeffe 2004b; Murphy and O'Conor 2006.
75. O'Conor 1998, 94–101.
76. Dyer 2007.
77. Oram 2008, 180–183.
78. Francovich 2008; Valenti 2008.
79. Hansson 2006.

CHAPTER 6

Town and Countryside:
Relationships and Resemblances

Christopher Dyer and Keith Lilley

Scholars ought to recognise that villages and towns resembled one another in their plans and architecture; that they were in constant contact; that they influenced each other; and that neither type of settlement can or should be considered in isolation. This volume is largely concerned with rural settlement. It compares the patterns of settlement in different regions and traces their development over eight centuries. This chapter does not attempt to deal with all aspects of urban settlements, but it aims to show that villages and hamlets need to be compared with towns and argues that we should be more fully aware of the contacts between town and country.

The chapter begins with an outline consideration of past research into country and town since the nineteenth century, and then proceeds to look at the differences and similarities, before turning to consider their connections and the ways that they have influenced one another. The chapter is based strongly on archaeological data, but also draws on topographical and documentary evidence, and will make reference to the understanding of urban landscapes, societies and economies that derives from the approach of historical geography and economic and social history.

Studying rural and urban settlements

Historians, archaeologists and geographers have tended to put the countryside and the town into separate compartments, and individuals often concentrate their work on *either* rural *or* urban subjects. Indeed, there are journals devoted to agricultural, rural and urban history, and societies and research groups focused on rural settlements and towns.

The nineteenth-century roots of rural history lie in the study of the institutions of manors and villages. Subsequently there has been more interest in the economic history of farming and its cycles of growth and decline, changes in the family and society, and in the cultural history of religion and peasant mentality. The archaeology and geography of the medieval countryside has developed, from an original concentration on the discovery and cataloguing of deserted villages, into a concern for nucleated and dispersed settlement and their place in the wider landscape.[1] The history of towns also began with writing in the period 1890–1936 on town constitutions, that is the origin and development of boroughs and guilds. In a great revival in the 1970s the urban economy and society, centred on such issues as occupations, trade regulation, oligarchy and conflict, came to the fore, and urban decline in the later Middle Ages emerged as a major field of controversy. Geographers applied theories of central place, urban hierarchy and hinterlands, and developed a very active interest in town planning and urban forms.[2] Urban studies in general have pursued themes of gender, identity and community, and were concerned with issues of rubbish disposal, pollution and cleanliness. Archaeological work on sites threatened by redevelopment was financed initially from the public funds and then from the developers of urban sites; such projects, in centres such as London, York, Lincoln and Perth, have made scholars aware not just of the potential for studying urban evolution and societies across time, but also the substantial losses of the urban archaeological resource through earlier, unchecked building development. As a result, however, archaeologists have made great strides in understanding material cultures, economies and environments in towns.[3]

A series of alternative narratives have explained the relationship between town and country and the overall dynamics of medieval society and economy. Since the nineteenth century the big story has been the rise of feudal society, centred on the domination of the peasantry by lords, which went into crisis and decline in the period after *c*. AD 1300. Towns could be seen as lying outside the essentially rural world of feudalism, and even as representing the forces of capitalism that eventually eroded the power of the aristocracy.[4] This view was eclipsed in the mid-twentieth century by an explanation of change which assumed that as most people and productive activities were located in the countryside, the relationship between population and agricultural land was central to understanding both society and economy. The most important vehicle for change lay in the growth of population up to *c*. 1300, followed by a decline caused by the over-exploitation of land by an excessive burden of people. Among those who put forward this Malthusian interpretation, towns were regarded as small-scale and unimportant.[5] Since the 1980s commercialisation has been given a more central and decisive role, and town and country have been seen as interacting and stimulating each other. The importance of towns has certainly been upgraded by the discovery that from the late thirteenth century near to a fifth of the English population lived in them – perhaps a million people.[6] Towns could be regarded as an integral part of feudal society: many were founded by lords, most were encouraged by them and many were patronised by them. After all, towns provided lords with a source of profit and power. In other words, after a long period in which towns looked separate, marginal, alien and in conflict with the rest of society, they are now regarded by scholars as complementing rural society and promoting productive exchange.[7]

Modern academic researchers working separately on rural and urban themes have much to learn from one another: specialists in environmental and artefact studies in towns are more than aware that almost all animals and plants were produced in the countryside, and many industries, such as pottery making, had a rural location. Meanwhile, the bones, seeds and potsherds which are found in greatest abundance among the accumulated rubbish in towns, inform us about the rural landscape's economy. An example of fruitful use of urban evidence to throw light on the land outside the towns has been the analysis of botanical material from town deposits, as at Cowbridge (Glamorgan) or Stone (Staffordshire), which shows how townspeople drew on the varied resources of the surrounding countryside for food, building materials, fuel, fodder and litter,[8] while analysis of the cattle bones in Norwich and Thetford as elsewhere has identified the different breeds kept in their hinterlands.[9] Historians and geographers in the case of the 'Feeding the City' project researched both the London sources and those for manors in the vicinity to investigate the capital's supplies of food and fuel in the later Middle Ages.[10] Architectural historians have discovered cross-currents between rural and urban housing traditions. In the 1960s a plausible case was made for believing that townspeople 'borrowed' rural housing types and then adapted them to their needs and the constraints of available space. Now it can be argued that urban houses were devised by town-dwellers and that their features, such as upper storeys and jetties, were imitated in various rural settlements.[11] Despite these fruitful examples, scholars do not, however, always take maximum advantage of the revealed comparisons and connections.

Distinguishing between towns and rural settlements

In view of the divide between those who are involved in urban studies and those who specialise in rural settlements, one might expect that the differences between towns and villages would be easily established, but this is not the case. It is a source of irritation when those who should know better fail to recognise the lower ranks of market towns and still call a settlement with a market place, numerous shops and craftsmen, plus continuous rows of houses and other urban characteristics, a 'village'. The language does not help, as until the eighteenth century the word 'town' could be applied to a rural settlement, and that is still the case in the United States. In the Latin of the Middle Ages the much-used word 'villa' could refer both to small agricultural settlements and even to the very urban Durham or Winchester. Sometimes it is said that definitions do not matter, but a precise terminology is a valuable aid to understanding the past. Defining differences should not lead to erecting barriers between the categories, but rather make it possible to pursue an informed analysis. However, that said, the problems should not be exaggerated, as the grey area of uncertainty applies to a relatively small number of places.

One approach is to devise a clear definition of a town or urban settlement, and then to regard settlements that are excluded as rural. A commonly respected and much repeated method of defining a town is to use occupations as the key, and therefore to regard a town as a place where the majority of the inhabitants pursued a variety of non-agricultural occupations.[12] It could be added to the definition that the settlement should be compact and permanent, so as to prevent the inclusion of a coalfield or an annual fair in the urban category. Some scholars would wish to add extra characteristics, such as the clear separation of the urban settlement from the countryside; or they might wish to amplify the idea of the compactness by referring to the settlement's distinctively concentrated plan. It is no longer possible to regard walls or legal privileges as necessary urban characteristics, and while most towns were larger than most villages, a minimum size such as a population of 300 would be difficult to apply consistently. Thus many villages with a basis in agriculture (such as in the Lincolnshire fenland) exceeded that figure, whereas places in Wales or Devon which clearly fit the 'urban' category in every other way dip below the figure of 300 inhabitants.

Another method of classifying settlements would be to arrange them in a single hierarchy:

Metropolis	*Urban*
Regional capital	
Provincial town	↑
Market town	
Village	↓
Hamlet	
Farmstead	*Rural*

The position that we might assign to each place in this hierarchy depends partly on settlement size and population, but also on occupations, functions, institutions and facilities. For example, a hamlet would be provided with a chapel as a place of worship, a village with a parish church, and a provincial town would contain a number of religious institutions. Worcester, for example, by the fourteenth century, had 12 parish churches, two hospitals, a number of almshouses, and a cathedral and large monastery. Friaries have been taken as an especially reliable guide to urban status, but the orders which managed them aimed to found establishments only in larger towns, where there were crowds of relatively poor people to receive the spiritual message of the friars, and where there was sufficient elite wealth to pay for their upkeep. Hence Worcester was provided with both a Dominican and Franciscan house, but it is striking that no friaries were inserted in the other smaller towns of its county, apart from a very small Augustinian establishment in the industrial town of Droitwich.[13]

Each rank in the hierarchy would connect with its surroundings in different ways and over varying distances: a hamlet's territory was restricted to the fields and pastures used by its inhabitants within a distance of perhaps 2 km, while a regional capital like York, Norwich or Bristol would be in regular contact with a hinterland consisting of smaller towns and rural settlements stretching over a radius of a 100 km and more.

The material culture of towns

Together with its occupations and its connections to its hinterland, the medieval town had a readily identifiable landscape: distinctive features of its physical appearance included a more or less continuous built-up frontage along the streets (something that would not have been seen in lower order settlements such as villages or hamlets), with buildings standing two or three storeys high, especially in the later Middle Ages, and built substantially from materials such as stone and brick, as well as timber (Figure 6.1). The commercial focus of the town was the market place (in some cases market places), with trading functions separated out deliberately, differentiating between livestock and foodstuffs. Markets might be equipped with selds or groups of shops, dedicated for the use of particular traders, such as a drapery for cloth sales or, most commonly, a shambles or butchers' row. As well as private domestic dwellings, the townscape would be characterised by public buildings and structures, built and maintained by civic institutions and organisations, and vying for visual dominance just as the churches, religious houses and castles sought to do. These civic buildings, which were not very numerous, included guild halls, town houses in Scotland, tollbooths and market crosses.[14] Towns that lay on rivers often had the responsibility of maintaining bridges, which could be combined with chapels and gates (and permanent shops and houses on some of the major urban bridges). Towns on the coast or navigable rivers would have wharfs, either privately developed or the result of public investment. Walls similarly were usually built by the municipal government, but sometimes (as in Edinburgh) sections of the wall were assigned to individuals or organisations within the town, so they were not an unambiguous expression of collective civic pride. The walls and gates could have a defensive function, but often they were also intended to impress visitors, and had a more practical day-to-day role as controlling traffic in and through the town. The many towns without walls closed off entry to the town at night with bars, barriers or chains strung across the principal street.[15] Beyond the gates and bars were suburbs, which might sometimes have separate administration, if they belonged to another lord. Some suburbs, at Bristol for example, were larger than the town itself.

Excavations in towns quite frequently reveal occupational diversity in the form of the detritus of crafts. To take a Scottish example, at Elgin we find the debris of bone- and antler-working, manufacturers using iron and copper alloy, together with less substantial evidence for a textile industry (those crafts based on organic material tend to leave little trace).[16] Standing buildings or house-plans at least can help demonstrate the varied social ranks characteristic of towns, with contrasts between large well-founded houses with many rooms, and modest one- or two-roomed dwellings of the poor. Excavations on sites with a degree of organic preservation, such as in Perth and Aberdeen in Scotland, give the strongest impression of intensity of occupation, with dwellings, often quite flimsy outbuildings, yards, rubbish pits, middens, latrines, and even animal pens and housing for cattle.[17] The picture is generally a positive one of the many varied activities which went to make up the urban economy, but far less attractive was the amount of rubbish and squalor which inevitably accompanied the cramming of many people into such a tightly packed space. Cess-pits contain invaluable evidence for urban diet including fruit stones and fish bones, but also show that the inhabitants were infested with intestinal parasites such as hook worms.[18]

Towns were centres of consumption by the wealthy, so their rubbish pits and middens are especially productive not just of human waste, but of finds, including copper-alloy dress fittings and ornaments, and pottery with a good proportion of decorated jugs. One is indeed much more likely to find in towns the imported wares, such as Saintonge jugs, Spanish lustre ware and German stoneware. The presence of wealthy consumers will be reflected in the bone assemblages, with their scarcity of very young animals, because they were not bred on site. Judging from the animal bones, townspeople ate a good deal of beef from prime cattle rather than those kept as working and dairy animals for many years. The quantity of finds varies from one region to another. Pottery and artefacts, which are found in such abundance in towns such as York and Lincoln, or in small towns in the north such as Bawtry, are very scarce in Penrith and Tynemouth nearer the Scottish border. In Scotland itself, instead of the great variety of late medieval pottery from a dozen different kilns which is characteristic of English urban sites, in a large town like Perth a local ware and white gritty ware from the east coast are predominant.[19] In the same vein, late medieval Aberdonians did not consume the prime beef cuts but the meat of rather elderly cattle that had served long as draught animals or milk producers.[20]

Commercialisation and colonisation

The commercialisation of the countryside through the creation of towns occurred throughout Britain and Ireland, and was not just a characteristic of lowland England. In Scotland a type of town, the burgh, was introduced in the reign of David I (1124–53) as part of a royal programme of promoting the methods of government and social organisation associated with the Anglo-Norman aristocracy. Before this undoubted deliberate campaign of town foundations, already proto-urban settlements had developed near prominent churches and monasteries, such as Glasgow,

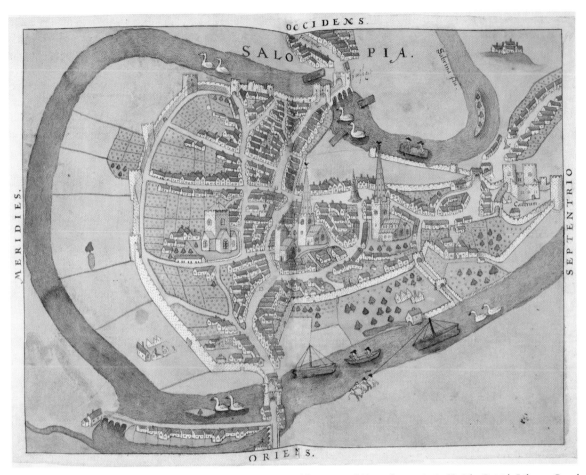

Figure 6.1. The topography of a late medieval town: Lord Burghley's map of Shrewsbury 1575. (© The British Library, Royal Ms. 18.D.III, f. 90)

St Andrews and Whithorn.[21] Similarly in Wales and Ireland a picture is now emerging of towns functioning from the early Middle Ages onwards; again, some of these places were associated with monasteries and early churches, as at Armagh and St David's, but many also acted as commercialised communities in their own right, attracting further trade and traffic through their roles as pilgrimage centres.[22] Such instances are often associated with a particular plan-form, characterised by a series of elliptical or circular enclosures with the monastic church at the centre, and the settlement (sometimes including a market place) located in the outer enclosure, or even outside it (Figure 6.2). Through aerial photograph and map interpretation more of these early monastic towns and settlements no doubt await discovery.[23]

As well as monastic towns, aristocratic elites in both Wales and Ireland created foci of administration and rule over their territories, and such centres provided a nexus for commercial activity and exchange, often drawing upon their agricultural hinterland. For example, the particularly fertile and agrarian economy of Ynys Môn (Anglesey) in north Wales was vital to the rulers of Gwynedd in the early and high Middle Ages, and at Rhosyr excavations have revealed a large manorial-type residence serving as a commotal (local government) centre for medieval Anglesey, which, during the twelfth and thirteenth centuries, provided an administrative and servicing central place for local Welsh rulers on the island.[24] At nearby Beaumaris an existing Welsh port and town called Llanfaes was deliberately removed

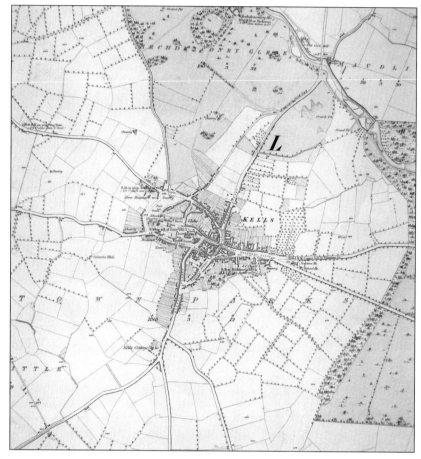

Figure 6.2. Kells, Co. Meath, an Irish 'monastic town'. (Extract from Ordnance Survey 6" map, first edition, courtesy Map Library, GAP, QUB)

by King Edward I in the 1290s to make way for the new English castle and town.

Thus, far from urbanism in medieval Wales and Ireland being a 'foreign import', brought in from England in the twelfth and thirteenth centuries, the recent work of archaeologists and historical geographers has shown that the commercialisation of both Welsh and Irish rural landscapes predated the conquest and colonisation of these lands by outside rulers. Nevertheless, the invaders remodelled many territories through the creation of new towns, alongside a re-organisation of the local landscape. A case in point is Flint, founded as part of Edward I's attempts to secure control of Gwynedd in the 1270s and 1280s:

here the local field-pattern of long strips, fossilised by field-boundaries, connect with the layout of the town, which is based on a rigid grid system comprising streets in parallel surrounded by a rectangular circuit of defences (Figure 6.3).[25] Noticeably, however, not all such 'planted' or 'new' towns in Wales (or Ireland) had such regular forms, and many were placed, like Beaumaris and Caernarfon (founded in 1283), close to or even on top of earlier focal settlements.[26] The variety of layouts of such 'new towns' is evident when their plans are studied comparatively, as has been done for the 'Norman towns' in south-west Wales and the later 'Edwardian' towns in North Wales.[27] Further comparative study of settlement forms here

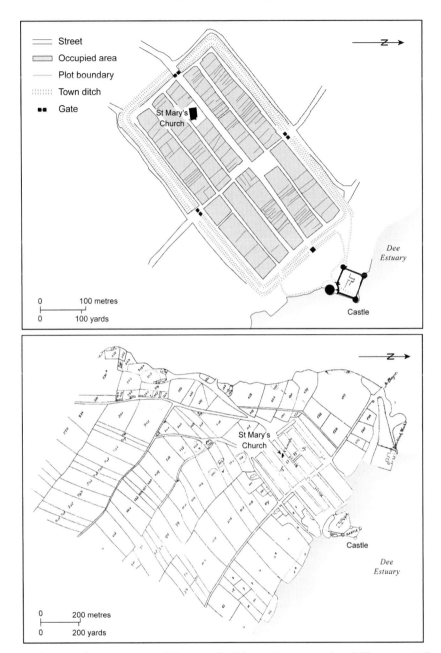

Figure 6.3. Plan of the Edwardian 'new town' of Flint, North Wales, and its surrounding field pattern. (Adapted from Lilley et al. 2005 and Boerefijn 2010)

and in Scotland and Wales is required, and while the Irish Historic Towns Atlas has done much to uncover the layouts of certain medieval centres, new evidence is still revealing traces of medieval towns embedded within the core of later urban settlements, as is the case with Newtownards in Co. Down – the place-name clearly offering a clue (Figure 6.4).[28]

Now that we recognise that older market centres

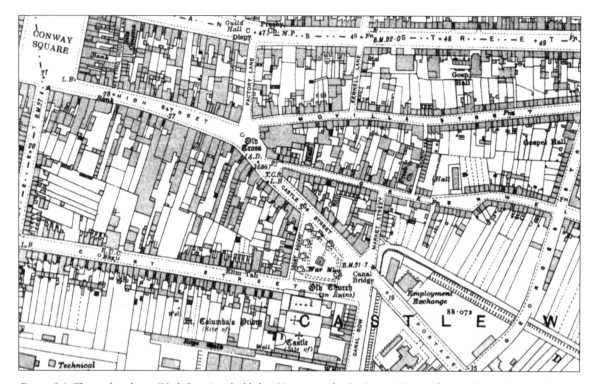

Figure 6.4. The medieval core (High Street) embedded in Newtownards, Co. Down. (Extract from Ordnance Survey 25″ map, second edition, courtesy Map Library, GAP, QUB)

and 'new towns' co-existed, a greater appreciation has emerged of the role that towns also served in processes of conquest and colonisation. Towns either functioned alongside castles as strongholds (e.g. Carrickfergus, Co. Antrim, and Pembroke, Dyfed) or outsiders were encouraged to join the new towns, particularly from England, and settle there as burgesses and traders. Such new towns thereby served a 'colonial' role (e.g. New Ross, Co. Wexford, and Newport, Pembrokeshire).[29] Not all such places were commercially (or militarily) viable, however, since weakly-developed rural hinterlands and problems of access and political instability meant that certain towns disappeared to become villages, or even disappeared completely as settlements, as occurred at Bere in Merionydd.[30] There were cases too, particularly in Ireland, where a charter of borough customs would be granted by a local lord, but so few people came to take up the privileges that the place remained rural in character.

Such 'deserted medieval towns' occur even in Scotland and England and ought to provide fruitful comparisons with the deserted villages and hamlets that often feature in the same areas. There is something very evocative in visiting an empty field where once a town stood, at such places as Newtown in the Isle of Wight and Roxburgh in the Scottish borders.[31] Failed medieval urban ventures are as a part of lowland England as they are of upland areas, and can be found in every part of these islands.

Market towns and market villages

In the fuzzy territory between villages and market towns lay a number of ambiguous and hybrid places. In England as well as Ireland were settlements called boroughs which failed to become urban. Some villages were granted a weekly market, and a market place was embedded in their settlement plan, but they attracted no more than handful of artisans or traders. There were some trading places or small ports (on the coast and on rivers), or centres of industry like cloth-making or mining villages, which again remained both small and devoid of a critical mass of those with varied non-agricultural occupations. The miners, fishermen, clothworkers or boatmen were part-timers with holdings of farming land. One example of a place which poses these dilemmas is Brinklow in north-east Warwickshire, set on a road connecting Coventry with Rugby, at the point where it crossed the Fosse Way which took traffic from central Warwickshire to Leicester. Now a village with a few shops and pubs, in the Middle Ages Brinklow had a market, castle and also, it seems, the special legal privileges that made it a 'borough', meaning that its tenants, who were free, paid a fixed cash rent to their lord. In their list of medieval boroughs, Beresford and Finberg noticed that in the early fourteenth century Brinklow was taxed at the urban rate and was thus 'styled a borough'.[32] Nearby places, such as Wolvey and Monks Kirby similarly had chartered markets, but without borough status, and for them there is limited evidence for craft and trade specialisation. At Brinklow, according to the occupations recorded in the lists of poll tax payers in 1379, among the 80 inhabitants one was identified as a turner and another as a badger or corn dealer, and surnames (which were becoming hereditary at this time, but still give some indication of occupation) include mason, weaver, smith, tailor, cook and fisher. In effect, Brinklow looks a little more urban than its near neighbours, but is distinctly inferior to the well-established borough of Solihull in the same tax list, where seven tax payers were described as craftsmen or traders, and more than 20 carried occupational surnames.[33]

Brinklow thus appears as a 'hybrid' place, somewhere between a town and a market village: it served its local rural hinterland as a trade and craft centre and thereby functioned like a town, yet it lacked some other key markers of urban status; hence, initially, its place of worship was a chapel rather than an independent parish church. Market villages were particularly numerous in England in the Middle Ages, and in some cases were speculative ventures fostered by local lords keen to earn revenues from their estates. Like Brinklow, many subsequently lost their markets and trading functions during the sixteenth and seventeenth centuries, and the spaces once set aside for their market places are now grassy greens in quiet villages.[34]

If we concentrate on the topographical and material evidence, there are various guidelines which might point to a place as having urban characteristics – if with all the necessary qualifications about the uncertainties of the evidence. A town ought to have a distinctive plan, particularly a relatively dense pattern of plots facing on to its streets; these patterns are often visible by inspecting nineteenth-century large-scale Ordnance Survey maps, such as those produced at 25 inches to the mile (1:2500). The plots usually form distinct series and are a reflection of past property-holdings fossilised for centuries by their boundary hedgerows and walls. Brinklow again provides a useful example of this distinctive urban form (Figure 6.5): its plan reveals two areas of different types of plots, one type in rows fronting on to the former market place and featuring large and spacious plots, with generous proportions, and the other type with smaller plots fronting on to a broad street extending southward from the market place. These different plot patterns most probably reflect two stages in the physical growth of Brinklow, one associated with the foundation of the market, most probably in association with the construction of the motte and bailey castle, and the other linked with the later borough status of the place as it developed urban pretensions.

In general, urban plots tended to be smaller in size, and especially narrower, than those found in rural settlements. They were often subdivided into two, three or four narrow plots, sometimes only 5 m wide. There was also within the urban plots a denser pattern of occupation and building, resulting from the addition of workshops, storage spaces or small houses for subtenants. The larger towns were composed of a number (i.e. more than two or three) of distinct 'plan-units', that is areas of streets and plots that each have a particular identifiable form reflecting stages of past growth. Towns at the upper end of the urban hierarchy, such as Coventry, had a greater number of these growth-stages, duly reflected in their urban layout, all of which to some degree originated from controlled development of rural lands at the urban fringe, resulting sometimes in a pattern of plots that reflected earlier cultivation strips.[35]

Rural settlement forms and village life

Rural settlements have many similarities with towns, but there are also important differences. We will begin with their topography and then consider

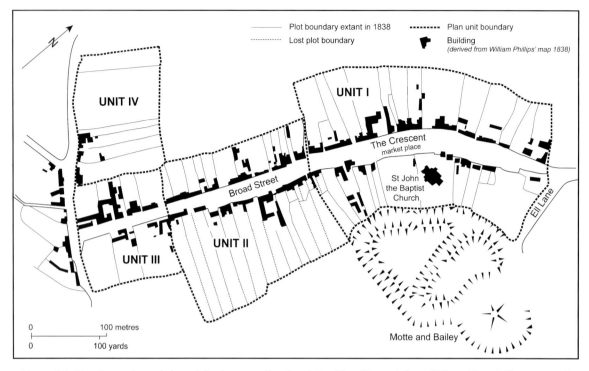

Figure 6.5. The plan and morphological development of medieval Brinklow, Warwickshire. (Adapted from Lilley 1993–94).

their buildings and economy. Village plans could be complex, both in terms of their forms as well as their topographical development. As Taylor showed, many settlements were 'polyfocal', with multiple parts.[36] Roberts has termed these 'composite' plans, as part of his classification of rural settlement forms.[37] In the case of villages, more so than in towns, caution has to be exercised in studying modern Ordnance Survey maps as evidence for the layout of medieval settlements: in towns, medieval features, such as plot patterns and streets, can be very enduring, whereas in rural contexts shrinkage, expansion and movement all can contribute to a settlement plan that seems to be very dynamic. Earthwork features on the ground often point to such changes, of course, but these are not typically shown on Ordnance Survey plans, so fieldwork and aerial photographs are used to build up a fuller picture of rural settlement morphology, in combination with plan-analysis. Such methods make it possible to discern discrete areas in the layout of villages, perhaps reflecting stages in settlement evolution or different landholdings or both.

A striking example of a village that changed radically over time is Akeley (Buckinghamshire) which now has a cluster plan as its most prominent feature, grouped around the site of the church and a small square (Figure 6.6). The cluster is linked to the street on which the manor house stands, by the road called Church Hill. A combination of test pitting and documentary research shows that by around AD 1300 the village consisted of Church End and South End, separated by a large green, and Church Hill did not exist. After 1350 South End was cleared of houses, and Church End developed as the principal settlement.[38]

Typically, where village plans are 'regular' in form, with relatively straight streets and toft-croft boundaries, it is assumed that they resulted from 'planned' development. Caution again is required, however, because 'irregular' forms are not necessarily a sign of a lack of planning: any number of reasons can account for differences in the shape of a village, including local site characteristics, the settlement's function and origins, and the decisions and whims of those (often unknown) groups or individuals who

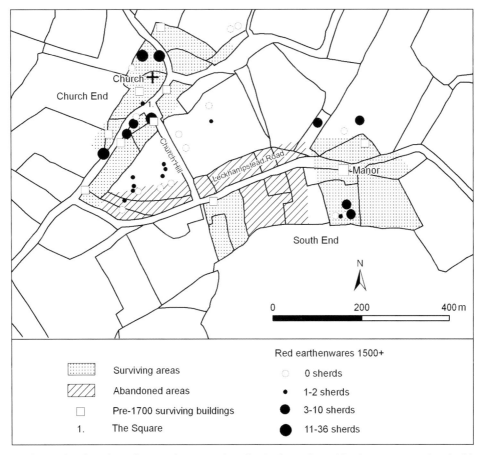

Figure 6.6. Akeley, Buckinghamshire, showing changes in the village's plan indicated by documents, standing buildings, pottery found in test pits, and documents. Based on the enclosure map of 1794. (Image courtesy of Richard Jones)

decided on the layout of villages or parts of them in the Middle Ages. The juxtaposition of manor house, or castle, or church, in relation to parts of the village may provide clues as to who influenced a settlement's development and form, but inferring from these topographical relationships that a village was planned by one particular lord or another is necessarily risky, not least because the layout of a village may well reflect as much the needs and desires of villagers as it did those of their overlord.

Peasant houses, either excavated or, more generally, inferred from visible earthworks, appear to have been relatively homogeneous in size and construction, suggesting an egalitarian social structure. Historians are aware of gradations of peasant wealth depending on the size of holdings, so that through much of

lowland England in the thirteenth and fourteenth centuries an upper rank of peasants had 30-acre yardlands, with others holding of 15 and 7 acres each ('half yardlands' and 'quarter yardlands'), and in addition there were many cottages and smallholdings. Often there would be a number of holdings of similar size, giving a degree of equality within parts of the village. An essential cultural unity is reflected in the similarities in ground plan of houses, with a standard division into two or three rooms, with a hall and inner sleeping and storage room, the chamber, and an occasional extra store room or space for food preparation, or (more rarely) stalls for animals under the same roof as the accommodation for humans. Adjoining the houses are buildings without hearths or signs of human occupation, presumably denoting barns and animal houses. The space between buildings was often occupied by sunken yards for animals, stores of fodder and muckheaps. There were public spaces, such as greens and streets, but the church or chapel was usually the only public building, apart from guildhalls in eastern England, and the church houses which tend to be most easily recognised in the west.

Rural sites have few finds directly deriving from agriculture, apart from small implements like weeding hooks, together with horseshoes among the iron objects, but the topography of the settlement, with the close proximity of fields and pastures, makes abundantly clear the connection between the inhabitants and the land. Most villages contain some evidence for crafts and trades, and occasionally a smithy has been excavated. From potting villages like Potters Lyveden and Stanion in Northamptonshire come kilns and the debris of wasters.[39] Otherwise the main craft, judging from finds of spindle whorls, seems to have been distaff spinning: this part-time activity for women, which could be continued while engaged in other tasks or while walking and talking, was very likely organised to supply yarn for specialist weavers beyond the village. Villages were probably not self-sufficient in manufactured goods, such as cloth, though they did carry out some crafts at home, as suggested by occasional finds of tools appropriate for carpenters or masons. The main foodstuffs were usually prepared within the community; bone debris suggests that they killed animals for consumption for themselves, rather than buying joints from a specialist butcher, and houses were sometimes equipped with bread ovens.[40] In almost every rural settlement ale could be bought from women who brewed both for domestic consumption and sale.

Small finds and animal bones are present in varying numbers, but are usually smaller in quantity and poorer in quality than those found in towns. There were also major regional differences. Finds, including pottery, were considerably scarcer in parts of Wales for example: excavations on an upland rural site at Cefn Graeanog in Caernarvonshire produced a mere handful of sherds of pottery and a few objects of iron or copper alloy, suggesting a material culture based on wood, leather and other organic materials rather than more durable ceramics and metals.[41] The differences between rural sites in general and towns may partly be the result of methods of rubbish disposal, as the rural middens (containing domestic rubbish such as potsherds as well as animal dung) will have been carried out to and spread on the fields. However, this does not explain why some rural sites have a more plentiful material culture than others.

An opportunity to make a direct comparison between living conditions in country and town comes from the analysis of human bones from cemeteries. The village churchyard at Wharram Percy can be compared with an almost contemporary urban example from York, that of St Helen-on-the-Walls. Both were receiving the majority of their burials in the period 1000–1550. They belong to the same region, and cranial statistics suggest that the populations were of the same physical appearance, and they were closely similar in height – the males averaged 169 cm or 5 feet 7 inches, and women 158 cm (5 feet 2 inches). Some of those buried may have belonged to the same families, as York recruited many immigrants from the villages on the wolds, including Wharram. The gender balance supports this connection, as the Wharram graveyard had a high proportion of males, whereas St Helen's contained more females, and we know that women were prominent among those who sought jobs in the city. Urban living conditions are reflected in the bones: the York burials were more likely than the country ones to show porotic hyperostosis, a pitting of the bones caused by episodes of serious infectious disease; the bones of town-dwellers more often than those of villagers had signs of periostitis, which is a build up of fresh bone after a crisis, such as a serious illness. Both conditions tell us that those living in a large city were likely to suffer infections associated with unhygienic and crowded conditions. Periostitis shows that people recovered from these diseases, and it is possible that the York population were so commonly exposed to illness that they developed a capacity to recover. The Wharram inhabitants, however, who encountered fewer threats in the relatively healthy rural environment, were more likely to die when they contracted diseases. Furthermore, evidence for sinusitis suggested that townspeople living in a smoky atmosphere suffered from respiratory problems. Rural women did more hard work, judging from their arm bones, signifying most probably that they laboured in the fields as well as in the yard and garden. Presumably towns offered the young women of the wolds villages a better life, where they could find employment, higher earnings and less arduous work, for which they were prepared to accept the risks of a less healthy environment.[42]

Connecting town and country

Having made comparisons and drawn distinctions between country and town, the point must be made that even in settlements that fall decisively on either side of the village/town divide, there are generic similarities between their plans in terms of streets and rows of houses.

Towns indeed had rural dimensions. They included peasants among their population, sometimes with houses interspersed with their artisan and trader neighbours as in Daventry in Northamptonshire, or sometimes in adjacent settlements like the Bond Ends found in the Midlands on the edge of towns, or the village called 'Old Shipston' immediately next to the borough of 'New Shipston' in Warwickshire.[43] Townsmen themselves might combine their work in trade, industry, administration or religion with part-time farming, as many towns, even those as large as Cambridge or Colchester, were surrounded with fields in which townsmen held strips of arable or the right to pasture animals. The most frequently encountered urban outbuilding was not a smithy or brewery, but a barn, for the storage of hay and crops bought for resale or consumption in the household, or for those produced on the household's own acres. Towns were in addition centres for horticulture, in which gardens were attached to the houses of a wide range of inhabitants, and were part of the facilities of institutions, but also were grouped at the edge of the town in separate plots.[44] Pigs scavenged in urban streets just as they rooted in villages, in both cases causing annoyance to the neighbours who suffered from their anti-social behaviour.

We can take a broader view by adopting a landscape approach to see how the types of settlement fit together in different environments and circumstances. Urban settlements, though often small in size, can be numerous in areas of dispersed settlement and in upland or woodland pays. An extreme example is Devon, where the rural settlements include nucleated villages in the south of the county, but which has a large number of hamlets and farms. About 50 towns have been identified there, which is double the normal

total in an English county (Figure 6.7). There are a number of explanations for this relatively high density of towns, including the problems of communication when roads were steep and narrow, and travel to market centres would have been inconveniently slow and arduous if the towns were as much as 20 km apart.[45] Since the lords of the countryside gained relatively low incomes from the infertile soil, and could not squeeze large amounts of rent from tenants whose incomes were also limited by the shortage of best-quality land, founding a borough with a market was a logical way to raise revenue from rents and tolls. The towns could benefit from, and in their turn stimulate, the spread of rural industries, and some Devon towns traded the tin and cloth which were produced in their hinterlands. Similarly, the emphasis on pastoral farming brought the peasants more often to market because they needed to sell their surpluses of animals, wool and cheese, and to buy grain and straw.

In a champion county like Leicestershire, where nucleated villages and corn growing predominated, there were only ten towns, though they tended to be larger than their Devon counterparts (Figure 6.8). The cultivators of the corn fields did not need to visit markets so often, especially as the majority were not much involved in industry. In such a context towns were distributed evenly, and their hinterlands sometimes conform with the rule devised by lawyers deciding if markets were too close to one another – they said that those using the market should expect to travel 6.66 miles, or 10.7 km.[46] A hinterland in a champion landscape would often contain 40 villages. Market towns are often found strung along the boundaries between areas with different rural economies, such as Melton Mowbray, which lay on the frontier which divided a river valley from upland wold country, where cultivators could bring for sale the products of their particular countryside. More dramatic differences encouraged the flourishing of towns around the edge of the breckland in Norfolk and Suffolk, for example, or along the Cotswold edge in Gloucestershire.

How, and in what circumstances, did country people interact with their urban neighbours? Villages and hamlets were by no means cut off from urban life, as the population sold agricultural produce in the town markets, and bought the goods that they could not make themselves, such as clothing. The

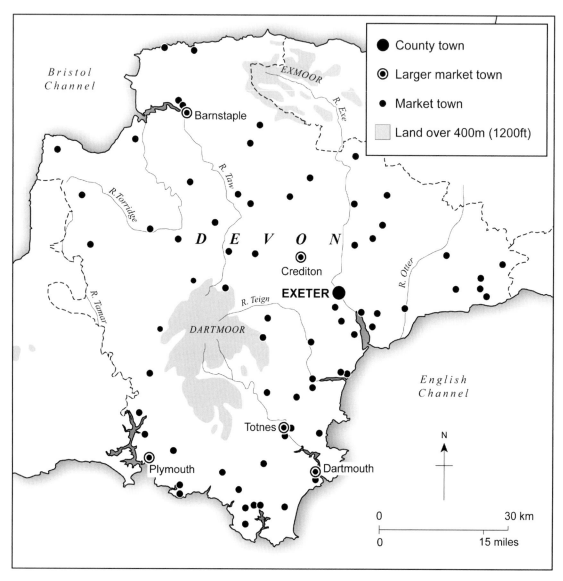

Figure 6.7. Towns in Devon.

main historical evidence of trading contacts comes from records of debts, and from the presence in towns of the artisans and traders whose business as smiths, shoemakers, cartwrights and grain dealers would depend on selling to and buying from the local rural population. Animal bones recovered by excavation indicate clearly the constant flows of foodstuffs into the towns, which in the case of meat would arrive on the hoof to be processed by the urban butchers.

In Scotland, where there was not much large-scale industry in towns, the whole economy depended on the collection in towns of hides, woolfells, wool, meat and salmon, which were then exported to England and the continent through the east coast ports.[47]

Metal goods, especially those made from copper alloy, were mainly manufactured in the towns, but percolated into the possession of peasants. Let us take as an example a village in Norfolk, Grenstein, which

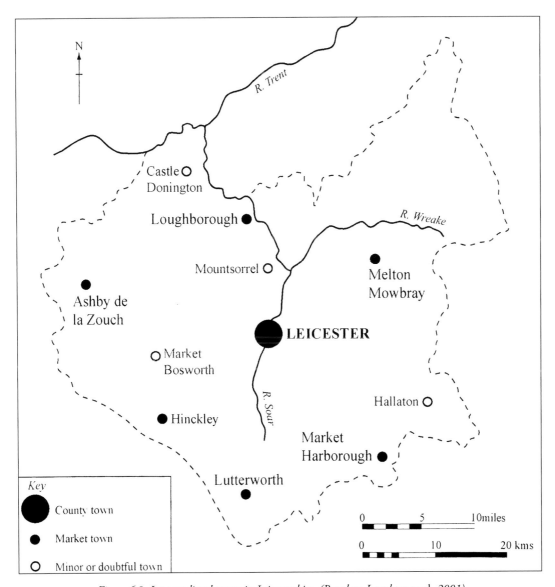

N

R. Trent

Castle O
Donington

Loughborough ●

R. Wreake

Mountsorrel O

Melton
Mowbray ●

Ashby de
la Zouch ●

LEICESTER ●

O Market
Bosworth

Hallaton O

R. Soar

● Hinckley

Market
Harborough ●

Key

● County town

● Market town

O Minor or doubtful town

Lutterworth ●

0   5   10 miles

0   10   20 kms

Figure 6.8. Late medieval towns in Leicestershire. (Based on Laughton et al. 2001)

lay about 8 km from two market towns, Fakenham and East Dereham, and 25 km east of a large town with a wide range of crafts and international trading links, King's Lynn.[48] Excavations of a house at Grenstein, occupied in the fourteenth and fifteenth centuries, yielded 26 objects of copper alloy, including buckles, strap ends and a piece of a cooking vessel, and a hundred iron artefacts, including knives, horseshoes, hinges, pieces of locks, and horseshoes (Figure 6.9).

Most items of metal when broken or worn could have been recycled, so these few dozen small pieces represent just a fraction of the dress accessories, kitchen utensils, farming gear and building fittings which this household once owned, and which were mostly made in towns and bought from urban markets and fairs. Of almost 6000 pieces of pottery, the majority came from pots made at the nearby rural centre of manufacture at Grimston in Norfolk, although these

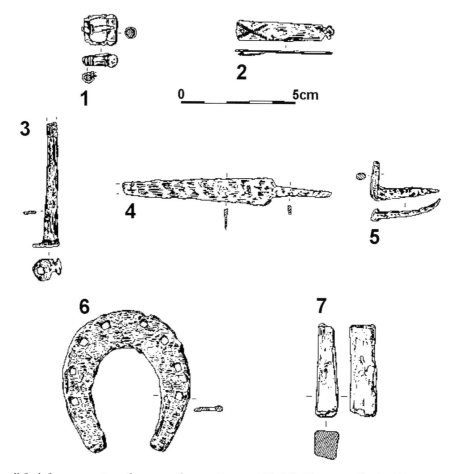

Figure 6.9. Small finds from excavations of a peasant farm at Grenstein, Norfolk. The copper alloy buckle (1) and strap end (2) would have been made in a town; the iron objects include some also likely to have been of urban origin: the knife (3) and the padlock key (4). The hinge (5) and horseshoe (6) might have come from a rural smith. The whetstone (7) came from Norway, probably through the port of King's Lynn. All of the objects are of the thirteenth to fifteenth centuries. (Images re-drawn from Wade Martins 1980b)

may still have been bought from a town market. Not all of the goods acquired by the peasants of Grenstein had local sources, as the pieces of millstone had been imported from the Rhineland, six hones (sharpening stones) had originated in Norway, and a few pottery vessels were of French and German manufacture. The peasants at least in a small way were thus involved in an international trading network, and the complexity of the chain of middlemen which brought such exotic items to a remote village hints also at some sophistication in the financial arrangements by which peasants obtained credit which enabled them to buy more expensive items. The excavations cannot tell us

about the peasants' purchases of objects made from organic materials, except that some of the metalwork was originally attached to textiles, leather and wood, so do help tell us something at least about clothing, belts and shoes, and furniture which has not survived in the ground. Documents meanwhile fill other gaps, notably in telling us of the garments, household textiles, harness and wooden vessels and implements which every household possessed.

Single households usually confined themselves to small and relatively cheap purchases, but collectively they could afford more expensive items: the churchwardens of rural parishes were paying for statues, processional crosses, books and organs for their parish churches, and these would be obtained from large towns. London bell-founders, for example, were supplying churches more than 100 km from the capital.[49] Rural consumers also needed on occasion specialist professional services, which were often provided by town-dwelling lawyers, medical practitioners and clergy.

Significantly, some non-agricultural products, such as pottery and building materials, went from the country to the town, as did bar iron and fuel such as firewood, coal, charcoal and turf. Urban industry would indeed have depended on the products of rural workers, most notably the clothworkers, such as spinners, who looked to urban clothiers for employment. When the textile industry was based in the country, the clothiers, weavers and dyers still expected to buy their dyestuffs, oil and other raw materials from the towns, and the finished cloth was then traded by urban merchants.

Documents provide evidence of migration, from surnames in the thirteenth century, and lists of serfs who had left the manor in the fifteenth; these show towns gathering people mainly from within a 16 mile (26 km) radius. But this was not a one-way traffic, since townspeople, both rich and poor, on occasion might set themselves up in the country, meaning that we can encounter villagers with such names as 'John de London'.[50]

Influences and borrowings

Rural life went through a profound change in the thirteenth century which persisted thereafter. The indirect impact of the growth of towns and commerce permeated every corner of village life: land was being bought and sold – with special intensity in East Anglia, but to some extent everywhere; rents were paid in cash, and lords increasingly regarded financial payments as the principal means by which they gained income from the peasants. Exchange within the village, for labour, goods and rent, was assessed in money, even if coins did not always change hands. Country dwellers came to think in terms of values and profit: they could measure a successful cultivator's performance in terms of an annual return in money, and they could put a price on land, produce and services.

Country dwellers were sometimes suspicious of the cunning of those who lived in towns, while townsmen thought that they were superior in culture and skill to their country cousins. But were towns really the main source of innovations? Certainly urban styles of architecture, such as the jettied upper storey, were adopted in the countryside entirely for stylistic reasons, as the jetty was an advantage in a crowded town, but unnecessary in the wide spaces of the village or farm. Fashions in clothes were adopted in the country through the influence of urban tailors. Nonetheless, some ideas flowed in the other direction, such as the windmill, which first appears in the countryside. In the case of settlement planning, there are generic similarities to be seen between villages and towns, with rows of plots and houses fronting on to streets in each. These resemblances might suggest that processes of village and town formation were going on at the same time, pointing to influences and connections between rural and urban settlement planning.

Villages and towns had much in common: they existed in the same environment of lordly authority and under the influence of the church. They shared a common culture, one dimension of which was revealed by a recent find from Perth, namely a fourteenth-century ivory knife handle carved with a 'maying' figure, reminding us that the typically rural celebration of May was also a feature of the cycle of festivals in towns, when maypoles were erected in the streets and people went into nearby woods and returned with greenery to decorate the houses.[51]

Conclusion

We need to maintain the distinction between country and town. Contemporaries thought the difference important, and it helps us to analyse settlements, and the landscapes and societies in which they functioned. Having said this, there will always be uncertainties and we will debate which label to attach to some places. We ought to study country and town together in order to gain as full a picture as possible and enrich our understanding, but in doing so we must be aware of the complexities of the interaction between town and country. People and goods moved back and forth between villages and towns and between markets. Towns varied in their distribution in areas of nucleated or dispersed rural settlement, and accordingly would have had different roles depending on circumstances. Although there was a native urbanising movement in Ireland, Scotland and Wales before AD 1100, the new towns mainly of the period AD 1100–1300 had a dominating aspect; lordship was strong in English towns, but we are growing more aware of the sense of common purpose and identity among townspeople, who claimed cultural, commercial and social superiority over their country neighbours. Towns generated new ideas and techniques, but country people could be as creative as their urban counterparts.

Further reading

The first major analysis of the makings and contents of medieval towns in Britain belongs, arguably, to M. W. Beresford, who followed his studies of rural settlement by publishing *New Towns of the Middle Ages. Town Plantations in England, Wales and Gascony* (London,

1967; reprinted Alan Sutton: Stroud, 1988). Few substantial syntheses exploiting archaeology as the main tool followed until Martin Carver's *Underneath English Towns* (London, 1984), followed by the fuller and more thematically organised volume by John Schofield and Alan Vince, *Medieval Towns* (London, 1994; new edition, 2003). Numerous valuable overviews of town periods, types and regions are covered in *The Cambridge Urban History of Britain, vol. 1: 600–1540* (Cambridge, 2000), edited by David Palliser. More compact, and drawing together documentary and historical geographical approaches, is K. D. Lilley, *Urban Life in the Middle Ages 1000–1450* (Basingstoke, 2002), while an excellent example of efforts to bring together the townscapes, landscapes and their interrelationships is K. Giles and C. Dyer (eds), *Town and Country in the Middle Ages: Contrasts, Contacts and Interconnections 1100–1500* (Leeds, 2005).

Notes

1. See Chapter 3.
2. Tait 1936; Reynolds 1977; Carter 1981; Slater 2000.
3. Schofield and Vince 2003, 212–242.
4. Pirenne 1925, 75–91.
5. Postan 1972.
6. Palliser 2000, 4.
7. Britnell 1993; Hilton 1982.
8. Dyer 2003b, 99–101.
9. Albarella 2005, 143–144.
10. Campbell *et al.* 1993.
11. Pantin 1962–63; Pearson 2005.
12. Holt and Rosser 1990, 4.
13. Baker and Holt 2004, 408–412; Knowles and Hadcock 1971.
14. Giles 2005.
15. Creighton and Higham 2005, 165–184.
16. Spearman 1988, 134–147.
17. Holdsworth 1987, 18–83; Murray 1982, 17–106; Coleman 2004.
18. Schofield and Vince 2003, 232–234.
19. Dyer 2003b, 108; Holdsworth 1987, 95–101.
20. Murray 1982, 234–235.
21. Dennison and Simpson 2000.
22. McCulloch and Crawford 2007; Soulsby 1983, 238–240.
23. Simms and Simms 1990; but see Valente 1998.
24. Longley 2010.
25. Lilley *et al.* 2007; Boerefijn 2010.
26. Williams-Jones 1978.
27. Lilley 1996; Lilley *et al.* 2005.
28. http://www.ria.ie/Our-Work/Research/IHTA.aspx for a current list of the Irish Historic Towns Atlases.
29. Lilley 1996 and 2000.
30. Soulsby 1983, 104–105.
31. Beresford 1967, 445–446; Martin and Oram 2007.
32. Beresford and Finberg 1973, 173.
33. Fenwick 2001, 649, 651, 653, 655–656.
34. Taylor 1982; Lilley 1993–94.
35. Lilley 1998.
36. Taylor 1977.
37. Roberts 1987, 127–150.
38. Page and Jones 2007, 143–144.
39. Steane and Bryant 1975; Chapman *et al.* 2008.
40. Richardson 2005, 164–167.
41. Kelly 1982a.
42. Mays *et al.* 2007, 89–192.
43. Brown 1991; Dyer 1992.
44. On such garden spaces in the city of Chester, for example, see Laughton 2008, 86–87.
45. Kowaleski 1995; Fox 1999.
46. Masschaele 1997, 61–67.
47. Ewan 1990, 72–80.
48. Wade Martins 1980, 127–157.
49. Laughton *et al.* 2001.
50. McClure 1979.
51. Hall 2005, 217–219; Phythian-Adams 1979, 167–176.

PART 2

REGIONAL AND NATIONAL SURVEYS

CHAPTER 7

South-East England: Forms and Diversity in Medieval Rural Settlement

Mark Gardiner

Regions and settlement forms

The south-east of England is not an area of sharply contrasting regions. It has few of the dramatic changes in relief which mark, for example, the boundaries of some regions in the north of Britain. This is reflected in the gradual transitions in the character of settlement and, when travelling across the South-East, many changes in the *pays* only become apparent over a period of miles. A comparison between the map of historical settlement regions drawn up by Roberts and Wrathmell and the map of 'natural areas' prepared by Natural England shows this lack of sharply defined regions most clearly.[1] The first is based on the Ordnance Survey Old Series one-inch maps which were compiled for south-east England in the early nineteenth century, but which, in part, reflect a medieval settlement structure; Roberts and Wrathmell identified various 'provinces' and 'sub-provinces' based upon the degree of nucleation or dispersal of settlement. The second was compiled from diverse sources, including geology maps, distribution records of species and habitats, and surveys of land utilisation. The natural area maps are just that – maps of the physical and non-human living world. The points at which these two types of boundary coincide are where there are sharp, well-defined changes in region reflected in the pattern of settlement. Where the boundaries diverge, the distinctions between adjoining regions are less pronounced (Figure 7.1).

Both maps pick out the boundaries of the North Downs, distinguishing that region from the North Kent Plain on one side and Vale of Holmesdale on the other; similarly, the South Downs is recognised by both and separated from the South Coast Plain and the Weald Greensand and Low Weald to the north. The two maps also identify the flat, almost tree-less expanse of Romney Marsh as a distinctive region. We can contrast these well-defined regions with the area of the Weald: there is almost no agreement on the line of the boundaries within the Weald; the common designations of the High and Low Weald, and Wealden Greensand are used in the natural areas map, but in the map of settlement provinces the quite different districts of the Western, Eastern and Southern Weald are presented. This suggests that the chalk downland and the marshlands exerted a strong influence on the medieval settlement form. The complex geology within the Weald does not seem to have been the determining factor in quite the same way and so left a less distinctive impression upon settlement within the region. Here other factors were dominant.

It is convenient to begin with those regions where the settlement types and environment were coincidental. The chalk downlands of south-east England, although comprising a similar geology, have very varied vegetation. It is dependent on whether the chalk is capped with a surface deposit of clay with flints which produces a heavy soil, or if it lacks the clay and has free-draining light Rendzina soils. The heavy clay soils on the downland were often wooded. Such soils are found in Sussex on the South Downs west of the Arun, which was briefly under forest law and used for hunting in the late twelfth century, and

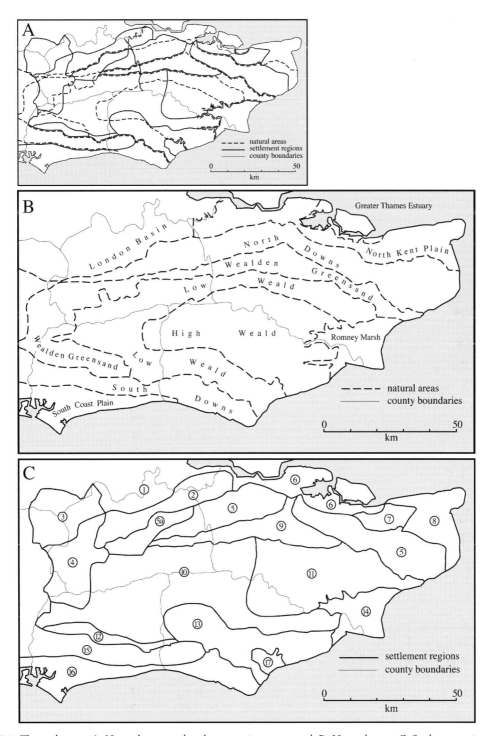

Figure 7.1. *The study zone. A. Natural areas and settlement regions compared; B. Natural areas; C. Settlement regions: 1: Mid-Thames village belt, 2: South Slope, 3: Thames Heath, 4: West Weald, 5: North Downs, 5a: High Downs, 6: Lower Thames, 7: Blean, 8: Canterbury – Thanet, 9: Vale of Holmesdale, 10: Western Weald, 11: Eastern Weald, 12: Greensand Bench, 13: Southern Weald, 14: Romney Marsh, 15: South Downs, 16: Coastlands, 17: Pevensey Marsh. (Source: A, B: map from Natural England, with permission; A, C: adapted from Roberts and Wrathmell 1995; Roberts and Wrathmell 2000)*

Figure 7.2. Lynchets and other earthworks of the deserted settlement of Monkton in West Dean parish, West Sussex (see Aldsworth 1979, 117–121). The remains of Monkton Farm, dating to the sixteenth or seventeenth century, lie at the far end of the field. The name of the settlement derives from its possession by the monks of Surrey abbey of Waverley. The alternative, and probably earlier name of the site was Northolt, the suffix of which refers to the wooded conditions in this area of the South Downs.

still retains extensive woodland.[2] A fine of AD 1231 gives a clear idea of the area south of Heyshott near Midhurst, describing the land granted as the woods of *Leweredescumb*, *Loppescumb* and *Pachescumb* with the pasture in between, and mentioning the hunting in the woods (Figure 7.2).[3] The North Downs too had a capping of clay which produced extensive woodland extending from eastern Surrey into Kent as far east as the A2 road between Canterbury and Dover.[4] There was much variation in the type of woodland on the Downs. *Chesteynwode* – Chestnut Wood in Borden – was notable for the number of sweet chestnuts which grew there, though oaks also flourished. However, the well-known yew woods of Kingley Vale near Chichester on the South Downs are neither prehistoric nor medieval in origin, as some have thought, but developed in the late eighteenth and early nineteenth century following a change

in agricultural practice.[5] One of the features of settlement in this area of Kent is the square manorial enclosures now set in the woodland. Examples have been recorded at Joyden's Wood (Bexley) and Chapel Wood (Hartley), and there are further enclosures elsewhere in north Kent, including Cozendon Wood (Northfleet), Well Wood (Aylesford) and perhaps Darenth Wood.[6] It is not the existence of these enclosures which is notable, since it is probable that many substantial, isolated manorial farmsteads would have been set in similar enclosures; but what is interesting is that so many should have survived in woodland. It seems that these manorial farms were established in the twelfth or thirteenth centuries in the period of high farming and were later abandoned, often in the fifteenth century according to the limited excavation undertaken, and their sites subsequently overgrown or planted with woodland.

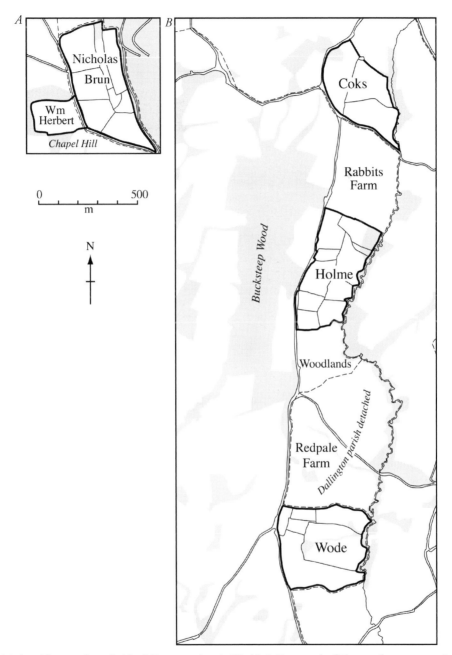

Figure 7.3. Medieval farmsteads on the North Downs and in the Weald. A: Farmsteads of Thorncroft manor near Crabtree Cottage, Mickleham in Surrey. The eastern virgate was a detached part of Leatherhead parish, and must have been established before the parochial boundaries were fixed in c. 1180. B: The farmsteads given to Battle abbey in the early twelfth century, bounded by the road to the west and stream to the east. These are outlined with a thicker line. Other probable tenements in different lordships are named (Source: A: after Blair 1991, fig. 16. B: from Gardiner 1995, fig. 19)

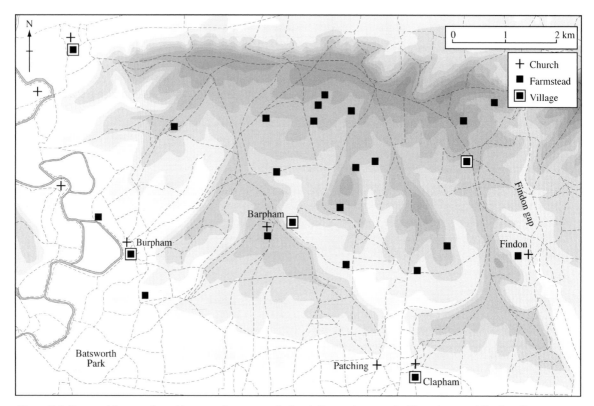

Figure 7.4. Scattered farmsteads and larger settlements on the South Downs between the River Arun and Findon. (Incorporating data from the West Sussex County Council HER)

The pattern of settlement on both the downland covered with clay with flints and in the areas of light Rendzina soils of the chalk was broadly similar. There was a low density of settlement, generally with isolated farmsteads (Figure 7.3A), although in the river valleys, where water was available and the soils were thicker, we find a number of villages. The nature of settlement and land-use on the Rendzina soils can be best illustrated by examining the downland west of the river Arun in Sussex. Many of the sites here were recorded by the local archaeologists Eliot and Cecil Curwen before the extension of ploughing in the Second World War[7]; work after the war by H. Ratcliffe-Densham and Eric Holden extended their work eastwards.[8] Figure 7.4 shows the distribution of late medieval sites, many of which were isolated farmsteads. These generally cluster in the centre of the downlands. By contrast, the land towards the southern edge of the downland and in the valley of the

river Arun was worked from villages situated in those more favourable spots. This area was not particularly important for sheep-raising which was practised more extensively east of Brighton. High on the downland in that area was a type of earthwork formerly known as 'valley entrenchments', forming large sheep enclosures of a type which also known from Wiltshire.[9]

The coastal marshlands form another distinctive area of landscape recognised on both the maps in Figure 7.1. The development of settlement on Romney Marsh, in particular, is now well understood (see Feature Box 1), though less work has been done on the Thames and the Pevensey marshes. Until recently all these marshlands were grazed by sheep, but this was a pattern which was only established in the fifteenth century when the economy moved decisively in favour of the production of wool. It led to the depopulation of the marshlands, since a single 'looker' or shepherd could managed many tens or even

Key Excavation: Lydd Quarry, Kent

Gravel extraction at Brett's Lydd Quarry on Romney Marsh enabled the stripping, recording and excavation of an enormous landscape measuring 1 km across and 600 m wide.[10] Rarely is it possible to work on such a scale and to examine not only individual farmsteads, but their wider setting. A pattern of ditched fields, trackways, farmsteads and embankments was uncovered through the excavations. As work proceeded, it became clear that the pattern of ditched fields present in 1991 before gravel extraction began was only the latest phase in the evolution of a landscape. The large fields present in the late twentieth century had been established 500 years before in response to the growth of sheep-raising on the marsh, but there was an earlier, medieval landscape which could be traced through excavation.

The first medieval occupation dating to the late twelfth to early thirteenth century was marked by the digging of ditches to act both as stock boundaries and for drainage. Natural tidal marsh creeks were also incorporated into the system to channel water. Three buildings belong to this phase: two were perhaps shepherd's huts and the third, a more substantial building, may have been a house.

The construction of embankments in the early thirteenth century to exclude tidal water opened new possibilities for agriculture. The field boundaries were re-organised and from the second quarter of the century permanent farmsteads were established. It proved very difficult to interpret these farms because the buildings constructed directly on the ground surface left little trace. Often the only indication of a building was the pattern of surrounding ditches and the absence of pits (Figure 7.5). Environmental evidence show that both cattle and sheep were kept and cereals cultivated. Fishing took place both in the freshwater channels in the marsh, but also at sea.

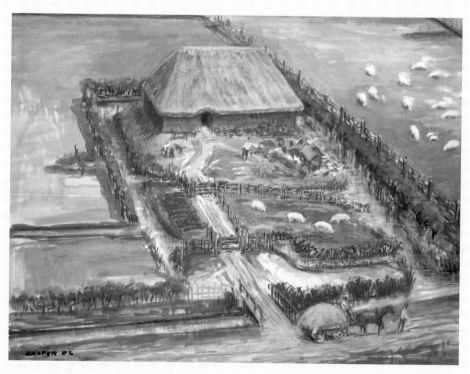

Figure 7.5. Reconstruction of a thirteenth-century farmstead at Lydd Quarry. (Painting by Casper Johnson © Archaeology South East, with permission)

A fall of population in the late thirteenth and fourteenth centuries has been suggested from the results of fieldwalking elsewhere on Romney Marsh and was also reflected in the excavations at Lydd Quarry. The reasons for this decline are not entirely understood, though flooding of the low-lying marshland and plague are obvious factors. Only a single farmstead, including a house of two rooms, was found from this period. One room was marked by a well-defined gravel spread and the other by a depression containing some pottery.

In the fifteenth or else sixteenth century the only house standing in the midst of the now regular pattern of large fields was a large building. This was occupied in 1552, when a survey was made of the area, by Thomas Harlakinden, who had purchased it or inherited it from Thomas Bregge. It was probably the same building which in 1471 had been described as 'the mansion house of John a Bregge'.[11] The site of the house was not excavated, though evidence of the presence of the building was discovered.

The excavations demonstrated the complexity of the changes which took place in the landscape in the late Middle Ages. The field pattern which survived up to the establishment of the quarry was very different to that created when the marsh was first farmed in the twelfth century.

hundreds of acres of pasture which will have required many more people when under arable cultivation.[12] The only larger centres on Romney Marsh were the towns of New Romney and Lydd and the market settlement at Brookland; Old Romney also seems to have been a village, though it was much reduced in size by the sixteenth century.[13]

We have already noted that the other regions in the South-East were less sharply defined. Among these was an area of favourable soils on the Lower Chalk and Upper Greensand at the foot of the scarp slopes of both the North and South Downs, a zone occupied by a string of settlements. The region was known in Kent and Surrey as the Vale of Holmesdale and is referred to by English Nature as the Wealden Greensand. Roberts and Wrathmell recognised Holmesdale and the Greensand Bench in West Sussex, but treated a larger area in East Sussex as the Southern Weald (Figure 7.1). Most of the settlement clusters were not large enough to merit the title of villages, but were certainly hamlets. There were also numerous isolated farms, because the tendency towards nucleation does not seem to have been strongly developed. Nevertheless, there were some villages in the late Middle Ages at, for example, Ightham and Wrotham in Kent and Alciston in East Sussex.[14] The settlements at the foot of the Downs lay within strip parishes which extended from the top of the chalk down to the Upper Greensand and beyond on to the poor soils of the Gault Clay and Hythe Beds. These were in narrow bands and presumably reflect earlier estates boundaries. Similar strip parishes in Oxfordshire seem to have originated

by the tenth century and the same chronology may apply in this area of the South-East.[15]

The boundary between the Low Weald and the Wealden Greensand on the one hand and the High Weald on the other is not always sharply marked, which is perhaps why the region was not separately distinguished by Roberts and Wrathmell. The Low Weald is a useful region to consider, as long as we remember that it does not have a homogeneous character. Various studies of the region suggest that the woodland was occupied at first during the early medieval period by animal herders, perhaps on a seasonal basis, and subsequently larger farms were established there. Some of these early farms seem to have been marked by arc-shaped boundaries, which have been identified in Surrey and across the border in West Sussex.[16] The pattern of settlement in the later Middle Ages was mixed, with many scattered houses and a few villages and hamlets; some land was worked in common fields, though their operation was quite unlike that in the Midlands: the common fields were not grouped into three large blocks, but into numerous smaller, hedged or fenced fields.[17]

At the centre of the Weald was a series of sandstone ridges, the most elevated of which produced large areas of heathland and wood, including the Dallington and Ashdown Forests. These uplands often had poor soils. The place-names Frant ('place overgrown with bracken') and nearby Verridge ('bracken ridge') suggest the character of land to the south of Tunbridge Wells. The same place-name element, Old English *fearn*, bracken, also occurs in Fair Ridge in Salehurst and Fairlight. The extent of woodland on the upland commons was dependent on the intensity of usage. By the late thirteenth century there were substantial areas of heath produced by the intensity of grazing and the practice of firing the vegetation to improve the 'bite'.[18] The demesne at Herstmonceux also included 80 acres described as heath, which were occasionally ploughed, but otherwise used as poor pasture. This practice of taking in poor land for a few years to use as arable before it reverted to pasture is also recorded on the demesnes of Battle Abbey and at Westerham.[19] Away from these heaths, the High Weald was dissected by narrow valleys or 'ghylls' which were commonly wooded. Small farmsteads were often bounded by these steep-sided ghylls, such as those at Bucksteep donated to Battle Abbey in the early twelfth century and still distinguishable on an eighteenth-century map of the Battle Abbey Estate (Figure 7.3B). The best land, however, lay in the broader river valleys where large tenements had been formed, very probably well before the Norman Conquest.[20]

The North Kent and South Coast Plains were both notable in the Middle Ages for the quality of their soils and the size of their demesnes which, like those of central southern England, were managed to grow large quantities of wheat, using labour supplied by the work-services owed by the villeins. A considerable proportion of the workforce lived in villages, but, equally, there were many isolated farmsteads. At Gillingham in Kent, in addition to the central village, there were hamlets and dispersed farmsteads; at Bosham in Sussex a similar situation is evident, along with a number of isolated farms with lands held in severalty lying to the north of the open fields.[21] While the best land in the area could be cropped every year, there were also low-lying areas near the coast prone to flooding and areas of 'shravey' soils near Chichester derived from flint gravels. To the north of Canterbury, the London Clay forms a distinctive area of higher land, the heavy soils of which were occupied by the Blean Woods which supplied fuel for the pottery kilns at nearby Tyler Hill.[22]

The final area to consider is the London Basin which Roberts and Wrathmell sub-divided into the separate regions of Thames Heath, the Mid-Thames Village Belt, and the South Slope. Various villages in this area, including Chertsey, Chobham, Egham and Putney, plus Sutton and Epsom which lie just beyond

the region, may have been laid out by Chertsey Abbey, perhaps in the mid-twelfth century.[23] Bagshot Heath and Chobham Common remained largely unsettled, but on the margins the pattern was more one of isolated farmsteads and hamlets.

The South-East lies outside the 'Village Belt' – or, as Roberts and Wrathmell term it, 'the Central Province' – that part of England in which late medieval settlement was predominantly in villages. There were, however, in some regions, a significant number of nucleated settlements: thus the Canterbury-Thanet region, the Vale of Holmesdale, the Coastlands, the South Slope and the Mid-Thames Village Belt were all notable for the number of hamlets or villages. By contrast, the interior of the South-East, particularly higher up on the Downs and within the Weald, were distinguished by the number of isolated farmsteads.

History of research

The South-East has not played a prominent part in debates on the development of rural settlement in Britain. It is an area, as observed, with complex patterns, containing both nucleated and dispersed settlement, which has discouraged simple generalisations. Until recently there was no university department of archaeology in the region, although Southampton and the Institute of Archaeology in London lie just beyond its edges. The medieval history of the countryside in this area has also been relatively neglected, though there have been some studies of seigneurial agriculture on the great estates.[24] As a result, the settlement of this area in the Middle Ages is significantly less well understood than much of the rest of southern Britain. This is particularly unfortunate because before the outbreak of war in 1939 very considerable progress had been made on the study of its medieval settlement patterns. The most prominent archaeological remains, and those which attracted the earliest interest, were the earthworks on the North and South Downs, which were largely prehistoric and Roman in date, but, in the process of surveying these, much valuable work was done in recording later remains: for example, H. S. Toms made extensive records in the Brighton area of 'valley entrenchments', a type of enclosure now recognised as late medieval or post-medieval sheep folds;[25] similar careful surveys were made of medieval farmsteads in the Burpham area of Sussex as part of the record of lynchets on the South Downs and on the earthworks in Joyden's Wood on the North Downs in Kent.[26]

In the post-war years attention shifted away from earthwork survey towards the excavation of sites with upstanding remains, again mainly on the downland. Much work was driven by the need to record sites in advance of development. For example, the construction of a housing estate at Tadworth in Surrey was preceded by excavations in 1952–54 of the Preston Hawe manor house, including its associated bakehouse, churchyard and drove roads.[27] A similar threat prompted the excavations at the deserted medieval village at Hangleton (West Sussex),[28] while a possible manor house at Joyden's Wood (Bexley, Kent) was also dug before it was destroyed by building works, revealing not only the complete plan of the hall, but also some of the outbuildings.[29] A different sort of threat, from ploughing, led to a small-scale excavation on a thirteenth-century farmstead at Bramble Bottom (East, Sussex) attached to one of Toms' 'valley entrenchments'.[30]

In Surrey, where the chalk Downs form a smaller part of the county and thus prominent earthworks were fewer, medieval settlement study tended to focus on moated sites. An early example of this was the work between 1946 and 1953 by the local history society at *Pachenesham* in Leatherhead.[31] The work took the form of trenching of the site, which makes the plan difficult to understand. Further excavations followed in the early 1960s on moated sites near Burstow Rectory at Hookwood in Charlwood, Lagham manor in South Godstone, and, more recently, at sites at Grayswood and Cobham.[32]

Postgraduate students of historical geography at London made a major contribution to other aspects in the early 1960s: thus Peter Brandon's study of the common fields and wastes of Sussex laid the basis for the understanding of the landscape of that county, while J. Gulley's study of the development of the Weald served a similar function across a relatively little explored region.[33] Alan Baker's study of fields of Kent explained their distinctive features.[34] As significant was E. M. Yates' examination of the landscape history of the north-west corner of Sussex.[35] The cumulative result was that by the end of the 1960s the groundwork for interpreting medieval settlement in the South-East had been laid.

The growing pressures of development led to the formation of full-time archaeological units in Sussex and Surrey in 1974, though the archaeology in Kent continued to be treated in an *ad hoc* manner. It seems apparent that medieval rural sites were not a major area of investigation for these units. However, the Easter training course for undergraduate students from London run by the Sussex unit took as its subject the landscape of Bullock Down near Eastbourne, which included a number of medieval farmsteads.[36] The published book on this area also included results from Martin Bell's programme of valley sections dug to study the history of land-use through the record of colluviation on the Downs.[37] Non-professional archaeologists continued to make an important contribution examining sites, both in advance of development and simply for research. For example, a medieval hall and its associated buildings at Brooklands in Surrey were excavated by the Walton and Weybridge Local History Society.[38] Significant work was undertaken by David Martin on moated sites in the Robertsbridge area of Sussex, by Fred Tebbutt in the Weald and by Eric Holden in the Adur valley of Sussex.[39]

In recent years the growing awareness of landscape history has led to a proliferation of field and archive-based studies, and it is only possible to mention a few of these. Understanding of the landscapes of Surrey and Kent have been transformed by the work of Blair in the former and Everitt in the latter, while Gardiner has clarified the development of the Weald in eastern Sussex.[40] Large-scale threats from the construction of transport links, minerals extraction and housing have been met by equally large archaeological investigations, which at last have begun to solve some of the problems raised by small-scale studies. Work in advance of the Folkestone terminal and the Channel Tunnel Rail Link and the proposed construction of Broad Oak reservoir have been particularly significant.[41] Notable are the studies on Romney Marsh which were stimulated by a research trust dedicated to its study, and where subsequent quarrying led to one of the largest excavations anywhere in the South-East, allowing many hectares of landscape to be examined (see Feature Box: *Key Excavation: Lydd Quarry, Kent*, p. 105).[42]

Processes of settlement growth and decline

The pattern of settlement in the early medieval period in this part of England, as elsewhere, remains comparatively obscure. There seems to have been no sharp break in the fifth century in the distribution of settlement, though clearly there was in the lifestyles of the inhabitants. Excavations on a number of Roman villas in Kent and Sussex have shown that settlement often persisted on the same spot even after the villa buildings went out of use; a recent discovery is the Roman villa at Beddingham in East Sussex where fifth-century 'Saxon'-style pottery was discovered in one building. However, over the next few centuries there was a gradual retreat from the upper parts of the downland. The Anglo-Saxon settlement at Rookery Hill, Bishopstone (Sussex), which had been established on top of Roman fields, was abandoned by the seventh century and that at Church Down, Chalton, just across the border in Hampshire, was deserted during the course of the eighth century. Sections cut across the downland valleys show that cultivation of the upper slopes ceased until the eleventh century and these probably reverted to pasture.[43] The absence of Anglo-Saxon pagan burials in the Weald has long indicated that the usage of this area declined, though it probably continued to be exploited for pasture, pannage and mast (grazing on acorns and beech nuts).

The excavated Middle Saxon sites at Millbrook and Friar's Oak (both Sussex) have provided evidence for small-scale metalworking in this region.[44] Longer-lasting settlements in the Weald may be marked by arc-shaped boundaries, which are of uncertain antiquity, though they predate the systematic division of the western end of the Sussex Weald which had to wait until the tenth century.[45] It is probable that about this time too the long strip parishes developed on the scarp slope of the North and South Downs (discussed above). By the late eleventh century the coastal areas of the South-East had some of the greatest concentrations of recorded population in England, particularly in eastern Kent and southern central Sussex.[46]

The period from *c.* AD 1000 to 1300 is marked by a continuing intensification of land-use as the population expanded further. This process is particularly well understood in two areas – the Weald and the coastal marshes – but we should not imagine

that these were the only areas affected. The shift from seasonal or temporary settlement to permanent occupation in the central Weald had occurred considerably before the turn of the millennium, and by 1100 the parochial structure was very largely in place, arguing for a reasonable-sized population.[47] It has been estimated that in the late eleventh century about one quarter of the area of the liberty of Battle, an area one league (2560 yards) in radius, was in cultivation. This figure is notable because the Battle area of eastern Sussex included some of the poorest lands in the region.[48] We can assume that an even greater proportion of land had been turned into enclosed fields elsewhere.

The process of assarting – the clearance of land of wood and scrub to create pasture and arable – was pursued with particular vigour in the thirteenth century. On the manor of Rotherfield in the centre of the Sussex Weald the cultivated area was increased in this way by 20 per cent in a period of 80 years in the late thirteenth and first half of the fourteenth century.[49] The story was similar on the coast where former tidal salt marsh was improved by embankment to be used for improved grazing or converted to arable. The process of embankment was far advanced by the opening of the thirteenth century, and such large areas had been won from the sea on Romney Marsh that new parishes were created at Brookland, Broomhill and Fairfield.[50]

The movement away from the tops of the Downs to the valleys which had taken place in the early Middle Ages was reversed and settlement was established there, often overlying prehistoric and Roman fields. This has been most comprehensively demonstrated at Bullock Down near Eastbourne, where, for 700 years, there was no occupation, but around 1250 new farmsteads were established at Kiln Combe and elsewhere. The settlements on the downland between the River Arun and Findon generally belong to this period (Figure 7.3). Larger settlements were also established on the margins of the Downs, most notably at Hangleton, where a village developed from about 1200 onwards. In Surrey, the pattern of downland colonisation seems to have been much the same, although the chronology may be different. Large-scale assarting of the woodland had been completed by the mid-twelfth century, though smaller clearances continued to be made.[51]

Figure 7.6. Excavations at Park Farm, Salehurst, a grange of Robertsbridge abbey (Gardiner et al. 1991). After the purchase of the land of the settlement, a grange with aisled hall (see here during excavation) was established on lands in the floor of the River Rother in eastern Sussex. The site of the abbey itself lies in the far distance.

The late Middle Ages saw an enormous growth in monastic holdings so that by 1279 – the date of the Statute of Mortmain which sought to control further grants of land to the Church – perhaps one third of England was in the possession of the Church. It is probable, however, that the proportion of Sussex and Surrey in monastic hands was less than that because there were fewer monasteries than in other counties and the estates of individual houses were smaller. In east Kent, where Christchurch Canterbury and the archbishop of Canterbury had many manors, the proportion may have been greater.[52] The large monastic estates were run like modern companies: investment was made in buildings, livestock and equipment in order to maximise the return from agriculture and minimise the loss through wastage and decay. Some of the monastic manors were simply lay lordships which had passed as such into the hands of the Church. Other holdings were carefully assembled through the accumulation of grants in free alms and, where necessary, through purchase of lands (Figure 7.2).[53] It was Cistercian practice to establish granges or home farms staffed by lay brothers (agricultural workers in religious orders), although the terrain of the South-East did not offer many opportunities for the formation of granges on areas of newly occupied or improved land (Figure 7.6); granges of this type were more typical of the uplands of northern England or Wales. However, the woodlands, heaths and marshlands of the South-East did provide some scope for expansion, not only for Cistercian houses, but also other monastic orders.

The Benedictine foundation of Battle Abbey was established in the eleventh century on the site of the Battle of Hastings. The monks were said to have been appalled by the location, but that, perhaps, was later rhetoric. In any case, they rapidly set about establishing a manor, a demesne farm and a town on the Wealden ridge.[54] The first Cistercian foundation in England in 1128 was at Waverley. Though the site of the abbey was in a pleasant location in a river valley, it was surrounded by poorer land; the monks set about improving the site and constructed mills there. Two years later they acquired land nearby at Wanborough where they established a grange. A barn belonging to the grange has been dated by dendrochronology to 1388 and the area of grange buildings is still marked by a 2 m high boundary bank.[55] The Premonstratensian order shared the Cistercians' enthusiasm for remote places, and founded houses at Durford in Rogate, Otham near Hailsham and at Bradsole near Dover in Kent. All of these places qualify as 'difficult' locations, and the site of Otham on the edge of marshes proved so bleak that, 30 years or so after its foundation, the abbey moved to Bayham on the Kent-Sussex border and the former site became a grange. These religious houses all brought investment to improve unpropitious carr, marsh and heath.

The period from 1300 up to the end of the Middle Ages was marked first by a cessation of growth in population and then a very rapid decline. Our understanding of this is complicated by the operation of the twin factors of changing environmental conditions and plague. The low-lying marshland at Pevensey and Romney Marshes had suffered in the floods of 1287–88 and although some land was recovered immediately after, much remained tidal marsh for the following two centuries. The disturbed conditions in the North Sea and English Channel had an impact over a wider area of low-lying coast in the South-East: for example, in 1341 considerable areas were reported to be flooded on the Sussex coast from Hove westwards and there were similar problems in the Thames estuary in Kent.[56] The second problem was the declining population resulting from plague. The sums paid in 'tithing penny' in central Sussex, a payment of a penny per adult male each year, suggest that not only had the population declined in the second half of the fourteenth century, but that it continued to fall from the 1440s, the period for which we have detailed records. Only in the 1490s were there the first signs of a modest recovery.[57] The effect of this on settlement is particularly clear in the court rolls of Herstmonceux where in 1380 presentments were made that at least 34 buildings on various villein tenements were ruinous or had fallen down. As tenants died from the plague, their lands were taken over by neighbours to create larger holdings and only a single house was necessary where previously there been two or more. This was a widespread problem, and has been recognised on many of the manors of Westminster Abbey across the Home Counties.[58]

Engrossment of holdings was one response to declining numbers of people. The shift to pastoral agriculture, which was a marked feature of the rural economy in this region in the fifteenth century, was both a response and also a cause of further depopulation.[59] Fewer people were required to look after stock than to till the fields, so that the demand for labour fell. On Romney Marsh the shift to sheep-grazing at the end of the fifteenth century was accompanied by a desertion of houses and the subsequent dereliction of churches as congregations fell away.[60] The shift to sheep-farming on the downlands has already been mentioned, although the details of this remain little studied. Fewer hands to work the land made it more difficult to maintain the hedgerows and in the Weald woodland and scrub reasserted themselves where land had fallen out of cultivation.[61] Manorial lords themselves were under pressure from declining agricultural prices and chose to concentrate their spending on a small number of houses. Although a few new gentry houses were built in the fifteenth century, other manor houses, both those surrounded by moats and those by hedges, were abandoned, with their sites sometimes becoming overgrown by woodland.[62]

It would be wrong to conclude the chronological account with the impression that the fifteenth century was only a period of decline, since by the end of the century there were signs of recovery and certainly early in the sixteenth century clear evidence emerges of improving conditions: thus, much of the area of marshland lost in the 1287–88 storms had been recovered by the 1470s; land was being cleared of wood to bring under cultivation in Iden (Sussex) in the 1470s; and in 1516 we hear that 60 acres of derelict land near Maidstone were brought back into cultivation.[63] It should be remembered that the low rents and weak demand for land was favourable for some. The number and size of surviving timber-framed houses recorded in Kent are testimony to the wealth of those who had sizeable landholdings (around 100 acres or more) and their ability to adapt to market conditions (see Feature Box: *Key Site to Visit*, p. 112). Even the casual visitor to the Low Weald is struck by the number of surviving timber-framed buildings. It some areas the numbers still standing are sufficient to have housed 20 per cent or even 30 per cent of the population in *c.* 1500. This suggests the

Key Site to Visit: Weald and Downland Museum, Singleton, West Sussex

The Weald and Downland Museum provides a vivid insight into the character of later medieval buildings in the South-East, by bringing together a series of buildings to illustrate the range of houses constructed in the region. Most are timber-framed structures of the fifteenth century: many more survive from this period than earlier centuries. A reconstruction of an excavated building from the Hangleton (Sussex) deserted village is exceptional, both because it was built of flint and because it dates from the thirteenth century. The reconstruction is based on the evidence from two buildings found in excavations and some elements of the structure, particularly the roof, remain conjectural. However, the most problematic element is whether it was a domestic cottage (which was the interpretation when it was first erected) or a bakehouse and ancillary to a main building.[64]

The best known of all medieval buildings at Singleton is the imposing Wealden house, 'Bayleaf', which originally stood at Chiddingstone. This type of building is not restricted to the Weald, though it is found in large numbers there. It is characterised by a recessed hall and two cross-wings, which are jettied out. Even by modern standards, the house provided a very substantial area of accommodation, suitable for a prosperous farmer. Rather unusually for a Wealden building, Bayleaf was built in two phases, the first about 1400–05 when the hall and the 'low' or service end were built; these must have been added to an existing structure. A century later this earlier structure was removed and a new chamber (bedroom) was built to match the one at the low end.

The final building discussed here is the cottage from Walderton (Sussex), though it is not immediately obvious from the exterior that it is of medieval origin. The building as it now stands is largely of seventeenth-century appearance, when the exterior walls were rebuilt in flint and brick, a new upper floor was inserted in the open hall and a brick chimney stack constructed. Little survived of the medieval phase below wall-plate level (the level of the bottom of the roof), because this had been removed during rebuilding. Traces of the timber frame were found when the building was taken apart, and further details were recovered from excavation. The first medieval building which can be described with any certainty comprised a hall, a service room and an overshot chamber (a bedroom which projected over the cross-passage). There must have been another pre-existing room beyond the hall, but no trace of it survived (Figure 7.7). The Walderton cottage is a reminder of how old houses were not treated as museum pieces by their owners, but were altered over the centuries and adapted to suit changing needs.

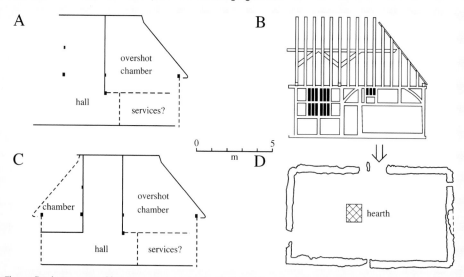

Figure 7.7. The medieval cottage at Walderton, now re-erected at the Weald and Downland Museum. A, B: section and elevation of fifteenth-century phase. Insufficient evidence survives to indicate the form of the left-hand end. C: section of building c. 1550. D: Plan of fifteenth- and sixteenth-century phases. (After Aldsworth and Harris 1982)

quality of building at the end of the Middle Ages and implies a degree of wealth in that region allowing the construction of enduring houses which subsequent generations found little need to replace.[65]

Gaps, directions and questions

It may not be immediately evident from the discussion above that our understanding of medieval settlement in this area of England is still very limited. The work so far has merely determined the potential of archaeological field survey, excavation, documentary research and the study of standing buildings to elucidate the complex histories of settlement, but in few places have these approaches been fully worked through. Certainly there have been no detailed settlement studies of the sort practised at Wharram Percy in Yorkshire, Whittlewood in Northamptonshire or Shapwick in Somerset. One reason for this may be that the South-East *appears* to be relatively well studied, while the opposite is in fact true. A second problem in the study of the South-East is the extraordinary diversity of the area, both in terms of its geography and its economic history: as outlined above, it lacks sharply defined regions, but does contain a great range of landscape types. One might also note the lack of good aerial photographic coverage, chiefly because of the extents of woodland and pasture and with soils not particularly conducive to the production of crop or soil marks.

The type of intensive settlement studies undertaken in other regions, which have been mentioned above, could profitably be employed in the South-East. The chosen area should have both nucleated and scattered settlement so that the contrasting forms could be examined. The methodologies for undertaking such work have worked out in the studies in other areas of England (see Jones and Lewis, this volume). What is lacking here is the sustained input of effort required to dissect a complex historical landscape. While no one area can stand for the South-East, an understanding of the settlement dynamics in one place would surely help us to suggest the processes elsewhere. Unfortunately, there is no immediate prospect of such a project, though there is much useful work being undertaken on a smaller scale, both field survey and excavation. Perhaps one of the most interesting recent

initiatives has been the development of landscape study of areas now covered by woodland; this is particularly important here because the South-East has a significant area covered by trees. The study of Dering Wood in Kent has shown the possibilities for elucidating the land-use history, as well as discovering relic features which have not survived elsewhere.[66]

Work on the local scale needs to be complemented by wider overviews. One way of approaching the settlement history of the region as a whole was suggested by Brian Short, who pointed out that there was a fundamental dichotomy between the coastal fringe, where historically much of the wealth of the South-East was to be found, and a less well developed interior.[67] It was not only that the better soils tended to lie towards the coastal margins of the South-East, but there were the regions with better contacts with the markets of London and continental Europe (Feature Box: *Key Theme*, p. 114). However, instead of thinking about it, as Short proposes, as a process of systematic exploitation of the interior by the margins, it is necessary to see it as a broader and perhaps more equal relationship. One way in which we might begin to provide a unified view of settlement development is to look at it in terms of capital flow – the movement of capital, in its widest sense to include human labour and materials, as well as the narrower measures of coin and credit, from region to region. An obvious example of this is the re-investment of the profits of commerce by London merchants in the purchase of land in the surrounding area.[68] London was not only a centre of wealth and consumption, but a place from which investment flowed to the surrounding area. The re-investment of the profits of trade was not limited to London, though it is most obvious there. Even small merchants in the Cinque Ports purchased land in the surrounding area, which are noted in 'billets', a class of document recording exemption from taxation; the same must have been true around all the towns in the South-East.

Clearly, then, the work of understanding the patterns and processes of medieval rural settlement has barely begun, and what has been outlined above is a merely statement of the stage we have reach in research, rather a definitive account. The South-East offers immense scope for future work, whether in the record office or in the field.

Key Theme: The Influence of the Market

The large towns and cities of the later Middle Ages provided important markets for agricultural produce and goods in the surrounding countryside. The most important of these was London which was well established as the pre-eminent town in England, and therefore in Britain, by the twelfth century.[69] Major urban centres had significant impacts on prices and land-use in their hinterland. Producers within the vicinity of a large town might have expected to receive a price which was close to the mean of the urban hinterland; but in areas where the demand of urban centres was less influential, it was the local prices in smaller markets which governed the amounts paid. Bruce Campbell and his associates have demonstrated this by examining the prices of wheat sold in the London region around the turn of the fourteenth century. Access to the metropolitan market was not necessarily advantageous to producers because competition could also depress prices, as it seems to have done in parts of Kent and Surrey. Prices there were higher away from the Thames and other supply routes.[70]

Supply to the London market was a major stimulus to the development of settlements along the banks of the Thames. It clearly was an important factor at Faversham and Sittingbourne which were key centres for the shipment of grain to the capital, but it also encouraged the development of markets at places with ready access to the Thames – such as Greenwich, Gravesend and Northfleet.[71] Building materials and fuel were also shipped up to London, while Limehouse was named after the lime kilns which prepared chalk shipped from Kent for buildings works; other settlements down the Thames at Deptford, Woolwich and Greenwich supplied fish to the capital.[72] Immediately around the city was a series of hamlets, some of them already established by the eleventh century, such as those at Bishopsgate, Stepney and 'No man's land' in Middlesex, occupied both by those who worked in the London and by those who grew vegetables for sale in the metropolis.[73] Just over London Bridge was its largest suburban settlement, at Southwark.[74]

Most major cities had suburban settlements situated beyond their walls, but closely tied to them through commerce. Canterbury had suburbs at Northgate, Westgate (Estursete) and St Martins, and even the rather moderate-sized town of Lewes had suburbs at Southover and over the River Ouse at Cliffe.[75] All major towns in Britain, therefore, had an impact to varying degrees upon the settlements both within their hinterland and those immediately beyond their walls.

In the South-East, the picture was particularly complex because rural communities looked not only to markets in the major towns in the vicinity, but also through the numerous ports to markets across the Channel in France and Flanders. Access to the continental markets dated from before the Conquest, but was stimulated by the increased contact after 1066. Further possibilities for trade opened with the taking of Calais in 1347: this English enclave was unable to trade with the surrounding and hostile French territory and was largely dependent on imports for fuel and all crops which could not be grown in the March – the territory surrounding the port. Calais's hinterland therefore embraced the much of the coastal district of the Kent and Sussex.[76]

The impact of commerce is also apparent through its role in encouraging the development of nucleated settlement. Examples of this from East Anglia and Cambridgeshire have been identified by Chris Taylor.[77] In the South-East it has been argued that trade preceded villages and led to their growth in the High Weald; village growth here took place so late that it could be traced in part in late thirteenth- and even fourteenth-century records.[78] It is more difficult to demonstrate when it took place earlier, though it does seem to provide a possible explanation for some villages in the South-East. One such place is West Tarring in Sussex. Excavations on a number of sites within Tarring found no evidence of settlement before the early thirteenth century.[79] The village has a curious plan and it is possible to suggest how it may have developed. Most of the roads, tracks, field and parish boundaries in this area of the coastal plain run N–S and E–W. The High Street approaching Tarring from the north deviated from the N–S line, a line which remained as a field boundary; instead, it turns towards the church and only resumes its alignment to the south (Figure 7.8). The church may have been an attraction for travellers, but it seems more likely that the reason for coming off the road was an early market in or close to the churchyard – a common location of commerce before ecclesiastical opposition to the practice developed in the first decade of the thirteenth century. A further sign of the early date of the market is that Tarring obtained no market grant, apparently holding the right by prescription, implying that it was of long-standing.[80] The house plots on the west side of High Street show clear evidence of a planned layout, and are aligned to the diverted road. The evidence is not decisive, but an early market preceding the planning of the village provides a possible explanation of the morphology.

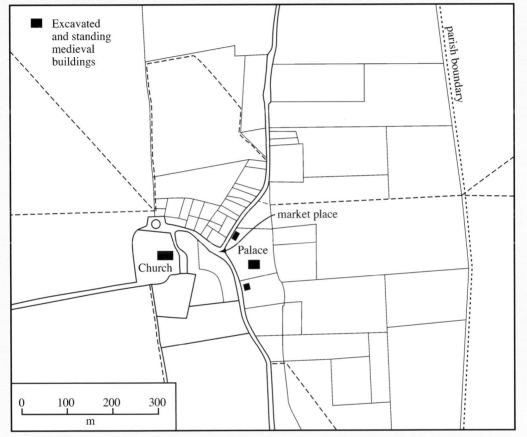

Figure 7.8. The road and field pattern of West Tarring, Sussex. (After the Ordnance Survey first-edition, six-inch map)

Further reading

The Early Anglo-Saxon period in Sussex and Kent is well covered by Martin Welch in his book, *Early Anglo-Saxon Sussex* (Oxford, 1983) and a chapter in J. Williams (ed.), *The Archaeology of Kent to AD 800* (Woodbridge, 2007). There is an up-to-date summary of the evidence for Surrey by John Hines in J. Cotton *et al.* (eds), *Aspects of Archaeology and History in Surrey: Towards a Research Framework for the County* (Guildford, 2004). They draw on the numerous cemeteries which have been excavated, but

the only settlement dating from the period before AD 700 dug in this area is at Bishopstone, which forms a complete volume of *Sussex Archaeological Collections* (115 (1977)). Rather intriguingly, recent excavations in the valley below that site have uncovered buildings occupied from the eighth century onwards, allowing a contrast to be drawn between the settlements of different periods. The later sites are published by Gabor Thomas as *The Later Anglo-Saxon Settlement at Bishopstone: A Downland Manor in the Making* (York, 2010). John Blair has provided the clearest guide to developments in the early Middle Ages in his study of *Early Medieval Surrey: Landholding, Church and Settlement Before 1300* (Stroud, 1991). The most ambitious and thorough-going interpretation of the process of medieval settlement on a county-wide scale is the study of Kent by Alan Everitt, *Continuity and Colonization: The Evolution of Kentish Settlement* (Leicester, 1986). This is a remarkable piece of work which encompasses a range of evidence, but it is in equal measure a frustrating study which is difficult to use. Kenneth Witney's work – *The Jutish Forest: A Study of the Weald of Kent from 450 to 1380 AD* (London, 1976) – is to that extent more valuable, for it can be criticised and tested.

There are a number of useful overviews which cover the late medieval period: Stuart Rigold's posthumous paper on Kent in P. E. Leach (ed.), *Archaeology in Kent to AD 1500* (London, 1982) is a stimulating, if now rather dated account, but written with such mastery of the evidence that it remains worth reading. Surrey

is covered by an analysis in 1984 by Denis Turner in J. Bird and D. G. Bird (eds), *The Archaeology of Surrey to 1540* (London, 1984), and another, more recent examination of manors and other settlements in the volume by Cotton cited above. Only for Sussex is there no summary of the evidence for the county as a whole, though Richard Jones' examination of castles – in D. R. Rudling (ed.), *The Archaeology of Sussex to AD 2000* (King's Lynn, 2003), interprets the term very widely to include a range of sites. Instead, it is necessary to refer to Peter Brandon's account, *The Sussex Landscape* (London, 1974) which requires correction in a number of details. More superficial pictures of various aspects of the South-East are provided by maps in the historic atlases published for Sussex – K. Leslie and B. Short (eds), *An Historical Atlas of Sussex: An Atlas of the History of the Counties of East and West Sussex* (Chichester, 1999) – and Kent – T. Lawson and D. Killingray (eds), *An Historical Atlas of Kent* (Chichester, 2004). There is no similar study for Surrey.

Notes

1. Roberts and Wrathmell 2000, 67 and fig. 1. Natural regions are from http://www.englishnature.org.uk/Science/natural/boundary.htm (accessed 10 November 2009).

2. For the predominance of sheep on the Downs in eastern Sussex, see Pelham 1934.

3. *An Abstract of Feet of Fines for Relating to Sussex from 2 Richard I to 33 Henry III* (Sussex Record Society 2), ed. L. F. Salzmann: no. 266. *Leweredescumb* was certainly on the Downs (see *Two Estate Surveys of the Fitzalan Earls of Arundel* (Sussex Record Society 67), ed. M. Clough: 106), and the other two woods very probably.

4. Everett 1986, 163; Blair 1991, 46.

5. *Calendar of Patent Rolls 1247–58*, 435, 502; *Calendar of Patent Rolls 1377–81*, 84; Tittensor 1980. For early consideration of the yew woods, see Watt 1926.

6. Joyden's Wood – Hogg 1934; Tester and Caiger 1958; Tester 1980. Chapel Wood, Hartley – Keen 1967; Philp 1973, 220–223; Proudfoot 1978; *Medieval Archaeology* 28 (1984), 225. Cozendon Wood – Caiger 1970. Well Wood – Philp 2006. Darenth Wood – Caiger 1964.

7. Curwen and Curwen 1922; 1923.

8. Ratcliffe-Densham and Ratcliffe-Densham 1961; Eric Holden unpublished notes; West Sussex HER. For an early fourteenth-century extent of the manor of Barpham, alias Bargham, see *Custumals of the Manors of Laughton., Willingdon and Goring* (Sussex Record Society 60), ed. A. E. Wilson, 73–78 which shows that there was about 150 acres of arable in demesne and extensive downland pasture for sheep.

9. For valley entrenchments in the Brighton area, see below and Barber *et al.* 2002, 135–140. For similar enclosures on the Wiltshire Downs, see Smith 2005.

10. Barber 2006; Barber and Priestley-Bell 2008.

11. Centre for Kentish Studies, U1043/M4; Lambeth Palace Library, MS 951/1, f. 166r.

12. Barber and Priestley-Bell 2008; Gardiner 1998.

13. Gardiner 1994.

14. Baker 1966a, 4–7, 13–14; Blair 1991, 55–58; Brandon 1974, 121–122; Yates 1961.

15. Blair 1991, 33–34; Hooke 1987; Yates 1961, 68–69.

16. Chatwin and Gardiner 2005, 36–37; English 1997.

17. Baker 1973, 425–420; Yates 1960, 37–39.

18. Gardiner 1996, 127.

19. Bishop 1938; Gardiner 1996, 126; Searle 1974, 278–286.

20. Gardiner 1995, 70–72, 82, 91–93.
21. Baker 1964, 21; West Sussex Record Office, Add. MS 2275 and Acc. 939. See also Blair 1991, 66–70.
22. Brandon 1971, 116–117; Cotter 1991.
23. Blair 1991, 58–60.
24. Searle 1974; Smith 1943.
25. Toms 1917; 1924; 1926.
26. Curwen and Curwen 1923, 10–30; Hogg 1934.
27. The excavation report remains unpublished. The excavation was noted in *Surrey Archaeological Collections* 53 (1954), xxvii–xxviii; 54 (1955), 157–158.
28. Holden 1963; Hurst and Hurst 1964.
29. Tester and Caiger 1958.
30. Musson 1955; Toms 1913.
31. Lowther 1983.
32. Burstow Rectory in Turner 1966; Hookwood in Turner 1977; Lagham manor in Ketteringham 1984; Grayswood in Graham and Graham 2000 and Cobham in Graham *et al.* 2005.
33. Brandon 1963; 1971; 1974; Gulley 1961.
34. Baker 1963; 1965; 1973.
35. Yates 1954; 1960.
36. Drewett 1982.
37. Bell 1981; 1989.
38. Hanworth and Tomalin 1990.
39. Holden 1980; Holden and Hudson 1981; Martin 1989 and 1990; Tebbutt 1981.
40. Blair 1991; Everitt 1986; Gardiner 1995.
41. Cross 1989; 1992; Glass 1999.
42. Barber and Priestley-Bell 2008; Eddison 1995; Eddison *et al.* 1998; Eddison and Green 1988; Long *et al.* 2002.
43. Bell 1977, 271; Bell 1983: 140; Drewett 1982, 213.
44. Butler 2000: 41–42; Tebbutt 1982.
45. Chatwin and Gardiner 2005; English 1997.
46. Darby 1977, figs 35, 36.
47. Everitt 1986, 204–205; Rushton 1999; Witney 1976, 104–153.
48. Gardiner 1995, 89–91.
49. Brandon 1969, 138.
50. Eddison and Draper 1997, 84–85; Eddison 2000, 69–73.
51. Blair 1991, 48–49.
52. See, for example, Donkin 1976, fig. 25.
53. On building investment on the nearby estates of the bishop of Winchester, see Langdon *et al.* 2003. For the acquisition of land in Kent, see Mate 1984.
54. Searle 1974, 44–88.
55. Service 2010, 212, 225; *Vernacular Architecture* 28 (1997), 146.
56. Bailey 1991; Baker 1966b, 4; Galloway 2009; Galloway and Potts 2007.
57. Mate 1991, 127–128.
58. East Sussex Record Office, ACC 3616/14; see also Searle 1974, 380–381; Harvey 1977, 273–274.
59. Mate 1987.
60. Gardiner 1998, 130–141.
61. Brandon 1969, 142–143; Searle 1974, 369–371.
62. Pearson 1994, 129. Examples of excavated moated and other manorial sites have been listed above. To these may be added the recently published site of Manston Road, Ramsgate, Hutcheson and Andrews 2009, 212–218. However, there remained continuing investment in manor houses, see, for example, Poulton 1998.
63. Gardiner 1998, 136; Du Boulay 1966, 228.
64. The Hangleton building is based on houses 3 and 11: Holden 1963, 85–94; Hurst and Hurst 1964, 109–111. Wrathmell 1989, 14 argues that these were bakehouses.
65. Pearson 1994, 125–127, 136–144.
66. Bannister 2002; Bannister and Bartlett 2009; Cross 1992.
67. Brandon and Short 1990, 12–14.
68. Thrupp 1948, 279–287.
69. Nightingale 1996, 92.
70. Campbell *et al.* 1993, 65–69.
71. Campbell *et al.* 1993, 101; Gardiner 2007a, 88.
72. Phillpotts 1999, 64–65.
73. Dyer 1994, 246.
74. Carlin 1996; McDonnell 1978.
75. Brent 2004, 138–145; Dyer 1994, 246; Tatton-Brown 1984, 10.
76. Burley 1958; Gardiner 2000; see, for example, *Accounts and Records of the Manor of Mote in Iden, 1442–1551, 1673* (Sussex Records Society 92), ed. M. F. Gardiner and C. H. C. Whittick, xiii; Pelham 1934.
77. Taylor 1982.
78. Gardiner 1997a.
79. Barton 1963; 1964; Bedwin 1979.
80. *Victoria County History of Sussex* 6, part I, 275.

CHAPTER 8

Central Southern England: 'Chalk and Cheese'

David A. Hinton

Introduction

The BBC decided some years ago that 'central southern England' should cease to exist for the purpose of its weather forecasts; sometimes it feels as if the same policy applies to landscape and settlement studies, with south-easterners reluctant to travel beyond Chichester, and south-westerners finding Exeter a good place to stop. Of course there are honourable exceptions, and by ignoring Sussex this chapter will open itself to the criticism that it fails to review the southern English chalk belt as a whole; but Mark Gardiner's paper (Chapter 7) on the South-East admirably covers this extra ground. Instead, my chapter deals with five counties – Berkshire, Dorset, Hampshire, the Isle of Wight, and Wiltshire – that have some geological coherence in that all are dominated by chalk downlands. These usually slope gently up from the south and end in a steep northern scarp. They are dissected by stream and river valleys that provide water, shelter, and at least a little meadow, making them the focus of rural settlement in all periods except when either population or taxation pressure is at its most extreme, or when climate is at its most benign. All the counties also have substantial tracts of clays and sands, mostly not naturally very fertile but useful for woods and commons; gravel terraces and narrow bands of Gault and Greensand are more attractive for arable cultivation. In the south, the coast provides some coherence – although Portsmouth, Langstone, and Chichester Harbours should really be treated as a whole – and to the north the crest of the Berkshire Downs marks a kind of frontier with the Upper Thames Valley, which is very different economically, and often politically. The River Kennet divides the Hampshire from the Berkshire Downs and by running into the Thames at Reading, draws east Berkshire into the Middle Thames orbit.

None of the five counties has deposits of metals like those that helped to create settlements on the moors of the South-West or in iron-ore rich forests like Dean or the Weald. Smelting of ferruginous stones seems not to have outlasted the ninth century, after which the only natural resources worth exploiting in any significant quantity were stone, notably Purbeck marble and Quarr limestone, and salt from the sea; clay was used for pot-, tile- and brick-making, but only the white clay on the Hampshire-Surrey border gave the region any advantage over others for ceramic production. Agriculture, including timber exploitation, was the main economic driver, with cloth manufacture the only craft that offered significant opportunities for growth. For the Isle of Wight, southern Hampshire, and Dorset, the sea formed a primary element in the development of trade and therefore of ports, notably Southampton. Yet fishing seems never to have had a significant economic role, so there was no equivalent to Yarmouth or Dover. Commercial advantage was offset in the fourteenth century by vulnerability to destructive raids by the French, as ships became better at transporting firstly armed attackers and subsequently cannon.

Medieval settlement research in central southern England since 1950

A review of research into the settlement patterns of the five counties since the Second World War should begin with a tribute to the Royal Commission on Historical Monuments, whose final Dorset volume appeared in 1975. By then its fieldwork had produced many earthwork surveys of deserted and shrunken medieval sites. At least as valuable, however, were the books and papers produced by its staff as individual authors: for example, Christopher Taylor's *Dorset* includes a chapter that remains useful for its demonstration of the parcelling-up of estates before the Norman Conquest, and the interrelationship of that process with the formation of parishes, manors, and tithings.[1] After Dorset, the Commission's attention was transferred to Wiltshire, where boundaries were a focus of the work of another of its staff, Desmond Bonney,[2] while Peter Fowler began his investigations of the landscape in and around West Overton, including its post-Roman aspects. Fowler's work included excavation of Raddon, a small farmstead mainly of the thirteenth/early fourteenth centuries, and therefore presumably an example of abandonment in the adverse circumstances of the second half of the latter; but the site also featured a few sherds of the seventh or eighth centuries AD, hinting that it might have started then as the cattle farm mentioned in a tenth-century charter, and was perhaps seasonally occupied; other boundary points include a *chiricstede*, 'church site', and 'Aethelferth's dwelling', probably sites already abandoned and illustrative of the fluidity of medieval settlement location.[3]

The final fruits of the Royal Commission's fieldwork were to be the study of the earthworks on the Salisbury Plain Training Area, which revealed how much survived within the army ranges: for the later Middle Ages, whole plans of sites (such as Imber), blocks of strip lynchets, and isolated downland barns and sheep-pens were recorded, reflecting changing population pressures and economic circumstances, as twelfth-/thirteenth-century expansion demanded more arable, and fourteenth-/fifteenth-century contraction favoured grazing.[4] Fieldwalking programmes that have produced comparable results include work in Hampshire.[5]

The area's first medieval settlement excavation was financed by a generous and anonymous benefactor as a training excavation at Holworth, Dorset, directed in the late 1950s by Philip Rahtz, who was then, like a few others, a professional peripatetic excavator, but who was to become one of the best-known post-Roman archaeologists, and a pioneer of open-area excavation – the Holworth project helped to convince him that, despite the time-consuming nature of such work and its unpopularity with impatient diggers, this technique of excavation provided the only means of understanding such sites fully (see Feature Box 1).[6] Another early excavation of a deserted medieval village was by John Musty and David Algar at Gomeldon, Wiltshire, still the only such site to have yielded a gold coin, although the interpretation of the main structure as a 'long-house', defined as a structure with humans living at one end and (at least in winter) animals at the other, under the same roof-line, has been called in question on grounds both practical – an internal drain may indicate a dairy, not a cow-shed – and cultural: this form of housing is not simply something found in any area where stock was reared, but seems geographically specific to the west.[7] Similar re-interpretation would place a dairy rather than a byre at one end of the early thirteenth-century 'long-house' at Raddon, with its successor making a clearer physical distinction between dwelling and farm activity, rather than between people and animals.[8]

Wessex's 1970s contributions to post-Roman rural settlement archaeology included the excavation initiated by Barry Cunliffe on the chalk ridge above Chalton, Hampshire – the first site to show unequivocally that the early Anglo-Saxons had not lived exclusively in squalid semi-sunken huts.[9] The site also showed that the inhabitants had access to supplies of substantial timber, and the time to cut and carpenter it. All the more surprising then is that sites like Chalton, into which considerable human and material investment had gone, were liable to be abandoned, in Chalton's case just before the opening of the period that is reviewed in this volume, but it is relevant because of the way that it showed that settlement was not stable. Subsequent rescue work at Cowdery's Down, Basingstoke[10] means that Wessex's Anglo-Saxon settlements remain part of national and international discussion. The removal of the very grand buildings at that site has raised the possibility that abandonment should be linked to generational

Key Excavation: Holworth

Part of one of the seven clearly visible tofts along the north side of the street at the deserted medieval settlement at Holworth (now in Chaldon Herring parish), Dorset (number 5 on the plan below), was excavated by Philip Rahtz in 1958, applying the open-area method for the first time to a British site of this kind (Rahtz 1959; RCHM Dorset 1970, 35–37). Consequently, ephemeral traces of buildings were located from spreads of rubble, showing that solid walls, post-holes or deep foundations were not the norm on such sites; this technique of excavation has been applied successfully at many other such sites subsequently. Usefully, Rahtz noted the difficulty of working with volunteers untrained in recording methods, which exacerbated some problems of interpretation. But even the most meticulous excavation cannot always reveal vestigial traces of where a timber rested on the ground, or the function of an area from which residues have been removed by later ploughing. In the toft excavated at Holworth, for example, it was not clear whether one complex of features represented an open-sided stable or a yard. It was also found that a structure identified as a two-roomed house because of the hearth inside it has less substantial walls than one identified as being for storage because of the carbonised grain in it.

The identifiable structures overlay earlier occupation, recognisable only from ditches, pits, and daub from

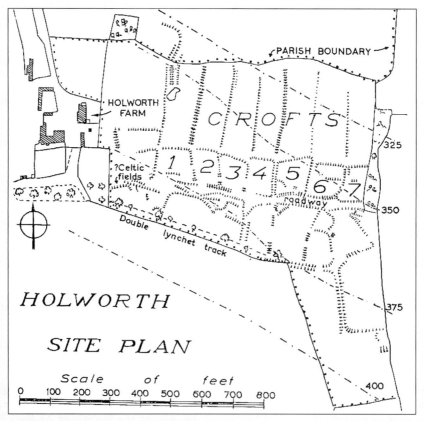

Figure 8.1. Plan of the earthworks of the deserted medieval settlement at Holworth in Dorset. (Illustration from Rahtz 1959; used by kind permission of the author and the publisher). Very sadly Philip Rahtz died during preparation of this contribution, but it is hoped that he would have been pleased to see Holworth contributing to this MSRG volume

a collapsed structure. The data were sufficient to suggest that the site came into use by the twelfth century, possibly earlier. The tofts may have been laid out in a replanning of the thirteenth century, probably initiated by the owner, almost certainly Milton Abbey. Rahtz recognised that the buildings of this period were stone-footed, and not built of posts driven into the ground – a structural change that has since been shown to have been widespread. He also identified various sub-phases in the subsequent centuries, providing a clue to the frequent adaptations that buildings underwent once their foundations allowed permanence.

Another feature of the later use of the site was the digging of deeper ditches, which resulted in the accumulation of soil in a bank on one edge of the toft, which before the excavation had been wrongly assumed to mark a collapsed structure; clearly what survives as earthworks at such sites cannot be taken as a direct guide to how they were formed. Whether deeper ditches resulted from a worsening climate, or more rearing of cattle and the need for more effluent removal, remains an issue of debate.

How long the site remained in use could be reassessed from the pottery. It is safe to assume that two stoneware sherds do not derive from occupation on that particular toft, but whether abandonment came in the later fourteenth century or the fifteenth, and whether all the tofts were abandoned at the same time, leaving only the single farm that is on the site today, are issues that remain open for discussion. The uniformity of the seven earthworks might favour a single process of desertion, but the much less regular remains on the south side of the street cannot as yet be interpreted and could result from later usage.

change and a means of preventing direct inheritance. Peter Fasham's discovery on the line of the M3 motorway of the spread-out settlement at Abbots Worthy amplified debate by demonstrating that on the chalklands such sites might be found in river and stream valleys deeply buried by alluvium, as well as on plateaux and ridges, so that the existence of many concealed parts of the settlement pattern must be allowed for.[11] Collingbourne Ducis, Wiltshire, has shown that abandonments are as likely to be eighth- or ninth-century as earlier, something that radiocarbon dates suggest also for Riverdene, Basingstoke.[12] In Berkshire, a different complexity was revealed by Grenville Astill and Sue Lobb, who showed at Wraysbury that in some places occupation may have shifted over much smaller areas than is implied by the total desertions on the chalklands, and that some present-day settlements have much earlier, though still post-Roman, antecedents, than was beginning to be thought likely.[13] New sites, such as at Ufton Nervet and Chieveley, were also coming into use, however, and other recent work in Berkshire has produced evidence of middle Anglo-Saxon traps for fish and eels, exploiting another resource.[14]

Cunliffe at Chalton discovered his site through fieldwalking. Unfortunately, Wessex is not the best area for this landscape archaeology technique, especially for anyone seeking early medieval evidence, since much of the pottery of the period is too friable to survive, as well as being too black to see easily in dark soil. Thus, despite not being staffed entirely by prehistorians, Stephen Shennan's fieldwalking team in East Hampshire collected only two sherds of Anglo-Saxon pottery, and various Berkshire projects have had similar problems.[15] More productive was the Avon Valley Archaeological Society's work, showing that there were fields on the gravel terraces from which Anglo-Saxon pottery could be recovered.[16] Small settlements may yet be located off the chalk, exploiting woodlands and clay soils.[17]

In the 1970s, various rural surveys were published,[18] but not enough to provide the overall coverage achieved for the five counties' towns. Road-building led to some excavation of later medieval sites, such as part of Popham and, at Easton Lane outside Winchester, of a surprisingly rare example of a late Saxon/early Norman rural enclosure.[19] Hatch Warren church and surrounding graveyard – and other settlement traces – were investigated as part of the expansion of modern Basingstoke, and Foxcotte because of the growth of Andover.[20] Attrition by the plough is not so eye-catching as destruction by earth-scraping for development schemes, however, and it is still much more difficult to find funding for sites that are not immediately threatened with total obliteration.

Current issues: (i) Fields and estates

Settlement patterns between the eighth and the eleventh centuries were affected variously by political and ecclesiastical change and taxation, by the depredations of Vikings and Normans, and by the growth of estate centres, coinage, and places of exchange. The first documentary mention of fields occurs in a Wessex law-code, that of King Ine of the turn of the seventh/eighth centuries, stating: 'If ceorls have a common meadow or other land divided into shares to fence…' This has been taken to show that open fields divided into strips and subject to uniform farming arrangements already existed, but modern commentators take it to mean careful management of the infield.[21] The archaeological problem is to recognise any traces of such arrangements, and here the evidence is thin. Laurence Keen identified long linear boundaries shaping the open fields of Dorchester, which are not on the same alignment as the Iron Age and Roman fields seen on air photographs; they must therefore be post-Roman and could be associated with the eighth-/ninth-century royal vill based at Fordington, outside the walls of the Roman town. If indeed middle Anglo-Saxon in date, those boundaries could provide a similar date for boundaries around Sherborne, also in Dorset.[22] Nothing similar has been claimed for the other four counties. Generally it is assumed that an infield/outfield system was practised, traces of which would presumably disappear if the settlement that it served was moved on. In a few cases, the large oval boundaries that are often early medieval have been identified, as for instance by Steve Clark on the Berkshire Downs, and by George Campbell in the forests and heathlands.[23] As in the New Forest, some may have been vaccaries, but they are not necessarily all of pre-Norman date.[24] In general it is rectilinearity that is recognised – including at Worth Matravers, Dorset, although the place-name 'worth' has been associated with such ovals elsewhere.

'Worth' and 'worthy' names can mean estate centres. Some have churches, like Martyr Worthy, Hampshire, an estate of the bishops of Winchester, where the Domesday Book record of 'a church' on a three-hide estate seems insufficient for a building that housed a very large Rood carving, still largely extant. Whether the bishops maintained a house there is unknown, but residences investigated at Faccombe-Netherton and Portchester show the investment that owners were prepared to make.[25] The first was on an estate owned by members of a well-to-do family, and something appropriate to their status is unsurprising. Portchester is often cited as illustrating the early eleventh-century *Rectitudines Singularum Personarum* document, which says that a ceorl who held five hides of land should become a thegn with a *burh-geat*, and a belltower; Cunliffe's excavations revealed a two-phase square masonry structure with graves adjacent to it, which could very well be the foundations for such a tower. Domesday Book for Portchester has three 'free men' holding three manors taxed for five hides in total; it seems likely that a five-hide estate had recently been sub-divided and that William Mauduit re-amalgamated it, presumably taking over also the residence inside the Roman fort. If one of the three 'free men' had lived in that, he was technically living above his station! The original 'thegn-worthy' five-hide unit is probably beyond reconstruction on a map – it need not even have been geographically unitary, since charters show that sub-divided estates were not necessarily immutable: the late Chris Currie argued that boundaries in and near Southampton were not always the same in the tenth century as in the eleventh, and at Corscombe, Dorset, two Sherborne charters show that a bloc of land was added to the estate between 1014 and 1035.[26] Another case of changing land-units seems to be provided by Shaftesbury Abbey's Kingston estate on the Purbeck peninsula. There are three purportedly Anglo-Saxon charters in the nuns' fifteenth-century cartulary, but one is extremely dubious; the other two have boundaries that imply the amalgamation of two estates that had been separate in the mid-tenth century. Furthermore, only parts of the boundaries are also those of the nineteenth-century parish, which included places recorded in Domesday Book, but which were not owned by Shaftesbury.[27] The ecclesiastical arrangement of Purbeck may have begun with the whole peninsula under the control of a church, perhaps British, in or near Wareham. The E–W division that probably placed the western part under a 'minster' at Corfe may have been the next stage (Feature Box: *Key Sites to Visit*, p. 123).

Key Sites to Visit: Corfe and Purbeck

Samuel Grimm did this drawing of Corfe Castle and its environs in 1790; a convenient lay-by now allows the same view to modern photographers, who do not realise that the road they are on is a *herepath* recorded in a tenth-century charter.

In AD 979, King Edward the Martyr was murdered *æt corfes geate*, probably at a royal residence built on the natural knoll in the gap through the chalk ridge. By 1066, Shaftesbury Abbey owned most of the land on the left side of this picture, but William the Conqueror coveted the knoll; Domesday Book (c. 1085–90) records that he acquired a hide of land from the abbey for a castle. He did not need it for military reasons as the road through the gap leads to nowhere of significance, so he probably admired its position. His successors certainly used it for their hunting parties, though sometimes also as a secure prison.

Figure 8.2. *Drawing by Samuel Grimm of Corfe Castle and its environs in 1790, looking north. (Picture from a manuscript in the British Library, Add. MS 15537, fol. 134, reproduced by kind permission of the Trustees)*

To the right of the castle, Grimm shows the tower of Corfe church, which has good claim to be on the site of an Anglo-Saxon minster. A small settlement must already have existed around it and become part of William's hide, since Shaftesbury made no claim later to any of the tenements in Corfe. Those who lived there in the late eleventh century escaped record in Domesday, however. By chance, Grimm's drawing captures another omission. As well as Shaftesbury's Kingston, several other manors farmed this valley. Their boundaries are not all certain, but either down along the stream or up at the top of the ridge ran that of a manor named Ragintone, valued in the 1080s at 40 shillings; no people were recorded as working for its Norman sub-tenant, although in 1066 nine thegns had held it 'freely'. By chance, another 1080s survey, the *Liber Exoniensis*, adds that the nine thegns were in fact still there, presumably a good deal less 'free' than before, but still farming the land.

The land in the foreground of Grimm's drawing probably fell within one or more of the five small Domesday units named Afflington, which implies the sub-division of a single holding belonging to a woman called Aelfrun. Alueron held one of its five parts in 1066, presumably a Norman rendering of the Old English name and implying that the sub-division was then still quite recent. Even if two of the units surveyed in the 1080s were worked by their holders and their families (for the other three were certainly too grand for manual labour), the recorded labour force only totalled ten, surely fewer than six hides all yielding small returns needed.

Afflington is still the name of a farm today, but that does not mean that all five Domesday manors were grouped at it. Nor did all nine thegns necessarily live together at modern Rollington. In other words, the survey tells us a lot about manors, but not about how many people lived and worked on them. Estimates based on Domesday Book put the total population at around two million, but local vagaries like these could well suggest something a lot higher.

By the early fourteenth century, Corfe was rated as a town, though it was probably smaller than a good many villages. Its people made a living from the castle and from stone quarrying at Purbeck, as well probably as agriculture. Grimm was standing on top of strata of good-quality limestone when he drew this picture, stone that can still be admired in the walls and on the roofs of many of the buildings in modern Corfe (Hinton 2002a).

An historical context for that could be the end of the seventh century and the Wessex kings' take-over of south Dorset; before that, the area seems to have been firmly 'British' since there are no 'Anglo-Saxon' cemeteries or objects, the Ulwell cemetery with its cist graves being very different from anything on, for instance, the Isle of Wight, despite a short sea crossing being all that separated them.[28] Teresa Hall has suggested that St Aldhelm may have re-organised the ecclesiastical structure then.[29] Thereafter, further sub-division occurred, the broadly N–S lines of several parishes suggesting an intention to provide a variety of different land types, which in turn strongly suggests the interests of estate owners. Some of this provision was subsequently lost, if the smaller parish units reflect later sub-divisions. These may have reflected estates, but not all estates became separate parishes, so that by Domesday the peninsula had a plethora of small manors. Discrepancies between their sizes and the terminology used of their holders have been discussed recently by Michael Costen, who, like many others, has tried to establish their boundaries, but whether they can all be mapped confidently is doubtful, because of many later foundations, as within Tyneham or Langton Matravers.[30]

Investigating the implications of place-names and charter boundary markers remains a fundamental way of assessing the late Saxon countryside.[31] A useful new on-line tool for any discussion of boundaries is the nation-wide plotting of nineteenth-century parish boundaries on to the modern Ordnance Survey map.[32] Sheet 179 instantly reveals the interlocking and overlapping of east Purbeck parishes which hint at an underlying Corfe *parochia*. Other sheets, notably 167 that predominantly covers the chalklands around Salisbury, are dominated by very long thin parishes at right angles to rivers and streams, often hinting at originally larger units from which they had been taken, and of course occasionally with charters to show the consonance of parish and estate unit.[33] Christopher Taylor showed by plotting tithing boundaries that the same was also true for sub-divisions of parishes in large parts of Dorset's chalklands.[34] Also common is for a long strip to be divided at the stream, giving both estates access to it, and leading to 'paired' settlements on each side, as in East and West Chisenbury, Wiltshire, or Shaftesbury Abbey's East and West Orchard in Dorset.[35] Not

obviously related to streams running through valleys are long strip parishes that run across the steep north scarp of the Hampshire downs into the clay vale of the Kennet, just as many on the north edge of the Berkshire Downs descend into the Ock Valley.[36]

In Hampshire, Roman roads seem to have been more influential than streams in the layout of parishes; surprisingly few on its chalklands are long and linear. That seems true of smaller units also: Alison Deveson's recent reconstruction of the tithings within Hurstbourne does not have them in parallel lines straddling the stream, or in pairs either side of it.[37] Some of the most complex interlocking and overlapping parishes are on the chalk/Kennet Valley interface.[38] Kingsclere looks as if it was Hampshire's largest nineteenth-century parish, with low-lying heath in the north, and high chalkland to the south; it had several detached portions lying beyond parishes to the east. That these did not result from relatively recent arrangements is strongly suggested by Hannington, a parish south of Kingsclere, for which there is an early eleventh-century charter (Figure 8.3).[39] The estate was even then in at least two parts, linked by a lane; Kingsclere parish surrounded its northern half on three sides. Yet Hannington was high on the chalk downs, where uninterrupted expanses of sheep grazing might have been expected, not small, complex units. Furthermore, the church, which has Anglo-Saxon features, is right on the estate boundary.

All this feeds into one of the major issues of present debate: when were open fields created, and is village nucleation associated with them? Domesday Book reveals ploughs and ploughlands in both Kingsclere and Hannington but not, of course, where the arable was located or how its cultivation was organised. Nineteenth-century maps show that there were open fields around Kingsclere itself, but give no hint of them on the downs. When the king wanted to enlarge his park on the interface of the downs and the valley in the thirteenth century, he had to buy up several very small parcels of land from a variety of owners, but no hint that they lay within open fields is given.[40] If Hannington was already so sub-divided by the beginning of the eleventh century, how much further back in time can the process of division have gone? Was there ever a time when landlords could have rearranged their estates and where their tenants lived

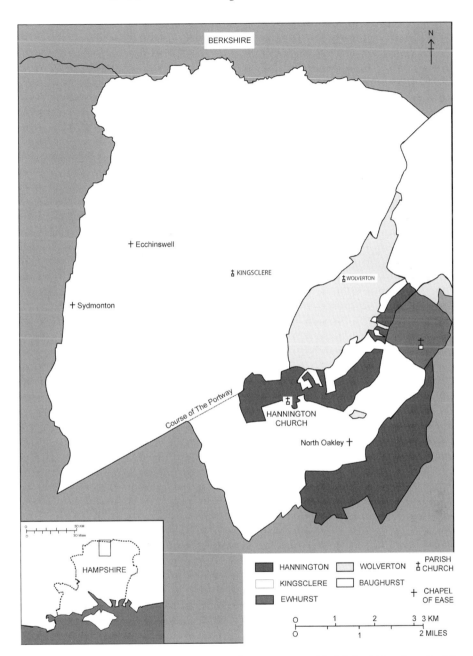

Figure 8.3. The parishes of Kingsclere and Hannington, Hampshire, reconstructed by Michael Hare from the tithe maps and an early eleventh-century charter. The charter has Hannington as a single estate, despite its different parts. By 1066, it was divided between two manors, but which had which parts is not made clear in Domesday Book. Such complexity, so high on the chalk downs, is unexpected – Hannington church is at 201 metres AOD, Kingsclere church at 95, and down in a valley with poor soils. The probability is that a large bloc called Clere had been divided; Highclere and Burghclere are both to the west. Kingsclere was then further sub-divided, with Hannington and other adjacent parishes taking its eastern part. Ecchinswell was a separate late Saxon estate, with a charter, but never became ecclesiastically independent of Kingsclere, unlike Hannington, and unchartered Wolverton and Ewhurst. (Plan from Hare 1979, fig. 1, reproduced by kind permission of the author and of the Hampshire Field Club and Archaeological Society)

Figure 8.4. Winterbourne Stoke, Wiltshire. The earthworks in the foreground suggest abandoned house sites, stretching along a village street, enclosed within a narrow valley formed by the River Till. It looks as if the church is typically close to a manor-house, but in this case the medieval manorial site seems to have been in a different part of the village The linear settlement pattern also looks typical of the chalklands, but may not be the whole story in this particular case. At the top of the photograph is a road at right angles to the street. This was a braid of the main routeway that is now the A344, and settlement may have been attracted to line along that as well as along the valley. When contraction came, people may have preferred to stay by the road to take advantage of passing trade. (Photograph by courtesy of Mick Aston)

in such a way as to create nucleated settlements and large open fields? In Wessex generally, large numbers of small units – whether legal manors or otherwise – may have been a barrier to nucleation, existing rights being much more difficult to overrule than in those parts of England which had been under Danish rule in the early tenth century, even if only briefly.

Purbeck was clearly an area of generally dispersed settlement, though Corfe, Bucknowle, and a few other places may have been big enough to be considered 'nucleated'. Corfe, however, was merely the largest of several scattered settlements within Shaftesbury's Kingston estate; the nuns did not set out to create a Midlands-type regime. Nevertheless, quite large blocks of open fields were a feature of the Purbeck peninsula (see Feature Box: *Key Theme*, p. 128). When these fields systems were laid out is not known; there are no charters for Worth Matravers, but those for Kingston of the tenth century do not suggest that ploughed lands ran up to any of the estate boundaries. On Wight, where Saxon charter coverage is particularly good, the same is true.[41] A Wiltshire charter has '*ealdan land sceare*' or 'old boundary of the

ploughlands', as a boundary marker, but 'old' here may mean an ancient lynchet, not a recently abandoned acre-by-acre system, though another marker, *for yrthe* ('as far as the ploughland'), does not hint at anything other than contemporary cultivation.[42] In Berkshire, on the edge of the downs, mentions of acres are made in some charters, as they are in Hampshire; in a few instances, therefore, ploughland with strips preceded the boundaries.[43] Recent work near the coast at Pennington, Hampshire, may have revealed the laying out of one such system with 20 m wide strips realigning an earlier pattern in the eleventh/ twelfth century, replaced by small enclosures at some point.[44] Twenty metres is too wide for a normal selion, however, so unless there were unditched sub-divisions, the system served some other purpose.

In general, the clays and heaths were too barren to be worth ploughing, and the chalks, gravels, and greensands were light enough for deeply cut drainage ditches between selions not to be needed. Consequently, this is not an area with much surviving evidence of ridge and furrow; where it survives at all, on the downs, the ridges are much lower than in the Midlands.[45] On some steep and uninviting slopes, however, as at Worth Matravers, prominent lynchets still show the amount of effort that went into cultivation. Ironically, another good set of surviving valley-side lynchets can be seen at Longbridge Deverill, a Glastonbury Abbey estate for which documentary evidence suggests that farming concentrated on grazing.[46] The extent of open fields is usually therefore revealed by post-medieval estate maps;[47] medieval documents may sometimes give the names of fields, furlongs, and strips, but rarely enough information for them to be mapped. The Langton Matravers evidence comes from a secular Inquisition; more usually it comes from Church cartularies. Such records sometimes give glimpses of the operation of field systems, but not about the introduction of common fields – i.e. open fields practising communal rotations and stinting.

Open fields extending out to the boundaries of manors or vills were usually associated with nucleated villages. Use of the early nineteenth-century Ordnance Survey maps to plot dispersed and nucleated settlements and to propose 'Provinces' and 'Sub-Provinces' from the results is a technique that may treat as non-nucleated too many of the long, linear villages characteristic of the valleys in central southern England (Figure 8.4), particularly if they are in 'interrupted' rather than continuous rows, and includes many places that were almost certainly not medieval in origin.[48] Doubt has been thrown on the validity of a similar study using a Wiltshire map of 1773, because that map was drawn up after most of the claylands had been enclosed, causing earlier nucleation to become dispersed.[49] Off the chalklands, commons and greens fringed by sixteenth-century houses take settlement evidence back before the maps, and show common-edge patterns to be at least very late medieval.[50] A contrast in ownership which saw more small manors on the claylands, with scattered places lost to documents when aggregated into vills for taxation purposes, is another factor.[51] Small secular manors are rarely documented, but one on the Isle of Wight suggests that the farming strategies pursued in the thirteenth century were similar to those on the bishop of Winchester's demesne, mixed farming with much consumed on the estate and by the household, with some sales.[52] The documented great estates indicate that this was the overall pattern throughout

Wessex until the fourteenth century, with different balances and chalkland emphasis on sheep.[53]

Current issues: (ii) Commerce, population and material culture

Great estates such as those of the bishops of Winchester created extensive documentation, leaving information about their management that is beyond the reach of archaeology. The accounting in them may disguise the full picture, however; questions about the validity of yield estimates when there is uncertainty over, for instance, whether tithes were included in the reckoning may give a false picture of returns, and peasant producers may have been more efficient than demesne workers.[54] One aspect of Wessex's documentation, however, is that tax and other records may reveal swings in profitability. Purbeck, for instance, shows up in the Domesday Book as fairly profitable; yet by the early fourteenth century it was one of the poorest areas in terms of tax assessments, and is characterised as having been in the land-use type with the lowest annual average. Nevertheless, it supported a large population – larger than the documents reveal, as the very poor were excluded from taxation (Feature Box: *Key Theme*, p. 128). All this was in an area where quarrying, salt-working, fishing, and exploitation of the heaths gave more diversity than in other parts of central southern England.[55] The Worth Matravers and other Purbeck lynchets look like fairly desperate expedients by peasants to stay alive and by lords to extract a bit of income from them. True, some of the local lords built themselves manor-houses which suggest that they were adept at being undertaxed, but they may not have been exceptional in that.

Lords had interests other than purely agricultural, of course. The kings' forests covered much of southern England.[56] The effect that this had on where people lived is hard to judge. Eviction may have been exaggerated, since it seems only documented for the New Forest, and even then its scale is uncertain, since the land could never have supported large numbers; Domesday Book reveals a very complicated pattern of holdings on the Isle of Wight dependent on Avon valley and Forest settlements.[57] The rights that surrounding settlements had in forests such as Bere gave useful extra resources, and, even if services were

Key Theme: Expansion and Retraction

Taken half a mile from where Samuel Grimm looked northwards in 1790 to draw Corfe Castle (Figure 8.2), this photograph (Figure 8.5) looks southwards over fields in Worth Matravers and out to sea. The scene is idyllic when blue sun and sea merge imperceptibly, but not when a gale is blowing salt-laden sea-mist inland, blighting the crops. Yet the series of terraced strips on the headland to the right were nevertheless thought worth the hard physical effort of creating, to give manorial tenants a little more arable land. It is assumed, though rarely proven, that 'lynchets' like these are a sign of land hunger and therefore rural settlement expansion in

Figure 8.5. Coast-edge lynchets at Worth Matravers in Dorset, part of the manors of Worth and Weston, both documented since Domesday. (See papers in Hinton (ed.) 2002. Photograph by courtesy of Mick Aston)

the twelfth and thirteenth centuries, and that their fossilisation under grass came with reduced population pressures, settlement retraction, and more demand for meat and wool, in the fourteenth and fifteenth.

The well-preserved system on the headland may well result from a medieval sequence, but the shallower lynchets on the slope to the left have a different story. Closer to the village, those strips were still being farmed in the old way when an estate map was drawn up in 1772. The 'common-field' system still gave various properties in the village the right to farm separate strips, intermingled with those of their neighbours. Some of the terraces seem to have been sub-divided into two strips, and the field in the foreground had already been turned into pasture, 'Cowleaze', by 1772. The correlation between what was surveyed then and a topographical survey carried out in 1991–94 is not quite exact, so the individual holdings cannot be reconstructed in their entirety; amalgamations can be traced through various surviving leases. Plans were already being mooted in 1752 to abolish the 'severalls', and the strips were probably not all being ploughed, unless labourers were coming from outside Worth village. Enclosure was not completed until the 1790s, however, and elsewhere on Purbeck a common-field system survived to be shown on the 1840s' Swanage tithe map; some elements of one are still worked on the Isle of Portland, to the west.

The field systems in the photograph belonged to two different manors, Worth and Weston, until 1752 when they were amalgamated. Domesday Book recorded three Orde/Wirde manors, so the original unit had probably already been sub-divided, with settlements at Weston, Worth, and Eastington (not in the picture). The largest, with land for twelve ploughs, was based around the church and pond at Worth. The *Liber Exoniensis* adds that Roger of Arundel, the 1080s holder, owned 250 sheep as well as pigs, woodland and a mill – the estate stretched a long way to the north, as well as down to the sea. Nevertheless, if the headlands were terraced and ploughed, so too probably was much of the flatter land to the north, as in 1840s Swanage, and as is recorded for medieval Eastington and nearby Langton. Consequently, arable reduced the grazing, producing a concomitant shortage of manure. Population numbers are not known, but another Purbeck manor, Steeple, was recorded variously in the early fourteenth century as having 345 acres and pasture for 200 sheep, or 528 acres; these supposedly sustained two free tenants, 22 customary tenants, and 22 cottagers – an average of 11½ fairly low-quality acres per family. Idyllic photographs disguise harsh medieval realities.

due in them, payments for work or supplies might also be available.[58] Castles were another imposition which were not an unmixed blessing, since small payments might be made for castle-guard and other duties; their direct effect on the development of rural settlements, however, was not great.[59] The introduction of the fallow deer increased the attractiveness of parks, which occur in all the Wessex counties and are part of discussions about their social and economic roles.[60] Fishponds were another status symbol, such well-known open waters as Fleet and Alresford ponds originating in this way. Because lords controlled water flows, a more commercial investment by them was in mills, better known from documents than from archaeology; investment in church institutions was for their souls, not to develop their settlement pattern.[61]

The extent to which the settlement pattern was affected by population growth, as opposed to the increase in people being contained within existing places, remains an issue. Certainly there was growth: Isle of Wight and Hampshire estimates comparing Domesday Book and the 1334 Lay Subsidy suggested that it was sluggish in the twelfth century, thereafter rising by 60 per cent.[62] It is difficult to chart the ebb and flow within existing villages, but work at Peasemore, Berkshire, by Steve Clark and local colleagues is encouraging. Individual sites also continue to be found, often enough where none was expected. An example of expansion on to the unpromising heathland south of the River Kennet in Berkshire has been provided by recent work at Meales Farm, with pottery from the later eleventh century onwards, and grain thought to have derived from a drier. Little medieval pottery was collected during fieldwalking in the area, however, which suggests that not much manure was spread, and therefore that cultivation was either brief or never very intensive.[63] On the whole, despite such examples, and again probably showing a difference between the chalklands and elsewhere, it seems that most medieval settlements in the five counties were already in being before the eleventh century.[64]

Commercial growth is also a factor. The rural peasants' role in this seemed slight, while the numbers of coins found outside towns amounted to little more than the very few found in their excavated buildings and under their church floors, the latter presumably mislaid offerings. However, metal-detection is showing that quite staggering numbers of coins were in fact being lost in country fields. Although we might imagine that a few were cast aside by an uncaring lord careering across his tenants' land after venison, it is difficult not to see most as the losses of ordinary people. Estimated totals from the Portable Antiquities Scheme in 2005 suggested that an average of nine coins for each year of the twelfth century had been recovered and reported, but by the end of the thirteenth the average was up to 30 coins for each year. This certainly indicates a very active and growing peasant involvement in coin use.

The most obvious evidence of consumption is provided by pottery. Duncan Brown has shown that small medieval rural sites, such as Wroughton Copse, near Marlborough, Wiltshire, have a much more limited range than urban or castle sites.[65] But that the finest imported vessels were not gracing peasants' houses may be less important than that their occupants could exercise at least some degree of choice between jugs and cooking-pots from different kilns at the local market, because they had the wherewithal to buy such things. Most of the jugs were glazed and decorated, indicating that the peasants could afford a bit more than the most basic kitchenware. Quantities are not unimpressive, either: an unusual survival, an unspread midden at West Meads, in central Dorset, contained some 525 early to mid-thirteenth-century sherds, in 14 different fabrics; 14,000 sherds were recovered in the single season of excavation at Holworth.[66] Points like these suggest commercial expansion,[67] and although lynchets and open fields can be read as representing hard graft, they would also have been a way of using extra family members to slight profit.

Another potential measure of prosperity is buildings: ground plans recovered from excavations at such sites as Holworth show thirteenth-century houses to have had stone footings and therefore the potential for timber-framed superstructures. These involve larger, carpentered timbers such as crucks (Figure 8.6) and denote therefore an investment beyond mere daub walls and lashed rafters. The number of peasant-level buildings surviving above-ground is inevitably few, but they too will have involved substantial timbers and framed carpentry, both of which had to be paid for. In Hampshire, where an extensive dendrochronological survey has

Figure 8.6. A cruck house in the Avon Valley at Ibsley, Hampshire. Many such well-built rural houses survive at least in part, and many have been dated by dendrochronology. In Hampshire, they range in date from early in the fourteenth century to the end of the fifteenth. The 'cruck frontier' runs through east Hampshire, i.e. no full crucks, with a single curved timber running from the ground to the apex, have been found in Sussex or Kent, for reasons still argued over – cultural, economic, topographical, even political and ethnic. (Photograph by the author)

been undertaken, the earliest known cruck house is in Bentley, dated to 1311/12.[68]

Although they cannot usually be attributed the sorts of precise dates needed for discussion of population growth in a particular 50–year period, the growth in the number of markets and fairs is certainly evidence of twelfth- and thirteenth-century expansion, and although many were small places, if they were successful they were duly taxed as towns, as Corfe was in 1332, this the smallest of Dorset's nine places taxed as boroughs (Feature Box 2).[69] Their growth presumably soaked up surplus people from the countryside, mostly villages in the immediate hinterland, like the seven Kingston *fugitivi* recorded in the early twelfth-century Shaftesbury Abbey survey, five of whom were certainly living in nearby Wareham, as probably was the sixth; only one other of the abbey's many estates had 'fugitives' recorded, and none of them was in a town. They must have existed elsewhere, a caution against over-reliance on the figures for demographic interpretation.[70] Density

in many towns was not great: in Dorchester, the open fields actually extended inside a good part of the Roman walls, and although some selions provided the outline of twelfth-century burgage plots, other parts were not enclosed until 1596.[71] In Hampshire, 51 places had a market of some sort at some time in the Middle Ages, but 13 of them were only worth £20 or less.[72]

Current issues: (iii) Politics and (de)population

Most of central southern England was not close enough to London to be much affected by the increasing political pulling power of the capital and the demand for great houses within reach of it. Only north-west Wiltshire, Salisbury, and Newbury really took advantage in the later Middle Ages of the new cloth industries that were partly caused by politics and the Hundred Years War; in terms of relative wealth, Hampshire and Dorset remained slightly below national wealth averages, whereas Wiltshire rose to fifth place in the county league table.[73] Inland waterways were not able to carry goods cheaply to new outlets, so the extra costs of carting limited marketing opportunities.

The king's wars caused taxation demands and new defence systems. Civil turmoil, partly a consequence of soldiers returning from France, was another problem affecting prosperity. It would be worth re-opening the subject of moats with this factor in mind; there have been excellent studies of them in all the five counties, and a clearer demonstration of the social and economic differences of the likely constructors would be useful. Water-filled moats have been drawn into discussions of the fear of crime and violence, being seen as providing extra defence against lawlessness. Where documentation exists, however, it suggests that such problems were endemic rather than episodic, although the 1381 Peasants' Revolt was a more extreme incident;[74] in general there was no great rush to fortify unmoated manor-houses.

Whether the impact of the Black Death created new problems, or exacerbated those already developing, remains arguable, but the extent to which the fourteenth and fifteenth centuries saw desertion and shrinkage of rural settlements caused directly or indirectly by population loss has been a major issue since Maurice Beresford's initial recognition of the question.[75] Total abandonment may have been less frequent than partial – Holworth retained a working farm, for instance (Feature Box: *Key Sites to Visit*, p. 123), and many Hampshire and Isle of Wight sites entered as 'deserted' are still to some degree active today. Many of Hampshire's total desertions were for post-medieval parkland creation around great mansions, though many may already have been much weakened; Berkshire's Hampstead Marshall is another example.[76] John Hare has shown from documentary evidence how one near-total abandonment occurred on a Winchester bishopric estate on the chalk, at Northington, where a village with at least 35 households had been reduced to four by 1485, when the manor became a single, tenanted, farm. Gomeldon, with good evidence of croft amalgamation, looks like a similar example. Other sites diminished more slowly, such as the one excavated at Foxcotte, which was still well-peopled in the sixteenth century. Hatch Warren, on the other hand (Figure 8.7), seems

to conform to the once-expected pattern of mid-fourteenth-century abandonment caused by the Black Death: in 1378 the parish was amalgamated with a neighbour because there was no-one living in it, and the excavation record is of a place petering out at that time. What does not conform, however, is the way that the archaeology shows some sort of brief re-use towards the end of the fourteenth century. Earthwork evidence of desertions and an isolated church may show a pattern of abandonment in Lockerley parish, Hampshire, of a type recognised in Norfolk: an early core, then scattered greens with new houses around them retained while the original focus was deserted, leaving only the church.[77]

Amalgamation of farms, as at Gomeldon and Northington, was a standard late medieval change. Tenants were hard to find. Central southern England is not known to have had any cases of enclosure driving out large numbers of reluctant workers; instead, gradual accommodation was probably the norm, though some may have been pressurised – as on some parts of the de Newburgh estate in south-east Dorset, but with the surprising compensation that in other parts of the same estate the amount of arable was actually increased.[78] Other changes included increasing rabbit breeding on the Wessex chalklands, as at Northington, providing fur and meat to meet new demand patterns. At Kington Magna, Dorset, new fishponds were superimposed upon some of the empty tenements, although the building of a west tower on to the church shows that the community was still viable.[79] 'Catch-works' to take water along a contour-line so that it could be released into the valley below may also have been introduced, for instance at Hale in the Avon valley in the 1520s, but is not distinguished archaeologically.[80] Sheep may have been more profitable in Wiltshire and north Dorset, and more grass for them was a benefit. The Northington case illustrates what was not untypical, that a few people could benefit from leasing estates that great lords had previously farmed themselves; lessees' building is a late medieval feature, notably in Hampshire.[81]

Conclusions

The term 'central southern England' has been used in this chapter's title partly because the original West

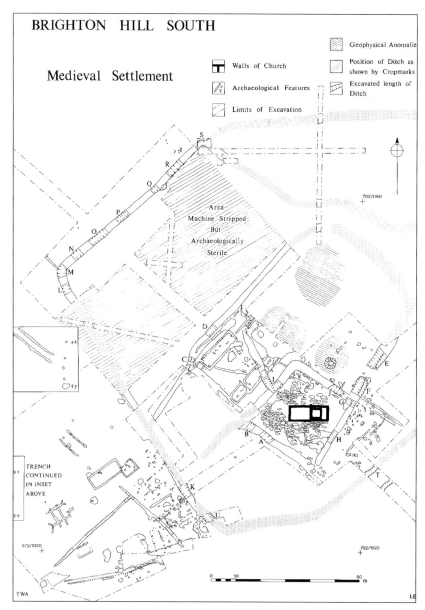

Figure 8.7. Hatch Warren, Basingstoke, Hampshire. Plan of the excavations around the two-cell stone church, its chancel probably enlarged to conform with new liturgical requirements in the thirteenth century for locating the main altar at its east end. Its surrounding graveyard was separated from secular life by a shallow ditch and probably by a fence. The larger foundations are identified as a hall and other buildings belonging to the lord of the manor, distinguished by a large enclosure from the smaller houses and structures to the south. Occupation need not have started before the Norman Conquest, and the archaeology is not inconsistent with documentary records that no-one was living in the parish in 1378, although some sort of late fourteenth-century usage occurred. (Plan from Fasham and Keevill (with Coe) 1995, fig. 40, reproduced by kind permission of Wessex Archaeology)

Saxon kingdom was differently constituted from the five counties considered in it, and also to avoid implying agreement that a 'West Wessex Sub-Province' within the 'Central Province', and an 'East Wessex' within a dispersed-settlement 'South-East Province' would have been meaningful during the Middle Ages.[82] Linear settlements on the chalk, the extent of open fields, the amounts of woodland, greens, marsh, and commons all argue against separating Dorset and Wiltshire from Berkshire, Hampshire, and the Isle of Wight, and make the five counties very different from the central Midlands. That the chalklands north of Dorchester were significantly different in kind from those north of Winchester is not proven, and the broken geologies of west Dorset and the Blackmoor Vale are not so very different from the Hampshire basin or the Kennet valley. Equally, to claim the existence of a 'central Wessex', significantly different from Sussex, and denying that north-east Berkshire did not belong within the Middle Thames, would be to try to create a false unity. Far better, therefore, is to think in terms of downland, forests, wood-pasture, marshland and commons,[83] in other words *pays*, as denoting what characterised central southern England, with varied ownership, the coast, and geopolitics also to be borne in mind.

Further reading

Of the very many books that deal with central southern England, or with parts of it, J. Thirsk (ed.), *The English Rural Landscape* (Oxford, 2000) takes the approach that seems best to suit the topic. D. Hooke's *The Landscape of Anglo-Saxon England* (Leicester, 1998) is an excellent introduction to the first millennium AD generally, and for the second millennium, Joe Bettey's *Wessex from AD 1000* (London, 1986) is outstanding. Interesting because it sees the area in a wide perspective, extending from Kent and London as far west as Dorset, is B. Short, *The South East* (London, 2006), and S. Turner reached into Wiltshire and Dorset in his *Making a Christian Landscape. The Countryside in Early Medieval Cornwall, Devon and Wessex* (Exeter, 2006).

More detailed work has been cited in the text, but M. Aston and C. Lewis (eds), *The Medieval Landscape of Wessex* (Oxford, 1994) deserves a separate mention, rather than just for its individual contributions. The five counties considered here fall into two different local government regions, and this is reflected in the recent English Heritage-sponsored 'Research Frameworks', which have led to useful environmental and other contributions; medieval Dorset and Wiltshire were not given much prominence in C. J. Webster (ed.), *The Archaeology of South West England* (Taunton, 2008), although it is a useful volume overall. Whether 'Solent-Thames' makes any coherence as a region is doubtful, but the individual period-by-period sections on Berkshire, Hampshire, and the Isle of Wight are generally good summaries, and are available through the website of Oxford Archaeology, www.thehumanjourney/index/projects

Much important work is of course published in county archaeological society journals: four of the counties have long had prestigious publications, and it is excellent that the Isle of Wight Society has recently been able to produce an annual periodical of equal quality. Monographs are also produced intermittently by most counties.

Notes
1. Taylor 1970.
2. Bonney 1966 and 1976, critiqued by Draper 2004.
3. Fowler and Blackwell 1998, 79–105; Fowler 2000, 37–38. It says much for the integration of documents and fieldwork that one of these charters, Sawyer no. 547, has been ascribed to Orton, Huntingdonshire, as well as to West Overton! Happily it is not crucial to Fowler's mapping of the boundaries.
4. McOmish *et al.* 2002, 109–134.
5. Shennan 1985, 91–103; Light *et al.* 1995; Stedman 2005.
6. Rahtz 1959; 2001, 78.
7. Musty and Algar 1986; Grenville 1997, 142–145; Gardiner 2000, 163–165.
8. Fowler and Blackwell 1998: 82; Fowler 2000, 121, 125.
9. Cunliffe 1972; Addyman *et al.* 1972.
10. Millett 1983.
11. Fasham and Whinney 1991.

12. Pine 2001; Hall-Torrance and Weaver 2003.
13. Astill and Lobb 1989.
14. Clark 2009, 10–11, 19; Mudd 2007.
15. Shennan 1985, 90–91; Clark 2009, 3.
16. Light *et al.* 1995.
17. Page 2009.
18. E.g. Groube and Bowden 1982; Basford 1980.
19. Fasham 1987; Fasham *et al.* 1989, 75–78; also now Crockett 1995.
20. Fasham and Keevill 1995, 76–148; Russel 1985.
21. Faith 1997, 79–80.
22. Keen 1984, 206, 236–238.
23. Clark 2009, 13; Campbell, G. 2008a; Campbell, G. 2007.
24. Smith 1999.
25. Fairbrother 1990; Cunliffe 1976.
26. Currie 1994; Barnard 1994.
27. Hinton 1994.
28. Cox 1988; radiocarbon dating allows the cemetery to have remained in use even into the tenth century, but it may have closed by the end of the eighth.
29. Hall 2000, 14–15.
30. Hinton 2002a: Frontispiece, 89, and appendixes 1 and 2.
31. E.g. Hooke 1998; Lennon 2009 for woodland in Wiltshire.
32. Kain and Oliver 2006.
33. Cf. Hooke 1998, 11, 65, 122; Acornley 1999, 54.
34. Taylor 1994.
35. Brown, G. 1996; Stacy ed. 2006, 11.
36. Hooke 1998, 74, 123–127.
37. Deveson 2009.
38. Kain and Oliver 2006: sheet 168.
39. Discussed by Grundy 1926, 112–116, and mapped by Hare, M. 1979, 193–195.
40. Sharland 2010.
41. Margham 2003.
42. Acornley 1999, 56–57.
43. Hooke 1987, 138–139; Hooke 1994, 92.
44. Moore *et al.* 2008.
45. Fowler and Blackwell 1998, 55–56, 74, and col. pls 10 and 15; McOmish *et al.* 2002, 111–115.
46. Gates 1996.
47. Chapman and Seeliger 2001.
48. Roberts and Wrathmell 2002, 5–12; Hinton 2002b for a critique of a small area and the difficulty of replicating their results.
49. Lewis 1994; Chandler 1996. See also now Lambourne 2010.
50. Edwards, B. 1995.
51. Hare, J. 1994a.
52. Page 1998.
53. Hare, J. 1994a, 160–162.
54. Stone 2005, 262–276.
55. Hinton 2002a; Campbell, B. 2000, 96.
56. Bond 1994.
57. Mew 2001.
58. Pile 1989; Munby 1985.
59. E.g. Hughes 1989 for Hampshire, Lewis 2000 for Wiltshire.
60. E.g. Mileson 2009.
61. Roberts 1986; Graham 1986.
62. Lewis and Fox 1995.
63. Lobb *et al.* 1986–90.
64. Lewis 2000.
65. Brown, D. 1997.
66. Rahtz 1959, 140; Hinton 2010, 103–104.
67. Langdon and Masschaele 2006.
68. Roberts 2008: 6.
69. Mills (ed.) 1971, vi and 102–106 (the assessment did not treat Sherborne as a borough, which seems anomalous); Hinton 2002c: Appendix 4.
70. Stacy (ed.) 2006, 130, 140.
71. Woodward *et al.* 1993, 8–9, 86–87.
72. Campbell, G. 2008b; see also Stamper 1996.
73. Miller 1991b, 149. Berkshire's position is complicated by the 1974 boundary changes; much of the prosperous Vale of the White Horse with its late medieval manor-houses and textile industry is now in Oxfordshire.
74. E.g. Watts 1982.
75. Beresford 1954.
76. Lewis 2000; Hughes 1994; Bonney and Dunn 1989.
77. Hare, J. 1994b; Musty and Algar 1986; Russel 1985; Fasham and Keevil 1995, 149–150; Edwards 1995.
78. Soane 1985.
79. Ross 1985.
80. Cook *et al.* 2003, 159–161.
81. Roberts, E. 1996.
82. 'West Wessex' and 'East Wessex' are terms used by Roberts and Wrathmell 2002, 44f.
83. This is the approach taken by the contributors to Thirsk (ed.) 2000.

CHAPTER 9

South-West England: Rural Settlements in the Middle Ages

Sam Turner and Rob Wilson-North

Introduction

The landscapes of South-West England have inherited a particularly rich legacy from the Middle Ages. This is not limited to major buildings like churches, castles and village sites, but also includes the fabric of many of today's lanes, farms and field boundaries. The work of archaeologists and historians suggests these landscapes have their origins in developments that took place well over a thousand years ago, but despite sustained research over the last half-century the details of how this happened remain far from clear.

'The South-West is almost another country...

...as well as being diverse in itself'.[1] The distinctive, elongated, irregularly tapering shape of the South-West peninsula gives some clue to the variety of its physical landscape and to its underlying geology. This topographical diversity contributes to the complexity of the historic landscape. Unusual factors are at play in the South-West peninsula: it is remote from the economic and political centres of power and influence, yet profoundly influenced by external factors through sea-travel. The sea exerts a strange effect, in that settlements irrevocably separated by miles of rough terrain were in reality often joined by a similar distance of sea. Small coastal settlements became disproportionately important because the remote and vast hinterland with its wealth of minerals, wool and other commodities needed the coast, and

the access to the wider world that it afforded, in order to thrive; there is sometimes interdependence between coastal settlements and those in the hinterland which can be reflected in the structure of land tenure.

The climate of the South-West is maritime, gentle, wet, sometimes unpredictable and highly localised. An oft-quoted saying which seems to be applied to a number of locations in the South-West is, '[on Exmoor] if you can see Dartmoor it's going to rain, and if you can't see Dartmoor it *is* raining'. The main uplands of Dartmoor, Bodmin and Exmoor exert a strong influence over the weather, the settlement patterns, communications and the agriculture of the region, but so too do the lesser uplands of the Quantock Hills, the Blackdown Hills and Mendip. Together they help to physically break up the region into an array of diverse mini-regions or *pays* (Figure 9.1). The geology of the region, like everything else, is complex and diverse, and for our purpose is best seen in terms of the landforms it presents on the surface. In broad terms, much of west Cornwall and south Devon comprises igneous rocks which contribute to the rugged and wild nature of the landscape, especially Dartmoor, Bodmin and some of the Cornish heaths. In north Cornwall, central and north Devon, the influence of sedimentary rocks is felt in a more undulating landscape varying from rolling countryside to intimate combes or valleys. Exmoor was forced upwards creating a generally level plateau with especially deeply incised valleys. The northern coasts are very rugged, while the southern coasts

Figure 9.1. *The Blackdown Hills, looking west across Luppitt Common. The sinuous boundaries of medieval enclosures lie on the valley sides and valley bottom; straight-sided post-medieval fields have been laid out on Luppitt Common above (part of the Common still lay unenclosed at the beginning of the twentieth century). The settlements of Greenway Farm (centre left, with smoke rising) and Luppitt (extreme right) were both first documented in Domesday Book, where they were recorded as small estates of one and two hides respectively in 1066. (Photo: Sam Turner, November 2005)*

are more accessible and therefore more amenable to coastal settlement.

The South-West as a whole is especially rich in a wide range of mineral deposits. These minerals in the underlying rocks – and the rocks themselves – gave rise to extractive industries across the region, principally for tin, iron and copper.

The high rainfall of the region means that peatlands, streams and rivers are an inescapable feature of the South-West, from expansive blanket peat on Dartmoor through the intimate valley mires on Exmoor to the deep lowland peats of the levels and 'moors' in Somerset. The abundance of water, from flashy moorland streams to the major rivers of the peninsula, has given rise to thousands of mills; even remote moorland farms harnessed water for processing crops and irrigating fields.

History of research

Documentary sources

Compared to some parts of England, the South-West does not seem particularly well-endowed with early documentary sources useful for understanding the medieval landscape.[2] Nevertheless, the region has benefited from detailed studies by some of the twentieth century's most important English landscape historians, prominent amongst them being members of the 'Leicester School' such as W. G. Hoskins and H. S. A. Fox, both native Devonians. In the years after World War II, a series of seminal studies was published that identified and discussed issues of key importance for the region, for example H. P. R. Finberg's *Tavistock Abbey* and Hoskins' *Devon*.[3] Like F. W. Maitland before them,[4] they recognised that the South-Western landscape was different in many ways to the better-known Midland counties. In *Devon*, for example, Hoskins drew attention to the fluctuating boundary of moorland-edge cultivation. The expansion of settlement in the uplands during the twelfth and thirteenth centuries provided a parallel for assarting in the Midlands, but Hoskins carefully pointed out that viewed over a longer period there had been several episodes of expansion and retreat.[5] Finberg wrote detailed discussions of Devon's agrarian practices based on documentary sources and highlighted distinctive features such as convertible husbandry and open strip fields, which he argued had once been virtually ubiquitous.[6] These subjects and many others were developed from the 1970s onwards by Harold Fox, whose intimate knowledge of the medieval records allowed him to illuminate a great diversity of themes with relevant references. His work on field systems fully exploited the documents to show how well-suited the medieval South-Western farming system was to the local environment.[7] His work on enclosure demonstrated how and why it progressed at different rates in different sub-regions and the consequences for local societies and economies.[8] Fox made fundamental contributions to many settlement-related topics, including work on the changing size and pattern of dispersed hamlets and farms,[9] and the origins, growth and significance of marginal settlements by the sea and on the moors.[10]

Fox recognised that in a landscape with dispersed settlements it was important to understand how and where farms and hamlets were located (this, he argued, was knowledge that medieval tax collectors might have benefited from, since the records suggest they repeatedly failed to levy taxes in some out-of-the-way settlements).[11] Studies of place-names in the South-West have contributed significantly to our understanding of medieval landscapes, not least because early forms can show which settlements existed at particular times, and these can often clarify the significance of names' original meanings. Related studies for Devon[12] and Cornwall were undertaken in the early twentieth century, though the latter was unfortunately not published.[13] For Cornwall, where place-names continued to be coined in the Cornish language well into the post-medieval period, more recent research by Oliver Padel and his colleagues in the Survey of Cornish Place-Names has updated, corrected

and greatly expanded on these early studies.[14] Sadly the other parts of the South-West have not benefited from such in-depth place-name research, which can make inter-regional comparisons difficult. In some areas, for example Exmoor and the other uplands, a lack of medieval documentary sources means the archaeological remains of many medieval settlements have no associated name or other written record.

Nevertheless, several studies have made extensive use of information derived from historical sources to illustrate the development of medieval settlement organisation in particular parishes or regions. For example, pioneering papers by Maurice Beresford on Cornwall, Harold Fox on Devon and Mick Aston on Somerset used lists of tenants or tax records to help locate settlements and analyse their development in the late Middle Ages.[15] This kind of work has helped to illustrate not only the desertion of medieval settlements before the modern era, but also the ways they contracted or expanded from hamlets or single farms at different times.

At a broader scale, historical and geographical data have been used to produce characterisations of medieval and later landscapes. A good example is provided by H. C. Darby and R. Welldon Finn's *Domesday Geography of South-West England*,[16] which presents a series of general maps for each county representing the distribution of population, livestock, different types of land-use and so on based on information in the great survey. Other characterisations have used more recent sources to provide county-wide coverage: thus, as part of their national survey of settlement patterns, Brian Roberts and Stuart Wrathmell have mapped the degree of nucleation and dispersion of settlement across the South-West based on nineteenth-century maps;[17] while recent historic landscape characterisations (HLCs) of Cornwall and Devon used nineteenth- and twentieth-century maps and air photographs to map a range of character types such as medieval enclosures and ancient woodland at a fairly detailed scale.[18]

Archaeology and physical remains

Excavations on medieval settlements began in the nineteenth century, but it was not until later that their date and significance were generally recognised (e.g. Trewortha, Bodmin Moor).[19] In the decades either side of World War II excavation, survey and

Key Excavation: Mawgan Porth, Cornwall

The early medieval settlements of the South-West are not well known, with the partial exception of one category
– coastal sites. Archaeologists have identified a range of different site-types in the region from fortresses to farms,
often first revealed as a result of coastal erosion. In the post-Roman centuries, major fortified settlements like Tintagel
in north Cornwall provided pivotal nodes of power. At the same time, beaches like Bantham and Mothecombe in Devon
provided venues for periodic trade and exchange between sea-going ships and local communities. Small settlements
such as the one excavated amidst the dunes or 'towans' of the north Cornish coast at Gwithian by Charles Thomas
provide evidence for continued occupation into the seventh century and later (Thomas 1958; Fowler and Thomas 1962;
Nowakowski *et al.* 2007). Another important site and probable late-Saxon royal centre was identified at Gunwalloe on
the Lizard (Jope and Threlfall 1956), and is now being researched by a team led by Imogen Wood.

The most fully excavated coastal settlement lies about 10 km south west of Padstow on the north coast of central
Cornwall (Figure 9.2). The site at Mawgan Porth was excavated over several seasons in the 1950s and again in 1974
(Bruce-Mitford 1997). Like several other coastal sites of this period from the region, it lay relatively undisturbed beneath
a covering of wind-blown sand. The site was first identified before World War II when trial trenches in advance of building
works revealed walls, pottery, fragments of bone and a skeleton, but it was not until 1948 that investigations

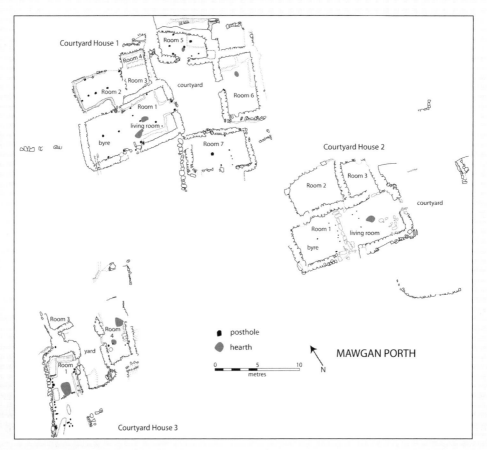

*Figure 9.2. Mawgan Porth, Cornwall: plan of the settlement and its 'courtyard houses'. The cemetery lay just to the north. (Redrawn by Sheila
Newton after Bruce-Mitford 1997, fig. 3)*

resumed; these were followed in the early 1950s by excavations organised on an impressive scale: over 120 volunteers were involved in 1952, and a light tramway was installed to remove spoil! The work revealed a hamlet of at least three 'courtyard houses', and a small cemetery. Each courtyard house consisted of several rectangular structures arranged around a central courtyard. The principal building in each of these units seems to have housed people at one end and animals at the other. They are similar in form to later medieval longhouses but laid out slightly differently with a drain at the corner of the long side. The buildings were made of stone-faced walls bonded with earth, which in places survived up to *c.* 1.5 m in height. Within many of the buildings the excavators identified stone-slab 'furniture' that probably represent seats, cupboards and beds. The buildings were heated by internal hearths and lit by small apertures like the triangular window in Courtyard House 1.

The site was dated by a stratified coin struck between AD 990 and 995. Although it is uncertain how long it had been inhabited before this, it likely originated at least in the later ninth century – this is consistent with the discovery of grass-marked pottery similar to that found at Gwithian which provided bowls, dishes and platters. The main ceramic assemblage comprised over 2000 sherds of so-called 'bar-lug' pottery, a distinctive type of cooking pot with ingenious internal 'bars' protected by 'lugs' to stop the suspension rope from burning through in the flames of the fire below. Numerous stone objects including hammerstones, whetstones and polishers were also discovered, along with shell and bone showing that the residents consumed a wide range of foodstuffs from land and sea. Encroachment of blown sand forced the inhabitants to abandon the site, perhaps in the later eleventh century.

Thirty metres or so uphill from the settlement a small cemetery was found. It consisted of 22 burials including both adults and a separate group of children. They were buried mostly in the stone-lined cists that are typical of the area from the late Iron Age into the later Middle Ages. Owing to its proximity to the settlement it has been assumed the two elements of the site were contemporary with one another, but it is unclear whether the cemetery would have also served a wider population or whether a small church or chapel could still lie hidden beneath the dunes.

publication began in earnest with fieldwork at early medieval sites like Mawgan Porth in mid-Cornwall (Feature Box: *Key Excavation*, p. 138), Gunwalloe and Gwithian in west Cornwall,[20] and later medieval settlements such as Beere near North Tawton and Dean Moor on southern Dartmoor.[21] These early excavations proved extremely fruitful and laid strong foundations for the study of both the pre- and post-Conquest periods, particularly in Cornwall. Their scope went beyond the remains of settlements to consider important topics such as field systems, as for example at Gwithian where an area of early medieval arable cultivation (probably ploughed) was excavated beneath later sand dunes.[22]

Perhaps encouraged by these early successes, archaeologists in the 1960s and 70s undertook a great deal of fieldwork on rural settlements across the South-West. Following on from the previous excavations at Mawgan Porth and Trewortha, longhouses were recognised as the standard dwelling-type at many sites including Old Lanyon, Garrow Tor, Tresmorn, Treworld, Okehampton Park, Hutholes and Houndtor.[23] This work established that longhouses were normally two- or three-room structures *c.* 10–15 m long and rarely more than *c.* 4.5 m wide. At several sites, longhouses were accompanied by barns with ovens for drying grain.[24] Survey work also began to identify large numbers of medieval settlement sites on the moors,[25] while intensive archaeological field survey analysed the surviving earthworks of medieval settlements and their fields, sometimes in conjunction with excavation.[26]

Much of this work focused on the uplands, where large-scale survey work has continued since the 1980s. The Royal Commission on the Historical Monuments of England (RCHME) carried out surveys using air photographic transcription and/or detailed fieldwork of Bodmin, Exmoor and parts of Dartmoor, and, following the merger with English Heritage in 1999, has continued with this sustained programme of investigation on the Quantock Hills and Mendip. These have greatly enhanced our understanding of the medieval uplands.[27] Some of the smaller uplands and some lowland areas have also benefited from the

Figure 9.3. Hutholes near Widecombe-in-the-Moor, Devon, under excavation in 1994. (Photo: © Tim Gent/Exeter Archaeology, November 1994)

attention of English Heritage's National Mapping Programme (NMP), in particular in Cornwall and Somerset. The NMP focuses on identifying and mapping archaeological sites visible on air photographs. The results in the lowlands tend to be richest for prehistory and the Romano-British period, perhaps because many settlements with medieval origins are still occupied. Nevertheless, the NMP has helped illuminate relationships between medieval and earlier patterns of settlement and land-use.[28] Medieval landscapes have also been investigated through scientific studies, including work on sedimentation in river valleys and on the ancient buried pollen record, with the moors most productive, since pollen is often well-preserved in upland bogs.[29] Over the last decade, however, scientists have also identified small bogs and other deposits in lower-lying areas that

have been suitable for geoarchaeological or pollen analysis.[30] This work has addressed important topics such as the intensification of medieval agriculture, the expansion of farming on the moors, and the origins of the South-Western agricultural system.

Significant programmes of excavation have continued, not least in response to major infrastructure projects such as the construction of reservoirs at Colliford (Cornwall) and Roadford (Devon).[31] Since the introduction of new planning guidelines in the early 1990s, the amount of archaeological fieldwork funded by developers has greatly increased. Because development sites tend to be outside the National Parks and therefore off the moors, such work has begun to allow archaeologists to redress the balance of knowledge between upland and lowland areas. Categories of both early and late medieval

Key Theme: Dispersed Settlement

The nature of the landscape of South-West England, with its broken topography and varied character, has deeply influenced the structure of rural settlement in the region. It seems as though changing political and economic systems frequently had little effect on the settlement pattern: neither Romans nor Normans made much detectable impact. Settlement patterns adapted gradually, with the moorlands remaining mostly unpopulated and a very varied pattern of largely dispersed settlements in the lower areas, ranging from individual farms, through small hamlets to nucleated villages. Our approach to studying the settlement patterns of the South-West should be to fully accept and embrace their variety and be prepared to accept the diversity of these sub-regional pays.

Settlements are considered 'dispersed' when they are scattered across the landscape, with farms standing individually or with a few neighbours. The smaller and more frequent such settlements, the more heavily 'dispersed' the settlement pattern is thought to be. Dispersed settlement patterns are typical of western Britain, Ireland and many other parts of Atlantic Europe (see, for example, Antoine 2005). The building block of the settlement pattern today is usually the individual farmstead, but in many places this is likely to be a simplification of an earlier pattern built primarily on hamlets (groups of two or more farms). The antiquity of hamlets might be sought in the late prehistoric enclosures which abound across Cornwall, Devon and into west Somerset, but so far any evidence for this remains elusive. It seems more likely that hamlets developed on new sites between the fifth and eighth centuries AD, though we lack much hard evidence in the form of excavated archaeological sites.

In some parts of the region large parishes have no central settlement and the parish church is sited within one of the hamlets. Some parishes (like North Molton or Chittlehampton in north Devon) have documented early origins and a nucleated village has grown up at their heart, but with a complex pattern of farmsteads and hamlets beyond. Intricate patterns of lanes connect the scattered elements of the settlement pattern forming a locally logical system, with wider networks of routes often holding higher ground, especially ridgeways, except when they cross rivers at fording points. Some other settlements – like Parracombe on Exmoor – are a conglomeration of elements and almost defy classification: part of the settlement is nucleated, while the other elements are several hamlets and a small grouping around the medieval church, which itself is away from the main focus of the village (Figure 9.4).

Figure 9.4. Parracombe, Exmoor, from the air (Photo © English Heritage. Crown copyright NMR 18528 27)

sites that were previously unknown in the region have been identified and professionally excavated (e.g. the metalworking site at Burlescombe in east Devon; a horseshoe-shaped early medieval structure at Stencoose, mid-Cornwall; and a moated site at Wonford, near Exeter).[32] Recent research excavations have been designed to address particular problems or questions arising from earlier work: a good example comes from the longhouse settlement of Hutholes on Dartmoor where recent re-excavation was designed to evaluate the results of previous work on upland settlements (Figure 9.3).[33] On the eastern borders of the South-West region, interdisciplinary research undertaken for the Shapwick Project has elucidated the growth of a nucleated village and open field system. The village at Shapwick seems to have replaced an earlier pattern of dispersed settlements in the late Saxon period (see Feature Box: *Key Theme*, p. 141). Nevertheless, it was only in certain parts of the region that nucleated villages became widespread, and even then dispersed elements were frequent: scattered farms and hamlets remained the most common settlement form throughout the Middle Ages.[34]

The final major strand of medieval settlement research in the South-West has been the study of standing buildings. While there are a great many late medieval buildings, the distribution of surviving domestic structures varies significantly across the region; in particular, relatively few medieval houses seemingly survive in Cornwall compared to Devon and Somerset.[35]

Late medieval and early modern longhouses survive in numbers and have become somewhat iconic, perhaps because they are part of a regional medieval building tradition well-attested through the excavated moorland sites. Such buildings are usually set across the slope with living accommodation in the uphill end separated by a passage from livestock in the downhill end, with a drain that passed out under the narrow end wall.[36] The great majority of both standing and excavated examples lie on the region's uplands, though recent work has begun to identify examples in other areas.[37] One problem with understanding the distribution of longhouses is that their original form is frequently obscured by conversion of the shippon (animal) end into accommodation for people, meaning that a building that was originally a longhouse might easily be taken for a two- or three-room cross-passage house – the other common type of late medieval rural house in the South-West.[38] Cross-passage houses appear to have been widespread in the lowlands but fewer have been excavated, perhaps because the great majority of sites have been continuously occupied.[39] Confusingly, longhouses and cross-passage houses share what is essentially the same floor plan, comprising a central cross-passage which separates a lower room (in longhouses the shippon) from a hall and usually an inner room beyond. The most reliable indicator that a building functioned as a longhouse is the central drain, but this may not be visible unless excavated. Detailed studies of larger rural houses have also provided valuable material for understanding the social, cultural and economic transitions from the Middle Ages to the early modern period. At Leigh Barton in the South Hams, for example, the expansion and subdivision of the building from the fifteenth century onwards illustrates how separate spaces were created for members of the family and their servants.[40]

Settlement morphologies and landscape use

Origins and processes of site growth
During the Roman period the settlement pattern of the peninsular South-West was dominated by farmsteads and hamlets enclosed with one or more banks and ditches. In Cornwall these are known as 'rounds', a word which often appears in field names or other place-names either in its English form, or as the Cornish prefix *ker, and frequently indicates the remains of such a settlement. In marked contrast to neighbouring parts of western England, there were very few Roman villas in Devon and Cornwall and most of those identified by archaeologists lie in the east of the region. The 'rounds' and other enclosed farmsteads seem to have been established in the late Iron Age but continued to be the normal form of settlement right through the Roman period and several were still inhabited during the fifth and sixth centuries. The best-known example is Trethurgy near St Austell, which was investigated in the early 1970s.[41] The excavations covered the whole of the interior and revealed a settlement that was inhabited into the sixth century. People lived in oval houses and used both locally produced and imported Mediterranean pottery. An increasing number of

similar sites inhabited during the post-Roman period has been identified, but evidence for their use generally disappears between the fifth and early seventh centuries.[42]

It remains unclear how widespread unenclosed settlements were in the Roman and post-Roman periods, although examples from Cornwall show they certainly existed (e.g. at Tremough[43]). From about the sixth century, however, archaeologists believe it was normal for hamlets and farmsteads to be unenclosed. Gwithian on the north Cornish coast provides one example, and a structure excavated at Stencoose may have formed part of such a settlement.[44] Unfortunately people in much of the South-West do not seem to have used pottery between the seventh and tenth centuries, which adds to the difficulty of identifying rural settlements. In Cornwall place-names provide relevant evidence, since scholars believe that certain name-elements were used during the early Middle Ages (e.g. *tre* and **bod*)[45] and the distribution of such names have been used to try and map zones of early medieval settlement.[46] Further east in Devon and Somerset scholars have so far only made brief forays into the significance of Anglo-Saxon place-names for early settlement patterns.[47] Unfortunately very few examples have been explored archaeologically, not only because they are hard to identify, but probably also because the majority of sites have continued to be occupied down to the present day.

Although the exact reasons for the move from enclosed to unenclosed settlements remain to be determined, it is evident that this was a time of profound change. Major processes that affected the lives of people in the South-West included the establishment of the kingdom of *Dumnonia* and the conversion to Christianity. Evidence from archaeology, place-names and increasingly from palaeoenvironmental studies all suggests that the landscape was re-cast with new settlement patterns and a new farming system. As noted above, agricultural historians like Finberg and Fox recognised the distinctive nature of the South-West's regime of 'convertible husbandry' and traced its signature in the medieval documents, but owing to the paucity of early texts it was unclear when it might have begun. Under convertible husbandry, fields were normally put down to grass but were ploughed up for arable crops on a long rotation (perhaps for a couple of

years once every 10–12 years).[48] This meant that on any given land-unit, most fields would usually be grass (and could be grazed by livestock), but a few were cultivated. As Finberg, Herring and others have argued most medieval arable in the South-West seems to have been farmed as strip fields.[49] This was a flexible system since it allowed extra fields to be dedicated to crops some years if necessary. A further element of flexibility was provided by outfields beyond the core farmland which were also cultivated in strips and could be brought into cultivation very occasionally (a practice that continued as part of this farming system into recent centuries).[50]

There are hints in early sources that aspects of this system were of some antiquity, although they probably related to the outfields rather than the core farmland. A mid-tenth-century charter from Ayshford and Boehill in east Devon refers to '…many hills that can be ploughed', and evidence for such fields may have been discovered at Bunning's Park on Bodmin Moor.[51] In the last decade, important scientific studies based on pollen preserved in wetlands have cast new light on this issue. This evidence has been interpreted to suggest that the palaeoenvironmental sequence shows there were major changes in the agrarian regime between the seventh and ninth centuries, which then remained relatively stable in later centuries. It seems probable that this was when the system of convertible husbandry first emerged, and that it continued throughout the Middle Ages and into recent times.[52] Archaeologists have argued that field patterns associated with settlements that are likely to have originated in the early medieval period are frequently aligned differently to those of earlier times. This hints that the field systems which were crystallised by enclosure in the later Middle Ages were based on the cropping units of early medieval times.[53] Occasionally documentary sources offer support to this idea, like the mid-eleventh-century Anglo-Saxon charter from Trerice in St Dennis which appears to describe the outer boundaries of a field system that survived into the twentieth century.[54]

In some areas, for example on the Lizard peninsula in Cornwall, there are geographical clusters of pre-Conquest charters that make grants of several tiny estates.[55] The places in question are usually identifiable in the medieval documents and indeed on the modern map, which suggests that many of the later medieval land-units were already in existence in the late Saxon period. It was also from this time that the use of ceramics became more widespread across the region, and as a result archaeologists have been able to identify increasing numbers of sites: in Cornwall distinctive 'grass-marked' and then 'bar-lug' cooking-pots may have been used throughout the early Middle Ages[56]; in Devon and western Somerset chert-tempered pottery was circulating in the towns from the tenth century and its use grew in the country from the eleventh.[57] It is important to note that many places mentioned in charters and later documents are not mentioned in the Domesday Book, which provides a reminder that in regions of dispersed settlement the great survey is far from a complete list of existing settlements. In fact, it seems likely that the number of settlements began to increase from the tenth and eleventh centuries, when new farms were established around the margins of existing fields and on the moorland edges.[58]

Various upland sites have provided evidence for farming on the moors around the time of the Norman Conquest (see Feature Box: *Key Site to Visit*, p. 145).[59] Even so, research suggests the speed at which the moorlands were colonised by medieval farmers should not be overestimated. In the 1980s David Austin raised questions over the interpretation of excavations on Dartmoor which argued that longhouses were commonly preceded by a phase of turf-walled buildings that could date back as far as the mid-Saxon period.[60] Recent re-excavation of Hutholes with this question in mind failed to identify any occupation phases preceding the late medieval stone house.[61] Combined with John Allan's analysis of the pottery from excavated Dartmoor sites (typically locally produced cooking pots and jugs), it seems certain that the main episodes of medieval settlement on the higher moorland took place *after c.* AD 1200.[62] New farms were also established in other areas during this period, and these were often sited in elevated positions compared to existing settlements (e.g. the excavated site 600 m uphill of Treworld, Lesnewth[63]). Although the exact chronology and mechanism remain uncertain, it seems likely that 'settlement splitting' was a common way of creating new farms in this period. The process involved the division of an existing land-unit and the construction

of one or more new farmsteads. Peter Herring has analysed this process at Brown Willy through field survey and documentary research and suggests it dates to the thirteenth century there.[64] Quite probably a similar process could account for the existence of so many farmsteads with shared names (e.g. 'Great' and 'Little' Tredinnick; 'West', 'Middle' and 'East' Lewarne; 'Higher', 'Lower' and 'Inner' Fawton, all in St Neot, Cornwall).

Status of peasants

Domesday Book mentions no free tenants in Devon and Cornwall, only *servi*, *bordarii* and *villani*. Some scholars have deduced from this and similar records that the South-West was dominated by oppressive systems of tenure.[65] While tenurial arrangements certainly varied between different times and places, it seems likely that the Domesday record does not fully reflect the prevailing system.[66] Ros Faith has argued that in addition to substantial landowners there was probably a considerable group of effectively free tenants in the eleventh century who were not recorded in Domesday but who paid their taxes through their neighbours' farms.[67] Certainly by the early fourteenth century, when documentary sources become more common, there are substantial numbers of free tenants in many places. The other major category of peasants in the later Middle Ages comprised 'conventionary' tenants who commonly held their leases for seven-year periods, after which they had to bid for them again.[68] The tenements of each hamlet or land-unit were probably divided into shareholdings between the tenants, explaining how the strip-field system was maintained over such a long period.[69] This communalism was a key element of South-Western farming life throughout the Middle Ages, and infrastructure like mills was sometimes referred to explicitly as 'common'.[70]

The flexible agricultural system of shareholding and convertible husbandry was well-suited for adapting to fluctuating population levels. As elsewhere in England, during the fourteenth and early fifteenth centuries a greatly reduced population and changing market forces led to engrossment, where individual farmers were able to acquire extra tenancies when they became vacant.[71] In parts of the South-West this facilitated the enclosure of former strip fields,

Key Site to Visit: Badgworthy, Exmoor – A Relict Medieval Landscape in Microcosm

On the northern side of Exmoor and in the remote, deeply incised valley of Badgworthy Water are the stony heaps of an abandoned village. You will be told that these are the remains of the Doone village made famous by R.D. Blackmore in his romantic – and fictional – novel *Lorna Doone*! What you are less likely to be told is that the remains are really those of an exceptionally well-preserved medieval village which was abandoned in the fifteenth century. Around 14 buildings, visible as low stone walls, can be discovered lying on the banks of the moorland streams. They are longhouses, cottages, stores and barns sited as the topography allows, and clearly not laid out in relation to a discernible road pattern. Some of the buildings have small paddocks or closes attached to them, and a few of the smallest structures may be better interpreted as animal pens. On the hillsides above are level terraces created for growing arable crops, areas of ridge and furrow ploughing and a number of extensive outfield enclosures stretching away from the area of the settlement, which were mainly used for grazing but which could be ploughed up from time to time as required.

The settlement at Badgworthy predates the Domesday Book (although it is not recorded in 1086), and the name refers to 'Baga's Farm' (Figure 9.5). The place is first documented in 1170 when the land was given to the Knights Hospitaller, and is described as being the land of the hermits of Baga Wordia. By the 1200s there was a priest named Elias and a chapel at the vill of Badgworthy and several tenements are mentioned. By 1423 the settlement was largely unoccupied and tenants could not be found to occupy it.

Possible clues to the earliest origins of the settlement lie all around in the form of prehistoric cairns and enclosures, showing that this area in particular has been settled and used for thousands of years. But perhaps a fundamental reason for the success of the settlement at Badgworthy in the 1200–1300s is its proximity to the former Royal Forest of Exmoor: the settlement lies only a few hundred metres from the Forest's northern boundary and access to the valuable summer grazing which it afforded. Reasons for the failure of the settlement can be found in the deteriorating climate towards the late medieval period and the overall population decline in England at this time following the Black Death. These two factors combined to present tenants at Badgworthy with the opportunity for an easier and more profitable life elsewhere in a less harsh environment.

Figure 9.5. Air photo of the desrted village of Badgworthy, taken by Damian Grady in April 2010. The view is westwards up a side valley of Badgworthy Water. The settlement remains are focused to the west of the confluence (© English Heritage 26646 018)

although in other areas (e.g. east Devon) this process had begun considerably earlier.[72]

Other rural settlements

While most medieval settlements in the South-West accommodated permanent farming communities, others were home to seasonal migrants like transhumant shepherds or people involved in other activities such as peat-digging and mining. Late medieval documents examined by Harold Fox record the seasonal movement of livestock from the lowlands to the moors,[73] showing that by the fourteenth century lowland farmers were paying drovers to take their stock up into the hills. That the practice grew out of earlier traditions of transhumance going back into the early Middle Ages is suggested by manorial links between grazing land on the moors and arable land in the lowlands.[74] In Cornwall the place-names *havos* ('summer dwelling') and *hendre* ('winter farm' or 'home farm') suggest similar links.[75] Few archaeological remains of early transhumants' shelters have been identified, although there are groups of stone huts on Bodmin Moor and excavated features at Houndtor that may be related.[76] Seasonal settlements existed in other places, for example on the coast where 'cellar' settlements provided a base for summer fishing. These often developed into post-medieval villages, squeezed tightly on to the strand or cliffs between the fields and the sea.[77]

Temporary shelters could also be associated with non-agricultural activities such as mining, tin-streaming and peat-digging. On Dartmoor drystone shelters are commonly found amid the earthworks of tin-working sites, sometimes built into the remains of prehistoric hut circles.[78] Medieval farms and fields could be destroyed or disrupted by tin-workings, though it should be remembered that farmers may also have been tinners and that tin-workings would quickly have reverted to rough pasture once exhausted.[79]

Deserted and shrinking settlements

Most of the medieval settlements excavated to date in the South-West were abandoned in the late Middle Ages. John Allan's careful analysis, however, showed that the majority were probably still inhabited late in the fourteenth century, and perhaps even into the fifteenth.[80] Even so, the excavated settlements are mostly located on the moors and other uplands, and their histories are not necessarily typical of the South-West in general or of its particular sub-regions, each of which is likely to have experienced somewhat different conditions. Fox's classic study of Hartland, in north-west Devon, showed how medieval settlements there did not simply disappear, but instead grew or shrank over time in response to particular conditions, sometimes contracting to single farms (which might then thrive), sometimes disappearing altogether.[81] Even on the high moors contraction may have been as common as outright desertion: Challacombe on Dartmoor provides a good example of a well-studied medieval hamlet that had dwindled to two farms by the late eighteenth century.[82] Where settlements dwindled it was relatively simple for any remaining tenants to accommodate the abandoned strips of vacant tenements under the regime of convertible husbandry: fewer cropping units would be cultivated each year, and each field would just be ploughed less often.

In lowland Devon relatively few settlements that were deserted in the Middle Ages have been located, perhaps because the region lacks the large earthwork complexes of former nucleated villages common in some other parts of England. Nevertheless, Richard Jones has noted that a growing number of sites have been identified in recent years.[83] Their archaeological potential remains virtually unexplored. Many thousands of settlements in the county shrank or were deserted in the post-medieval period, and they too represent a rich and very much neglected archaeological resource. A cursory comparison of the first edition Ordnance Survey 6-inch maps with their modern equivalent shows that around 300 settlements have been deserted in east Devon alone since about the mid-nineteenth century (Figure 9.6). About half of these seem likely to have been medieval in origin judging by their place-names and the form of the fields, paddocks and lanes that surround them. Some could be very ancient indeed, like Higher Gatcombe and/or Lloyd's Gatcombe in Colyton – *Gatcumba* was first recorded in 1086.[84]

Future research

The pace of research on medieval settlement in South-West England has been steady and yet there seems

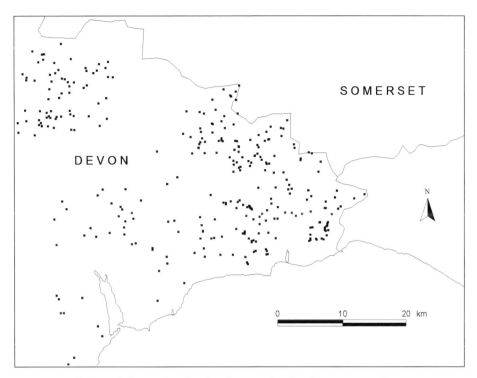

Figure 9.6. Deserted medieval and post-medieval settlements in east Devon.

to be a lack of emphasis on some fundamental areas. Recent reviews for the South-West Archaeological Research Framework have identified many challenges that lie ahead.[85] For the purposes of this overview, it is appropriate to highlight just a few of the most pressing gaps in our knowledge.

Perhaps the most glaring problem is the dearth of excavated early medieval settlements. Farms and hamlets of the twelfth to fourteenth centuries have been investigated in reasonable numbers, although there has been a distinct emphasis on investigation of upland sites and more fieldwork off the moors would greatly increase our knowledge. But it is the centuries before the Norman Conquest where the lack of knowledge based on archaeological evidence is most serious. This is a particularly acute problem since we believe it was in this period that much of the structure of the medieval and modern landscape was first established. Although some post-Roman settlements have been excavated (mostly in Cornwall, e.g. Trethurgy), almost none dating to between the seventh and ninth centuries have been investigated

archaeologically. It seems probable that many such sites lie beneath farms and hamlets that are still occupied, and that this continued use, combined with a lack of easily identifiable material culture, has so far rendered them more or less invisible to archaeologists. This seriously frustrates our ability to understand the origins and development of the region's medieval landscape.

In the absence of archaeological evidence, place-names have been used (especially in Cornwall) to try to fill the void; however, this is hard in other parts of the South-West because the rest of the region generally lacks up-to-date analysis of its medieval place-names. Given that many early medieval sites are likely to be perpetuated in later medieval settlements, we might attempt to approach these problems through places recorded in later records. There is a need to focus research on the origins of isolated farmsteads where they are documented in the later Middle Ages (for example through the fourteenth-century Lay Subsidies). How much older than this are they and what are their origins? What physical evidence can be found in the orchards and paddocks around such farmsteads? What can be gleaned from farms like this which were abandoned in the eighteenth or early nineteenth century and which have therefore escaped later enlargement and amalgamation?

By building on such work we could also address questions about the development of settlement patterns in different regions. One pressing question concerns the process of 'settlement splitting' by which it seems likely a pattern of dispersed hamlets was further fragmented in the later Middle Ages. The form and material culture of settlements beyond those ordinarily occupied by free and bond tenants are still poorly understood: Harold Fox drew attention to people such as landless labourers, squatters and other migrants like transhumant herdspeople, but their cottages and shelters have seldom been investigated or even identified by archaeologists.

The great variation in South-Western settlement patterns visible by the later Middle Ages is sure to be closely related to these problems. In Somerset the detailed, long-term fieldwork of the Shapwick Project helped to identify both the origins of the village and elements of the dispersed settlement pattern that preceded it. Further west we do not presently understand why nucleated settlements are found in some areas and not others, nor do know when they originated. In this respect there is also a need to explore systematically the connections between individual settlement components and field systems. For example, why do tiny hamlets and small villages in north Devon and west Somerset sometimes have elaborate and extensive open field systems when there was, seemingly, little pressure on space? How did regional specialisation in late medieval agriculture affect developing settlement patterns, and to what extent did such trajectories of change have roots in earlier periods?

Finally, we know relatively little about the origins and development of the lanes and trackways which form such characteristic elements of the landscape of the South-West. These are fiendishly difficult to study beyond systematic recording, but by understanding how they related to settlement patterns and landscape resources such as arable fields, pasture and the sea we might better appreciate both the long-term development of the landscape and how it was experienced by people in the Middle Ages.

In general terms, our research might usefully consider how medieval communities experienced, lived in and altered their landscapes. We currently only have a limited knowledge of the extent to which physical and environmental constraints affected people's actions in different periods. Existing cultural features from settlements, fields and roads to broader administrative patterns must have provided a framework that channelled much activity along particular lines. It is important to analyse the extent to which people operated in inherited landscapes, and to understand why they were able or compelled to change the landscape in particular ways at particular times. To provide useful analyses of these questions we need interdisciplinary approaches that go beyond individual sites or narrow themes; our research will provide more satisfying interpretations when it combines a broad range of approaches to illuminate the full contexts of rural life and how people shaped their societies in the Middle Ages.

Further reading

General introductions to the historic landscapes of the South-West can be found in Roger Kain and William Ravenhill's monumental *Historical Atlas of South-West England* (Exeter, 1999) and Kain's *England's Landscape: The South West* (London, 2006).

Introductions to the medieval uplands are available in Sandy Gerrard's *Dartmoor* (London, 1997), Hazel Riley and Rob Wilson-North's *Field Archaeology of Exmoor* (Swindon, 2001) and Nicholas Johnson and Peter Rose's *Bodmin Moor: An Archaeological Survey. Vol. 1: The Human Landscape to c. 1800* (London, 1994). John Allan discusses settlements and their abandonment in his article 'Medieval pottery and the dating of deserted settlements on Dartmoor' (*Devon Archaeological Society Proceedings*, 52, 141–147). The history of medieval settlement is discussed in a series of important articles by Harold Fox in *The Agrarian History of England and Wales, Vol. III, 1348–1500* (Cambridge, 1991). Recent articles on various aspects of the medieval landscape including field systems and crop rotations, mining, churches and castles can be found in Sam Turner's *Medieval Devon and Cornwall* (Macclesfield, 2006). The South-West Regional Research Framework provides a good overview and source of bibliographic references (Webster 2008).

Notes

1. Roberts and Wrathmell 2003, 57.
2. Hatcher 1988a, 383–384.
3. Finberg 1951; Hoskins 1954.
4. Maitland 1897, 39.
5. Hoskins 1954, 69–73.
6. For convertible husbandry see Finberg 1951, 104–106; for strip fields (and Braunton Great Field in particular), Finberg 1949; and see also Flatrès 1949; Rawson 1953.
7. Fox 1973; 1991a; 1991b.
8. Fox 1972; 1975; 1989a.
9. Fox 1983a.
10. Fox 1994; 2001; 2006; forthcoming.
11. Fox 2003.
12. Blomé 1929; Gover *et al.* 1931–32.
13. Gover 1948.
14. Padel 1985; 1988; 1999; see also Svensson 1987.
15. Beresford 1964; Fox 1983a; Aston 1983; 1989.
16. Darby and Welldon Finn 1967.
17. Roberts and Wrathmell 2000.
18. Herring 1998; Turner 2007.
19. Baring-Gould 1891; 1892.
20. Mawgan Porth: Bruce-Mitford 1997; Gunwalloe: Jope and Threlfall 1956 and Thomas 1963; Gwithian: Thomas 1958 and Nowakowski *et al.* 2007.
21. Beere: Jope and Threlfall 1953; Dean Moor: Fox 1953.
22. Fowler and Thomas 1962.
23. Old Lanyon: Beresford 1994; Garrow Tor: Dudley and Minter 1962–63; Tresmorn: Beresford 1971; Treworld: Dudley and Minter 1966; Okehampton Park: Austin 1978; Hutholes and Houndtor: Beresford 1979; for summary of Cornish evidence see Preston-Jones and Rose 1986; for Dartmoor: Gerrard 1997.
24. Henderson and Weddell 1994, 135–138.
25. Linehan 1965; Gawne 1970.
26. Fleming and Ralph 1982; Herring 1986 and 2006a; Austin *et al.* 1980.
27. See, for example, Riley 2006; Riley and Wilson-North 2001; Gerrard 1997; Pattison 1999; Johnson and Rose 1994.
28. Young 2006.
29. Caseldine and Hatton 1994; Gearey *et al.* 1997; Caseldine 1999.
30. Foster *et al.* 2000; Fyfe *et al.* 2003; Fyfe 2006; Barnett *et al.* 2007.
31. Colliford: Austin *et al.* 1989; Roadford: Henderson and Weddell 1994.
32. Burlescombe: Reed *et al.* 2006; Stencoose: Jones 2000–01.
33. Gent 2007.
34. Gerrard and Aston 2007; Aston 1994.
35. E.g. Chesher and Chesher 1968; Alcock and Laithwaite 1973; Preston-Jones and Rose 1986, 148–150.
36. Beacham 1990.
37. E.g. at Stonaford, North Hill: Herring and Berry 1997.
38. Child 1990.
39. E.g. Brown and Laithwaite 1993; Allan and Langman 2002.
40. E.g. Leigh Barton: Brown 1998; Keynedon Barton: Waterhouse 2000.
41. Quinnell 2004.
42. Turner 2006b, 72–75.
43. Gossip and Jones 2007.
44. Nowakowski *et al.* 2007; Jones 2000–01.
45. See Padel 1985: 223–225.
46. Rose and Preston-Jones 1995; Turner 2006b: 74–79.
47. Padel 1999.
48. Herring 2006b, 68–69.
49. Herring 2006b; Turner 2007, 32–56.
50. Fox 1973.
51. For the Ayshford and Boehill charter see Finberg 1971; Sawyer 1968: S.653; for Bunning's Park see Austin *et al.* 1989, 229–230.
52. Fyfe *et al.* 2004; Fyfe 2006; Rippon 2007.
53. Rose and Preston-Jones 1995; Herring 2006b.
54. Herring and Hooke 1993; Sawyer 1968, S.1019.
55. Hooke 1994; Turner 2006b, 164.
56. Bruce-Mitford 1997, 71–80.
57. Allan 1984; e.g. Dyer and Collings 1999.
58. Turner 2006b: 79–81, 89–93; Faith forthcoming.
59. E.g. Bunning's Park: Austen *et al.* 1989; Brown Willy: Herring 2006a.
60. Austin 1985a; cf. Beresford 1988.
61. Gent 2007.
62. Allan 1994.
63. Dudley and Minter 1966.
64. Herring 2006a.
65. Fryde 1996, 209–219.
66. Hatcher 1988b, 677.
67. Faith 2004, 77–78.
68. Hatcher 1988b, 676–678.
69. Fox and Padel 1998, lxxxiii–xciii.
70. Herring 2006b, 47–57.
71. Fox 1991c.
72. Fox 1972.
73. Fox 1994.
74. Fox 2006; forthcoming.
75. Herring 1996, 35–37.

76. Herring 1996, 37–39; forthcoming; Beresford 1979, 110–111.
77. Fox 2001.
78. Gerrard 1994.
79. Newman 2006, 138–141.
80. Allan 1994, 145.
81. Fox 1983a.
82. Pattison 1999.
83. Jones 2010, 9–11.
84. Thorn and Thorn 1985, 51,13.
85. Webster 2008, particularly chapters 10–12.

CHAPTER 10

Wales: Medieval Settlements, Nucleated and Dispersed, Permanent and Seasonal

Robert Silvester and Jonathan Kissock

The Welsh landscape

Wales is a land of contrast and variation. Less than a sixth the size of England with a surface area of just over 8,000 square miles, it stretches for nearly 137 miles from Point of Ayr in the north to the coast around Barry above the Bristol Channel in the south, and for over 110 miles between St David's Head in the west and the English border by Monmouth in the east. At the lowest altitudes, the coastal fringe and some of the major river valleys provide fertile zones comparable with lowland England, while the heartlands are its extensive ranges of rolling hills, moorlands and mountains. The Welsh landscape has been described countless times, with entire books devoted to the topic.[1] We offer here a brief descriptive outline only, sufficient to establish the backdrop to the patterns of medieval settlement in the country (Figure 10.1), but not to examine how the landforms and geology have affected those patterns.

Wales presents a mountainous central spine, generically termed the Cambrian Mountains, which runs for almost the entire length of the country but is in places deeply indented. Snowdonia in the north and the Brecon Beacons in the south offer the highest mountain ranges in southern Britain, and between are highlands appearing as elevated, rounded plateaux, interrupted by deep valleys. Out to the west, the peninsulas of Llŷn in the north and Pembrokeshire to the south border the sweeping arc that is Cardigan Bay. The coastal plains along the south coast extend from Pembrokeshire through Glamorgan to Monmouthshire, while in the north the much narrower coastal strip is partnered by the lowland island of Anglesey.[2] Finally, down the eastern side runs the borderland (the Marches in the Middle Ages) where the hills are broken up by the major river valleys of the Severn, Wye, Usk and Dee. More than a quarter of Wales lies at over 300 m above sea level, and two counties, Brecknock and Radnorshire, have virtually no land falling below 100 m.

The oldest rocks of Pre-Cambrian age are to be found in the west, on Anglesey and on the adjacent Llŷn peninsula and again in the extreme south-west, exemplifying the general northeast to southwest trend in the older rocks of the country. Cambrian rocks are the next oldest, in the north-west and along the west side of the country into Meirionydd. Large parts of north-east and central Wales from Denbighshire through Montgomeryshire, Radnorshire and Cardiganshire down into Pembrokeshire are of Ordovician and Silurian age. Further south Devonian sandstones and grits appear in Brecknock, and to the south are overlain by Carboniferous Limestone and Coal Measures. Similar rocks occur in the north running from the Dee Estuary southwards to the Wrexham area. Younger sediments of the Permian and Triassic underlie the northern lowlands bordering on the Cheshire Plain, and also edge the Severn Estuary. Successive glaciations have affected Wales, the most recent one covering the whole country other than parts of Pembrokeshire. Glacial till has been deposited across the southern lowlands, the northern borderland and Anglesey.

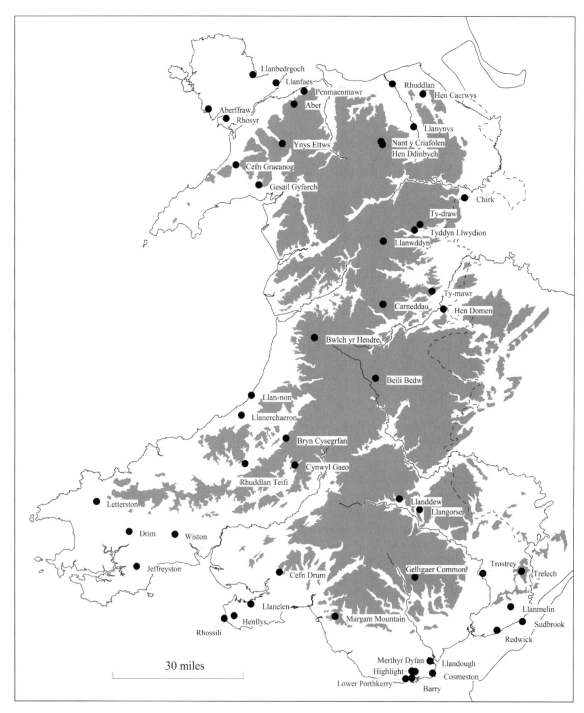

Figure 10.1. Location map of the main sites in Wales mentioned in the text.

Settlement morphologies

Given the size of the country and the varied topography and geology, it is not surprising that the medieval centuries witnessed considerable variation in the form of medieval settlement and also in the combinations in which these various forms now appear. At the same time, some morphological types reveal remarkable consistency across the many different regions of the country.[3] We outline these forms first and comment on their visibility and survival before considering how research on medieval rural Wales has developed and the main themes of recent and current investigation.

Standing buildings

Standing buildings do survive from the medieval period in Wales, but in far fewer numbers than in England. Those that remain are the houses of the upper and middle classes, the gentry and yeomen.[4] Half-timbered hall-houses from the fifteenth and sixteenth centuries are prevalent in the Welsh borderlands, spreading westwards but not as far as the coast. Longhouses are generally associated with the yeoman class and housed farmers and their stock under one roof. In the late medieval period they are evidenced in the borderland, though known survivals are infrequent. Some hall-houses had integral byres and so functioned as longhouses. Exceptional are the tower houses found primarily in Pembrokeshire in the far south-west and only very occasionally elsewhere.[5]

Platforms

While standing buildings have not survived in great numbers, their archaeological counterparts are commonplace. Two basic types need explanation: the platform and the long hut, terms which are simply descriptive, without cultural or chronological nuances.[6] Following their initial recognition in Glamorgan in the early 1930s, platforms (or 'platform houses' as they were then termed)[7] were identified too in the north-west of Wales; but it is only in recent years that their distribution has been revealed more widely across large parts of the country. They are uncommon only in the south-west lowlands, in much of the north-east, in Monmouthshire and on Anglesey.[8] What remains to be established

is whether they spread across the border into the hills of Shropshire and Herefordshire or represent a specifically Welsh phenomenon. The platform is an obvious response to the topography: set into a hillside, generally though not invariably perpendicular to the contours, material was dug from the back and thrown forward to project a level platform out above the natural slope. Detailed analysis of those in Glamorgan found that they ranged in length from 5.5 m to 32 m.[9] Ubiquitous elements are the sloping face at the front of the platform (the apron) and the scarped face at the rear (the fan), while on occasions a bank known as a hood was constructed around the top of the fan to deflect surface water away from the platform.[10] The platform's angle to the natural slope restricted the amount of sub-surface water that flowed on to the platform and was undoubtedly a primary reason in the design. Of course, the corollary is that a medieval building constructed on flat ground would not require a platform and where stone was not the constructional medium, there will be no surface trace of that building.[11] The prevalence of platforms in some areas may thus create a distorted picture of medieval settlement; except in upland regions where preservation levels are high, the platform is not likely to be the only representative of medieval settlement, but rather the only visible one.

Some platforms are featureless, but others display the low foundations of rectangular buildings on them. Paired platforms occur, though rarely more, and very occasionally platforms are wide enough to take two or more buildings. Some platforms still support dwellings, though how common a feature this is it is difficult to determine as architectural historians have generally been little inclined to highlight this aspect of a building.[12] Platforms can occur at any altitude and in any farming context (Figure 10.2).[13] Few have been dated, although a late thirteenth- to early fourteenth-century origin has been inferred from documentary sources for one group on Resolven Mountain (Glamorgan), and Gresham felt able to link some of his platforms to historically attested houses of medieval date, though whether we should accept his view that platforms in the north-west did not appear until the later twelfth century is open to debate.[14] Recent excavations have shown that platforms support the fifteenth-century hall-houses at Tŷ-mawr (Montgomeryshire) and Tŷ-draw (Denbighshire), the former created for an even earlier, thirteenth-century building.[15]

Long huts

Platforms that still display the foundations of buildings take us to the second morphological type: the long hut. First adopted by the Royal Commission in Caernarvonshire, this simple term was coined to cover what may well constitute a range of building types, but which, from the visible remains, usually appear to be unsophisticated, rectangular structures with low foundation walls, simple entrances and occasional internal partitions, and which range in length from around 5 m to well over 20 m.[16] Primarily a feature of the uplands and occurring in their hundreds across Wales, they represent both permanent and seasonal dwellings. What makes them stand out is the use of stone, giving form and height to their foundations. Excavation, however, can readily reveal a more complex structure, as is shown for instance on Gelligaer Common (Glamorgan). Many other comparable buildings were of course of less durable material: thus excavations at Beili Bedw (Radnorshire) revealed three buildings with earthen or turf walls and at Llanerchaeron (Cardiganshire) a clod-walled house was recognised. Many of the numerous platforms without visible physical structures on them presumably reflect the use of timber or perhaps turf.[17]

Longhouses

A third type, the longhouse, is strictly an architectural term, adopted where animals and their human owners lived in a single building with contiguous living quarters and byre under one roof. Many long huts may have been longhouses, but distinguishing them just from their field remains is virtually impossible, even where compartments are visible, for it requires the corroborative signs of drains and stalls, evidence that normally only comes from excavation. For this reason a recently published distribution plan of longhouses in Wales is misleading – only in the south-west were longhouses posited from field evidence, producing a skewed and wholly spurious picture of their distribution across the country.[18] The longhouse is best evidenced late in the medieval period; Suggett describes them in Radnorshire in the sixteenth century.[19] But there can be little doubt that

longhouses existed in Wales as they did in south-west England in earlier centuries, and one of the tales in the *Mabinogion*, variously attributed to anytime between the late eleventh and early thirteenth centuries, clearly describes such a building.[20]

Settlement groupings

How do these morphological types manifest themselves in the Welsh landscape? The most visible medieval form is the individual farm, collectively creating a dispersed settlement pattern across much of Wales. The majority of medieval dwellings stood alone, accompanied only by ancillary structures, their closes and fields. Seasonally occupied settlements are similarly dispersed across the Welsh uplands, often in great numbers, and showing as both huts and platforms. Nucleated settlements of medieval date, whether hamlets and villages, appear in some southerly regions of Wales. In Pembrokeshire, small planned settlements reflect foreign influences, while a thorough survey of Glamorgan recorded 29 examples of deserted and shrunken villages. Eighteen of these were identified by excavation or by earthworks, the remainder being assumed from historical sources. Most were considered a result of Anglo-Norman manorialism, with Cosmeston the best-known example.[21] Further north in Brecknock, earthworks around existing settlements in the Usk and Wye valley also point to early nucleation.[22] The historian's take on nucleation is not wholly in accord with the archaeological evidence. Claimed as reasonably ubiquitous across the country, the Welsh bond hamlet (for which see below) has generally failed to materialise in the archaeological record.

There is, too, evidence for a class of sites, intermediate between the nucleated and dispersed forms, in the form of a *rhandir*, whereby sharelands lay at the centre of a group of dwellings scattered around the periphery. Evidenced in the historical record, this is occasionally manifest in surface remains.[23]

Semi-nucleated groups of dwellings and platforms also appear in the hills, if rather sparsely. The only excavated example – Hafod Nant y Criafolen (Denbighshire) –was attributed a sixteenth-century date on the evidence on the finds, while other groups have been noted in Cardiganshire and in neighbouring parts of Brecknock such as the Elan Valley and most recently on Mynydd Epynt. That these represent

Figure 10.2. The late prehistoric hill-top enclosure of Castell-y-blaidd near Llanbadarn Fynydd, Radnorshire, accompanied by medieval platform sites with their enclosures, one in the centre distance, the other in the same field as the prehistoric earthwork, but off to the right and adjacent to a stream. (© Clwyd-Powys Archaeological Trust: 92-c-508)

Figure 10.3. The moated site at Lightwood Green, south-east of Wrexham, surrounded and overlain by ridge and furrow. (© Clwyd-Powys Archaeological Trust: 04-c-001)

groupings of *hafodydd* seems probable, though this has been disputed, and indeed it is a measure of the uncertainty that the authors of this chapter hold rather different views on the issue.[24]

Moated sites are a special case. In comparison to England, they are not common in Wales: the number of known sites is well under 200, with the majority in the lowlands along the English border and on the coastal plain of Glamorgan (Figure 10.3). Few have been excavated. Thorough analyses by Jack Spurgeon appeared in the 1980s and little can presently be added to these at a regional or national level, although a thesis on moats in the south and south-east was completed at Newport more recently.[25]

History of research

The history of the study of medieval rural settlement in Wales is a curious one of advance, stagnation and gradual recovery. Compared with the situation in England, research is still at a preliminary stage.[26] In the decades either side of the beginning of the twentieth century, Ordnance Survey surveyors and Royal Commission investigators were recording, though not necessarily comprehending, the remains of medieval settlements.[27] The classic platform settlement at Beili Bedw in Radnorshire was, for instance, described in the Commission's *Inventory* as 'a confused mass of earthworks – mounds, banks and enclosures – … which from superficial observation only, it is difficult to arrive at any conclusion concerning their origin. It seems evident that they were not thrown up for military purposes, and they may possibly be due to agricultural operations.'[28] More coherent research commenced in the 1930s when Cyril and Aileen Fox reported on their fieldwork on Margam Mountain (Glamorgan) and Aileen excavated several platforms to reveal house foundations on Gelligaer Common in the same county.[29] Though these excavations were the first to demonstrate the nature of the platforms, the limited fieldwork failed to reveal just how common were platforms in the Welsh hills; sufficiently unusual were they felt to be at the time that the discovery of a couple of sites in Radnorshire merited their own publications. With the exception of two isolated pieces of work in Glamorgan,[30] it was left to the Welsh Royal Commission to demonstrate their prevalence, with Colin Gresham and his colleagues working in the north-western counties of Caernarvonshire and Meirionydd, and other Commission staff studying Glamorgan more intensively.[31]

Following the Foxs' lead, it might have been anticipated that sustained, long-term excavation projects delivering clear, published results would have materialised after the second World War, but strangely they did not. Indeed, medieval dwellings seem largely to have emerged only as a by-product of the excavation of prehistoric sites initially in the south-east of the country and more recently in the north-west.[32] Some settlement investigations did take place in the 1960s through to the 1980s, but they were never numerous. In 1961–62, for instance, after the platform settlement at Beili Bedw was damaged by ploughing, Leslie Alcock excavated three of the earthworks, each revealing a rectangular stone building, and two yielding pottery of the fifteenth to sixteenth centuries.[33] At much the same time a medieval house platform was examined in the nucleated settlement of Hen Caerwys (Flintshire), one of only a handful of known medieval sites in the north-east of Wales.[34]

In the 1960s, though, it was the south-east that came to the fore, with a series of projects undertaken by the Barry and Vale Archaeology Group. Between 1964 and 1969 they worked at Highlight or *Uchelolau* in the Vale of Glamorgan.[35] This was one of the largest excavation projects in Wales in terms of the area of excavation and the range of structures revealed included ecclesiastical, domestic and ancillary buildings. The village appears to have comprised a series of crofts along a roadway, a moated manor house which stood a little way from the village itself, and the church which lay at the north-western extremity of the settlement. Though constructed in the first half of the thirteenth century, the church contains a twelfth-century font. Other buildings included a wooden mill standing astride a stream, which produced twelfth- and thirteenth-century pottery. Evidence of four houses was recovered, two represented by house platforms within large crofts and viewed as evidence for an expansion of the settlement in the thirteenth century. The manor house was one of the most thoroughly excavated examples of its kind in south Wales, its long structural history stretching from the late twelfth century down to the fifteenth century.

A scattered group of homesteads at Barry, occupied from the twelfth to the second half of the fourteenth century and perhaps typical of many settlements in the Vale of Glamorgan, was excavated by the same archaeology group from 1962 onwards, with further excavation by the Glamorgan-Gwent Archaeological Trust in 1977.[36] Unlike Highlight the site at Barry was of no great size. Three houses were excavated:

one had middens outside both doors and produced a range of ironwork and ceramics dating from the late thirteenth to mid-fourteenth century; two others, dating from the period *c.* 1200–1250, had been replaced before 1300 by substantial stone dwellings. Other excavations occurred at Lower Porthkerry, Llandough and Merthyr Dyfan.[37] Further west on the Gower peninsula, excavations at Rhossili in 1980 revealed the remains of a stone house eroding into the sea; a house at another be-sanded Gower village, Pennard, was excavated a few years later; and a single thirteenth- and fourteenth-century farmstead building, which was initially a church that went out of use *c.* 1210, was excavated at Llanelen between 1973 and 1985.[38]

The few upland settlement excavations were generally less informative, providing more in the way of structural data than of the material culture of the inhabitants, and allowing little certainty about the chronology. So little datable material came from sites such as Penmaenmawr and Aber, both in Caernarvonshire, that it is quite possible, though unprovable, that none of them was established until the seventeenth century![39]

1971 marked something of a watershed in medieval settlement studies in Wales, not through a shift in emphasis or intensity but through the appearance of Lawrence Butler's still valuable synthesis of the work that had been completed up to the late 1960s.[40] Broader analyses since that time have been rare. We can identify David Austin's discussion of the excavation of dispersed settlements, where Wales featured alongside south-west England in the *Festschrift* for Maurice Beresford and John Hurst, but others have been disappointing in their tightly focused historical approach.[41] Settlement studies of course have continued, and varying approaches can be identified.

Excavation has in general been carried out on a sporadic basis. In the north, Richard Kelly excavated a twelfth- to thirteenth-century farmstead at Cefn Graeanog at the head of the Llŷn Peninsula

---

Key Excavation: Cefn Graeanog

Cefn Graeanog lies in north-west Wales where the mountains of Snowdonia drop down to the Llŷn Peninsula, at a height of around 130 m OD. Mineral extraction in the late 1970s enabled the complete excavation of a farmstead unit, with four buildings lying side by side on a single large platform.[42] The buildings had low stone foundations, presumably supporting wooden walls. One of the central buildings had a laid floor and an off-centre hearthstone shattered by fire; its stone walls had been preceded by a timber building on roughly the same axis. This produced a remanent magnetic date of 1240±30, which coincided with the radiocarbon date from a pit beneath the hearth of 1240±70. Beside it was a barn where flotation produced the charred remains of oats and species that might have been used for animal bedding or fodder. The two buildings lying outside these were interpreted as a stable and possibly a byre. Finds were few: two sherds of cooking pot, two iron objects, a spade and a blade and some broken nails, hones and whetstones, a spindle whorl and a lead ring. The buildings do not appear to have been destroyed or burnt, and the excavator argued that they had been abandoned and probably dismantled in an orderly fashion, having been occupied for possibly much less than a century. The farm had been established close to the best soils in the locality and the charred plant remains reveal the cultivation of oats and wheat, though there seems to be no evidence of an associated field system.

Why then is Graeanog significant? Probably because, in the absence of evidence, we might assume it to be typical of its kind even if it appears rather unusual in having so many buildings on the same platform; because it has been almost entirely excavated, not just the farmhouse but the ancillary structures that accompanied it; because of the recovery of evidence relating to its arable economy; because it is a lowland rather than an upland farmholding and there can thus be no debate as to whether it was seasonally or permanently occupied; and, notwithstanding this, because the paucity of finds that came from the excavation reinforces the view that the material culture of even permanent farms is slight; and finally because, along with the majority of the other excavated settlement sites mentioned in this overview, it was occupied for only a few generations at the most.

Figure 10.4. Llanddew, near Brecon, one of the small medieval nucleated settlements in the lowlands around the Usk Valley. (© Clwyd-Powys Archaeological Trust: 05-c-124)

(Caernarvonshire), the buildings of the farm being set on a large platform (see Feature Box: *Key Excavation*, p. 157).[43] At the opposite end of the country, a major programme of excavations at the village of Cosmeston (Glamorgan) was carried out between 1977 and 1987, and it is hoped that a full report will appear by 2015.[44] Trelech, in northern Monmouthshire, has also been the subject of a long-term excavation programme; although now no more than a village, the structures examined here formed part of what once was one of the largest towns in medieval Wales.[45] A survey of Cefn Drum, an upland ridge north-west of Swansea at less than 250 m above sea level, was followed by the excavation of platforms and rectangular structures, but interpretation here was hampered by the almost complete absence of artefacts; the only date was a radiocarbon determination from material recovered from a possible corn-drying kiln.[46] Most recently, in 2006, a previously unrecognised deserted village was found at Henllys in central Gower. Survey, geophysical prospection, limited excavation and an extensive programme of hedgerow analysis have all taken place there.[47]

In Cardiganshire, Austin examined several buildings associated with pillow mounds at Bryn Cysegrfan in 1979, but no datable finds were recovered and the only chronological indicator was provided by a single radiocarbon date from below one of the mounds which gave a date around the fourteenth century. Two decades later part of a medieval settlement was examined at Llanerchaeron in the same county, which produced pottery and a coin of the fourteenth century.[48]

The picture presented in recent annual editions of *Archaeology in Wales* published by the Council for British Archaeology also makes disappointing reading. The emergence of developer funding in the 1990s looks to have had an intermittent impact: a few smaller settlements, particularly in south-east Wales – as for instance at Llanddew near Brecon (Figure 10.4) and Redwick near Newport – have witnessed some advance in the understanding of their layout and chronology, but the number is few.

If excavation has been only an occasional contributor to our knowledge of medieval rural settlement, field survey has made steady advances. Work for the Royal Commission's Caernarvonshire volumes published in the 1950s and 1960s was followed by assessments of Glamorgan from 1960 and in part Breconshire, while preparatory fieldwork in Radnorshire went unpublished.[49] Other field surveys have included that of Ardudwy on the Meirionydd

Key Theme: Exploiting the Uplands

The uplands of Wales have been exploited on an extensive scale since prehistory. At what altitude the uplands begin depends on the observer, for upland is in one sense a relative concept, reliant on defining present and past unenclosed commons and waste which in some regions such as the south-west may drop to 180 m above sea level or even lower, though most archaeologists would probably settle for 240 m or even 305 m OD. Farms that were permanently occupied in the medieval period can be found well above 305 m – some of those on the western edge of the Berwyn Mountains studied by one of the writers were located at up to 420 m above sea level, in some cases well beyond the limits of modern enclosure. However, as with the moorlands of south-western England, arable farming at such altitudes was potentially precarious, and the critical circumstances of the fourteenth century ending in the Glyndŵr rebellion undoubtedly had an effect on such settlements, even if the scale is a matter for debate.

Stock-farming was different. The evidence is more elusive and relies rather on historical documentation than on archaeological recognition. But the vaccaries or cattle ranches of the great lords and princes have on occasions been picked out in the upland landscapes, usually defined by boundary banks, and perhaps used on an all-the-year round basis, and Longley has drawn attention to the upland pastures (*ffriddoedd*) that were used by royal estates.[50] Similarly there are upland granges and allied sites such as the Llanwddyn Hospitium above Lake Vyrnwy and Hen Ddinbych on the moors of Mynydd Hiraethog, both of which probably saw permanent use.[51]

These though are exceptional, and the exploitation of the Welsh uplands is generally viewed in terms of the summer grazing and seasonal settlement that is associated with the term *hafod*.[52] Seasonal use of the uplands during prehistory has been posited on often slim evidence, but in the post-Roman era the similarities in the Cornish and Welsh terms for both the winter residence and the summer hut validate the belief that the languages reflected practices common to both areas prior to the expansion of Wessex.[53] Seasonal grazing of the uplands was widespread across Wales in the medieval period and was still practised sporadically in remote areas of the north-west into the eighteenth century. There are occasional written references to the practice and to the summer houses themselves, but the term *hafod* occurs frequently as a place-name in some regions (though in some areas it is supplanted by another term, *lluest*).[54] Above all it is the substantial number of huts and platforms that are found in upland valleys and on hillsides, often at a considerable distance and at a higher altitude than the permanently occupied farms and their landholdings (Figure 10.5). Mostly the huts are scattered along valleys, but in Cardiganshire and adjacent parts of Brecknock and Radnorshire, occasional nucleations are encountered. The single excavated group – Hafod y Nant Criafolen in Denbighshire – appears to be unique in that region. Generally, the stock were allowed to wander freely on the adjacent upland pastures, and the only appendage to a *hafod* would have been a small enclosure, perhaps used for young animals or for some cultivation, though regional variations do occur, as with the stone-built cold stores found in the Brecon Beacons.

Figure 10.5. A hafod in a remote valley in the Elan Valley uplands in Brecknock. (Photo © Clwyd-Powys Archaeological Trust: 94-022-022)

coastal fringe, of the Mynydd Du and Fforest Fawr region of the Brecon Beacons, of Blaencaron in Cardiganshire and the Preselis in Pembrokeshire,[55] and to these geographically focused studies in upland regions can be added more site type-oriented studies on the long huts of the Black Mountain in eastern Carmarthenshire and upland agricultural settlements.[56] In contrast there has been relatively little assessment of non-nucleated settlements in the farmed landscapes at lower altitudes, although that undertaken in Castle Caereinion (Montgomeryshire) in conjunction with the work at Tŷ-mawr (see below) is an exception which demonstrates the potential.[57]

In 1989 when Cadw commenced funding the Uplands Initiative (which passed to the Welsh Commission in 1992), there was no specific focus on medieval remains in the uplands, but the recognition of medieval rural settlements and their post-medieval successors has been one of the major gains in a programme which is still continuing after 20 years.[58] More recently, between 1995 and 2004, the four Welsh Archaeological Trusts embarked upon what was termed the 'Deserted Rural Settlement Project', again sponsored by Cadw. The remains of nearly 3000 deserted settlements, a considerable number of them previously unknown, were rapidly recorded as part of a field-based study that aimed to enhance the current level of understanding of upland rural settlement and to record sites which were becoming increasingly vulnerable to destruction.[59] Several hut sites were also excavated, though only on a small scale. In the context of this chapter, the examination of Ynys Ettws in Caernarvonshire added another example through radiocarbon dating to the short list of broadly dated medieval *hafodydd*, while Gesail Gyfarch at Penmorfa near Porthmadog offered a rare excavation of a platform site.[60]

Historical research into medieval rural settlement revolved around the work of two eminent Welsh historians in the post-war era, T. Jones Pierce (d.1964) and Glanville Jones (d.1996). The former used native law books and Edwardian documents to unravel the nature of Welsh rural medieval society, its institutions and also the tenurial systems, primarily in north-west Wales but also in Cardiganshire. Jones, though best known for his concept of the multiple estate, assessed settlement patterns in relation to topography and soils, and attempted to equate them

with the tenurial systems described in the literature.[61] Jones tried with varying success to identify these patterns of tenure in the Welsh landscape in a string of publications, and others too have combined documentary and archaeological approaches: Colin Gresham, Tony Carr on Anglesey and, more recently, David Longley.[62] Throughout, the emphasis has been very much on north-west Wales.

The study of medieval houses has been intermittent and, on the evidence of publication, mostly conducted on a county basis, although this probably obscures the many unpublished surveys of individual buildings conducted by the Welsh Royal Commission. While it might be argued that the elucidation of vernacular architecture commenced with Hughes and North's *The Old Cottages of Snowdonia* at the beginning of the twentieth century and continued with Iowerth Peate's ethnographic approach to architectural development in Wales,[63] it was the book-length study of Monmouthshire houses by Sir Cyril Fox and Lord Raglan that represented a new beginning, a ground-breaking work that was the 'most ambitious work on farmhouse architecture that had up till then been published in Britain'.[64] It has been succeeded by county surveys from the Welsh Royal Commission of Glamorgan, and more recently Radnorshire,[65] together with other significant studies of Brecknock and Meirionydd (Figure 10.6).[66] Over all of these towers Peter Smith's monumental *Houses of the Welsh Countryside* which will provide a basis for vernacular building studies well into the future.[67] Two other trends can be discerned. One seen primarily in Montgomeryshire has been the integration of standing building analysis with archaeological excavation, witnessed first on the hall-house at Tŷ-mawr, at Tyddyn Llwydion and most recently at Tŷ-draw.[68] The other is geographically broader, namely the Royal Commission's dendrochronological programme which providing enviable precision in the dating of late medieval timber buildings across eastern Wales.[69]

Processes of site growth

Origins
The centuries immediately after AD 800 are poorly represented in the record, with little to be added to the last assessment more than twelve years ago.[70] Almost

Figure 10.6. Medieval platforms near Glascwm, Radnorshire. The farmhouse occupies a platform, with others left of centre, cut into the hillside. (Photo © Clwyd-Powys Archaeological Trust: 97-007-010)

invariably a starting point is the Welsh law books which appeared in manuscript form in the thirteenth century, but incorporated material from an earlier age, the various redactions emerging from the laws of Hywel Dda who died in the mid-tenth century. Amongst other things they define the patterns of land administration and settlement through what has been termed 'a paradigm rather than an ideal, still less a precisely accurate reflection of how things were'.[71] Complicated by variations in the different geographical redactions, the laws define the *trefi* (townships) with their specific number of homesteads. In simplified form, the *tref* initially constituted the house (later sometimes termed the *hendref*) and land of the freeholding head of a family, which, through partible heritance, was subsequently subdivided into the holdings of closely related families within the same administrative area.[72] In time this could result in a dispersed pattern of farms, at times spread girdle-fashion around the perimeters of arable fields, which were subdivided into strips or quillets. The shareland was known as a *rhandir*, a term that might also include the dwellings (or *tyddynodd*) around it.[73]

Additionally, in each major administrative district (or commote), the king, or sometimes the powerful local lord, maintained a court (*llys*) supported by a *maerdref*, an administrative and estate centre comprising demesne land and a bond settlement for the unfree estate workers. This, it is generally accepted, would have been a nucleated settlement. Furthermore, there were hamlets, seemingly without an equivalent term in Welsh, which might accommodate bond or free tenants, and free men themselves might have bond tenants.[74]

Transferring or translating the concepts of the law books to the landscape is not straightforward. Groups of *trefi* forming larger administrative units termed *maenorau/maenolau* have been distinguished on Anglesey and more recently on the Cardiganshire/ Carmarthenshire border.[75] On Anglesey the royal *maerdref* of Aberffraw had seven bond hamlets, each comprising perhaps nine to fifteen households, the lordly estate of Conysiog no less than nine, with their general locations known from the place-names attached to modern farms and other settlements, while the *maerdref* at Llanfaes might even be classed as a town given its 120 households spread over 90 acres.[76]

Now as in the past the problem is what is diagnostic and what is typical. High-status settlements such as royal courts (*llysoedd*) and their associated bond settlements (*maerdrefi*) may well go back to these early centuries. But demonstrating this is entirely another matter, for the datable examples in the north-west of Wales, where research through documentary research and excavation has been most advanced, as at Rhosyr in south-west Anglesey, cannot take us back beyond the twelfth, or at best the eleventh, century.[77] The term *llys* appears quite commonly in place-names but few outside north-west Wales have been subject to the level of scrutiny afforded Cynwyl Gaeo (Carmarthenshire) and Rhuddlan Teifi (Cardiganshire).[78] And a suggestion that *llysoedd* were deliberately selected as the locations for later castles has yet to be demonstrated in more than a handful of cases across north Wales.[79] Other excavated, higher-status sites by their nature look to be atypical: the crannog in Llangorse lake (Brecknock), Viking Llanbedrgoch (Anglesey) and the Anglo-Saxon *burh* at Rhuddlan (Flintshire).[80]

Of lower status, it appears, are the proposed oval post-and-wattle huts found in the area of the later castle bailey at Trostrey (Monmouthshire) with a radiocarbon date of the eleventh/twelfth century,[81] though confirmation awaits full publication of all the Trostrey excavations. But at Drim (Pembrokeshire), a wattle-walled round hut on the site of an earlier farmstead produced a date of the seventh to ninth century AD.[82] Is it unduly optimistic to speculate on the basis of such slim evidence on the emergence of a characteristic Welsh house type as Edwards has done?[83] What is plain is that such sites have been uncovered by chance not design, and that even if the house as a type is accepted, the nature of the settlements that incorporated them remains to be established.

The Norman intervention in Wales led to further components in the settlement mix. As we have seen, the nucleated hamlet or village was not a concept alien to Wales, but it was the Marcher Lords who over time originated the most visible manifestations of it. Thus, in the extreme south-west, planned villages were laid out in the early twelfth century as a result of Flemish communities being settled in what became the Pembrokeshire landsker region, Wizo and Lettard founding Wiston and Letterston respectively (Figure 10.7).[84] More speculatively, the organisation of radial holdings around churchyards as at Jeffreyston could have led to some degree of nucleation.[85] On the coastal plain of Glamorgan and Monmouthshire, villages also emerged in the post-Conquest era, Cosmeston being the best known of these, but others, whether planned such as Whitson or developing organically as at Redwick, have been distinguished in the Gwent Levels.[86] Survey work around modern villages in Brecknock and Radnorshire has also revealed numbers of settlements which have shrunk – if the earthworks of platforms are a guide.[87] Not every village has them, but they are sufficiently common to suggest that in the valleys of the middle Wye and Usk and the adjacent hills, nucleation was relatively normal. Such relict traces are absent further north in Wales: modern villages with historic churches at their heart are common enough, but evidence of the medieval aggregation of dwellings around them is sparse; very few have pre-seventeenth-century houses in them, while the marked increase in developer-funded evaluations, though random in nature, has generally produced little medieval material, other than in those areas of settlement nucleation already noted. This is not to claim that there are no medieval villages in mid- and north Wales, rather that they are presently elusive.

If the physical evidence for village nucleations is localised in certain areas, the historical concept of the bond hamlet is ubiquitous, from the beginning of our period through to the twelfth and thirteenth centuries, when it is generally held that these nucleated settlements were in decline, a process exacerbated in the fourteenth century by climatic deterioration, plague and, at the end of the century, the Glyndŵr rebellion.[88] Bond communities can be observed as shadowy entities in the pattern of nucleal land at Llanynys in the Vale of Clwyd (Denbighshire); the evolutions of the bond hamlets of Rhosyr and

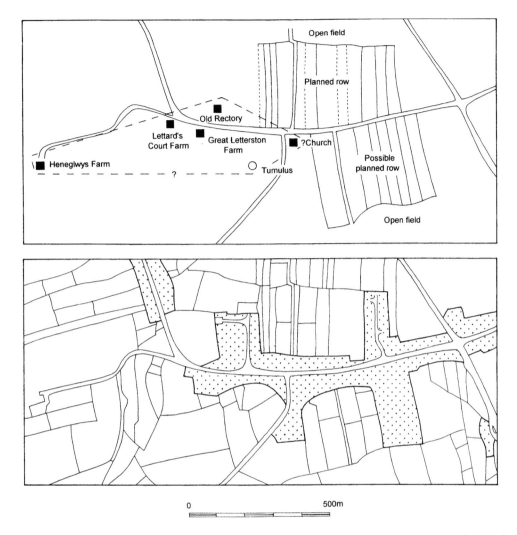

Figure 10.7. Letterston. Above, the settlement in c. 1110, reconstructed with a clear planned row to the north of the central pathway, and a similar one on a slightly different orientation on the southern side, though this could have resulted from the incorporation of open-field plots into the village plan. To the west stands a group of three major farms, the church and the rectory. These may represent an earlier, pre-village focus of elite and ecclesiastical settlement (Heneglwys = old + church.). Below, in c. 1990, the two planned rows are still evident although modern building work has taken place, represented by the stippled areas.

Aberffraw on Anglesey have been described in detail; and others have been recognised at Llanon above Cardigan Bay in the west of the country.[89] Beili Bedw in western Radnorshire may be one of the very few such hamlets observable on the ground, the 15 or more platforms representing several groups of dwelling with outbuildings. Courtney, in publishing the earlier excavations, preferred to see it as evidence of a free community, but admitted the possibility

that it could be a late-dated bond settlement.[90] What, however, seems certain is that this was not a seasonally occupied settlement. Bond communities declined in size during the fourteenth century and surviving bondmen finding their responsibilities too onerous fled to other areas, leading to the decay of bond and demesne settlements and their lands.[91] *Maerdrefi*, where they had acquired added significance as market centres, emerged as English-style boroughs,

Key Site to Visit: Gelligaer Common

It might be considered backward-looking to highlight a group of sites that first came to prominence more than 70 years ago, but Gelligaer Common, south-west of Merthyr Tydfil and north of Caerphilly, has several points to recommend it. The platforms have played a prominent role in identifying and unravelling the history of Welsh rural settlement in the medieval era, yet also remain a matter of debate. Some scholars see them as permanently occupied upland farms as their excavator, Aileen Fox, originally argued; others follow Iorwerth Peate's contention that they were the remains of seasonal settlement. The authors of this paper are in opposing camps on this.[92] The advantage of Gelligaer Common is that visitors can go and look for themselves, for the sites are established on an upland common without access restrictions and where the earthwork remains are still highly visible.

Platforms lie on either side of the broad ridge which forms Gelligaer Common. Fox designated one set of two excavated in 1936 as Dinas Noddfa (also known as Gelligaer West), the other of three platforms excavated in 1938 as Graig Spyddyd (Gelligaer East). They are in fact only 2 km apart, and there are other platforms to the north and south, the Royal Commission recording six groups and two single examples.[93] Most lie just above the boundary between the modern enclosed ground and the common, a not infrequent feature in south and mid-Wales. Both sets of excavated platforms are around 395 m OD with the ridge between them cresting at up to 470 m OD and the valley floors below around 200–230 m OD. We have noted the contrast between the excavations, namely that Dinas Noddfa produced virtually no artefacts, while the occupation at Graig Spyddyd could be securely dated by its finds to the thirteenth to fourteenth centuries. Full details of dimensions and the like can be found in the excavation reports and the Royal Commission *Inventory* and here we should note that the principal buildings in the two platform groups were 17–18 m long, but, while the smaller house at Dinas Noddfa was entirely of timber, the larger had drystone walling; and those at Graig Spyddyd had wall bases of stone slabs and turves. Internal arrangements differed too and hearths were found only at Gelligaer East (Figure 10.8).

What is missing, however, is a contextual plan of either set of platforms.[94] South of the platforms at Dinas Noddfa is a pair of enclosure banks running up the hill, fading out in a scatter of clearance cairns that may or may not be contemporary.[95] Gelligaer Common East appears to be devoid of any associated features. Both sets of platforms have faint ridging on the slopes around them, but it has been argued in the case of the eastern group that the ridging respects and probably post-dates the platforms.

particularly in north Wales: Aberffraw (Anglesey) and Chirk (Denbighshire) can be cited as examples.[96]

Nucleated settlements, whether hamlets, villages or towns, were always in a minority; dispersed settlement was the norm, and where recognisable in physical form it is likely to be post-Conquest in origin.[97] As in England the twelfth to fourteenth centuries were undoubtedly times of significant population and settlement growth, both generally attested,[98] but also recognisable from specific excavations yielding datable material as at Cefn Graeanog and Gesail Gyfarch (Caernarvonshire) Gelligaer Common (Glamorgan), Llanerchaeron (Cardiganshire) and an unpublished platform site at Carneddau (Montgomeryshire).[99]

Increasingly common in Welsh Wales as the

descendants of the original founder spread out were the 'girdle' settlements. In the landscape of north-east Wales this pattern has been recognised at Caerwys on the Flintshire plateau where nineteenth-century farms mirrored their medieval predecessors, with arable quillets lying between them.[100] As earthworks, similar settlements have been recorded on the western edge of the Berwyn (Meirionydd) and above Lake Vyrnwy in northern Montgomeryshire.[101]

There was a further stage in settlement growth. On the rebound from the disasters of the fourteenth century, settlement again expanded.[102] It has been argued that individual farms emerged on the lands of old bond settlements, presumably in both upland and lowland contexts. The three timber

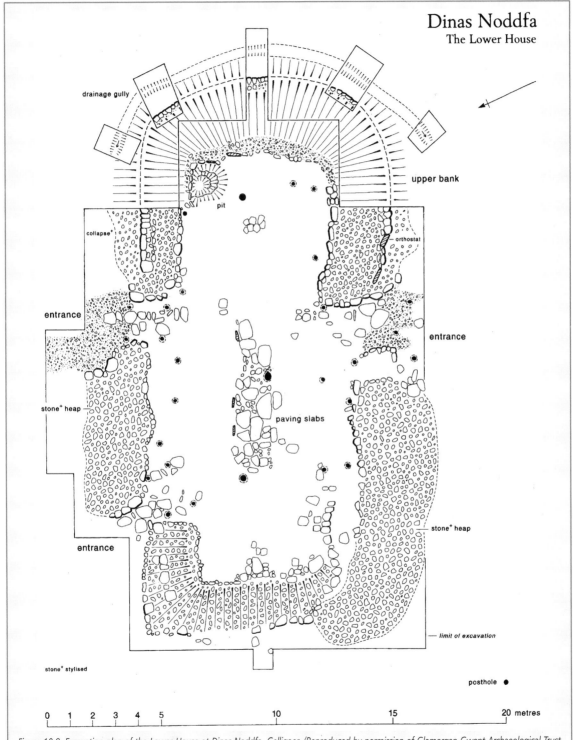

Dinas Noddfa
The Lower House

drainage gully

upper bank

collapse

pit

orthostat

entrance

entrance

stone⁺ heap

paving slabs

stone⁺ heap

entrance

limit of excavation

stone⁺ stylised

posthole ●

| 0 | 1 | 2 | 3 | 4 | 5 | | 10 | | 15 | | 20 metres |

Figure 10.8. Excavation plan of the Lower House at Dinas Noddfa, Gelligaer. (Reproduced by permission of Glamorgan-Gwent Archaeological Trust Ltd and the Council for British Archaeology)

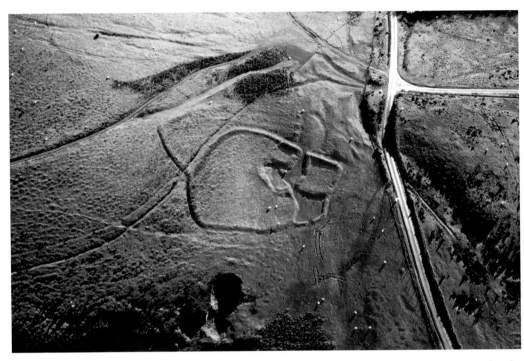

Figure 10.9. Moelfre City, Radnorshire. A platformed farmstead surrounded by its enclosures, probably of late medieval or early post-medieval date. (Photo © Clwyd-Powys Archaeological Trust: 05-c-229)

farmhouses in northern Montgomeryshire and southern Denbighshire, all hall-houses, where archaeology has been coupled with building analysis and dendrochronology all tell a story similar in outline if different in the details: Tŷ-mawr in Castle Caereinion was platform-built in 1460, though it appears to have had a thirteenth-century predecessor; Tŷ-draw in Llanarmon Mynydd Mawr, also on a platform, was erected about 1480, utilising what must have been an existing cultivation lynchet; and Tyddyn Llwydion in Pennant Melangell was erected in 1554 sealing plough marks beneath it.[103] Richard Suggett has argued on the basis of substantial numbers of dendrochronological dates from buildings across Wales for a significant horizon in new building in the fifteenth century, and as with Tŷ-draw it is likely that many were on new sites.[104] One of the writers has argued that the emergence of now abandoned farms with long huts at the heart of groups of surrounding appended enclosures in the mid-Wales border counties is a fifteenth-century phenomenon (Figure 10.9), a view based in part on the perceived

chronology of Beili Bedw.[105] Similarly, in the vicinity of Tŷ-mawr, relict earthworks mark other medieval farms in similar topographical positions that did not prosper, while new farms emerged with similar patterns of appended fields that were certainly in existence in the earlier sixteenth century. And in upland Cardiganshire recent detailed work on the land holdings of Strata Florida Abbey points to the establishment of a group of dispersed farms prior to the Dissolution.[106]

Seasonal settlement almost certainly followed a broadly similar trajectory. Similar terms for the home farm and the summer settlement in Old Cornish – *hendre* and *havos* – and in Welsh – *hendre* and *hafod* – signal common roots and comparable activity pre-dating the end of the seventh century AD when Wales was divorced from the south-west peninsula by the westwards expansion of Wessex.[107] Identifying such early settlement sites remains no more than an aspiration at present. The chronology of *hafodydd* (or in north Wales, *hafotai*), their clustering or isolation, their relationship with another upland settlement form, the *lluest,* and indeed even their function, have all been debated in the recent past.[108] Very few summer huts have been dated by excavated finds: dwellings on Gelligaer Common (Glamorgan) were thought to have been occupied between the twelfth to fourteenth centuries; but at Hafod Nant y Criafolen (Denbighshire) and Bwlch yr Hendre (Cardiganshire) later, sixteenth-century dates seem likely. On the Gwent Levels the place-names Somerton and Summerhill may point to the existence of summer pasture in an area where the medieval episode of drainage lasted from 1113 down to 1295.[109] As yet there is little substantive evidence to support any suggestion that *hafodydd* or their sites were long-lived – where examined their life-span appears to have been short.

Land use

Most settlements, nucleated or dispersed, practised mixed farming to a varying degree in the medieval era. Cultivation was undoubtedly of considerable significance, even in the hills – a view supported by the sporadic palaeoenvironmental evidence.[110] At an early date, and certainly well before the Conquest, arable land formed arguably the most important element of any landholding, and Glanville Jones took this further by claiming that the location of dwellings was conditioned by the availability of arable land, which, in his words, was the scarce factor of production.[111] Yet, overall, field and enclosure systems have attracted little attention. The two contrasting papers on Wales in *Studies of Field Systems in the British Isles* (1973), where Glanville Jones's paper focused strongly on the historical documentation for the north, while Margaret Davies examined the nature and distribution of systems in south Wales, coupled with Dorothy Sylvester's pioneer work on the border counties undertaken a few years earlier, failed to ignite much interest, and there has been relatively little published work since.[112] Open-field systems were prevalent in the manorialised lowlands of south Wales in the Gwent Levels, the Wye Valley around Monmouth and in the Usk Valley of Brecknock.[113] It has even been suggested by one of us that some of the strips fields in Pembrokeshire had their origins in co-axial field systems of the Bronze Age.[114] If the Anglo-Norman field systems are an under-researched phenomenon, the smaller areas of open-field agriculture associated with settlements in the Welshries, which were usually set higher into the hills, have been all but been ignored, even though there is general acceptance that they were extensive.[115] One of the present writers has examined the fields that emerged contiguous to settlement on the upland pastures of mid- and north Wales, though these are relatively few in number.[116]

Ridge and furrow appears to be localised. Wrexham Maelor, the eastern projection of historic Flintshire, was carpeted with cultivation ridges, an extension of the patterns across the Cheshire Plain. In south Wales it appears to be much more sporadic, and there is little of it for instance in the open fields of the Usk Valley to the east of Brecon.[117] In north-west Wales it was estimated that 10 per cent of the settlement sites encountered during a recent survey had cultivation ridges nearby. This figure is probably exaggerated by their coincidence with later, post-medieval cultivation, although there is genuine medieval ridging as at Cae'r Mynydd, Aber and on the Great Orme near Llandudno, both in Caernarvonshire.[118] Cultivation ridging has a long history going back into the pre-Conquest era; excavations at the late eleventh-century motte and bailey of Hen Domen (Montgomeryshire) revealed ridges below the bailey, perhaps associated with the adjacent, but very slight, platforms of a late Saxon vill.[119]

Focusing attention on open-field agriculture is, however, to ignore the numerous field and enclosure systems that developed around individual farms, particularly in the later medieval period. Over large parts of Wales stock-farming was of considerably greater importance, though the archaeological and landscape record rarely presents any visible facets of this activity, other than in the enclosures and their boundaries. Exceptions could come in the form of the vaccaries that were established by the princes and lords to provide beef, and the sheep farms geared to the production of wool: vaccaries of the lordship of Brecon in the Brecon Beacons can be identified on the ground, as can some of those of the princes of Gwynedd in Snowdonia; similar settlements have recently been identified in both upland and lowland Gower. [120]

Desertion

Decline and abandonment were as much features

of the settlement cycle as growth. However, while the effects may be visible in the earthwork record, only excavation provides a chronology. Events of the fourteenth century undoubtedly took a heavy toll of the population and must have generated considerable desertion. But while sites such as Gelligaer Common and the nucleated houses at Beili Bedw could have been abandoned in that century, it is best to avoid the temptation of consistently attributing the desertion of arable farms in uplands such as the western edge of the Berwyn Mountains to these factors, let alone that of the abandoned farms of medieval appearance at lower altitudes. One such lowland farm, Cefn Graeanog, may well have been occupied only in the thirteenth century, but others at both higher and lower altitudes could have lasted or even been established rather later than the fourteenth century.[121]

Gaps, directions, questions

An entire article might of course be devoted to the subject of gaps and problems, but here we touch on just three of the major issues. Firstly, the infrequency of excavation, whether upland or lowland, remains one of the fundamentals critical to the evolving study of medieval settlement in Wales, and it should be obvious from the foregoing that this is no minor problem. There is no shortage of medieval settlement sites in Wales; indeed, large numbers survive with good physical preservation. Excavations of course provide us with details of plan and construction, both of which can only be surmised from fieldwork, with associated artefact collections, with the materials of dating and with complementary palaeoenvironmental data on the economy. All of these aspects are currently badly under-represented in the record. The unpredictability of artefact recovery is an additional problem: the comparative richness of Hafod Nant y Criafolen contrasts with the sparsity of Bryn Cysegrfan, Cefn Drum and Cefn Graeanog; and even the two excavations on Gelligaer Common, separated by no more than a couple of kilometres, produced very different material assemblages.

Secondly, there has been a heavy bias in site identification: the emphasis of discovery has been very much in the uplands. But it is the lower lands with their better soils where more affluent and longer lasting settlements might be expected, and where the relationship with the agricultural setting will be better determined.

And, finally, a regional bias in the narrative of the last few pages should have become apparent to the reader. The well-established tradition of melding documentary analysis with landscape and archaeological research is largely focused on the north-west of Wales; relatively little has been done elsewhere, and this certainly needs to be rectified.

Further reading

The earliest modern survey of deserted medieval settlement in Wales was provided by L. A. S. Butler in *Deserted Medieval Villages: Studies*, edited by M. W. Beresford and J. G. Hurst (1971). A more recent overview is provided in Kathryn Roberts (ed.) in *Lost Farmsteads: Deserted Rural Settlements in Wales* (York, 2006) and there is a wide-ranging set of essays from a conference in Bangor: N. Edwards (ed.), *Landscape and Settlement in Medieval Wales* (Oxford, 1997). The Glamorgan material is presented in the Welsh Royal Commission's *Glamorgan Inventory, Volume 3, Part 2* (London, 1982), and from the same year David Robinson's paper can also be recommended for Glamorgan and adjacent Monmouthshire. Unravelling the historical evidence and marrying it with that from archaeology and the landscape has an illustrious history in north-west Wales (Jones Pierce, Glanville Jones, Gresham, Carr and others), if sometimes densely written, but David Longley's work (2001; 2004) provides a clear assessment of current thinking. Other regions of Wales lag behind north-west Wales in this respect, but Bezant (2009) has recently completed some work in the south-west. Buildings are covered in Peter Smith's massive tome on the whole of Wales, while a recent and accessible study of a single county is that for Radnorshire (Suggett 2005), both products of the Welsh Royal Commission's deep involvement in building recording. Arguably, the most important site-specific reports are those on Beili Bedw (Courtney 1991), Cefn Graeanog (Kelly 1982), Hafod Nant y Criafolen (Allen 1979) and Tŷ-mawr (Britnell 2000).

Notes

1. See, for instance, Howe and Thomas 1968; Brown 1960; and for a shorter exposition Bowen 1989.

2. There is some merit in staying with the old historic counties for locational purposes, though this may cause some problems for readers familiar only with such modern inventions as Gwynedd (formerly Anglesey, Caernarvonshire and Meirionydd) Powys (Montgomeryshire, Radnorshire and Brecknock) and Neath Port Talbot (part of Glamorgan). Wales has undergone two county re-organisations in the recent past, in 1974 and again in 1996. CBA Wales' annual journal, *Archaeology in Wales,* reproduces helpful maps of the old and the new on its inside covers.

3. E.g. Thomas 2001, 175.

4. Smith 1989, 95; see also RCAHMW 1982, 119–213 for a county survey.

5. Smith 1989, 98; Fox and Raglan 1951–54; Wiliam 1992, 6.

6. These simple terms were adopted by the committee that oversaw the Cadw-funded study of deserted rural settlements in Wales which started in 1995, for which see Roberts 2006a. While not necessarily universally accepted, they form convenient descriptive labels which have been adopted by the four regional Historic Environment Records and appear in an increasing number of publications.

7. The term was introduced by Cyril Fox in the 1930s – see Gresham 1963, 273. It is now evident, however, that not every platform will have carried a house; some will have supported ancillary structures.

8. Fox 1937; Gresham 1954; RCAHMW 1982, 17; Roberts 2006b, fig 9.2a.

9. RCAHMW 1982, 19.

10. Hoods appear to be an optional extra, often met with in Caernarvonshire and in Glamorgan, but uncommon in east Wales: Gresham 1954.

11. Rarely, a platform shows as a raised area on flat ground. One or two instances are known for instance in the Brecon Beacons, but they are exceptional. See also Gresham 1954, 40.

12. Smith 1989, 114; also Longley 2006, 65.

13. Peate 1946; Gresham 1963, 273.

14. RCAHMW 1982, 7; Gresham 1954, 38, 43.

15. For Tŷ-mawr see Britnell and Dixon 2001, 77; also Silvester 2006, 24; for Tŷ-draw: Britnell *et al.* 2008.

16. RCAHMW 1956; 1982, 43–68.

17. Courtney 1991, 242; Evans 2003.

18. Roberts 2006b, fig 9.2c.

19. Suggett 2005, 19.

20. Kelly 1982a, 883, citing Jones and Jones 1948; Davies 1982, 211.

21. RCAHMW 1982, 215–243.

22. Silvester 1997a.

23. Silvester 2006, 23.

24. Briggs 1985, 304.

25. RCAHMW 1982, 69–120; Spurgeon 1981; 1991; Travers 2004.

26. Edwards 1997, 5.

27. Silvester 2006, 14.

28. RCAHMW 1913, 143.

29. A. Fox 1937, 247–268; 1939: 163–199; C. Fox 1939, 295. Martin Locock re-examined this work in 2006, 50–55. See also RCAHMW 1982, 17; Robinson 1982, 96.

30. Green 1954; Morris 1954.

31. Gresham 1954; RCAHMW 1982, 17–42.

32. Nash-Williams 1933; 1939; Savory 1954–55; Longley 1991.

33. Courtney 1991.

34. Rogers 1979.

35. Thomas 1966, 63–66; 1967, 82–83; 1970, 88–92.

36. Thomas and Dowdell 1987, 94–137; Thomas and Davies 1970–72, 4–22.

37. Robinson 1982, 98. Though written nearly 30 years ago, this is still the best synthesis on medieval settlement excavations in south-east Wales, and includes a useful corpus of house plans.

38. Davidson *et al.* 1987, 244–269; Lees and Sell 1984, 44–52; Schlesinger *et al.* 1996, 104–147.

39. Griffiths 1954; Butler 1963.

40. Butler 1971.

41. Austin 1989b; Owen 1989b.

42. Kelly 1982a.

43. Kelly 1982a.

44. A series of interim reports exists – Sell 1982, 32–36; Newman and Parkhouse 1983, 1–13 and 1985, 31–51. Cardiff University is working on the archive, and John Hines expects a full publication by 2015, as reported in the *Society for Medieval Archaeology Newsletter* 43 (April 2010), 20.

45. The most recent reports are Howell 2004, 22–23 and 2006, 49–52.

46. Kissock 2000; Kissock and Johnston 2007.

47. Kissock and Anthony 2009.

48. Austin 1988; Evans 2003.

49. The work on the Caernarvonshire Inventories was supplemented by very occasional, small-scale, problem-oriented excavations for which see Austin 1989b, 236. The later county inventories did not benefit in this way.

50. Longley 2006, 75.

51. Silvester 1997; Gresham *et al.* 1959.

52. Whether this should be termed transhumance (or

even short-distance transhumance as Austin called it (1989b, 235)) is little more than a question of terminology. That it occurred cannot be doubted, even though there have been some attempts to question it (see for instance Kelly 1982a, 886).

53. Herring 2009, 47; Silvester 2010, 152.
54. Davies 1984–85.
55. Kelly 1982b; Leighton 1997; Williams and Muckle 1992; for Preseli there are unpublished interim reports from 1983 to 1985 for which see Sambrook 2006, 84.
56. Ward 1991; Silvester 2000.
57. Silvester 2001.
58. Some of the results are highlighted in Browne and Hughes 2003.
59. Roberts 2006: *passim*.
60. Smith and Thompson 2006, 117.
61. Jones Pierce's papers are usefully brought together in Pierce 1972. There is no equivalent collection for Glanville Jones but most of his papers are referenced within the volumes edited by Edwards (1997) and Roberts (2006).
62. Gresham 1963, 276.
63. Hughes and North 1908; Peate 1946.
64. Fox and Raglan 1951; the quotation is taken from Peter Smith's introduction to the second edition of 1994, iv.
65. For Glamorgan: RCAHMW 1982 and 1988. For Radnorshire: Suggett 2005. The law books represent one of the basic historical texts for Wales. Three groups of manuscripts relating to different geographical regions of Wales and classed as the Venedotian, Gwentian and Dimetian Codes were first compiled in the thirteenth century. Traditionally the laws themselves were compiled and rationalised by Hywel Dda in the mid-tenth century (see Davies 1982, 203).
66. The Brecknock study by S. R. Jones and J. T. Smith appeared in five successive volumes of the county journal *Brycheiniog* between 1963 and 1969. Merioneth: Smith 2001.
67. Smith 1988.
68. Britnell 2001; Britnell and Suggett 2002; Britnell *et al.* 2008.
69. Suggett 2003; 2004.
70. Edwards 1997, 2.
71. This section gives little idea of the complexities of settlement and tenurial arrangements which changed through time, and probably differed across Wales. Other relevant terms such as *cantref*, commote, *gwely* and *gafael* are not considered here because of a lack of space, but have been elucidated fully in the past by Glanville Jones, Jones Pierce and others. The

quotation is from Longley 2004, 290. Both that paper and more particularly Longley 2001, 39–43 give clear descriptions of the complexities of the settlement hierarchy, and are arguably the most accessible and recent commentaries on settlement and land tenure within the Welsh laws and other medieval documents. Other earlier commentaries include Glanville Jones 1985; Carr 1982; Thomas 2001.

72. Thomas 2001, 177.
73. Jones 1985, 163.
74. Longley 2001, 44.
75. Longley 2004, 295; Bezant 2009.
76. Carr 1971–72, 172; Longley 2001, 41, Carr 1982, 144, 231–237.
77. Longley 1997. See also Johnstone 2000.
78. Jones 1994; Bezant 2009, 65.
79. Longley 1997, 43.
80. Redknap 2004; Redknap and Lane 1999; Quinnell and Blockley 1994, 208–213.
81. Mein 1994, 71.
82. Edwards and Lane 1988, 68–69.
83. Edwards 1997, 4.
84. Kissock 1997, 127.
85. Kissock 1997, 133.
86. Rippon 1996, 45.
87. Silvester 1997a.
88. Longley 2001, 45.
89. Jones 1973, 346; Longley 2001, 46–59; Jones 1985, 161–163; for Llanon, Jones 1985, 165–167.
90. Courtney 1991, 250. In passing, Courtney's geographically wide-ranging discussion of this important site demonstrates inadvertently just how impoverished is our knowledge of the structure and organisation of medieval settlement in mid-Wales.
91. Pierce 1972, 39–57; Carr 1982, 327–330.
92. Fox 1939; Peate 1946, 128, n. 2; Locock 2006, 52–55; Silvester 2010, 153–154.
93. RCAHMW 1982, 27–31.
94. Locock 2006, fig 3.7 provides a distribution plan of the platforms on the east side of the common.
95. Locock 2006, 54.
96. Jones 1985, 168.
97. The term post-Conquest carries varying implications in Wales. In the border counties and south Wales, it has a broadly similar chronology to England, with AD 1100 a reasonable starting date. Not so in north-west Wales where it is Edward I's conquest of the Welsh princes two centuries later, culminating in the Statute of Rhuddlan in 1284, that is usually cited. This can also lead to confusion over what is and isn't classed as early medieval.
98. Longley 1991.

99. Smith and Thompson 2006, 117.
100. Jones 1985, 163–164.
101. Silvester 2006, 23.
102. While historians may not afford the same degree of significance to each of these three factors, the decline in population can hardly be doubted. Useful summaries include that of Thomas 2001, 170–172. The impact on settlement patterns is considered in Silvester 2010.
103. Britnell 2001, 58–62; Britnell and Suggett 2002, 150–152; Britnell *et al.* 2008, 162.
104. Suggett 2004.
105. Silvester 2006, 28–29; Courtney 1991.
106. Silvester 2001; Fleming and Barker 2008.
107. Herring 1996, 35; Silvester 2010, 152.
108. E.g. Ward 1997; Sambrook 2006.
109. Kissock 2008, 87, n. 48.
110. Caseldine 2006: 144.
111. Jones 1989, 179; Jones 1996, 168.
112. Jones 1973, 430–439; Davies 1973; Sylvester 1969.
113. Kissock 2008, 76; Silvester 2005.
114. Kissock 1993.
115. See, for instance, Thomas on Merioneth, 2001, 210–211.
116. Silvester 2000.
117. Davies 1973, 491.
118. Longley 2006, 64, 68; Aris 1996, 67.
119. Barker and Higham 1982, 6–7; Barker and Lawson 1971.
120. Davies 1978, 116; Jones 1969, 38–39; Kissock 2001, 63–66.
121. Kelly 1982a; Silvester 2010.

CHAPTER 11

Ireland: Medieval Identities, Settlement and Land Use

Audrey Horning

Introduction

A core concern in addressing the character of land use and settlement in medieval Ireland is the extent and nature of the influences brought by the Anglo-Normans, beginning with a series of military incursions in the late twelfth century and culminating in the establishment of a form of English governance based in Dublin. The newcomers introduced manorial settlement, new types of agricultural practices, religious practices and architectural forms. Although the Anglo-Norman invasions were once considered a monolithic process of cultural conquest marked by Gaelic acculturation, more recent investigations have highlighted dynamism in the cultural interplay between Gaelic and Anglo-Norman societies as marked through processes of continuity and change. While addressing settlement forms throughout medieval Ireland, this chapter pays particular attention to archaeological evidence from the north and west which is contributing to a revised understanding of the character of Gaelic settlement in the wake of the Anglo-Norman incursions to the eve of the sixteenth- and seventeenth-century English and Scottish plantations (Figure 11.1).

Regional geographic context

Broadly speaking, Ireland's landscape, a product of glaciation, is marked by a ring of coastal upland zones surrounding a central lowland region characterised by an underlying carboniferous limestone geology. This lowland area is drained by the 386 km-long River Shannon, which has provided a key transportation and communication corridor throughout Ireland's 7,000–year human history. A classic feature of the northern half of the island is the band of drumlins, or small rounded hillocks, that characterise lands from Strangford Lough in the east across to the Atlantic coasts of Donegal and Sligo. A profusion of small lakes and boglands characterises the lowland zones between and around the drumlins – a landscape that has challenged movement and has duly been interpreted as a barrier separating the northern portion of the country from the south and south west.[1] Ireland's topography helps to explain its historical division into four provinces: Ulster in the north, Leinster in the east, Connacht in the west, and Munster in the south. Distinctions have also long been drawn between the agriculturally productive lowland regions in the south and east of the country – regions arguably most influenced by their proximity to Britain – and the wetter, boggier, and rockier lands of the north and north-west.

From an environmental perspective, settlement in medieval Ireland underwent severe challenges during the Little Ice Age of the thirteenth century and the epidemics of the fourteenth century. Population decline and settlement abandonment encouraged the growth of woodlands, many of which were recorded along the boundaries of individual lordships on maps of the sixteenth century, serving as effective defensive barriers as much as territorial markers.[2] Palynological studies have revealed considerable variation in the character of woodland in late medieval

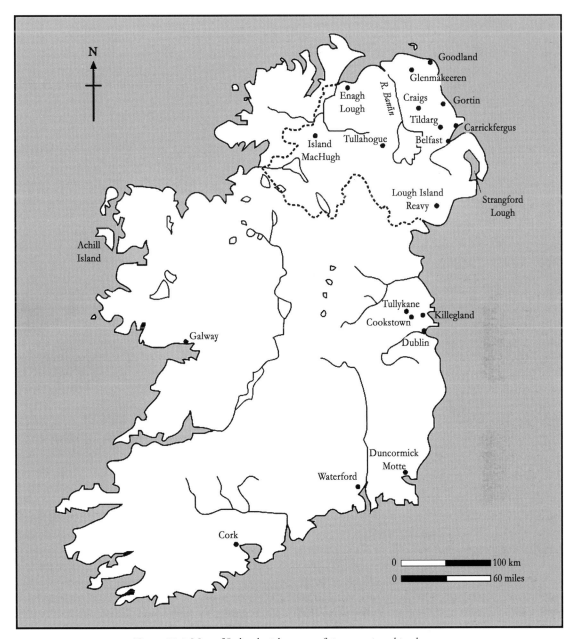

Figure 11.1 Map of Ireland with names of sites mentioned in the text.

Ulster. For example, pollen profiles from Garry Bog near Ballymoney in Co. Antrim indicate a medieval landscape characterised by light woodland cover and the cultivation of mixed cereals;[3] by contrast, areas of extensive woodlands covered portions of north-west Co. Armagh in the late medieval period.[4] Certainly the existence of considerable tracts of woodland in zones subjected to intensive English plantation in the late sixteenth and early seventeenth centuries, such as the escheated Desmond lands of Munster and much of the province of Ulster, served as economic incentives for entrepreneurial planters. Thus the documented forest of Glenconkeyne along the River Bann supported the timber industry of the early seventeenth-century London Company plantation settlements. Such forested tracts were not the norm, however, with far more land under cultivation or employed for pasturage.

Pictorial and cartographic sources from the sixteenth and early seventeenth century help to illuminate the physical character of Ireland at that date. John Derricke's 1581 *Image of Ireland* depicts a wealth of mature trees, while the cartographer Thomas Raven's 1622 mapping of London Company lands in the new County Londonderry and, in 1625, of Scottish estates in Co. Down emphasises natural resources such as forests, navigable waterways, fish, deer, and rabbits. However, such representations were often political in function and cannot therefore be taken at face value.[5] More importantly, they cannot necessarily be assumed to reflect the appearance of the landscape in the centuries between the arrival of the Anglo-Normans and the intensification of English interest in Ireland in the wake of the Reformation.

Reconstructing the character of this landscape during the medieval period is instead dependent upon the interrogation of a range of sources, not least of which is a deciphering of the development of the townland system. A townland is the smallest cadastral unit in modern Ireland, with its origins pre-dating the imposition of English plantation from the late sixteenth century as underscored by its appearance in plantation-period efforts to codify and administer Gaelic lands. Townlands themselves were not uniform in size, but rather correlated to complex territorial divisions rooted in both political and economic values. As such, plantation administrators often found their efforts to divide and grant lands to new settlers hampered by this lack of uniformity, with some grantees receiving vastly more acreage than was originally intended.[6]

Townlands formed part of a much larger system of land use responding to medieval political divisions. In late medieval Ulster, for example, land divisions ranged from the largest, the *ballybetagh*, through to the quarter, the *ballyboe* (sometimes *tate* or *poll*), to the smallest, sometimes recorded as *sessagh, gort, gallon*, or *pottle*. Research by Thomas McErlean suggests that the modern townland, averaging between 200 and

400 acres in size, most likely corresponds with the ballyboe unit of division.[7] A similar system operated in Connacht, where land was divided into the baile, then quarter, then (at the townland level) the *cartron* or *gnive*. Lands in Leinster and Munster evidently lacked the ballybetagh or baile-sized unit, and instead were assessed in units of quarters and a townland-level unit variously termed a ploughland, cowland, cartron, martland, carrowmeer, or colp. Along with the use of terms such as cowland and ploughland, also common in England, the absence of the baile or ballybetagh from Leinster and Munster can be attributed to Anglo-Norman influence. Overall, the system of land assessment and division functioned to facilitate the exaction of taxes and tributes by the Gaelic lords, as implied by the nomenclature (e.g. 'ballyboe' likely derives from 'baile bó', or 'cowland'). Ballybetaghs and ballyboes can be understood to correspond with clan or sept territories, within which land was subject to periodic redistribution. Within the ballybetagh, as suggested by McErlean, could be found the full range of land types necessary to support cattle-raising and grain (most often oat) cultivation.[8]

History of research

Medieval settlement in Ireland has not suffered from a lack of attention, as exemplified by numerous studies on Irish castles and medieval towns; yet, at the same time, some very basic questions remain about the actual character of non-elite rural settlement. A central question for many scholars of medieval Ireland is the extent to which it can be considered an English colony (see Feature Box: *Key Theme*, p. 175) – an appellation which clearly explains the comparatively late development of medieval Irish archaeology compared to the examination of earlier periods. In the new Irish state of the twentieth century, Nationalist imperatives ensured that medieval Irish castles were unpopular subjects of study because of their association with English domination.[9] Given that perspective, it comes as little surprise that the development of the study of medieval Ireland took hold sooner in Northern Ireland. Such would also be the case for early efforts at studying Irish post-medieval archaeology.[10]

Early studies focused almost exclusively upon architectural analyses and upon identifying differences between Anglo-Norman and Gaelic

Key Theme: Colonialism

Scholars are divided as to whether colonialism represents an apt or even appropriate description of the character of relations between England and Ireland in the period from the late twelfth century through to the strengthening of England's grasp on the island under Henry VIII and the forces of the Reformation. Throughout this period, English control was principally centred on Dublin, with English laws and rights only extending to segments of the population. Colonialism itself has been defined simply as a 'system of domination', a definition that could be applied to the extension of Anglo-Norman control over portions of Ireland in the medieval period.[11] However, contemporary understandings of colonialism are very much coloured by the character of European Atlantic expansion in the early modern world, characterised by extensive dislocation of indigenous peoples by settler communities. Such colonisers often operated under the principle of '*res nullius*' and were motivated by religious as well as economic ideologies.[12] Such was not the case for medieval Ireland, where the Anglo-Norman invaders did not perceive of the lands as either empty or 'morally' theirs for the taking. Unlike the Norman invaders who conquered the territories of England and Wales, the Anglo-Norman adventurers who made their way to Ireland in the twelfth century did not replace native legal systems nor did they dominate with a wave of settlers; even Dublin, the most English of Ireland's medieval settlements, experienced considerable Gaelic influences.[13] So, whether or not medieval Ireland can easily be considered a colony, processes of colonialism nonetheless marked the character of cultural relations on and beyond the island. Therefore, insights gained from postcolonial scholarship regarding cultural identities can be usefully, if carefully, employed to understand the exchanges and influences between Anglo-Norman and Gaelic society.

forms. Contemporary politics inevitably influenced some of the interpretations made as to the significance and impact of the arrival of the Anglo-Normans: for example, the work of scholars such as Goddard Orpen and Annette Otway-Ruthven has been viewed as overly coloured by their Unionist politics, which led to visions of the Gaelic world as backward and archaic by comparison to that of the Anglo-Normans.[14] As a consequence, there was a presumption that many of the changes brought about by the Anglo-Normans were positive, bringing political and economic advancement to Irish society as expressed especially through the medium of architecture. Earlier Nationalist theorists were not immune to their own judgments about the perceived absence of Gaelic castle building discussed by Orpen and Otway-Ruthven: L. C. Beaufort, for example, argued that the stone defences of the Anglo-Normans were 'cowardly' and unsuited to the 'noble Celt'.[15] Reaction against these stark portrayals characterises much work on medieval Irish settlement since the 1970s, with studies emphasising the close links between Gaelic Ireland and the continent and a consequent downplaying of the impact of Anglo-Norman settlement. Such

a construction, however, itself runs a similar risk of oversimplifying cultural complexity.

Another way of viewing medieval rural settlement in Ireland allows for considerations of the dynamism as well as the ambiguity that can arise from the meeting of different cultures in colonial or proto-colonial contexts. While eschewing construction of pre-Anglo Norman Ireland as 'backward', Kieran O'Conor has recently argued for the continuing existence of particularly Gaelic forms of building, settlement patterning, and landscape use after the twelfth-century invasions.[16] Hence the continued use of crannógs (artificial islands), ráths and caisels (circular enclosed settlements), and moated sites for lordly seats, as opposed to masonry castles or timber palisaded mottes, reflects Gaelic cultural realities. Such realities also included the practice of tanistry, whereby a lordship could be inherited by any male member of a clan, as well as the practice of periodic land redistribution. Both practices discouraged lavish architectural expenditure by lords who were never assured of maintaining their seat. Another contributing factor was the nature of Gaelic warfare, which was less reliant upon defensive structures and more focused upon employing defensive elements of the natural landscape.

Of late, the increased use of Gaelic literature and a more sophisticated understanding of the structure of the Gaelic *oireacht* or lordships have helped to clarify the roles of elites and the organisation of Irish political life, while also undermining the common belief in the stark contrast between the Gaelic Irish and the Old English in the late medieval period, even if no consensus has yet been reached.[17] For both Anglo-Norman and Gaelic-dominated regions, the study of individual lordships has proven to be one of the more effective ways of understanding the nature and evolution of settlement types. It is clear that the incoming Anglo-Norman overlords did not uniformly remove or replace native lordships and settlements. Even at the height of Anglo-Norman power in the thirteenth century, O'Conor argues, 'there was widespread Gaelic Irish lordly survival, not just in parts of the island that lay outside the direct control of the Anglo-Normans, but also within the bounds of the colony itself.'[18]

In Gaelic Ireland, political power was held by hereditary chieftains or lords who maintained influence through control of inherited territories and via a complicated system of mutual obligation. Society was structured by kin relationships, both familial and fictive, but the individual nature of those social relationships could vary between lordships. In many lordships, customs of fosterage and gossipred provided a means of ensuring loyalty and affinity between non-related families, usually at the elite level. In fosterage, a child was sent, often for a fee, to be raised by another family, a practice intended to ensure lifelong obligation. The custom of gossiprid rested upon a pledge of fraternal bond between a client and a lord, cementing expectations of patronage and service that challenged any effort by a central administration to govern lordships.[19] Thus by the fourteenth century, as interpreted by Terry Barry, Ireland was characterised by a '"patchwork" of lordships' and by a 'multiplicity of regional frontiers.'[20] These regional frontiers correlate to the often fluid boundaries of individual lordships. Therefore, the level of measurable differences between Anglo-Norman and Gaelic lordships in the fourteenth and fifteenth centuries was highly variable.

Settlement morphologies and landscape use

Anglo-Norman manorial settlement

The variable influence of Anglo-Norman and Gaelic lordships is clearly expressed across the medieval Irish landscape in terms of the character of settlements and the ways in which the landscape was used. As noted above and as discussed by Terry Barry and Oliver Creighton in this volume (Chapter 5), the twelfth-century Anglo-Norman invaders brought with them the idea of manorial-style settlement, re-designing and developing settlements following that model. Manors were often situated near to a parish church, as was the case for 45 out of 60 known manorial centres in Co. Dublin.[21] Nucleated settlements also often grew up around a motte, as at Duncormick motte, Co. Wexford. Expanding from the initial defended settlement, these manorial centres generally featured a church, a mill and a bakery, and a range of agricultural units such as granaries, barns, dovecotes, fishponds, and rabbit warrens.[22] Outside of the manorial centres, free tenants began constructing moated sites, or defended farmsteads, beginning in the second half of the thirteenth century. Upwards of 1,000 moated sites have so far been identified, predominantly concentrated in the south-east and south of the country, but also identified in areas outside of Anglo-Norman control.[23]

Moving beyond the manorial centres, the material lives of the medieval non-elite remains a consistently under-researched topic. Their lack of visibility has led some archaeologists to question our ability to ever appreciate non-elite life: 'all strata of secular society beneath the castle-owning élite… are very difficult to isolate in the archaeological record. In consequence, archaeologists cannot draw from their own reservoir of data to speak independently and authoritatively about any subtle distinctions of social class and economic dependence around which mediaeval Gaelic society was organized.'[24]

The situation may not be quite so bleak, however. Recent discoveries from developer-led excavations ('compliance excavations' in Ireland) in Co. Meath, within the territory granted to the Anglo-Norman Hugh de Lacy by Henry II in 1172, include several small-scale timber-built medieval settlements attributable to free tenants, cottars, and possibly unfree Irish tenants, or betaghs. At Tullykane, Co. Meath, archaeologists uncovered a small late thirteenth- to early fourteenth-century domestic complex consisting of ephemeral traces of two structures associated with a series of pits, ditches, and burned spreads. Of particular interest is the fact that Tullykane does not lie near any known manorial centre, thereby underscoring the existence (and persistence) of dispersed settlement. The predominance of locally made glazed wares produced after the fashion of Ham Green led the excavators here to suggest that the site was most likely occupied by English rather than by Irish free tenants.[25] Similar may be the case of the thirteenth-century farmstead recently excavated at Killegland, Co. Meath: while seemingly not part of a nucleated settlement, the building was situated close to a known mill and a posited medieval church, and a nearby fifteenth-century tower house may have been constructed atop the remains of a thirteenth-century manor. The medieval farmstead itself was undefended and comprised (traces of) three sub-rectangular structures, partially drystone-built, a cobbled haggard or farmyard, and drainage ditches.[26]

Another small domestic compound of the thirteenth century was located at Cookstown, Co. Meath, incorporating an earthfast house, blacksmith's forge, timber workshop and garden area. These were all sited adjacent to a ráth, or circular enclosed settlement, possibly implying continuity in occupation as well as in cultural identity. Also on de Lacy lands, this site was similar to that at Tullykane in not being situated near a manorial centre. The recovered faunal and archaeobotanical remains pointed to a reliance on cattle husbandry, garden crops such as peas and beans, and possibly some cereal cultivation.[27] The small scale of the site and its limited artefact assemblage suggests, in contrast to Tullykane and Killegland, that it may have been occupied by individuals 'below the level of free tenants,' and of either English or Irish identity.[28]

Gaelic rural settlement

Archaeological and documentary evidence indicate that the implementation of a manorial settlement pattern was effective predominantly in south-east Ireland. This is not to say, however, that Gaelic settlements were in any way static or unchanging, nor indeed that nucleation was aberrant, only that Gaelic ideas of land use and landholding continued

to hold sway. Such practices emphasised pastoralism and the periodic redistribution of lands which were held not by individuals but by lineage groups or clans. Yet even these practices could accommodate some of the new forms of settlement. It takes no great leap of imagination to find commonalities between the Irish circular enclosed ráth and a rectangular moated site.

Simplistic notions of 'evolutionary' change, in which the Gaelic Irish slowly accommodate themselves to the new settlement forms introduced by the Anglo-Normans, clearly do not stand up to scrutiny. Recent research in fact emphasises dynamism in the continued use of settlement forms once associated predominantly with the early medieval period, i.e. ráths, caisels, and crannogs (Figure 11.3). As noted by Elizabeth FitzPatrick, 'enclosed settlements of ráth and caisel type are the most ubiquitous, abundant, and lesser understood features of the Irish cultural landscape'.[29] Over 45,000 of these circular enclosures have been identified throughout the Irish landscape, often generically subsumed under the label of 'ring-fort'. Excavated examples are numerous, and summarised in Matthew Stout's *The Irish Ringfort*. Stout concluded that, as a monument type, 'ring-forts' chiefly date to the early medieval period.[30] However, while it seems secure that many were constructed during this period, growing evidence suggests that many continued to be occupied or employed into the seventeenth century.

Late medieval lordly residences

From the late fourteenth century on, the territories associated with individual lordships were physically protected by increasing numbers of tower houses. Tower houses, effectively stone castles reliant upon the vertical stacking of primary chambers for four or more storeys, were constructed both by Anglo-Norman and Irish lords, and served as defensive residences and centres of lordly power most often expressed through the mechanism of hospitality (Figure 11.4). Estimates suggest that anywhere from 2,900 to 7,000 masonry castles may once have stood in Ireland, the majority of which were of tower house form.[31] In function, their verticality corresponded to increasing levels of privacy the higher one ascended. The ground floor often exhibited defensive features such arrow slits and later gun loops, and space for a guard or doorkeeper.

Key Excavation: Tildarg

Seasonal settlement or Gaelic moated site?

At Tildarg in Co. Antrim (Figure 11.2) a site situated at an elevation of nearly 275 m on the slopes of Big Collin illustrates the challenges of identifying and interpreting the material traces of rural medieval Ulster settlement. Consisting of an earthen enclosure measuring approximately 65 x 36 m and demarcated by a 5–6 m wide bank and 5–6 m wide fosse, the structure incorporates traces of three building platforms. Minimal sampling of the site was conducted in 1982 by Nick Brannon. A medieval date for the earthwork was suggested by a reference in an early seventeenth-century land grant to 'the old fort of Tullaghdarge', and while excavation of a cross-section of the ditch elicited no chronological evidence, dating evidence was obtained from partial excavation of one house platform. Revealed to be a sub-rectangular mud- and stone-walled structure measuring approximately 16 x 6 m, the building was interpreted as a dwelling on the basis of the recovery of sherds of coarse pottery and the discovery of a hearth on the western wall. Radiocarbon dating of the ash in this hearth produced a calibrated date range of AD 1185–1375. The excavator speculated that the thirteenth-century date correlated to a period of climactic warming when settlement at such a relatively high elevation may have been more attractive than in

Figure 11.2 Aerial view of Tildarg. (Image courtesy of the Northern Ireland Environment Agency)

later centuries. Alternatively, the site could relate to seasonal transhumance, serving as a locale for summer cattle pasturage. In support of this latter interpretation, Brannon argued that the dwelling may have relied upon a cruck roofing system based upon the lack of evidence for either a stone or earthfast timber foundation. Because cruck timbers are independent, such a building could arguably have been dismantled and then rebuilt seasonally.[32]

An alternative explanation comes from Kieran O'Conor.[33] Drawing upon evidence from elsewhere in Ireland, he suggests that Tildarg most closely resembles a moated site, or a farmstead defended by a rectangular enclosure. Such sites are traditionally associated with Anglo-Normans, given that their highest numbers correlate to areas with extensive Anglo-Norman settlement in the south-east of Ireland. However, O'Conor has also identified Gaelic-built examples in areas that remained outside of the Anglo-Norman sphere of influence, such as Cos. Roscommon, Leitrim and Clare.[34] If Tildarg is a moated site, it is the only known example in Ulster. Yet, as can be seen from the continued use of ráths, the idea of a defended farmstead sits comfortably within Gaelic settlement. How culturally significant was the use of a circular rather than rectangular form?

Ground-floor space also generally served for storage, of both munitions and domestic supplies, while upper-level chambers included one or more halls and, on the top floor, private sleeping chambers. Tower houses were

often protected by a bawn, or defensive enclosure, and accompanied by a range of dependencies, sometimes including, in the words of the late sixteenth-century Old English intellectual Richard Stanihurst 'fairly

Figure 11.3 Bivallate ráth, Rough Fort, Co. Down. (Photo: author)

Figure 11.4 Kildavnet tower house, Achill Island, Co. Mayo. (Photo: author)

large and spacious halls, constructed of a compound of potter's earth and mud'.[32]

It is clear that both the Gaelic and Anglo-Norman elite engaged in tower house construction. But are there discernible differences in tower house form that can be attributed to ethnic identity? In 1951, Harold Leask cited the use of wicker centring as a peculiarly Gaelic practice, while more recently Rolf Loeber has suggested that the use of mural rather than newel staircases may be an Ulster Gaelic trait, while the use of wooden floors rather than stone vaulting characterised Gaelic tower houses in the midlands.[36] However, such differences probably more readily relate to regional differences rather than to any ethnic preferences in form. Rather than looking to original constructional details as fossilised ethnic markers, it may instead be more productive to consider the potential variability in the use and alteration of such structures according to social and legal traditions. Rory Sherlock argues that the Gaelic practice of partible inheritance influenced the internal subdivision of tower houses, citing both architectural and documentary evidence.[37] The province of Ulster stands out for its comparative dearth of tower house construction, which has been attributed to the continuing use of crannógs, or artificial islands, as seats of lordly authority. For example, a crannóg in Lough Catherine, Co. Tyrone, known as Island MacHugh, served as a notable lordly centre and residence for the O'Neills during the late medieval period.[38] Finds of sixteenth-century German stoneware as well as querns and whetstones are recorded for Lough Island Reavy crannog, Co. Down, suggesting potential domestic use punctuated by military activity, as attested to by the presence of cannonballs and musket balls.[39] As a secondary note, the presence of German stoneware from Lough Island Reavy underscores the active participation of the Gaelic elite in continental trade. Excavation of a crannóg in Lough Henry, Co. Down, reportedly yielded a late medieval helmet and fragments of chain mail, possibly associated with the documented occupation by Tool McPhelim McIvor in the early seventeenth century.[40]

However, it would be false to assume that the Ulster Irish had no knowledge of or ability to construct tower houses, as tower houses were prominent on the Ards Peninsula of Co. Down, where they were erected by Old English lords, and in the urban settlements of Newry and Carrickfergus. In the fifteenth and sixteenth centuries, the Gaelic O'Cahans, whose territory was confiscated by the Crown in 1608 and transformed into the Londonderry Plantation, constructed a series of tower houses at strategic locations: overlooking the River Roe were the castles of Limavady and of Dungiven, while another tower house stood near Coleraine, where the River Bann flows out to the sea. Yet while the O'Cahans relied upon tower houses in these locales, archaeological and documentary evidence shows that they continued to use a crannóg in Enagh Lough – although anecdotal evidence from the early twentieth century suggests that a tower house may also have been constructed on one of the two islands in the Lough; this awaits archaeological confirmation.[41] Similarly, in the sixteenth century, the O'Neills constructed a tower house on the aforementioned Island McHugh crannóg, attesting to a continuity of purpose. That both crannóg and tower house forms were employed simultaneously late in the sixteenth century informs us of the ability of Gaelic society to selectively retain 'old' practices while incorporating 'new' elements.

Finding the non-elite

Moving beyond the elite residences including tower houses and the still poorly understood reuse or adaptation of enclosed settlements such as ráths and caisels, where can we find the homes of the tenants? One possible avenue for research into the experiences and material signature of non-elite Irish is to tease out truth from overstatement in sixteenth-century accounts of Irish 'nomadism' through examining evidence for rural settlement. In attempting to impose the rigours of plantation upon these Ulster natives, Lord Deputy Arthur Chichester decreed in 1608 that the Ulster Irish were to be 'drawn from their course of running up and down the country with their cattle… and are to settle themselves'.[42] While Chichester and other commentators characterised the Irish as rootless and wandering, in reality these characterisations appear to be a deliberate misunderstanding of the practice of seasonal transhumance, known in Ireland as booleying. Under this system, cattle would be moved between lowland and upland pastures according to the season – a practice that continued through the nineteenth century in parts of Ireland. Such long-established patterns of seasonal movement took place within a clearly defined territory, in contradiction to the English emphasis on nomadism.[43] Surviving evidence of medieval Gaelic field systems in Connacht meanwhile hints at the extensive and organised creation and exploitation of grasslands to support often sizeable cattle herds, while evidence for the cultivation of cereal crops can be found in Gaelic areas as well as those under firm Anglo-Norman control.[44]

Examination of a selection of sites associated with transhumance in Ulster highlights the complexity, challenge and promise of using so-called booley sites as a way of improving our understanding of late medieval rural life. Often associated with the practice of booleying are single-room structures with occasional annexes, built of stone or sod, possessing no chimneys or windows, and situated in clusters on high ground near water.[45] While documentary and oral historical sources confirm the seasonal use of some of these structures in the eighteenth and nineteenth centuries, it remains an open question as to whether these structures and locales may also have medieval roots. Re-analysis of 38 Co. Antrim sites listed as booleying locales on the Northern Ireland Sites and Monuments Record revealed that few exhibit any clear chronology, with excavations at a number of such sites in Ulster yielding only chronologically ambiguous deposits. Most, conceivably, could date anywhere from the thirteenth century to the nineteenth century.[46] For example, two small (2 m²) sub-rectangular structures were recorded and excavated in Ballyutoag townland, Co. Antrim, in 1996, but were devoid of any finds;[47] similarly, in 1982 a sub-rectangular stone and sod building measuring 7.4 × 3.6 m was excavated adjacent to the Carnlough River in Gortin townland, Co. Antrim, but again no artefacts were recovered from the structure to pinpoint its occupation more precisely than to the broad period AD 1000–1700. Recent re-analysis of the site by Mark Gardiner raised the possibility, on the basis of the size and solid construction of the house as well as the presence of associated cultivation ridges, that

the structure was associated with permanent rather than seasonal habitation.[48]

Also in north Co. Antrim, investigations in Glenmakeeran townland recorded three sub-rectangular sod-built houses (Figure 11.5). One of these was excavated to reveal a structure of approximately 10.2 × 5.2 m of sod-wall construction and with a central hearth. Finds included six sherds of everted rimware, or Ulster coarse pottery, a ware type dateable only generally to the period of the thirteenth through seventeenth centuries.[49] More extensive settlement evidence emerged at another upland Co. Antrim site, at Craigs, including cultivation ridges and field boundaries possibly associated with a nearby sub-rectangular dwelling, again implying that the site served as a more permanent base than merely one tied to seasonal cattle pasturage. Finds here also consisted entirely of Ulster coarse pottery, but they were augmented by radiocarbon dates suggesting a sixteenth- to seventeenth-century date range.[50]

Perhaps the most well-known, if least understood, upland Co. Antrim site encompasses the traces of over 100 earthen structures on the grassy cliffs above Murlough Bay in Bighouse, Goodland, Knockbrack, Torglass and Tornaroon townlands.[51] Excavations in the 1940s and 1950s sought to prove that the huts were of Neolithic date but instead recovered medieval and post-medieval materials. The density of house remains and evidence for alignment cast doubt on the presumed association with transhumance. Cartographic data pinpoint the locale as a site where beacons were lit in the late sixteenth century to attract Scottish forces from the Mull of Kintyre, visible in the distance, while documentary sources imply that the space served as a plantation settlement associated with the Scottish earl of Antrim, Randal MacDonnell. Excavation of one structure in 2007 recovered only a single sherd of Ulster coarse pottery, leaving interpretation of the date, cultural affiliation and function of the site still ambiguous.[52] A further complication for understanding medieval rural settlement in this part of Ulster is the very close relationship of north Co. Antrim with south-west Scotland, as inhabitants of both lands shared linguistic and cultural traditions. As detailed by Chris Dalglish in Chapter 16 of this volume, evidence from the Highlands and Islands for the same period

Figure 11.5 Excavations at Glenmakeeran. (Image courtesy of the Northern Ireland Environment Agency)

emphasises dispersed settlement and seasonality, with site types very similar in appearance and in a shared paucity of diagnostic ceramics.

More extensive evidence illuminating the lives of the non-elite medieval Ulster tenantry was recovered from a site at Portmuck on the north-eastern side of Islandmagee on Belfast Lough. Here, another sub-rectangular dwelling with an internal width of 4.8 m was uncovered in association with a boundary wall and a series of ditches; it also lay near an ecclesiastical site. Artefacts were more abundant than in the north Antrim examples cited above, perhaps reflecting the proximity of Belfast Lough and the major medieval settlement of Carrickfergus. The ceramics assemblage (comprising 532 sherds, but with a low estimated vessel equivalent of 3.46) was dominated by glazed jug fragments, possibly manufactured in or around Carrickfergus, where a thirteenth-century pottery kiln was excavated in the 1970s. Like Tullykane, discussed earlier, the preference for English-style glazed wares may relate to the cultural identity of the Portmuck inhabitants. Of note, however, is the

presence of a total of 49 sherds of locally produced Ulster coarse pottery, reflecting some blending of material traditions.

Conclusion and future directions

There is no shortage of unexplored or barely explored aspects of the study of late medieval Irish rural settlement. Research over the last 15 years in particular has made it clear that simplistic understandings of the Anglo-Norman invasions of the twelfth and thirteenth centuries as a monolithic process of cultural conquest deny the evident social and political complexity evident on the island. While historically assumed to have supplanted native leadership in all but the least economically productive areas of the country, such as upland and boggy regions, the incoming Anglo-Norman overlords clearly did not uniformly remove or replace native lordships and settlements. Even at the height of Anglo-Norman power in the thirteenth century, as argued by O'Conor, 'there was widespread Gaelic Irish lordly survival, not just in

Key Site to Visit: Tullahogue (Tulach Óg)

Tullahogue exemplifies one of the key themes in the study of rural Ireland in the medieval period, namely the material expression of Gaelic culture and the extent to which continuity emerges as a guiding characteristic. An extensive circular hilltop enclosure situated approximately 4 km to the south-south east of Cookstown in Co. Tyrone, this site may have had prehistoric origins but is best known for serving as the inauguration site for the northern O'Neills, or Cenél Eóghain, from the eleventh century onwards. As it survives today (Figure 11.6), the enclosed area of the site measures approximately 80 m in diameter. Archaeological surveys in the mid-nineteenth century and the 1940s uncovered evidence to suggest the existence of a series of banks and ditches. However, recent re-evaluation of the evidence by Elizabeth FitzPatrick instead suggests that the site was originally surrounded by a single bank and ditch, and was likely constructed 'for ceremonial purposes during late prehistory.'[53]

Tullahogue appears to have served in a range of different capacities from its initial construction through to the present day. FitzPatrick's analysis indicates that following its establishment as a ritual site, Tullahogue served as a royal ceremonial centre for the kingdom of Airgialla and then as a residential centre for the O'Neill (Uí Néill) kings of Ailech beginning in the eleventh century (from when rare documentary references begin).[54] For the next 200 years, during and beyond the period of the initial Anglo-Norman incursions elsewhere in Ireland, the site maintained its function as an O'Neill inauguration and residential centre. From the mid-thirteenth century, the site was occupied by the O'Neill stewards, the O'Hagans (Uí Ágáin), who played a significant role in the inauguration ceremony itself. Following the destruction of the Leac na Rí (the stone inauguration seat) by the English forces of Mountjoy in 1601 and the subsequent submission of the Ulster leader Hugh O'Neill to the English crown in 1603, the site's key role ceased. In the early years of the Ulster Plantation the defensive qualities of the site commended itself for the establishment of a dwelling constructed by a planter by the name of Lyndsay. Sometime after the 1620s, additional banks and ditches were constructed, either for military purposes or as part of a designed landscape.

Recent geophysical survey, while hampered by early modern agricultural activity, identified a series of anomalies that may relate to the use of the site for the noted inauguration ceremonies: the presence of high-resistance anomalies at the entrance way to the site may relate to the existence of a formalised gateway structure at the entry, while the presence of 'a number of large, subsurface features' suggested by readings from an area outside of the fort may correlate with the former location of the Leac na Rí.[55] To date, no further subsurface testing has been carried out at the site. Those who visit today, however, cannot fail to be impressed not just by the scale of the monument but also by its visibility in the landscape and the extent of the views that can be enjoyed from its summit of what had formerly been the heartland of the O'Neill lordship.

Figure 11.6 Tullahogue today. (Photo: Northern Ireland Environment Agency)

parts of the island that lay outside the direct control of the Anglo-Normans, but also within the bounds of the colony itself.'[56] A continuing focus on the character and functioning of individual lordships and their associated settlements provides a valuable microscalar approach to elucidating the experiences of all those present in medieval Ireland, be they of Gaelic or Anglo Norman heritage, or of elite or non-elite status. Similarly, a reconsideration of sites presumed to be associated with seasonal transhumance may take us closer to an understanding of both economic and cultural practices which in the north of Ireland clearly overlap with Scottish traditions of the same period. Finally, as the dust settles in the wake of the demise of the Celtic Tiger, the results of countless developer-led excavations which encountered medieval remains throughout the island can now be interpreted and synthesised. A far more nuanced portrait of settlement in medieval Ireland will be the inevitable result.

Further reading

The best synthesis of settlement in medieval Ireland remains the 1998 Discovery Programme monograph by Kieran O'Conor, *The Archaeology of Medieval Rural Settlement*. A more recent publication that augments this study is the 2010 volume edited by Christiaan Corlett and Michael Potterton, *Rural Settlement in Medieval Ireland in the Light of Recent Excavations,* which brings together 16 short contributions detailing the results of compliance excavations, including an important range of sites associated with non-elite occupation. Another Discovery Programme monograph, *The Dublin Region in the Middle Ages: Settlement, Land-Use and Economy* edited by Margaret Murphy and Michael Potterton, provides a comprehensive overview of history and archaeology in the Dublin region from the eve of the Anglo-Norman invasions through to the late medieval period. For valuable considerations of Gaelic life and settlement, see the essays in *Gaelic Ireland: Land, Lordship and Settlement 1250–1650* edited by Patrick Duffy, David Edwards and E. FitzPatrick, plus FitzPatrick's 2009 article in *Medieval Archaeology*, 'Native enclosed settlement and the problem of the Irish 'ring-fort", and Niall Brady and Kieran O'Conor's 2005 article 'The later medieval use of crannogs in Ireland', published in *Ruralia*. For castles and tower houses, see Tom McNeill's 1997 *Castles in Ireland*, but with a more recent perspective on tower houses provided by Rory Sherlock's *Journal of Irish Archaeology* article 'Cross-cultural occurrence of mutations in tower house architecture: evidence for cultural homogeneity in late medieval Ireland?' (2006).

Notes

1. Aalen *et al.* 1997, 7–19.
2. Nicholls 2001, 202–203.
3. Hall and Bunting 2001.
4. Nicholls 2001.
5. Andrews 1997; Klein 2001.
6. Robinson 1984; McErlean 1983.
7. McErlean 1983.
8. McErlean 1983.
9. Or, as wryly noted by Tom McNeill 1997, 2, 'were unwelcome guests at the academic feast'.
10. Donnelly and Horning 2002.
11. Osterhammel 1995.
12. Gosden 2004.
13. Booker 2010.
14. Orpen 1911–20; Otway-Ruthven 1980. For discussion, see McNeill 1997, 1–2; Donnelly 2007; Tierney 2004, 186.
15. Beaufort 1828; Tierney 2004, 186.
16. O'Conor 2005.
17. Duffy *et al.* 2001b. Old English is the term used to signify descendants of the Anglo-Normans in Ireland.
18. O'Conor 2005: 211.
19. Fitzsimmons 2001.
20. Barry 1995, 227.
21. Murphy and Potterton 2010, 169; Simms and Fagan 1992, 93.
22. DeHaene 2009; Murphy and Potterton 2010, 171.
23. O'Conor 1998, 2000, 92; Barry 1977; 1988a; 1988b.
24. O'Keeffe 2004a, 20.
25. Baker 2009, 1, 9.
26. Frazer 2009, 109–124.
27. Clutterbuck 2009.
28. Clutterbuck 2009, 35.
29. FitzPatrick 2009, 271.
30. Stout 1997; see also Comber 2008.

31. Donnelly 2001, 8; Leask 1951, 153–162; Barry 2000, 119.

32. Brannon 1984; 1988.

33. O'Conor 1988, 88–89.

34. See Finan and O'Conor 2002 for a consideration of a moated site at Cloonfree, in Co. Roscommon.

35. Richard Stanihurst 1569, cited in Stoppard 1909, vol. I, 266.

36. Leask 1951, 87; Loeber 2001.

37. Sherlock 2006.

38. Brady and O'Conor 2005, 129–130.

39. Mallory and McNeill 1991, 292; Dickinson 1964, 276.

40. *Archaeological Survey of County Down* 1966, 184.

41. Davies 1941; McNeill 2001, 346–347.

42. *Calendar of State Papers of Ireland* 1608–1610.

43. McErlean 1983. For a consideration of booleying on Achill Island, see McDonald 1992 and 2009.

44. For discussion of field systems, see O'Keeffe 2000, 80.

45. As originally based on the work of Graham 1954 and Estyn Evans 1945. See also O'Conor 2002. For a general overview of booley-type sites, see Rathbone 2009, and for a consideration of booley sites in the Mourne Mountains, see Gardiner 2010b.

46. Horning 2002, 2004.

47. MacSparron 2002; Williams 1984.

48. Gardiner 2010a.

49. Williams and Robinson 1983; MacSparron 2007.

50. Williams 1988.

51. Horning 2004; Horning and Brannon 2004.

52. Horning and Brannon 2007.

53. FitzPatrick 2004, 147.

54. FitzPatrick 2004, 141, 148.

55. Trick and McHugh 2006.

56. O'Conor 2005, 211.

CHAPTER 12

The Midlands: Medieval Settlements and Landscapes

Richard Jones and Carenza Lewis

Defining 'the Midlands'

Defining the Midlands is a challenge because it is an area which is mostly lacking clear geographical divisions and its boundaries have consequently been drawn along different lines depending on frames of reference. Here, however, 'the Midlands' has been taken to encompass 15 counties from five different local government regions: Derbyshire, Leicestershire (including Rutland), Lincolnshire, Northamptonshire, and Nottinghamshire (East Midlands region); Herefordshire, Staffordshire, Shropshire, Worcestershire and Warwickshire (West Midlands region); Buckinghamshire and Oxfordshire (South-East England region); Bedfordshire and Hertfordshire (East of England region; and Gloucestershire (South West Region). This area, which could perhaps be better termed 'the greater Midlands', including as it does both core and peripheral regions of the traditional Midlands zone is, of course, at one level a function of a prosaic need within this volume to divide the country up into regions for discussion, and in no way seeks to suggest that these 15 counties constitute a meaningful distinct culture-historical *pays*. Although covering such a large region in a single chapter creates some difficulties, it does also deliver some benefits: encompassing the diverse areas of the 'greater' Midlands highlights the 'fuzziness' of most historical/geographical/cultural boundaries and allows us to compare and contrast settlement patterns within and beyond the traditional boundaries of the core Midlands *pays*.

Historically, the concept of a Midlands distinct from other English regions did not find voice until the very end of the Middle Ages. The term was first used by Oliver Bokeham in his topographical work *Mappula Angliae* shortly before 1475 but further references remain relatively scarce before the nineteenth century.[1] Generally those seeking to characterise England's regional variation have done so not in terms of administrative units, but in terms of its different landscapes, the shape of its settlements, and the materials used in the construction of buildings. The Midlands was champagne country, a rich arable-growing region where open-field farming predominated, where tree cover was sparse, and where villages tended to be large and nucleated.[2]

Today the historic Midlands core is easily recognisable, but its peripheries are very much more difficult to establish. Traditional midland counties of Leicestershire, Northamptonshire, Rutland, Staffordshire and Warwickshire are fringed by those such as Derbyshire and Nottinghamshire to the north and Herefordshire and Shropshire in the west, where the residents in more remote parts might well not consider themselves Midlanders. Similarly, in Lincolnshire, some would exclude the Fens. Symptomatic of the difficulties involved in establishing the precise extent of the Midlands is the fact that those who have explored aspects of the region's medieval history have variously included and excluded from their deliberations the counties of Worcestershire and Cheshire (south of the Mersey), and likewise all or parts of Bedfordshire, Buckinghamshire, Gloucestershire, Hertfordshire and Oxfordshire.[3]

The Midlands, then, is perhaps about feel and the realisation of preconceived ideas rather than anything more tangible or visible. It is also about recognising that different cultural zones will have different boundaries and that all of these will change over time. In looking at the evidence for medieval rural settlement in the Midlands, we are looking not at one phenomenon, not even at a complex mosaic, but at an ever-changing kaleidoscopic pattern. Thus, for the medievalist, the imposition of an exact geographical delimitation of the Midlands is not necessary, and it could even be a hindrance to understanding.

Midland topographies

As we have defined it, the Midlands covers more than a quarter of England, from the Welsh borders to the Wash and from Gloucester to Hull. Inevitably, for such a large part of a topographically varied country, it includes a range of landscapes, including moorland, fen, forest and coastline as well as extensive tracts of 'champion' mixed farming land. Crucially, it spans traditional highland and lowland zones, defined by Cyril Fox as divided by a line running approximately from the Severn to the Trent,[4] and likewise crosses the boundaries of the 'ancient' and 'planned' landscape divisions proposed by Rackham,[5] and the 'central province' defined by Roberts and Wrathmell.[6] In respect of its fluvial landscape, the Midlands faces in many directions, drained by major rivers including the Severn and its tributaries running south-west into the Severn Estuary, and the Trent and its tributaries draining north-east into the Humber estuary. To the south-east the region empties into the Thames estuary and into the Wash via the Great Ouse.[7] The Midlands is thus a largely inland region, with Lincolnshire the only county with a coastline. But this mostly landlocked region is not without its drama. In the north-west, the southern limits of the Pennines give much of Derbyshire a rugged upland character. Here, expanses of limestone moorland, both open and enclosed, are punctuated by the outcropping rocky eminences of the White and Dark Peaks where the Dove has carved its limestone gorge, and the Severn does likewise at Ironbridge in Shropshire. The imposing bulk of Kinder Scout dominates the Dark Peak just as the Malvern Hills cast their late-afternoon shadow over the Severn flood plain.

To the west lie the large urban conurbations of the midland industrial heartlands of Birmingham, the Black Country, the Potteries and Coventry.[8] To the east and south are the coalfield regions of Derbyshire, Nottinghamshire and Leicestershire, characterised by a softer hilly landscape of wooded valleys and coalfield village farmlands with riverside meadows.[9] Further east again are the gently undulating wolds of Leicestershire and Lincolnshire with their legions of quietly verdant deserted rural settlements. From High Leicestershire, one looks north-west to the granite boss of Charnwood forest, the oldest rocks in England, and south into the champion vales of the river Welland. From the northern dip slope of the Chilterns, Midland England, stretching as far as the eye can see, appears laid out at your feet. Viewed from below, few can fail to appreciate the local significance of the Lincoln escarpment or the wild and rugged nature of Shropshire's Stiperstones (Figure 12.1). By way of further contrast, the flatness of the Lincolnshire fens creates vast skies and offers distant horizons, providing an extreme of a different order through their monumental scale. Thus wide vistas afford scenes of enormous contrast.

The classic Midland scene, characteristic of its core counties, is one that is topographically soft. It is a landscape that undulates; its soils are unctuous, deep brown or luxuriously red in hue, and stick to your feet. The major rivers which pass through – the Severn, Avon, Trent, Welland, Nene, and Great Ouse – have quietly eroded away at the glacial boulder clay cap, pushing back their valley sides, easy in gradient, to reveal the solid bedrock below. Periodically (and, in recent years, more regularly it would seem) they break their banks to wash across their wide flood plains depositing rich alluvium in the process and adding verdure to their water meadows. The Midland landscape may not be monumental or picturesque, it may not have attracted the attention of Romantic poets or artists, nor much more than passing comment by those such as John Leland, Daniel Defoe and Celia Fiennes who wrote of their journeys through the region, but it did impress itself on the minds of those who settled, divided and worked the land in the early medieval period.[10]

Old English place-names, perhaps more than any other historic source, reveal the close relationship that developed between people and their surroundings

Figure 12.1. Stiperstones, Shropshire. Rising to over 500 m, the Stiperstone ridge with its rocky outcrops, its shattered quartzite scree, and moorland is one of the wildest parts of the Midlands landscape. In the Middle Ages the area offered rough grazing for communities located on its periphery as well as important lead deposits which were worked in places such as Shelve. Monastic interests saw many parts of this upland landscape brought under cultivation. (Photo © Paul Stamper)

during the post-Roman centuries. The rolling nature of the Midlands core inevitably means that names referring to hills and valleys are less prominent than in areas of strong relief, but the subtle folds of the land were carefully noted and came to be used as the markers of place.[11] The term *ofer/ufer* was used to describe a flat-topped ridge with convex shoulder, as found in a group of place-names around Droitwich – Over, Hadzor, Pridzor, and Becknor. The term *ora* 'bank' is found in the Oxfordshire place-names of Stonor and Chinnor as well as elsewhere; the term *scelf* 'shelf' is found regularly compounded with *tūn* in the modern form Shelton in the counties of Bedfordshire, Nottinghamshire, Shropshire and Staffordshire, and as Shilton in Leicestershire, Oxfordshire and Warwickshire.[12] Terms such as *beorg*, a rounded hill, *clif*, a cliff or river bank, and *dun*, hill or upland expanse, find common usage across the Midlands; whilst in Hockerton in Nottinghamshire can be

found a unique presumed element **hocca*, taken to mean a softly rounded hill.[13] Physical topography, however, was only one marker of place. In many instances, place-namers turned to the 'look' of their surroundings for their cues. The wooded nature of the Warwickshire Arden is reflected in the concentration of *lēah* names, a complex term which appears to have shifted over time from 'forest/wood' to 'glade/clearing' or may have been used to describe a wood pasture environment.[14] Notable clusters of other woodland terms, *wudu, graf, holt, fyrhth, hangra, hyrst* and *sceaga* can be found in the Chilterns.[15] Beyond these major names, field and furlong names – recorded in large numbers from the later Middle Ages – reveal the intimate knowledge possessed by the Midland peasant regarding the colour and quality of soils, and with the trees, plants and animals with which they shared the land. Such names, of course, help us to connect directly with the former inhabitants of the medieval

Figure 12.2. Norwell, Nottinghamshire. A classic single-street nucleated village of the Midlands with the church of St Lawrence standing at the eastern end of the settlement. In the Middle Ages the village was divided between three prebendal manors of nearby Southwell minster accounting for the three moated sites found within the settlement itself. Two other moated sites lie outside the village associated with the hamlets of Willoughby and Norwell Woodhouse. (Photo © Michael Jones)

villages and farmsteads of the Midlands in which we still live, and remind us that in contemplating the landscape we share much in common with them.

Landscape *pays* and settlement morphologies

Anyone with even a cursory knowledge of rural settlement studies is likely to associate the core Midlands area with the 'champagne' or 'champion' region of England – defined as such by John Leland and William Harrison in the sixteenth century – which is typified by the presence of nucleated villages surrounded by open arable landscapes (Figure 12.2). Maitland, writing at the end of the nineteenth century, described this broad band of central England as a 'countryside of villages' and much of it is coincident with that in which Gray identified the medieval practice of two- and three-field

farming, a form of agriculture he named 'the Midland System'.[16] Whether termed 'champagne', 'planned' or 'central', much settlement in the core areas of our Midlands region is today typified by large villages, clustered around the parish church and surrounded by carefully planned rectangular fields that result from the Parliamentary Enclosure of former common fields.[17] The geographical extents of these elements of champion England actually differ significantly,[18] demonstrating the futility of attempting to map the limits of the champion region as such, but it is clear that a substantial part of the Midlands – those parts of Oxfordshire, Bedfordshire, Northamptonshire, Leicestershire, Nottinghamshire and Lincolnshire which lie between the Chilterns and the Humber estuary and away from the coast – fall within the central champion belt, whichever criteria are used.

Much of our knowledge and understanding of the medieval pattern of settlement in the Midlands, as elsewhere, has tended to start with the analysis of the earliest post-medieval evidence for settlement form taken from nineteenth-century county maps and Ordnance Survey maps. These have allowed the general characteristics of settlement to be assessed across the Midlands in a number of 'top down' projects.[19] They reveal a settlement pattern in the core champion regions that was predominantly (although not exclusively) nucleated, a term which belies the variation in layout that individual villages might actually adopt, as studies of Oxfordshire and Warwickshire settlement plans have shown.[20] Likewise the term tends to obscure different processes and chronologies we now know to lie behind the formation of these places. Much of what can be gleaned from these late sources, of course, reflects post-medieval changes. In the coalfield landscapes of western Leicestershire, for instance, earlier patterns of settlement are difficult to detect under more recent settlement dominated by mining and industry. The centre of the elevated Charnwood region of Leicestershire contains many isolated farmsteads of probable post-medieval origin and appears likely to have been densely wooded and largely devoid of settlement in earlier times; here the nineteenth-century settlement pattern is characterised by long chains of settlement, including irregular rows, single farmsteads and tiny regular planned units, whose separate elements are difficult to untangle. By contrast, the main valleys of the Soar, the Wreake and the Sence contain nucleated settlements, mostly taking the form of linear rows aligned parallel with the valleys in which they are sited. Some of these extend for more than a kilometre and may include more than one smaller medieval settlement. In other Midland landscapes post-medieval processes might lead to very different outcomes: in the south Pennines and northern and western Nottinghamshire, for example, industrialisation encouraged the growth of nucleations, while in Staffordshire the reverse was the case as dispersed settlements grew up around focal points such as furnaces and surface mines.[21]

While archaeological investigation, including earthwork survey,[22] fieldwalking and excavation in many Midland rural nucleated settlements, has proved that the majority of existing settlements had already established themselves in the Middle Ages,[23] one must still proceed with extreme caution

when reconstructing their earlier forms. For even where post-medieval changes can be ruled out, later medieval village plans do not necessarily reflect earlier arrangements. Although it is certainly the case that many villages can display remarkable stability in layout across the centuries, examples such as Wicken in Northamptonshire and Lillingstone Lovell in Buckinghamshire demonstrate that replanning in the thirteenth and fourteenth centuries could be undertaken both rapidly and wholesale, thus both misleading us and depriving us of a sense of what these places looked like in earlier periods.[24] That said, it cannot be doubted that across the champion Midlands the classic later medieval village arrangement was a tight cluster of buildings containing church and manor house together with regular-sized peasant tofts and crofts of similar width and length to their neighbours. Nearly all surveyed nucleated settlements in Northamptonshire comprise, at least in part, a number of rectangular plots arranged along one or both sides of a linear street as a single or double row linear settlement, with buildings close to the central street and yards and gardens behind.[25] This is borne out by the earliest extant map of an English village, that of Boarstall in Buckinghamshire, dating to the 1440s, which shows just such an arrangement, the settlement surrounded by its open fields made up of interlocking furlongs, and beyond woodland and pasture.[26] In other parts of the Midlands, land given over to the plough had been extended to the very edges of parishes and manors before the agricultural crises of the early fourteenth century so that up to 90 per cent of available land had been brought under cultivation.[27]

Boarstall lay in Bernwood Forest, one of a string of royal jurisdictions that in the twelfth and early thirteenth centuries ran almost continuously from Oxfordshire (Wychwood) through north Buckinghamshire, Northamptonshire (Whittlewood, Salcey, Rockingham) into Rutland.[28] Other parts of the Midlands were similarly defined legally including Sherwood in Nottinghamshire, Peak Forest covering large parts of northern Derbyshire, and in Staffordshire and Warwickshire the forests of Kinver, Feckenham, Cannock and Arden. Although open-field farming was practised in many of these forests (medieval forests need not be wooded, although the majority of the Midland examples were), they still act as a reminder that the medieval landscape of the Midlands was far from homogeneous and contained much which would not be considered archetypically 'champion'. Even at its geographic centre, there are landscapes that do not fit easily into any landscape characterisation. The intermixing of nucleated and polyfocal villages with smaller hamlets, isolated farmsteads, granges and moated sites in Whittlewood, for example, from which open fields were worked in an area which continued to retain significant stands of trees through to the end of the Middle Ages, has led to this landscape being described as a hybrid because it combined elements of both champion and woodland regions (Figure 12.3).[29]

Using early medieval woodland place-names, it is possible to suggest that a couple of centuries before the Norman Conquest, only a thin strip of predominantly open landscape ran through the Midlands counties, but that by 1086, this had already been greatly expanded through clearance (the early stages of the process attested perhaps by *lēah* and *wald* names) so that by the time of the great survey its assessors were recording large numbers of plough-teams across the region symptomatic of large-scale arable cultivation.[30] The assarting of woodland in the Midlands increased in pace through the twelfth and thirteenth centuries, which, in part, explains why it is often so difficult to draw the distinction between the champion and woodland zones: their boundaries were never static or distinct but tended to grade into one another over time. Even in the Midland core the colonisation and clearance of woodland seems to have promoted the foundation of new settlements, often dispersed in nature; thus by the middle of the fourteenth century hamlets and farmsteads had become intercalated with larger villages across large parts of the Midlands.

Move in any direction from the inner Midlands and polyfocal or dispersed settlements become far more common. This is certainly the case in Bedfordshire and Cambridgeshire.[31] In Gloucestershire to the south-west, nucleated villages such as Bibury can be found,[32] but large settlements are as likely to have adopted a more polyfocal appearance such as Roel,[33] or to be so spatially fragmented as to be described as 'non-villages'.[34] Further north and west into what Rackham deemed the 'ancient' countryside,[35] and Roberts and Wrathmell the 'North and West Province',[36] dispersed settlement begins to dominate.

The medieval development of landscapes of hamlets and farmsteads can be followed in detail in places like Pendock and Hanbury in Worcestershire[37]: in Hanbury by *c.* 1300 and as a result of the dual and related processes of tree clearance and the subdivision of manors, a complex pattern of dispersed settlement had developed across this parish; many of the new centres took 'end' and 'green' names, the former belonging to an earlier phase of expansion than the latter. Nor is Hanbury an isolated case. 'Green' names, in fact, are commonly encountered not only in the West Midlands, but also on the Cheshire Plain, in parts of the Cotswolds, and in the counties of Bedfordshire and Hertfordshire, presumably attesting to a similar expansion of settlement in these regions across the medieval centuries (Figure 12.4).

From the mid-fourteenth century, the expansion of settlement at Hanbury turned to retreat as properties were abandoned, a long attenuated process which would continue well into the eighteenth century and beyond. A similar trajectory of desertion can be traced, albeit with important local and regional differences, cutting across all the Midlands landscape *pays*. Late colonised landscapes such as the wolds of Gloucestershire, Leicestershire and Lincolnshire were particularly affected by depopulation, in part due to famine and plague but more regularly as a result of the shift from arable to pastoral farming.[38] The story is often more complex than the ghostly remains of former village sites suggest, however: tax returns for Cold Newton in Leicestershire, whose surviving earthworks appear to indicate massive shrinkage in the late medieval and early modern period, reveal that it was the village and not the people that disappeared; those inhabitants who had once occupied the abandoned tofts and crofts simply moved out to farms in the newly enclosed landscape of the former open fields of the nucleated village. Nevertheless, across the Midlands, levels of settlement abandonment are high against the national picture, with many in decline in the period after 1350. This process produced particularly strong clusters of desertions in eastern Leicestershire, Northamptonshire and Lincolnshire where they number between 15 and 25 per cent of the settlements that once existed in the Middle Ages.[39] Other areas such as the Humber wetlands, Lincolnshire fens and the southern Pennines seem to have been less affected.

Figure 12.3. Wicken, Northamptonshire. Formerly two villages, Wick Hamon and Wick Dive, these two separate entities were unified in the sixteenth century to create a single settlement. The village lay within the bounds of the royal Forest of Whittlewood before being disafforested by the end of the thirteenth century. This accounts for the survival of considerably more woodland (visible in the background) than was usual in this part of the Midlands where open-field farming often extended to the limits of manor and parish by the beginning of the fourteenth century. (Photo © Mike Aston)

Figure 12.4. Hazleton, Gloucestershire. The nucleated village with its church stands at the head of a minor tributary of the river Windrush. Lower Barn, one of a number of dispersed settlement elements found within its parish, lies in the foreground. Woodland is largely confined to the steep valley sides and higher ground. The fieldscape of ancient and post-medieval enclosure comprises both hedge and dry stone walls typical of the Cotswolds. (Photo © David Aldred)

Such a brief pen sketch of the medieval settlements and landscapes of the Midlands inevitably simplifies the reality, flattening out or even hiding important local variations in settlement form and the precise chronology of landscape development. But it nevertheless begins to reveal that the lack of topographic and soil restraints in the Midlands has allowed different types of farming to develop successfully, and has always ensured that this landscape has been in a permanent process of change as farmers have reacted to changing demographic and economic circumstances. This is reflected in the choices that they made regarding the types of settlements in which they lived. There never has been one Midlands landscape; rather there have been many, often co-existing together at the same period and always in a state of perpetual flux. Within this continuum, however, the medieval centuries stand out as a period of particular change encompassing both the birth of the village and in many instances their demise, and the introduction of communal farming systems and the early beginnings of their enclosure. Making sense of these developments has been hard won and it is to the history of research in the Midlands that we now turn.

Medieval settlement research in the Midlands: an historical overview

Scholarly enquiry into the origins and development of medieval settlement is one in which the Midlands has played a leading role: it stands out in the field of rural settlement studies for a number of reasons. Some of these are to do with historical processes, with the region notably divided for parts of the early medieval period between the Danelaw and 'English' England. But what really attracted attention to the region is the extent and quality of the survival of easily visible remains of deserted rural settlements. This is complemented, in many instances, by good documentary records and, in the east of the region, by a well-understood pottery sequence which spans the whole of the period from the late Roman to the modern day. As a consequence, much attention has been focused on the study of rural settlement and the region is widely recognised as one of the great crucibles for the study of such phenomena in the medieval period. Following the earliest period

of interest in deserted medieval villages when attention was given to identifying and listing sites, to dating desertion and investigating the character and development of medieval domestic buildings and village plans, attention turned in the 1970s and 1980s to the question of how, when and why these settlement forms appeared in the English landscape. Covering such a vast region and so much related research, it is impossible to provide a comprehensive account in the limited space this volume inevitably allows; the following is thus more a review of some of the key discoveries and case studies in the region over the last century.

It is mostly true to say that the interests of those antiquarians interested in the medieval period, in the Midlands as elsewhere, did not turn to those of rural settlement until the middle decades of the twentieth century. One exception to this rule were the archaeological excavations undertaken at Woodperry in Oxfordshire and published in 1846, where the aim was to 'search for a church, churchyard and village, supposed to have formerly existed'; this was achieved, with the added bonus of discoveries of Roman features and finds.[40] Nearly 40 years later, Frederic Seebohm used evidence from the Hertfordshire parishes of Hitchin and Much Wymondley to ignite debate as to the origins of the English rural village and the open-field system with which, he contended, it was integrally linked.[41] This debate has continued ever since, but there was no immediate rush of interest in excavating Midlands rural settlement sites in a period when most antiquarian activity in Britain remained firmly focused either on earlier periods or on edifices of Church, state and aristocracy, or restricted themselves to art historical or, of course, documentary enquiry. This prevailing lack of interest amongst scholars and antiquarians in medieval rural sites led C.V. Charlton to comment with unconcealed disappointment during his 1909 excavations at Mallows Cotton in Northamptonshire that 'only medieval dwellings were revealed...' on a site he suspected to be a Roman camp.[42] It is not a little gratifying that Mallows Cotton later became part of the Raunds project, one of the most important medieval settlement projects of the twentieth century (see Feature Box: *Key Project*, p. 194).[43] Although interest in archaeological sites of medieval date began to increase in the early decades of the twentieth

Key Project: Raunds, Northamptonshire

Raunds, a small town located a little to the east of the Nene Valley in north-east Northamptonshire, has been one of the iconic sites for rural settlement and landscape studies for more than 30 years. Ten years of excavation in the north of the present village started in 1976 in response to threatened development and gradually expanded to cover thousands of square metres on three main sites on both sides of the valley. Here were uncovered not only the remains of scores of buildings ranging from large timber halls to minor ancillary structures spanning more than a millennium from AD 450 onwards, but also an otherwise entirely unknown church and associated graveyard of late Anglo-Saxon origin[44] and numerous ditches. In 1985 the focus of investigation expanded, ultimately to encompass 40 km² of the historic landscape around the town. The Raunds Area Project[45] was one of the major cutting-edge British landscape research programmes of the later twentieth century. Its objective was not only to provide a context for the rescue excavations in the town but also, of much wider relevance, to extrapolate from this research to advance more generally knowledge and understanding of the character and process of the development of the English landscape. The Project was designed from the outset to be large-scale, interdisciplinary and multi-period and would be a model of historic landscape investigation, avoiding the pitfalls and limitations of earlier, less formally scoped or holistically planned landscape projects.

Around 3,000 ha were fieldwalked (more than 70% of the project area) and four other major sites were excavated (including the deserted medieval hamlet of West Cotton).[46] This provided a solid empirical base for the reconstruction of spatial and chronological patterns of settlement and land use across a range of land types from sub-alluvial floodplain to boulder clay plateau. Despite some limitations, such as the lack of opportunity for excavation on any of the boulder clay sites, this evidence showed that settlement and agriculture increased in intensity from the early Roman period before declining from the second century AD, especially on the boulder clay, a period which was apparently accompanied by an early phase of settlement nucleation within the valley. In the early/middle Anglo-Saxon period settlement was more dispersed but continued to show a preference for river valley sites while not altogether withdrawing from the clay plateau, of which substantial areas continued to be cultivated using an infield/outfield system. An open-field system was instituted at some point in the period between the ninth and twelfth centuries, while a period of population expansion led in the twelfth and thirteenth centuries to the creation of new minor settlements rather than an infilling of open spaces in existing villages. The widespread desertion of village fringes and complete abandonment of the hamlets in the fourteenth and fifteenth centuries was accompanied by a reversion to grassland in much of the region. Assertions made by archaeologists involved in the project such as 'there is no simple development from Roman villa to medieval manor',47[87] 'boulder clay constitutes no hindrance to a champion landscape',[48] or 'the Saxon folk movements and subsequent adjustments greatly affected the local landscape',[49] have never shied away from controversial or difficult questions.

Within Raunds itself, repeated reinterpretations of the excavated evidence over more than 20 years have enhanced this picture, as identified dispersed 'untidy' areas of settlement of early Anglo-Saxon date both sides of the stream could be seen to have been variously reorganised or abandoned in the middle Saxon period before apparently being replanned fairly rapidly in the early tenth century, thereby creating a nucleated settlement with regularly laid-out blocks of rectangular plots defined by linear boundary ditches. Raunds has thus become a key site in debates as to the Midland origins of both the nucleated village and the open-field system, and it has even been suggested that this replanning occurred in the wake of the 'reconquest' of the region by the kingdom of Wessex, when 'the basis of the late Saxon reorganisation was the establishment of a coordinated and consistent land allocation to all members of society'.[50] The process behind this physical reorganisation has been characterised as 'a sudden and dramatic event', carried out as a rapid, staged process of laying out successive blocks of several plots at a time, in which 'the two processes of settlement and field system reorganisation may well have been introduced as a single package'.[51]

Some might consider that the archaeological evidence is sometimes too slight to bear the heavy weight of some of the historical inferences placed upon it by the editors of the published volumes, but none would deny the immense value of such a detailed and expansive body of evidence to medieval settlement studies. The unique nature of the investigations at Raunds, combining wide landscape perspectives with detailed long-term excavations within a currently occupied rural settlement, allied to the vision of those who assessed and interpreted such a huge volume of evidence while not shirking from using it to tackle wider historical questions, have driven debate forward to make Raunds supremely important for medieval settlement studies within the Midlands region and, indeed, far beyond its borders.

century, this remained almost exclusively rooted in remains of 'elite' monuments, with interest focused chiefly on presenting to the public the ruins of castles and monasteries, whose stone walls or footings, whether unearthed or (preferably) upstanding, could easily be appreciated by the inexpert eye. One Midlands exception to this rule was in Lincolnshire, where a list of known deserted medieval villages was published by Foster and Longley as early as 1924.[52]

Things were soon to change, however, in the wake of one technical innovation, aerial photography, which was particularly crucial in the Midlands where remains of former settlements often survive as well-defined earthworks. In 1925 O. G. S Crawford published an aerial photograph of the deserted medieval village of Gainsthorpe in Lincolnshire, which proved a revelation.[53] Deserted rural settlements, even those as well-preserved as Gainsthorpe, are often difficult to appreciate from ground level; even the most pronounced earthwork remains of hollow-ways and buildings can be incomprehensible and thus invisible to those used to viewing their medieval archaeology as upstanding ivy-clad walls, as James Bond amusingly reminded us as late as 1989.[54] From the air, however, the dramatic nature of the evidence for deserted rural settlements could be appreciated for the first time: at Gainsthorpe the lonely outlines of abandoned streets and tofts containing deserted houses with their entrances and dividing walls clearly visible can all be seen as a lightly shrouded 'ghost' village. The value of aerial photography as a tool for investigation of the medieval landscape, rather than just for its vivid illustration, was subsequently demonstrated in the study of the field systems on which medieval rural settlement depended: in 1938 the Orwins included an aerial photo of arable strip fields at Crimscote in Warwickshire to support their argument for the medieval date of such features.[55]

The Midlands were to prove the perfect nursery for the newly emerging discipline of medieval settlement studies in the inter-war years. Excavations at Seacourt, then in Berkshire and now Oxfordshire, had revealed 'loosely constructed and heavily robbed' buildings.[56] By the end of the 1940s, W. G. Hoskins had published lists of deserted sites in Leicestershire and carried out excavations on medieval settlement earthworks at Hamilton,[57] and Maurice Beresford had published his extensive account of deserted villages in Warwickshire which combined documentary research with field investigation, in order to prove that large numbers of medieval settlements had been abandoned since that time – contradicting the then still-prevailing view that settlement since the high medieval period had been largely static.[58] The date of 18 June 1948 can perhaps be identified as the moment when the starting gun for medieval settlement studies in the Midlands (and, indeed, much more widely) was fired, when economic historians and archaeologists (including Michael Postan, Beresford, Rodney Hilton and Grahame Clark) together visited Hoskins's excavations at Hamilton and other earthworks near Leicester, setting the scene for the interdisciplinary approach which has typified medieval rural settlement studies ever since.[59]

In 1952 the Deserted Medieval Village Research Group (DMVRG) was founded by Maurice Beresford and John Hurst. This provided a major stimulus for programmes of identifying and recording medieval settlements in the Midlands, where pronounced earthwork remains are often easy to see, much of it carried out by amateurs (Figure 12.5). In Gloucestershire, for example, just 15 deserted medieval settlements were known in 1954, but this number nearly doubled to 28 in the next five years and had increased more than fourfold to 67 by 1968[60] – an achievement whose value was considerably enhanced

Figure 12.5. Lower Shuckburgh, Warwickshire. Light snow picks out settlement earthworks and the ridge-and-furrow of the village's medieval open fields which extends outwards from the medieval village boundary. The deserted village of Upper Shuckburgh stands a mile to the south-east in the grounds of Shuckburgh Park. (Photo © Northamptonshire County Council, reproduced by permission of NCC Archives and Heritage Service/Glenn Foard)

by Don Benson's pioneering work incorporating it promptly into one of the earliest county Sites and Monuments Record (SMR).[61] Jack Golson began work on deserted medieval villages in Lincolnshire in 1951,[62] while Hoskins published the plans of seven deserted village sites in Leicestershire in 1956.[63] In 1957 H. P. R. Finberg produced a seminal paper on Withington in Gloucestershire which suggested that some medieval estate boundaries might be essentially contiguous with those of the Roman period, pointing towards a more nuanced view of the impact of the forces of continuity and change in the first millennium AD.[64]

The impact of the DMVRG was directly acknowledged in one of the earliest published excavations of the deserted village, namely Riseholme in Lincolnshire, which appeared in *Medieval Archaeology* in 1960.[65] This model excavation report (for its time) includes a hachured earthwork survey which shows the settlement to have been laid out either side of a central street, with a discussion contrasting this linear arrangement to the clustered arrangement displayed by Hoskins's Leicestershire sites and the suggestion that 'if enough surveys from different areas can be collected it may well be possible to make comparisons between them and arrive at certain conclusions about

Key Theme: Nucleation

Enquiry into the origins of the English village has dominated the study of medieval rural settlements in the Midlands for more than a century.[66] Though there is now general agreement about when villages first began to take shape in the landscape – between the eighth and twelfth centuries AD – and that they represent a fundamental reorganisation of an earlier pattern of dispersed settlement, the related questions of why and how they formed continue to elude full resolution. Greater chronological precision has unquestionably brought with it the opportunity for more detailed exploration of the prevailing conditions which may have encouraged village nucleation; however, that the processes involved were complicated and might vary from place to place is surely reflected in the number of different models that have been proposed.

Fieldwork in Northamptonshire during the 1970s to 1990s led to the idea of a 'Great Replanning' of the landscape at a relatively early date.[67] Based on the discovery beyond the later village core of abandoned farmstead sites which produced no material evidence postdating AD 850, it was proposed that nucleation had largely been completed by this date. This chronology permitted village formation to be linked to the fragmentation of large estates and the creation of smaller territorial units. The relocation of the farmsteads to a single settlement focus allowed the laying out of extensive open fields. The capital investment required in this reorganisation, it was suggested, was dependent upon the growth of the market economy and encouraged by the development of new urban centres. In their earliest phases the internal arrangement of these emerging nucleations was rather untidy. At some later point, perhaps in the tenth century, many village cores and open-field systems were replanned, producing more regular toft and croft arrangements and the familiar structure of interlocking furlongs and strips.[68]

Implicit in the Northamptonshire model is the notion that initial nucleation was a widespread phenomenon that took place both early and quickly. In other words, nucleation was seen as an 'event' rather than a protracted 'process'. Lewis, Mitchell-Fox and Dyer's study of four East Midlands counties took the opposite view:[69] they suggested that the evidence pointed in the direction of a much slower evolutionary process. Nucleation may have been initially forced on communities as they sought to tackle problems caused by a rapidly filling landscape. As farms began to lock together, movement through the landscape and access to resources such as woodland and pasture became problematic. Nucleation and the laying out of communally farmed fields provided one solution. In the absence of these negative stimuli, they suggested that elsewhere, once the village model had proved effective, other communities adopted this because of the benefits it brought, in a process of nucleation through emulation. In certain parts of England, and in the Midlands especially, the conditions for these innovative responses prevailed from the mid-ninth to the mid-thirteenth century, an episode they termed the 'village moment'. Thereafter the social, economic and cultural circumstances which stimulated nucleation had disappeared and the period for further village nucleation had passed.

Both these models advocate change. In Whittlewood, however, considerable continuity was exhibited between pre- and post-nucleation settlement patterns, many of the latter growing out from existing settlements with long pre-AD 850 histories.[70] These villages might grow or contract, but their basic structure – whether a single nucleated centre or a polyfocal layout – reflected earlier arrangements.

The identification of a relatively late nucleation date – post 850 – fits better with the evolutionary model without dismissing the possibility that elsewhere nucleation might have occurred in the eighth century and first half of the ninth. A distinction might be drawn between precocious nucleation associated with high-status sites and estate centres, the very sites that proponents of the Northamptonshire model had concentrated on, and a later phase of nucleation linked with settlements occupying lower rungs of the settlement hierarchy as the Whittlewood examples tended to be.

Most recent models of nucleation have tended to underplay the influence of the environment with one notable exception. Williamson's study of eastern England (including some Midland counties) correlated settlement forms with different types of soils and varying patterns of land use.[71] Clayland and large blocks of meadowland encouraged nucleation since this aided the efficient mustering of the labour, crucial since the conditions under which these could be easily ploughed or mown were limited to only a few days of the year. Where meadow was divided into small patches, settlement would tend to disperse accordingly. Farming considerations also lie behind a further recent model, based on an examination of place-names in –thorp, which suggest that these small hamlets might represent an intermediate phase between full dispersion and full nucleation. Rather than moving directly to a single focal point of settlement, the main village centre was initially served by a small number of satellite centres each attached to, and from which was worked, one of the open fields of the new farming system.[72]

housing patterns on a regional basis'.[73] This was followed by a summary of the documentary evidence which consciously avoided the temptation to 'spread the net too widely and to digress' but did include a cogent presentation of material pertaining to the decline of the village in the fifteenth and sixteenth centuries. One building was excavated and proved to be a two-celled stone-footed tile-roofed structure with a hearth at one end and a possible byre at the other: this was one of the first found in England to be identified as a longhouse, previously considered to be exclusive to western Britain. No evidence pre-dating the twelfth century was recovered, while the date of abandonment was cautiously suggested as mid-fourteenth century, on the basis of an absence of pottery post-dating *c.* 1350.

Another important excavation was that of Upton in Gloucestershire, which took place between 1959 and 1973.[74] Here, detailed excavation revealed not only the presence of a longhouse, but also a series of alterations that had been made to the original building in the thirteenth and fourteenth centuries to create separate accommodation for humans and animals in a move away from the traditions of the longhouse. There was, however, little evidence for settlement planning found at Upton, which lacked a regular layout or any clearly defined plot boundaries; its size and layout are more suggestive of a hamlet than a nucleated village. Potentially, the absence of crofts may reflect a practice of keeping animals away from the core of the settlement.[75] Further north, excavation by Guy Beresford at Barton Blount in Derbyshire revealed evidence for regular toft and croft boundaries of probable eleventh-century date.[76]

Once out of the bottle, there was no stopping the genie of medieval settlement studies in the Midlands. Accounts and inventories of deserted settlement sites were produced across the region in rapid succession throughout the 1960s and early 1970s in Annual Reports of the DMVRG, local journals and monographs: added to Beresford's 1946 list for Warwickshire came Shropshire, Oxfordshire and Northamptonshire between 1964 and 1966,[77] Staffordshire and Worcestershire in 1971[78] and Herefordshire in 1972.[79] This process of identification and listing was able to proceed at such speed because most of it was based on field survey rather than excavation. This could be completed rapidly and – crucial for those in the early years working with little professional training – without causing any damage, since mistakes of identification, if made, could easily be corrected by a later visit or further investigation. One classic example is Harry Thorpe's analysis of Wormleighton in Warwickshire.[80] This study combined evidence from aerial photography, field survey and documentary research to identify regular planned blocks of tofts and crofts, streets, ridge-and-furrow, moated sites, fishponds and water meadows and to show how the latter succeeded the former as the medieval nucleated village became depopulated.

Field survey is an investigative technique well-suited to the study of medieval rural settlement in the Midlands, where earthwork sites are widespread and are, or, at least, were, well-preserved. The value of such an approach was demonstrated by the work of the Royal Commission on the Historical Monuments (RCHM, later Royal Commission on the Historical Monuments of England (RCHME)) in Northamptonshire, where the entire county was ultimately encompassed in a programme of analytical earthwork survey. The majority of sites recorded in detail were settlements of medieval and later date, and of these, most represented the remains of rural settlement. This work was crucial in three respects. First, in recording in detail the earthwork remains of scores of deserted and shrunken villages it allowed the extent of settlement contraction to be fully appreciated. Secondly, in presenting so many case studies of settlements, both deserted and still-occupied, whose pre-modern plan could be reconstructed, the RCHME volumes enabled medievalists to appreciate the wide variety of forms adopted by medieval rural settlements, and assess the type and extent of planning within settlements over a wide area and a diversity of landscape types. Plumpton is one example out of many where the RCHME plan shows the settlement, which then comprised little more than a church, manor house and rectory to lie within the remains of an earlier small regularly planned linear row settlement;[81] and at Isham, survey demonstrated the continuation of three parallel village streets, traces of others to the south of the village, and remnants of toft and croft boundaries forming a continuous settlement from the church and manor house in the west to the mill situated on the river Ise 150 m to the east.[82] Thirdly, the data provided further incontrovertible evidence for the dynamic, changing character of rural settlements in the south Midlands in the medieval and post-medieval periods. Similar earthwork survey work by R. F. Hartley in Leicestershire around the same time,[83] and by RCHME in West Lindsey (north-west Lincolnshire) a decade later,[84] complemented Milton Keynes Archaeological Unit (MKAU) parish surveys in north Buckinghamshire, resulted in the medieval settlement remains in the south and east Midlands being arguably the most extensively recorded in Europe.[85]

Another significant discovery resulting from this work was that many of the Midland settlements were not nearly as old as had long been supposed. The deserted village of Faxton in Northamptonshire is sited on good ground, has a name which includes the *–tūn* element considered likely to indicate Anglo-Saxon origin, combined with a possible Scandinavian personal name, and is recorded in Domesday Book with a population perhaps 60–80 people.[86] It was thus assumed to have been of Anglo-Saxon origin, and this was the prevailing assumption regarding medieval villages in general. However, extensive excavation found no evidence anywhere in this large, complex settlement, for any occupation pre-dating *c.* AD 1150, and it showed how part of the village was not laid out until *c.* AD 1200. It was clear that the serfs, villeins and bordars listed under the entry for Faxton in 1086 were not living on the site of the later medieval village, which was revealed as a

post-Norman foundation. Excavations at nearby Wythemail and Lyveden showed the same pattern, and similar observations, with finds discovered during excavation or field survey pointing towards a late foundation date, were made at numerous other deserted medieval village sites.[87] The overturning of previous assumptions of the antiquity of medieval villages was given added impetus by discoveries made during fieldwalking, another archaeological technique which has revolutionised understanding of settlement evolution. Fieldwalking in Northamptonshire, David Hall and others discovered numerous small concentrations of pottery dating to the fifth to ninth centuries in many of the fields around the nucleated villages, indicating a pre-village pattern of dispersed settlement.[88] At Brixworth, for example, eight or more such sites were scattered across the parish, all abandoned before AD 850 and overlain by the open fields of the nucleated village which replaced them.[89] Complementing this came discoveries of settlements of ninth- and tenth-century date which had no evidence of later occupation, such as at Fladbury in Worcestershire, where excavation on a previously unknown site led to the discovery of ninth-century settlement including a timber building.[90]

Significantly, the programmes of earthwork survey by RCHME, MKAU and Hartley directed attention also towards still-occupied settlements. This broadening of focus was stimulated both by a shift in scholarly interest away from settlement desertion and towards the origins of medieval settlements and by a growing awareness of the threat posed to medieval settlement remains from building development. Perhaps the best-known single development threat, and certainly the largest in terms of the area which it covered, came from the last and largest of the post-war new towns of Britain, Milton Keynes in Buckinghamshire. Designated in 1967, this town's network of roads, settlement and services was thrown across 82 km² of previously mostly rural land. Existing villages were incorporated more or less intact into the new town, but vast swathes of open countryside, including archaeological sites of all dates, were covered by new construction. Although some sites were preserved as open space, innumerable others were destroyed, but the development did also ultimately provide unparalleled opportunities for field survey across hundreds of hectares of landscapes within the development area, much of it densely covered with ridge-and-furrow and other earthworks of medieval date, and for excavation of a number of deserted medieval rural settlements.[91] These ranged widely in size, form and history. Caldecotte on the south-east of the development area was a small hamlet on the edge of the parish of Bow Brickhill, in an area of predominately nucleated settlement.[92] The medieval settlement comprised two areas of remains adjacent to an area devoid of earthworks which was interpreted as a green. Excavation of a block of four tofts detached from the rest of the small settlement showed them to have been a late thirteenth-century extension to the settlement laid out over twelfth-century fields. It remained in occupation for less than a century, with no finds post-dating the mid-fourteenth century: it was under cultivation once more by the late fourteenth century. On the west side of the development area settlement at Tattenhoe, in contrast, apparently came into existence in the late eleventh century, probably as a polyfocal settlement on two separate locations.[93] In the later thirteenth century it was extended and/or reorganised as a nucleated settlement extending for approximately 500 m south-east from the church and nearby moated complex. The settlement was abandoned by the later fifteenth or early sixteenth century. At nearby Westbury-by-Shenley, nearly a kilometre of dispersed settlement was surveyed and either excavated or stripped; here, most of the habitative plots were laid out in the twelfth century or later over ridge-and-furrow, a factor which is likely to account for the regular layout of these tofts, which largely lack defined crofts; they may instead have backed on to less regularly defined enclosed small fields. Most were abandoned in the fifteenth or sixteenth centuries.[94] Great Linford, on the northern fringes of the development area, was a much bigger settlement which expanded in the late twelfth century into crofts which generally continued in occupation until the mid-seventeenth century.[95] These four sites from across the Milton Keynes development area thus neatly illustrate the diversity of settlement form and history of this part of the Midlands.

Recent research

Research in the Midlands towards the end of the last century was dominated by a number of extensive surveys. Extensive fieldwalking across Leicestershire has produced interesting results, particularly for discussions of the levels of continuity and discontinuity of settlement patterns across the transitional post-Roman centuries, although the full analysis of the data recovered and their full implications have yet to be realised.[96] Very significant has been David Hall's long-term study of open-field systems in Northamptonshire, based on extensive documentary enquiry and field survey, which brought with it the concept of large-scale landscape replanning.[97] He identified 'long furlongs' running over several kilometres which appeared to ignore parish divisions which, when combined with the evidence for the abandonment of early medieval dispersed settlement patterns before AD 850 carried the implication that villages were nucleating and open fields were being laid out in the context of small estates rather than individual manors. At a later point – the tenth century is often cited – it was suggested that both villages and open fields might be reorganised, with settlement layouts exhibiting more regular and neat arrangements thereafter, while long furlongs might be subdivided to form the more familiar pattern of smaller interlocking furlongs.[98] Important details and new discoveries that helped to develop this idea were provided by the long-running excavations and field survey undertaken at Raunds in the same county, the results of which cannot be underestimated and which are summarised in the Feature Box: *Key Project*, p. 194.

Results from Raunds can be compared with those from Yarnton in Oxfordshire.[99] Here the development of a number of settlements has been traced from early Saxon times onwards. Settlement shows a degree of continuity between the Romano-British and early medieval periods. But the arrangement of Sunken-Featured Buildings which occupied these sites in the fifth through to the sixth centuries exhibits little sign of internal organisation and few permanent boundaries. There was expansion in the seventh century, with settlement having the tendency towards transience and shift. By this stage the surrounding landscape appears to have supported a mixed economy of grazing land and arable fields. Signs of more permanent settlement – post-built structures, ditched and fenced enclosures, and more dense concentrations of buildings – begin to appear after AD 700. This chronology parallels that seen at another of the key Midland sites of Catholme in Staffordshire.[100] At Yarnton and its neighbour Worton there is evidence for both the intensification and diversification of agriculture in the vicinity in the second half of the ninth century. New crops such as rye and hemp were being grown, while levels of alluviation in the Thames valley rose substantially indicating the presence of large tracts of exposed ploughsoil. Within the settlements free-threshing wheat and barley were being processed, and valuable manures curated in middens. Into the late Saxon period, the focus of settlement shifted slightly on to the site of the modern village, a move which was also accompanied by a replanning of the middle Saxon settlement and the laying out of new enclosures. Excavations here also help to chart the effects of the late medieval downturn in climate, the early fourteenth-century agricultural crises and successive waves of plague and other epidemics.

While excavation on Midland sites has shown that two or more settlements might share very similar histories, other recent studies reveal that even within a small area, settlements might develop along very different lines. The ongoing debate surrounding the origins of the village is summarised in Feature Box: *Key Theme*, p. 197, but here we must briefly mention two inter-related studies which have contributed much to this debate. The thorough examination of the historical and existing archaeological evidence for settlement and landscape development in the four East Midland counties of Leicestershire, Northamptonshire, Buckinghamshire and Bedfordshire led Lewis, Mitchell-Fox and Dyer to reconsider the processes that lay behind medieval settlement formation, publishing their results as *Village, Hamlet and Field* in 1997. Against the revolutionary model developed earlier in Northamptonshire they proposed a more evolutionary model that saw villages forming between AD 800 and 1200. This survey forcefully reminded us of the diversity of settlement types found in the Midlands during the Middle Ages. By giving equal attention to the development of hamlets and single farmsteads, and not treating the nucleated village in isolation, they set the exploration of medieval settlement in the Midlands on a new footing. The challenge of explaining these complex patterns was taken up in a detailed examination of both nucleated

and dispersed settlement forms found in Whittlewood Forest in north-east Buckinghamshire and south-west Northamptonshire, an area whose potential had been first recognised during the four-county survey.[94] This research sought to answer a number of questions, central among which were why did nucleated villages form in some places and not in others, and why did some places fare better than others (it was not simply the diversity of settlement form that the area contained that mattered here, but the fact that the area contained a mix of surviving, shrunken and deserted sites)?[102] Combining documentary, cartographical, archaeological, architectural and environmental evidence, the story that emerges from this study is that while many local communities were subject to very similar internal and external pressures across the medieval centuries, the solutions that they might adopt to the working of the land and the mode of communal living might often be very different. The principal conclusion drawn was that nucleated and dispersed settlements should not be viewed as entirely separate categories of medieval settlement but rather as alternative and interlinked outcomes of the same processes. The revelation at Whittlewood that each place has an individual developmental biography might well signal the end of the quest to find a universal model for village nucleation, at least in the terms that that enquiry is currently framed.[103] If so, then Woodperry and Whittlewood represent the alpha and omega for medieval village studies both in the East Midlands and across the country more generally.

Looking to the future

Despite the central position the Midlands has held in the development of medieval settlement research and medieval archaeology more generally, and despite the number of intriguing lines of enquiry Midland-based studies continue to throw up, the region has in recent years rather fallen out of favour with scholars, who have quite rightly turned to other parts of the country which have received less attention. As a result, new insights are emerging and a more balanced, and truly national, picture can start to be drawn.[104] But while it is certainly the case that the Midlands remains more intensively studied than other regions, it would be plainly wrong to imply that it was better understood as a result. As successive studies have shown, each

Key Site to Visit: Ingarsby, Leicestershire

To go to Ingarsby, one of those sites visited by the 1948 group, is to follow in the footsteps of the pioneers of medieval settlement studies. Hoskins acknowledged that it was the identification of the deserted village remains here (and their resemblance to the plan of Bingham in Nottinghamshire produced by Allcroft in his *Earthwork of England*) that helped him to identify others elsewhere.[105] But Ingarsby's interest does not rest entirely with the well-preserved earthworks, impressive though these are, since a detailed pre- and post-desertion history can be reconstructed from documentary sources. The greater part of the manor was granted to Leicester Abbey in 1352 and further acquisitions ensured that by the 1460s the Abbey held all 48 of its 24-acre virgates; in 1381 the Poll Tax reveals around 12 families in residence, all but one economically dependent upon the Abbey. In 1469 the whole manor was enclosed: arable was converted to rich grazing, the open fields replaced by paddocks and closes, and the village deserted and replaced with a monastic grange. After the Dissolution, Ingarsby was sold to the Cave family who were almost certainly responsible for the construction of Old Hall which stands to the north of the former village site. But to visit Ingarsby is not simply to look back to a golden era of deserted village studies but to consider how far we have come over the last 60 years and how we now understand these sites. In 1950 all the earthworks were considered to relate to the abandoned village, the regular arrangement of terrace-ways, hollow-ways and prominent boundaries of tofts and crofts, ensuring that the settlement layout was deemed to be 'fairly clear'.[106] Old Hall, surrounded by a moat and located beyond the village, was thought not only to stand on the site of the grange but to preserve parts of its late medieval buildings. More recent assessments, based on the size and morphology of some of the earthworks, suggest in contrast that what was formerly thought to be the south-west quarter of the medieval village may well be the remains of the later monastic grange; moreover, many of the other visible earthworks, particularly the dam and lake in the valley bottom, the triangular mound in the south-east corner, and the angled banks to the south, probably represent garden features laid out over the former village as the landscape of Old Hall was 'recast in a developed ornamental garb in the sixteenth and seventeenth centuries'.[107]

The stories emerging from detailed survey of the earthwork remains of deserted villages may be becoming more complex, but this only serves to enhance rather than diminish the powerful hold these places have on our imagination. Even if many of the earthwork features at Ingarsby may not be associated with the village at all, this does not stop us thinking about the community that once did live here, helped in this instance by Hoskins's lyrical prose penned about this spot:

Today sheep graze over the turf that covers the homes of Thomas Bytyng and Joan his wife, of Thomas Webster and Matilda, and Richard Scheperd and his wife Agnes; and lapwings rise up from the grass-covered lanes where Alice and Margery and Juliana stood and gossiped on a far-away summer morning while the larks sang above the growing corn; or where on a black, frosty night the north wind, smelling of snow, nipped round the corner of the barn, and John Lynseye "blew upon his nail" as he returned from the cows, thinking of his bed and Cecily his wife, waiting for him with hot pease gruel.[108]

To this colourful scene we can now add the grazier monks with their flocks of sheep and herds of cattle, and later still imagine the Cave family as they promenaded leisurely around their gardens, perhaps pausing to contemplate the old village remains from the vantage point of their new elevated viewing mounds (Figure 12.6).

time the evidence is reconsidered, existing theories have been found wanting and in need of partial or full replacement. This intellectual investigation needs to continue. A century of carefully considered exploration in this region provides the perfect foundation for the development of new conceptual frameworks to advance our understanding of what is clearly an intricate subject. Just as it might be observed that the Midlands has been in the vanguard of every major settlement and landscape shift over the last two millennia and that the future direction of the English countryside is likely to manifest itself first here too,

Figure 12.6. Ingarsby, Leicestershire. The high ground lying east of the county town of Leicester is deserted village country. While the region suffers from its relatively exposed position and does not enjoy the best soils, the medieval period saw settlement colonisation and intensive arable cultivation. No single factor accounts for the number of abandoned sites found here; however, post-medieval conversion to grass and emparkment played their part as communities were either moved off the land or were alternatively moved elsewhere within the near vicinity. (Photo © Richard Jones)

so we might predict that the next paradigm-shifting step forward in scholarly enquiry relating to medieval rural settlement studies will again find its footing in this fascinating and bewilderingly complex region.

Further reading

Useful regional surveys setting the medieval settlements and landscapes of the Midlands within a longer timeframe can be found in Hooke (2006) who deals with the West Midlands, and Stocker (2006) who treats the East Midlands. A sense of the variety of landscape *pays* in the wider Midlands can be found in Thirsk's *An Illustrated History of the English Rural Landscape* (2000), republished in 2002 under the title *Rural England* (2000), particularly Fox's contribution on the Wolds; Dyer, Hey and Thirsk on lowland vales; and Dyer on woodlands and

woodland-pasture. These are complemented by three other books, Van de Noort's (2004) exploration of the Humber wetlands, Barnatt and Smith's (2004) survey of the Peak District, and Foard *et al.*'s *Rockingham Forest* (2009). Settlements and landscapes of the early medieval period are carefully considered in Hooke's *The Landscape of Anglo-Saxon England* (1998) and Blair's *Anglo-Saxon Oxfordshire* (1994).

Those wishing for a place-name perspective should consult Gelling and Cole's *The Landscape of Place-Names* (2000). Anyone craving more detail is guided towards a number of recently published large-scale surveys and excavations. Of these we recommend *Village, Hamlet and Field* (Lewis *et al.* 2001), Yarnton (Hey 2004), Whittlewood (Jones and Page 2006), Raunds (Audouy and Chapman 2008; Parry 2006), and West Cotton (Chapman 2010).

Notes
1. Horstman 1887; OED.
2. Harrison quoted in Roberts and Wrathmell 2000, 15.
3. Beckett 1988; Darby and Terrett 1971; Gelling 1992; Hooke 2006; Lewis *et al.* 1997; Rowlands 1987; Stafford 1985; Stocker 2006.
4. Fox 1932.
5. Rackham 1986.

6.   Roberts and Wrathmell 2002.
7.   Phythian-Adams 1996.
8.   Hooke 2006, 159–202.
9.   The Landscape Character of Derbyshire (Derbyshire County Council) (www.derbyshire.gov.uk/environment/conservation/landscapecharacter) accessed Nov. 2009.
10. Toulmin Smith 1910; Cole and Browning 1962; Hillaby 1983.
11. For the use of toponyms in the Chilterns, see Gelling and Cole 2000, 289–316; for Shropshire see Gelling 1990–2006; and for Derbyshire see Cameron 1959.
12. Gelling and Cole 2000, 143–219; Ford 1976.
13. Watts 2004, 308.
14. Gelling 1974.
15. Gelling and Cole 2000, 166–168.
16. Maitland 1897; Gray 1915.
17. Rippon 2008, 1.
18. See Rippon 2008, fig 1.2 where the author juxtaposes four maps of England showing the extents of Parliamentary Enclosure (after Gonner 1912), two- and three-field systems (after Gray 1912), ancient and planned countryside (after Rackham 1986), and predominantly nucleated settlement pattern (after Roberts and Wrathmell 2000).
19. E.g. Lewis *et al.* 1997; Roberts and Wrathmell 2000.
20. Bond 1985; Roberts 1982a.
21. Roberts and Wrathmell 2000, 47, 56
22. E.g. Hartley 1984; 1987; 1989; 2008; RCHM 1975; 1981; 1982; 1984; Everson *et al.* 1991. Most notably, work carried out in Northamptonshire by David Hall, and in south Leicestershire by Peter Liddle and his team – notably at West Cotton, Raunds, Faxton (Northamptonshire); Barton Blount (Derbyshire); Great Linford, Tattenhoe, Westbury, Caldecote (Buckinghamshire); Upton (Gloucestershire); Riseholme (Lincolnshire).
23. E.g. Jones and Page 2006.
24. Jones and Page 2006; Page and Jones 2007.
25. RCHM 1979; 1981; 1982.
26. Skelton and Harvey 1986, 211–220.
27. Hall 1995.
28. See Schumer 1984; 1999; Broad and Hoyle 1997; Jones and Page 2006; Pettit 1968.
29. Jones and Page 2003; for discussion of polyfocal settlements see Taylor 1977.
30. Roberts and Wrathmell 2000, fig. 24.
31. Brown and Taylor 1989; Taylor 1995.
32. Dyer 2007.
33. Aldred and Dyer 1991.
34. Dyer 2002b.

35. Rackham 1986.
36. Roberts and Wrathmell 2000; 2002.
37. Dyer 1991; 1994.
38. Fox 1989; 2000.
39. Dyer and Jones 2010; Roberts and Wrathmell 2000, 48–49.
40. Wilson 1846.
41. Seebohm 1883.
42. RCHM 1975, 81.
43. Parry 2006.
44. Boddington 1996.
45. Parry 2006.
46. Chapman 2010.
47. Parry 2006, 95.
48. Parry 2006, 129.
49. Parry 2006, 274.
50. Audouy and Chapman 2008, 52.
51. Audouy and Chapman 2008, 53.
52. Foster and Longley 1924.
53. Crawford 1925.
54. Bond (1989) refers to an ingénue visitor on one of his field trips in Oxfordshire who, quite unable to see the village streets and houses he had enthusiastically pointed out, admitted the experience had reminded her of the fable of the emperor's new clothes.
55. Orwin and Orwin 1938.
56. Bruce Mitford 1940; Biddle 1961–62.
57. Hoskins 1946.
58. Beresford 1945–46; Bond 1989, 132.
59. Gerrard, 2003, 103; Dyer and Jones 2010, xvii.
60. Beresford and Hurst 1971, 187–188.
61. Bond 1989, 131.
62. Society of Antiquaries, Interviews with Fellows: J. G. Hurst, www.sal.org.uk, accessed 12 July 2010.
63. Hoskins 1956.
64. Finberg 1957.
65. Thompson 1960.
66. See Rippon 2008, chapter 1, for a useful summary of the historiography.
67. Brown and Foard 1998.
68. Hall 1995.
69. Lewis *et al.* 1997.
70. Jones and Page 2006.
71. Williamson 2003.
72. Cullen *et al.* 2011.
73. Thompson 1960, 98.
74. Hilton and Rahtz 1966; Rahtz 1969b: Rahtz and Watts 1984.
75. Astill and Grant 1988, 48.
76. Beresford 1975.
77. Gaydon and Rowley 1964: Appendix E; Allison *et al.* 1965; 1966.

78. Bate and Palliser 1970–71; Dyer 1971.
79. Hickling 1971–72.
80. Thorpe 1975.
81. RCHM 1982, 165–167.
82. RCHM 1979, 100–101.
83. Hartley 1983; 1984; 1987; 1989.
84. Everson *et al.* 1991.
85. Croft and Mynard 1993.
86. RCHME 1981, 119–124; Gover *et al.* 1975, 124–125.
87. Hurst and Hurst 1969; RCHME 1975.
88. Foard 1978.
89. Hall and Martin 1979.
90. Taylor 1983, 128–130.
91. Croft and Mynard 1993; Mynard 1994.
92. Zeepvat *et al.* 1994; Lewis *et al.* 2001, 52.
93. Ivens *et al.* 1995.
94. Ivens *et al.* 1995.
95. Mynard and Zeepvat 1992.
96. Bourne 1996; Bowman and Liddle 2004.
97. Hall 1995.
98. Brown and Foard 1998.
99. Hey 2006.
100. Losco-Bradley and Kinsley 2002.
101. Lewis and Mitchell-Fox 1993.
102. Jones and Page 2006, 24.
103. Jones 2010b.
104. E.g. Rippon 2008. Symptomatic of this shift of emphasis was a recent series of five AHRC-funded workshops entitled *Perceptions of Medieval Landscapes and Settlements* that contained not a single contribution based on Midland lowland England!
105. Hoskins 1950, 79.
106. Hoskins 1950, 79; Hoskins 1956, 46–47.
107. Everson and Brown 2010, 52–56.
108. Hoskins 1950, 79.

CHAPTER 13

Cambridgeshire and the Peat Fen: Medieval Rural Settlement and Commerce, *c.* AD 900–1300

Susan Oosthuizen

Introduction

The origins and development of medieval settlement in Cambridgeshire have been well explored, principally by Christopher Taylor, both in overview and through a series of important case studies.[1] The range and detail of this body of scholarship, still widely accepted, allow a different approach here: building on Taylor's work, this chapter explores the influence of rivers and canals on the location and morphology of rural medieval settlement in the Cambridgeshire peat fens between about AD 900 and 1300 where, as in western Suffolk and Norfolk, 'most of the villages along the fen-edge had any number of small staithes and hythes to facilitate the loading and unloading of boats'.[2]

Strikingly, the Cambridgeshire peat fens appear to be one of the few English regions in which water transport remained dominant throughout the Middle Ages.[3] This is not difficult to explain. The great fenland rivers linked Lincolnshire, Northamptonshire, Huntingdonshire and Cambridgeshire with Rutland, Leicestershire and Bedfordshire in the west, Buckinghamshire, Hertfordshire and Essex in the south, and Suffolk and Norfolk in the east across the fenland basin (Figure 13.1).[4] Furthermore, the comparative cheapness of carriage by water was most explicit in the fens, where the necessity to skirt large tracts of marsh often made road journeys particularly indirect.[5] The network of natural watercourses which drained the fen had, by the mid-thirteenth century and probably some time before, been augmented by a large number of artificial waterways, locally called 'lodes', most of which (with their catchwater drains)

exhibited at their landward ends at least one hythe, frequently several, supplemented by small private cuts which led up into individual properties.[6] Rivers and canals were indeed interlinked in a complex and far-ranging pattern, which extended both the range of goods traded, and the areas from and to which goods could be supplied.[7]

Regional geography

The peat fens cover about 4,000 km^2, providing a delta not only for the major river systems of the east Midlands (the Nene, Ouse and Welland), along which the tides could be felt up to 48 miles inland, but also for the rivers of the south and east: the Cam (Granta), Lark, Little Ouse, Wissey and Nar.[8] The floor of the fen basin generally undulates between a few metres below or above sea level, within inland verges which frequently lie at around 5 m above Ordnance Datum, the winter floodline; only in a few places does it rise to form clay and gravel 'islands' which rise above 5 m above OD – some substantial, like Ely, Chatteris and March, and others smaller, like Quanea, Apesholt or Shippea.[9] Raised areas of peat bog had begun to form from the sixth millennium BC between sea level and the 5 m contour where the fen basin was permanently damp or flooded for extended periods in autumn, winter and spring; by the eleventh century AD, it had reached a depth of around 3 m and continued to grow until drainage in the seventeenth century, forming large tracts of wetland between the islands and the fen-edge.[10]

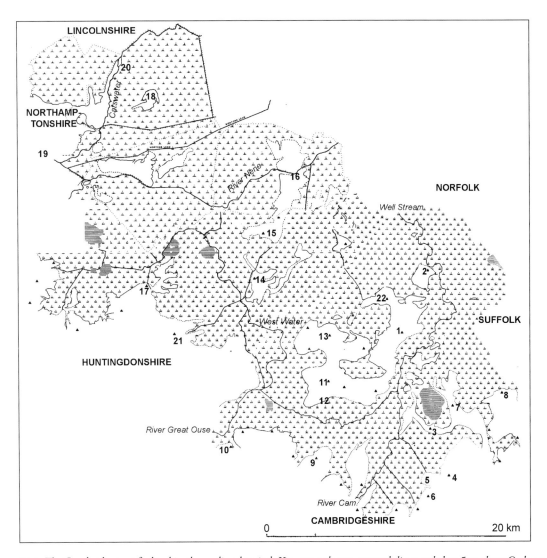

Figure 13.1. The Cambridge peat fenland in the medieval period. Key: areas shown as marsh lie at or below 5 m above Ordnance Datum, the winter floodline. Triangles denote the major settlements in medieval parishes. North is to the top of the page. 1. Ely. 2. Littleport. 3. Wicken. 4. Burwell. 5. Reach. 6. Swaffham Prior. 7. Soham. 8. Isleham. 9. Cottenham. 10. Swavesey. 11. Haddenham. 12. Aldreth. 15. Doddington. 16. March. 17. Ramsey. 18. Thorney. 19. Peterborough. 20. Crowland. 21. Somersham. 22. Little Downham (Reproduced with permission from Hall 1987, 65; Hall 1992, 102; Hall 1996, 160)

Such low-lying land, sensitive to minor variations in water-level and too damp for arable cultivation, could nonetheless support a wide range of rich, natural resources: grazing for large herds of cattle and sheep, as well as reeds, rush and sedge, hay, woods, peat and vast quantities of fish and wildfowl. This productive environment appears continuously exploited from prehistory onwards.[11] Medieval customs of intercommoning between vills seem so ancient that they may even have pre-dated the establishment of the seventh-century monastic estates at Peterborough, Crowland and Ely.[12]

The cohesive geography of the region appears to have been reflected in physical patterns of settlement and land-use. Medieval field systems in the fen parishes tended to be divided into a multiplicity of irregular subdivisions, like those in East Anglia: the Bishop of Ely's demesne at Doddington in 1251, for example, was made up of ten fields with names like Byrswrong, Estcroft and Akermanslond, while in only five of his fenland estates were arable fields arranged in the regular two or three divisions of the Midland System.[13] On the other hand, settlement throughout the fen was predominantly nucleated, even along the eastern edge of the fen in west Norfolk and Suffolk.[14] By the late eleventh century nucleated settlements largely took the form of a single focus (for example, Witchford, or Yaxley, Hunts.) or polyfocal clusters like Haddenham (with its additional nuclei at Hinton, Linden End, Aldreth, and Hill Row), Burwell (including Church End, High Town, Newnham, and North Street) or March (made up of Knight's End, Town End, West End, Well End, and High Street, Westry, and *Estwode*). Many settlements contain one or more regular planned elements, each characterised by properties of uniform area arranged into blocks which share front and back boundaries (the latter often labelled Back Lane), into which the parish church is often integrated. Some are explored in more detail below. Informal settlement with no sign of planned settlement is less common: the almost deserted settlement at Fenton in Huntingdonshire (first documented in 1236), for example, seems to have grown up along one side of a small green near the head of Fenton Lode, itself first mentioned in the early thirteenth century.[15]

Transport and trade by water in the medieval peat fens

That waterways were used for trade and transport in Anglo-Saxon England (and earlier) is well established: although hythes were first recorded in the later ninth century when documentary evidence becomes more common, archaeology consistently demonstrates the everyday quality of river-borne trade throughout the period.[16] Water transport in the fens expanded after the Norman Conquest and especially from the later twelfth century, building upon and extending many already old trading patterns.[17]

The importance to the development of medieval commerce of access to and transport by water

has been demonstrated in Essex, where a good proportion of post-Conquest markets were located at coastal ports.[18] Watercourses supporting similar inland trading networks have been described as a 'dendritic path'.[19] This phrase is particularly apt for the Cambridgeshire peat fens where rivers and canals linked a subtly differentiated hierarchy of places of greater or lesser importance through formal or informal trading networks, which might be regular, seasonal or intermittent, and local, regional, national or international.[20] By the twelfth century, for example, King's Lynn (Norfolk) had become a leading national and international port at the mouth of the river Ouse through which passed salt, grain, lead and wool as well as spices, wine and luxury goods.[21] More regional networks emerge in the carrying duties imposed by the Bishop of Ely on his customary tenants: thus those from his manor at Doddington were required to transport goods across an area bounded by Cambridge, St Ives and Ramsey (both Hunts.), and Peterborough (Northants.), while those from Wilburton additionally went to King's Lynn and Brandon (Suffolk).[22] Nor did local exchange necessarily require formal outlets, since evidence from Ramsey (see Feature Box: *Key Excavation*, p. 209) and the Suffolk Breckland demonstrates that informal trade could be as vibrant and complex as that in places with a market grant.[23]

Opportunities to travel by water were almost ubiquitous across fenland by the High Middle Ages.[24] The fenny environment and manorial carrying duties meant that most free and customary tenants, many of whom owned their own boats, were required to travel by water for their manorial lords, while the small cuts which lead up to many medieval properties from the lodes demonstrate the extent to which they also used waterborne transport on their own accounts. The fen offered such men a wider range of employment than those in predominantly arable parishes, including the possibility of exploiting fen products either directly for sale or after processing:[25] reeds, grazing, rushes, sedge, osiers, fish and wildfowl each contributed to the relative prosperity of peasant communities here.[26] Even the landless were better off: at Waterbeach, for example, 'men with little or no land could support themselves through their rights over the extensive common pastures and fens, listed in 1340 as fodderfen, turffen, fodderlot and

Key Excavation: Ramsey

Little is known about the construction of the lodes, or the maintenance of water levels within them. At Ely, their sides were revetted with oak timbers secured by a wattle fence. Ponds and tanks at Ramsey (and Burwell) may have been holding tanks intended to restore water levels behind flash-locks or sluices after use, although chamber- or lift-locks are known from the late twelfth century. Ramsey is one of the few fen-edge settlements where the relationship between a settlement and its canal has been explored in detail through excavation (Figure 13.2).[27] The estate centre for one of the major fenland abbeys, notorious for their wealth, and the site of a medieval planned town and market, it is atypical of the minor rural settlements of the region which have principally been explored by fieldwork.[28]

The settlement lies on a promontory reaching northward from Huntingdonshire into the peat fen, linked to the mainland by a narrow neck of land to the south, and bounded on the west by the Bury Brook, and by peat fen to the north and east. The Abbey was founded in the late tenth century, and became 'one of the richest in the fens – Ramsey the Golden'.[29] The depredations of the Anarchy in the mid-twelfth century may have stimulated

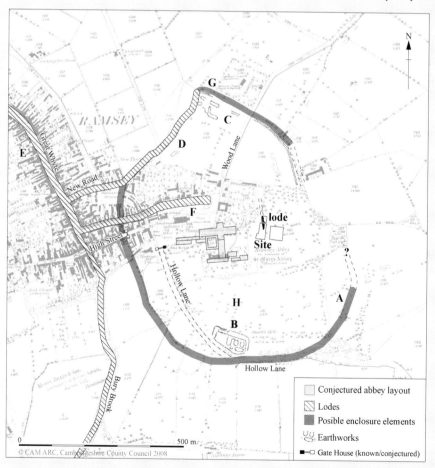

Figure 13.2. Ramsey. Interpretative map, showing possible elements of the Ramsey Abbey precinct enclosure and lodes in relation to the 1891 Ordnance Survey map (1st edition). A. Excavations 2004 and 2006. B. Booths Hill. C. Earthworks. D. Ditch or channel. E. Great Whyte. F. Little Whyte. G. Northern limit of abbey precinct. H. Three-celled structure and double ditch (Reproduced with permission from Spoerry et al. 2008, 176)

the Abbey into investment in a series of commercial developments in order to regain its earlier wealth, and included a substantial replanning of the landscape both inside and outside the precinct. In the mid- to late twelfth century the Bury Brook was canalised (becoming Ramsey Lode), leading to Ramsey Mere and thence to the Nene; Ramsey Lode was widened at the fen-edge to create hythes on either bank (the area called the Great Whyte); and a causeway was constructed across the fenny meadows that bordered the Bury Brook, including a bridge (replaced in stone in the thirteenth century) to facilitate road access to Huntingdon and Peterborough. Since High Street continued the alignment of the causeway right up to the Abbey gates, it became the main access route into the town. The Abbey obtained a market grant in about 1200 when a market place may have been laid out between High Street and Little Whyte, and at the same time a planned settlement was laid out on either side of the High Street, flanking the market place.

   The success of the market at Ramsey may be judged from the construction, in the early or mid-thirteenth century, of two large additional lodes leading east from the Great Whyte to new wharves within and on the edge of the precinct (perhaps replacing an earlier lode further to the east). Where the more northerly of these secondary lodes met the precinct boundary, excavations have revealed traces of what may be a crane and storehouse; these structures may be related to the import of Barnack stone for the extension and refurbishment of the monastic church and the domestic buildings, as well as for more general trade – the Abbey exported corn, wool and tile from its own manufactures, as well (perhaps) as riding horses.

sheeplot'.[30] Pottery, another seasonal (though not specifically a fenland) craft, offers further insight into distribution and production: in 1070 Hereward 'the Wake' is said to have disguised himself in order to infiltrate the Conqueror's camp by borrowing from an itinerant potter his torn and dirty clothes, his stock of pots, and his small boat.[31] Whether or not this story is true, it indicates how such small producers and sellers were so common as to be unremarkable – a conclusion perhaps supported by the wide dispersal of Ipswich and then St Neots and Thetford wares across the fenland basin between the eighth and eleventh centuries.[32]

   The primacy of carriage by water for these activities has led to a consensus that, in Cambridgeshire, a 'primary function' of the lodes was trade and transport.[33] The section that follows examines this conclusion through the morphology of medieval settlement in the Cambridgeshire peat fens first through planned commercial centres, and second through rural settlement.

Planned commercial centres

The planned market towns of the fens, laid out between about AD 1000 and 1300, are so well known as to be type-sites.[34] I do not, therefore, intend to linger upon them here, except to establish

the influence of access to water on their locations and plans. Generally speaking, such planned towns were formally established on or alongside existing settlements, where grants for markets and fairs had already successfully been achieved or where trade was already taking place.[35] They tended to be laid out along riverbanks where water- and land-routes intersected, providing a focus for traffic from a wide hinterland. Frequently, substantial investments were made for improving such nodal points through the canalisation or embankment of rivers, and/or the improvement of roads by the construction of substantial bridges or causeways.[36] In the fens, the integration of port and market seems to have been an additional premise of such foundations. The choice of suitable locations appears therefore to have been made on the basis of three criteria: (i) the opportunity to capitalise on traffic passing along the major rivers of the region; (ii) an identification of appropriate intersections of road and water; and (iii) a site allowing as short a distance as possible between the market and the port, thus reducing or eliminating the costs of transporting goods to or from the river to the market.

   The successful examples are famous: King's Lynn (Norfolk) was founded c. 1096;[37] St Ives (Hunts.) was reinvented as a centre for commerce around 1107–1110, at the same time that a new bridge was constructed over the Ouse to funnel traffic into the town;[38] Ely underwent a similar metamorphosis between 1109 and 1131 through a series of strategic investments – the award of a seven-day fair (almost certainly formalising an earlier market), the deliberate diversion of the Ouse in order to bring river traffic right up to the island at Ely, and the construction of a causeway between Ely and Stuntney, bringing road traffic from Suffolk and north-east Cambridgeshire into the port;[39] and at Crowland (Lincs.), the river Welland was diverted in the late Saxon period to run through the centre of a planned settlement laid out outside the monastic gates.[40] By about 1200, when a market was granted, the Abbots of Ramsey laid out a planned market and settlement integrated with their newly constructed lode (the Great Whyte) from which they appear to have traded in tile, horses, cattle, grain and other produce.[41] Not all planned markets were successful: Reach was a collaborative foundation by the abbeys of Ely and Ramsey of, perhaps, the early twelfth century, and is the best-known Cambridgeshire example to have failed – to the extent that it did not develop into a local market and does not even appear in the list of inland ports in England between 1294 and 1348, although its annual fair survived into the modern period.[42]

The priors and bishops of the large monastic estates who founded these towns were not the only manorial lords with aspirations to commercial success. The attempts of minor lords to emulate them can be seen in the thirteenth- and fourteenth-century market grants made to rural fen-edge settlements which were connected to the larger rivers by lodes.[43] The location and layout of these settlements reveal that comparable criteria were applied to the choice of their sites: the possibility of enticing passing river traffic down the lode; the intersection of road and water transport systems; and the potential for ensuring close proximity of market and hythe. Most such foundations were relatively unsuccessful, perhaps because lodes were in practice *culs-de-sac* and had few intersections with major land routes. Swavesey, for example, had evidently been a trading centre for at least two centuries before it received a formal market grant in 1244, since the name itself records a hythe (*Suauesheda*, 1086).[44] The grant more or less coincided with the construction of two large docks, around which burgage plots were laid

out and to which the settlement focus appears to have shifted.[45] At Cottenham, the rector rather than the manor of Crowland acquired a market grant in 1265, either capitalising on the hythe behind his rectory at the north end of the settlement, or constructing it at the same time.[46] The market may have been held in the wide street which separated the rectory from the church, and appears to have stimulated the development of a new settlement focus over arable strips nearby.[47] There is little to distinguish the morphology of such settlements, with their formal market places and the regularity of their planned messuages, from similar places elsewhere on the uplands – except for the inclusion of a hythe in their settlement plans. In both cases, lordship and commerce came together to influence settlement form and development either by creating an extension to an existing village or by re-forming its layout.[48]

On the other hand, there are two, or perhaps three, places in fenland which never received a market grant, but which nonetheless achieved a moderate commercial success – Littleport, March and (possibly) Aldreth. All three appear to have been initiatives of the Bishop of Ely intended to exploit and control existing trading activities, while protecting the major markets at Wisbech and Ely. Of the three, only Littleport was a vill in its own right in 1086, the other two being subordinate to other centres; and all lie either on the boundaries of the Ely estates or facing a significant area of fen.

A planned settlement was laid out at Littleport on the banks of the Old Croft River, possibly in the eleventh century, almost certainly replacing earlier ribbon development.[49] It was set out around a large rectangular open space, bordered on the north by the river and its riverbank hythes (whose alignments are still preserved in Hythe Lane). The church lay at the south-west corner of this space, and was itself flanked to the south and east by regular, planned blocks.[50] The initial nucleation at March may have been around the parish church of St Wendreda at Town End;[51] by the mid-thirteenth century, a sizeable planned focus (*Mercheford*) had appeared well over 1 km to the north at a ford over the river Nene, now redirected in an artificial course across, rather than around, the island on which March stands.[52] Aldreth lies where a substantial medieval causeway across the fen enters the Isle of Ely. The maintenance of the causeway formed part of the labour dues of very many fenland vills – a substantial investment by both the Abbots and Bishops of Ely.[53] The boundaries of 15 properties lying in a block along the eastern side of the catchwater drain at the head of Aldreth Lode, together with their shared Back Lane, suggest a planned settlement, although the aratral (reversed S) curves of their boundaries perhaps show that they were laid out over former open-field strips. The only evidence that such planning was intended as a commercial centre is that, by the nineteenth century, this area was called The Borough. A large triangular hythe survives in the angle where lode and catchwater meet, and a large triangular green at the head of the causeway.[54] Aldreth appears, though, always to have been a small, insubstantial place.

The history of Reach at least may demonstrate the inhibiting influence on the development of a trading settlement of a location at the end of a lode where it was more difficult to attract passing traffic compared with settlements along the major rivers, even if (as at Aldreth) there was a link to a major through-route. March and Littleport, perhaps because they lay on substantial natural watercourses, grew into large villages even without market grants and connections with the upland by road; however, being isolated by the surrounding fen before drainage in the seventeenth century, they never expanded into trading centres which could rival the planned towns. They do show how nuanced the effects of communications by water might be in the commercial development of the fens.[55]

The peasantry and commercial development

It is clear that peasants also generally understood the importance of waterborne transport to the local economy. Freeholders and lords, for example, together constructed the thirteenth-century lode and hythe on the northern edge of Landbeach;[56] in 1376 villagers at Swaffham Bulbeck 'asserted their immemorial right to carry merchandise along [Swaffham Lode] by boat … while Cambridge men were using boats on it *c.* 1435'.[57] This importance is also evident in the gradual colonisation of common-field strips along the catchwater drains leading into the lodes which can be seen in many fenland settlements like Aldreth, Reach, Burwell, Wicken and Isleham, or along the northern

bank of the Nene at March. Many of the properties backing on to these watercourses still contain the remains of private cuts.[58] On the other hand, the public pools and hythes which survive along such catchwaters in many of the places already cited may have been dug by communities for their own use, rather than at the direction of lords, since many are not in any sort of proximity to manorial centres. At Isleham, for example, while it is true that both manor house and priory were each served by their own cut leading up from the catchwater, there were at least two other larger quays which were most easily reached either from public roads or from peasant tofts created by encroachment on open or agricultural land.[59]

Participation in local or regional trade, either by selling fen products or by undertaking some craft specialisation based on them, seems to have been so common as to be unremarkable.[60] The larger proportion of tenants listed in the Ely Coucher Book in 1251, for example, had no surnames, while the surnames which distinguished the remainder recorded the conventional occupations of any village, fen or upland (shepherd, cowman, etc.). Indeed, only a few had craft names – like the weaver and felter at Wilburton, or the harness-maker at Lyndon in Haddenham.[61] An even smaller number were listed as merchants or traders. Some, such as Osebius *mercator* at Bottisham or Raduly *mercator* at Burwell in 1279, were based in settlements with a market; many vills without a market in 1251, however, also included similar men, such as John *mercator* at Stretham, John *le Chapman* in Doddington, and Peter *chapman* in *Merchforde*.[62] A *hoker*, perhaps a hawker, lived in Willingham at the same date.[63] As in Breckland, there is some evidence of specialists in transport, like the *maryner* based in Haddenham in 1251, Adam *seman* at Isleham in 1279, or the carters at Somersham, March and Fen Ditton in 1251.[64] Such men were mostly customary tenants, although, perhaps significantly, a few paid a commuted rent, like Vincent *mercator* at Littleport in 1251. Trade must have been an integral part of daily life even though it is difficult to quantify.[65]

Smaller rural settlements

Despite all the evidence for medieval peasant trade and transport along the lodes and rivers of the

Cambridgeshire fens, a significant difficulty soon becomes apparent when one moves to consider the relationship between the lodes and rural settlement. Generally speaking, medieval settlement in or on the edge of the peat fens was not focused on the lodes – most, in fact, was separated from them by some distance. Where settlement was polyfocal, it was the subordinate hamlets that lay in proximity to the hythes rather than the major centre in each community where the church and manor(s) were located. Take, for example, the best known of the Cambridgeshire lodes – those running from the Cam towards the eastern fen-edge: Bottisham Lode, Swaffham Lode, Burwell Lode and Wicken Lode. The churches and older manorial centres of the medieval settlements at Bottisham, Swaffham Bulbeck, Swaffham Prior, Burwell and Wicken lie between 1.5 and 3 km from the ends of their respective lodes. The lodes' ends were far more likely to be characterised by minor, peasant settlement which remained small. In Bottisham, for instance, a secondary settlement actually called Lode had developed around a small triangular basin at the lode's end by the mid-twelfth century.[66] At Swaffham Bulbeck, the earliest known settlement focused on the lode is a late twelfth-century Benedictine priory, which may itself have formed the focus for a lesser settlement called Newnham by the late fourteenth century.[67] The medieval manor house and settlement around the early thirteenth-century church at Swaffham Bulbeck is about 2.5 km from the Lode. Swaffham Prior lies almost halfway between the landfalls of Swaffham Bulbeck and Reach lodes. The twelfth-century church and castle at Burwell appear to succeed a mid- to late Anglo-Saxon settlement focus about 3 km south of the end of Burwell Old Lode.[68] Although two subsidiary foci lay a little way to the north, the first was closer to the church than to the lode, and the second (North Street, 1351) was the result of the gradual colonisation of open-field strips along the catchwater drain which fed the lode, and was at least 1 km from the end of the lode.[69] Although Burwell was one of 62 'important inland ports' in England between 1294 and 1348, this is not reflected in its settlement plan when compared with, for example, Cambridge, Ely or St Ives.[70]

The problem of the connection between settlement and lodes receives more force from Taylor's twin conclusions that medieval settlement along the fen-edge tended to be polyfocal, and that each focus had ancient antecedents.[71] If this interpretation is correct, then settlement foci in each parish should be distinguished as dominant and subordinate, rather than primary and secondary. Thus, at Bottisham there were eight or nine settlements in the twelfth and thirteenth century, each with some evidence for earlier origins;[72] similarly, each of the four medieval manor houses at Swaffham Prior lay close to the site of a Roman settlement.[73] The Bishop of Ely's manor at Doddington included Wimblington and March, both recorded well before the Norman Conquest, while the three components of Haddenham – Linden End, Hill Row and Haddenham – were each mentioned in Domesday Book, yet Aldreth (at the end of the lode) was not recorded until the late twelfth century.[74] In no case was the dominant settlement located at the end of the lode; nor, as commerce expanded during the High Middle Ages, did indicators of dominance (manorial centres, churches, the major proportion of the population) shift towards the lode. Opportunities for trade and the ease of transport offered by the lodes seemingly had little general influence on the region's rural settlement pattern, in contrast to the effects of market grants on some upland villages.

Even a market grant was not necessarily sufficient to change this pattern. Late thirteenth-century market grants were made at both Bottisham and Burwell, though most probably the market in each took place some distance from both the lode's end and the catchwater drains:[75] the Bottisham market was presumably held on the widened village street in front of the church; that at Burwell was 'at the manor' of Robert Tybotot, which might mean the site of the manor house in the widening south end of the High Street near the church.[76]

The distinction between planned commercial centres and rural villages cannot be explained in terms of lack of access to water or lack of use of watercourses for transport. Almost every fenland community had the opportunity to develop the means for waterborne transport and almost all seem to have taken it. By the mid-thirteenth century there was a multiplicity of man-made watercourses across the fenland basin connecting uplands with rivers which might be several miles distant across the fen (see Feature Box: *Key Theme*, p. 214). In 1251 the fens around Doddington alone, for example, were crossed by *Sumershamlode*,

Key Theme: Landscape Management and the Fenland Economy

The undrained peat fen supported a landscape of interlaced, watery micro-environments – meadow, reed, rush, sedge, osiers, wood and peat – linked by watercourses, and interspersed with lakes and meres. It is often assumed that this landscape provided its rich harvests with little or no significant human intervention. Nonetheless, there is plentiful contemporary evidence to the contrary of the careful and deliberate use of cropping regimes, timetables for access, and techniques of water management aimed at the maximised exploitation of a wide range of non-arable crops, each dependent on a specific micro-ecology, harvested for long-term environmental sustainability.[77]

The higher parts of the fen (the 'hards') were perhaps only a metre or two above their surroundings and usually peat-free, but provided poorer quality grazing for non-dairy herds throughout most of the year. On lower grounds closer to Ordnance Datum rich natural water meadows 'were dry in summer, and the winter floods, provided they did not last too long, served only to make the meadow richer for the following summer', offering two mowings of the rich whiteseed grass called 'fen hay'.[78] There was rough pasture in overgrown carr fen, while wetter areas could be exploited in varying cropping rhythms for reed, rush, sedge, osiers, wood or peat. In many fenland parishes the local specificity of such qualities is preserved in their names: Smithyfen (1343 Cottenham, smeeth, 'marsh in smooth lowlying land'), Frith (1326 Landbeach, 'winter fodder, brushwood', including rough pasture), Stacks (1251 Willingham), Hasse (1404 Soham, hassuc, 'coarse grass'), Foderfen (1325 Soham), Horsecroft (1343 Soham), or Segfrythfen (1345 Wicken, 'sedge fodder fen').[79] The greatest physical risks to this economy were winter floodwaters which might not arrive, or might not recede, in time for grass to receive its maximum benefit, depriving the dairy herds of their early 'bite'. Unseasonal flooding in late spring, summer or early autumn posed yet another hazard.

From the late Anglo-Saxon period onwards there was widespread construction of canals, drains and ditches, to assist the flow of water across flat landscapes that were otherwise slow to drain, and of catchwaters to carry upland floodwater straight into canals or the major rivers, and re-routing or straightening of existing watercourses.[80] They all demanded consistent maintenance and, sometimes, further construction (Figure 13.3).

Figure 13.3. Soham Lode passing eastwards through East Fen Common. (Photo © Hugh Venables, and licensed for reuse under the Creative Commons Licence, http://www.geograph.org.uk/photo/2061916)

Such works were not undertaken in order to extend arable, but to regulate the length of time that grasslands lay inundated and hence to maximise the productivity of natural water meadows. When the Well Stream was blocked at Upwell in the early fourteenth century, fens and meadows were drowned as far away as Thorney and St Neots, and complaints were not about the flooding of reclaimed arable land, but about interference with the degree of control that men expected to be able to exert over seasonal levels of water in their pastures.[81]

Here is the wider context of the lodes and catchwaters – useful for trade and transport, but perhaps more generally constructed to allow the management of water across an almost level, slow-draining landscape.

Wilberwykelode, Traveslode, Hymelode, Cokeslode and *Danelode*, while *Edyvelode, Wertelode* and *Alderhelode* lay across the marshland between the southern uplands and the Isle of Ely at Wilburton.[82] Scope for using boats, punts and other craft on these canals was extended by the catchwater drains which ran from each lode's landward end along the contours of the winter floodline. Langdon suggests that the lodes were used as 'feeders' for long-distance trade along the rivers.[83] Although he has also proposed that national trade along these secondary routes might have been intermittent or seasonal, evidence from the Suffolk Breckland suggests that they were fairly consistently used for local or regional transport throughout the year; indeed, lists of the carrying duties of the Bishop of Ely's customary tenants are not differentiated by season, implying that these tasks might be required at any time.[84]

That such artificial waterways were well used by boats is attested by the innumerable landing places which were recorded by the mid-thirteenth century both as place-names and as surnames.[85] They also survive as field monuments in a variety of forms: as substantial artificial promontories facing on to a lode, and bounded on either side by a cut large enough to take a fair-sized craft (for example at Burwell and Reach); as triangular or rectangular basins in which boats might turn as well as tie up (as at Lode, Isleham and Willingham); as hythes or wharves along one or both sides of the landward end of a lode (like those at Wicken, Little Downham and Swaffham Bulbeck); and as relatively minor, narrow cuts which led from a lode or its catchwater feeder on to the tofts of medieval peasants, as can still be seen at Burwell, Reach and March.[86] Some of these vessels will have been large enough to be sea-faring.[87]

Taylor's work on small rural markets has forcefully

demonstrated the extent to which they focused on maximising the advantages of communications with traders, consumers and other markets.[88] Yet, at the point of intersection of water and road, rural settlement in the peat fens generally remained subordinate, small and (relatively) impoverished in contrast to the layout of the planned towns. There was no shift of manorial focus, for example, from Waterbeach to Clayhithe, Cottenham to Church End, Wicken to Wicken Lode, Little Downham to Downham Hythe, Witcham to Witcham Hive, Isleham to Waterside, or from the manor house at Linden End in Haddenham to Aldreth. The populations clustering around the hythes generally tended to be small, poor and economically marginal (although there were a few exceptions like Lode which contained some prosperous trading families from the mid-twelfth to the early thirteenth centuries).[89] At Little Downham in 1311, for instance, Moricius *atte Hethe*, Nicholaus *atte Hethe* and Thomas *atte Hethe* were all paupers, too hard-up to contribute towards the maintenance of the causeway from Coveney; and a high proportion of those presented in the manorial courts came from Downham Hythe: Avicia *atte Hith* was fined for breaking the assize of ale, Simon Morice made an illegal fishweir in the water of the hythe, and Moricius was fined for the illegal sale of 200 turves.[90] It may be that 'villages on the fen edge provided important debarkation posts for the passage of goods', but if wealth was created by movement and sale of goods along the fenland waterways, this is not usually reflected in the settlements around the hythes themselves.[91] Methwold Hythe, Suffolk, mentioned by 1277, 'produced nothing other than a couple of concentrations of unexceptional medieval material' even though the settlement was large enough to have its own church, while at Little Downham hythe

Figure 13.4. Witcham. Key: yellow: area of hythe; purple: medieval church and churchyard; red: medieval site of manor; orange: core medieval settlement; blue: medieval catchwater drain. (Ordnance Survey 1884, Sheet XXXV SE, 2½":1 mile, with amendments)

excavation has uncovered some evidence of imports yet almost none of settlement.[92]

Two examples, at Witcham and Wicken, one on the fen-edge, the other on the Isle of Ely, one without and one with a medieval market grant, illustrate the problem. Witcham (Figure 13.4) remained one of the demesne manors of the monastery at Ely, and later the Dean and Chapter, from the tenth to the twentieth centuries. It was never particularly productive of arable crops, but produced fair returns of wool and skins from the sheep which grazed on the fen.[93] In the thirteenth century the site of the manor lay some distance to the east of the settlement.[94] By the time of Parliamentary enclosure in 1838, settlement in the parish lay in two nuclei: a strongly nucleated settlement called Witcham, and two cottages at Witcham Hive (hythe) about 1.5 km north of the village.[95] The major

settlement at Witcham is dominated by a large, fairly regular rectangle bounded by Hive Lane on the west, High Street on the south, and Back Lane on the north. If surviving properties in 1838 are any indicator, the block may have been divided into about 13 properties, each of approximately the same width, into which the thirteenth-century church (and the post-medieval manor house) appears to have been a later insertion.[96] There is a relatively close correspondence between this figure and the 12 leaseholding sokemen on the manor in 1086 which might just indicate that nucleation and settlement planning occurred in the eleventh or early twelfth centuries, although there is currently no archaeological evidence to reliably establish this inference.[97] The vicissitudes of multiple phases of population growth and decline seem to have resulted in further expansion over the arable fields to the south

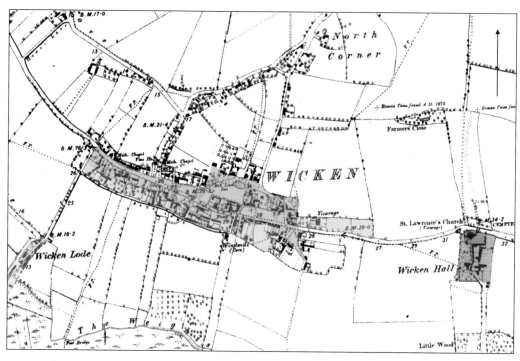

Figure 13.5. Wicken. Key: yellow: area of hythe; purple: medieval church and churchyard; red: medieval site of manor; orange: core medieval settlement; blue: medieval catchwater drain. (Ordnance Survey 1884, Sheet XXXV NE, 2½":1 mile, with amendments)

of the High Street and, by the twelfth century, to the west of Hive Lane; further medieval settlement, later deserted, lay to the east.[98] Although by 1838 the greater number of dwellings lay opposite the church on the southern side of the High Street, the irregular back boundary to these properties, and uncertainty about the western and eastern limits to the block within which they lie, suggests that they fossilise later stages of the flow and ebb of population expansion, decline and shift across the settlement and its open-field strips over the past 800 years.[99] The hythe lay at Witcham Hive on a catchwater drain to the north of the settlement and was first documented in 1251; Agnes *atte hethe* lived there in 1306.[100] In 1838 just two cottages were present of which only one remains; but there is no evidence to suggest that settlement there was ever substantially larger.[101] The point is, of course, that the initial nucleation was detached from the hythe and that, even if the hythe were a later development, it does not appear in any period to have exerted any significant pull on population in the parish.

The site of the pre-Conquest and medieval manor at Wicken (Figure 13.5) and the church which it owned lie together about 800 m to the east of the core of the nucleated settlement. A few cottages line the end of Wicken Lode, about the same distance to the south-west of the centre of the village.[102] The medieval settlement, both in planned and in informal arrangements, appears focused on a long W–E green between the two.[103] The ten half-yardlanders and 13 quarter-yardlanders of 1279 may have been accommodated in a long block facing north on to the High Street (whose western end was called North Street in 1413), bounded at the rear in 1840 by Back Lane.[104] In 1331 the manor received the grant of a market which may have taken place on the green, where two pits containing medieval pottery have been found.[105] Several fifteenth-century houses and other archaeological evidence confirm that the site of the village remained fairly fixed throughout the medieval period. By the later fifteenth century dwellings had begun to encroach upon the northern boundary of the green, a process which continued into the nineteenth century.[106] As at Witcham, the lode may have had little influence on the settlement pattern, either in the medieval period or after.

Exploring the problem

How might the apparent indifference of rural settlement to the potential of waterborne transport be explained, when the benefits were so clearly recognised elsewhere? The produce of the estates of the Abbey and of the Bishop of Ely still had to be conveyed to the markets at Ely, Wisbech or Sutton, and to other parts of the estate (as the carrying services emphasise), even if monastic lords did not wish to establish markets in other parts of the Isle which might grow to rival their nominated commercial centres. And a man who had to undertake carrying duties for his lord, and/or had common rights in the fen, would still have to move bulky fenland products – bundles of reed or sedge, boatloads of fish or wildfowl – from the hythe back to his messuage, to the manorial centre, or outside the settlement. The costs of transferring goods between boats and carts on land could, over just a short distance, begin to nullify savings gained by carriage by water.[107] The closer that both manor house and messuage were to the water, the cheaper and more efficient transport would be and the greater any surplus.

A number of potential explanations present themselves. First, perhaps a combination of surface geology and the relationship between the settlement and the winter floodline could create conditions which might inhibit a settlement of any size? While attractive at the outset, this possibility is soon dispelled by an examination of the maps of the Geological Survey.[108] Second, perhaps the lodes post-dated settlement nucleation? It is certainly true that the origin of most of the lodes is obscure, and that lodes were being constructed throughout the medieval period[109]; but, on the other hand, a fair volume of documentary and archaeological evidence exists to show at least some of the lodes were in active use before the Norman Conquest.[110] The most authoritative conclusion is that of Hall, who suggested, on the basis of extensive fieldwork, that the north-east Cambridgeshire lodes 'are of late Saxon or early medieval date'.[111] Most Cambridgeshire settlements were nucleated between

AD 950 and 1250.[112] The polyfocal arrangements at Haddenham, for example, seem fixed by the late tenth century when Haddenham, Hill Row, Hinton and Linden were all listed in a charter.[113] An eleventh- or twelfth-century date has been suggested for settlement planning at Witchford, Wilburton, Wicken, Littleport and Witcham.[114] Both the lodes and settlement nucleation therefore appear to have been developments of more or less the same period, in the later part of which there was rapid, if uneven, expansion of trade by water.[115] Settlement planning elsewhere has demonstrated how willing lords were to divert roads towards a market or around a park, or to lay out a market at a distance from a settlement. The diversion of an existing land-route towards a lode's end would certainly have been straightforward if a pre-existing lode had been regarded as an enticing location for settlement. Settlement shift towards the sites of new medieval markets in the uplands demonstrates the potential for similar processes in the fens, even if a lode was constructed after the settlement pattern had become reasonably fixed. The relative chronology of lodes and settlement history cannot explain the disjunction between the location of manorial centres and churches, and the ends of the lodes.

Alternatively one might argue that peasants did not understand the potential for transport and trade offered by the lodes. However, this seems extremely unlikely given, for example, the carrying services on the Bishop of Ely's manors which were explicitly intended to be undertaken by water. Certainly at Ramsey (Hunts.), smallholders and landless peasants regularly communicated within a region made up of 'a cluster of four to five neighbouring vills', and wealthier peasants operated within a region at least 17 miles in diameter, while others have calculated that local trade generally operated in a radius of ten miles.[116] Traders from the hamlet at Lode were able to accumulate a noticeable volume of wealth by the 1160s.[117] The physical evidence of small, private cuts leading up into peasant tofts from the catchwater drains at places like Reach, Isleham and Burwell often occurred where there was secondary ribbon development on arable land or encroachment on open spaces (see Feature Box: *Key Sites to Visit*, p. 219). Although they support Gardiner's contention that new foci for waterborne trade were generally the result of peasant rather than lordly activity, they do not

Key Sites to Visit: Reach and Burwell

There is a wealth of evidence on the ground for anyone wishing to explore the landscape of medieval water-management along the fen-edge. It is fragmentary, with some elements preserved better in some places, and others more visible elsewhere. Taken as a whole, however, they allow the visitor to reconstruct with some accuracy the extent of such works in the medieval fen. Two sites within a few miles of each other along the north-east Cambridgeshire fen-edge are suggested here: Reach and Burwell.[118]

As Reach Lode nears its landfall, about 100 m from the fen-edge, it divides, capturing between its arms a long, narrow promontory of higher ground. This was a huge medieval hythe reaching NNE into the fen and connected at its landward end with the site of a large planned market, also medieval, now partly obscured by encroachment. The canal along the eastern side of the promontory is now much less obvious than that to the west. A small footbridge leads south-westwards from the hythe across one of the arms of Reach Lode to the fen-ward side of the water, and it is possible to follow the catchwater drain which runs along the fen-edge, draining the upland into the lode. Careful scrutiny of the banks on the landward side of the drain reveals the remains of minor cuts along which small boats were once taken up on to the properties which lined it.

At Burwell, a few miles to the north-east, lie perhaps the most complete remains of a medieval canal system anywhere in the fens (Figure 13.6). The traveller should make for Hythe Lane in the northern part of the village, and begin his explorations by walking westwards down that lane towards the fen-edge. Hythe Lane was once, as its name suggests, a public landing place (although not the only one in Burwell). Originally it had the same structure as that at Reach: a piece of land made into a promontory by a large ditch on either side along which boats could tie up. The southern ditch has disappeared, obscured by recent building, but that on the north still survives as a large (generally dry) cut.

On the west Hythe Lane and its northern ditch meet the catchwater drain (The Weirs) which, as at Reach, runs along the fen-edge into Burwell Lode. A footpath takes the explorer across to the fen-ward side on to a track which runs on top of a raised bank along the Weirs to its junction both with Burwell Lode and with a second catchwater leading down from the north. Once more, careful examination of the riverbank on the landward side

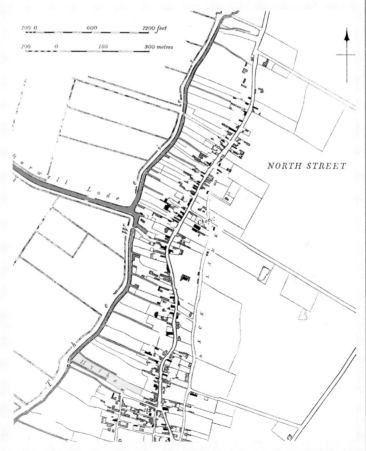

Figure 13.6. Lode, medieval catchwater drains, and private cuts at Burwell. Key: yellow: area of hythe; blue: lode, medieval catchwater drains, and private cuts. (Reproduced with permission from RCHM 1972, fig. 25, with amendments)

of the Weirs reveals the remains, some more complete than others, of small private cuts which once led some distance into the properties which lined the canal, a number of which continued to be used well into the nineteenth century. A small promontory hythe survives at the junction of the Weirs and Burwell Lode, where a bridge leads the explorer back into the village and the aptly named Anchor public house.

appear to represent a substantial shift in settlement towards such new places.[119]

A third possibility is that trade only occurred if there was a market grant and that the lodes were otherwise only used for transport within a manor. This proposition can quickly be dismissed: the presence of traders in mid-thirteenth-century settlements without a market grant has already been demonstrated, and it is clear that peasants of all status and in all communities showed some engagement in trade.[120]

Britnell has noted that 'even over short distances trade benefited from roads or water communications *of above average quality*'.[121] Perhaps the quality of transport along the lodes was too poor for a sufficient volume of trade and transport to develop? There are, for example, records of summer water shortages preventing the passage of laden boats as at Cottenham in 1431; and in the early eleventh century Cnut had to come to Ely by wagon rather than by boat because 'of the excessive frost and ice in the locality, the marshes and meres being frozen all around'.[122] On the other hand, it is difficult to know how frequent or exceptional such events were. The multiplicity of hythes and landing places along the lodes suggests that water transport was an intrinsic part of medieval working life in the fens, and the evidence for carrying services and for trade are all consonant with the conclusion that the 'most convincing evidence for extensive navigation' is between the eleventh and the thirteenth centuries.[123] Yet, although this was the same period in which settlement was particularly subject to planning, the connection between rural settlements and their lodes remains tenuous.

Perhaps again, it was the character of existing activity where the lodes made landfall that inhibited settlement at that point? Gardiner has suggested that 'new ports did not grow at estate centres or places of feudal administration, but at new places' or at places where trading and/or industrial activity was already well established.[124] This certainly appears to be true for the larger, planned commercial centres of

the Middle Ages, but it is difficult to recognise the smaller, fenland settlements in this description. There can be little doubt of the extensive activity each rural community undertook within the fens, or of the primary and secondary products resulting from this activity; 'trading and/or industrial activity' even if only on a local scale surely happened in nearly every rural settlement in the peat fens, but the lodes and hythes did not provide the magnet for settlement.

Silvester has noted that along the west Norfolk fen-edge settlement patterns changed in the late Saxon and medieval periods, shifting away from the fen-edge.[125] The argument for a move away from the fen-edge is, however, more difficult to sustain in the Cambridgeshire peat fens. While there *are* some places where settlement lies at a greater distance from the fen-edge, these can almost always be explained by the local topography – such as the steepness at Wilburton and Sutton of the slopes of the islands rising out of the fens. On the other hand, medieval settlement at Swaffham Bulbeck, Burwell, Isleham, Willingham and Landbeach does run along the fen-edge – but at a distance from the lodes.

That some hythes may have been intended to serve several places might explain why they were rarely located at the point of production.[126] Fen Ditton is a good example of this: it was a major 'local collecting centre' for the sale of grain from the Ely manors, even though it never had a market grant or developed into a trading centre.[127] There, the settlement lay alongside a river rather than a lode, and at least one and probably two substantial hythes were integrated into the settlement plan.[128] The Crowland manor at Cottenham was famously a collecting centre for its Cambridgeshire estates, yet the manorial centre was not located near the head of the lode, and the market grant went to the rector rather than the manor.[129] If manorial ports were carefully managed, this does not explain why peasants who engaged in more local trade did not begin to focus their settlement on their local hythes. Why did small clusters of houses at places like

Downham Hithe or Witcham Hive, which served only one settlement centre, or larger developments like Burwell North Street or Lode which served several settlement foci, never develop into central places themselves? This is not, of course, to argue that every small hythe had the potential to become a large trading centre; that is plainly not a feasible proposition. But the question nevertheless remains why, if lodes and hythes were so central to trade, and if trade was such an integral part of everyday life in the medieval fenland, the dominant centres of settlement in each parish were not located at the lodes.

Conclusion

There are clearly, then, problems in attempting a functional explanation for the distance between hythes and the dominant medieval rural settlements of the Cambridgeshire peat fens. Access to waterborne transport does not seem to have been a primary consideration in the location of the dominant settlement in rural vills either at the time of their foundation or later, unlike the major commercial centres of the day. This is not to argue that the exploitation of fenland products and access to markets were not important to medieval peasants and their lords – just that they were not important *enough* to outweigh the pull of other factors. Perhaps more fruitful directions for explaining this phenomenon are those of peasant productivity, commercialism and entrepreneurship, an investigation of the perspectives of peasants who might have been planning for subsistence and/or leisure rather than for wealth?[130] Both Chayanov and Boserup, for example, suggested that peasant productivity was proportionate to the levels required for subsistence.[131] Dodds has reported recent research suggesting that peasant arable output may have been higher than that of the demesnes given the availability of familial labour, the probable higher level of enthusiasm for the task, and the availability of all household waste, including their own, for manuring their fields.[132] As has already been argued, the contribution of the fen to the peasant economy through pasture for cattle and sheep, and the cropping of reeds, sedge, peat and so on were likely – just as in the seventeenth century – to assure greater levels of wealth for peasants with low acreages of arable land. Medieval peasants along the fen-edge may have

been able to achieve acceptable levels of subsistence, protected against the worst effects of land-hunger and population increase before 1300 by a combination of the higher productivity of their arable land, the variability of rich fen resources, and ready waterborne access to local and long-distance trading networks. They may, by contrast with their upland counterparts, have been able to practise rather than dream about 'a preference for greater leisure'.[133] As Dodds has observed, 'having the capacity to raise productivity is not the same as actually doing so'.[134] Among the villagers of Montaillou, for example, it was important for the head of a household 'to be a good neighbour, but not to kill himself with work', wherever possible shortening 'the working day into half a day'.[135] The consistent distances between smaller medieval centres and the landward ends of the Cambridgeshire lodes suggest that perhaps medieval peasants were as alive as we are to a 'work-life balance'. Although the lodes clearly played an important part in the fenland economy once they had been built, in many places the production of a surplus through trade and transport does not necessarily appear to have provided the principal motivation for their initial construction.[136]

Further reading

Readers wishing to explore the origins and development of medieval settlement will inevitably begin with the seminal work of Christopher Taylor. Since so much of Taylor's work has centred on Cambridgeshire, the scholarship of medieval settlement studies is interwoven with exemplars from this county. The best overview of the discipline is still that of *Village and Farmstead* (London, 1983). An interest in planned settlement and the origins of moats underpins *West Cambridgeshire* (RCHME, 1968); the expansion of settlement forms a major focus of *North-East Cambridgeshire* (RCHME, 1972). RCHME volumes on Northamptonshire and Lincolnshire are as important, exploring the reasons behind change and continuity in settlement morphology. A series of papers on the influence on medieval settlement of market grants, of pasture, and of the designed landscapes of parks and gardens appear in *Landscape History*, the journal of the Society for Landscape Studies, and many more in volumes of the *Proceedings of the Cambridge Antiquarian Society*.

For those interested in the impact on settlement of wetland ecology and environment, two publications by H. C. Darby provide an essential starting point – his *Medieval Fenland* (Cambridge, 1974) and *The Draining of the Fens* (Cambridge, 1956). The results of parish-based studies of the history of the fen landscape for the English Heritage Fenland Project, using methods pioneered by David Hall (who also completed much of the survey), were reported in *East Anglian Archaeology*, especially volumes 35 (1987), 45 (1988), 56 (1995) and 79 (1996).

Few activities are as enjoyable as exploring existing or deserted settlements on foot. Two books will set any reader off with informed enthusiasm: although now achieving the venerability of age, neither has yet (in this writer's mind, at least) been surpassed – Maurice Beresford's *History on the Ground* (Cambridge, 1957) and Christopher Taylor's *Fieldwork in Medieval Archaeology* (London, 1974).

Acknowledgements

Christopher Taylor, David Hall, Dr Nicholas James, Dr Mark Gardiner, Professor Michael Chisholm and Dr Paul Spoerry kindly read and commented on earlier drafts, but mistakes and misconceptions remain my own.

Manuscript sources

CA	Cambridgeshire Archives	
Haddenham	Parish Survey, 1806	TR836/E/A-B
Haddenham	Tithe map, 1869	578/P1
Littleport	Inclosure Map, 1836	R57/31/40/108
March	Map, c. 1680	R51/23/3
March	Tithe map, 1840	R51/28/1
Wicken	Draft Inclosure Map, 1840	152/P19
Wicken	Inclosure map, 1840	Q/RDc 69
Witcham	Draft Inclosure map, 1838	152/P20
Witcham	Inclosure Map, 1839	R52/10/17
CCC HER	Cambridgeshire County Council Historic Environment Record	
CUL	Cambridge University Library	
EDR/G3/27	Ely Coucher Book, 1251	

Published primary sources and printed maps

| DB | *Domesday Book: Cambridgeshire*, A. Rumble (ed.) 1981: Phillimore, Chichester |

LE	*Liber Eliensis: A History of the Isle of Ely*. Janet Fairweather (trans. and ed.) 2005, Boydell: Woodbridge
OS	Ordnance Survey of Great Britain, First edition, 6 inches to the mile
Aldreth	Sheet XXIX SW, 1886
Littleport	Sheet XXII SE, 1885
March	Sheet XVI NW, 1886
Wicken	Sheet XXXV NE, 1886
Witcham	Sheet XXV SE, 1887
OS GS	Ordnance Survey Geological Series, 1:50 000: Southampton
Sheet 158	Peterborough (158)
Sheet 159	Wisbech (1995)
Sheet 172	Ramsey (1995)
Sheet 173	Ely (1980)
Sheet 187	Huntingdon (1975)
Sheet 188	Cambridge (1981)
Sheet 189	Bury St Edmunds (1982)
Rot. Hund.	*Rotuli Hundredorum 1279*, Volume II, 1818, London

Notes

1. RCHME 1968, 1972; Taylor 1974a. Christopher Taylor was the principal author of the settlement analyses in the RCHME volumes on Cambridgeshire, and has also published extensively on settlement in south Cambridgeshire. A sample of his output is represented in the bibliography. See also Ravensdale 1974 and 1986; Oosthuizen 1993, 1994, 1997, 2002.
2. Figure 13.1; Bailey 1989, 153.
3. Edwards and Hindle 1991; Edwards and Hindle 1993; Langdon 1993; Jones 2000; Langdon 2000.
4. Carus-Wilson 1964, 195; Summers 1973, 13.
5. Masschaele 1993.
6. RCHME 1972, lxv–lxvi; Taylor 1995b; Spoerry *et al.* 2008, 185–196.
7. Britnell 1992: 86, 114; Bailey 1989, 143–158; Jones 2000, 61.
8. Hall 1992, 3–6; Elstobb 1793, 28, 91–92; Summers 1973, 10–13, 18.
9. All place-names are in Cambridgeshire unless otherwise noted.
10. Hall 1992, 6–8.

11. Blinkhorn 2005; though see also Hall 1987, 1992, 1996.

12. Neilson 1920, xl–xlix; Miller 1951, 13, 43; Raftis 1957, 153.

13. CUL EDR/G3/27; Miller 1951, 80. The manors with two or three fields were Little Downham, Linden (Haddenham), Sutton, Wilburton and Littleport.

14. Silvester 1993, 37.

15. Mawer and Stenton 1926, 211; Hall 1992, 54.

16. Hooke 2007, 40–41. See also, for example, RCHME 1972, 43 and 81–82; Hall 1996, 35 and 174; Fowler 1931–32, 1932–33, 1934; Carr *et al.* 1985; Milne and Goodburn 1990; Good *et al.* 1991; Cole 2007.

17. Britnell 1992, 79; Metcalf 2003, 47; Palmer 2003; Barrett *et al.* 2004; Gardiner 2000a, 84; Gardiner 2006b, 36; Spoerry *et al.* 2008, 173.

18. Britnell 1981, 18–19.

19. Gardiner 2007a, 88.

20. Silvester 1993, 34–38; Langdon 1993; Gardiner 2007a.

21. Owen 1984, 42, 49–50; Campbell *et al.* 1993, 181.

22. CUL EDR/G3/27; Darby 1974, 101–106. Regional and local products can be glimpsed through those which the Bishop of Ely required to be carried by water between his manors, or between his manors and the ports: cheese, building timber, underwood and firewood, grain, hay, sheaves of reeds, wood and underwood, mill stones and livestock: CUL EDR/G3/27.

23. DeWindt 1987, 194–195; Bailey 1989, 143–158; Britnell 1992, 97–99.

24. DeWindt 1987; Bailey 1989, 157–158.

25. Bailey 1989, 158–191.

26. Darby 1974, 22–38; Spufford 1974; Britnell 1992, 114.

27. The material in this box is based chiefly on Spoerry *et al.* 2008.

28. For example: RCHME 1972, parish essays; Hall, 1987, 1992, 1996; Silvester 1988, 1991, 1993; Hayes and Lane 1992; Oosthuizen 1993; Taylor 1995b.

29. Spoerry *et al.* 2008, 173.

30. *VCH Cambs.* 9, 250.

31. LE II: 106.

32. Blinkhorn 2005, 62–65; Cherry 2001, 200–203; Spoerry *et al.* 2008, 203; though see Hall 1987, 103.

33. Hall 1996, 112; Gardiner 2006b, 36; Bond 2007, 181–182.

34. E.g. Owen 1984; Beresford 1967; Beresford and St Joseph 1979.

35. Beresford 1967, 100; Owen 1984, 7.

36. Beresford 1967, 105–109, 136; Edwards and Hindle 1991, 133.

37. Owen 1984, 7–9. Professor Chisholm points out that Boston (Lincs.) was, of course, as important.

38. Beresford 1967, 456; Beresford and St Joseph 1979, 182–183.

39. Fowler 1932–33, 22; *VCH Cambs.* 4, 36–37; Taylor 1995b, 273; Hall 1996, 39–40; Darby 1974, 108–109.

40. Hayes and Lane 1992, 200–202; Langdon 1993, 5.

41. Spoerry *et al.* 2008, 180, 199–205.

42. Taylor 1995b; *VCH Cambs.* 10, 225–227; Langdon 1993, 5.

43. Medieval market grants to rural settlements in the Cambridgeshire peat fens were made at Bottisham (1298–99), Burwell (1277), Cottenham (1265), Fordham (by 1233), Rampton (1270), Sutton (1311), Swaffham Prior (1309), Swavesey (1244), and Wicken (1331), Letters 2003.

44. *VCH Cambs.* 9, 377 and 390; Reaney 1943, 172–173.

45. Ravensdale 1974, 145 fn.

46. *VCH Cambs.* 9, 63.

47. Ravensdale 1974, 122.

48. Taylor 1982, 21.

49. Hall 1996, 27; see also Hall 1996, 76; Silvester 1993, 38; Johnson 1995.

50. CA Littleport R57/31/40/108; OS Sheet XXII SE.

51. Pestell 2004, 93.

52. Hall 1987, 46; Taylor 1995b, 272–273; *VCH Cambs.* 4, 116; CUL EDR/G3/27.

53. Darby 1974, 109–111.

54. CA Haddenham TR836/E/A–B; CA Haddenham 578/P1; OS Sheet XXIX.

55. March eventually grew into a substantial small town in the post-medieval period encouraged by fen drainage, which allowed connections by road for the first time, only receiving its market grant in the seventeenth century.

56. Ravensdale 1974, 26–27, 127, and 1986, 37; Taylor 1995b, 267; Reaney 1943, 180.

57. *VCH Cambs.* 10, 263, my additions.

58. E.g. RCHME 1972, 43, 89–90; Taylor 1995b, 267; Oosthuizen 1993.

59. Oosthuizen 1993, 31–32.

60. De Windt 1987; Biddick 1987; Bailey 1989, 158–166.

61. CUL EDR/G3/27.

62. *Rot. Hund.* II, 488 and 499; CUL EDR G3/27.

63. CUL EDR G3/27.

64. Bailey 1989, 154; *Rot. Hund.* II, 505.

65. CUL EDR/G3/27.

66. Reaney 1943, 131.

67. *VCH Cambs.* 10, 249–250.

68. RCHME 1972, 41.

69. Taylor 1974a, 76–77; Reaney 1943, 188–189.

70. Langdon 1993, 5.

71. Taylor 1974a, 54–69.
72. Taylor 1974a, 58–59.
73. RCHME 1972, 115, 128–129.
74. Hall 1992, 72; *VCH Cambs.* 4, 112–113; DB 5:52–54.
75. *VCH Cambs.* 10, 213; Letters 2003.
76. *VCH Cambs.* 10, 343–344.
77. Oosthuizen in prep.
78. Darby 1974, 62.
79. Reaney 1943, 150, 174–176, 180, 198–204, 344, 367.
80. Cook *et al.* 2003.
81. Dugdale 1662, 301–306.
82. CUL EDR/G3/27.
83. Langdon 2007, 3.
84. Ibid.; Bailey 1989, 153–155; CUL EDR/G3/27.
85. For discussions of medieval boats: Friel 1995, 35; Goodburn 1991; Greenhill and Morrison 1995.
86. Taylor 1995b, 267; Oosthuizen 1993; RCHME 1972 parish sections. Gardiner 2007a, 85, has suggested a useful typology of ports ('a settlement, the economy of which was substantially based on river- or seaborne traffic'), hythe ('site adjoining a river without a significant settlement at which boats may be pulled up or moored'), and landing places ('anywhere a boat might be grounded, pulled up or moored'). This does not help in fenland, however, in distinguishing between, on the one hand, Aldreth or Swaffham Bulbeck, each of whose hythes was associated with some settlement (how large does a settlement have to be to be 'significant'?), but where that settlement was subordinate to a centre elsewhere in the parish; and on the other hand somewhere like Witcham or Little Downham whose hythes were all but deserted by settlement, yet may have supported similar volumes of traffic.
87. *VCH Cambs.* 9, 391.
88. Taylor 1982.
89. *VCH Cambs.* 10, 192.
90. Coleman 1996, 33–35, 73.
91. Bailey 1989, 154.
92. Silvester 1993, 37; CCC HER.
93. *VCH Cambs.* 4, 173.
94. Reaney 1943, 245; Hall 1996, 51.
95. CA Witcham 152/P20 and R52/10/17.
96. Ibid.
97. In 1086 there were 12 sokemen holding on average around 18 acres each, two *villani* with ten acres each and two with five acres each, four *cottari* and two *servi*, DB 5:62.
98. CCC HER.
99. CA Witcham 152/P20 and R52/10/17; OS Sheet XXV SE.
100. CUL EDR/G3/27; Reaney 1943, 245.
101. CA Witcham 152/P20 and R52/10/17; OS Sheet XXV SE.
102. By the fourteenth century the parish contained at least four other nuclei at Upware, Thornhall, Spinney and Dimmock's Cote: Reaney 1943, 203–205.
103. *VCH Cambs.* 10, 553. See also Wicken 152/P19 and Q/RDc 69; OS Sheet XXXV NE.
104. *Rot. Hund.* II, 504. A figure not substantially different from the 11 *villani* and 8 *bordarii* in 1086. DB 14:74; CA Q/RDc 69, 1840.
105. CCC HER.
106. CCC HER; Wicken 152/P19 and Q/RDc 69; OS Sheet XXXV NE.
107. Langdon 1993, 7.
108. OS GS Sheets 158, 159, 172, 173, 187, 188, 189.
109. Silvester 1993, 36–37; Hall 1992, 40.
110. See. for example, Mawer and Stenton 1926, 185, 216; Hart 1966, 164, 38; RCHME 1972, lv; Hall 1996, 114; Cherry 2001, 200–203; Blinkhorn 2005, 62–65; LE 1: Prologue and II, 53, 102.
111. Hall 1996, 112.
112. Taylor 1974a; 1992, 8; Oosthuizen 1994; 1997.
113. Reaney 1943, 231–234.
114. Above; Oosthuizen 1994.
115. Barratt *et al.* 2004, 627, 630; Britnell 1978, 188.
116. DeWindt 1987, 188, 191; see also Britnell 1992, 82–83; Biddick 1987, 291.
117. *VCH Cambs.* 10, 192.
118. The text in this box is largely drawn from RCHME 1972.
119. Gardiner 2000a, 84.
120. DeWindt 1987; Biddick 1987; Bailey 1989, 158–166.
121. Britnell 1981, 20.
122. *VCH Cambs.* 9, 51; LE II, 85.
123. Jones 2000, 72.
124. Gardiner 2000a, 84.
125. Silvester 1991, 38.
126. Gardiner 2007a, 91.
127. Miller 1951, 86; *VCH Cambs.* 10, 118.
128. RCHME 1972, 49, 63.
129. Page 1934; *VCH Cambs.* 9, 63.
130. Dodds 2008, 80–87.
131. Chayanov, cited in Dodds 2008, 84; Boserup 1965.
132. Dodds 2008, 80–87.
133. Dodds 2008, 86.
134. Dodds 2008, 87.
135. Le Roy Ladurie 1978, 340, 339; see also Dodds 2008, 81.
136. Cf. Oosthuizen 2000.

CHAPTER 14

Norfolk, Suffolk and Essex: Medieval Rural Settlement in 'Greater East Anglia'

Edward Martin

The physical setting

'Greater East Anglia' is a useful way of describing the territory that lies between the Thames estuary in the south and the Wash in the north, with a long North Sea coastline on the east and a land border on the west that, in the Middle Ages, ran through wet fenland for much of its northern half. The addition of Essex to Suffolk and Norfolk (the two counties normally accepted as constituting East Anglia) not only makes a coherent geographic unit, but it also makes the area's human geography more understandable. Recent studies have shown that there is a previously unrecognised cultural boundary running through Suffolk.[1] When Norfolk and Suffolk are considered alone, there is an imbalance towards the northern part of the unit; this is redressed if Essex is added as a southern counterbalance.

The region's lowland English landscape, despite Noel Coward's gibe about the flatness of Norfolk, is generally one of gently rolling countryside. Its solid geology consists of strata that dip gently from west to east, with the oldest (Jurassic) deposits exposed in the west and the youngest (Neogene) in the east. Chalk underlies most of the western half of the area, but disappears under Crag sands in the eastern parts of Suffolk and Norfolk, and London Clay in eastern and southern Essex. These largely soft materials – chalk, uncemented sands and clays – were planed by the ice-sheets of the great Anglian Glaciation (*c.* 475,000 to 425,000 years ago) and when the glaciers retreated they deposited a thick mantle of chalky boulder clay or till (greatest in the Chedburgh/Rede area of Suffolk where thicknesses in excess of 50 m have been proved by boreholes) over much of the central heart of the region. Much of this till was derived from Kimmeridge Clay deposits gouged out of the Fen Basin, admixed with chalk. On either side of the central clay plateau, which is one of the dominant features of the East Anglian landscape, there are extensive sand deposits formed through a mixture of the surface weathering of underlying material and of glacially derived outwash and wind-borne sands or fine loess. These give rise to the distinctive sub-regional landscapes of Breckland (north-west Suffolk/south-west Norfolk), the Sandlings (south-east Suffolk), the Good Sands (north-west Norfolk) and the Rich Loam District (north-east Norfolk) (Figure 14.1).

The drainage pattern is predominantly one of broad-valleyed rivers that flow east or south-east, often ending in significant coastal estuaries: the Crouch, Chelmer and Colne in Essex; the Stour forming the Essex/Suffolk border; the Gipping, Deben, Alde and Blythe in Suffolk; the Waveney forming part of the Suffolk/Norfolk border; and the Yare, Bure and Ant in Norfolk. The main exception is on the western edge of the region, where the Great Ouse and its tributaries – the Lark, the Little Ouse and the Wissey – drain northwards through the Fen Basin into the Wash. Some of the wider interfluves can have significant water problems, either a lack of it, as in the sandy soil areas of Breckland or the Sandlings, or too much, as in some parts of the clayland plateaux where the

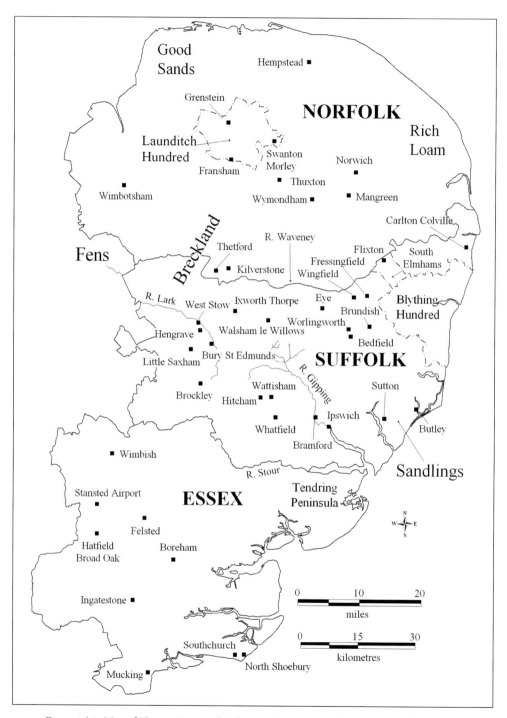

Figure 14.1. Map of 'Greater East Anglia' showing the principal places mentioned in the text.

gradient is slight or where there are actually concave depressions, resulting in poor drainage. This of course has significant implications for agricultural potential. Until the advent of modern irrigation techniques, large parts of the sandy soil areas were unsuitable for arable crops because of summer moisture deficits. Instead, those areas had large heaths that were primarily used as sheep pastures. On the clays, good drainage was the vital factor for arable farming and this naturally occurred where the land sloped, as in the more dissected parts of the plateaux in south Suffolk and Essex. The flatter parts of the clayland had to wait until the introduction of effective under-field drainage before realising their arable potential. Buried drainage trenches filled with stones, woody material and straw, called 'Hollow-ditching' or 'thorough-draining', are mentioned as a 'late invention' in 1727 and were in widespread use by the end of the eighteenth century, but it was the introduction of long-lasting fired-clay tile or pipe drains in the early nineteenth century that made the greatest difference (*draining tyles* were certainly in use at Playford in Suffolk by 1817, but their cost inhibited their greater adoption until the repeal of the tile tax in 1833).[2] Before then the dominant use of these clayland plateaux was as cattle pastures, having often progressed from woodland to wood-pasture and then to open grassland.

The landscape and its settlement morphologies

In common with most of lowland England, East Anglia has a farmed landscape, and can even claim an iconic 'Englishness' through its depiction in the works of artists such as John Constable and Thomas Gainsborough. Today it has few areas of dramatic scenery or extensive wildernesses, though in the past it had a share of the huge eastern England fens (largely drained and parcelled into fields in the seventeenth and eighteenth centuries), zones with extensive sandy heaths (much reduced and converted into farmland or forestry plantations in the nineteenth and twentieth centuries) and coastal marshes (progressively drained and enclosed for farming from the Middle Ages onwards, but now threatening to revert through the erosion of coastal defences).

If now thought of as a mainly rural area, East Anglia was in fact one of the most populated regions of England by 1086 (and throughout the Middle Ages) and one of the wealthiest – in terms of taxable wealth in 1334, Norfolk ranked third out of 39 English counties, Suffolk was sixth, and only Essex trailed at twenty-sixth.[3] Most of East Anglia had arable land values above the national average and included some of the highest value.[4] To this farming wealth was added a growing importance as a cloth-producing area. Woollen cloths were already being produced there in 1200, but the trade grew substantially in the fourteenth century, so much so that Suffolk became the pre-eminent textile manufacturing county in England in the fifteenth century.[5] The wealth generated by this trade resulted in the building of magnificent churches in 'wool towns' such as Lavenham and Long Melford.

The level of population in medieval East Anglia can come as a surprise because, in general and compared to the midlands, East Anglia has a dispersed settlement pattern, though there are variations in the level of dispersion.[6] The lowest levels of dispersion are to be found on the western side, particularly in north-west Suffolk and west Norfolk, and in the Sandlings of south-east Suffolk and the Tendring peninsula of north-east Essex. In these areas the farmsteads are more likely to be collected into villages and hamlets. Elsewhere the farmsteads characteristically lie at intervals along the winding lanes, each set within its own group of fields. Noticeably, there is also a recurrent pairing of medieval churches and manorial halls, usually in prime valley-side locations close to a water supply. Where there are water-retentive soils, these halls are often surrounded by water-filled moats. On the clay plateaux farmsteads are also often found fringing the edges of greens, some extant and some now reduced to enclosed 'landscape ghosts'. These greens (also called commons or tyes) were communal pastures that ranged in size from under an acre to several hundred acres.

Building materials

The geological background gave only limited opportunities for good building materials. In a few areas the sands are cemented, as in parts of the Lower Cretaceous deposits on the western fringe of Norfolk, giving rise to a sandstone, called carstone, which was widely used as a building material in western Norfolk.

The Crag Sands of eastern Norfolk and Suffolk are also occasionally sufficiently cemented to be used as a building stone, as in the tower of Chillesford church in Suffolk. Outcrops of hard chalk, termed clunch, were exploited on the western edge of the area, both for vernacular buildings and for church interiors – sources include pits at Lakenheath in Suffolk, Thetford in Norfolk and at Burwell, Barrington and Orwell in Cambridgeshire. The chalk deposits were also burnt to create lime for mortar and plaster. The Eocene London Clay deposits of south Suffolk and Essex contain calcareous mudstone concretions, called septarian nodules or just septaria. Although these weather badly, they were extensively used in the building of Colchester and Orford castles, as well as many churches. Across southern Suffolk and Essex the sporadic sarsen boulders (residual hard fragments or 'clasts' from a layer of otherwise uncemented or poorly cemented Palaeocene sand) were favoured for the foundations of some of the medieval churches. Otherwise, the numerous flints from the chalk provided the main building stone for the region. The irregular flint nodules were usually set, unmodified, in generous beds of mortar giving a relatively rough appearance. But, from the early fourteenth century, struck flints with smooth black or grey surfaces and often shaped into regular squares were frequently applied to churches as a decorative facing called flushwork. Often this was combined with imported white Lincolnshire limestone to create elaborate black and white patterns.[7]

The most important building material for domestic use was, however, timber and particularly oak. The earliest surviving timber-framed buildings date from the late twelfth century, but by then the tradition was already well established.[8] East Anglia, and Suffolk and Essex in particular, has one of the highest concentrations of medieval timber-framed buildings in England; but framed buildings leave little trace in the ground, as was revealed in the medieval settlements of Grenstein and Thuxton in Norfolk, where the buildings were mainly defined by gaps in the cobbling of the associated yards.[9]

The twelfth century also saw the region's huge clay resources starting to be exploited for brick-making.[10] The full potential of this material was realised around 1270–80 with the construction of Little Wenham Hall in Suffolk – this being probably the earliest English building constructed mainly of brick.[11] By AD 1600 bricks were strongly rivalling timber as the preferred material for houses in this region.

History of research in the region

Research on East Anglia's medieval archaeology and landscape initially lagged behind work on its prehistory, which had a very long and high-profile history extending back to the eighteenth century with John Frere's momentous recognition that the deposits and flint tools he saw in a brick pit in Hoxne, Suffolk, belonged 'to a very remote period indeed, even beyond that of the present world'.[12] Progress owed much to three strands of work originating in the mid-twentieth century. In 1955, Keith Allison published a survey of deserted medieval villages in Norfolk, having been inspired by the national work on DMVs by his friend and tutor, Maurice Beresford, who in turn had been inspired by his Cambridge tutor, John Saltmarsh, who had suggested medieval settlement desertion as an explanation of the numerous ruined churches in the Norfolk part of Breckland.[13] These works further inspired a number of other Norfolk-centric studies.[14] The dating of settlements was crucially aided by John Hurst, a co-founder with Beresford of the Deserted Medieval Village Research Group in 1952. In 1956–57 he produced the classification of the region's Middle and Late Saxon pottery: the first, named as Ipswich Ware, was dated to *c.* AD 650–850; and the latter, named Thetford Ware and St Neots Ware, to *c.* AD 850 to the twelfth century.[15] Thirdly, the publication of W. G. Hoskins's *The Making of the English Landscape* in 1955 was the inspiration for a number of county-based landscape studies in the next few decades.[16]

Aspects from all three of these strands, together with the new strand of systematic fieldwalking, were brought together in the 1970s in Peter Wade-Martins's study of settlement patterns in Launditch Hundred in Norfolk.[17] Fieldwalking surveys by individuals and groups formed an important element of the settlement research in the next 30 years, some published but with others only accessible through the county Historic Environment Records (HERs).[18] The 1970s also saw the establishment of county council-based archaeological services in all the East Anglian counties and, linked to these, the beginning of the influential *East Anglian Archaeology* monograph series. Despite this, excavations targeted specifically on medieval rural sites in this region have not been particularly numerous or large scale.[19]

When the Moated Sites Research Group produced its first national total for moats in 1978, those in this region comprised 24 per cent of the 5,307 then known. Essex with 548 and Suffolk with 507 had by far the largest county totals – Yorkshire, in third place, trailed with 320 and Norfolk, with only 206 was equal-seventh with Bedfordshire.[20] The county totals since then have grown – Essex had 855 in 1997, Norfolk had 'about 800' in 2005 and Suffolk can now muster at least 925 – but it is likely that East Anglia has retained its national dominance.[21]

The ubiquity of moats in Essex was no doubt a major factor in its early lead in the study of moats. It was an Essex antiquarian, Isaac Chalkley Gould, who played a key part in the formation and running of the Ancient Earthworks and Fortified Enclosures Committee of the Congress of Archaeological Societies which, in 1901, produced the first classification scheme for earthworks, with moats as Category F.[22] Gould advocated the inclusion of earthworks into the *Victoria County History* volumes, contributing to the first Essex volume and several others; he also was advocating a survey of Essex moats shortly before his death in 1907 and had already produced a list of nearly 400.[23] A fellow enthusiast, Charles Wall, wrote a guide to the different classes of earthworks and penned the earthworks section of the first volume of the Suffolk VCH, noting that in its number of moats Suffolk was 'especially remarkable', with no less than 505.[24] Two of the first national studies of moats, in 1910 and 1935, drew attention to the large number of moats in East Anglia, but were more concerned with the history of the houses within the moats than with the significance of the moats.[25] It was not until well into the second half of the twentieth century that East Anglian moats started to be studied again, but even then the number of excavated examples was, and is, surprisingly small.[26]

Despite being distinctive features of the East Anglian landscape, greens seem to have excited little historical or archaeological interest in this region before the 1960s, though the settlement significance of greens had been recognised elsewhere.[27] Interest in greens, initially in landscape terms, was sparked

by the Royal Commission on Common Land 1955–58, the national survey of commons 1961–66 and the influential publications arising from them, together with the Commons Registration Act of 1965.[28] The frequency of the occurrence of greens in East Anglia, and something of their character, was noted by both Smith and Dymond, but the first archaeological approach to their origins came with Wade-Martins's work in Launditch Hundred, where, from fieldwalking evidence, he suggested that there had been a major 'shift of settlement' from *nuclei* around the churches to the green edges from the twelfth century onwards.[29] Peter Warner's 1987 study of Blything Hundred in Suffolk was critical of Wade-Martins's reliance on pottery to date greenside settlements and he instead used a more documentary-based approach, though he too has been criticised for putting too great a reliance on a few finds of Late Saxon metalwork and the presence of medieval churches on a very small number of greens to suggest an origin for greens in the ninth or tenth centuries.[30] He did, however, acknowledge that these continued to develop in the eleventh, twelfth and early thirteenth centuries. Susan Oosthuizen has also canvassed a Saxon origin for greens in Cambridgeshire, based on topographical analysis, but fieldwork in Suffolk has tended to reinforce the view that greenside settlements start in the twelfth century, while similar work in Norfolk indicates possible origins in the eleventh century.[31]

The Anglo-Saxon settlement origins

Two of the most extensive and influential excavations of Early Anglo-Saxon settlements in England took place in this region: at Mucking on a Thames-side gravel terrace in southern Essex, and at West Stow on a low sandy knoll beside the River Lark in Suffolk.[32] At West Stow the settlement comprised three groupings of halls and sunken-featured buildings, interpreted as three family units. This settlement gradually decayed in the seventh century, with 'new' settlements being established elsewhere in the vicinity.[33] This was seen as an example of the 'Middle Saxon Shift', whereby settlements were moved from light but relatively poor soils to heavier but richer soils – a move that could also be linked with the Christianisation of the population and the establishment of churches as settlement *foci*.[34] At the larger Mucking settlement it was suggested, instead, that there had been a constant but slight drift of about ten households along the terrace, which could have been incorrectly interpreted as a series of separate settlement clusters of different dates.[35] Parallels were drawn with the *Wandersiedlungen* ('wandering settlements') that have been identified in the Continental homelands of the Anglo-Saxons, where they appear to be part of a tradition that stretches back to the Iron Age.[36] However, more recently, the Mucking interpretation has been challenged and an alternative model of two contemporaneous and static settlement *foci* has been proposed.[37] Irrespective of which of these two interpretations is correct, it does seem that the settlement area was abandoned in the seventh or eighth century.[38] Similar end dates are suggested for several of the more recently excavated Early Saxon settlements in the region, for instance Carlton Colville, Eye and Flixton in Suffolk and Kilverstone in Norfolk.[39] Fieldwalking in south-east Suffolk has similarly shown only small amounts of Ipswich Ware (starting *c.* AD 720) on the earlier Saxon sites.[40]

Little attention has, however, been paid to the fact that all the substantial Early Saxon settlements that could be described as villages or hamlets are either located on the Thames estuary or to the north of the 'Gipping Divide' (see Feature Box: *Key Theme*, p. 236; Figure 14.2). There is a distinct lack of evidence for this type of settlement in south Suffolk and north Essex. Only two of the 31 sites examined in connection with the major Stansted Airport expansion (1986–91) in north-west Essex produced evidence of Early Saxon occupation, and both had only minimal quantities; but environmental evidence from the same area indicates a very open landscape with mixed farming in the period AD 530–680.[41] One explanation could be that the settlements are less archaeologically visible because they are significantly smaller – individual farmsteads rather than the hamlets/villages of the other areas.

For the subsequent Middle and Late Saxons periods there is, overall, much less in the way of excavated settlement evidence at the ordinary domestic level. Excavated sites of these periods are mainly aristocratic and/or monastic – such as at Brandon and Butley in Suffolk.[42] One of the exceptions is an isolated building found *c.* 100 m to the north of Takeley church in the Stansted environs in north-west Essex, which has produced a radiocarbon date of cal. AD 670–880.[43] The proximity to a medieval church is probably significant, for fieldwalking from 1983–88 of a sample area of 134 km² in south-east Suffolk showed that all the major scatters of Middle Saxon Ipswich Ware were located near the medieval parish churches.[44] This in turn matched the findings of earlier fieldwork in Norfolk.[45]

Burhs and the hall-and-church complexes

There are, however, some significant Middle Saxon sites that are not near an extant church, as was discovered on the White House Industrial Estate in the northern outskirts of Ipswich in Suffolk (see Feature Box: *Key Excavation*, p. 232; Figure 14.3). This site, with its enclosure containing both buildings and a cemetery, may be a precursor of the hall-and-church complexes that that are a strong and recurrent feature of the East Anglian landscape.[46] These hall-and-church complexes often consist of a roughly square area that contains a church in one quarter, as can be seen at Wattisham in Suffolk, where the churchyard nestles in the north-west corner of a square enclosure of 7.2 acres, defined by a simple ditch, that contains Wattisham Hall and its barns. Similar layouts appear at Brockley (see Feature Box: *Key Site to Visit*, p. 242; Figure 14.4), Sutton (7.8 acres) and Wingfield (4.7 acres).[47] At North Shoebury in Essex a complex of about 6 acres was partially excavated and was found to contain an inner sub-rectangular enclosure with sides that were roughly parallel with those of the outer one; the inner enclosure was defined by a ditch 4 m wide and 1.5 m deep which contained an area of at least 1.3 acres, with its north-western corner seemingly overlapped by the rectangular churchyard (the exact relationship was not confirmed by excavation). The lower fills of this ditch produced eleventh-/twelfth-century pottery.[48] This inner enclosure, with its slightly overlapping churchyard, is reminiscent of the Late Saxon (*c.* AD 950–1139) settlement excavated at Trowbridge in Wiltshire, where a small rectangular churchyard abutted the north-east side of partially excavated but probably sub-rectangular enclosure of about an acre that contained a post-hole building,

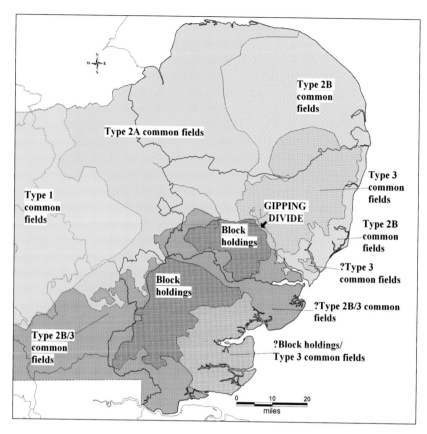

Figure 14.2. Map of the medieval farming regions of Greater East Anglia. This is an interpretative map drawing on historic landscape characterisation mapping together with other historical, cartographic and geological data (developed from Martin and Satchell 2008: fig. 35). Key: Type 1 common fields are the 'classic' two- or three-field systems found in the midlands; Type 2 are similar but less strictly regulated and frequently with larger numbers of fields (subtype A are closer to Type 1, and B to Type 3); Type 3 are the least regulated, often limited in extent and usually enclosed very early. Block holdings are groupings of hedged fields belonging to one owner or tenant (otherwise called 'land in severalty').

both enclosures being defined by ditches that were *c.* 2 m wide and up to a metre deep.[49]

There are further parallels in the layouts excavated at Raunds Furnells in Northamptonshire, where a roughly square area of about 2 acres contained both a Late Saxon (estimated here as *c.* AD 900–1200) timber hall complex and a cemetery with a small church. The complex was defined, and internally subdivided, by lengths of ditches, none of which were wider than 1.5 m or more than 0.7 m deep. The church probably went out of use in the thirteenth century, being superseded by the church of a twin

complex situated about 250 m to the south-east, across the valley of the Raunds Brook. This complex was also only partly excavated, but superficially its churchyard formed a similar, but larger (*c.* 4.7 acres) sub-rectangular complex with its adjacent manor, the Burystead.[50]

The occurrence of the name Burystead at Raunds provides a link to the elusive Late Saxon thegnly fortifications called *burhs*. A possession of a *burh* by a person of noble rank is implied in the laws of the Anglo-Saxon kings and more explicitly in an early eleventh-century tract called *Geþyncðo* on the

Key Excavation: Middle and Late Saxon Settlement site on the White House Industrial Site, Ipswich, Suffolk

Excavations here in the 1990s revealed a D-shaped enclosure that measured approximately 80 x 100 m (approximately 2 acres) within which were two rectangular building, with a third building just outside it (Figure 14.3).[51] This settlement overlay an earlier Iron Age and Roman settlement and was characterised by Middle Saxon Ipswich Ware (4.2 kg), with lesser amounts of Late Saxon Thetford Ware (2.5 kg) and Early Medieval Ware (0.7 kg), suggesting that the settlement was most active from about AD 720 to 850, but was then in decline down, possibly, to the twelfth century. The northern part of the enclosure also contained a small cemetery with 16 certain graves and a few possibles. These contained

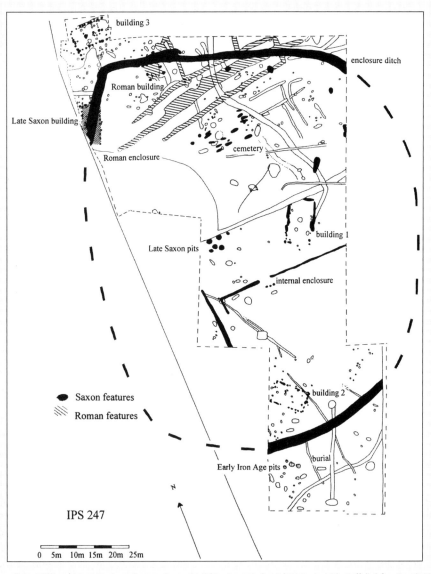

Figure 14.3. Plan of the Middle and Late Saxon settlement site on the White House Industrial Estate, Ipswich, Suffolk (after Caruth 1996: fig. 103)

bodies with their heads to the west, suggesting that they were Christians. Two of the graves were radiocarbon dated, yielding dates of AD 870–1050 and 890–1020. No associated church or chapel was identified, though there were both gaps and uncertain structures in the vicinity that might have accommodated one. The settlement could have been in existence at the time of Domesday Book, but it is not immediately recognisable. Then and later it formed a part of the parish of Bramford, whose medieval church lies about a kilometre to the south-west of the enclosure, on the other side of the River Gipping. By the nineteenth century the site was unoccupied farmland, but it could have been the predecessor of Lovetofts, a farmstead 500 m to its south-east. This was the site of one of the sub-manors of Bramford, taking its name from its first recorded holder, a royal administrator named John de Lovetot (c. 1236–1294), but with no certain history before his possession of it.

Early medieval Bramford was a major but complex royal estate, containing two churches – one at Bramford itself and the other at what is now Sproughton – as well as possessing the berewicks of Burstall and Albrihtestou.[52] The last named has possible parallels with the White House site in that Middle Saxon pottery has been found near the site of its medieval chapel (long gone) dedicated to St Albright (possibly to be identified as St Æthelbeort, the King of East Anglia martyred in AD 794), which is in turn is only about 350 m from the Early Saxon cemetery (active from the sixth to, possibly, the early eighth century) excavated at Boss Hall.[53] It is possible that both the White House site and Albrihtestou are examples of arrested development of Middle/Late Saxon sites towards a fully developed hall-and-church complex.

qualifications for thegnly status. (Note: the words in round brackets, below, only occur in one version of the text.):

> If a *ceorl* [farmer] prospered so that he had fully five hides of his own land, (church and kitchen), bell (house) and *burh-geat* [*burh* gate], seat and special office in the king's hall, then was he henceforward entitled to the rank of thegn.[54]

Burhs should therefore have been as numerous as the thegns certainly were, yet the accepted examples were surprisingly few, such as Goltho in Lincolnshire, Sulgrave and perhaps Earls Barton in Northamptonshire.[55] The number of examples has risen slightly in recent years, but can perhaps still be counted on the fingers of two hands.[56] A large part of the problem probably lies in the expectation by archaeologists for *burhs* to have substantial fortifications. They may, however, have been more usually 'defended' by simple ditches and hedges/fences. Thus the ditch excavated at the White House site only measured 2.8 m wide × 1.4 m deep, while that at North Shoebury was only slightly larger at 4 × 1.5 m. The modest nature of 'private' *burh* defences is further suggested by several eleventh-century references to *burhheges* ('*burh* hedges').[57] The principal 'show' might have been reserved for the gate, hence

the emphasis on the *burh*-gate in the qualifications for thegnhood. This would make the *burh* much more like the *curtis* or enclosed house yard of the Germanic law codes, where the enclosure was both a protective fence and a legal definition of property rights.[58] A definition of a *burh* – and probably its derivatives (*burh-stall*, *burh-stede* and *burh-tun*) too – as the enclosure around a noble person's house, rather than as a strongly fortified place, would solve some of the problems that place-name scholars have had in explaining some of the names where *burhs* seem to be associated with women or even priests. This would also explain the Middle English use of the term to mean 'a manor house' or an 'estate'.[59] It may well be significant that in the southern part of this region (Essex, south Suffolk – also Middlesex, Berkshire, Hertfordshire and Cambridgeshire) the manors associated with hall-and-church complexes are frequently dignified with the suffix 'bury' – as, for instance, Felsted Bury in Essex.[60]

Overall, there is a suggestion that modest Late Saxon hall enclosures of one or two acres that were considered *burhs* by their owners, often with abutting churchyards with private chapels, were enlarged in the early medieval period (eleventh to twelfth centuries) to accommodate more farmstead buildings and associated yards, together with the larger churchyards that served the enlarged chapels that had become parish churches, to form the hall-and-church complexes of four to nine acres that are recognisable on modern maps.

In some parts of England it is possible to discern a framework of early large parishes (termed *parochiae* by modern historians) that were served by teams of priests operating from important central churches known as *minsters* (Old English *mynster*, derived from Latin *monasterium,* meant both a monastery and a major church served by a group of clergy).[61] In East Anglia the pattern seems to have been seriously disturbed by the period of Viking rule; for instance, the minster that was founded by St Botolph at Iken in Suffolk in AD 654 was probably destroyed by the Vikings in the winter of 869/70, as may have been the rich monastery at Barking in Essex.[62] However, some minsters survived or were refounded, since tenth-century wills indicate minsters at Barking and Mersea in Essex, and Bury St Edmunds, Hoxne, Mendham, Stoke-by-Nayland and Sudbury in Suffolk.[63] Several other minsters can be inferred from the Domesday record on account of their large endowments: for instance, St Peter's in Ipswich (720 acres), St Mary's in Thetford (712½ a. and four dependent churches), Blythburgh (240 a. and two dependent churches), Eye (240 a.) and Long Melford (240 a.). In the case of Wymondham in Norfolk, a minster has been postulated to explain a massive parish of 10,950 acres that forms the hub for an encircling wheel of 19 parishes.[64]

In the tenth and eleventh centuries the number of churches grew much greater as thegns founded their own churches, so much so that King Edgar issued an ordinance in AD 959–63 to regulate the tithes that were owed to the 'old minsters' in the face of competition from churches that thegns had established on their own lands.[65] There may have been a genuine religious intent for these foundations, but one suspects that the incentive for thegns to have their own churches was as a visible confirmation of their status, as the eleventh-century qualifications for thegnhood clearly indicate. It is in this context that the hall-and-church complexes came into being, the family cemeteries in or adjacent to the *burhs* being enhanced by the addition of a chapel or church. The Suffolk section of Domesday Book lists no less than 418 churches, the greatest number for any English

county – perhaps justifying the county's nickname of 'Silly [Old English *sælig* 'blessed'] Suffolk'. More significantly, this means that four out of every five of the known medieval churches were then in existence. It also implies that the framework of major settlements, particularly the hall-and-church complexes, was largely established by 1086; although smaller numbers of churches are recorded for Norfolk (only 274) and Essex (a mere 17), it is likely that it is true for the region as a whole.

Nucleated and dispersed settlements

Some hall-and-church complexes grew into hamlets or villages, but large numbers in the East Anglian landscape remained as small units. These sometimes excited speculation that they were the remains of deserted villages, but as early as 1954 Maurice Beresford had noted that the search for deserted villages in Suffolk was 'complicated by the occurrence of the isolated church as a normal feature, with farms scattered or gathered at a Green some distance from the parish church'.[66] This very dispersed settlement pattern has been confirmed by the mapping work of Roberts and Wrathmell, who noted low numbers of nucleated settlements (hamlets, villages, market towns) in most of East Anglia (notably in Essex, Suffolk and southern Norfolk), contrasting a figure of 55 nucleations per 25 × 25 km square with figures of 70–80 in the English Midlands, where the nucleated settlements were not only more numerous but larger. It is only in north-western Essex, the western fringes of Suffolk, western Norfolk, with smaller areas in the Broads of north-east Norfolk, the Sandlings of south-east Suffolk, and the Tendring peninsula of north-east Essex that the settlement pattern is significantly more nucleated.[67] These are also the areas of East Anglia where the evidence for the former existence of common fields is strongest.[68] The causal link between common fields and nucleated settlements has been clearly demonstrated in the English midlands, where both are well evidenced.[69]

Stephen Rippon has argued recently that the nucleated settlements of northern East Anglia resulted from the replacement of an earlier dispersed settlement pattern by nucleated villages from the eighth century onwards – a movement that was associated with the emergence of common fields.[70] However, as noted above, there seems to have been a pre-existing tendency for 'villages' in this northern area and what Rippon has seen as coalescing settlements may in fact just be moving settlements. The wandering tendency of these settlements may have been slowed down by the agricultural intensification that starts around the eighth century and which seemingly led to a greater formalisation of field systems and property boundaries. In some areas this led to the emergence of common fields by the tenth century, but not in all areas, especially in southern Suffolk and Essex, where a dispersed settlement pattern with isolated farmsteads surrounded by their own fields has continued down to the present day (see Feature Box: *Key Theme*, p. 236).

A corollary of this uneven distribution of nucleated settlements is that deserted medieval villages in East Anglia are almost exclusively a feature of its northern part, and especially of Norfolk, particularly its western half. In this, and in its much higher proportion of common fields, Norfolk is more like the English midlands than the rest of East Anglia. The greatest concentration of deserted settlements and abandoned churches is in Breckland, where the prevalence of dry sandy soils tended to make some of the settlements marginally viable.[71] Tying down the reasons for desertions is difficult, because on examination many of the examples dwindled slowly, probably for a variety of reasons – economic, climatic and social. Similarly, the date of the desertions is often not medieval, but comes in the sixteenth, seventeenth or eighteenth centuries, when emparking was a significant factor.[72]

Greens and tyes

A more widespread and very distinctive feature of the medieval East Anglian landscape was its greens – areas of common pasture surrounded either densely or intermittently by houses, depending on the green's size (Figures 14.4 and 14.5).[73] Although widespread, these greens, also called 'tyes' in the southern part of the region, are very much a feature of the clayland parts of East Anglia and are most frequently found on heavy clay soils with poor natural drainage, as is commonly found on the flat or even concave interfluves of north Suffolk and south Norfolk. Before the widespread introduction of under-draining in the

nineteenth century, this land was difficult to cultivate successfully, but could be relied on to produce good crops of grass. Greens therefore tend to be situated on the higher ground on the margins of parishes, away from the slopes and valleys where the best arable land was to be found and where the manor house and church were more likely to be located. Where the interfluves are large the greens are correspondingly large, as was the huge Allwood Green in north Suffolk that covered some 530 acres (215 ha) on the edges of five parishes including Walsham-le-Willows. Narrower interfluves, such as those in south Suffolk, resulted in smaller, more linear greens, such High Street Green in Great Finborough. The smallest greens, often under five acres, tend to be the triangular ones associated with crossroads where three roads meet, as at Swanton Morley in Norfolk.[74] Less closely associated with settlement are the heathy commons that occur on the dry sandy soils and the wet riverside commons that often have a fen or marsh component.

Woods tend to occur in the same topographical positions as greens, and some greens actually have 'wood' names, as in the case of Allwood Green already mentioned, which was recorded as *Aldewude* ('old wood') *c.* 1220.[75] This strongly suggests a close relationship between greens and woods. Continual grazing of wooded waste or wood-pasture could have prevented tree regeneration, leading to a gradual conversion from wood to pasture. Preserved in the List of Benefactors of Bury Abbey is a story about Ulf, son of Manning, who lived just before the Norman Conquest. He revoked his father's gift of land to the abbey and was promptly bitten by a snake; in fear of his life, he offered the monks a choice of either Syleham or Chippenhall in Fressingfield, both in Suffolk. The monks chose Chippenhall because 'it abounded in woods'.[76] In 1066 there was wood for 160 swine at Chippenhall, which had been reduced to 100 by 1086. By the eighteenth century there was virtually no woodland at Chippenhall, but there was, and still is, a fine green, with the partial ghost of another green close by. A progression from a common wood to a green is suggested by Manwood Green (*Man(e)wode(s)grene* 1272) in Hatfield Broad Oak, Essex, for the name means 'the green at the common wood'.[77] A similar progression from Handley Wood to Mill Green took place at Ingatestone in Essex.[78]

The only 'green' in East Anglia to be mentioned

in Domesday Book is Mangreen (*Manegrena*) in Norfolk, just south of Norwich. The name is clearly *gemaen-grene*, 'the common green', but confusingly, Mangreen does not now appear to have a green. On the whole, however, place-name evidence, both nationally and locally, suggests that greens were rare before the twelfth century. The archaeological

evidence from Suffolk, mainly from the fieldwalking of deserted sites around the margins of greens, as at Greshaw Green in the South Elmhams and around Rush Green in Bardwell/Stanton, also points to a twelfth-century starting-point for green-edge settlements.[79] Fieldwalking around greens in Norfolk offers similar results, with the late eleventh or twelfth

---

Key Theme: East Anglia's fields

The first in-depth analysis of East Anglia's field systems came in 1915 as a part of the magisterial survey of English field systems by the American scholar Howard Gray.[80] Despite his undoubted brilliance, Gray had to confess that 'The early field system of few English counties is so difficult to describe as that of Essex'.[81] For most of the twentieth century there was little archaeological interest in the region's historic field systems and most of the continuing analysis was provided by agricultural historians who, perhaps heeding Gray's warning, tended to concentrate more on the safer territory of Norfolk, which more closely resembled the expected model derived from the Midlands.[82] An archaeological interest in fieldscapes was awakened by the work of Paul Drury and Warwick Rodwell in Essex in the 1970s. Through 'landscape analysis' of areas with markedly rectilinear field systems, as in the Dengie peninsula and in the Chelmer valley, they put forward theories that these could be Roman in date and that they pointed 'to agricultural management on a grand scale'.[83] These theories were challenged by the work of T. J. Wilkinson and Stephen Rippon in south Essex, who suggested medieval or Saxon dates for similar systems.[84] The idea of early agricultural management on a grand scale reappeared, however, in Tom Williamson's influential 1987 study of the extensive co-axial field systems on the claylands of north Suffolk and south Norfolk, which he suggested pre-dated the Roman road that crosses them, a theory that has provoked a considerable amount of debate.[85]

The significance of the co-axial systems was one of the strands examined in the recent English Heritage-sponsored 'Historic Field Systems of East Anglia Project'.[86] This concluded that although co-axial systems do exist, they are not vast terrain-oblivious entities as has been claimed; instead they are individual smaller panels running at right angles to the main water courses and have a drainage purpose. They probably have varying dates and purposes: some may incorporate prehistoric elements, but others are more likely to be late Saxon or early medieval. Importantly, they are not automatic indicators of early land allotment. The Project's case studies suggested that 'locational' analysis involving soil type, drainage potential and access to water is a more certain way of identifying the areas most likely to have been used for early agriculture.

A more significant finding was the differing importance of individually owned and enclosed 'block holdings' (or land in severalty) and common or 'open' fields. In general terms, block holdings were found to be most prevalent in the south of the region, while common fields were more evident in the north and west, but could still form a minority part of the available farmland (Figure 14.2). A correlation was found with two types of 'ancient countryside' identified though Historic Landscape Characterisation mapping: a northern area with field systems that had layouts that were co-axial to a greater or lesser degree, and a southern area with field systems that were mainly 'random' in their arrangement, having no dominant axes. The boundary between the two approximated to the line of the Gipping valley through the centre of Suffolk, leading it to be termed 'the Gipping Divide'. Once identified, this 'divide' was found to re-occur in datasets that related to human culture rather than to the physical world – for instance, in place-names (e.g. the term 'tye' for a green is only found in the southern area); in medieval dialect (a differential pronunciation of 'f' and 'v'); in vernacular carpentry traditions (notably the frequency of queenpost roofs in the northern area and their scarcity in the south); and probably in inheritance customs.[87] This suggests that the observed 'divide' is the complex result of both natural causes and human history.

centuries perhaps the starting point there.[88] However, the presence of Saxo-Norman Thetford-type ware on some green-edges in Norfolk has led Williamson to suggest that common-edge settlement was already taking place by the time of Domesday Book.[89] A large part of the dating problem is the uncertain ending of the Thetford Ware tradition. Hurst originally argued that it ended in the twelfth century, and the early twelfth is perhaps the best advance on that dating.[90] Rogerson's fieldwalking in Fransham, Norfolk, produced 13 sites on or near green edges that he dated to the eleventh century, 38 sites of the twelfth century and 53 of the thirteenth, suggesting a gradual start somewhere in the eleventh century, but much greater activity in the twelfth and thirteenth centuries. John Ridgard's documentary study of Worlingworth Green, Suffolk, found only three of the 'older' tenements (defined by higher labour services and sizes expressed in ware acres) that may stem from the Domesday villein holdings, but ten molland ('rent-land') and five free tenements that are more likely to have been created in the twelfth, thirteenth or early fourteenth centuries – recommending that this was the main period of the green's formation.[91]

The relationship of greens to churches is also significant. The vast majority of Suffolk's churches were in existence by 1086, yet churches rarely occur in association with large greens (those at Mellis and South Elmham St Michael being notable exceptions), though there are slightly more associations with small greens (as at Badley, Brockley, Hartest and Palgrave). All this strongly indicates that greens are secondary, post-Norman, elements in the landscape, an impression reinforced by the peripheral position of many greens within their parishes. The fast-growing population in the 200 years or so before the Black Death resulted in great pressure to take into cultivation former areas of 'waste', including woodland and wood-pasture. The Statute of Merton (1236) allowed manorial lords to enclose and improve wastes, so long as they left sufficient common grazing for their free tenants, whose rights they could not extinguish.[92] It seems likely that greens were, in effect, such areas of reserved common grazing, established when the surrounding waste was converted into farmland. Most probably the land least suitable for arable conversion would have been chosen for the common pastures.

Fieldwalking evidence has been used to propose settlement shifts from original nuclei around the churches to newly founded greens at several places in Norfolk.[93] At Ixworth Thorpe in Suffolk it seems that a settlement, suggested by a scatter of Saxo-Norman pottery in a field adjacent to the now isolated Norman church, moved in the twelfth century some 700 m northward to Thorpe Green.[94] However, this may not be an example of a substantial nucleated settlement moving, but just of a manorial hall moving, as seemingly in this case, to a new moated site on the green. At All Saints South Elmham, fieldwalking found very little around the existing, isolated, hall-and-church complex to indicate that there was ever a more substantial nucleated settlement there.[95] The formation of the settlement around the large green half a mile the east, which fieldwalking indicates was there by the thirteenth century, cannot therefore be easily explained as a settlement shift from the church area; a more complex re-ordering of settlement seems to be in evidence. It may be that the establishment of greenside settlements was driven more by a population increase, leading to a transfer of people from established farmsteads to new ones, but not replacing them in a 'settlement shift'.

At Worlingworth, also in Suffolk, there is such a degree in the regularity to the landholdings on the former Great Green that deliberate planning looks likely.[96] It is probably significant that it was owned by the great Benedictine abbey at Bury St Edmunds, which is notable for its early involvement with town-planning.[97] Regularity is likewise apparent at two other greens owned by this abbey: Melford Green at Long Melford and The Green, Palgrave. The regular shape of the greens at Scole and Thelveton in Norfolk also suggests that they were planned creations.[98]

Moated sites

As already noted, another characteristic feature of the clayland areas of East Anglia is its moated sites, numbering in excess of 2,500 across the three counties – a concentration unmatched elsewhere in England (Figure 14.6). This is partly because the boulder clay plateaux and, to a lesser extent, the London Clay areas of south Essex and the river valleys, have the necessary water-retentive subsoils for the construction of successful water-filled moats, but it is also, crucially,

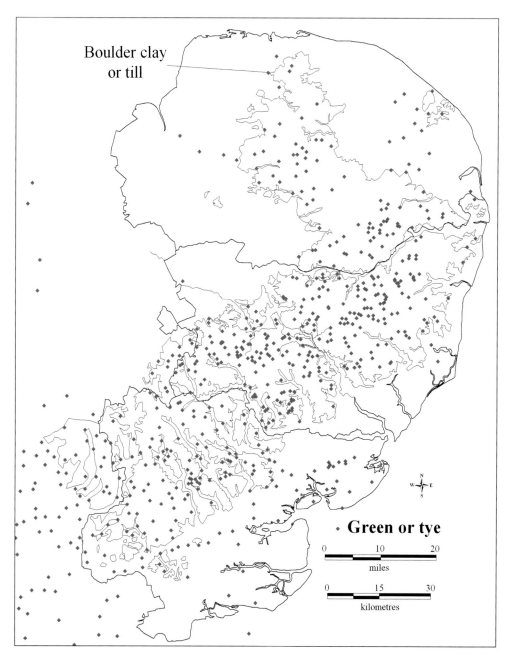

Figure 14.4. Map of greens and tyes in Greater East Anglia. This shows the place-name evidence for existing or former greens and tyes and their strong relationship with the areas with clay soils.

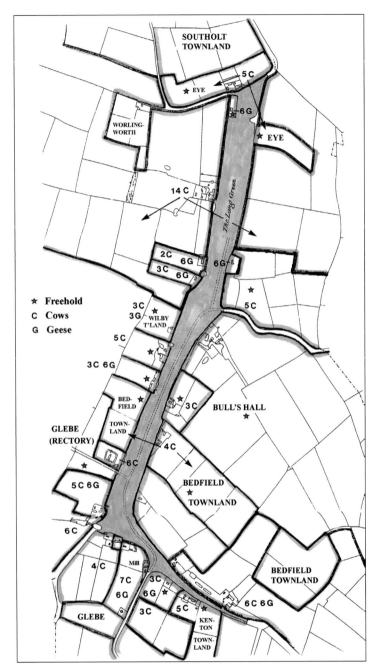

Figure 14.5. Map of Long Green in Bedfield, Suffolk. This shows the common grazing rights belonging to the farmsteads surrounding the 32-acre green, as recorded at its enclosure in 1853 (Suffolk RO(I) 105/1/3.8). The number of properties belonging to nearby parishes may be an indication of former wood/pasture rights in this area. The map shows two moated sites on the green: Bull's Hall (a sub-manor) and the Rectory, both being about half an acre in size. The positioning of the rectory on the green may be related to a land grant of c. 1230 to the parson 'upon which he built his dwelling house' (Eye Priory Cartulary no. 287) and the further acquisition by the parson of a messuage 'for the enlargement of the dwelling house of the rectory' in 1332 (Cal. Pat. 1330-4, 260) may relate to the construction of the moat. (Adapted from the tithe map of 1842)

a reflection of the high number of people who wanted a moat.

The possession of such a defended residence was closely linked in the medieval mind with concepts of lordship and social status: great lords had their castles, while lesser members of the free classes (knights, esquires, clergy and freehold farmers) had, where conditions were suitable, moated houses.[99] Although inspired by castles, the defensive banks and walls of true castles are characteristically absent on moated sites where the 'defences' are limited to the broad but water-filled moat that surrounds the central platform – this is an important distinction, since the building of 'real' castles tended to be controlled by the king and was largely restricted to the great barons, whereas the building of moated sites with only token defences seems to have been less controlled.[100] This parallels the situation in the Champagne district of France where its medieval counts actively sought to control the amount of fortification that their under-tenants could employ on their residences – shallow moats were acceptable, but only the simplest of walls, fences or hedges.[101] Moats were there closely associated with the seigneurial class and were clearly status symbols. Similarly, in Holland, moats denoted freehold farms, which, by the fifteenth century, were referred to as *ridderhofstaden* ('knightly homesteads'); their importance for status is revealed in a lawsuit of 1465 when the defendant attempted to prove his *ridderlijke* ('knightly') status by asserting that, although he had sometimes driven a horse and cart on his farm, he had only done it for pleasure and that he clearly belonged to the knightly class because he lived on 'a moated site with bridges and a gate'.[102]

East Anglia was generally an area of complex lordship, with most parishes containing more than one manor – four or five not being uncommon.[103] As a result, small manors, with demesnes of 75 acres or less, were of quite frequent occurrence.[104] Small manors were already a feature of the area by 1086, with Maitland commenting that Domesday Book demonstrated that 'the sixty acre manor was very common in Essex [and] the thirty acre manor was no rarity in Suffolk'. To him, these were 'so small that we, with our reminiscences of the law of later days, can hardly bring ourselves to speak of them as manors'.[105] The distinction between a small manor and a free tenement was therefore not a clear one then

or later, but both were very numerous in East Anglia, especially in the clayland areas.[106] The principal manorial sites and the parsonages are frequently near the church in the core of their parishes, but the minor manors and free tenements are often in a peripheral position and similar in appearance. The size of the moated enclosures is also a reflection of social rank: principal manorial sites tend to be larger (an acre or more – see Feature Box: *Key Site to Visit*: p. 242), while minor manors, parsonages, and free tenements are usually smaller (around half an acre).

At Felsted in Essex there are numerous dispersed farmsteads of medieval origin, but it is the freehold farms rather than those held by customary tenure that are distinguished by moats.[107] At Hitcham in Suffolk a moated site of 0.4 acre at Oak Tree Farm on the northern edge of the parish has a history showing that it belonged to a 60-acre free tenement belonging to the bishop of Ely's large manor there. Freeholders formed a major component of East Anglia's social structure from the Domesday period onwards, and are particular numerous in the clayland areas.[108] The numerous manorial lords and freeholders are the major reason for so many moats in East Anglia – namely the coming together of a group of people wishing to have a visible symbol of their status and, in the claylands, a relatively simple way of doing this by excavating a moat. At Brundish in Suffolk all the land in the parish was reported as being freehold in 1844 and within it there are no less than nine moated sites.[109]

The clerical connection with moats is most clearly seen with rectories, as at the deserted rectory site at Wimbotsham in Norfolk (0.6 acre) and the former (but still occupied) rectories at Ringshall (0.5 acre) and Whatfield (0.4 acre) in Suffolk.[110] At Whatfield, the glebe terrier of 1613 describes the site as containing 'one dwelling house, with a Bake-house, an orchard lately planted, a garden, & a kitchin-yard, all within a moate… and a Gate-house lately buylt, at the entrance of the moate'. Outside the moat were 'one great Barne for corne, & one lesse Barne for haye, a Stable, & a Cart-lodge & henne-house lately buylt, all in the outward yard betweene the moate and the pond on the backside of the Barnes, next the Parsonage lane'.[111] This description could have fitted many moated sites, for it was usual for the house and the garden to be on the moated platform, but for the farm buildings to lie outside in a separate yard.

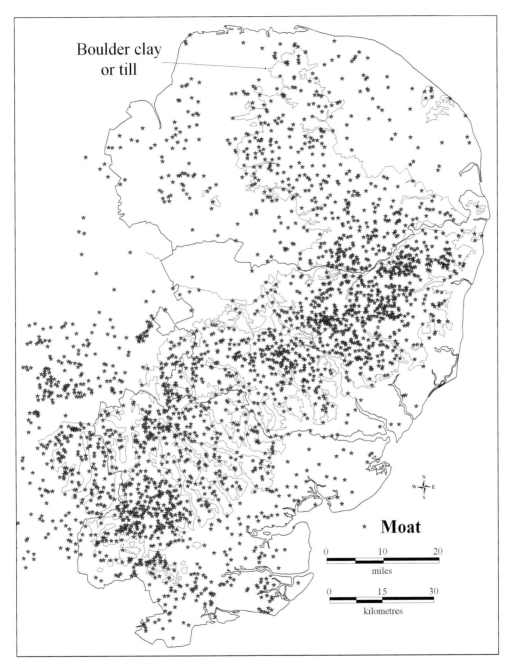

Figure 14.6. Map of moated sites in Greater East Anglia. (After Martin and Satchell 2008: fig. 27, with the addition of the areas with clay soils)

Key Site to Visit: Brockley Hall Moated Site, Suffolk

Brockley Hall in Suffolk is a timber-framed aisled hall with a contemporary cross-wing that has been dated by dendrochronology to within a year or two of 1319. This stands near the centre of a rectangular moated site of 1.2 acres with an entrance causeway on its north side (Figure 14.7). The approach to the entrance is flanked by a yard containing the farm buildings, and the north-east corner of the moat abuts the small rectangular churchyard, and on the north side of churchyard there is another much smaller moated site (0.3 acre), now deserted, which may originally have contained the house of the rector. The whole group forms a distinct and roughly rectangular church-and-hall complex of some 8 to 9 acres which, in the early fourteenth century, formed the knightly residence of Sir Alexander de Walsham, who was both lord of the manor and patron of the church.[112] The field adjoining this complex was, perhaps significantly, named as Burgate Field in 1846.[113]

In his native parish of Walsham-le-Willows, Sir Alexander's kinsman held a small manor on the eastern periphery of the parish called High Hall, which has a moated site of 0.6 acre, whilst a freehold tenement on the southern edge of the same parish has a moat enclosing 0.4 acre.[114]

Access: This moated site is still occupied (as are many in East Anglia) and not open to visitors; however, the frontal area of its moat can be viewed by visitors to the adjacent church. The big ogee-headed recess in the south wall of the church may be the tomb of Sir Alexander de Walsham, who died in 1335.

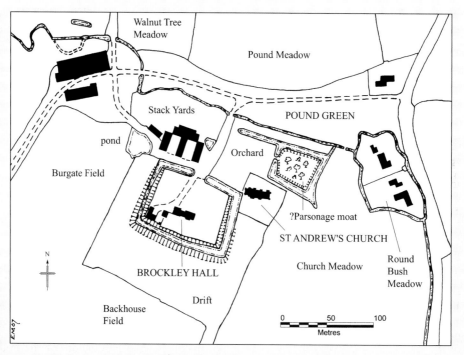

Figure 14.7. Map of the moated site at Brockley Hall, Suffolk. The early fourteenth-century aisled hall stands near the centre of the large rectangular moat, with the parish church at one corner and a probable parsonage moat close by. The farm buildings, although not medieval, are in the traditional position: outside the moat but flanking the approach to the house. The other buildings on the periphery of Pound Green are twentieth-century in date. The field names are taken from the 1846 tithe apportionment.

Figure 14.8. Crow's Hall, Debenham, Suffolk. This moated manor house takes its name from a late thirteenth-century owner named John Crowe. However, the extant buildings are mainly sixteenth-century, and particularly from the time of a major rebuild c. 1560 by Sir Charles Framlingham (1544–95), a kinsman and probable godson of Henry VIII's favourite, Charles Brandon, Duke of Suffolk. About two-thirds of the complex was demolished in the eighteenth century and the upper part of the gatehouse was removed. The brick revetting of the sides of the moat only occurs on the front parts of the site and was clearly a display feature. The bridge was approached from the left through a large base court lined on one side by a very long range of fifteenth- and sixteenth-century barns and ancillary buildings, and on the other by a dovehouse and orchard.

There often seems to have been a conceptual progression from the public, work-related barn yard in front of the moat, to a more select area on the moated platform in front of the house (sometimes separated from the yard, as at Whatfield, by a gatehouse), to a more private, garden or orchard area behind the house. This may in part have been a protective, gender-related division between the adult male activity area in the barn yard, and more secluded female and child-related areas in the vicinity of the house and particularly to its rear, where there was a safe zone bounded on three sides by a moat and by the house on the fourth. At Bruisyard Hall, formerly a nunnery of the Poor Clares, it is only the rear area of the site that is moated, presumably to ensure the privacy and seclusion of the nuns.[115] An ultimate example of this is at Shelley Hall in Suffolk, where a house of the 1520s is unmoated, but the garden to the rear is enclosed within its own moat.[116]

Moats are usually wide, 5 m plus, but relatively shallow. It is not unusual for the front section of the moat to be wider and longer than the other sides (as at Columbyne Hall in Stowupland, Suffolk), thereby maximising their visual impact to visitors. If an additional brick revetment was added to the later moats, this too was often done on the sides most likely to be seen by visitors, as at Crow's Hall in Debenham, Suffolk (Figure 14.8).[117] As already noted, the clay dug out to form the moats was not used to form banks or ramparts; rather, it was often used to increase the height of the internal platform, as at Southchurch Hall in Essex.[118] This may have had the dual intent of making a solid foundation for the house and of making the house more prominent.

For over 30 years the inception of the moat construction tradition has been set to the period AD 1150–1200, but this has been on very insecure foundations. Partly this is because the simple

Norman earthwork castles of the ringwork type have been seen as providing the inspiration for moats or at least for the small proportion that are circular these were, naturally therefore, viewed as the earliest moats.[119] However, a review in the 1980s of the dating evidence from an admittedly limited number of examples moat excavations suggested that most moats were constructed in the thirteenth or fourteenth centuries.[120] Within East Anglia, the dating evidence in Table 14.1 has been accumulated from excavations, dendrochronology and documents.

The dating evidence is mainly from pottery, which unfortunately does not give very precise dates; in addition, care needs to be taken with dates from older reports. There is also a problem separating pre-moat occupation material on several sites – the moats themselves seldom produce direct evidence because they tended to be cleaned out at regular intervals. The East Anglian evidence suggests that although moats may have started in the twelfth century, there is stronger evidence for the thirteenth and fourteenth centuries, which is in keeping with the national picture. It must be significant that this period also saw the emergence, around AD 1200, of knights as a distinct social class on the bottom fringe of the nobility, instead of just being horse soldiers. By 1300 an additional layer had been added below

the knights of esquires: men of 'good families' who had pretensions to some sort of noble status;[121] these new 'nobles' had an avid interest in visible symbols of their nobility, which found one expression in a rapidly growing use of heraldry to express status and lineage from about 1250. This interest in heraldry was expressed not only on the shields of the knights but also on their horse harness, their seals, their buildings, their tiled floors and their tombs. Its widespread adoption necessitated the production of identifying aids in the form of 'rolls of arms' – in effect, catalogues of the nobility – that were produced from the 1250s onwards into the fourteenth century.[122] The construction of moats would have been another way of visually signalling status and the available dates suggest that moats became popular at exactly the same time as there was an increase in the use of heraldic symbols. The powerful social signal conveyed by a moat still continues to be understood and moats certainly continued to be constructed into the first half of the sixteenth century, as the above documented examples indicate.

Conclusions

In 1980 Peter Wade-Martins identified four distinctive features of the East Anglian landscape and posed some questions about them:[123]

Site	Report	Date	Pre-moat activity
Boreham, Essex[124]	2003	12th–13th centuries	10th–13th centuries
Wimbotsham, Norfolk[125]	2003	Late 12th–14th centuries	Mid to late 12th century
Southchurch Hall, Southend, Essex[126]	2006	Early 13th century; hall dendro. date of 1321–63	12th–13th centuries
Brome, Suffolk[127]	1970	13th century	11th–12th centuries
Blood Hall, Debenham, Suffolk[128]	1968	13th–14th centuries	?12th century
Cedars Field, Stowmarket, Suffolk[129]	2004	13th–14th centuries	11th–12th centuries
Exning, Suffolk[130]	1976	13th–14th centuries	10th–early 12th centuries
Hempstead, Norfolk[131]	1978	13th–14th centuries	11th–12th centuries
Tiptofts, Wimbish, Essex[132]	1999	Building dendro. date c.1282–1327	
Brockley Hall, Suffolk[133]	2007	Hall dendro. date 1319	
Little Saxham Hall, Suffolk[134]		1505 building account	Yes
Hengrave Hall, Suffolk[135]		1525–26 building account	Yes
Colchester Hall, Takeley, Essex[136]	2004	?17th century	12th–13th centuries

Table 14.1. Dated moated sites in East Anglia.

a) the large numbers of isolated churches – why are so many churches isolated? Does a church far removed from its village demonstrate the movement of a population from a site near the church to a totally different one near the existing village?

b) the hundreds of scattered hamlets – why so many?

c) village greens, many of which were enclosed in the nineteenth century – what proportion of villages were truly 'green' villages in the Middle Ages and at what time did the 'green' settlement become such a distinctive village form, and for what reasons?

d) the highest density of moated sites in England – how to explain this high density in East Anglia and how to determine at what date they were created?

Thirty years later, we can perhaps offer some answers, though there can be different answers depending on which part of the region is being examined, for it is now clear that there is not just one landscape history for East Anglia and certainly not for 'Greater East Anglia'. The recognition of an important cultural division – the 'Gipping Divide' – running through the centre of the region has shown that it is no longer safe to assume that what is true in one area is true for another. Taking the observed large number of isolated churches as an example, these, in the northern part of the region (particularly in Breckland), may be indicative of deserted villages, but in much of the rest of the region they are nearly always a symptom of the generally dispersed settlement pattern, as are the observed 'hundreds of scattered hamlets'. The origins of this dispersed pattern are still not totally clear, but there are indications that it has a very long history. The 'isolated churches' in those areas usually indicate hall-and-church complexes, either fully intact or merely minus their hall component. Many of these hall-and-church complexes have a likely origin in the thegnly *burhs* of the later Saxon period, but probably saw an increase in the size of both the hall and the church component in the century or two after the Norman Conquest.

The model of a widespread settlement shift from settlement nuclei around churches to the edges of greens also seems in need of modification in the light of evidence suggesting that many hall-and-church complexes were stable but relatively small settlement units, and therefore unlikely to be the sole source of people for the new greenside settlements. The frequent location of greens on the poorer land of their

localities should show that they are areas of secondary settlement and the weight of evidence at the moment points to a late eleventh- to thirteenth-century horizon for their establishment. The size of the greens is closely linked to the size of the interfluves on which they stand, further emphasising their relationship with land quality. Greens are very variable in their shapes and often have irregular outlines, suggesting that an initial shaping in relation to topography has frequently been modified by encroachments and lapses; only in a few cases is there a regularity which might reveal deliberate planning.

Although moats do provide a modicum of protection to the structures they surround, it was their capability to convey a visual message of rank that likely made them so attractive to those on the lower rungs of nobility. It seems that, initially, moats were dug to give castle-like visual properties (with the implicit lordly message that castles proclaimed) to manorial halls that were frequently part of pre-existing hall-and-church complexes; these were then copied by people who, though lower in social rank, still had claims to be of part of the free classes. Although the dating framework is still weak, it does seem that the thirteenth and fourteenth centuries were an active time for moat creation, making them contemporary with the widespread adoption of that other powerful visual indicator of status – heraldry. The large number of moated sites in East Anglia can therefore be attributed to the conjunction of a landscape with extensive areas of water-retentive soils with a large number of manorial lords and freeholders in search of something that would proclaim their status.

The above answers still of course contain a number of uncertainties and so future research should be directed to answering a new set of questions and research aims:

a) the 'Gipping Divide' and other sub-regional divisions – how true are these, can we further define them and how can we explore their origins?

b) the church-and-hall complexes – can we provide more conclusive evidence for their origins and development?

c) the dispersed settlement pattern – its origins need further exploration as does the question of its 'archaeological visibility' in earlier periods; what are its implications for social organisation and landscape development across the medieval period?

d)   moated sites – can more be done to clarify their dating and to elucidate the variety of forms and sizes?

e)   the number of archaeologically explored medieval houses is still surprisingly small – do we need to refine excavation techniques for identifying them and understanding their construction methods?

f)   greens, tyes and commons – research into their origins and development needs to take into account the different types of common pasture that are represented in this broad grouping; can more be done to bring together both archaeological and documentary evidence?

The answering of these questions will require a synthesis of many strands of information – archaeological, historical, architectural, as well as geological and palaeo-environmental. Much has already been achieved, but, as described above, much more definition is required to properly understand the society and the economics that drove the development of the landscapes and settlements of medieval Greater East Anglia.

Further reading

Syntheses of the archaeology and history of medieval Greater East Anglia are not numerous, but Professor Tom Williamson's volume on *East Anglia* in English Heritage's multi-volume series on *England's Landscape* (London, 2006) is an excellent general introduction to its landscape history. Medieval East Anglia was also the principal focus of his earlier *Shaping Medieval Landscapes. Settlement, Society, Environment* (Bollington, 2003). The origins of the East Anglian landscape also form a component of Stephen Rippon's *Beyond the Medieval Village. The Diversification of Landscape Character in Southern Britain* (Oxford, 2008). Beyond these, the choice largely comes down to either studies of particular counties or particular themes.

The county historical atlases for Suffolk and Norfolk – D. Dymond and E. Martin (eds), *An Historical Atlas of Suffolk* (Ipswich, 1999) and T. Ashwin and A. Davison (eds), *An Historical Atlas of Norfolk* (London, 2005) – contain much of relevance to the medieval period. For the beginning of the period there are useful county syntheses by Tom Williamson and Peter Warner – *The Origins of Norfolk* and *The Origins of Suffolk* (Manchester, 1993 and 1996). For Essex, there is John Hunter's *The Essex Landscape. A Study of its Form and History* (Chelmsford, 1999) and the period essays in O. Bedwin (ed.), *The Archaeology of Essex. Proceedings of the Writtle Conference* (Chelmsford, 1996). On a more thematic level, there is E. Martin and M. Satchell's *Wheare most Inclosures be. East Anglian Fields: History, Morphology and Management* (Gressenhall, 2008) and Professor Bruce Campbell's collected essays that contain much about medieval farming in Norfolk: *Field Systems and Farming Systems in Late Medieval England* (Aldershot, 2008). For more a strictly historical approach, there is Professor Lawrence Poos's *A Rural Society after the Black Death. Essex 1350–1525* (Cambridge, 1990) and Mark Bailey's *Medieval Suffolk. An Economic and Social History, 1200–1500* (Woodbridge, 2007).

For detailed information about individual sites, the monograph series *East Anglian Archaeology* is a rich source of information, with 134 volumes published since 1975. Important articles can also be found in the journals of the county archaeological societies – *Essex Archaeology and History*, the *Proceedings of the Suffolk Institute of Archaeology and History* and *Norfolk Archaeology*.

Notes

1.   Martin 2004, 7; Williamson 2006, 28–30; Martin 2007, 128–130; Martin and Satchell 2008, 195–206; Martin 2008, 346–356; Rippon 2008, 138–140.

2.   Raynbird 1849, 50–51, 124–125; Thirsk and Imray 1958, 40.

3.   Glasscock 1976, 139, 141; Darby 1976, 45–46; Dyer 2002a, 95, 359. For more detailed economic histories of the region see Poos 1991 and Bailey 2007.

4.   Campbell 2000, 351–353.

5.   Sutton 1989; Poos 1991, 58–72; Dymond and Martin 1999, 140–141; Britnell 2003; Bailey 2007, 158, 270.

6.   Roberts and Wrathmell 2002, 29.

7.   Hart 2000.

8.   Walker 1999b, 21. For a fuller discussion of the regional tradition see Stenning and Andrews 1998.

9.　Wade-Martins 1980b, 117–118, 126; Butler and Wade-Martins 1989, 24–32.
10.　Ryan 1996.
11.　Martin 2002.
12.　Frere 1797.
13.　Saltmarsh 1941; Beresford 1954; Allison 1955.
14.　Wade-Martins 1980a, Cushion *et al.* 1982; Davison 1988; Butler and Wade-Martins 1989; Cushion and Davison 2003; Davison 2005.
15.　Hurst 1956b and Hurst and West 1957. More recently Paul Blinkhorn (1999 and forthcoming) has moved the start of Ipswich Ware to *c.* AD 720. For East Anglian medieval pottery, see Jennings 1981; Pearce *et al.* 1982; Wade-Martins 1983; Leah 1994; and Spoerry 2008.
16.　Dymond on Suffolk (1968) and Norfolk (1985), Scarfe on Suffolk (1972), Yaxley on Norfolk (1977), Hunter on Essex (1999) and, most ambitiously, Williamson on East Anglia as a whole (2006).
17.　Wade-Martins 1971, 1975 and 1980b.
18.　Lawson 1983; Williamson 1986; Hardy and Martin 1987–89; Silvester 1988 and 1991; Newman 1989; Davison 1990; Davison and Green 1993; Savery *et al.* 1994; Rogerson *et al.* 1997; West and McLaughlin 1998; Rogerson 2000. HER accessible material includes the work of Roy Colchester in Mendlesham, Suffolk, in the 1970s.
19.　Wade 1997, 47. Some exceptions are Martin 1976; Rogerson and Adams 1978; Wade-Martins 1980a; Wilkinson 1988; Brooks 1992; Wymer and Brown 1995; Medlycott 1996; Anderson 2003; Shelley 2003; Havis and Brooks 2004; Brown 2006.
20.　Aberg 1978a, 3.
21.　Hunter 1999, 128; Rogerson 2005, 68; Suffolk Historic Environment Record 2009.
22.　*Report of the Congress of Archaeological Societies*, 1901, Appendix II.
23.　*Victoria County History of Essex*, vol. I, 1903, 275–314; Gould 1905.
24.　Wall 1908; *Victoria County History of Suffolk*, vol. I, 1911, 584–585.
25.　Tristram 1910; Hopkins 1935.
26.　Cook 1960; Trump 1961; Owles 1968; Paine 1969; Rahtz 1969a; West 1970; Christie 1972; Horsey 1973; Ward and Marshall 1972; Martin 1976; Hedges 1978; Dollin 1986; Martin 1999b; Anderson 2003; Clarke 2003; Cushion and Davison 2003; Shelley 2003; Havis and Brooks 2004; Brown 2006.
27.　Thorpe 1965.
28.　Hoskins and Stamp 1963; Denman *et al.* 1967.
29.　Smith 1964, 127–128; Dymond 1968, 29–30; Wade-Martins 1975, 152–153; 1980b, 90.
30.　Warner 1987, 17–18; Martin 1995, 174.
31.　Oosthuizen 1994 and 1998, 100; Hardy with Martin 1987 and 1988; Savery *et al.* 1994; Davison 1990, 71–72; Williamson 1993, 169; Rogerson 1996, 62.
32.　Hamerow 1993; West 1985.
33.　West 1985, 168, 170.
34.　Arnold and Wardle 1981; West 1988; Hamerow 1991.
35.　Hamerow 1993, 86–87.
36.　Hamerow 1991; 2002, 104–105; Hedeager 1992, 190–191.
37.　Tipper 2004, 39–52.
38.　Hamerow 1993, 86.
39.　Lucy *et al.* 2009; Selkirk and Boulter 2003; Caruth 2008; Garrow *et al.* 2006.
40.　Newman 1992, 34.
41.　Havis and Brooks 2004, 346, 354, 537–538.
42.　Carr *et al.* 1988; Fenwick 1984.
43.　Timby *et al.,* 2007, 153–155.
44.　Newman 1992, 34.
45.　Wade-Martins 1980b, 84; Lawson 1983, 75.
46.　Rippon 1996, 124; Dymond and Martin 1998, 88; Martin and Satchell 2008, *passim.*
47.　Aitkens *et al.* 1999, 393; Martin and Satchell 2008, 133.
48.　Wymer and Brown 1995, 53.
49.　Graham and Davies 1993, 34, 37, 42.
50.　Boddington 1996, 2, 5; Audouy and Chapman 2008, 11, 37, 54, 75–76, 95.
51.　Caruth 1995 and 1996; Reynolds 1999, 141, 144.
52.　Dugdale 1846, III, 266 no. XXIII.
53.　Newman 1993; Scull 2009, 307–212, 327–328.
54.　Attenborough 1922, 83; Whitelock 1955, 432; Williams 1992.
55.　Higham and Barker 1992, 49–50; Welch 1992, 124–125.
56.　Reynolds 1999, 129–135; Creighton 2002, 70.
57.　Williams 1992, 227.
58.　Rivers 1977, 150, 152–153; Hamerow 2002, 85–86.
59.　Smith 1956, I, 58–62; Parson and Styles 2000, 74–88.
60.　Reaney 1935, 565; Martin and Satchell 2008, 13, 143.
61.　Blair 1988 and 2005.
62.　Blair 2005, 296; Martin 1978; Rippon 1996, 122.
63.　Whitelocke 1930: wills of Bishop Theodred AD 942x951, Ealdorman Ælfgar 946x951 and his daughters Æthelflæd 975x991 and Ælfflæd 1000x1002.
64.　Pestell 2004, 195–196.
65.　Whitelock 1979, 431.
66.　Beresford 1954, 386.
67.　Roberts and Wrathmell 2000, 8, 41–42.

68. Martin and Satchell 2008, 210.
69. Roberts and Wrathmell 2002, 82.
70. Rippon 2008, 193–194, 198.
71. Allison 1955, 125; Batcock 1991, 12.
72. Davison 1988, 1–2, 101–105; Sussams 1996, 86–88.
73. Martin 1995; Roberts and Wrathmell 2002, 54–56; Martin and Satchell 2008, 15–17.
74. Martin and Satchell 2008, 51–54, 92, 178.
75. Martin and Satchell 2008, 190 n. 116.
76. Hervey 1925, II, 291.
77. Reaney 1935, 41.
78. Martin and Satchell 2008, 153.
79. Martin *et al* 1986: 147–150; Martin *et al* 1991, 263–265.
80. Gray 1915.
81. Gray 1915, 387.
82. Postgate 1962 and 1973; Campbell 1980 and 1981a, b and c; and Holderness 1984. Britnell was one of the few to tackle Essex fields – see Britnell 1983, 1988 and 1991.
83. Drury 1978; Drury and Rodwell 1978 and 1980; Rodwell 1978 and 1993.
84. Wilkinson 1988; Rippon 1991.
85. Williamson 1987 and 1998b; Peterson 1990; Warner 1996: 44–53; Hinton 1997; Martin 1999a: 52–58.
86. Martin and Satchell 2008, 214–216.
87. Martin 2007 and 2008; Martin and Satchell 2008.
88. Wade-Martins 1980b, 86–88; Davison 1990, 71–72.
89. Williamson 1993, 169.
90. Hurst 1957, 29; Rogerson and Dallas 1984, 123, 126.
91. Ridgard 1983, 15–17, 54–55; Dymond and Martin 1999, 86–87; Martin and Satchell 2008, 118–119.
92. *Statutes of the Realm,* vol. I (London, 1810), 2–3; Titow 1969, 205.
93. Wade-Martins 1975, 141–143; 1980, 88.
94. Martin *et al.* 1994, 205–207.
95. Hardy with Martin 1987, 235.
96. Martin and Satchell 2008, 119.
97. Fernie 1998; Gauthiez 1998.
98. Martin and Satchell 2008, 109.
99. Crouch 1992, 257–273.
100. For a dissenting view of the defensive role of moats see Platt 2007, 99–100.
101. Bar 1981, 92.

102. Hoek 1981, 192.
103. Douglas 1927, 3.
104. Campbell 2005; Bailey 2007, 27–29.
105. Maitland 1897, 111, 118.
106. Martin and Satchell 2008, 12–15, 79, 95, 123, 147–148, 171. In 1086 the 'free peasantry' comprised more than 25% of the population to the north of the 'Gipping Divide', but less than 25% to its south – Darby 1971, 361. For the numerical distribution of freeholder voters in Suffolk in 1705, see Dymond and Martin 1999, 102–103.
107. Martin and Satchell 2008, 148.
108. Dymond and Martin 1999, 102–103; Williamson 2006, 45–47; Martin and Satchell 2008, 221.
109. *White's Directory of Suffolk* 1844, 453; Suffolk Historic Environment Record nos BUH 001–008 and 013.
110. Shelley 2003.
111. Suffolk Record Office, Bury St Edmunds, E/14/4/1.
112. Aitkens *et al.* 2007, 390.
113. Suffolk Record Office, Bury St Edmunds: T130/1,2.
114. Martin and Satchell 2008, 171.
115. Colman *et al.* 1995, 375.
116. Martin 1998.
117. Martin *et al.* 1993, 108, 110.
118. Brown 2006, 140.
119. Le Patourel 1978, 41; Le Patourel and Roberts 1978, 46, 51; Higham and Barker 1992, 194–199.
120. Wilson 1985, 27–28.
121. Crouch 2005, 238–252.
122. Wade-Martins 1980b, 3–4.
123. Coss 2003, 138–140.
124. Clarke 2003.
125. Shelley 2003.
126. Brown 2006.
127. West 1970.
128. Owles 1968.
129. Anderson 2004.
130. Martin 1976.
131. Rogerson and Adams 1978.
132. Tyers 1999.
133. Aitkens *et al.* 2007.
134. British Library Add.MS 7097, *f.* 175.
135. Cambridge University Library: Hengrave Deposit 80.
136. Havis and Brooks 2004.

CHAPTER 15

Northern England: Exploring the Character of Medieval Rural Settlements

Stuart Wrathmell
with a contribution by Robert Young

Patterns of settlement in northern terrains

The relationship of soils and topography to medieval settlement forms and farming strategies has been the subject of much debate over the past decade,[1] and for this reason the first part of the present chapter covers both terrain and settlement morphology. The accompanying map (Figure 15.1) depicts the distribution of different forms of rural settlement as they existed across northern England in the mid-nineteenth century: it shows 'nucleated' settlements – towns, villages and hamlets – as size-graded black dots, and areas of 'dispersed' settlements – single farms and small groups of farms and cottages – by means of different densities of shading. Sparse distributions of dispersed farms and cottages are indicated by lighter shading; heavier shading marks denser distributions.[2] What emerges from this exercise is not a series of mutually exclusive distributions, but varying proportions of nucleated and dispersed settlement across different regions. To the east of the Cheviots and the Pennine uplands the predominant settlement form is the village, interspersed with mainly low densities of dispersed settlement. To the west, there is a much greater emphasis on dispersed homesteads and a more uneven and restricted distribution of villages.

It should be emphasised at once that the map is based on Ordnance Survey maps of the mid-nineteenth century – this is not a distribution of medieval settlement. Densities of both villages and dispersed farmsteads will have changed dramatically in some places since the end of the Middle Ages. One

clear example is the high density of both dispersed settlements and large villages and towns in parts of Lancashire and the West Riding of Yorkshire (as they then were), a phenomenon undoubtedly linked to the rapid industrial development which these areas witnessed from the sixteenth century onwards. On the other hand, the national distribution of deserted medieval villages, mapped from detailed county-by-county records, follows quite closely the band of territory – defined at a national scale as the Central Province – where nucleated settlement predominated in the mid-nineteenth century. Examples of deserted villages are largely absent from areas to the west of the Central Province, in what has been defined at a national level as the 'Northern and Western Province'.[3] In general, post-medieval developments in the North have blurred the pattern and shifted the weightings, but they have not overturned or obscured entirely the earlier distinctions.

A closer examination of the accompanying map reveals some obvious correlations between settlement forms and terrain. The North York Moors, for example, stand out as a 'hole' in the distribution of villages in the Central Province, in terms of both the nineteenth-century mapping and the distribution of known deserted medieval villages. More detailed studies have confirmed that in the Middle Ages these upland moors were characterised by dispersed settlement.[4] On the other hand, there are also regions that show a distinct lack of correlation between settlement forms and terrain. For example, the very marked variations in terrain southwards from the

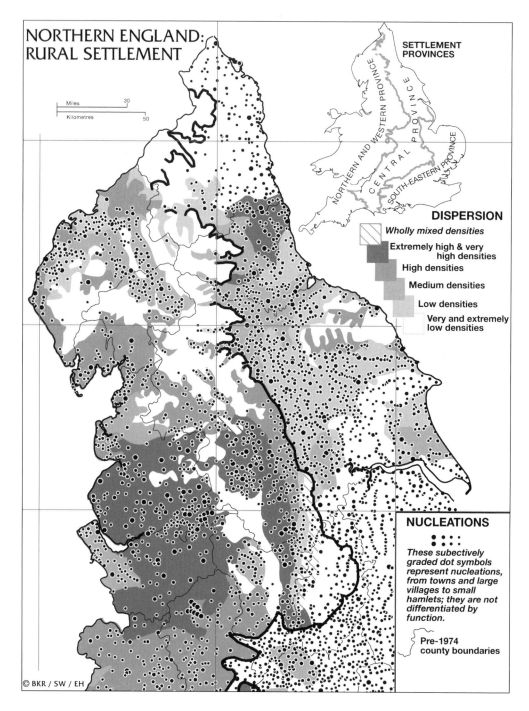

Figure 15.1. Map of settlement in northern England in the mid-nineteenth century; with villages and towns marked by dots, and differing densities of dispersed settlement by shading. (© Brian Roberts)

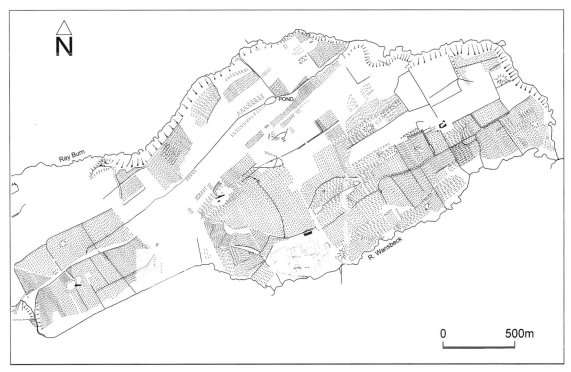

Figure 15.2. Plan of West Whelpington township, Northumberland, made in 1979, showing the deserted village site by the river Wansbeck, and surviving ridge-and-furrow marking the community's open-field arable lands. (Image by Howard Mason)

North York Moors as far as the Humber estuary are largely ignored by the relatively uniform arrangements of settlement and land use which have been identified in numerous local studies.

Starting in the middle of this area, the thin, chalky soils of the Yorkshire Wolds were occupied in the main by village settlements supported by extensive open-field cultivation; by the thirteenth century, only relatively minor stretches of permanent grassland remained. In many of its townships – the territorial units supporting distinct communities – very long open-field strips, the basic elements of land holding, stretched all the way from the township boundary to the homestead enclosures on each side of the village. It might be thought that this was some kind of specific arrangement appropriate to the creation of communities on the light soils of the Wolds. On the contrary, it is precisely the same arrangement as that which characterised medieval communities to the south and east of the Wolds, on the heavy clayey loams of lowland Holderness. Furthermore, the same

characteristics – villages with long, uniform lands – can be seen on the more fertile soils of the Vale of Pickering to the north of the Wolds, in townships such as Middleton by Pickering.[5]

Within the northern part of the Central Province, therefore, the land-use model characterised by single village settlements set within extensive open-field arable land proved adaptable – and was evidently worth adapting – to a wide range of terrains and varied mixes of farming resources. At one end of the region was the open-field township of Eske in Holderness, its village settlement now largely deserted, occupying alluvium and boulder clay at or just above sea level. At the other end was the open-field township of West Whelpington in Northumberland (see Feature Box: *Key Excavation*, p. 252; Figure 15.2), created on the edge of extensive upland moors, the now completely deserted village set on a craggy outcrop about 215 m above sea level.[6]

In the Northern and Western Province, however, this model was less frequently employed, whatever

Key Excavation: West Whelpington

West Whelpington, on the edge of open moorland in mid-Northumberland, is the most extensively excavated medieval village site in northern England. The settlement site was dug over a period of 15 years in advance of its destruction by quarrying. In all, about 14,000 m² were excavated, representing about 20% of the whole site. By the time quarrying ceased, in 1976, a total of 95 buildings had been investigated, ranging in date from the late eleventh or twelfth century, when the village was probably created, to the early eighteenth century, when it was finally depopulated.

In its first two centuries of occupation, the village seems to have accommodated over 30 farmsteads, but few details of these had survived the settlement's later redevelopment. Only at the west end of the village, which was abandoned completely in about 1320, were twelfth- to thirteenth-century buildings revealed with any clarity. This partial abandonment, and the need for subsequent redevelopment on the rest of the village site, can be attributed to successive devastations inflicted by the Scots after the battle of Bannockburn in 1314. Scottish depredations are documented across the parish, and there were signs that several thirteenth-century buildings had been burnt out. Moreover a small coin hoard, hidden in the corner of a barn abandoned at this time (Building 14: Figure 15.3), had been deposited in the period 1311–20 and never reclaimed.

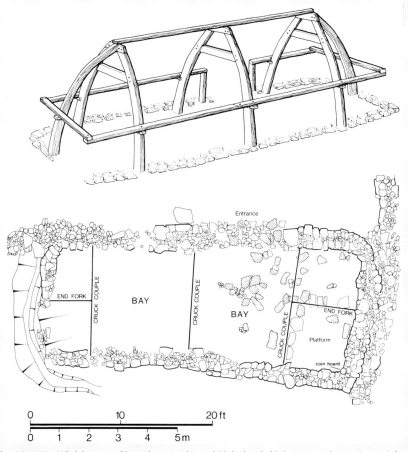

Figure 15.3. Building 14 at West Whelpington, a thirteenth-century barn which had probably been erected around a cruck-framed superstructure. A coin hoard hidden in its south-east corner wall, deposited between the years 1311 and 1320, presumably marked its abandonment. (Drawing by Chris Philo)

The re-development of the village in the fourteenth or early fifteenth century seems to have created – or perhaps re-created – rows of tofts along the north and south sides of the village green. There were continuous rows of houses along the frontages of the tofts with various outbuildings immediately behind them. The houses were of 'longhouse' form: a paved cross passage separated the living room with its hearth stone from the byre; the latter was marked by a central paved and stone-kerbed drain running down the axis of the room, with cattle standings to either side (Figure 15.4). These longhouses seem to have been created to a standard plan and this, together with their uniform layout, strongly suggests an overall design. There are indications that the village shrank in size during the fifteenth to seventeenth centuries, and the rows of longhouses were gradually replaced by smaller numbers of discrete farmsteads occupying the same sites and reusing the earlier structures. The last of these were finally abandoned around 1720, to be replaced by a smaller number of farmsteads located in other parts of the township.

A survey of archaeological remains in the township, carried out in 1979 after the end of the excavations, indicated that most of it had been under ridge-and-furrow in medieval and early post-medieval times, except for an area of moorland at the west end (Figure 15.2). The overall distribution of ridge-and-furrow indicated the extent of the village's open fields, which continued in use down to the later seventeenth century. These were then replaced by enclosed fields, the tenants of which straightened and subdivided, and in some places even ploughed at right-angles across the broad medieval ridges.[7]

Figure 15.4. *The north-west block of tofts at West Whelpington, showing the kerbed byre drains and hearths of a row of late medieval longhouses, with a superimposed post-medieval building in the foreground and outbuildings to the left. (Photo © Stuart Wrathmell)*

the terrain. Nucleated settlements originating in medieval times are largely confined to coastal fringes, except for a distinctive wedge of village territory in Cumbria, extending from the Solway Plain south-eastwards along the Eden valley. This 'outlier' to the Central Province has been linked to the radical changes that followed the Norman takeover of this area in 1092, when William II is recorded as having sent many peasants there, with their wives and cattle, to cultivate the land.[8]

Elsewhere in the Northern and Western Province the dominant pattern is of townships with far more restricted and irregular areas of open field (often called 'townfields') and far larger proportions of their territories given over either to enclosed fields (held by one person or a few individuals), or to communal reserves of pasture, moor and marsh.[9] The homesteads from which these lands were farmed were often established in marginal locations, to facilitate access to contrasting but complementary resources: they might be scattered around the periphery of the townfield or blocks of enclosed fields, or clustered at the junction of arable and pasture enclosures. Such locations can be seen in Hunsterson township, Wybunbury parish, Cheshire (Figure 15.5), and at Tunley in Wrightington, Lancashire. They are also evident at Liversedge in West Yorkshire, and at Braithwaite in Cumbria, and can again be seen in the distributions of thirteenth-century farmsteads and associated enclosures on the North York Moors.[10]

There have been numerous attempts to explain why nucleated villages came to predominate in some parts of England and not in others,[11] and this is not the place to add to them. It is, however, worth noting two characteristics of the provincial patterning. First, the nucleated village seems, on the whole, to be characteristic of townships where a very large proportion of the territory has at some stage been incorporated into the open-field arable land, and where, therefore, a distribution of farmsteads on its periphery may no longer have represented a convenient arrangement.[12] It had, indeed, become necessary in many places to establish an area of permanent pasture within the settlement – the village green – to create what was, in effect, a reverse pattern of marginal settlement, presumably to facilitate stock management. Secondly, the pattern of peripheral settlement evident in the Northern and Western Province can also be seen in the South-eastern Province, despite the enormous differences in the topography and soils of these two parts of England (see inset, Figure 15.1). Was this a 'base' settlement and land-use pattern that had once extended throughout the area defined here as the Central Province as well as through the provinces on each side; and one that had, at some point or in successive stages, been eroded and ultimately superseded by nucleated villages with extensive open fields? Or were the characteristics

of the Central Province that eventually promoted medieval village settlements present long before their creation, perhaps in the prehistoric period?

There is a further significant element in the northern settlement pattern that has yet to be discussed: seasonal settlement. The vast tracts of upland pastures in the Pennines, the Cheviots and the Cumbrian fells were sufficiently distant from lowland communities to encourage transhumance: the movement of cattle from lowland townships to these high pastures for the summer months. This in turn required the creation of temporary settlements of huts – known in the North as shielings – for the people who were sent to look after the herds.[13] Though the best documentary and archaeological evidence for such practices comes from the uplands close to the Scottish borders, where they continued into the seventeenth century, there are indications of transhumance at a much earlier period in areas such as Cheshire and central Lancashire.[14]

The twelfth and thirteenth centuries saw a general diminution of the areas used for seasonal pasturing as a result of the expansion of permanent settlements. It is signalled by place-name evidence, for example in township or farm names incorporating 'shield', 'scale' or 'erg', and by residual linkages between upland and lowland townships.[15] Colonisation sometimes involved a lengthy process of assarting – taking in new fields from open pastures and woodland – around the edges of existing settlement nuclei, with new hamlets established in the newly formed fields. In other areas there may have been more rapid, planned programmes of farm creation, as appears to have occurred at Goathland on the North York Moors and at Wythop in Cumbria.[16]

The more intensive use of upland pastures is evidenced not only by the establishment of new tenanted farms, but also by the creation of ranches to accommodate the lord's own animals. Vaccaries, demesne stock farms supporting large herds of cattle, were established by both lay and ecclesiastical lords.[17] They are recorded, for example, in the thirteenth and fourteenth centuries in the upland forests of Bowland, Copeland, Derwentfells, Skipton, Weardale and Wyresdale. In Cumbria they were often set in dalehead locations.[18] Bercaries, or sheephouses with associated enclosures, were also established. These include the well-known excavated example belonging

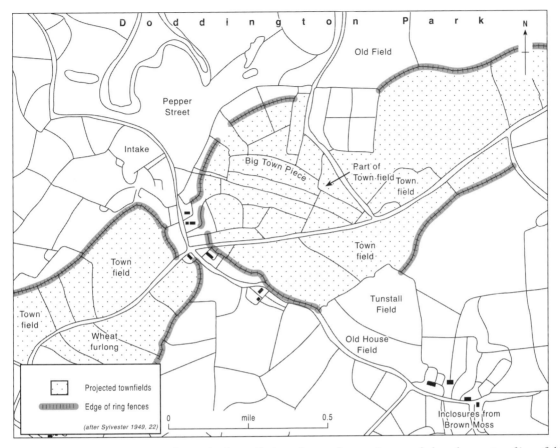

Figure 15.5. Plan of Hunsterson township, Wybunbury, Cheshire, showing farmsteads scattered along the margins of 'townfields' reconstructed from field names and field boundaries. (Drawing by Brian Roberts, after Dorothy Sylvester)

to Bolton Priory on Malham Moor in Craven,[19] which is discussed, along with a selection of other investigations on both village and farm sites, in the next section of this chapter.

Archaeological investigations in northern England

The exploration of villages

Northern England can lay claim to the earliest recorded excavation of a deserted medieval village. It was carried out before 1812 at Barden in Wharfedale, North Yorkshire, by the Rev. Thomas Dunham Whitaker (1759–1821). Whitaker was a renowned antiquarian and topographer of both Yorkshire and Lancashire,[20] and the second edition of one of

his finest works, *The History and Antiquities of the Deanery of Craven*, contains details of 'an abandoned and forgotten village' about 4 km west of Bolton Abbey. He describes the traces of the village street, the enclosures and tofts along each side of it, and the 'marks of the plough' (presumably ridge-and-furrow) in the heather-covered land beyond.[21] Within the enclosures he identified the sites of paved cow-houses and dwellings, and he organised the excavation of house sites to determine whether their plan forms were similar to those of extant old houses in the neighbourhood. He believed that the visible remains of stone walls still stood to their original height, and that they 'must have supported slender crooks or poles, forming a roof for the thatch', similar to those that still survived (and survive still) in the nearby hamlets of Barden and Drebley. He attempted to date the village's occupation with reference to the vill names recorded in Domesday Book.[22]

His thoughts on this site anticipated much of the research agenda developed in more recent studies of deserted villages in the North: the dating of occupation and, by inference, of settlement desertion; the plan forms and uses of the abandoned houses and their structural relationship to surviving buildings in the vernacular traditions of the region; the identification of outbuildings within the homestead enclosures; the route-ways and enclosures that articulated the settlement, and their relationship to the cultivated lands that supported its inhabitants.

Whitaker's investigations represent just one of several false starts in the history of deserted medieval village studies: it was not until the early 1950s that the historical and archaeological exploration of deserted medieval villages was promoted into the mainstream of academic research.[23] Once again, Yorkshire witnessed some of the earliest work, notably the publication of lists of 'lost villages' in the county's three Ridings, and the beginning, in 1950, of excavations at the village site of Wharram Percy on the Yorkshire Wolds (Figure 15.6). It was here that the Deserted Medieval Village Research Group was founded in August 1952.[24] The Wharram Research Project continued its excavations for 40 years, producing what is unquestionably the largest assemblage of data and finds from any medieval village excavation: no less than 100 sites were dug, ranging from trial trenches to open area excavations; almost 140,000 fragments of animal bone were recovered, as well as over 40,000 pieces of pottery. This project, for long the flagship of the Research Group, was immensely influential not only in Britain but also across the Continent; it has been described by one leading scholar as the most important archaeological excavation of any period since 1945.[25]

Maurice Beresford's initial trenching at Wharram Percy, as at other deserted villages in Yorkshire, was designed to elicit a date for occupation and therefore depopulation. He saw the arrival of John Hurst, in 1952, as an opportunity to gain access to expertise on the dating of medieval pottery to further this objective. Hurst's research aim was, however, rather different: the excavation of a complete house site to gain a better understanding of the lives of medieval peasants.[26] The house site Area 10 was selected

because it was close to the excavation base in surviving nineteenth-century labourers' cottages. In the event, it proved to be a less than ideal choice in terms of this specific research aim, in that the location had been occupied by manorial buildings until the mid-thirteenth century.[27]

Hurst's strategy was followed in many other deserted village excavations, both on the Wolds and beyond, thanks mainly to his influence from within the Ministry of Works. For example, it was the Ministry that excavated in the largely depopulated village of Riplingham, near the southern end of the Wolds, in 1956–57. Here, the best-defined earthwork house site was the one chosen for excavation; but as the house proved to have continued in occupation into the eighteenth century, a second one was opened up to try to gain a picture of a medieval house untrammelled by later modifications.[28]

Northwards, the lower Tees Valley of County Durham witnessed, in the 1960s, another clutch of medieval peasant house excavations. The sites of three buildings were investigated at the deserted village of West Hartburn in 1962–68 (Figure 15.7), generating valuable plans of two houses and what was perhaps originally a bakehouse or brewhouse associated with one of them. Contemporary work at the deserted village site of West Whelpington, in the upper reaches of the Wansbeck valley in Northumberland, was again focused very much on the sites of buildings visible as earthworks; many were houses but some proved to be barns and other ancillary structures (Figures 15.3 and 15.4).[29]

This widening of objectives, which saw the excavation not only of houses but also of ancillary buildings, had already taken place at Wharram by the end of the 1950s. In Area 10 a large part of the earthwork enclosure – the toft – which contained the first fully excavated building, had been opened up to reveal a wide range of other structural remains as well as external surfaces and boundaries. It was decided, therefore, to excavate another complete toft, towards the southern end of the village site, and to compare the results.[30] The focus had widened from the house to the farmstead – a unit that would arguably give a much broader picture of the lives of Wharram's farming families. The excavation of Area 6 did, indeed, provide this picture, though it was only much later that the latest remains in Area 6

Figure 15.6. Aerial view of Wharram Percy village site from the north, taken in 1979. The excavation is in the North Manor precincts, with the west range of tofts and crofts running southwards from it, and the north range running eastwards. The compartments of the east row are just visible on the far side of the white track. (Courtesy of NMR [APR 1449/22])

Figure 15.7. House D at West Hartburn in the Tees valley, after excavation. Breaks in the walls towards the centre mark a cross passage, with the putative byre at the far end of the building and the living room in the foreground. (Photo © Alan Pallister)

were identified as a house and barn set opposite each other against the toft boundaries, with a gated yard between them. A similar, broader strategy can also be seen in the 1971–72 excavations in the deserted village of Cowlam, only 11 km from Wharram. Here again, the intention was to explore the outbuildings and associated yards within the toft as well as the dwellings – even though it proved, in the event, difficult to assign functions to them.[31]

The early 1970s also saw more extensive excavation on village sites in the Tees Valley and central County Durham, such as at Tollesby, on the south side of the Tees, where both buildings and the yards behind them were explored. Larger-scale work was carried out on the southern edge of the East Durham plateau, with excavations at the shrunken village of Hart (mainly the manorial enclosure) and at the deserted village of Thrislington.[32] Thrislington again featured the excavation of a manor house, though this time one that was unanticipated. On the northern row of the village a series of adjacent tofts was also investigated, not just the buildings on their frontages but also the areas behind them. Toft C, the most comprehensively excavated, contained a possible barn, a well-worn sunken yard behind the buildings on the toft frontage, and a garden.[33] The extent of excavation at Thrislington, combined with the plan of the rest of the village known through earthworks, provided an opportunity to measure the widths of the tofts to establish whether they were laid out at a single time to demarcate equal-sized farmholds. The plan form and dating evidence suggested in this case the creation of a regular-row village in the late twelfth or early thirteenth century.[34] Work at Wharram Percy and West Whelpington was also extensive enough to permit the development of hypotheses on the origins and growth of these villages. Their stories are told elsewhere in this chapter.

The only other northern village to have provided significant excavation data on regular-row development is Wawne, on the clay just north of Kingston upon Hull, where salvage recording after the bulldozing of earthworks took place in 1961. In this case a row of tofts and houses seems to have been laid out in the fourteenth century.[35] The conditions under which recording took place and the style of the resulting plan of the remains, make it difficult to compare Wawne with other sites. For example, the absence of

evidence for toft divisions is probably a result of the bulldozing, as toft partition boundaries are clearly present on a 1946 air photograph of the earthworks; and the sunken yards to the rear of the houses were perhaps not that much different from those at other northern village sites, including Thrislington.[36]

With the exception of Whitaker's village site at Barden, all the settlement excavations outlined thus far have been carried out in locations in the Central Province. The Northern and Western Province has witnessed a significant number of investigations, but as will be evident in the next section of this chapter, these have been focused almost exclusively on the well-preserved earthwork remains of upland hamlets and farmsteads in areas that are now open moor and fell. It is hard to refute the claim that the North-west as a whole has been largely ignored by those concerned with medieval settlement research.[37] Tatton in Cheshire is one north-western deserted village that has seen open-area excavation – a rarity, on both counts. Its excavated remains look very different from those discussed above: at Tatton, the buildings were indicated by patterns of post-holes and little else, and the enclosures were marked by successive phases of ditches.[38] Its characteristics have more in common with the clay-land village sites of the Midlands than with the stone-formed remains of northern settlements.

The exploration of hamlets, farmsteads and shielings

In terms of upland farmsteads, hamlets and shieling sites, the investigations carried out since the 1950s have had a reasonably broad geographical spread, covering both sides of the Pennines, the Cumbrian fells, the Cheviots and the North York Moors. They have also demonstrated a broad chronological spread, with examples ranging in date from the late eighth or early ninth century down to the sixteenth and seventeenth centuries. At least four groups of excavated sites are thought to pre-date the Norman conquest: Simy Folds in County Durham, Bryant's Gill in Cumbria, and two in North Yorkshire, on Gauber High Pasture (Ribblehead) and Malham Moor (Malhamdale), with further possible examples in the upper Lune valley.[39] Some of these pre-Norman farm sites were unanticipated discoveries made during broader surveys of upland landscapes; in the case of the Gauber High Pasture site, the specific focus had been Romano-British field systems and settlements.[40] Post-Conquest sites, too, have been identified in the main during multi-period surveys, as in Redesdale, Northumberland and on Levisham Moor in the North York Moors.[41] In contrast, Wensleydale has seen extensive survey work focused on the full spectrum of medieval settlements – villages, hamlets, farmsteads, vaccaries, bercaries, even horse studs. The Royal Commission's survey of shieling sites in north-east Cumberland and north-west Northumberland was much more closely constrained.[42]

Beyond the pre-Norman sites, there have been relatively few excavations of dispersed settlement remains, though two of them, carried out in the 1950s, were contemporary with the earliest village excavations. The one that focused on Malham Moor in Craven uncovered a medieval farmstead that seems to have produced pottery of the twelfth to fourteenth centuries, as well as the full ground-plan of a bercary belonging to Bolton Priory.[43] The other, north-west of Malham, near Sedbergh, was one of a number of dispersed hamlets and farmsteads. The site excavated in 1955–58 was located at Underbank, and comprised a house and what were probably two ancillary structures. Pottery dated its occupation to the fifteenth and sixteenth centuries.[44] More recently there has been further work near Sedbergh, in the western Howgill Fells.[45] Further north, a possible shieling site in Bewcastle area was subject to rescue recording in the 1970s.[46]

Though this list of excavations at dispersed settlements could be extended to cover several other small-scale interventions, in Northumberland and elsewhere, it would still be a relatively short one when compared with the record of work on village settlements. It is also clear that the kind of detailed landscape survey that would place these remains in a wider geographical and chronological context has rarely been attempted. This, and a number of other suggestions for further work on northern medieval settlement sites, will form the final part of this review.

Current understanding and future directions for research

Research in villages

In the early 1950s John Hurst set out a two-part strategy for investigating deserted medieval villages, a strategy that was to inform the activities of the Deserted Medieval Village Research Group, the Ministry of Works and their successor organisations for many years to come. The first part was effectively a sampling strategy: the complete excavation of at least one house site in each village, in order, amongst other things, to 'provide the architect with the answers to some of his questions about house construction and plan'. This led on to a more general question: 'What were the peasant houses of medieval England really like…?' The other element of the strategy had the aim of 'completely stripping a whole village'. The then current excavation of Area 10 was intended to test whether Wharram Percy should be continued as the 'whole village' excavation.[47]

The excavations noted earlier in this chapter represent by no means a complete record of work that has taken place in the North. Nevertheless, they still indicate considerable progress with the first part of Hurst's strategy. Significant numbers of excavated medieval peasant house plans are now available for study, though their distribution is very uneven. This is because the two separate elements of the strategy, of sampling one house site in each village, and of excavating a deserted village comprehensively, became blurred over time, notably when it came to be recognised that the house was only one of a group of buildings and other structural components that together constituted the 'peasant' farmstead.

A large proportion of the relevant building plans comes from the most extensively excavated village site, at West Whelpington, where the fourteenth- and fifteenth-century farmhouses conformed to the 'longhouse' type, with living room and cattle byre under one roof, separated by an entry cross-passage. The hearth was in the centre of the living room, indicating the absence of a loft. The byres were identified on the basis of their axial paved and stone-kerbed drains (Figure 15.4). Similar plans were identified at West Hartburn (Figure 15.7), though here, as at Wharram Percy House 6, evidence for the function of the non-heated room was ambiguous.[48] It now seems likely that the longhouse tradition was confined to particular regions of England, rather than being represented across the whole country.[49] On the basis of documentary evidence and excavation, northern England was clearly one of the regions that were home to the longhouse tradition.[50]

Key Theme: 'Planned' Villages in the North

All medieval settlements have been 'planned', in the sense that individuals or groups of people have at one time or another decided to place buildings in particular locations and to create associated enclosures of particular forms and sizes in specific places. What distinguishes northern England from the rest of the country is the high percentage of its villages that display geometric regularity in their plan forms: rows of homestead enclosures – the village tofts – of uniform length and sometimes width, which look as though they were created in single acts of planning (Figure 15.8). It has been estimated that about 80 per cent of northern villages provide evidence of such planning. In some places, the whole village has a regular plan, typically two rows of tofts facing each other on either side of a street or green. Elsewhere, a 'regular-row' element may be just one part of a more complex settlement plan that bears witness to a longer and more intricate development. They key questions are: when were such regular elements created; who created them – the lord(s) of the manor or the community itself; and why? It is very difficult to answer any of them, for the earliest accurate plans available for most northern villages date to the late eighteenth and nineteenth centuries. Regular plan elements could have been created a few years or a few centuries before the date of the first accurate plan, or conceivably as much as a thousand years earlier.

For a few villages there are detailed plans dating to the late sixteenth and early seventeenth centuries, and there is physical evidence in the form of earthworks marking the sites of villages abandoned before the end of the Middle

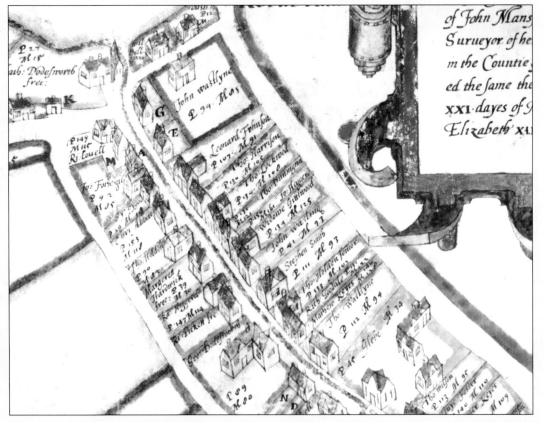

Figure 15.8. The two-row core of Settrington village in the Vale of Pickering, Yorkshire, as it appeared on a plan of 1600. A stream flows through the narrow green separating the rows, which may have been established at different times. (Paul Gwilliam; courtesy of Sir Richard Storey, Bt)

Ages. For the most part, however, those wishing to analyse village morphology have been compelled to try to relate the various elements they have detected in nineteenth-century plans to patterns of landholding recorded much earlier, namely in charters and written surveys. For the North, with its paucity of documentary evidence before the twelfth century (and with most of the region's vills absent from Domesday Book), the tendency has been to ascribe regular village plans to the century and a half after the Norman conquest, and to link them to re-colonisation after successive phases of devastation caused by Normans, Scandinavians and Scots. That position is now being rethought.

The idea of village planning was very probably around for the whole of the period covered by this book. In Yorkshire, evidence is emerging from Wharram Percy's archaeological record that its earliest row could have been created in the ninth century. In Cumbria, row villages in the Eden valley may have been established after the Norman takeover of 1092. In the main, the urge to create regular-row villages had probably dissipated by the thirteenth century, but a few seem to represent more recent foundations. Thus, in Northumberland, Halton Shields is a single-row village probably created in the early sixteenth century, and East Thriston, a two-row village, may have been established a few decades later.[51]

Turning to the post-medieval phase of occupation at West Whelpington, the sixteenth and seventeenth centuries saw modifications to the longhouses that created 'hearth-passage' plans comparable to ones known from documentary sources and surviving buildings.[52] The hearth was moved from the centre of the living room to a position against the partition wall which separated the room from the entry passage. It was furnished with a firehood, enabling the rest of the room to be lofted over. The more substantial partition wall created a clearer separation between the living room and the entrance passage and byre end of the building, in precisely the same manner as that recorded in the early nineteenth century by Rev. John Hodgson, the antiquarian and vicar of Kirkwhelpington, when describing the local 'inferior' type of farmhouse. It is a change that can also be seen at West Hartburn and Wharram Percy.[53]

In terms of their plan forms and use, therefore, some of the house sites excavated since the 1950s have been located reasonably well within vernacular traditions. The same is true of the methods and materials used to construct them, with wattle-and-daub or clay walls set on stone foundations, and thatched roofs supported by cruck or post-and-truss frames (Figure 15.3).[54] Beyond that, there has been a growing recognition of evidence for outbuildings, including substantial barns, and for ancillary domestic buildings such as bakehouses and brewhouses.[55]

The first part of Hurst's strategy has, therefore, been progressed some distance in northern England,

even though the investigations carried out thus far could hardly claim to provide adequate representation for all parts of the North. There are, in particular, questions as to whether the longhouse form was ubiquitous in the medieval North, and whether it was the antecedent form to the post-medieval 'lobby-entry' house plan – where the main doorway gave access to a lobby on one side of the hearth place – as well as to the hearth-passage plan, where the entry gave access to a passage running behind the hearth place. Documentary sources for the Vale of York and archaeological evidence from Wharram Percy suggest that, in at least some parts of Yorkshire, longhouses preceded lobby-entry houses;[56] but we lack excavated buildings that demonstrate structural conversion from the one to the other.

As an extension to the house sampling strategy, progress in understanding the toft enclosures – the units that framed much of the daily life of the farming families – has been far less satisfactory. Though excavations on village sites have, since the 1960s, generally extended well beyond individual house sites, they have failed to provide an adequate record of the material culture contained within a complete toft. This is true even of the most extensive excavations at villages like Cowlam (Areas 1–4) and Wharram Percy (Area 6), where excavation in the end failed to reach all areas of the yards, trackways and gardens, and often omitted the toft boundaries themselves where (at least on the evidence of Area 6 at Wharram) much of the domestic refuse may have been dumped.[57]

There remains a need to uncover complete tofts, selected not on the prominence of the relevant earthworks but on the basis of detailed analysis of earthwork and geophysical surveys that would allow the excavation to become an integral element of a broader investigation. All too often in the past, the selection of areas for excavation has actually preceded detailed earthwork and geophysical survey. Given the costs of excavation and particularly of post-excavation, the process of selection needs to be far more purposeful and informed than it has sometimes been in the past.

The second part of Hurst's strategy is yet to be realised, with no more than 20 per cent of any northern village site explored. Inferences can be drawn with regard to the formation of some elements in village plans. There are blocks of tofts and crofts which seem to have been created as single acts of planning, as at Wawne, Thrislington and West Whelpington, but inferences such as these are a long way from allowing us to develop hypotheses relating to overall village development: their stages of growth; how and when they originated, and what they replaced. The most extensively excavated site, West Whelpington, may have been created no earlier than the twelfth century in a location that had been largely unoccupied since the Roman period.[58] This archaeological interpretation accords with the village's marginal location and its name: it seems most likely to have been a new township carved out of the vill of neighbouring Kirkwhelpington, the medieval parish centre, at a relatively late period.

The suggested development of West Whelpington usefully demonstrates some of the more general biases in the excavation data that have arisen because of the criteria used to select northern village sites for investigation. Many of the complete or near complete depopulations – those sites usually targeted for excavation – took place in relatively minor settlements, often small outlying villages established as dependencies of estate centres. This applies not only to West Whelpington but also at West Hartburn, a minor settlement in Middleton St George parish and Thrislington, which probably started as an outlier of Middleham.[59] Such settlements are not only potentially relatively late foundations; they also frequently lack any depth of documentation.

Wharram Percy might at first sight appear to be a very different case, given that it was the centre of a medieval parish covering a number of neighbouring townships as well as Wharram Percy itself. Nevertheless, it too may well have begun as a minor upland community, perhaps originally a seasonal settlement supporting summer grazing for the longer-established communities in the Vale of Pickering to north. Its emergence as a parochial centre, perhaps in the late tenth or eleventh century, does not signify an early importance as an estate centre; it seems to have resulted from _ad hoc_ arrangements.[60]

This does not, however, detract from Wharram's importance as a research project, for its longevity and scope have enabled us, for once, to speculate meaningfully on the village's origins and early development. To elaborate an earlier comment, this has been made possible not so much though direct excavation strategy (which in this case had many other objectives), but as a result of remarkably detailed and informative earthwork and geophysical surveys carried out by English Heritage a decade _after_ the end of the excavation programme. The geophysical survey has identified a group of curvilinear settlement enclosures of very different form from the rectangular tofts and crofts marking the medieval village, leading to further analysis and re-revaluation of excavation data.

In short, the earliest element of the village defined by earthworks – a row of tofts forming its western side, probably originating in the Anglo-Scandinavian period – replaced an adjacent group of Middle Saxon curvilinear settlement enclosures that had perhaps grown out of one or two original farmsteads or shielings. Thus settlement nucleation came about through accretion, and it preceded a phase of replanning that generated the earliest part of the medieval village. The level of confidence in this hypothesis has been increased by the recognition that this pattern is repeated elsewhere on the Yorkshire Wolds and beyond, a number of so-called Butterwick-type enclosure groups being replaced by more ordered village layouts which have in many cases survived down to the present day.[61] It may be that at least the northern part of the Central Province was already set on its own, distinctive trajectory at the time these Butterwick-type settlements were created, some time in the seventh or eighth century.

Key Site to Visit: Wharram Percy

The 40-year programme of excavations at Wharram Percy, on the Yorkshire Wolds about 10 km south-east of the town of Malton, has made this the best-known deserted medieval village in the country. It is in the care of English Heritage, which has provided some signage to help visitors appreciate what was once there, and it can be visited free of charge. Visitors cannot drive up to the site, but there is a car park about 500 m to the east, near Bella Farm, from where a track can be followed down into the valley, across a stream and into the area that once housed upwards of 30 farming families. The track itself is the first archaeological feature of interest: it is part of a cross-valley routeway that has been in use continuously since prehistoric times.

The layout of the medieval village is fairly simple: there were two rows of houses, tofts and crofts facing each other on the east and west sides of a triangular village green which tapered towards the south (Figure 15.6). At the north end of the green was a further row of farmsteads with, at its west end, the precincts of a large manorial homestead. None of this is easy to see from the valley because of the topography of the site: the green was formed on the steep valley side, and while the houses and crofts of the east row of the village can be traced as earthworks along the valley towards the nineteenth-century cottages, the west and north rows of farmsteads lie at a much higher level, along the edges of the chalk plateau above the valley.

Some of the sites of excavated medieval buildings have been marked out in the grass on the plateau edge, but more accessible are the sites of the post-medieval farmhouse and its outbuildings on either side of the surviving cottages, the foundations of the vicarage beyond them, and finally the unroofed but largely intact church of St Martin. Beyond the church and its graveyard the former village pond has been re-created. It is fed by a number of springs, and seems originally to have supplied power to a water mill used to grind corn.

The earliest part of the medieval village, the west row, was probably established in the ninth century; the graveyard seems to have been created late in the tenth century, and the first church a little later still. The village continued to expand after the Norman conquest; a larger church was built on the site of its more modest predecessor, and later modified on several occasions. From the late fourteenth century onwards, Wharram's population started to decline and by the early sixteenth century very few farmsteads remained. The seventeenth and eighteenth centuries saw a single farmstead on the old village site, along with the vicarage, and new farmsteads being built elsewhere in the township, on what had been the former village's open fields. The most significant of the tens of thousands of objects recovered from the excavations have been illustrated in the 13 published volumes of the Wharram project.[62]

Research in dispersed settlements

The story of settlement research in the northern uplands displays many of the strengths and weaknesses of village research over the past 60 years. While a number of individual houses have been excavated, and some, like Underbank, linked to vernacular traditions of housing through plan form and inferred structural characteristics,[63] for many, again like Underbank, documentary evidence is practically non-existent. Furthermore, excavation has rarely been extended to ancillary buildings and yards, let alone to whole farmsteads; and there have been few detailed surveys of features in the wider landscape outside the

settlement area – enclosure banks, areas of ridge-and-furrow and so on – at least in any systematic way that would facilitate detailed analysis.[64]

This last omission is perhaps all the more surprising given the preoccupation of many investigations with determining whether the sites were shielings or permanent settlements, and if the latter, whether these were tenanted hamlets and farms or seigneurial vaccaries or bercaries. Criteria for distinguishing shielings were developed by the Royal Commission in the 1960s: they were 'simple huts without any associated contemporary enclosures and scattered singly or in clusters along the streams that cross the

Figure 15.9. Medieval upland settlement on Alnham Moor, Northumberland. The two rectangular earthworks mark the sites of possible shieling huts, but nearby ridge-and-furrow suggests more permanent habitation at some point in the Middle Ages. (Photo © R. Young)

remoter moors'.[65] These were broadly the criteria used in upper Teesdale, where buildings with associated enclosures were identified as farmsteads, and those without as shielings, especially when grouped together in hamlets presumably occupied by several households.[676]

Yet a medieval turf-walled building on Black Lyne Common in Bewcastle, Cumbria was identified as a shieling because of its (supposedly) flimsy structure, despite having associated enclosures.[67] Furthermore, whatever the durability of its structure, its plan form is very similar to that of a medieval building identified as a farmhouse on Malham Moor.[68] A medieval building at Crosedale in the Howgills, again with possibly associated enclosures, was identified both as a shieling *and* as a monastic bercary.[69]

There is clearly a need to clarify definitions, but perhaps an element of confusion is inevitable (see Figure 15.9). It is evident from township and farm names that shielings often became the sites of permanent hamlet settlements, as at Linshiels and Aldenshiels in the upper Coquet valley of Northumberland;[70] but there were also occasions when permanent settlements reverted to shieling status. A 1604 survey of North Tynedale recorded that there had once been 'husband farmes and cottages' at

Grindon, but that there remained only the 'grownd worke' of the houses, the area now being used as common and 'sheildinge ground'.[71]

One particular plan form that deserves further investigation is that associated with some of the upland farmsteads assigned to the pre-Norman period. In upper Teesdale, the Simy Folds farmsteads contain long narrow buildings with rounded corners and distinctive paved gable entries. Similar buildings have also been identified elsewhere in Teesdale.[72] Furthermore in Yorkshire, Building A at Gauber High Pasture was recorded as a long, narrow rectangular structure with rounded corners and paved entrances in each end wall.[73] As the excavators of both sites recognised, these buildings have affinities with Norse house plans, in terms of their dimensions and internal features.[74] This recognition has prompted the suggestion that the Simy Folds structures were built by Norse farmers who had reached this area from the Eden valley of Cumbria[75] – an intriguing speculation given the morphology of some settlement enclosures and buildings discovered in the upper Eden and upper Lune valleys.

Smardale South Demesne lies in the Eden valley less than 30 km south-west of Simy Folds. Here two small, adjacent groups of curvilinear (or sub-rectangular) enclosures appear to have comparable size ranges (about 25–30 m across) to the Simy Folds enclosures; and though the Simy Folds enclosures are not agglomerated in the same way, they have similar shapes. Furthermore, and again as at Simy Folds, rectangular buildings have been recorded in the Smardale enclosures, prompting the suggestion that these may have been the sites of farmsteads occupied until the period of village formation associated with the Anglo-Norman takeover.[76] Though there is some debate about the Smardale remains, several other farmstead sites have been recorded less than 10 km to the north-west of Smardale, on Orton Scar, that are closely comparable to the 'Viking' farmstead at Gauber High Pasture, Ingleborough.[77]

Conclusions

Excavating significant parts of large medieval villages can nowadays be a very expensive activity; even more so after the creation, over the past two decades, of a commercially determined value for archaeological expertise. It is, therefore, harder than ever to envisage the realisation of John Hurst's ambition for the excavation of a complete village site. Is this a bad thing? Not necessarily. A complete village excavation might generate sufficient information to delineate its origins, growth and character, but this would lead inevitably to a need to excavate more villages completely, so as to determine how typical the findings were, both within the same region and beyond.

If the future for research on northern sites (as elsewhere) is one of small-scale interventions, these should be located within broader frameworks, designed to test hypotheses developed through the systematic analysis of detailed cropmark, geophysical, earthwork and documentary surveys related to both settlement and township. This has happened at Wharram, but largely retrospectively through the requirements of a lengthy post-excavation programme, and thanks to the participation of English Heritage. The Wharram excavation archive may be pre-eminent in the quantity and range of data available for re-examination, but a similar process of re-analysis applied to other past excavations, combined with new fieldwork on sites that partially survive using the improved investigative technologies and methodologies now available (including test-pitting, plan analysis, etc.), might offer opportunities for re-assessing medieval settlements and for generating new ideas of origins, growth and change. The cost of such programmes can be contained to some extent by involving local communities in the research, with the added dividend of increasing community awareness and appreciation of their local historic environment. The Historic Village Atlas Project for Northumberland (see below) is one example of what can be achieved through such an approach.

Further reading

A valuable guide to the broad characteristics of medieval settlement in northern England, and to the methods used by scholars in defining and analysing them, is Brian Roberts's *Landscapes, Documents and Maps. Villages in Northern England and Beyond AD 900–1250* (Oxford, 2008). There are two excellent regional surveys for north-west England, namely Nick Higham's *A Frontier Landscape: The North West in the Middle Ages* (Macclesfield, 2004), which focuses on Lancashire and Cheshire, and Angus Winchester's *Landscape and Society in Medieval Cumbria* (Edinburgh, 1987). For the uplands as a whole in the later Middle Ages and beyond, Winchester's *The Harvest of the Hills* (Edinburgh, 2000) is highly recommended. Several useful summaries of excavations on North-east village sites can be found in *Medieval Rural Settlement in North-east England*, edited by Blaise Vyner and published by the Architectural and Archaeological Society of Durham and Northumberland (1990). For the best-known deserted village excavation, Wharram Percy, the most useful general summary is still Maurice Beresford and John Hurst's *Wharram Percy Deserted Medieval Village* (London, 1990).

The Northumberland National Park Authority Historic Village Atlas Project 2003–04

Robert Young

In 2003, before Carenza Lewis saw the full fruits of her Cambridgeshire community fieldschools and Michael Wood produced his 2010 TV series documenting the community-based study of Leicestershire's Kibworth Village, Northumberland National Park Authority (NNPA) initiated its own, innovative approach to the study of historic settlements: *The NNPA Historic Village Atlas Project.* It proved to be a highly successful collaboration between the NNPA and local communities, funded by the Heritage Lottery Fund, and the NNPA Sustainable Development Fund. As NNPA Archaeologist at the time I finalised the project brief, raised the grant aid, and managed the project, but all of the hard work was carried out by the Newcastle-based consultancy *The Archaeological Practice,* in association with a vast number of enthusiastic National Park residents.

The Project

While the dictionary definition of ATLAS appears as: *'A bound collection of maps'* and *'Any volume of tables charts or plates that systematically illustrate a subject'*, our own *NNPA Historic Village Atlas* was, and is, much more than a gathering of materials. NNPA officers in general have always promoted an approach to understanding history and archaeology rooted in local communities and driven by community groups, working with professional historians and archaeologists. Our principal aim in the Atlas project was to turn passive consumers of 'expert' opinions into active producers of their own historical and archaeological stories to create an organic whole. We wanted to instil confidence in local groups to organise future archaeological projects. We also aimed to produce:

i) an illustrated historical summary of each selected village, based on maps and showing village development within the surrounding landscape;
ii) 'archaeological sensitivity maps' that would help to plan future village development without damaging archaeological remains;
iii) a summary report on the development of the National Park's historic villages, and a general account of historic settlement patterns throughout the area.

The following sites were chosen for the study, based on their potential, their known archive evidence and physical data, and active local groups:

Akeld	Hethpool
Alnham	High Rochester
Alwinton	Holystone
Byrness	Ingram
Elsdon	Kilham
Falstone	Kirknewton
Great Tosson	Tarset
Greenhaugh	West Newton
Harbottle	

What further distinguished these from other 'archaeological' sites was the fact that they are still occupied today, and consequently are continually maintained and modified by active communities to meet the changing demands of modern life.

The project drew on archaeological data, buildings surveys, an excellent series of air photographs, maps, documents and old photographs as its main information sources – all standard landscape archaeology fare. But what made the project 'special' at the time was a series of public meetings and workshops, and an oral history project that brought members of the local community into contact with professional archaeologists.

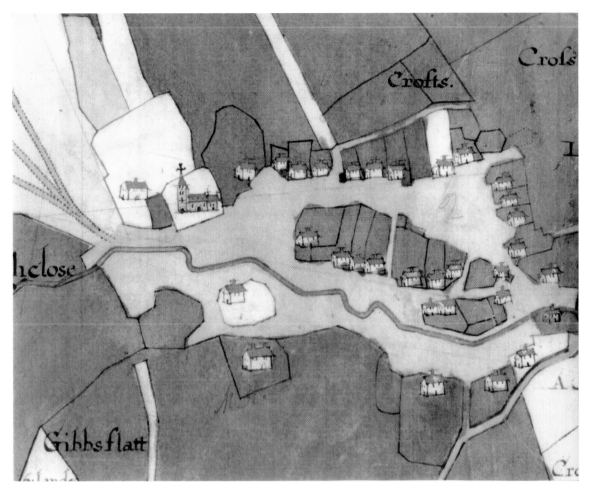

Figure 15.10. Plan of Alnham village from an estate map of 1619 (courtesy of the Estate and Collection of the Duke of Northumberland)

One of the main highlights was the wealth of historic map data unearthed in the region's various libraries, Record Offices and private collections including that of the Duke of Northumberland; some of this material goes back to at least the sixteenth century. Of particular importance were the eighteenth- and nineteenth-century County Maps, seventeenth- to nineteenth-century Estate Maps, the Parliamentary Enclosure Surveys and Tithe Maps and various editions of OS maps. Extracts from all of these appear throughout the Atlas and they give a fascinating view of the rapid rate of change within the villages and their landscapes in a relatively short

space of time. The project also produced its own archaeological distribution maps for each village. At Alnham, for example, a comparison of the 1619 Estate survey (Figure 15.10) with the eighteenth-century Enclosure Map, and the air photographs revealed that several of the seventeenth-century boundaries and the foundations of buildings shown on the maps still survive in the landscape today.

In 1987 John Grundy produced a report on *The Historic Buildings of the Northumberland National Park*. Here, for the first time, all of the supposed 'historic' buildings within the Park were graded in terms of their national and regional importance. In addition, the Historic Village Atlas Project produced up-to-date photographs of the exterior of each identified 'historic' building in the villages.

Undoubtedly, the real innovation came with the level of community involvement that the project engendered. Nine public consultation events were organised over the year at which people were encouraged to bring maps, plans and old photographs for consolidation into individual 'village archives'. Some of the material was absolutely fascinating: at one meeting in Elsdon village, for example, we were presented with a bill of sale and deeds for a single rigg within a large field – but this was not a medieval transaction and instead was something which happened in 1946!

All local schools were informed about the work, as were Parish Councils, and an oral history project ran in conjunction with the public consultations. Over 60 interviews were recorded about various aspect of village life. The results of the research were widely distributed and, in addition to libraries, schools, etc., copies of village reports were placed in pubs and cafes

where both locals and tourists alike could learn more about the individual sites.

The Project subsequently served as a springboard for community led, historic environment projects in the National Park. The 'Atlas' has helped planning and development control decisions, and it has also provided a baseline document from which further studies, enhancing the understanding and enjoyment of the National Park's historic villages, might be developed. Local history groups now exist in Elsdon, Harbottle and Holystone villages and the work also stimulated the activities of the Tarset Archive Group. The overall 'Atlas' approach has since been adapted to locations elsewhere in Northumberland, as well as in County Durham and North Yorkshire.

Summaries of all village reports are available on the NNPA website: http://www.northumberland nationalpark.org.uk/understanding/history archaeology/historicvillageatlas.htm. These should stand as a lasting testimony to the importance of community involvement in the study of village development and evolution.

Notes

1. E.g. Williamson 2003.
2. Roberts and Wrathmell 2002, 29, fig. 1.14.
3. Roberts and Wrathmell 2002, 9–11, figs 1.3–1.5.
4. Harrison 1990.
5. Harvey 1982; Wrathmell forthcoming; Roberts 2008, fig. 4.6.
6. English and Miller 1991, 14–18; Evans and Jarrett 1987, 199–210.
7. Jarrett and Wrathmell 1977; Evans *et al.* 1988.
8. Roberts 1989–90, 25–38.
9. Sylvester 1956, 23–26; Higham 2004, 62–63; Winchester 1987, 68–77.
10. Sylvester 1949, 1, 13–24; Atkin 1985, 173–175; Roberts and Wrathmell 2002, 90–99; Winchester 1987, 69–70, 82–83; Harrison 1990, 22, fig. 3.
11. E.g. Taylor 2002, 53–71.
12. See Higham 2004, 126.
13. Winchester 2000, 91, fig. 4.4.
14. Higham 2004, 29–30.
15. Higham 2004, 29–30; Winchester 1987, 3, 93.
16. Higham 2004, 75–78; Harrison 1990, 20–25; Winchester 1987, 39–41.
17. Winchster 2000, 10–13 and fig. 1.9.
18. Winchester 1987, 6, 42; Higham 2004, 114–118.
19. Raistrick and Holmes 1962, 20–23.
20. Mayfield 2003.
21. Whitaker 1812, 237.
22. Raistrick 1976, 33–34; Whitaker 1812, 237–238. The writer is preparing a more detailed discussion of Whitaker's discoveries.
23. See Beresford and Hurst 1971, 80–83.
24. Beresford 1952–54; Beresford 1986, 22–23; Hurst 1986, 8.
25. Taylor 2010, 5.
26. Beresford 1986, 22–23; Beresford and Hurst 1971, 76–78, 87.
27. Beresford and Hurst 1990, 92; Andrews and Milne 1979, 29–33.
28. Wacher 1966, 608.
29. Pallister and Wrathmell 1990, 67–71; Evans and Jarrett 1987, 203–204.
30. Andrews and Milne 1979, ix.
31. Andrews and Milne 1979, 44–45; Wrathmell 1989, 23–33; Hayfield 1988, 33, 84–90.
32. Heslop and Aberg 1990, 79–88; Austin 1976, 69–132; Austin 1989a.
33. Austin 1989a, 15, 65–80.

34. Austin 1989a, 167–173.
35. Hayfield 1984, 43, 46, 50.
36. Hayfield 1984, 43, pl. 1, 49; Austin 1989a, 70–71.
37. Higham 2004, 8–13.
38. Higham 1998–99, 79–101.
39. Coggins *et al.* 1983; King 2004,335–338; Higham 1979, 34–37.
40. King 1978, 21.
41. Charlton and Day 1979; Hayes 1983.
42. Moorhouse 2003; Ramm *et al.* 1970.
43. Raistrick and Holmes 1962, 18–23.
44. Addyman *et al.* 1963, 29–35.
45. Hair *et al.* 1999.
46. Richardson 1979.
47. Hurst 1956a, 251, 270.
48. Pallister and Wrathmell 1990, 66; Wrathmell 1989, 28.
49. Gardiner 2000b, 163–168.
50. See Harrison and Hutton 1984, 10–15.
51. Roberts 1987; Roberts and Wrathmell 2002; Roberts 2008.
52. Wrathmell 1984, 30–31.
53. Hodgson 1827, 189; Pallister and Wrathmell 1990, 70; Wrathmell 1989, 26.
54. Wrathmell 1989, 3–4.
55. E.g. West Hartburn House C. Pallister and Wrathmell 1990, 71.
56. Harrison and Hutton 1984, 10–15; Neave 2010, 356–357.
57. Hayfield 1988, fig. 4; Andrews and Milne 1979, fig. 1; Wrathmell 1989, 32, fig. 23.
58. Evans *et al.* 1988, 140.
59. Pallister 2007, 25–27; Austin 1989a, 4, 10.
60. Roffe 2000, 14–15; Wrathmell forthcoming.
61. Wrathmell forthcoming.
62. Beresford and Hurst 1990; Wrathmell forthcoming. See tabulation of reports on p. 30 of this volume.
63. Addyman *et al.* 1963, 33–35.
64. See, for example, the plea in Coggins 2004, 329.
65. Ramm *et al.* 1970, 2.
66. Coggins 1992, 81.
67. Richardson 1979, 24–25, fig. 4.
68. Raistrick and Holmes 1962, fig.14.
69. Hair *et al.* 1999, 141–143, 154–156.
70. Hodgson 1827, 388, note; Charlton and Day 1979, 219, note.
71. Sanderson 1891, 72.
72. Coggins 1992, 77–82; Coggins 2004, 325.
73. King 1978, 21; King 2004, 340.
74. E.g. Jarlshof Houses 3, 6 and 7. Hamilton 1956, 137–139 and pl. 27a, 160–164 and pls 33a–b; see also Dalglish, Chapter 16, this volume.
75. Coggins 2004, 331.
76. Roberts 1993, 438–441, 445, 452–453.
77. Higham 1979, 35, fig. 4.3.

Scotland's Medieval Countryside: Evidence, Interpretation, Perception

Chris Dalglish

Introduction

My entry point for this discussion of the medieval Scottish countryside is a question: what do we mean by Scotland? I have chosen to consider all of modern Scotland, because archaeology is organised in the present along national lines and because the country's modern borders were established before AD 1600, yet I am conscious that it was only during the later medieval period that much of the north and west came under Scottish dominion. Whether or not the medieval archaeology of these areas can be described as 'Scottish' is of more than semantic (or pedantic) importance: perceptions of the Scottish landscape and research traditions in Scottish archaeology have been coloured more than a little by national narratives rooted in the concerns of the kingdom's heartlands in the east and south.

Here, I wish to adopt a critical perspective, questioning divisions and traditions in the scholarship of the medieval countryside. I begin by considering the constructed nature of Scotland's geography and link this to a review of past research and a description of the development of the subject, while also seeking to understand its relationship with its intellectual and social context. The largest section of the chapter presents a summary of current understandings and interpretations of the evidence, and in this, I try to capture something of the complexity of what was evidently a varied and dynamic past. I end by considering questions for a future archaeology of the medieval Scottish countryside and, in particular, by reflecting briefly on the potential for an archaeology

which is more critical in its outlook and capable of developing a subtle understanding of the connections between local particularities and broader historical processes.

The geographical context

Scotland, as perceived, is a country of two parts: the Highlands and the Lowlands, separated by the Highland Boundary Fault, which runs from Arran in the south-west to Stonehaven in the north-east (Figure 16.1). Scotland north of the Fault is mountainous with a lower-lying coastal fringe. The interior is studded with fresh-water lochs and cut by glacial straths and glens. The coastline is indented with sea lochs, and the archipelagos of Orkney, Shetland and the Inner and Outer Hebrides lie to the north and west. South of the Fault are low-lying plains, hills and a less fragmented coastline. The hills and broad valleys of the Southern Uplands traverse the country from west to east, defined to the north by the Southern Upland Fault, beyond which lies a wide rift valley: the Midland Valley of Scotland.

The Highland/Lowland characterisation of Scotland seems natural – the topography either side of the Highland line is dramatically different – and its uncritical acceptance has conditioned archaeological and historical thinking, since discussions of settlement tend to concern themselves with one region or the other and search for characteristic regional types and patterns. It is too commonly assumed that the different physical conditions of each region caused

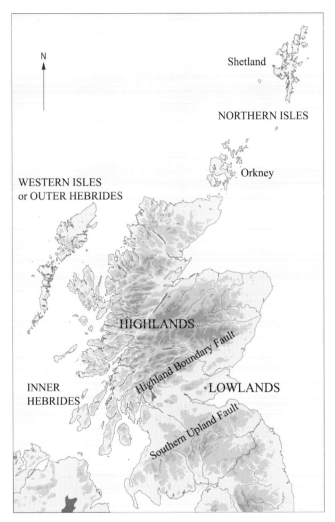

Figure 16.1. Map of Scotland showing the main geological features and geographical divisions mentioned in the text.

people to live in quite different ways: the Highlands are often presented as a marginal upland zone suited to pastoral farming; the Lowlands as fertile ground naturally suited to the production of crops. Superficial generalisations such as these lend a coherence and uniformity to each region by working from topographic and geographic averages. They convey value judgements about each region (e.g. as marginal or productive) and make such judgements appear natural and inevitable by tying them to seemingly objective physical traits of the landscape.

We should adopt a questioning stance towards the notion that we can understand Scotland as two distinct and coherent physical environments and the idea that we can interpret the human history of the Scottish countryside simply in terms of adaptation to differing environmental conditions. There are clearly many other contrasts in the Scottish landscape: thus the mountainous and peat-dominated interior of the Highlands contrasts with the fertile machair (shell sand) plains of the west; the hills of the Southern Uplands differ markedly from the plains of the Midland Valley, and even this division is confused by the fact that neither area is topographically uniform. Such variation means that there are districts which are only ambiguously 'Highland' or 'Lowland' in character and which can be, and have been, assigned to either region.

The process whereby this complexity has been simplified and reduced is clear when the problem is approached from an historical perspective. 'Highland' and 'Lowland' are not eternal facts but concepts which emerged in the Middle Ages and which are not in evidence much before the fourteenth century.[1] The circumstances surrounding their emergence include the retreat of the Gaelic language from the Lowlands and its resulting association with Scotland north and west of the Highland line, the centralising and expansionist ambitions of a Scottish kingdom whose heartlands lay in the south and east (with much of the north and west beyond Scottish control), and the related perception that the Lowlands were 'civilised', while the Highlands and Islands were savage and barbarous. Literature emerging from the Scottish Court identified the Highlands as distinct, with its own character, language and customs and this two-fold Highland/Lowland divide was later reiterated and developed in the culture and literature of Renaissance, Enlightenment and Romantic Scotland.

We must, therefore, be sensitive to the complexities of the relationship between people and environment in medieval Scotland. There are differences in settlement and land-use, and we might understand these in part by considering differences of physical geography, but we should also be attentive to the cultural origins of our perceptions of the Scottish countryside and the influence these preconceptions have had on scholarship.

Medieval settlement research

In constructing the Highlands and the Lowlands, settlement, landscape and life in each region have been reduced to an essence: variation and dynamism are overlooked in favour of a coherent 'Highland' or 'Lowland' past. Such essentialism is not characteristic of all research, but it has been common, and it has been most evident in relation to the Highlands: the Highland past has been mythologised in both the academic and the public mind. During the Victorian era, Scottish archaeologists showed little concern for the medieval countryside, for two main reasons: first, the discipline's primary interest was prehistory; second, there was a belief that there had been a

social and cultural stasis in rural, especially Highland Scotland from the Iron Age to the modern era.[2] This assumption was a deeply rooted one. Indeed, already during the medieval period, literature cast the Highlands and its inhabitants as wild and untamed, linking perceptions of geography and society.[3] In the eighteenth century, Enlightenment theorists built on these prejudices, holding that all societies developed along a set evolutionary path and concluding that Lowland Scotland was one step behind England, and the Highlands were further back still.[4] In the nineteenth century, national consciousness was founded on the Romantic conviction that the essence of Scottish society had been preserved in pure, primitive, authentic form in rural Scotland, especially in the Highlands.[5] In this context, archaeologists saw little point in the direct investigation of the medieval rural past, as that past could be known through archaeological studies of the Iron Age or ethnographic studies of the Victorian present.

After the First World War, the study of historic settlements and landscapes did begin to develop with the emergence of the new discipline of Folk Life studies.[6] However, the primary focus here was the recent past of the eighteenth and nineteenth centuries and Folk Life scholars concerned themselves with the study of traditional (read 'conservative') life. It continued to be assumed that the medieval rural past could be understood without direct investigation because centuries-old traditions had survived into a more recent age.

In the 1950s and 1960s, discontentment with this thesis of historical stasis grew and this was articulated by Horace Fairhurst, who questioned the prevailing method of projecting 'into a more distant past the conditions prevailing in the early eighteenth century'.[7] Fairhurst was a geographer with archaeological interests and, in 1961, he became the first head of the Department of Archaeology at Glasgow.[8] His approach combined archaeological, geographical and historical interests and he argued that knowledge of the pre-modern countryside should be founded on evidence not assumption. From this time, medieval settlement archaeology began to emerge as a recognisable concern in Scotland. This is broadly synchronous with the development of the subject elsewhere, and Fairhurst's origins as a geographer are important in understanding why. Elsewhere in Britain, medieval settlement archaeology gathered momentum in the 1930s as part of a wider interest in the history of everyday life.[9] There was a blurring of the divisions between history and geography with growing interest, on both sides, in local and regional patterns of geography, climate, settlement and agriculture. In Scotland, Fairhurst and his contemporaries began their careers in this context and their agenda makes sense in terms of the broader direction of their subject.

Yet, despite widespread recognition of a gap in archaeological knowledge regarding Scottish medieval settlement, little progress was made for some time; indeed, archaeologists continued to express anxiety about this failing into the 1990s.[10] There are a number of reasons we can give for this. Firstly, the survival of settlement sites has been adversely affected by the efficiency and intensity of later agricultural improvement, which appears to have been thorough in its re-ordering of the landscape.[11] The evidence can, therefore, be fragmentary and difficult to locate. Secondly, fieldwork undertaken to address the medieval settlement problem was limited in the decades after 1960 (there was a reduction in the volume of medieval settlement research in the UK as a whole at this time[12]). Thirdly, with the benefit of hindsight, we can see that the methodologies employed in the search for medieval settlements were themselves part of the problem; a few medieval sites were found in the 1950s and 1960s, but these were accidental discoveries where medieval remains lay on top of or within prehistoric monuments which formed the real focus of attention.[13] Where the discovery of medieval settlement evidence was the primary objective, fieldworkers tended to hope that such evidence would survive directly underneath eighteenth- or nineteenth-century structures.[14] This strategy was never likely to be productive: settlements appear to have been fluid and dynamic, moving and shifting location and changing form, and the construction of buildings from turf and wood has resulted in ephemeral, fragile and elusive remains.

Added to all this is a phenomenon recently dubbed the 'ghettoisation' of Viking and late Norse archaeology.[15] The Viking and late Norse periods are temporally coincident with the medieval period in Scotland, but confined to areas of Scandinavian settlement and rule in the far north and west. The archaeology of these regions has tended to be studied in separation from 'Medieval Archaeology' in Scotland and, as a result, the literature bemoaning a lack of knowledge about medieval settlement has tended not to acknowledge the much fuller settlement evidence which has been emerging from Scandinavian Scotland for some time.[16]

Since the early 1990s, changes in archaeological perspective and method and in the circumstances of archaeological practice have led to a transformation in our understanding of the medieval countryside. One key development has been the onset of developer-funded archaeology: limited resources were available for rural archaeology in the 1970s and 1980s, but this situation changed in the 1990s with the publication of government policy on the treatment of archaeological remains in the planning process, requiring developers to provide for the investigation and recording of archaeological remains likely to be affected by their proposals. The resulting increase in archaeological fieldwork has led to the identification of a number of medieval settlement sites, several of which have now been excavated.[17]

Coincidently, archaeologists began to shift their attention from the investigation of individual sites to the understanding of wider landscapes. The Royal Commission on the Ancient and Historical Monuments of Scotland (RCAHMS) now routinely combines field survey with the analysis of aerial photographs, maps and other sources in the investigation of large areas, and it has achieved some success in the identification of medieval settlements, field systems and other landscape features.[18] Others have combined landscape survey with excavation to identify, date, characterise and contextualise medieval settlement sites.[19] Adoption of a landscape approach has also been central to a new confluence of disciplines, bringing together archaeologists, historical geographers, environmental historians and others for the study of the historic countryside.[20]

Study of the medieval countryside has seen significant change in the last two decades, with a raised profile, the adoption of a landscape perspective and a reinvigorated concern for interdisciplinary dialogue. However, these changes have not been universal and the divide remains between medieval archaeology and Viking/Norse archaeology. Each of these subjects tends to maintain its own distinct research networks, to pursue its own concerns and use its own methods.

Key Theme: Settlement and Environment, Woodland and Forest

Archaeologists, historians and others have begun to take serious interest in the interaction of humans and the environment in medieval Scotland. In particular, recent decades have seen a number of studies of the relationships between settlement, farming, woodlands and forests and these have analysed archaeological landscapes alongside making effective use of documentary sources and palaeo-environmental data such as pollen.[21] This area of research is important, amongst other things, because it provides us with information on the different demands placed on resources in the medieval countryside and, in allowing us to understand how access to such resources was contested and negotiated, it generates valuable insights into the nature of medieval society.

A good example of this is the archaeology of the medieval forest.[22] The term 'forest' has a particular meaning in this context: forests were legally-defined hunting reserves, created either by the king or under licence by barons. Forests were being created from the early twelfth century and were eventually to be found across southern, central and eastern Scotland (e.g. the southern forests of Ettrick, Jedburgh and Liddesdale) and in parts of the Highlands as well (e.g. the forests of Atholl, Mamlorne and Mar); many were associated with royal or baronial castles or hunting lodges. Forests were managed to maintain habitats within which game, particularly deer, could flourish and this created the potential for conflict with other uses to which the same land might be put, such as grazing and crop-rearing. Forest laws prohibited actions such as woodland clearance, grazing, muir-burn and settlement, unless such actions were licensed. There is documentary evidence for the creation of licensed forest clearings known as 'assarts' in the twelfth to fourteenth centuries, and it is likely that many assarts will not be known to us because none of the local forest administrative records, known as Forest Rolls, survive for Scotland. We can enhance the documentary evidence by identifying the archaeological remains of deer park enclosures and assarts on the ground (Figure 16.2). In places like Annandale, Southdean and Liddesdale in southern Scotland, settlements have been located lying within large earthen dykes formed from a bank and external ditch. These boundaries most likely represent assart enclosures: placing the ditch on the forest side of the boundary, creating a higher obstacle on that side, would help to prevent deer from entering the farm but allow them to return to the forest if they did happen to stray. Assarts are attempts to accommodate different practices within forest areas by allowing farming to take place within defined and controlled limits.

Viking and late Norse archaeology has experienced a boom in settlement research but this has focused largely on the investigation of settlement sites:[23] the primary form of fieldwork is excavation and there are particular interests in the analysis of artefacts, architectural remains and environmental evidence.[24] Archaeologists of Viking/Norse Scotland and of medieval Scotland are all concerned to investigate interactions between people and their environment, but each group approaches this subject in a different way: medieval archaeology surveys and analyses field systems and other landscape features; Viking/Norse archaeology analyses fish and animal bones and other evidence preserved in domestic middens.

These archaeologies have followed separate paths and each has a distinct alignment, with archaeologists of Norse Scotland looking to the North Atlantic, including Scandinavia, Iceland and Greenland, and archaeologists of medieval Scotland looking elsewhere in Britain and to Continental Europe. At a deep level, the separation of the two subject areas is sustained by the 'national' character of historical writing. The heartland of the medieval kingdom of Scotland lay in the south and the east and large parts of the west and north lay beyond Scottish borders until late in the medieval period: Norway ceded the Hebrides to Scotland in 1266, along with the Isle of Man; Orkney and Shetland remained Norwegian until 1468/69. In other parts of the north and west, and after 1266 and 1468/69, Scottish sovereignty was acknowledged but the Crown often struggled to exercise any real authority. The concern of much Scottish history has been the story of Scotland's emergence, expansion and consolidation as a kingdom. In this story, the west

Figure 16.2. Aerial photograph of the deer park enclosure known as 'Buzzart Dikes' in Perth & Kinross. This bank-and-ditch earthwork (running left to right in foreground) encloses an area of about 86 ha. (Photograph © Crown Copyright: RCAHMS. Licensor www.rcahms.gov.uk)

and north are marginal and peripheral or they feature as problem territories to be won and subdued.[25] One result therefore is that the archaeology of the north and west, and particularly the islands, is frequently dislocated from discussions of medieval Scotland.

Settlement and landscape: evidence and interpretations

In partial correction of this dislocation, the following discussion begins with a summary of the evidence for Scandinavian Scotland. Two further sections discuss the evidence from other areas, from 'champagne country' and from upland Scotland; together, these sections provide an overview of the period between *c.* AD 800 and 1400. A fourth section discusses the late medieval period (the fifteenth and sixteenth centuries)

when the *baile* or *toun* (i.e. 'township') became the typical form of settlement across Scotland.

Scandinavian Scotland

With the exception of the trading centre at Whithorn, the settlement evidence associated with Scandinavian Scotland is concentrated in the far north and west.[26] Shetland, Orkney and the northern mainland (Caithness and Sutherland, perhaps south to the Moray Firth) fell within the Earldom of Orkney, which was under Norwegian suzerainty for much of the medieval period; numerous settlements of this period have been identified and investigated in the Northern Isles and on the northern tip of the mainland. In the west, the chain of islands stretching from Lewis to the Isle of Man also came to answer to the Norwegian Crown; but here the archaeological evidence for Viking and late Norse settlement is confined to the Western Isles.

The Viking period extends from *c.* AD 800, when Viking raids are first documented, to the eleventh century, and the late Norse period extends from the eleventh century to the fourteenth (although the end date is fluid: Norway ceded the west to the Scottish Crown in 1266, but the Northern Isles remained Norwegian until 1468/69). In archaeological terms, the first clear evidence for Viking-period settlement dates to *c.* 850, and some would argue that it is hard to place much of the evidence before *c.* 950.[27] One of the questions which have dominated research in this field is the extent to which there was continuity in settlement. Pre-Viking settlements were typically isolated farmsteads with cellular buildings, with plans variously described as 'jelly baby', 'figure-of-eight' and 'shamrock' in form (Figure 16.3). In contrast, Viking and late Norse buildings are often reminiscent of contemporary Scandinavian architecture: long rectangular hall-houses (with large central hearths and sometimes built-in benches along the walls) or longhouses (byre-dwellings where humans and animals lived under the same roof). However, any assertion that a clear change in architectural style represents a discontinuity in settlement driven by Viking invasion is complicated by a number of factors: on some sites, indigenous and Scandinavian styles of architecture and material culture mixed; and many 'Viking' or 'Norse' farmsteads have been built directly on top of or very close to pre-Viking ones, sometimes even retaining existing structures in use. A case in point is South Uist, where recent work has identified over 20 Viking/Norse settlements, many belonging to settlement mound clusters which also contain mounds of Middle Iron Age (100 BC–AD 300) and Late Iron Age (AD 300–800) date.[28] Here, good evidence exists for a long continuity in settlement pattern, with minor shifts in location around well-established focal points. Even where such continuity in location has not been established, the overall settlement pattern appears to have remained one of isolated farmsteads, with small building clusters composed of the main farmhouse and its outhouses. These farmsteads were a focus for mixed arable and pasture farms and for fishing, and their inhabitants appear to have come from all points on the social spectrum.

There are exceptions to this general pattern and a number of settlements appear to have developed into more complex entities. At Jarlshof in Shetland (see Feature Box: *Key Site to Visit*, p. 278), a single farmstead with a two-room rectangular house and associated outbuildings developed through time with the addition of further houses and outbuildings as the site grew to accommodate an extended family. At Bornais in South Uist, a number of settlement mounds lie in a cluster: the Viking/Norse phase of occupation comprised perhaps five farmsteads, and this nucleated settlement may have evolved from a single farmstead. Bornais may even have been a political centre; this was certainly true of one other larger-than-normal settlement, namely the Brough of Birsay in Orkney, a centre of the Norse earldom.

Champagne country

The other part of Scotland for which we have a reasonably coherent and well-supported model of medieval settlement is the low-lying part of the Lowlands from Aberdeenshire in the north to the border with England in the south. This area fell within the medieval kingdom and, during the twelfth and thirteenth centuries, landholding there was feudalised, new forms of estate centre were introduced, and the settlement and farming landscape was transformed.

Alongside castles, local estate centres of this period tend to take the form of enclosed manorial sites. Around 100 moated enclosures have been identified, scattered across the Lowlands.[29] The ditches enclosing these sites are often square or rectangular in plan and it is assumed they would have enclosed a group of buildings (few sites have been excavated and few of these excavations have explored the interior of the enclosure). Many of these enclosures, which date to the twelfth to fourteenth centuries, are likely to represent the administrative cores of new feudal estates, some belonging to the lay nobility and gentry and some to the Church. Non-moated manorial sites are also found, although many of these have been associated with the monastic orders, which were significant landholders; many of their estates were administered from granges, where farming produce was collected for further distribution.[30]

In the twelfth and thirteenth centuries, the wider countryside was also transformed, taking on characteristics like nucleated settlement and open-field farming to thus resemble 'champagne' or 'champion'

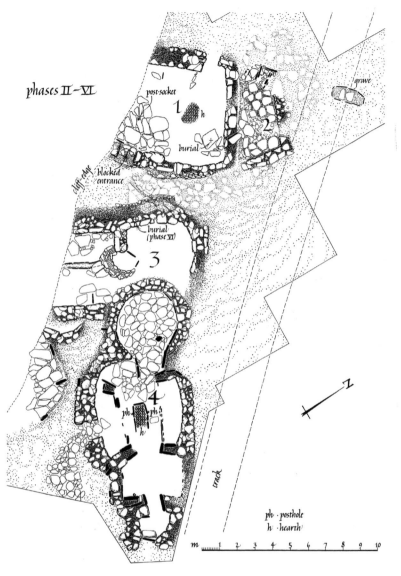

Figure 16.3. Plan of the excavated settlement at Buckquoy, Orkney. A Pictish-period building with an anthropomorphic, 'jelly baby' form occupies the south-eastern part of the trench (building 4 on the plan). Several rectilinear buildings representing successive Viking-period farmsteads lie to the north-west (buildings 1 and 3 on the plan). Parts of these later buildings have been lost to erosion along the cliff edge. (Plan © Crown Copyright: RCAHMS. Licensor www.rcahms.gov.uk)

landscapes elsewhere in northern Europe.[31] These characteristics are found in the lower-lying parts of the eastern Lowlands from the English border in the south to Aberdeenshire and Moray in the north, also extending into Lanarkshire and eastern Ayrshire in central Scotland. Nucleated villages and open-field

farming may have developed first in (or perhaps even before) the eleventh century in south-east Scotland, which was part of Anglo-Saxon Northumbria for a time. Elsewhere, they are to be associated with the emergence of demesne farming in the twelfth and thirteenth centuries. Under this system, landholders

Key Site to Visit: A Norse Settlement at Jarlshof in Shetland

Jarlshof,[32] on Sumburgh Head in Shetland, owes its name to Walter Scott who visited in 1814 when the only feature visible was a seventeenth-century laird's house (Figure 16.4). Scott imagined Jarlshof ('Earl's Mansion') as a seat of the earldom of Orkney. Subsequent events have complemented Scott's imaginary perception of the place: in the late nineteenth century, a storm revealed archaeological remains along the shore and excavations then and in the 1930s and 1940s have revealed a complex site with a sequence of structures dating from the prehistoric and historic eras, including an impressive grouping of Viking and late Norse buildings. In 1925, Jarlshof was given to the State by its owner and it is open to the public, featuring the most extensive remains of a Viking/Norse site currently visible anywhere in Britain.

Jarlshof is a multi-period site, with Neolithic houses, a complex of Bronze Age buildings, Iron Age dwellings including a broch, a Viking/Norse farm and a later laird's house. The Viking-period farm was built close to the ruins of the broch and is likely to have been established in the ninth century AD. Its focus is a long, rectangular house containing a hall, with a large central hearth and raised wooden platforms along the walls (for seating, sleeping, working), and a kitchen, with a central hearth and an oven. The outbuildings associated with this hall-house include a barn or byre, and two smaller buildings interpreted as a smithy and a bath-house or *hof* (cult building). Later, additional houses and outbuildings were constructed, although there may have been no more than two houses inhabited at any one time, suggesting that Jarlshof was home to an extended family rather than any larger community. In the eleventh century, the style of architecture changed and the longhouse, with byre and dwelling under one roof, came to replace the separate house and outbuilding. The presence of byres indicates that cattle were a component of the economy here, and animal bones from the site also include sheep and pigs as well as domestic and wild birds, whales, seals and fish, including cod, saithe and ling. Analysis of the fish bones suggests that deep-sea fishing was practised. As yet, no associated cemeteries are known for any of the phases at Jarlshof.

Figure 16.4. Aerial photograph of the multi-period settlement of Jarlshof, Shetland. A series of circular, prehistoric structures overlooks the beach on the right hand side of the image. These structures are partially overlain by the ruinous Early Modern laird's house (the tallest unroofed structure in the photograph). Inland lie the foundations of a number of rectilinear Viking/Norse buildings. (Photograph © RCAHMS (John Dewar Collection). Licensor www.rcahms.gov.uk)

Figure 16.5. Aerial photograph of the village of Midlem, Scottish Borders. The houses occupy long, thin, rectangular plots (tofts) stretching back from the central open space of the village green. (Photograph © Crown Copyright: RCAHMS. Licensor www. rcahms.gov.uk)

worked their land directly rather than leasing it out and direct farming required a labour force, housed in village settlements, and discouraged the division of land with walls or hedges.

Unlike England, Scotland has few apparent deserted medieval village sites – their absence or invisibility testament to the thorough manner in which the Scottish countryside was transformed in subsequent centuries. As a result, the character of the Scottish medieval village has to be teased out from disparate sources: some villages, like Midlem in the Scottish Borders, are still inhabited; others survived long enough to be depicted on post-medieval maps; medieval documents give us some information on settlement organisation; and the extent of village development can be plotted by mapping characteristic place-names elements like 'ton' (as in Duddingston). Added to this is a small but growing body of archaeological evidence: some village sites have been identified through fieldwork and aerial survey in the Borders and the Lothians; other villages may have

been ploughed flat, but their remains survive below ground and have been identified by field-walking for ploughed-up artefacts (e.g. Springwood Park in the Scottish Borders) or by archaeological evaluation in advance of development (e.g. Archerfield, East Lothian and Dreghorn, Ayrshire).[33]

These sources provide evidence for nucleated villages of varying sizes and forms but, to generalise, the ground was normally divided into a series of adjacent plots or tofts, each occupied by houses and other buildings and used for domestic, horticultural, agricultural or industrial purposes. Buildings were constructed from a range of materials, including clay and turf, wood and stone. In some villages, like Midlem (Figure 16.5), the tofts were arranged around a central open space or village green, while in others, like Rattray in Aberdeenshire,[34] they were strung out along a single road. Villages could stand alone or develop in association with a castle, moated enclosure or grange, church or chapel.

Village populations provided labour and needed

to exploit adjoining lands for their sustenance, and accordingly evidence for some of their farming practices has survived in the form of rig-and-furrow cultivation remains, visible as earthworks where they have escaped modern cultivation and as cropmarks on aerial photographs where they have not (Figure 16.6). These rigs are the result of repeated ploughing of the same ground using a mouldboard plough: they are broad and high and they have a characteristic 'reverse-S' shape, the curve resulting from the way in which the plough has been turned at the end of each rig. Rigs of this type are often grouped into blocks, known as 'butts' or 'furlongs', which can vary from 100 m to over 200 m in length. Prehistoric forms of rig are known in Scotland, and there indications that plough-formed rigs were being created from the mid-first millennium AD. However, there is no evidence to suggest that these forms were ancestral to medieval reverse-S rig: like village settlement, with which it is associated, reverse-S rig was perhaps introduced to Northumbrian south-east Scotland sometime before the eleventh century; otherwise it is to be associated with the twelfth- and thirteenth-century reorganisation of the landscape described above.

Upland Scotland

The champagne model is not applicable to all parts of the Lowlands and, across the Highland line, the rich settlement evidence of the far north and west is not replicated everywhere. This means that significant parts of Scotland cannot be understood by generalising from the evidence outlined above. To further appreciate the likely complexity of the medieval Scottish countryside, we can consider three districts: the eastern Highlands, the uplands of the Borders and of Dumfries and Galloway in the south, and Renfrewshire and eastern Ayrshire in central Scotland. These are districts where medieval settlement appears not to have taken village form, or where additional types of settlement have been found alongside villages.

Robert Dodgshon has combined historical, cartographic and archaeological evidence to propose that dispersed farmsteads and enclosed fields were typical of the west Highlands and Islands prior to the late Middle Ages.[35] The dispersed settlement pattern proposed by Dodgshon is consistent with the Viking and Norse evidence outlined above, and the

early medieval archaeology of the eastern Highlands also indicates a dispersed pattern, although the architectural detail is different there. Of principal interest here is a distinctive type of structure called the Pitcarmick building (after a site of that name).[36] Pitcarmick buildings have been found in upland Perthshire and Angus, where they lie singly or in clusters of two or three in areas of rough pasture or moorland, away from the lower ground favoured by medieval villages and by post-medieval and modern settlement. Pitcarmick buildings are long and rectilinear, with rounded or angled ends and turf or turf-and-stone walls (Figure 16.7). They are usually broader at one end and many have a partially sunken floor, perhaps indicating that they contained both a byre and a dwelling. The excavation of one of these buildings at North Pitcarmick returned a seventh- to ninth-century AD radiocarbon determination and a smaller structure built on top of this building is tenth to eleventh century in date. What we appear to see here is an early medieval episode of settlement in upland areas, followed by the retreat of settlement to the lower ground and the use of upland areas for shieling (transhumance, associated with small structures known as shieling huts). This medieval shift from permanent to seasonal occupation has been identified elsewhere in Perthshire,[37] and recent work in Aberdeenshire, even if it has not identified any Pitcarmick buildings, has recorded rectilinear structures of possible medieval date in similar moorland locations.[38]

Upland parts of Dumfries and Galloway and of the Scottish Borders have also yielded evidence of dispersed settlement and transhumance.[39] The remains of long rectangular stone-and-turf buildings, often with an adjacent enclosure and sometimes accompanied by additional buildings, have been identified in a number of upland locations. Although little or no excavation has been undertaken, documentary evidence suggests that these structures represent farmsteads which were well-established by the fourteenth century. Just as in the Highlands, upland locations in the south also provide evidence of shieling in the form of shieling huts, many of which should be medieval in date.

In Ayrshire and Renfrewshire, the medieval settlement evidence is sparse, but we can point to three excavated sites of non-village character. About 50 years ago, Frank Newall excavated a prehistoric

Figure 16.6. Aerial photograph showing cultivation rigs and terraces at Braemoor Knowe, Scottish Borders. In places, the open-field cultivation remains have been flattened by later ploughing; they survive best on the higher, rougher ground in the centre of the photograph. (Photograph © Crown Copyright: RCAHMS. Licensor www.rcahms.gov.uk)

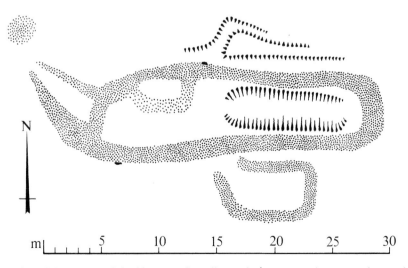

Figure 16.7. Survey plan of the Pitcarmick building at Ashintully, Perth & Kinross. This is a good example of the type: long and rectilinear with rounded ends; the depression in the eastern half of the interior may indicate the location of a byre. (Plan © Crown Copyright: RCAHMS. Licensor www.rcahms.gov.uk)

'homestead' at Knapps in Renfrewshire and found that it had been re-used in the medieval period, when a thick, sub-circular stone wall enclosed a cobbled yard, a byre-dwelling and a series of outbuildings.[40] Newall argued that this farmstead dated to the fourteenth or fifteenth century. He also excavated a second prehistoric site in Renfrewshire which returned evidence of medieval occupation: the Iron Age fort of Wall's Hill.[41] Excavations there encountered a rectangular building, of fourteenth-century date, divided into a central living space, a byre and a third chamber. More recently, development-led excavations at Laigh Newton in East Ayrshire have identified a plough-truncated medieval settlement comprising a sub-circular palisaded enclosure (perhaps a yard or pen) and an adjacent ditched boundary enclosing sunken stone-and-turf and timber buildings and a possible grain-drying kiln.[42] Pottery and radiocarbon dates indicate fourteenth- and fifteenth-century occupation.

Baile and toun: the late Middle Ages

The story of rural medieval settlement appears to have been a dynamic and complex one, with the introduction of new architectural idioms in the Scandinavian north and west, the development of nucleated settlement and open-field farming in parts of the Lowlands and the abandonment of established upland settlements and their replacement by shielings in both the Highlands and the Lowlands. To further complicate the picture, we can add two other processes: the emergence of the township (*baile* in Gaelic; *toun* in Scots) as the predominant settlement form, and the expansion of open-field farming throughout the country. These changes differ from the ones already discussed because they affected all parts of Scotland.

While some nucleated Lowland villages are still inhabited today, this is rare outside of south-east Scotland. Throughout most of 'champagne country', these villages appear to have been deserted or to have reduced in size – the excavated examples at Springwood Park, Rattray and Archerfield are cases in point.[43] Episodes of village desertion or shrinkage may have happened at various times, but there is evidence that this became a wider process in the late medieval period. Springwood Park (see Feature Box: *Key Excavation*, p. 283) experienced abandonment or

severe contraction from the late fourteenth century, and Rattray was in decline from the fifteenth. Documentary and place-name evidence indicates the splitting of landholdings in this period, which is clearly seen in the emergence of multiple farms with the same name but with different prefixes such as 'easter' and 'wester' or 'upper' and 'lower'.[44] Various explanations have been offered for this disaggregation of settlement, centring on the decline of demesne farming and its replacement by a rent-based economy and on an evident drive to take in new lands.[45] (Perhaps the latter explains the development of farmsteads in the late medieval period at Knapps, Wall's Hill and Laigh Newtoun.)

At the same time that large nucleated villages were shrinking or becoming deserted, we see the opposite trend elsewhere in Scotland. Dodgshon has argued that the dispersed settlement pattern of the western Highlands was replaced from the late medieval period, gradually and in a complex manner, by a pattern of nucleated townships.[46] He proposes that nucleation was tied to the introduction of feudal habits of landholding and land assessment, which appeared later in the west than in the east and south, although (as Dodgshon recognises) the diversity and fluidity of settlement forms throughout the late medieval and modern periods suggests that there is no simple, singular explanation of the situation. Recent work in the Western Isles has provided some archaeological evidence which supports or complements the suggestion that there was a broad shift in settlement pattern at this time. Thus survey and excavations in the Loch Olabhat area of North Uist have indicated the replacement of a dispersed with a nucleated pattern of settlement in the late Middle Ages.[47] On South Uist, the late Norse settlements at Bornais and Cille Pheadair were both abandoned in the thirteenth or fourteenth century.[48] Subsequently, settlement probably shifted inland: the township lying inland from Viking/Norse Bornais has produced artefacts dating to the period from the sixteenth to the nineteenth centuries, and South Uist as a whole seemingly experienced a gradual process of settlement shift inland in the late medieval and post-medieval periods.[49] Elsewhere in the west, the evidence for townships does not extend back any further than the late medieval period, a case in point being the excavated sixteenth-century township which extends

Key Excavation: Springwood Park: A Deserted Medieval Village

Springwood Park, near Kelso in the Borders, is one of the few Scottish deserted medieval villages to have been excavated.[50] Nothing of this site is visible on the ground surface: it was identified through scatters of pottery ploughed to the surface and partially excavated by Colin Martin in 1966 and as part of the 'Borders Burghs Archaeology Project' (funded by the Manpower Services Commission) in 1985–86. There is no direct medieval documentation for the village, but we know that it was on land which pertained to the lords of Maxwell and lay close to the medieval town of Roxburgh (this burgh – the principal market and administrative centre of the central border region – was itself deserted in the late medieval period). The distribution of pottery on the surface suggests that the village site represents a large 'suburban' settlement, possibly with more than one street, lying adjacent to a bridge to Roxburgh over the River Teviot. The economy of the settlement appears to have rested on a mixed farming regime, weighted towards cereal cultivation (wheat, barley, rye, oats) and cattle.

The excavations revealed one part of the settlement, occupied from the late twelfth to the fourteenth century and comprising several buildings and their yards fronting on to an open area or street on the slope of an old river terrace (Figure 16.8). Three main periods of occupation were identified. In Period I (c. AD 1150–1250) the excavated area contained at least two adjacent plots or 'tofts' divided by a ditch. These tofts were occupied by timber-framed buildings supported on earth-fast posts, probably with walls of a perishable material like wattle-and-daub and thatched roofs. In Periods II (c. 1250–1300) and III (c. 1300–50) the two tofts continued to exist, but not without change. In Period I, the buildings were aligned N–S; in Period II they were re-aligned to run E–W; in Period III they were returned to a N–S alignment. Also in Period III, the space between the houses was filled in to create a continuous row of buildings, and this perhaps suggests that there was some pressure on space. In contrast to the earth-fast post structures of Period I, the buildings of Periods II and III were cruck-framed, with clay walls on stone footings and thatched roofs. All of the Period III buildings had cobbling at their northern ends, suggesting that they were byre-dwellings. This was not the case with the Period II houses, where cobbling was associated with the hearth. The artefacts recovered during the excavations relate to the domestic and agricultural aspects of the settlement, and they provide evidence for the combing, spinning and weaving of wool for cloth (a traditional rural industry). The pottery assemblage was dominated by cooking pots and storage jars of types local to the region, demonstrating links to local markets, no doubt accessed through the adjacent town of Roxburgh.

Figure 16.8. Excavations in progress at Springwood Park, Scottish Borders, during the mid-1980s. The foundations of a row of medieval buildings can be seen extending along the far edge of the trench. (Photo © Piers Dixon)

over an area of *c.* 1 ha, occupying most of the island of Eilean Mor on Loch Finlaggan, Islay.[51]

Settlement patterns appear to have been in flux throughout the late medieval and early modern periods and the overall trend was towards the *baile* or *toun* as the predominant settlement form, smaller than the medieval village but larger than the farmstead and typically organic or irregular in plan form with of clusters of houses, outbuildings and yards. Associated with the emergence of the township is the spread of open-field farming. Open-fields were characteristic of champagne areas of the Lowlands for much of the medieval period and, Dodgshon argues, open-field farming likely led to the demise of enclosed field systems in the west Highlands and Islands from the late medieval period onwards.[52] By the eighteenth century, and in many places long before, unenclosed rig-and-furrow cultivation had become the norm.[53]

Questions for a future archaeology of the medieval Scottish countryside

When considered on the national scale, there are clearly gaps in our empirical understanding of Scotland's medieval rural archaeology: some parts of the country have rich settlement evidence; others have little or none; and some periods are better covered than others. Despite this, past work has done much to alter our knowledge of medieval settlement and landscape and we are now far from the position described by Horace Fairhurst in 1960, when assumption not evidence underpinned our understanding of the subject.

I could conclude this review by pleading for more work to add detail to the patterns outlined above and to fill the geographical and chronological gaps, but I think it is more important to offer some thoughts on the philosophy and practice of future research. The first is that future research must be critical in nature, questioning perceptions, preconceptions and traditions of inquiry. I have noted the manner in which national narratives have inflected research, not least in constructing divisions between medieval and Viking/ Norse archaeologies; in doing so, my intention has not been to argue for a new, fully integrated and uniform archaeology of the medieval countryside, rather I wanted to suggest that current practices cannot go unquestioned, and neither can the traditions from

which they stem. In discussing national narratives, I have also argued against perceiving Scotland in simple bipolar terms, as Highland and Lowland in geography and culture. Again, my intention here has not been to prescribe a new categorisation of medieval landscape and society, with a greater number of smaller regions each characterised by their own settlement forms and farming practices, but to call the process of categorisation into question and to indicate the complexity of this past. For me, the aim should be to value and capture that complexity. But the question is: how do we do that?

A key to this may be the problem of understanding how local particularities articulate with broader historical processes. We are in a better position than ever to understand the character, details and subtleties of medieval farms, villages and their landscapes. Over the last 20–30 years, there have been important developments in practice as archaeologists and others have asked new questions of the medieval countryside and mobilised new methods and techniques to provide some of the necessary answers: landscape archaeology has situated settlements in their local environments, provided evidence for a range of routine farming practices and discovered previously unrecognised archaeological forms like the Pitcarmick building; excavations on Viking and Norse settlements have approached questions of farming practice and economy from a different angle, undertaking intensive studies of midden deposits; and multiple disciplines have collaborated under the banner of environmental history, exploring human interactions with woodlands and other locales. These strands of work have laid strong foundations for future approaches to the subject, and additional interpretive power will no doubt emerge when they are employed in concert, rather than in separation.

The ability to investigate sites and landscapes in such detail does not of itself generate understanding, and many studies lack a convincingly critical perspective on the manner in which we connect archaeological data to historical narrative. In some work, there is a tendency to tie material change (or continuity) rather simplistically to questions of ethnicity, constructing cultural histories in which artefacts and architectural idioms serve as signifiers for particular groups like Vikings, Picts and so on.[54] In other work, patterns in the archaeological data are explained by tying them to contemporary (but not necessarily connected) historical events. Such interpretations could be subjected to a more rigorous critical interrogation and challenged with a more sophisticated grasp of the articulation between local particularities and broader processes. The particular and the general are not effectively linked by stating simply that X example is a case of Y process. Rather, we need to understand how broader processes played out in particular cases, seeking to stay attuned to variability as well as commonality. We need to ask questions such as: 'how did feudal principles articulate with the lives and routines of this particular farming community?' (There is a subtle but significant difference here from the statement 'the character of this settlement is a result of feudalisation'). To pursue the articulation of local particularity and broader process further, there is much that can be gained from considering recent discussions in post-medieval archaeology, where a dialectical approach to interpretation has gained some currency.[55]

Further reading

Historic Scotland has published a series of concise and well-illustrated introductions to Scottish archaeology including Piers Dixon's *Puir Labourers and Busy Husbandmen: The Countryside of Lowland Scotland in the Middle Ages* (Edinburgh, 2001), Robert Dodgshon's *The Age of the Clans: The Highlands from Somerled to the Clearances* (Edinburgh, 2002) and Olwyn Owen's *The Sea Road: A Viking Voyage Through Scotland* (Edinburgh, 1999). Viking and late

Norse settlement is reviewed more extensively in J. Graham-Campbell and C. Batey's *Vikings in Scotland* (Edinburgh, 1998).

A series of articles by Piers Dixon provides more in-depth discussion of the medieval Lowlands, including his 'Settlement in the hunting forests of southern Scotland in the medieval and later periods' (1997) and 'Champagne country: a review of medieval rural settlement in Lowland Scotland' (2003). The latter is published in S. Govan (ed.), *Medieval or Later Rural Settlement in Scotland: 10 Years On* (Edinburgh, 2003), which contains other useful overviews, syntheses and discussions, including Strat Halliday's 'Rig-and-furrow in Scotland' and Olivia Lelong's 'Finding medieval (or later) settlement in the Highlands and Islands: the case for optimism'. Two useful discussions of settlement and field systems in the Highlands and Islands are Dodgshon's 'West Highland and Hebridean settlement prior to Crofting and the Clearances: a study in stability of change?' (1993a) and 'West Highland and Hebridean landscapes: have they a history without runrig?' (1993b).

Acknowledgements

My thanks to Piers Dixon for proposing me to write this paper, for offering some suggestions on the content and for providing the photograph of the excavations at Springwood Park reproduced as Figure 16.8. Thanks to RCAHMS for supplying the images reproduced as Figures 16.2–16.7, to Ingrid Shearer for the base map used in Figure 16.1 and to Katinka Stentoft for her assistance in creating the final map.

Notes

1. Withers 1992, 143–145; Newton 2009, 59–65.
2. Dalglish 2003, 15–22.
3. Withers 1992, 143–145.
4. Berry 1997; Kidd 1993.
5. Withers 1992, 145–156.
6. Dalglish 2003, 23–27.
7. Fairhurst 1960, 73.
8. Caird and Proudfoot 1987.
9. Gerrard 2003, 56–89.
10. E.g. Yeoman 1991; 1995, chapter 8.
11. Dixon 2003, 54.
12. Gerrard 2003, 138.
13. E.g. Newall 1960; 1965.
14. Fairhurst's own excavations are a case in point here: Fairhurst 1968; 1969.
15. The phrase is Olivia Lelong's: Lelong 2003, 8.
16. For a summary of excavations undertaken up to the 1990s, see Graham-Campbell and Batey 1998.
17. E.g. Laigh Newton, East Ayrshire (James *et al.* 2007); Archerfield, East Lothian (Hindmarch 2006).
18. E.g. Dixon 1994; RCAHMS 1990.
19. E.g. the *Ben Lawers Historic Landscape Project* (Atkinson (ed.) 2004; 2005) and the *SEARCH* project

in the Western Isles (Sharples and Parker Pearson 1999).

20. See Dalglish 2009 for a discussion of the relationships between these different disciplines.
21. E.g. Davies and Watson 2007; Dixon 1997; Smout (ed.) 2003.
22. Dixon 1997.
23. See Graham-Campbell and Batey 1998; Barrett 2008 for overviews.
24. In addition to the above, see Sharples (ed.) 2005: 7.
25. McDonald 1997, 254; plus Armit 1996: 4–6 on the influence of ideas of marginality on the archaeology of the Western Isles.
26. Overviews include Barrett 2008; Graham-Campbell and Batey 1998, chapters 9–11; Morris 1998; Sharples and Parker Pearson 1999.
27. Parker Pearson *et al.* 2004b, 129.
28. Sharples and Parker Pearson 1999.
29. Alexander 2000; Banks *et al.* 2009, 16–26; Coleman and Perry 1997; Stronach 2004; Yeoman 1998.
30. Hall 2006; Dixon 2003.
31. Dixon 2003; cf. also Halliday 2003.
32. See Ritchie 2003 for a recent summary.
33. See Dixon 1998 on Springwood Park; Hindmarch 2006 on Archerfield; Addyman 2004 on Dreghorn.
34. Murray and Murray 1993.
35. Dodgshon 1993a; 1993b.
36. RCAHMS 1990; Lelong 2003.
37. Lelong 2003, 7.
38. RCAHMS 2007.
39. Dixon 2003.
40. Newall 1965.
41. Newall 1960.
42. James *et al.* 2007.
43. Dixon 1998; Murray and Murray 1993; Hindmarch 2006.
44. Dodgshon 1981.
45. Dixon 2003, 55–56; Dodgshon 1981.
46. Dodgshon 1993a.
47. Armit 1996, 208–213.
48. Sharples and Parker Pearson 1999, 51–55.
49. Parker Pearson *et al.* 2004b, 161.
50. Dixon 1998.
51. Caldwell and Ewart 1993; cf. also Caldwell *et al.* 2000.
52. Dodgshon 1993b.
53. Halliday 2003.
54. See Barrett 2008 on this interpretive tradition in Viking and late Norse archaeology.
55. E.g. Orser 2009; Johnson 2006; Dalglish 2009.

PART III

RESEARCH METHODS

A Practical Guide to Investigating Medieval Rural Settlements

Carenza Lewis

Introduction

The countryside of Britain contains the remains of tens of thousand of medieval rural settlements, some now entirely deserted, a few surviving as islands of antiquity within some of the last century's largest new towns, and many thriving as villages of varying size or as small towns. Preceding chapters of this volume show how much is now known about their origins and development. They also show how that knowledge has built up, in a creditably cumulative manner, as again and again, hard work combined with hard thinking have opened up new areas of research which have in their turn pointed to new avenues of enquiry. It is easy to forget that this is the result of barely half a century's study: even today, the study of medieval rural settlement remains a young discipline. The combined pace and breadth of these advances has been made possible by the wide range of approaches which have been brought to bear on the subject, and, notably, by the many researchers involved in recording and investigating medieval settlement, from a variety of disciplines – and from none. Indeed, it has been a hallmark of rural settlement studies that the work of scholars from the fields of archaeology, history, geography, economics, anthropology, ecology and landscape studies has been complemented, particularly in the early 'pioneer' years, by long hours of work put in by voluntary enthusiasts. Many have searched field and fen, moor and molehill for evidence of lost settlements, submitting their findings to the *Annual Reports* of the Deserted Medieval Village Research Group, as these in turn fed the nascent

county Sites and Monuments Records of the 1960s and 1970s.

The 60 years and more that have elapsed since Maurice Beresford first set foot on the quiet earthworks of Wharram Percy have seen many transformations in the way the study of medieval rural settlements has been approached and, almost as importantly, in the backgrounds of those who have carried out this work. The numbers of professional historians and, in particular, archaeologists, were swelled enormously by the expansion of the higher education sector in the 1960s and by changes in legislation and practice surrounding archaeological sites in the 1970s and 1980s, particularly those under threat from development. Consequently, it might seem reasonable to assume that all that can be known about medieval rural settlements has now been discovered and that this volume represents a grand, final exegesis at the end of medieval settlement history, to turn a phrase.

In fact, the truth could not be more different, as the chapters of this book in fact make apparent. Even today, when the ranks of heritage professionals are probably at their greatest extent and there seems to be ever less room for the 'amateur', there is still much to be contributed by anyone who has the time and commitment, unconstrained by targets and budgets, to search court rolls or stubble fields for the myriad pieces of the multi-layered jigsaw that is rural settlement studies.

This Appendix aims to help those who have been inspired by this volume to carry out their own historical and archaeological investigations into medieval settlements. It offers guidelines for a number of methods which can significantly advance knowledge and understanding, but which have little or no impact on the historical or archaeological evidence being investigated, and in particular do not risk breaking into undisturbed stratified archaeological layers. They can thus be carried out by those with little or no professional training as there is minimal risk of damage to unique and irreplaceable historic resources. All approaches covered here require minimal financial outlay and can be flexibly adapted to make best use of whatever time and manpower resources are available. A short account of how to carry out each type of investigation to appropriate standards in order to produce useful information is supplemented by references to other, more detailed, works which can be consulted for further detail.

This chapter excludes any activity which might cut into undisturbed, intact archaeological deposits. Any trench more than 20–30 cm deep dug in a rural settlement is likely to disturb pre-modern deposits, and on any given spot there is an approximately 10% chance of encountering a 'feature' (such as a pit, wall, ditch, floor surface etc) which requires a practised eye to recognise and a good understanding of stratigraphy (the relationship between different features and layers in the ground) to excavate properly. If this is not done competently, the information which would otherwise enable these to be identified, characterised and dated will be lost, and as both the feature itself and its relationship with the layers around it are inevitably destroyed by the process of excavation, this can never be re-investigated and so both feature and knowledge are lost forever. As it is never possible to be certain where intact archaeological deposits will survive, it is recommended here that methods which risk damaging such deposits should not be attempted by those with no previous experience or training.[1] Even 'test pit' excavations, which only disturb very small areas (typically 1 m^2) and can significantly advance understanding of settlement development,[2] should not be attempted by those without previous experience of excavation without making arrangements for on-site archaeological supervision or pre-excavation training in test pit excavation and finds recognition. They are, however, a very useful method for investigating within occupied settlements, which should be

considered if appropriate archaeological expertise is available.[3] Geophysical survey[4] is also excluded from this Appendix as it requires specialist equipment which requires considerable experience to operate and interpret the results.[5]

The methods outlined here range from desk-based research that can be carried out at home to activities involving on-site finds collection. It is vital to stress that the most important priorities in any research are: (1) to ensure the correct methodology is followed so that the results are valid; (2) to ensure that the results are recorded and reported properly so that they can be studied effectively by the original researcher and by others, in both the short and longer term; and (3) to ensure records and materials are stored or archived properly. In addition, it is important not to start any project unless you know you have the time, facilities, resources (including manpower) to see the work through to completion and to record and report the findings.

The following pages aim to ensure that the reader can achieve these aims in whichever investigations they choose to undertake. Indoor, desk-based research (internet and documentary research) is here followed by a range of outdoor techniques, with non-intrusive approaches (such as building and earthwork survey) followed by invasive procedures which involve some, fairly limited, disturbance of the physical evidence. Of these techniques, intrusive approaches are usually the most difficult to organise and liable to incur significant costs, notably in identifying finds, which may require the professional services of an expert. With all the approaches described below, while technical methods can be learned relatively easily, the knowledge required to fully analyse the results and appreciate their implications will always take much, much longer to acquire. However, any information, once collected properly, can always be analysed again and again, so this should not put off anyone with less than a lifetime's experience from having a go at their own data collection using any or all of the approaches below.

Part 1. Desk-based investigation

Internet research

Today, the most immediately accessible starting point for research into a medieval settlement is, for most people, the internet. An increasingly vast amount of relevant information is available here, but as with everything on the internet, it is advisable to proceed with caution. Simply typing a village name into a search engine may, in lucky instances, immediately turn up a list of sites containing copious quantities of meticulously researched reliable information about the known history of the settlement, supported by accurate references to works of known academic credibility – but it is much more likely to offer you a minimal Wikipedia entry and a list of local plumbers! In either case, it is important to check that the websites being consulted actually relate to the settlement in question – names such as Sutton, Bourne, Newport, Thorpe, Kirby, Downton and so on are very common, occurring several times in many counties across Britain, and even seemingly more unusual names are likely to occur in more than one place.

Even once it has been established that the website in question does indeed refer to the settlement under investigation, there are still many caveats: some sites are very much more useful to the serious researcher than others. Some towns, villages and even hamlets may have their own websites which contain historical and archaeological information about the settlement and its surroundings, which has been carefully researched and is entirely reliable. But for other villages their websites may be misleading or simply wrong, drawing on local traditions rather than facts. Any sites that are pursuing an obvious agenda are likely to contain suspect information: such sites may range from otherwise well-intentioned ones campaigning on environmental issues to more fantastical endeavours seeking to use historical or archaeological evidence to 'prove' some whimsical (but passionately held) notion about the final resting place of King Arthur or the Holy Grail.

As a general rule, websites of national and local government organisations (usually ending with .gov. uk) can be used with some confidence as being likely to contain reliable information. The most useful of these are, in most cases, those which allow the online visitor to search original historic sources. Links from such websites will often be useful, not least because the authority creating the link will usually have checked the validity of the linked site. Sites run or sponsored by British universities (usually ending .ac. uk) should also be of value. Below are a few sites, all free to access, which can be recommended as first ports of call when researching medieval settlements, as providing information, or sources of information, which is likely to be useful and reasonably accurate. A search of these will provide an indication of the extent of historical and archaeological research that has been conducted on any given site to date, some idea of the potential for future investigation, and allow some preliminary data collection, sorting and analysis to be carried out. In online research, like any other research, it is, of course, crucially important to take careful note of the exact details of every site visited, and ensure that all downloaded information can be traced back to its source (this will, of course, also aid referencing and help avoid plagiarism).

The National Archives website (http://www. nationalarchives.gov.uk/) is the site of the UK government's official archive, covering England, Wales and the United Kingdom. It is easily navigable and provides some advice about sources for researching villages and hamlets, and access to a limited number of primary sources, with a bias towards recent material, which can be searched online. Via this site, it is possible to trace other sources held by the National Archives of relevance to a particular settlement but not available online. The holdings of the National Archives of Scotland, which include records created by Scottish government from the twelfth century until the present day, along with private records created by businesses, landed estates, families, courts, churches and other corporate bodies can be searched online, but not viewed, at http://www.nas.gov.uk/. For Wales visit the site http://www.cadw.wales.gov. uk/ and www.rcahmw.gov.uk/, and for Ireland go to both http://www.nationalarchives.ie/ and http:// www.proni.gov.uk/ (the website of the Public Record Office for Northern Ireland). Of note also is http:// www.visionofbritain.org.uk/index.jsp, created by the University of Portsmouth, which enables online searches of various sources including early Ordnance Survey maps.

British History Online (http://www.british-history.ac.uk/) is the website created by the Institute of Historical Research and the History of Parliament Trust to support the learning, teaching and research of academic and personal users. The site provides access to the Institute's digital library which includes some of the core printed primary and secondary sources for

British medieval and modern history. If a settlement has been covered by the Victoria County History (VCH), British History Online is increasingly likely to contain the entry in full (including references). In earlier volumes, the emphasis will be on the 'establishment' history of manorial descents and church patronage, while for more recent entries, a more rounded local history including some archaeological evidence is likely to be available. For places which have not been covered by the VCH, the return on a search on British History Online may be disappointing, but it is nonetheless always a good starting point.

If seeking archaeological rather than historical evidence, the best starting point is usually the Heritage Gateway website (http://www.heritagegateway.org.uk/gateway/). This product of collaboration between English Heritage and the Association of Local Government Archaeological Officers (ALGAO) is a portal intended to provide integrated online access to local and national heritage information resources. From it, it is possible to perform live searches of a number local and national datasets. The most useful is likely to be the online access this gives to local authority Historic Environment Records (HERs, formerly known as Sites and Monuments Records or SMRs). Although not all local authorities have yet made their HERs available online, the Heritage Gateway site is immensely useful for those places that are included as it provides details of all known archaeological sites, monuments, excavations, surveys and other evidence, listed by county and parish. The site also provides access to Listed Buildings Online database, which includes information about all standing buildings listed as of architectural or historic interest. Other useful datasets accessible via Heritage Gateway are the NMR Excavation Index guide to many of the archaeological excavations and interventions carried out in England, and the PastScape collection of information about England's archaeological and architectural heritage. While not all information in the latter datasets is available to read online, an online search will enable you to establish whether a visit to the office holding the information will be worthwhile. Likewise, the index of the English Heritage archive of photos, plans, drawings, reports and publications on archaeology, listed buildings, aerial photography and social history, including the records of the former

Ordnance Survey archaeological recording team and the Royal Commission on the Historical Monuments of England (RCHME), can be searched online at http://www.englishheritagearchives.org.uk/, although little material is yet available to view.

Websites with satellite images of the modern land surface such as Googlemaps (http://maps.google.co.uk/) may offer much for the online researcher, especially anyone with aspirations to carry out fieldwork, providing a photographic image of Britain from the air and showing the present disposition of settlement and landuse. A modern rectified vertical photographic image of any location can be viewed easily and quickly at almost any scale by zooming in from a national map with a few clicks of the mouse. Basic modern map information is superimposed over the photographic imagery so it is easy to check the location of any features of interest that may be visible. Although the photography is not carried out with archaeological aerial survey in mind, it does, of course, require clear visibility with no cloud cover, so most of the images are sunlit, which can show up earthwork remains of deserted and shrunken settlements well; likewise soil- and cropmark sites may be clearly visible if conditions were favourable. Furthermore, pockets of land within currently occupied rural settlements which may which have potential for test pit excavation can also be spotted in this way (Figure A.1). Most of Britain is covered to a very good level of resolution, and although less-populated areas and especially uplands are often only available at lower resolution, this is improving all the time. The archaeological interpretation of aerial photographic images is discussed in more detail below.

Compiling information from reliable internet sources in this way will enable the careful researcher to begin to build up a corpus of information pertaining to the history settlement or area under investigation.

Documentary research

The medieval period in Britain is, of course, a period for which written records exist, and from *c.* AD 1200 onward these were created and curated in increasing numbers, both by national institutions such as the Crown, the exchequer and the courts of justice, and locally by sheriffs, boroughs, guilds, manors and religious institutions. Historical sources which may provide information about medieval settlements fall into two types: (1) 'Primary' sources are original written records such as Domesday Book, court rolls, wills, taxation records, etc. For medieval settlement study, some of the most promising are records of taxes levied nationally which may include a considerable amount of detail about the payees. Generally, however, material relevant to individual settlements will be found in the records of local institutions such as manors. (2) 'Secondary' sources are descriptive or analytical historical treatises written some time after the period being described. These include classic historical works such as Maitland's *Domesday Book and Beyond* (1871), local histories, and works of modern scholarship, such as the chapters in this volume.

Primary sources for history can be divided into national and local sources, with the latter likely to be of most interest to the aspiring historian of any given settlement. Below are summarised the main types of records and the types of information they might contain.[6]

National primary sources of most value for settlement research will include legal (chancery) records, accounting (exchequer) records and judicial records, all made or kept by the Crown. Legal records include those detailing the terms and conditions by which land or privileges granted directly by the king were held, which were often re-examined every time estates changed hands, either as a result of death or some other royal motive. These can contain valuable information about leading families, their households and local custom and practice in rural land management. Exchequer records include those drawn up to record the value of crown landholdings and details of national tax. The most famous of the former is the Domesday Book survey compiled on the orders of William I to establish the value of all his newly acquired English lands. The thirteenth-century Hundred Rolls provide some similar information for a more limited number of places. From the mid-twelfth century, records of the accounts of lands in royal possession are contained in the Pipe Rolls and their subsidiary documents. These may yield information such as income derived from estates and costs of building works. In many cases, these may provide the earliest documentary evidence for the names of subsidiary and minor places. Port Records and Royal Forest Eyres may also be of use for settlements

under the jurisdiction of these institutions. Other useful records are those detailing the yield from national taxes levied when the crown was short of funds: thus, for example, the Lay Subsidy of 1334 and the Poll Tax of 1377 provide pre- and post-Black Death snapshots which include the names of all payees by manor (although it must be borne in mind that as the former was a tax on wealth and the latter a per capita tax, the information is not directly comparable). Records relating to the administration of justice which are useful for local history are the Feets of Fines, effectively conveyancing documents, drawn up to record the private transfer of property, usually land. These can include genealogical and topographical information. Court Records (Eyre and Assize Rolls) include details of serious crimes in both town and country.

Key local primary historical sources for settlement studies include manorial estate and court records. These may include 'surveys' of demesne lands (those farmed directly by the lord), 'extents' detailing land farmed by tenants as well, 'terriers' describing landholdings topographically, accounts of incomes and expenditure, and records of the proceedings of manorial courts where justice for all but the most serious disputes and felonies would be administered. For those places lucky enough to have a good collection of surviving manorial records (often, but not uniquely, manors held by major landholders such as Glastonbury Abbey or the Duchy of Lancaster), there is a wealth of detail to be recovered about various aspects of medieval life and livelihoods, from decades-long year-on-year records of crop yields and prices to records of single incidents such as an accidental drowning in a village pond. The value of these resources has long been appreciated and many of the most comprehensive manorial records have been already been well worked over, and in many cases form the basis of published secondary historical sources such as village histories.

The first challenge for the aspiring settlement researcher usually lies in finding where information which needs to be consulted is held. The local studies section of good city libraries will often be a good starting point, especially for some of the secondary sources and published editions of primary sources. County Record Offices (CROs) usually also have published sources available for consultation as well as more recent primary historical records relating to their locality. Original versions of primary sources of medieval date may very occasionally be found locally in CROs, but these tend mostly to contain manorial records or 'estate papers' (relating to management of estates, but not courts) of post-medieval date only. However, these latter sources may well include records and maps which can be immensely useful to the study of medieval settlements, including eighteenth- and nineteenth-century Enclosure and Tithe maps. Many original manorial and estate records of medieval date are held in national institutions such as the National Archives (formerly the Public Records Office – PRO) (http://www.nationalarchives.gov.uk/) and the British Library's Department of Manuscripts, and are thus perhaps less easily accessible. Beyond these, other primary sources containing information pertaining to individual places may be contained in other repositories, including those of the universities of Oxford and Cambridge or in private hands in the libraries and muniment rooms of great houses. If this is the case, information can be very difficult to track down, although the National Archives is a good starting point. Even once located and accessed, original primary sources rarely have material arranged in such a way that makes it easy to find what one is looking for, even if one has good reason to believe it is there. Pot-luck searches for a particular name or place are likely to be frustrating and fruitless.

In general, consulting original primary sources of medieval date is usually impractical for all but a very few dedicated and experienced individuals who know the sources very well and have the skills to navigate their way through bulky parchment rolls and then to interpret medieval handwritten Latin. However, many valuable and key primary sources have been published in transcribed, translated (if necessary) and sometimes edited in order to make them available for a much greater number of people. These include many volumes produced by the Public Records Office and by institutions such as the Pipe Roll Society, the Royal Historical Society, and the Record Commission. Phillimore Press, for example, has performed an immensely useful service through its national 'History from the Sources' series. This includes comprehensive publication of Domesday Book (in both the original (abbreviated) Latin and modern English) in county-by-county volumes. At

a more local level, many regions are well served by long-running series of edited volumes produced, often in great numbers, under the aegis of county record societies such as the Wiltshire Record Society (originally the Records Branch of the Wiltshire Archaeological and Natural History Society). Such volumes (normally indexed) should be present in larger libraries with a local and county history section, or will be available on loan if requested.

Historical evidence should, of course, be interpreted with great care: it is important always to remember that medieval written records were created for a wide range of reasons, none of which had the settlement historian of the twenty-first century in mind; and also to be aware that historical records can be biased, misleading (sometimes intentionally so) and incomplete.[7] Every novice historian will soon encounter frustrating gaps and apparent inconsistencies in the evidence they examine, and these problems can be a challenge even to professional historians, let alone those with less experience. However, gradually building up a corpus of fully referenced historical information which can be organised chronologically (with the earliest information and events first), or thematically (with a series of sections on, for example, the history of the church, the manors, the people of the village, landscape forms and so on) can produce the beginnings of a useful and enlightening settlement history.

Historic map analysis

As noted above, many local record offices contain maps among their collections and, although most are post-medieval in date (seventeenth-century or later), many will contain valuable information about medieval rural settlements and landscapes. Comparing and transcribing information such as field boundaries, roads and buildings from historic maps of different dates allows the layout and changing form of earlier settlements and landscapes to be reconstructed.[8]

For some places, early estate maps may survive; these may show one manor or more. In most local record offices, maps relating to Enclosure and the commutation of Tithes are likely to be the most numerous and most detailed. Enclosure maps were created as a result of Parliamentary acts of Enclosure and mostly date to the eighteenth century onwards. These acts re-organised the medieval open fields into new enclosed fields and often laid out new roads to provide access to them.[9] Tithe maps were drawn up as part of the Tithe Commutation Act of 1836. This replaced 'in kind' payment (such as performing work for the tithe owner) for rights to farm land with cash rents, and in order to establish how much rent should be paid, the extent of tithe-able land had to be accurately measured and mapped, and details recorded of the land-owner, tenant, name or description of the land and rent payable for every piece of land in the parish.[10] Maps associated with Enclosure records and Tithe surveys alike are drawn at a large scale – a typical map covering a single parish can easily be 2 m across and contain a lot of detail. They will show the location of all features – buildings of all kinds, field boundaries, woods, roads and so on – in the landscape at the time the survey was made, before many of the most significant changes of the last two centuries: some of these features may be of medieval origin.

From the early decades of the nineteenth century, detailed Ordnance Survey (OS) maps are available: crucially these show the pattern and form of settlement before the advent of the railways and before significant expansion of many settlements which took place across the nineteenth and twentieth centuries, particularly in industrial areas. The 1:63,360 (1 inch to the mile) series can be informative, but the most useful for the settlement historian are usually the 1:10,560 series (6 inch to the mile), which inevitably contain much more detail of the layout of settlements and the rural landscape. Local Record Offices may hold copies of these maps.

To transcribe historical map data, drafting film should be laid over the historic map and all features traced onto it. These can then be transcribed onto a copy or tracing of the modern Ordnance Survey map. Features common to both the modern and historic maps can be identified, and the correct position of vanished historic features established by relating the position of these to features on both maps with a scale ruler or dividers. A new map is thus created, showing vanished historic features in their correct geographical position. If a number of historic maps are available, this process can be repeated for each one, with more recent historic maps providing reference points for features on older historic maps. Once all maps have been transcribed, it is then possible to

begin to carry out a 'regressive analysis' whereby later features can be removed (such as train lines or new enclosure field boundaries) or altered (in the case of roads or property boundaries which have been interrupted or diverted by later property additions). In this way, the earlier arrangement of the settlement or landscape can be gradually reconstructed, albeit increasingly speculatively in the case of earlier periods. Documentary evidence may contribute to this process, for example by dating features or providing evidence for the likely size of settlements based on the number of individuals taxed.[11]

Aerial photograph analysis

Aerial photographs can be an immensely illuminating source for the study of medieval settlements. At the very least, an aerial image of any settlement always provides a fuller and different view to that possible from the ground or by looking at maps, which can often lead to new insights. In many cases, however, aerial images are even more valuable for the traces of former settlement or other medieval activity they may reveal, potentially enabling entire landscapes of settlement, fields, and lanes to be reconstructed in a fraction of the time required to do the same from ground level (albeit in less detail).

As discussed above, contemporary aerial imagery of Britain is available via the internet. However, while this can provide an indication of areas of potential interest, rarely will it be at a good enough level of resolution to allow features of archaeological interest to be plotted and analysed in detail, and conditions at the time of photography may not always have been ideal to allow the features to show up well. Furthermore, much archaeological evidence visible from the air at the end of World War Two has been considerably eroded or even erased by subsequent ploughing, leaving little to be seen with any clarity on contemporary images. Aerial images most likely to contain data of interest to the medieval settlement researcher are those taken specifically to record archaeological remains, and historic images which show the landscape before recent damage. Such images may be available in local Record Offices, local HER offices and in some archaeological units, especially those attached to local government offices such as county councils and unitary authorities. In addition, the National Monuments Record (NMR) holds a vast archive of aerial photographs for England, including a collection of vertical black and white images of unparalleled value taken by the RAF in the late 1940s, which covers almost the entire country. The Royal Commissions for the Ancient and Historical Monuments of Scotland and Wales respectively hold collections of archaeological aerial images for their territories. The Cambridge University Centre for Aerial Photography (CUCAP) also holds a large repository of air photos of Britain, many taken by one of the greatest exponents of archaeological aerial photography, J. K. St Joseph. Some of these collections have online indexes which will allow the settlement researcher to establish where relevant information is held, although usually a visit to the repository in question will be needed to actually examine the images.

Archaeological features can appear in a range of different forms, depending on conditions on the ground.[12] With care, it may be possible to distinguish whether a feature visible from the air is a wall, ditch, platform or hollow, even if it has been ploughed flat. Features not been completely levelled by ploughing will show as earthworks, or humps and bumps in the ground. These will show most clearly in low sunlight. By noting the direction from which the sun is shining (by checking what direction shadows of trees are falling), it is possible to work out whether features are raised or depressed. As features running in the same direction as the sun will tend not to show up very well; it is best, if possible, to consult several photos taken at different times of day.

Buried archaeological features which have been completely levelled may nonetheless show up on aerial photographs as soil-marks, crop-marks or parch-marks. Soil-marks are features visible in soil bare of vegetation, such as arable fields after ploughing. In these conditions, features which have been cut into the ground, such as ditches or pits are likely to show up as darker than the surrounding area, as they will have a greater depth of soil in them. Buried banks or walls are likely to be lighter as they will have a thinner layer of soil on top of them. The exception to this rule is in landscapes such as fens, where water channels may show up as lighter than the surrounding dark peat as they have filled up with lighter silt. Crop-marks are features visible in growing crops: crops over cut features (thus filled with deeper deposits of soil)

will grow more vigorously, while those over buried built-up features such as walls, banks and platforms (overlain by less soil) will be relatively stunted in their growth. In spring and early summer, cut features are likely to show as areas of darker, thicker crop, and built features as lighter, thinner crop. The higher growth of crops overlying cut features may even create a false 3-D image, as cut features (that are actually depressions) will appear as areas of raised crop. Once the crop starts to ripen, however, the pattern changes, as stunted plants overlying built-up walls and so on will ripen before their richly nourished neighbours overlying cut features. Once the crop is all ripe, such distinctions will usually vanish. Parch-marks are created when grass overlying buried feature dies off differentially in dry conditions: grass overlying think layers of soil covering buried walls will die off sooner than that growing in deeper soils over cut features. A very dry, hot summer can often reveal, even just for a few days, archaeological features never seen before.

Once features of interest have been identified they can be copied or transcribed so they can be related to the OS map of the area under investigation (and of course it is always worth checking whether this has already been done before devoting hours of time to it!). Transcribing archaeological features is fairly easy if the photograph is a vertical image, taken looking directly down onto the features. (These are routinely taken for surveying purposes, and the RAF photos of the 1940s are all true verticals, with overlapping images taken to create stereoscopic pairs and to avoid the need to use the edges of the images, where some distortion will be present). To transcribe information from aerial photographs, a tracing should be made of the modern Ordnance Survey at a scale of 1:1000 (for a village) or 1:2500 (for a larger area such as an entire parish). Using field boundaries and buildings visible on both map and photograph as reference points, dividers and/or a ruler can be used to measure in the position of archaeological features onto the map. The small amount of distortion at the edges of photographs can be corrected in transcription by checking measurements in several directions. A new map is thus created, showing aerial photographic features in their correct geographical position. A magnifying glass can help when looking at fine detail on photographs, and if stereoscopic pairs of prints are available (taken to produce three-dimensional images), then a stereoscope (perhaps available to borrow) will enable earthworks and other upstanding features to be seen in 3-D.

Oblique aerial photographs are much more difficult to transcribe, because some features and distances will appear artificially foreshortened, but only in certain directions, and the extent of foreshortening will not be consistent across the whole image (the greater the distance of the feature from the lens, the greater the foreshortening). Accurate photogrammetry (correcting distortion to produce an accurate image) requires considerable experience and/or software packages and is effectively beyond the scope of non-experts. However, a useful approximation of the form of archaeological features can be made by using dividers to measure proportional distances in relation to features on OS maps. It is hugely helpful if several images of the archaeological feature are available, taken from different directions, as severe distortions in one image will be less severe in others.

The real skill, of course, comes in interpreting the features, identifying their likely date and character (village, manorial site, fishponds, etc.) and reconstructing the sequence of activities which created the observed features.[13] This only comes with experience, and in some cases it can be impossible to date features without excavation. Boxworth in Cambridgeshire is just one example of a village where an area of earthwork remains thought to represent former medieval settlement were revealed by excavation to be of predominantly Roman date.[14]

Part 2. Field investigation

A wide range of methods exist for field investigation into the physical remains of medieval settlements which can be both fascinating and produce entirely new information of great value to the medieval settlement historian for relatively little financial outlay, while causing no damage at all to the building or site under investigation. At the outset, however, it should be noted that, as with any activity which involves actually visiting a site, it is important to make personal safety and responsible behaviour top priorities. Permission should always be sought before entering land or property, and it is usually advisable to at least attempt to make contact before taking photographs. Risk assessment, health and safety responsibilities,

and insurance are all aspects of modern life which need careful thought before rather than during or after practical activities, particularly if these are being arranged for others to take part in, when risk assessments should always be carried out.[15] The Council for British Archaeology has access to policies specifically tailored to archaeological fieldwork.[16]

Earthwork survey

In places where settlement has contracted or shifted site during or after the medieval period and little cultivation has taken place since, the remains of former settlement may survive in pasture fields as upstanding earthworks, with the sites of houses, property boundaries and lanes preserved as a palimpsest of platforms, depressions, linear banks and troughs and holloways.[17] In areas where stone is widely available for building, traces of stone footings may be visible. Making a detailed measured plan of the exact form of such features not only records the extent of the abandoned settlement remains but, if done well, also produces a plan which will enable the form, function and even relative dates of the different elements of the remains to be established.[18] An experienced survey team working in good conditions may be able to complete a hectare in a day, but even a more novice team should be able to complete an area that size in a couple of weekends. Earthwork survey requires a team of at least two people, and a third can speed progress. If more than three people are available additional teams should be created to work on different parts of the site.

Earthwork survey involves recording changes in level which can be very slight – indeed, some of the most crucial information can come from very subtle features – and so it is best carried out when grass or other vegetation cover is short, which will often be in winter, spring or autumn. Earthwork survey should ideally be done after examination of historic maps and aerial photographs (and transcribing information as necessary), but a reconnaissance visit in advance of earthwork survey is nonetheless essential in order to establish the current extent of the earthworks and plan which areas are to be surveyed, at what scale, and identify any obstacles which may be present (such as livestock in fields, obstructions to visibility or access across different parts of the site). It is, of course, vital to keep to public roads and footpaths until landowners and tenants have been identified and agreed arrangements for access to fields. The scale at which the earthwork survey should be drawn is important as it will affect the amount of detail which can be collected and depicted. Drawing at a larger scale is easier for the novice draftsman, and can allow more detail to be shown, but smaller scales have the advantage of allowing a larger area to be depicted in a reasonably sized plan. The scale used for earthwork surveys is, of course, very different to that used on excavations which will often be planned at 1:10 or 1:20. Most earthwork sites are unlikely to measure less than 100 m in most directions, and so planning must be carried out at a smaller scale, which is in any case entirely justified by the lack of very fine detail which is present on excavated features. Commonly used scales for planning earthwork surveys are 1:500, 1:1000 and 1:1250. A decision as to which of these scales to select should be based on the assessment of the total area to be surveyed, the site complexity, and the ultimate purpose of the resulting information. For instance, earthwork remains within a small field less than 150 m square, could be drawn at 1:250, but if that field lies on the edge of an occupied village half a kilometre long and if the final intention for the plan of the earthworks is to be included on a plan of the whole settlement, then it would be better to draw at 1:1000 or 1:1250 scale. 1:500 is often used as a reasonable compromise. It may be possible later to change the scale of surveyed plans either by redrawing or by photographic copying (the latter is quicker and easier, although may cause some distortion).

On starting the survey the first task is to establish a series of fixed points from which all other measurements will be taken; this allows the finished plan to be tied into the OS. The easiest route is to create a 'baseline' along the centre of by marking out two points on the ground, one at either end of the site. In a rectangular field, the points would be sited midway along each of the shorter sides. These should be marked on the ground in a manner that will remain visible for the duration of the survey, taking into account the possibility that unexpected factors may delay this beyond its original intended time. Wooden or plastic survey pegs, flags on steel pins or spray-painted crosses are all acceptable ways of marking these baseline points (but do check that the landowner is happy for spray-paint to be used). This base line

can then be drawn onto the plan (positioned so that the site will not extend off the edge of the sheet!). The position of extant earthwork features can then be measured in by measuring from this baseline. A measuring tape should be laid out along the baseline, and another tape used to measure from it at right-angles or 'off-sets' to the tops and the bottoms of the slopes defining the earthwork features. Ensuring these right-angles or offsets are accurate is important. Measurements are then recorded on the plan, usually as dots which are then joined up once a series of points defining a platform, ditch, bank or other feature, have been marked. A set square or protractor should be used to ensure the off-set points are drawn on the plan in the correct place. It is good practice (and useful if something needs to be rechecked) to write the actual measurements on the plan as well as marking the spot with a pencil dot. Once completed, the dots can be joined up and direction of slopes shown using 'hachures'.[19] On large sites it will usually be necessary to lay out subsidiary baselines to measure from in order to cover the whole site, especially if it ranges across more than one field.

Much of the process of identifying observed features and analysing their relationships with others is carried out during the survey, which can thus often involve lengthy discussion between team members. Plans should be annotated to reflect these observations, including the identification of drawn features (e.g. 'bank', 'holloway', 'house platform', etc.), and any spatial or stratigraphical relationships they may have with other features.

Transcribing surveyed earthwork data onto copies of OS maps allows earthwork remains in different parts of the same settlement to be compared and analysed as part of the whole settlement, rather than in isolation. It is helpful to bring into the field a copy of the OS map at the largest possible scale in order to ascertain which features must be recorded in order to link the 'divorced' earthwork survey with the OS. Field boundaries should always be plotted. The plan made in the field from the measurements should be drawn up in ink (or scanned and drawn on computer) as soon as possible after survey is completed, with features from the modern OS map included so that the surveyed earthworks are fitted into the existing map. Once this is completed, the next stage is to try to identify and analyse any relationships between earthwork and modern features in order to tease out the earlier plan and development of the site. If this information can be combined with that from other investigations, the picture is likely to be much more complete, and much more informative. As with all methods of settlement investigation, the interpretation and analysis of the recorded information is where the greatest skill and knowledge is required, and nothing beats experience for developing this.

Historic building survey

Standing secular[20] buildings, if present, can be a highly important part of the evidence for medieval rural settlement studies: it is now known that many more buildings of medieval date survive in Britain than was until recently supposed. While most 'great' houses of any antiquity are likely already to have been recorded and analysed in some detail, lesser buildings such as smaller houses or cottages and industrial and agricultural buildings will often have had little or no attention, and in some cases buildings of medieval origin still remain to be identified as such behind more modern-looking (e.g. Victorian and Georgian) facades and repairs. Building survey can be done at two levels – extensive and intensive. In many instances, the second of these will follow on from the first.[21]

(i) Extensive building survey

Extensive building survey involves making a basic record, from the exterior, of all buildings within the study zone (village, parish or area) which are likely to be of interest. In the case of extensive building survey carried out to advance understanding of the development of the medieval settlement, it is in principle best to record *all* buildings, although in practice it is common to exclude those which are obviously new builds of the last century, especially on exclusively modern estates. As well as providing rough dates to all the built structures, it means you may be able to plot where possible post-medieval settlement extensions to a medieval core have occurred.

An extensive building survey should create a record for each building which includes the following information: its address, its type (domestic residence, farm building, industrial, etc.), its aspect (which way the front or main door faces) and overall orientation, its construction materials, and any dated feature (such as a plaque over a door or on a chimney stack – this is where binoculars may come in useful). A photograph should be taken, and an annotated sketch of salient features should be made. Notes should record the form of roofs, doorways and windows (and the frame material of windows), the number of storeys, the plan form of the house, the way it is linked to its neighbours, the material used for walling and roofing, and any extensions.[22]

(ii) Intensive building survey

Intensive standing building survey involves making a detailed, measured plan of the interior and exterior of a building which will help date it and reconstruct its chronological development in much more detail. This will of course require the owner's permission for access to the building: this can often provide a useful opportunity to enquire about any knowledge, plans or old photographs they may have relating to their home. Working with a building, best practice is to conduct a running survey where measurements within all rooms on each floor are linked by a single tape-line running the entire length of the house (akin to the baseline used in an earthwork survey), laid through interconnecting rooms or along a single linking corridor. A sketch plan with measurements should be made of the horizontal ground plan of each room and all vertical sections (i.e. internal wall surfaces). When recording the plan of each room, measure the length of all walls, and the position of windows and doorways. Also measure all diagonals across the room, and the depth of any recesses and fireplaces. When recording internal sections, measure the floor-to-ceiling height of each wall and all architectural features such as doors, windows, mullions, lintels, and timber sills, beams, posts, rafters, purlins and so on. Use a spirit level and string fixed to a vertical surface (this is where Plasticene or similar material comes in useful) to create a horizontal baseline and measure from this to ensure varying ground surfaces are recorded. Use a plumb line (again, this can be temporarily fixed in position using Plasticene) to create a vertical baseline and use this to check how far off the vertical line walls and architectural features are. Details of features within architectural timbers such as pegs, mortices and joints should be recorded, drawn, described and photographed, with a scale used in all photographs. Annotations will record important observations such as missing peg holes or hidden joints.

Upper storeys should be related to ground floor plans via the staircase(s). Roof spaces should also be included in the survey: they can be particularly valuable as they often contain early timber features which may be covered up elsewhere in the building, although access may be much more difficult here. External elevations should be measured and drawn in the same manner as internal ones, although at upper storey levels measurements may have to be taken from ladders, through windows, or estimated.[23]

Intensive building survey sketch plans should be drawn up to scale in ink or on computer as soon as possible. It is a standard convention that the thickness of lines indicates their importance: walls are more important than window frames, for example, and should be depicted using a thicker line.

Part 3. Intrusive field investigation

Planning an intrusive archaeological investigation
Methods of intrusive (or destructive) archaeological investigation described here differ from the non-intrusive methods described above as they involve leaving the site under investigation in a permanently changed state, as a result of removing archaeological artefacts from it. Such changes will affect future interpretations of the site, so it is of fundamental important that all activities which are intrusive/destructive to an archaeological site must have plans in place before the activity commences to ensure that (1) the location of all finds is recorded to an appropriate level of precision; (2) all finds of archaeological significance are identified by someone competent to do so reliably; and (3) all discoveries are reported to the appropriate local HER or SMR office for the area in which the fieldwork has been carried out. By ensuring these arrangements are carried out, a permanent record of the results of the investigations will be entered onto the HER/SMR so that others will be able to find out about them. Although it is doubtless self-evident to readers of this volume, it can never be stressed too often that a programme of activity which removes medieval finds from a site (however well-intentioned at the outset) has the potential to leave the site lacking any evidence for its medieval date which, if the finds are not reported, may lead to all knowledge of its existence being permanently lost. While the information such an exercise yields can justify this being done, it can only do so if the results are located, identified and reported properly. It is recommended that anyone considering undertaking any of the activities described in this section involve a professional archaeologist in at least an advisory capacity in order to ensure that everything is carried out correctly.

Finds must also be looked after properly: most finds (with the exception of metal finds) should be gently washed in water, air-dried until complete dry, marked to indicate where they came from and stored in clear polythene re-sealable bags with the name and location of the site, the date the finds were made and where on the site they came from marked in permanent ink.[24] They should then be identified by someone with the expertise and experience to do so competently. It is important also to be aware of the laws regarding the discovery of so-called 'treasure' items. In Scotland the Crown has the right to claim, on behalf of the nation, any object or coin found in Scotland and all finds, with the exception of Victorian and twentieth century coins, must be reported to the Treasure Trove Unit at the National Museums of Scotland for assessment (http://www.treasuretrovescotland.co.uk/). In England and Wales the law is different and the situation regarding reporting of finds much more complicated. In summary, finders are required to report all gold and silver objects, and groups of coins from the same finds, which are over 300 years old, to a coroner for the district in which they are found (http://www.finds.org.uk/). In mitigation of this complexity, the Portable Antiquities Scheme (PAS) employs a number of finds liaison officers to help with the process of ensuring that items defined as 'treasure' are reported correctly. Details of these for each area can be found at http://finds.org.uk/contacts.

At the planning stage, it is therefore imperative to decide exactly how the location of the activities/find-spots is to be recorded, who is going to identify archaeological finds, and to whom this should all be reported. The level of any costs (such as specialist pottery identification) should be established, and funding put in place to ensure these can be met. It is also important to decide how the results are to be written up, who is going to do this, and (again) whether this will incur any costs. It is advisable to contact the county HER office in advance of work being started in order to inform them of the activity

Figure A.1. Test-pitting in a back garden in Pirton, Hertfordshire (Photo © Catherine Ranson, Access Cambridge Archaeology)

that is being planned: this allows those responsible for curating the historic environment to offer advice if needed, monitor progress if required, and plan for accessing the results of archaeological investigations to the HER. In addition, plans must made for processing finds (e.g. washing and marking them) and also for storing them. Plans should also be made for in disposing of finds which are not be kept: discarding quantities of medieval tile which have been recovered in volumes too large to be retained, for example, if done in a place away from the original find-site, may lead a field-walker of the future to surmise the presence of a settlement where none, in fact, existed.

Field-walking

Field-walking involves collecting archaeological evidence from field surfaces not covered by vegetation. Within medieval settlement studies, field-walking is likely to have one of two aims: (1) to establish whether and where a medieval site is present, or (2) to identify the extent, date and possible character of medieval activity across a site.[25]

Field-walking is usually carried out on fields under regular cultivation while the ground is not obscured by crops. For the results to have value, it is important to ensure an even coverage of the area to be field-walked, and to record carefully and report exactly what has been found where. The larger the

Figure A.2. Field-walking near Bures in Suffolk, March 2011. Line marking and walking are in progress with attentive horses in the background. Each 10 m stint was examined for 15 minutes (Photo © Catherine Ranson, Access Cambridge Archaeology)

area that can be covered, the more valuable the results will be – changing settlement and land-use in parishes where all arable fields have been walked will offer more insights than those where only a couple of fields have been covered, and regions where a dozen adjacent parishes have been comprehensively field-walked are particularly informative. If possible, field-walking should be carried out on ploughed and harrowed soil which has been 'weathered' by rain for as long as possible, since this washes off loose soil thereby leaving artefacts more visible. The visibility of items of archaeological interest will also be affected by light conditions: failing daylight on a winter's afternoon is an obvious problem, but so is bright angled sunlight, as it creates deep shadows which can obscure finds from view. Overcast days offer the best conditions for field-walking. As with earthwork survey, field-walking requires a careful advance visit or recce to establish the location and parameters of the areas selected for field-walking, and to decide on what method of field-walking is to be used. Field-walking should always aim to cover large areas, although if this sounds daunting it is important to remember that every programme has to start somewhere. Novice field-walkers should be shown examples of the types of materials expected to be recovered: making them aware of the colour, shapes, of sherds, flints, etc. will help encourage them to pick up all items rather than focusing on

favoured types or period-specific artefacts (which can otherwise happen). As different individuals will often be differently skilled at noticing finds, it is good practice to record the names of those who have walked each area.

A number of basic methods described below can be considered for archaeological field-walking, but all inevitably require the locations from which the finds have been recovered to be recorded and planned. As in an earthwork survey, the simplest and most effective way to do this is to establish a baseline along the longest axis of the field to be walked, and mark out grids or lines at right angles from this baseline. Field boundaries should be measured and added to the drawn plan so that the distribution of material recovered can be tied into the Ordnance Survey map and thus to the wider landscape and to the results of other research that has been carried out. The baseline points should be marked in a way that will enable them to remain visible for the duration of the field-walking: it should be borne in mind that field-walking can be repeated to good effect on the same field in successive years, and so it may be advisable to use permanent features such as gateposts or measured-in points along fence-lines as baseline points. Garden canes or ranging poles can both be used to mark out subsidiary points on grids or lines. Canes are cheaper than ranging poles, and can be made more visible by adding coloured tapes of flags to one end, making these easier for walkers to see and thus keep within the limits of their allocated search area.

To carry out a grid field-walking survey, the field is divided into square grids with each grid given a unique identification number, usually an alphanumeric code based on its position in the field. Deciding on the size of the grid should be done at planning stage, as this affects the speed and accuracy of the results (small grids of 10 × 10 m enable the results to be plotted with more accuracy but take longer to lay out, and on a big site can also lead to a lot of time being spent in areas which may produce little or nothing in the way of finds). Once established, the whole area of each grid is then searched for a set period of time, with finds placed in re-sealable polythene finds bags marked with the grid identification number in permanent ink. The most common finds are likely to be pottery, stone, bone, metal and ceramic building material (brick and tile – known to archaeologists as 'CBM').

Grid walking in this way enables the whole surface of the field to be searched, but it can take a long time and can also generate enormous quantities of finds that are likely to be unfeasibly expensive to analyse and store. Because of this, collection is almost always restricted to a sample of the visible material. This can be done in one of three basic ways: by restricting (1) the time allowed for collection, (2) the range of finds to be collected, or (3) the area to be searched. It is possible to combine two or even all three of these approaches to enable useful results to be produced while a large area is still being covered. In restricting the time spent on collection, each grid is searched for a fixed period of time only (NB the same amount of time should be spent searching each grid in order to make the results comparable across all the grids) – 30 person minutes is usually likely to produce a representative sample of surface material from a single 10 × 10 m grid square.

Restricting the range of finds to be collected can be achieved simply by omitting material of little or no interest to the aims of the investigation. Thus, if the aim of the field-walking is to advance understanding of medieval settlement and land-use, it is sensible to exclude items such as modern building material (brick, tile, concrete, metal sheeting, asbestos, etc.) or anything made of plastic from the collection. Conducting a field-walk to collect only pottery may well be justified on some sites. This strategy can be

used effectively as long as the project records state clearly what material has been collected and/or excluded. A compromise is to collect all artefacts in the first instance, and assign an experienced individual capable of distinguishing ancient material from modern to sort through each finds bag on site and then return specified unwanted material to where it was collected from.

As an alternative (or an addition) to limiting the type of artefacts targeted for retrieval, it is entirely acceptable to decide not to search every bit of the field. Selecting which areas are to be searched involves developing a valid sampling procedure: this is, of course, easier said than done, as any mathematician, pollster or market researcher will confirm. In field-walking (as in any sampling), the aim should be to ensure reasonably even coverage with no large gaps. Applying too regular a pattern incurs the theoretical risk of misrepresentation: searching the site of a settlement whose linear street plan coincided with the line-walking grid is an obvious, although relatively unlikely risk, which can nonetheless be minimised by adding a number of occasional extra search areas, randomly distributed across an otherwise regular pattern.

Another way in which the scale of the task can be reduced is by subdividing large grid squares into smaller ones and walking only some of these: thus searching one in ten of the smaller squares would give an overall coverage of 10%. Another solution is to use a larger grid, to get an initial indication of which areas are more productive, followed by a subsequent survey using small grids laid out over areas of particular interest. Line walking is another method for reducing the area to be walked; this requires field-walkers to scan 1.5 m or 2 m corridors or 'stints' either side of lines marked out at right angles to the base line, again for a set period of time. This method was used very effectively in the east Midlands to cover large areas of land.[26] The distance between the lines are usually between 10 m, 15 m, 20 m and 30 m, depending on the area to be covered, the level of resolution required of the collected data and the amount of time available. Each stint should be no more than 10 m to 20 m long, after which a new stint should be started. A new stint should then be started along the same line, until the end of the field is reached. Using this method, lines set 15 m apart with each walker scanning a 1.5 m wide band covers 10 % of the surface area of each field being searched. Whatever method of field-walking is used, areas of the same size should be searched for the same amount of time, and the names of the searchers and the date, time and prevailing soil, weather and light conditions should be recorded for each grid or stint walked. Once the field-walking has been completed and the finds processed and identified, they can be plotted onto a map of the field(s) that have been searched.

Metal detector survey

The use of metal detectors on sites of historic interest is a thorny issue, as metal detectors used in the wrong way have caused terrible damage to many archaeological sites. Unlike field-walking, where a visual scan locates finds are already on the surface and collection involves no disturbance to the ground, metal detectors can and do locate buried objects, and recovery of these inevitably involves disturbing the ground surface. Even in cultivated fields, where the soil is being disturbed by ploughing to a depth of perhaps 20 cm or more on a regular basis, it is all too easy to break into undisturbed deposits when seeking the source of the siren whine from one of the more powerful metal detectors. Metal detecting should not be carried out in pasture fields, where the likelihood of damaging undisturbed deposits will be close to 100%. Medieval settlements are generally considered (on the basis of excavations of such sites) unlikely to yield significant numbers of metal finds of a type which will significantly advance knowledge and understanding of the settlement over and above that gained from field-walking. Moreover, the attendant risks are high: they are, first, the likelihood of damaging sub-surface deposits which will be expensive to stabilise, and second, the risk that the act of retrieving finds of other dates will denude the site of significant information for future generations.

In addition, excavation on medieval sites shows that the most numerous metal objects are likely to be ferrous, and surveys should therefore not screen out ferrous signatures. However, in electing to scan medieval settlement sites for ferrous objects as well as those of other metals, the likelihood is that an impractically vast number of positive readings will be recorded. Overall, current understanding suggests that field-walking is a safer and more effective way of advancing knowledge and understanding of the date and character of medieval settlements sites than metal detector survey. That said, use of metal detectors in conjunction with field-walking may increase the number of retrieved objects, and the study of items such as coins recovered by metal detectorists has been shown to have the potential to significantly advance understanding of aspects of life in medieval settlements such as the use of money.[27] It is here considered that, on balance, the use of metal detectors may sometimes be of some use in advancing the study of a medieval settlement, but that their use should always be open to question and, if embarked upon, should be carefully controlled.

Metal detector surveys in the investigation of medieval settlement sites should always be carried out in conjunction with field-walking, using the same grid to locate find spots. All metal objects should be recorded, including ferrous items. Ideally, only objects which are visible on the surface should be collected: this has the advantage firstly of not risking disturbing intact archaeological deposits, and secondly of allowing the object to be identified without any disturbance to the ground surface taking place. In this way, obviously modern items need not be retained. In no circumstances should any digging be carried out below 20 cm. Objects which are selected for retention should be processed in the same way as finds from field-walking, with the caveat that most metal finds should not be washed with water. Metal finds can be very unstable hence difficult and expensive to stabilise and conserve: The costs of doing this must be considered when deciding whether to carry out such a survey. It should also be borne in mind that finds of gold or silver or groups of coins are likely to qualify as treasure and should be reported to the local coroner or PAS Finds Liaison Officer.

Molehill survey

Archaeological molehill surveys involve finding, identifying and recording items of archaeological interest that have been brought to the surface by the action of moles. Molehills are not very big, but in some fields large mole populations can create hundreds of hills across wide areas, and if this is the case they can provide the only opportunity to establish the date and distribution of archaeological material on land set permanently to grass.[28] On a deserted settlement with a high density of pottery (and an equally high density of moles), simply kicking over the odd molehill during a recce visit could well reveal evidence which will give some hints as to the date of occupation. A more sophisticated approach can yield greater dividends.

As with any other survey, for a molehill survey to have archaeological value, it is crucial to record what has been found and where it has been discovered. In a field or garden smaller than a tenth of a hectare it is not essential to record the exact location where archaeological finds have been present as long as the plot is clearly identified. However, even working in an area this small it is certainly better to record where the finds have come from to within at least 10 m, and in larger plots this is essential. Ideally (and it is essential in larger fields) one should set up a baseline or grid for recording molehill locations which can be tied into the National Grid. If there are very large numbers of molehills over a large area, then a sampling procedure similar to that used in field-walking can be used, with the number of molehills within each grid square being limited to a pre-determined, standard number, such as ten molehills per 10 m^2.

Shovel-pitting
Shovel-pitting is a useful technique in mole-free pasture fields, or indeed in areas of woodland, where field-walking will be ineffectual, since, instead of scanning the exposed surface of the topsoil over a wide area, shovel-pitting means a much smaller area of topsoil is excavated at regular intervals and then searched for finds.[29] As with all other fieldwork, the sites for shovel-pitting need to be sited to ensure as representative and even a coverage as possible using a grid or line method, and tied into the OS. The distance between shovel-pits will depend on the amount of time and labour available, but laying out a 25 m grid with pits dug at every node will give a reasonable level of cover and ensure that no scatters of material greater than 25 m in diameter should be missed. Each shovel-pit must be given a unique identifying number, which is derived from its position on the 'x' and 'y' axes of the grid.

Shovel-pits should not be dug below a depth of 20 cm, below which buried features may lie, undisturbed by any previous episodes of ploughing, in the subsoil. The aim is to search a standard amount of soil from each shovel-pit: *c.* 30 litres (i.e. two average-sized buckets) of soil per shovel-pit is acceptable. Excavated spoil should be sieved through the standard 10 mm mesh, although in dry clay soils it is usually easier and quicker to search by hand, breaking up large clods of soil as necessary. Finds from each pit should be bagged separately and marked with the shovel-pit reference number in permanent ink.

Garden soil survey
Away from fields, garden soil survey involves searching cultivated garden soils – i.e. flowerbeds and vegetable patches – for finds. While it would be very unwise indeed to base any reconstruction of a settlement's development solely on the evidence from a garden soil survey, nonetheless, research at Shapwick in Somerset in the 1990s indicated that in most cases the distribution of pottery in cultivated garden soils in fact mirrored that from excavations in the village.[30] Garden soil survey may therefore be recommended as an approach to be considered as it is the only one which can collect datable finds from within currently occupied rural settlements. It is also a very effective away of engaging local residents, as they can get involved in collecting finds from their own property while gardening. As with other methods, no digging should penetrate beyond 20 cm below the surface. Soil can be sieved through a standard 10 mm mesh sieve, as this is likely to increase number of finds retrieved. If a large enough number of residents can be persuaded to allow finds to be collected from their gardens, a distribution pattern can be arrived which may provide interesting insights into the development of the settlement.

Part 4. Completing a programme of research

Synthesis and analysis
The approaches described above cover a wide range of activities which have the potential to yield a great deal of information which will transform understanding of the places in which they have been carried out. Although each activity can be undertaken independently, much more will be learnt if a number of different approaches are used, and the results synthesised. For example, documentary research might help identify the likely date at

which earthwork remains of former settlement were abandoned, estate maps and air photos may help define the extent of the site, while building surveys and garden soil surveys may hint at the earliest settlement around, say, the church in a nucleated village, whose outlying moated manorial sites may be found during aerial photographic transcription and dated by field-walking, which may also locate early dispersed settlements which predate the foundation of the village. As evidence from different documentary sources is sorted and ordered and data from field investigations are fitted into maps of settlements and landscapes, the chronological and spatial development of the study area will gradually begin to become clearer. As it does, new questions will present themselves and these in turn will lead to new avenues of enquiry.

Reporting the results

Anyone who carries out research into medieval settlements should always seek to disseminate the results, to allow all who are interested to benefit from new knowledge gained. This applies to any research, but is a particular obligation in the case of investigations which have involved disturbing or removing archaeological deposits. The results should all be written up and a copy of the report given to the county HER. In a long-term project lasting several years, it is good practice to submit interim statements detailing main findings of interest to the HER in order that this information will not remain out of the public arena for too long. There are also annual regional publications by the CBA, such as *South Midlands Archaeology*, which appreciate short, summary reports on field activities and some documentary-based research results. Significant outcomes should be reported in *Medieval Settlement Research* and any county journal – and hopefully these will no doubt act as spurs for other researchers to continue to build and enhance our understanding of the rich and varied landscape image of medieval Britain and Ireland.

Further reading

Much literature exists to guide researchers of medieval rural settlement studies whether in office, archive or field, but a few works merit highlighting here. *The Shapwick Project* by C. Gerrard and M. Aston

(Leeds, 2007) is perhaps the best starting point, being a comprehensive volume covering ten years of investigations into a single parish, which used most of the techniques described in this appendix, and many more; it shows just what can be achieved. J. Chandler's *Codford: Wool and War in Wiltshire* (Chichester, 2007) meanwhile presents the results of (mostly historical) research carried out by members of the public in collaboration with staff of the Victoria County History.

In terms of setting the scene and introducing important case studies as background reading and for setting out research ideas and questions, the reader should look at M. Beresford and J. Hurst's *Deserted Medieval Villages* (Lutterworth, 1971) and *Wharram Percy. Deserted Medieval Village* (London, 1990). D. Hooke's edited volume *Medieval Villages: A Review of Current Work* (Oxford, 1985) was a seminal publication, while more recent works by C. Lewis *et al.*, *Village, Hamlet and Field: Changing Medieval Settlements in Central England* (Manchester, 1997) and R. Jones and M. Page, *Medieval Villages* (Macclesfield, 2006) bring the subject up to date. C. Dyer's *Standards of Living in the Later Middle Ages* (Cambridge, 1989) very effectively combines historical and archaeological evidence. Recommended short introductions to medieval settlement studies include the Shire publications by B. Roberts, *Village Plans* (Princes Risborough, 1982) and T. Rowley and J. Wood, *Deserted Villages* (Princes Risborough, 1982), while C. C. Taylor's *Village and Farmstead* (London, 1983) and M. Aston's *Interpreting the Landscape* (London, 1985) are longer but very readable, aimed firmly at engaging the non-specialist. T. Rowley's *Villages in the Landscape* (London, 1978) and B. Roberts' *The Making of the English Village* are strong introductions, but perhaps more appropriate for those with an established interest. RCHME volumes for Dorset, Northamptonshire and West Lindsey provide excellent case studies for earthwork survey-based investigations in different parts of England. For fieldwork and map-based survey of medieval and later settlements in Wales and Scotland, see K. Roberts (ed.) 2006: *Lost Farmsteads* (York, 2006), J. Atkinson *et al.*, *Townships to Farmsteads* (Oxford, 2000) and RCHAMS (2002).

Various publications provide information about how to carry out investigations into medieval settlements and landscapes. R. Muir's *How to Read a Village* (London, 2007) is an excellent general introduction to techniques and approaches; J. L. Gaddis (2004, Oxford) outlines historical method and practice, while P. Riden's guide to *Record Sources for Local History* (London, 1987) is a very useful practical guide to the primary sources for local history. See also J. Richardson, *The Local Historian's Encyclopedia* (New Barnet, 1974). S. Hollowell, *Enclosure Records for Historians* (Chichester, 2000) and R. Kain and H. Prince, *Tithe Surveys for Historians* (Chichester, 2000) are good introductions for those looking at Tithe and Enclosure records. For buildings look to R. W. Brunskill, *Illustrated Handbook of Vernacular Architecture* (London, 1971) and *Traditional Buildings of Britain* (London, 1981), and try to get hold of English Heritage's *Understanding Historic Buildings. A Guide to Good Recording Practice* (Swindon, 2006). For air

photography, researchers should first look over the classic M. Beresford and J. K. S. St Joseph, *Medieval England. A Cambridge Air Survey* (Cambridge, 1958, revised ed. 1979) and then look at both D. Riley, *Aerial Archaeology in Britain* (Princes Risborough, 1996) and D. R. Wilson, *Air Photo Interpretation for Archaeologists* (Stroud, 2000). Invaluable for work in the field itself, for interpreting earthworks and undertaking field-walking, are publications by A. E. Brown, *Fieldwork for Archaeologists and Local Historians* (London, 1987) and *Unravelling the Landscape* (Stroud, 1999), the latter an immensely useful collection of papers by RCHME practitioners and edited by M. Bowden. Good guides to finds processing and identification which will be invaluable to all those engaged in any activities which involve collecting finds include Shopland (2006), McCarthy and Brooks (1988) and Orton *et al.* (1993) on pottery, and Hobbs *et al.* (2002) on metal finds.

Notes

1. Archaeological excavation should never be attempted without adequate supervision by experienced persons competent to ensure that any and all deposits are excavated, recorded and reported properly. For those wanting to know more, Barker 1977 remains an excellent guide which introduces readers to excavation in all its complexities, in the process underlining the need for competent on-site supervision.

2. Lewis 2007 and www.arch.cam.ac.uk/access/ for details of the results of test pit excavations in more than 30 currently occupied rural settlements in eastern England.

3. Lewis 2007 includes a description of the methods used for carrying out test pit excavations in currently occupied rural settlements by novices under archaeological supervision, which could be effectively used by those without archaeological supervision but with previous archaeological experience adequate to allow features to be recognised and excavated correctly.

4. See Oswin 2009 on geophysical survey for archaeologists.

5. See Christie *et al.* 2010b, however, for an example of amateur groups who have been able to carry out geophysical survey by working alongside academic and professional field archaeologists to map the open

spaces of the town and environs of Wallingford. Valuable work has also been carried out in eastern England by the Archaeology RheeSearch Group, a group of amateur enthusiast former students on a University of Cambridge extra-mural course (http://www.rheesearch.org.uk/)

6. Richardson 1974 and Riden 1987 detail the main types of primary historical sources for medieval Britain.

7. Gaddis 2004 and Partner (ed.) 2005 provide interesting recent introductions to the issues surrounding the interpretation of medieval historical documents and the writing of historical accounts using such records.

8. Howell 1983 offers an example of retrogressive settlement plan reconstruction using maps and documents pertaining to Kibworth Harcourt in Leicestershire. Howell's work on Kibworth is also discussed in Roberts 1987.

9. Hollowell 2000.

10. Kain and Prince 2000.

11. RCHME volumes for Dorset and Northamptonshire provide many good examples of historic map data interposed onto modern maps, as do many of the Victoria County History volumes.

12. Wilson 2000; Riley 1996.

13. Wilson 2000 and Beresford and St Joseph 1979 are

excellent guides to identifying, interpreting phasing and dating medieval features from aerial photographic evidence.

14. Taylor 2003.
15. The Health and Safety Executive *Essentials of Health and Safety at Work* provides an outline of requirements for safe working
16. The Institute for Archaeologists has basic risk assessment guidelines available at http://www.archaeologists.net/codes/ifa.
17. See RCHME volumes for Northamptonshire and West Lindsey for examples of earthwork surveys which have been used to reconstruct settlement development
18. See Bowden 1999 for further information about how to carry out analytical earthwork survey.
19. Brown 1987; Bowden 1999, 167–174 give further guidance and examples.
20. The architectural investigation and recording of churches is not included here as it is considered too specialised, but a good introduction to this subject is Cocke *et al.* 1996.
21. The key guides for undertaking recording of historic buildings remain Brunskill 1971 and Swallow 1993.
22. Brunksill 1971 provides a useful pro-forma for classifying and recording these features during extensive building survey. See also the English Heritage guide *Understanding Historic Buildings* (2006).
23. Brunskill 1981.
24. Shopland 2006 on finds processing; Griffiths *et al.* 1990 on drawing finds; Hobbs *et al.* 2002 on metal finds; Dorrell 1989 on photography.
25. Davison 1990 is an excellent case study reconstruction the development of settlements in Norfolk using archaeological field-walking and also has a useful short summary of the methods used.
26. Jones and Page 2007.
27. Naylor and Geake 2010, 396–398 report on a promising project looking at the monetisation of medieval England by studying coin finds reported by metal detectorists to the PAS.
28. Bowden 1999, 116–118 flags an archaeological molehill survey on an Iron Age hill-fort and medieval sheep fair site at Yarnbury in Wiltshire.
29. Gerrard and Aston 2007 provide further information about archaeological shovel-pitting.
30. Gerrard and Aston 2007, 261–265.

Bibliography

Aalen, F. H. A., Whelan, K. and Stout, M. (eds) 1997. *Atlas of the Irish Landscape*, Cork University Press: Cork.

Aberg, F. A. 1978a. 'Introduction', in Aberg (ed.), 1–4.

Aberg, F. A. (ed.) 1978b. *Medieval Moated Sites*, Council for British Archaeology Research Report 17. London.

Aberg, F. A. and Brown, A. E. (eds) 1981. *Medieval Moated Sites in North-West Europe*, British Archaeological Reports International Series 121. Oxford.

Acornley, J. 1999. 'The Anglo-Saxon charter boundaries of Coombe Bissett', *Wiltshire Archaeological and Natural History Society Magazine* 92, 53–59.

Addyman, P. V. 1965. 'Late Saxon settlements in the St Neots area: I. The Saxon settlement and Norman castle at Eaton Socon, Bedfordshire', *Proceedings of the Cambridge Antiquarian Society* 58, 38–52.

Addyman, P. V. 1969. 'Late Saxon settlements in the St Neots area: II, the Little Paxton settlement and enclosures', *Proceedings of the Cambridge Antiquarian Society* 62, 59–93.

Addyman, P. V. and Leigh, D. 1973. 'The Anglo-Saxon village at Chalton, Hampshire: second interim report', *Medieval Archaeology* 17, 1–25.

Addyman, P. V., Leigh, D. and Hughes, M. J. 1972. 'Anglo-Saxon houses at Chalton, Hampshire', *Medieval Archaeology* 16, 13–31.

Addyman, P. V., Simpson, W. and Spring, P. 1966. 'Two medieval sites near Sedbergh, West Riding', *Yorkshire Archaeological Journal* 41, 27–42.

Aitchison, N. 2006. *Forteviot: A Pictish and Scottish Royal Centre*, Tempus: Stroud.

Aitkens, P., Easton, T. and Martin, E. 1999. 'Wingfield', *Proceedings of the Suffolk Institute of Archaeology and History* 39, 3, 392–397.

Aitkens, P., Kirkham, A. and Martin, E. 2007. 'Brockley and Whepstead', *Proceedings of the Suffolk Institute of Archaeology and History* 41:3, 389–393.

Albarella, U. 2005. 'Meat production and consumption in town and country', in Giles and Dyer (eds), 131–148.

Alcock, L. 1988. 'The activities of potentates in Celtic Britain, AD 500–800: a positivist approach', in Driscoll and Nieke (eds), 22–46.

Alcock, L. 2003. *Kings and Warriors, Craftsmen and Priests in Northern Britain AD 550–850*, Society of the Antiquaries of Scotland: Edinburgh.

Alcock, N. and Laithwaite, M. 1973. 'Medieval houses in Devon and their modernization', *Medieval Archaeology* 17, 100–125.

Aldred, D. and Dyer, C. 1991. 'A medieval Cotswold village: Roel, Gloucestershire', *Transactions of the Bristol and Gloucestershire Archaeological Society* 109, 139–171.

Aldsworth, F. G. 1979. 'Three medieval sites in West Dean parish', *Sussex Archaeological Collections* 117, 109–124.

Aldsworth, F. G. and Harris, R. 1982. 'A medieval and seventeenth-century house at Walderton, West Sussex, dismantled and re-erected at the Weald and Downland Open Air Museum', *Sussex Archaeological Collections* 120, 45–92.

Alexander, D. 2000. 'Excavation of a medieval moated site in Elderslie, Renfrewshire', *Scottish Archaeological Journal* 22:2, 155–177.

Allan, J. 1984. *Medieval and Post-Medieval Finds from Exeter, 1971–80*, Exeter City Council: Exeter.

Allan, J. 1994. 'Medieval pottery and the dating of deserted settlements on Dartmoor', *Devon Archaeological Society Proceedings* 52, 141–147.

Allan, J. and Langman, G. 2002. 'A group of medieval pottery from Haycroft Farm, Membury', *Devon Archaeological Society Proceedings* 60, 59–73.

Allcroft, A. H. 1908. *Earthwork of England: Prehistoric, Roman, Saxon, Danish, Norman, and Medieval*, Macmillan: London.

Allen, D. 1979. 'Excavations at Hafod y Nant Criafolen, Brenig Valley, Clwyd, 1973–4', *Post-Medieval Archaeology* 13, 1–59.

Allen, T. 2004. 'Swine, salt and seafood: a case study of Anglo-Saxon and early medieval settlement in north-east Kent', *Archaeologia Cantiana* 124, 117–135.

Allerston, P. 1970. 'English village development: findings from the Pickering district of North Yorkshire', *Transactions of the Institute of British Geographers* 51, 95–109.

Allison, K. J. 1955. 'The lost villages of Norfolk', *Norfolk Archaeology* 31, 116–162.

Allison, K. J., Beresford, M. W. and Hurst, J. G. 1965. *The Deserted Villages of Oxfordshire*, Leicester Department of English Local History, Occasional Papers, 1st Series 17. Leicester.

Allison, K. J., Beresford, M. W. and Hurst, J. G. 1966. *The Deserted Villages of Northamptonshire*, Leicester Department of English Local History, Occasional Papers, 1st Series 18. Leicester.

Anderson, S. 2003. *A Medieval Moated site at Cedars Field, Stowmarket, Suffolk*, East Anglian Archaeology Occasional Papers, 15. Ipswich.

Andrews, D. and Milne, G. 1979. *Wharram. A Study of Settlement on the Yorkshire Wolds. Vol. 1. Domestic Settlement, 1: Areas 10 and 6*, Society for Medieval Archaeology Monograph Series 8. Leeds

Andrews, J. H. 1997. *Shapes of Ireland: Maps and their Makers 1564–1839*, Geography Publications: Dublin.

Antoine, A. 2005. *La maison rurale en pays d'habitat dispersé de l'Antiquité au XXe siècle*, Presses Universitaires de Rennes: Rennes.

Archaeological Survey of County Down 1966, HMSO: Belfast.

Aris, M. 1996. *Historic Landscapes of the Great Orme*, Gwasg Carreg Gwalch: Llanrwst.

Armit, I. 1996. *The Archaeology of Skye and the Western Isles*, Edinburgh University Press: Edinburgh.

Arnold, C. and Wardle, P. 1981. 'Early medieval settlement patterns in England', *Medieval Archaeology* 25, 145–149.

Ashwin, T. and Davison, A. (eds) 2005. *An Historical Atlas of Norfolk* (3rd edn), Phillimore: Chichester.

Astill, G. G. 2009. 'Anglo-Saxon attitudes: how should post-AD 700 burials be interpreted?', in D. Sayer and H. Williams (eds), *Mortuary Practices and Social Identities in the Middle Ages. Essays in Burial Archaeology in Honour of Heinrich Härke*, Exeter University Press: Exeter, 220–233.

Astill, G. G. and Grant, A. 1988. *The Countryside of Medieval England*, Blackwell: Oxford.

Astill, G. G. and Lobb, S. J. 1989. 'Excavation of prehistoric, Roman and Saxon deposits at Wraysbury, Berkshire', *Archaeological Journal* 146, 68–134.

Aston, M. 1970–72. 'Earthworks at the Bishop's Palace, Alvechurch, Worcestershire', *Transactions of the Worcestershire Archaeological Society* 3rd Series, 3, 55–59.

Aston, M. 1983. 'Deserted settlements on Exmoor and the Lay Subsidy of 1327 in west Somerset', *Proceedings of the Somerset Archaeological and Natural History Society* 127, 71–104.

Aston, M. 1985. *Interpreting the Landscape: Landscape Archaeology and Local History*, Batsford: London.

Aston, M. (ed.) 1988a. *Medieval Fish, Fisheries and Fishponds*, 2 vols., British Archaeological Reports British Series 182. Oxford.

Aston, M. (ed.) 1988b. *The Medieval Landscape of Somerset*, Somerset County Council: Bridgwater.

Aston, M. 1989. 'The development of medieval rural settlement in Somerset', in Higham (ed.), 19–40.

Aston, M. 1992. *Aspects of the Medieval Landscape of Somerset*, Somerset County Council: Taunton.

Aston, M. and Lewis, C. (eds) 1994. *The Medieval Landscape of Wessex*, Oxbow Books: Oxford.

Aston, M. and Rowley, T. 1974. *Landscape Archaeology: An Introduction to Fieldwork Techniques on Post-Roman Landscapes*, David and Charles: Newton Abbot.

Aston, M., Austin, D. and Dyer, C. (eds) 1989. *The Rural Settlements of Medieval England*, Blackwell: Oxford.

Atkin, M. A. 1985. 'Some settlement patterns in Lancashire', in Hooke, D. (ed.), 170–185.

Atkinson, J. A. (ed.) 2004. *Ben Lawers Historic Landscape Project: Annual Report 2003–2004*, GUARD: Glasgow.

Atkinson, J. A. (ed.) 2005. *Ben Lawers Historic Landscape Project: Annual Report 2004–2005*, GUARD: Glasgow.

Atkinson, J. A., Banks, I. and MacGregor, G. (eds). *Townships to Farmsteads. Rural Settlement Studies in Scotland, England and Wales*, British Archaeological Reports British Series 293. Oxford.

Attenborough, F. L. 1922. *The Laws of the Earliest English Kings,* Cambridge University Press: Cambridge.

Audouy, M. and Chapman, A. (eds) 2009. *Raunds: The Origin and Growth of a Midland Village AD 450–1500. Excavations in North Raunds, Northamptonshire 1977–87*, Oxbow Books: Oxford.

Austin, D. 1976. 'Fieldwork and excavation at Hart, Co. Durham, 1965–75', *Archaeologia Aeliana* 5th Series, 4, 69–132.

Austin, D. 1978. 'Excavations in Okehampton Deer Park, Devon, 1976–1978', *Devon Archaeological Society Proceedings* 36, 191–239.

Austin, D. 1984. 'The castle and the landscape', *Landscape History* 6, 70–81.

Austin, D. 1985a. 'Dartmoor and the upland village of the south-west of England', in Hooke (ed.), 71–79.

Austin, D. 1985b. 'Medieval archaeology and the landscape', *Landscape History* 7, 53–56.

Austin, D. 1988. 'Excavations and survey at Bryn Cysegrfan, Llanfair Clydogau, Dyfed, 1979', *Medieval Archaeology* 23, 130–165.

Austin, D. 1989a. *The Deserted Medieval Village of Thrislington County Durham. Excavations 1973–1974*, Society for Medieval Archaeology Monograph 12. Lincoln.

Austin, D. 1989b. 'The excavation of dispersed settlement in medieval Britain', in Aston, Austin and Dyer (eds), 231–246.

Austin, D. 2007. *Acts of Perception: A Study of Barnard Castle in Teesdale*, 2 vols., Architectural and Archaeological Society of Durham and Northumberland Research Report 6. Durham.

Austin, D. and Walker, M. J. C. 1985. 'A new landscape context for Houndtor, Devon', *Medieval Archaeology* 29, 147–152.

Austin, D., Daggett, R. and Walker, M. 1980. 'Farms and fields in Okehampton Park, Devon: the problems of studying medieval landscape', *Landscape History* 2, 39–57.

Austin, D., Gerrard, G. and Greeves, T. 1989. 'Tin and agriculture in the middle ages and beyond: landscape archaeology in St Neot parish, Cornwall', *Cornish Archaeology* 28, 5–251.

Bahn, P. and Renfrew, C. 2002. Archaeology: Methods, Theories and Practice, Thames and Hudson: London.

Bailey, M. 1989. *A Marginal Economy?*, Cambridge University Press: Cambridge.

Bailey, M. 1991. '*Per impetum maris*: natural disaster and economic decline in eastern England, 1275–1350', in B. M. S. Campbell (ed.), *Before the Black Death: Studies in the 'Crisis' of the Early Fourteenth Century*, Manchester University Press: Manchester, 184–208.

Bailey, M. 2007. *Medieval Suffolk. An Economic and Social History, 1200–1500*, Boydell: Woodbridge.

Baker, A. R. H. 1963. *The Fields Systems of Kent*, unpublished PhD thesis, University of London.

Baker, A. R. H. 1964. 'Open fields and partible inheritance on a Kent manor', *Economic History Review* (2nd Series) 17, 1–23.

Baker, A. R. H. 1965. 'Some fields and farms in medieval Kent', *Archaeologia Cantiana* 80, 152–174.

Baker, A. R. H. 1966a. 'Field systems in the Vale of Holmesdale', *Agricultural History Review* 14, 1–24.

Baker, A. R. H. 1966b. 'Some evidence of a reduction in the acreage of cultivated lands in Sussex during the early fourteenth century', *Sussex Archaeological Collections* 104, 1–5.

Baker, A. R. H. 1973. 'Field systems of southeast England', in Baker and Butlin (eds), 337–429.

Baker, A. R. H. and Butlin, R. A. (eds) 1973. *Studies of Field Systems in the British Isles*, Cambridge University Press: Cambridge.

Baker, C. 2009. 'Tullykane, Co. Meath: a medieval rural settlement', in Corlett and Potterton (eds), 1–18.

Baker, N. and Holt, R. 2004. *Urban Growth and the Medieval Church. Gloucester and Worcester*, Ashgate: Aldershot.

Banks, I., Duffy, P. R. J. and MacGregor, G. 2009. *Archaeology of Landscape Change in South-West Scotland, 6000 BC–AD 1400. Excavations at William Grant and Sons Distillery, Girvan*, Society of Antiquaries of Scotland: Scottish Archaeological Internet Report 32. (http://www.sair.org.uk/sair32/). Accessed 27/09/2010.

Bannin, E. B. 2002. *Archaeological Survey*, Kluwer: New York.

Bannister, N. R. 2002. 'The management of Dering Wood, Smarden, since the medieval period: archaeological and documentary evidence', *Archaeologia Cantiana* 122, 221–236.

Bannister, N. R. and Bartlett, D. 2009. 'An initial investigation of an early routeway and boundary, possibly prehistoric, in Bedgebury Forest', *Archaeologia Cantiana* 129, 295–312.

Bar, M. 1981. 'Research on the medieval fortified house in eastern France: the moated sites of the Champagne', in Aberg and Brown (eds), 87–101.

Barber, L. 2006. *Medieval Life on Romney Marsh, Kent: Archaeological Discoveries from around Lydd*, Heritage Publishing: King's Lynn.

Barber, L. and Priestley-Bell, G. 2008. *Medieval Adaptation, Settlement and Economy of a Coastal Wetland: The Evidence from around Lydd, Romney Marsh, Kent*, Oxbow Books: Oxford.

Barber, L., Gardiner, M. and Rudling, D. 2002. 'Excavations at Eastwick Barn', in D. Rudling (ed.), *Downland Settlement and Land-Use: The Archaeology of the Brighton Bypass*, Archetype Publications: London, 107–140.

Baring-Gould, S. 1891. 'An ancient settlement on Trewortha Marsh', *Journal of the Royal Institution of Cornwall* 11, 57–70.

Baring-Gould, S. 1892. 'Ancient settlement at Trewortha', *Journal of the Royal Institution of Cornwall* 11, 289–290.

Barker, P. 1966. 'The deserted medieval hamlet of Braggington', *Transactions of the Shropshire Archaeological Society* 58, 122–139.

Barker, P. 1977. *Techniques of Archaeological Excavation* (3rd edn 1993), Batsford: London.

Barker, P. and Higham, R. 1982. *Hen Domen, Montgomery*, Royal Archaeological Institute: London.

Barker, P. and Lawson, J. 1971. 'A pre-Norman field system at Hen Domen, Montgomery', *Medieval Archaeology* 15, 58–72.

Barnard, J. A. 1994. 'The boundaries of two Anglo-Saxon charters relating to land at Corscombe: a commentary on the paper by Grundy (1935)', *Proceedings of the Dorset Natural History and Archaeological Society* 116, 1–9.

Barnatt, J. and Smith, K. 2004. *The Peak District*, Windgather Press, Oxford.

Barnes, G. and Williamson, T. 2006. *Hedgerow History:*

Ecology, History and Landscape Character, Windgather Press: Oxford.

Barnett, C., Scaife, R. and Cooke, N. 2007. 'Iron Age to Saxon landscape and landuse change in the Taw Valley: evidence from an infilled river channel at Little Pill Farm, Sticklepath Hill, near Barnstaple', *Devon Archaeological Society Proceedings* 65, 15–34.

Barnwell, P. 2004. 'The laity, the clergy and the divine presence: the use of space in smaller churches of the eleventh and twelfth centuries', *Journal of the British Archaeological Association* 157, 41–60.

Barnwell, P. S. and Palmer, M. (eds) 2007. *Post-Medieval Landscapes. Landscape History after Hoskins, Vol. 3*, Windgather Press: Oxford.

Barrett, J. H. 2004. 'Beyond War and Peace: the study of culture contact in Viking-age Scotland', in Hines *et al.* (eds), 207–218.

Barrett, J. H. 2008. 'The Norse in Scotland', in S. Brink and N. Price (eds), *The Viking World*, Routledge: Oxford, 411–427.

Barrett, J. H., Locker, A. M. and Roberts, C. M. 2004. '"Dark Age Economics" revisited: the English fishbone evidence AD 600–1600', *Antiquity* 78, 618–636.

Barrowman, R. C., Batey C. E. and Morris, C. 2007. Excavations at Tintagel Castle, Cornwall 1990–1999, Oxbow Books: Oxford.

Barry, T. B. 1977. *Medieval Moated Sites of South-East Ireland*, British Archaeological Reports British Series 35. Oxford.

Barry, T. B. 1987. *The Archaeology of Medieval Ireland*, Methuen: London.

Barry, T. B. 1988a. The Archaeology of Medieval Ireland, Routledge: London and New York.

Barry, T. B. 1988b. 'The People of the Country… dwell scattered': the pattern of rural settlement in Ireland in the later Middle Ages', in J. Bradley (ed.), *Settlement and Society in Medieval Ireland*, Boethius Press: Kilkenny, 345–360.

Barry, T. B. 2000. 'Rural settlement in Ireland', in T. Barry (ed.), *A History of Settlement in Ireland,* Routledge: London, 110–123.

Barry, T. B. 2006. 'Harold Leask's "single towers": Irish tower-houses as part of larger settlement complexes', *Château Gaillard* 22, 27–34.

Barry, T. B. 2008a. 'The origins of Irish castles: a contribution to the debate', in C. Manning (ed.), *From Ringforts to Fortified Houses*, Wordwell: Bray, 33–40.

Barry, T. B. 2008b. 'The study of medieval Irish castles: a bibliographic survey', *Proceedings of the Royal Irish Academy* 108, 1115–1136.

Barton, K. J. 1963. 'Worthing Museum notes', *Sussex Archaeological Collections* 101, 9–27.

Barton, K. J. 1964. 'Excavations in the village of Tarring, West Sussex', *Sussex Archaeological Collections* 102, 20–34.

Basford, H. V. 1980. *The Vectis Report. A Survey of Isle of Wight Archaeology*, Isle of Wight County Council: Newport.

Batcock, N. 1991. *The Ruined and Disused Churches of Norfolk*, East Anglian Archaeology, 51. Gressenhall.

Bate, P. V. and Palliser, D. M. 1970–71. 'Suspected lost village sites in Staffordshire', *Transactions of the South Staffordshire Archaeological and Historical Society* 12, 31–36.

Baugh, G. C. (ed.), 1998. *VCH Shropshire Volume 10, Wenlock, Upper Corvedale, and the Stretton Hills*, Oxford University Press: Oxford.

Beacham, P. (ed.) 1990. *Devon Building*, Devon County Council: Exeter.

Beacham, P. 1990. 'The longhouse', in Beacham (ed.), 46–59.

Beaufort, L. C. 1828. 'An essay on the state of architecture and antiquities, previous to the landing of the Anglo-Normans', *Transactions of the Royal Irish Academy* 15, 101–242.

Beckett, J. V. 1988. *The East Midlands from AD 1000*, Longman: London.

Bedwin, O. 1979. 'Excavations at South Street, West Tarring. 1978', *Sussex Archaeological Collections* 117, 234–237.

Bell, M. G. 1977. 'Excavations at Bishopstone', *Sussex Archaeological Collections* 115, 1–291.

Bell, M. G. 1981. *Valley Sediments as Evidence of Prehistoric Land-Use: A Study Based on Dry Valleys in South East England*, unpublished PhD thesis, University of London.

Bell, M. G. 1983. 'Valley sediments as evidence of prehistoric land-use on the South Downs', *Proceedings of the Prehistoric Society* 49, 119–150.

Bell, M. G. 1989. 'Environmental archaeology as an index of continuity and change in the medieval landscape', in Aston, Austin and Dyer (eds), 269–286.

Bell, R. D. and Beresford, M. W. 1987. [Wharram III] *Wharram Percy: The Church of St Martin*, Society for Medieval Archaeology Monograph 11. Maney: London.

Beresford, G. 1971. 'Tresmorn, St Gennys', *Cornish Archaeology* 10, 55–73.

Beresford, G. 1975. *The Medieval Clay-land Village: Excavations at Goltho and Barton Blount*, Society for Medieval Archaeology Monograph 6. Leeds.

Beresford, G. 1979. 'Three deserted medieval settlements on Dartmoor: a report on the late E. Marie Minter's excavations', *Medieval Archaeology* 23, 98–158.

Beresford, G. 1987. *Goltho. The Development of an Early*

Medieval Manor c. 850–1150, English Heritage/ HMSO: London.

Beresford, G. 1988. 'Three deserted medieval settlements on Dartmoor: a comment on David Austin's reinterpretations', *Medieval Archaeology* 32, 175–183.

Beresford, G. 1994. 'Old Lanyon, Madron: a deserted medieval settlement. The late E. Marie Minter's excavations of 1964', *Cornish Archaeology* 33, 130–169.

Beresford, G. 2009. *Caldecote. The Development and Desertion of a Hertfordshire Village*, Society for Medieval Archaeology Monograph 28. Leeds.

Beresford, M. W. 1945–46. 'The deserted villages of Warwickshire', *Transactions of the Birmingham Archaeological Society* 66, 49–106.

Beresford, M. W. 1952. 'The lost villages of Yorkshire, part II', *Yorkshire Archaeological Journal* 38, 149, 44–70.

Beresford, M. W. 1953. 'The lost villages of Yorkshire, part III', *Yorkshire Archaeological Journal* 38, 150, 215–240.

Beresford, M. W. 1954a. *The Lost Villages of England*, Lutterworth Press: London.

Beresford, M. W. 1954b. 'The lost villages of Yorkshire, part IV', *Yorkshire Archaeological Journal* 38, 151, 280–309.

Beresford, M. W. 1964. 'Dispersed and grouped settlement in medieval Cornwall', *Agricultural History Review* 12, 13–37.

Beresford, M. W. 1967. *New Towns of the Middle Ages. Town Plantations in England, Wales and Gascony*, Lutterworth Press: London.

Beresford, M. W. 1986. 'A draft chronology of deserted village studies', *Medieval Settlement Research Group Annual Report* 1, 18–23.

Beresford, M. W. and Finberg, H. 1973. *English Medieval Boroughs. A Hand-List*, David and Charles: Newton Abbot.

Beresford, M. W. and Hurst, J. G. 1971. *Deserted Medieval Villages: Studies*, Lutterworth Press: Guildford and London.

Beresford, M. W. and Hurst, J. G. 1990. *Wharram Percy: Deserted Medieval Village*, English Heritage/Batsford: London.

Beresford, M. W. and St Joseph, J. K. S. 1958. *Medieval England. A Cambridge Air Survey*, Cambridge University Press: Cambridge.

Beresford, M. W. and St Joseph, J. K. S. 1979. *Medieval England: An Aerial Survey*, Cambridge University Press: Cambridge.

Beresford, M. W., Hurst, J. G. and Sheail, J. 1980. 'M. V. R. G.: the first thirty years', *Medieval Village Research Group Annual Report* 28, 36–38.

Berry, C. J. 1997. *Social Theory of the Scottish Enlightenment*, Edinburgh University Press: Edinburgh.

Bettey, J. H. 1986. *Wessex from AD 1000*, London: Longman.

Bewley, R. H. 1995. 'A national mapping programme for England', *Luftbildarchäologie in Ost- und Mitteleuropa*, Forschungen zur Archäologie im Land Brandenburg, 3, 13–22.

Bezant, J. 2009. *Medieval Welsh Settlement. Archaeological Evidence from a Teifi Valley Landscape*, British Archaeological Reports British Series 487. Oxford.

Biddick, K. 1987. 'Missing links: taxable wealth, markets, and stratification among medieval English peasants', *Journal of Interdisciplinary History* 18, 2, 277–298.

Biddle, M. 1961–62. 'The deserted medieval village of Seacourt, Berkshire', *Oxoniensia* 26/27, 70–201.

Bishop, T. A. M. 1938. 'The rotation of crops at Westerham, 1297–1350', *Economic History Review* 1st Series, 9, 38–44.

Blair, J. 1988. *Minsters and Parish Churches: the Local Church in Transition 950–1200*, Oxford University Committee for Archaeology Monograph 17. Oxford.

Blair, J. 1991. *Early Medieval Surrey: Landholding, Church and Settlement Before 1300*, Alan Sutton: Stroud.

Blair, J. 1994. *Anglo-Saxon Oxfordshire*, Sutton Publishing: Stroud.

Blair, J. 1996. 'Palaces or minsters? Northampton and Cheddar reconsidered', *Anglo-Saxon England* 25, 97–121.

Blair, J. 2005. *The Church in Anglo-Saxon Society*, Oxford University Press: Oxford.

Blair, J. (ed.) 2007. *Waterways and Canal-Building in Medieval England*, Oxford University Press: Oxford.

Blair, J. and Ramsey, N. (eds) 2001. *English Medieval Industries*, Hambledon: London.

Blinkhorn, P. 1999. 'Of cabbages and kings: production, trade, and consumption in middle-Saxon England', in M. Anderton (ed.), *Anglo-Saxon Trading Centres: Beyond the Emporia*, Cruithne Press: Glasgow, 4–23.

Blinkhorn, P. 2005. 'Early to Mid Saxon pottery', in R. Mortimer, R. Regan and S. Lucy (eds), *The Saxon and Medieval Settlement at West Fen Road, Ely: The Ashwell Site*, East Anglian Archaeology 110. Cambridge, 62–65.

Blinkhorn, P. W. forthcoming. *The Ipswich Ware Project: Ceramics Trade and Society in Middle Saxon England*, Medieval Pottery Research Group Special Paper. London.

Blomé, B. 1929. *The Place-Names of North Devonshire*, Appelbergs Boktryckeri Aktiebolag: Uppsala.

Boddington, A. 1996. *Raunds Furnells. The Anglo-Saxon Church and Churchyard*, English Heritage Archaeological Reports 7. London.

Boerefijn, W. 2010. *The Foundation, Planning and Building of New Towns in the Thirteenth and Fourteenth Centuries in Europe*, privately printed: Amsterdam.

Bond, C. J. 1974. 'Deserted medieval villages in Warwickshire: a review of the field evidence', *Transactions of the Birmingham Archaeological Society* 86, 85–112.

Bond, C. J. 1985. 'Medieval Oxfordshire villages and their topography: a preliminary discussion', in D. Hooke (ed.), 101–123.

Bond, C. J. 1989. 'Grassy hummocks and some stone foundations: fieldwork and deserted medieval settlements in the south-west midlands', in Aston, Austin and Dyer (eds), 129–148.

Bond, J. 1994. 'Forests, chases, warrens and parks', in Aston and Lewis (eds), 115–158.

Bond, J. 2007. 'Canal construction in the early middle ages: an introductory review', in Blair (ed.), 153–206.

Bond, J. and Tiller, K. 1997. *Blenheim: Landscape for a Palace*, Sutton: Stroud.

Bonney, D. 1976. 'Early boundaries and estates in southern England', in Sawyer (ed.), 72–82.

Bonney, D. and Dunn, C. J. 1989. 'Earthwork castles and settlement at Hamstead Marshall, Berkshire', in Bowden, Mackay and Topping (eds), 173–182.

Booker, S. 2010. 'An English City? Gaelicization and cultural exchange in late medieval Dublin', in S. Duffy (ed.), *Medieval Dublin X*, Four Courts: Dublin, 287–298.

Boserup, E. 1965. *The Conditions of Agricultural Growth: The Economics of Agrarian Change under Population Pressure*, Chicago: Aldine.

Bourne, J. (ed.) 1996. Anglo-Saxon Landscapes in the East Midlands, Leicestershire Museums Arts and Records Service: Leicester.

Bowden, M. 1999. *Unravelling the Landscape: An Inquisitive Approach to Archaeology*, Tempus: Stroud.

Bowden, M., Mackay, D. and Topping, P. (eds), *From Cornwall to Caithness*, British Archaeological Reports British Series 209. Oxford, 173–182.

Bowen, D. Q. 1989. 'The Welsh landform', in Owen (ed.), 27–44.

Bowen, H. C. 1961. *Ancient Fields*, British Association for the Advancement of Science. London.

Bowman, P. and Liddle, P. 2004. *Leicestershire Landscapes*, Leicestershire Museums Archaeological Fieldwork Group: Leicester.

Bradley, R. 1989. 'Herbert Toms – a pioneer of analytical field survey', in Bowden, Mackay and Topping (eds), 29–48.

Bradley, R. 2006. 'Bridging the two cultures – commercial archaeology and the study of Prehistoric Britain', *Antiquaries Journal* 86, 1–13.

Brady, N. 2003. 'The Discovery Programme's Medieval Rural Settlement Project, 2002–2008', *Medieval Settlement Research Group Annual Report* 18, 23–26.

Brady, N. and O'Conor, K. 2005. 'The later medieval use of crannogs in Ireland', *Ruralia* 5, 127–136.

Brandon, P. F. 1963. *The Common Lands and Wastes of Sussex*, unpublished PhD thesis, University of London.

Brandon, P. F. 1969. 'Medieval clearances in the East Sussex Weald', *Transactions of the Institute of British Geographers* 48, 135–153.

Brandon, P. F. 1971. 'Demesne arable farming in coastal Sussex during the later Middle Ages', *Agricultural History Review* 19, 113–134.

Brandon, P. F. 1974. *The Sussex Landscape*, Hodder and Stoughton: London.

Brandon, P. F. and Short, B. M. 1990. *The South-East from AD 1000*, Longman: Harlow.

Brannon, N. F. 1984. 'A small excavation in Tildarg Townland, near Ballyclare, County Antrim', *Ulster Journal of Archaeology* 47, 163–170.

Brannon, N. F. 1988. 'Medieval mountain-side enclosure: Tildarg, Co. Antrim', in A. Hamlin and C. Lynn (eds), *Pieces of the Past*, HMSO: Belfast, 70–71.

Brent, C. 2004. *Pre-Georgian Lewes: c. 890–1714. The Emergence of a County Town*, Colin Brent Books: Lewes.

Brewster, T. and Hayfield, C. 1988. 'Cowlam deserted village: a case study of post-medieval village desertion', *Post-Medieval Archaeology* 22, 21–109.

Briggs, S. 1985. 'Problems of the early agricultural landscape in upland Wales, as illustrated by an example from the Brecon Beacons', in D. Spratt and C. Burgess (eds), *Upland Settlement in Britain*, British Archaeological Reports British Series 143. Oxford, 285–316.

Britnell, R. H. 1978. 'English markets and royal administration before 1200', *Economic History Review* 31, 2, 183–196.

Britnell, R. H. 1981. 'Essex markets before 1350', *Essex Archaeology and History* 13, 15–21.

Britnell, R. H. 1983. 'Agriculture in a region of ancient enclosure, 1185–1500', in A. Gransden (ed.), *Nottingham Medieval Studies* 27, 37–55.

Britnell, R. H. 1988. 'The fields and pastures of Colchester, 1280–1350', *Essex Archaeology and History* 19, 159–165.

Britnell, R. H. 1991. 'Farming practice and technique: Eastern England', in Miller (ed.), 194–210.

Britnell, R. H. 1992. *The Commercialisation of English Society 1000–1500*, Cambridge University Press: Cambridge.

Britnell, R. H. 2003. 'The woollen textile industry of Suffolk in the later Middle Ages', *The Ricardian* 13, 86–99.

Britnell, W. J. (ed.) 2001. 'Tŷ-mawr, Castle Caereinion', *Montgomeryshire Collections* 89, 1–242 (special issue on Tŷ-mawr).

Britnell, W. J. and Dixon, P. 2001. 'Archaeological excavations at Tŷ-mawr, Castle Caereinion', in Britnell (ed.), 55–86.

Britnell, W. J. and Suggett, R. 2002. 'A sixteenth-century peasant hallhouse in Powys: survey and excavation of Tyddyn Llwydion, Pennant Melangell, Montgomeryshire', *Archaeological Journal* 159, 142–169.

Britnell, W. J., Silvester, R. J., Suggett, R. and Wiliam, E. 2008. 'Tŷ-draw, Llanarmon Mynydd Mawr, Powys – a late-medieval cruck-framed hallhouse-longhouse', *Archaeologia Cambrensis* 157, 157–202.

Broad, J. and Hoyle, R. (eds) 1997. *Bernwood: Life and Afterlife of a Royal Forest*, Harris Papers, 2. Preston.

Brooks, H. 1992. 'Two rural medieval sites at Chignall St James: excavations in 1989', *Essex Archaeology and History* 23, 39–50.

Brooks, H. 1993. 'Fieldwalking and excavations at Stansted Airport', in J. Gardiner (ed.), *Flatlands and Wetlands: Current Themes in East Anglian Archaeology*, East Anglian Archaeology 50. Norwich, 40–57.

Brown, A. E. 1987. *Fieldwork for Archaeologists and Local Historians,* Batsford: London.

Brown, A. E. 1991. *Early Daventry*, University of Leicester Department of Adult Education: Leicester.

Brown, A. E. and Foard, G. 1998. 'The Saxon landscape: a regional perspective', in P. Everson and T. Williamson (eds), *The Archaeology of Landscape. Studies Presented to Christopher Taylor*, Manchester University Press: Manchester, 67–94.

Brown, A. E. and Taylor, C. C. 1989. 'The origins of dispersed settlement; some results from fieldwork in Bedfordshire', *Landscape History* 11, 61–81.

Brown, A. E. and Taylor, C. C. 1991. *Moated Sites in Northern Bedfordshire: Some Surveys and Wider Implications*, Vaughan Papers in Adult Education 35. Leicester.

Brown, D. 1997. 'Pots from houses', *Medieval Ceramics* 21, 83–94.

Brown, E. H. 1960. *The Relief and Drainage of Wales*, University of Wales Press: Cardiff.

Brown, G. 1996. 'West Chisenbury: settlement and land-use in a Chalk Downland landscape', *Wiltshire Archaeological and Natural History Society Magazine* 89, 73–83.

Brown, N. 2006. *A Medieval Moated Manor by the Thames Estuary: Excavations at Southchurch Hall*, East Anglian Archaeology 115. Chelmsford.

Brown, R. A., Colvin, H. M. and Taylor, A. J. 1963. *The History of the King's Works, Volumes I and II: The Middle Ages*, HMSO: London.

Brown, S. 1998. 'Recent building recording and excavations at Leigh Barton, Churchstow, Devon', *Devon Archaeological Society Proceedings* 56, 5–108.

Brown, S. and Laithwaite, M. 1993. 'Northwood Farm, Christow: an abandoned farmstead on the eastern fringe of Dartmoor', *Devon Archaeological Society Proceedings* 51, 161–184.

Brown, T. *see* Brown, A. E.

Browne, D. M. and Hughes, S. (eds) 2003. *The Archaeology of the Welsh Uplands*, RCAHMW: Aberystwyth.

Bruce-Mitford, R. 1940. 'The excavations at Seacourt, Berkshire, 1939', *Oxoniensia* 5, 31–41.

Bruce-Mitford, R. 1997. *Mawgan Porth. A Settlement of the Late Saxon Period on the North Cornish Coast. Excavations 1949–52, 1954, and 1974*, English Heritage: London.

Brunskill, R. W. 1971. *Illustrated Handbook of Vernacular Architecture*, Faber and Faber: London.

Brunskill, R. W. 1981. *Traditional Buildings of Britain* (3rd edn 2004), Gollancz: London.

Burley, S. J. 1958. 'The victualling of Calais 1347–65', *Bulletin of the Institute of Historical Research* 31, 49–57.

Butler, C. 2000. *Saxon Settlement and Earlier Remains at Friars Oak, Hassocks, West Sussex,* British Archaeological Reports British Series 295. Oxford.

Butler, L. and Wade-Martins, P. 1989. *The Deserted Village of Thuxton, Norfolk*, East Anglian Archaeology 46. Gressenhall.

Butler, L. A. S. 1963. 'The excavation of a long hut near Bwlch yr Hendre', *Ceredigion* 4, 400–407.

Butler, L. A. S. 1971. 'The study of deserted medieval settlements in Wales', in M.W. Beresford and J. G. Hurst (eds), *Deserted Medieval Villages*, Lutterworth Press: Guildford, 249–269.

Cadman, G. 1983. 'Raunds 1977–1983: an excavation summary', *Medieval Archaeology* 27, 107–122.

Caiger, J. E. L. 1964. 'Darenth Wood: its earthworks and antiquities', *Archaeologia Cantiana* 79, 77–94.

Caiger, J. E. L. 1970. 'Cozendon Wood, Northfleet', *Archaeologia Cantiana* 85, 204–207.

Caird, J. and Proudfoot, B. 1987. 'Obituary: Dr. Horace Fairhurst', *Scottish Geographical Journal* 103, 2, 109.

Caldwell, D. H. and Ewart, G. 1993. 'Finlaggan and the Lordship of the Isles: an archaeological approach', *Scottish Historical Review* 72:2, 146–166.

Caldwell, D. H., McWee, R. and Ruckley, N. A. 2000. 'Post-medieval settlement in Islay: some recent research', in Atkinson, Banks and MacGregor (eds), 58–68.

Cameron, K. 1959. *The Place-Names of Derbyshire*, 3 vols., English Place-Name Society: London.

Campbell, B. M. S. 1980. 'Population change and the genesis of commonfields on a Norfolk manor', *Economic Historical Review* (2nd Series) 33, 1, 174–192.

Campbell, B. M. S. 1981a. 'Commonfield origins – the regional dimension', in T. Rowley (ed.), *The Origins of Open-Field Agriculture*. Croom Helm: London, 112–129.

Campbell, B. M. S. 1981b. 'The extent and layout of common fields in eastern Norfolk', *Norfolk Archaeology* 38, 5–32.

Campbell, B. M. S. 1981c. 'The regional uniqueness of English field systems? Some evidence from eastern Norfolk', *Agricultural Historical Review* 29, 16–28.

Campbell, B. M. S. 2000. *English Seigniorial Agriculture*, Cambridge University Press: Cambridge.

Campbell, B. M. S. 2005. 'Medieval manorial structure', in Ashwin and Davison (eds), 52–53.

Campbell, B. M. S., Galloway, J. A., Keene, D. and Murphy, M. 1993. *A Medieval Capital and Its Grain Supply*, Historical Geography Research Series 30. Queen's University Belfast and Centre for Metropolitan History: London.

Campbell, E. 2007. *Continental and Mediterranean Imports to Atlantic Britain and Ireland, AD 400–800*, Council for British Archaeology Research Report 157. York.

Campbell, E. and Lane, A. 1993. 'Excavations at Longbury Bank, Dyfed, and early medieval settlement in South Wales', *Medieval Archaeology* 37, 15–77.

Campbell, G. 2007. 'The Peter Serle Chilworth estate map of 1755', *Hampshire Field Club and Archaeological Society Newsletter* 47, 12–16.

Campbell, G. 2008a. 'The royal forest of Bere', *Hampshire Field Club and Archaeological Society Newsletter* 50, 17–18.

Campbell, G. 2008b. 'Location, location, location, and the medieval Hampshire markets', *Hampshire Field Club and Archaeological Society Newsletter* 50, 13–16.

Carlin, M. 1996. *Medieval Southwark*, Hambledon Press: London.

Carr, A. D. 1971–72. 'The extent of Anglesey, 1352', *Transactions of the Anglesey Antiquarian Society* 150–272.

Carr, A. D. 1982. *Medieval Anglesey*, Anglesey Antiquarian Society: Llangefni.

Carr, R. D., Tester, A. and Murphy, P. 1988. 'The middle-Saxon settlement at Staunch Meadow, Brandon', *Antiquity* 62, 235, 371–377.

Carter, H. 1981. *The Study of Urban Geography* (3rd edn), Edward Arnold: London.

Carus-Wilson, E. 1964. 'The medieval trade of the ports of the Wash', *Medieval Archaeology* 6–7, 182–201.

Caruth, J. 1995. *Archaeological Assessment Report, New Hewlett Packard Building, White House Industrial Estate, Ipswich. IPS 247*, Suffolk County Council Archaeological Service Report No. 95/23.

Caruth, J. 1996. 'Ipswich, Hewlett Packard plc, Whitehouse Industrial Estate', *Proceedings of the Suffolk Institute of Archaeology and History* 38, 4, 476–479.

Caruth, J. 2008. 'Eye, Hartismere High School', *Proceedings of the Suffolk Institute of Archaeology and History* 41, 4, 518–520.

Carver, M. 2008. *Portmahomack: Monastery of the Picts*, Edinburgh University Press: Edinburgh.

Caseldine, A. 2006. 'The environment and deserted rural settlements in Wales: potential and possibilities for palaeoenvironmental studies', in Roberts (ed.), 133–153.

Caseldine, C. 1999. 'Environmental setting', in Kain and Ravenhill (eds), 25–34.

Caseldine, C. and Hatton, J. 1994. 'Into the mists? Thoughts on the prehistoric and historic environmental history of Dartmoor', *Devon Archaeological Society Proceedings* 52, 35–47.

Chandler, J. 1996. Review of Lewis (1994), *Wiltshire Archaeological and Natural History Society Magazine* 89, 154–155.

Chandler, J. 2007. *Codford: Wool and War in Wiltshire*, Phillimore: Chichester.

Chapelot, J. and Fossier, R. 1985. *The Village and House in the Middle Ages*, University of California Press: Berkeley.

Chapman, A. (ed.) 2010. *West Cotton, Raunds: A Study of Medieval Settlement Dynamics AD 450–1450. Excavation of a Deserted Medieval Hamlet in Northamptonshire, 1985–89*, Oxbow Books: Oxford.

Chapman, H. and Seeliger, S. 2001. *Enclosure, Environment and Landscape in Southern England*, Tempus: Stroud.

Chapman, P., Blinkhorn, P. and Chapman, A. 2008. 'A medieval potters' tenement at Corby Road, Stanion, Northamptonshire', *Northamptonshire Archaeology* 35, 215–270.

Charlton, D. B. and Day, J. C. 1979. 'Excavation and field survey in upper Redesdale: part II', *Archaeologia Aeliana* 5th Series, 7, 207–233.

Chatwin, D. and Gardiner, M. F. 2005. 'Rethinking the early medieval settlement of woodlands: evidence from the western Sussex Weald', *Landscape History* 27, 31–49.

Cherry, J. 2001. 'Pottery and tile', in Blair and Ramsey (eds), 189–210.

Chesher, V. and Chesher, F. 1968. *The Cornishman's House*, D. B. Barton: Truro.

Child, P. 1990. 'Farmhouse building traditions', in Beacham (ed.), 32–45.

Christie, N., Creighton, O., Edgeworth, M. and Fradley,

M. 2010a. '"Have you found anything interesting?" Exploring early medieval and medieval urbanism at Wallingford: sources, routes and questions', *Oxoniensia* 75, 35–47.

Christie, N., Edgeworth, M., Taylor, J. *et al.* 2010b. 'Mapping Wallingford castle', *Medieval Archaeology* 54, 416–420.

Christie, P. 1972. *Moats in West Suffolk*, unpublished paper.

Clark, S. 2009. 'Early medieval Berkshire (AD 400–1066)', in *Solent-Thames Regional Research Frameworks, Berkshire*, website hosted by Buckinghamshire County Council. http://www.buckscc.gov.uk/bcc/archaeology/solent_framework.page?.

Clarke, H. B. 1998. 'Proto-towns and towns in Ireland and Britain in the ninth and tenth centuries', in H. Clarke, M. Ní Mhaonaigh and R. Ó Floinn (eds), *Ireland and Scandinavia in the Early Viking Age*: Four Courts Press: Dublin, 331–380.

Clarke, R. 2003. *A Medieval Moated Settlement and Windmill, Excavations at Boreham Airfield, Essex, 1996*, East Anglian Archaeology Occasional Papers 11. Chelmsford.

Clutterbuck, R. 2009. 'Cookstown, Co. Meath: a medieval rural settlement', in Corlett and Potterton (eds), 27–48.

Cocke, T., Findlay, D., Halsey, R., Williamson, E., Williamson, G. and Rust, D. 1996. *Recording a Church: An Illustrated Glossary*, CBA: London.

Coggins, D. 1992. 'Shielings and farmsteads: early rectangular buildings in upper Teesdale', *Durham Archaeological Journal* 8, 77–83.

Coggins, D. 2004. Simy Folds: Twenty Years On', in Hines *et al.* (eds), 325–334.

Coggins, D., Fairless, K. J. and Batey, C. E. 1983. 'Simy Folds: an early medieval settlement site in upper Teesdale, Co. Durham', *Medieval Archaeology* 27, 1–26.

Cole, A. 2007. 'The place-name evidence for water transport in early medieval England', in Blair (ed.), 55–84.

Cole, G. D. H. and Browning, D. C. (eds) 1962. *Daniel Defoe. A Tour through the Whole Island of Great Britain*, Dent and Sons: London.

Coleman, C. 1996. *A Court Roll of the Manor of Downham, 1310–1377*, Cambridge Record Society: Cambridge.

Coleman, R. 2004. 'The archaeology of burgage plots in medieval Scottish towns: a review', *Proceedings of the Society of Antiquaries of Scotland* 134, 281–324.

Coleman, R. and Perry, D. 1997. 'Moated sites in Tayside and Fife', *Tayside and Fife Archaeological Journal* 3, 176–187.

Colman, S., Griffin, F., Lawrence, R. and Easton, T. 1995.

'Huntingfield and Bruisyard', *Proceedings of the Suffolk Institute of Archaeology and History* 38:3, 372–376.

Comber, M. 2008. *The Economy of the Ringfort and Contemporary Settlement in Early Medieval Ireland*. British Archaeological Reports International Series 1773. Oxford.

Cook, H., Stearne, K. and Williamson, T. 2003. 'The origins of water meadows in England', *Agricultural History Review* 51, 155–162.

Cook, P. J. 1960. *Moated Settlements in the Blackwater Region*, unpublished BA thesis, University of Oxford.

Cooper, N. (ed.) 2006. *The Archaeology of the East Midlands: An Archaeological Resource Assessment and Research Agenda*, University of Leicester: Leicester.

Corlett, C. and Potterton, M. (eds) 2009. *Rural Settlement in Medieval Ireland*, Wordwell: Dublin.

Cornwall County Council, 1996. *Cornwall Landscape Assessment*, Cornwall County Council: Truro.

Cosgrove, D. and Daniels, S. 1988. *The Iconography of Landscape*, Cambridge University Press: Cambridge.

Coss, P. 2003. *The Origins of the English Gentry*, Cambridge University Press: Cambridge.

Costen, M. (ed.) 2007. *People and Places. Essays in Honour of Mick Aston*, Oxbow Books: Oxford.

Costen, M. 2007. 'Anonymous thegns in the landscape of Wessex', in Costen (ed.), 61–75.

Cotter, J. 1991. 'The medieval pottery and tile industry at Tyler Hill', *Canterbury's Archaeology 1990–1991*, Canterbury, 49–56.

Cotton, J., Crocker, G. and Graham, A. (eds) 2004. *Aspects of Archaeology and History in Surrey: Towards a Research Framework for the County*, Surrey Archaeological Society: Guildford.

Courtney, P. 1991. 'A native-Welsh mediaeval settlement: excavations at Beili Bedw, St Harmon, Powys', *Bulletin Board of Celtic Studies* 38, 233–255.

Cox, B. 1975–76. 'The place-names of the earliest English records', *Journal of the English Place-Name Society* 8, 12–66.

Cox, P.W. 1988. 'A seventh century inhumation cemetery at Shepherd's Farm, Ulwell, near Swanage, Dorset', *Proceedings of the Dorset Natural History and Archaeological Society* 110, 37–47.

Crawford, A. 1985. *C. R. Ashbee: Architect, Designer and Romantic Socialist*, Yale University Press: London.

Crawford, O. G. S. 1923. 'Air survey and archaeology', *Geographical Journal* 61, 342–360.

Crawford, O. G. S. 1925. 'Air photograph of Gainstrop, Lincs', *Antiquaries Journal* 5, 432–434.

Crawford, O. G. S. and Keiller, A. 1928. *Wessex from the Air*, Clarendon Press: Oxford.

Crawford, S. 2009. 'Settlement and social differentiation',

in P. Stafford (ed.), *A Companion to the Early Middle Ages: Britain and Ireland c. 500–1100*, Blackwell: London, 432–445.

Creighton, O. H. 2004. '"The rich man in his castle, the poor man at his gate": castle baileys and medieval settlements in England', *Château Gaillard* 21, 25–36.

Creighton, O. H. 2005a. 'Castles and castle-building in town and country', in Giles and Dyer (eds), 275–292.

Creighton, O. H. 2005b. *Castles and Landscapes: Power, Community and Fortification in Medieval England*, Equinox: London (1st edn 2002, Continuum: London).

Creighton, O. H. 2009. *Designs upon the Land: Elite Landscapes of the Middle Ages*, Boydell and Brewer: Woodbridge.

Creighton, O. H. and Higham, R. A. 2004. 'Castle studies and the "landscape" agenda', *Landscape History* 26, 5–18.

Creighton, O. H. and Higham, R. A. 2005. *Medieval Town Walls. An Archaeological and Social History of Urban Defence*, Tempus: Stroud.

Croad, S. 1989. 'Architectural records in the archives of the Royal Commission on the Historical Monuments of England', *Transactions of the Ancient Monuments Society* 33, 23–44.

Crockett, A. 1995. 'Excavations at Montefiori new halls of residence, Swaythling, Southampton, 1992', *Proceedings of the Hampshire Field Club and Archaeological Society* 51, 5–57.

Croft, R. A. and Mynard, D. C. (eds) 1993. *The Changing Landscape of Milton Keynes*, Buckinghamshire Archaeological Society Monograph Series 5. Buckingham.

Cross, R. 1989. 'Documentary studies and landscape history around Folkestone', *Medieval Settlement Research Group Annual Report* 4, 20–21.

Cross, R. 1992. 'Broad Oak Water', *Canterbury's Archaeology 1991–1992*, 42–45.

Crouch, D. 1992. *The Image of Aristocracy in Britain, 1000–1300*, Routledge: London.

Crouch, D. 2005. *The Birth of Nobility. Constructing Aristocracy in England and France 900–1300*, Pearson Longman: Harlow.

Cullen, P., Jones, R. and Parsons, D. N. 2011. *Thorps in a Changing Landscape*, University of Hertfordshire Press: Hatfield.

Cumming, E. and Kaplan, W. 1991. *The Arts and Crafts Movement*, Thames and Hudson: London.

Cunliffe, B. 1972. 'Saxon and medieval settlement pattern in the region of Chalton, Hampshire', *Medieval Archaeology* 16, 1–12.

Cunliffe, B. 1973a. 'Manor Farm, Chalton, Hampshire', *Post-Medieval Archaeology* 7, 31–59.

Cunliffe, B. 1973b. 'Chalton, Hants: the evolution of a landscape', *Antiquaries Journal* 53, 173–190.

Cunliffe, B. 1976. *Excavations at Portchester Castle. Vol. II. Saxon*, Society of Antiquaries: London.

Currie, C. K. 1994. 'Saxon charters and landscape evolution in the south-central Hampshire basin', *Proceedings of the Hampshire Field Club and Archaeological Society* 50, 103–125.

Curwen, E. and Curwen, E. C. 1922. 'Notes on the archaeology of Burpham and the neighbouring downs', *Sussex Archaeological Collections* 63, 1–53.

Curwen, E. and Curwen, E. C. 1923. 'Sussex lynchets and their associated field-ways', *Sussex Archaeological Collections* 64, 1–65.

Cushion, B. and Davison, A. 2003. *Earthworks of Norfolk*, East Anglian Archaeology 104. Gressenhall.

Cushion, B., Davison, A., Fenner, G., Goldsmith, R., Knight, J., Virgoe, N., Wade, K. and Wade-Martins, P. 1982. *Some Deserted Village Sites in Norfolk*, East Anglian Archaeology 14. Gressenhall, 40–101.

Dalglish, C. 2003. *Rural Society in the Age of Reason: An Archaeology of the Emergence of Modern Life in the Southern Scottish Highlands*, Kluwer/Plenum: New York.

Dalglish, C. 2009. 'Understanding landscape: interdisciplinary dialogue and the post-medieval countryside', in Horning and Palmer (eds), 233–254.

Darby, H. C. 1936. *An Historical Geography of England before AD 1800*, Cambridge University Press: Cambridge.

Darby, H. C. 1952–67. *The Domesday Geography of England*, 5 vols., Cambridge University Press: Cambridge.

Darby, H. C. 1971. *The Domesday Geography of Eastern England*, Cambridge University Press: Cambridge.

Darby, H. C. (ed.) 1973. *A New Historical Geography of England*, Cambridge University Press: Cambridge.

Darby, H. C. 1974. *The Medieval Fenland*, David and Charles: Newton Abbot.

Darby, H. C. (ed.) 1976. *A New Historical Geography of England before 1600*, Cambridge University Press: Cambridge.

Darby, H. C. 1977. *Domesday England*, Cambridge University Press: Cambridge.

Darby, H. C. and Terrett, I. B. 1971. *The Geography of Midland England*, Cambridge University Press: Cambridge.

Darby, H. C. and Welldon Finn, R. 1967. *The Domesday Geography of South-West England*, Cambridge: Cambridge University Press.

Dark, P. 2000. *The Environment of Britain in the First Millennium*, Duckworth & Co.: London.

Darlington, J. (ed.) 2001. *Stafford Castle: Survey, Excavation and Research 1978–1998, Volume I – The Surveys*, Stafford Borough Council: Stafford.

Davidson, A. F., Davidson, J. E., Owen-John, H. S. and Toft, L. A. 1987. 'Excavations at the sand-covered medieval settlement at Rhossili, West Glamorgan', *Bulletin Board of Celtic Studies* 34, 244–269.

Davies, A. L. and Watson, F. 2007. 'Understanding the changing value of natural resources: an integrated palaeoecological-historical investigation into grazing-woodland interactions by Loch Awe, western Highlands of Scotland', *Journal of Biogeography* 34, 10, 1777–1791.

Davies, E. 1984–85. 'Hafod and lluest : the summering of cattle and upland settlement in Wales', *Folk Life* 23, 76–96.

Davies, G. 2010. 'Early medieval "rural centres" and west Norfolk: a growing picture of diversity, complexity and changing lifestyles', *Medieval Archaeology* 54, 89–122.

Davies, M. 1973. 'Field systems of south Wales', in Baker and Butlin (eds), 480–529.

Davies, O. 1941. 'Trial excavation at Lough Enagh,' *Ulster Journal of Archaeology* 3rd Series, 4, 88–101.

Davies, R. R. 1978. *Lordship and Society in the Marches of Wales, 1282–1400*, Oxford University Press: Oxford.

Davies, W. 1982. *Wales in the Early Middle Ages*, Leicester University Press: Leicester.

Davison, A. 1988. *Six Deserted Villages in Norfolk*, East Anglian Archaeology 44. Gressenhall.

Davison, A. 1990. *The Evolution of Settlement in Three Parishes in South-East Norfolk*, East Anglian Archaeology 49. Gressenhall.

Davison, A. 2005. 'Medieval settlement desertion', in Ashwin and Davison (eds) 88–89.

Davison, A. and Green, B. 1993. *Illington: A Study of Breckland Parish and its Anglo-Saxon Cemetery*, East Anglian Archaeology 63. Gressenhall.

DeHaene, G. 2009. 'Medieval rural settlement beside Duncormick motte, Co. Wexford', in Corlett and Potterton (eds), 59–66.

Denman, D. R., Roberts, R. A. and Smith, H. J. F. 1967. *Commons and Village Greens*, Leonard Hill: London.

Dennison, E. and Simpson, G. 2000. 'Scotland', in D. M. Palliser (ed.), *The Cambridge Urban History of Britain, Vol. 1, 600–1540*, Cambridge University Press: Cambridge.

Department of the Environment. *List of Buildings of Special Historic and Architectural Interest*, DoE, No. 24. HMSO: London.

Deveson, A. M. 2009. 'The *ceorls* of Hurtsbourne revisited', *Proceedings of the Hampshire Field Club and Archaeological Society* 64, 106–115.

DeWindt, A. R. 1987. 'Redefining the peasant community in medieval England: the regional perspective', *Journal of British Studies* 26, 163–207.

Dickinson, C. W. 1964. 'Co. Down: Lough Island Reavy', in 'Medieval Britain in 1962 and 1963', *Medieval Archaeology* 8, 276–277.

Dixon, P. J. 1994. *Southdean, Borders: An Archaeological Survey*, RCAHMS: Edinburgh.

Dixon, P. J. 1997. 'Settlement in the hunting forests of southern Scotland in the medieval and later periods', in G. De Boe and F. Verhaeghe (eds), *Rural Settlements in Medieval Europe*, Instituut voor het Archeologisch Patrimonium: Zellik, 345–354.

Dixon, P. J. 1998. 'A rural medieval settlement in Roxburghshire: excavations at Springwood Park, Kelso 1985–6', *Proceedings of the Society of Antiquaries of Scotland* 128, 671–751.

Dixon, P. J. 2003. 'Champagne country: a review of medieval rural settlement in Lowland Scotland', in Govan (ed.), 53–64.

Dodds, B. 2008. 'Output and productivity: common themes and regional variations', in B. Dodds and R. Britnell (eds), *Agriculture and Rural Society after the Black Death*, University of Hertfordshire Press: Hatfield, 73–88.

Dodgshon, R. A. 1981. *Land and Society in Early Scotland*, Clarendon Press: Oxford.

Dodgshon, R. A. 1993a. 'West Highland and Hebridean settlement prior to Crofting and the Clearances: a study in stability of change?', *Proceedings of the Society of Antiquaries of Scotland* 123, 419–438.

Dodgshon, R. A. 1993b. 'West Highland and Hebridean landscapes: have they a history without runrig?', *Journal of Historical Geography* 19, 4, 383–398.

Dollin, B. W. 1986. 'Moated sites in north-east Norfolk', *Norfolk Archaeology* 39, 3, 262–277.

Donkin, R. A. 1976. 'Changes in the early Middle Ages', in H.C. Darby (ed.), *A New Historical Geography of England before 1600*, Cambridge University Press: Cambridge, 75–135.

Donnelly, C. J. 2001. 'Decline and adaptation: the medieval Irish tower house in early modern County Limerick,' in G. Malm (ed.), *Archaeology and Buildings*, British Archaeological Reports International Series 930. Oxford, 7–17.

Donnelly, C. J. 2007. 'Thomas Johnson Westropp and his study of the medieval towerhouses of Counties Clare and Limerick', in C. Manning (ed.), *From Ringforts to Fortified Houses: Studies on Castles and other Monuments in Honour of David Sweetman*, Wordwell: Dublin, 131–142.

Donnelly, C. J. and Horning, A. J. 2002. 'Post-medieval

and industrial archaeology in Ireland: an overview', *Antiquity* 76, 557–561.

Doran, L. 2004. 'Medieval communication routes through Longford and Roscomon and their associated settlements', *Proceedings of the Royal Irish Academy* 104C (3), 57–80.

Dorrell, P. 1989. *Photography in Archaeology and Conservation* (2nd edn 1994), Cambridge University Press: Cambridge.

Douglas, D. C. 1927. *The Social Structure of Medieval East Anglia*, Oxford Studies in Social and Legal History, Vol. IX. Clarendon Press: Oxford.

Dransart, P. 2008. 'Prospect and excavation of moated sites: Scottish earthwork castles and house societies in the late twelfth to fourteenth centuries', *Château Gaillard*, 23, 115–128.

Draper, S. 2004. 'Roman estates to English parishes? The legacy of Desmond Bonney reconsidered', in R. Collins and J. Gerrard (eds), *Debating Late Antiquity in Britain AD 300–700*, British Archaeological Reports British Series 365. Oxford, 55–64.

Drewett, P. F. 1982. *The Archaeology of Bullock Down, Eastbourne, East Sussex: The Development of a Landscape*, Sussex Archaeological Society: Lewes.

Driscoll, S. T. and Nieke, M. R. (eds) 1988. *Power and Politics in Early Medieval Britain and Ireland*, Edinburgh University Press: Edinburgh.

Drury, P. J. 1978. *Chelmsford Excavations I: Excavations at Little Waltham 1970–1*, Council for British Archaeology Research Report 26. London.

Drury, P. J. and Rodwell, W. 1978. 'Investigations at Asheldham, Essex: an interim report on the church and the historic landscape', *Antiquaries Journal* 58, 133–151.

Drury, P. J. and Rodwell, W. 1980. 'Settlement in the later Iron Age and Roman periods', in D. G. Buckley (ed.), *Archaeology in Essex to AD 1500*, Council for British Archaeology Research Report 34. London, 59–75.

Du Boulay, F. R. H. 1966. *The Lordship of Canterbury: An Essay on Medieval Society*, Nelson: London.

Dudley, D. and Minter, E. M. 1962–63. 'The medieval village at Garrow Tor, Bodmin Moor, Cornwall', *Medieval Archaeology* 6–7, 272–294.

Dudley, D. and Minter, E. M. 1966. 'The excavation of a medieval settlement at Treworld, Lesnewth, 1963', *Cornish Archaeology* 5, 34–58.

Duffy, P., Edwards, D. and FitzPatrick, E. (eds) 2001a. *Gaelic Ireland: Land, Lordship and Settlement 1250–1650*, Four Courts Press: Dublin.

Duffy, P., Edwards, D. and FitzPatrick, E. 2001b. 'Recovering Gaelic Ireland, 1250–1650', in Duffy *et al.* (eds), 21–76.

Dugdale, W. (ed.) (repr.) 1846. *Monasticon Anglicanum*, Vol. III, London.

Dugdale, W. 1662. *The History of Imbanking and Drayning of divers Fens and Marshes, both in Foreign Parts and in this Kingdom and of the Improvements thereby.* Alice Warren: London.

Dyer, C. 1971. 'DMVs in Worcestershire: an interim report on work in the county and a classified list', *Medieval Village Research Group Annual Report* 19, 5–7.

Dyer, C. 1985. 'Power and conflict in the medieval English village', in D. Hooke (ed.), 27–32.

Dyer, C. 1989. *Standards of Living in the Later Middle Ages. Social Change in England c. 1200–1520*, Cambridge University Press: Cambridge.

Dyer, C. 1990. 'Dispersed settlements in medieval England. A case study of Pendock, Worcestershire', *Medieval Archaeology* 34, 97–121.

Dyer, C. 1991. *Hanbury: Settlement and Society in a Woodland Landscape*, University of Leicester Department of English Local History Occasional Papers 4th Series 4.

Dyer, C. 1992. 'Small-town conflict in the later middle ages: events at Shipston-on-Stour', *Urban History* 19, 183–210.

Dyer, C. 1994a. 'Dispersed settlements in medieval England: a case study of Pendock, Worcestershire', in Dyer, 47–76.

Dyer, C. 1994b. *Everyday Life in Medieval England*, Hambledon Press: London.

Dyer, C. 1995. 'Sheepcotes: evidence for medieval sheepfarming', *Medieval Archaeology* 39, 136–164.

Dyer, C. 2002a. *Making a Living in the Middle Ages. The People of Britain 850–1520*, Yale University Press: New Haven and London.

Dyer, C. 2002b. 'Villages and non-villages in the medieval Cotswolds', *Transactions of the Bristol and Gloucestershire Archaeological Society* 120, 11–35.

Dyer, C. 2003a. *Making a Living in the Middle Ages: The People of Britain 850–1520*, Penguin Books: London.

Dyer, C. 2003b. 'The archaeology of medieval small towns', *Medieval Archaeology* 47, 85–114.

Dyer, C. 2007a. 'Landscape and society at Bibury, Gloucestershire to 1540', in J. Betty (ed.), *Archives and Local History in Bristol and Gloucestershire*, Bristol and Gloucestershire Archaeological Society: Bristol, 62–77.

Dyer, C. (ed.) 2007b. 'Perceptions of medieval landscape and settlement', *Medieval Settlement Research Group Annual Report* 22, 6–31.

Dyer, C. 2007c. 'The ineffectiveness of lordship in England, 1200–1400', *Past and Present* 195 (Supplement 2), 69–86.

Dyer, C. 2009. 'Excavations and documents: the case of Caldecote, Hertfordshire', *Medieval Settlement Research* 24, 1–5.

Dyer, C. and Jones, R. (eds) 2010. *Deserted Villages Revisited*, University of Hertfordshire Press: Hatfield.

Dyer, M. and Collings, A. 1999. 'Archaeological assessment and recording at Homefield Farm, Thurlestone', unpublished Exeter Archaeology Report No. 99.61, Exeter Archaeology: Exeter.

Dymond, D. 1968. 'The Suffolk landscape', in L. M. Munby (ed.), *East Anglian Studies*, Heffer: Cambridge, 17–47.

Dymond, D. 1985. *The Norfolk Landscape*, Hodder and Stoughton: London.

Dymond, D. 1998. 'A misplaced Domesday vill: Otringhithe and Bromehill', *Norfolk Archaeology* 43, 1, 161–168.

Dymond, D. and Martin, E. (eds) 1999. *An Historical Atlas of Suffolk* (3rd edn), Suffolk County Council: Ipswich.

Eddison, J. (ed.) 1995. *Romney Marsh: The Debatable Ground*, Oxford University Committee for Archaeology: Oxford.

Eddison, J. 2000. *Romney Marsh: Survival on a Frontier*, Tempus: Stroud.

Eddison, J. and Draper, G. 1997. 'A landscape of medieval reclamation: Walland Marsh, Kent', *Landscape History* 19, 75–88.

Eddison, J. and Green C. (eds) 1988. *Romney Marsh: Evolution, Occupation and Reclamation*, Oxford University Committee for Archaeology: Oxford.

Eddison, J., Gardiner, M. F. and Long. A. (eds) 1998. *Romney Marsh: Environmental Change and Human Occupation in a Coastal Lowland*, Oxford University Committee for Archaeology: Oxford.

Edelen, G. (ed.) 1994. *The Description of England, the Classic Contemporary Account of Tudor Social Life, by William Harrison*, Constable: London.

Edwards, B. 1995. 'Hampshire village survey', *Medieval Settlement Research Group Annual Report* 10, 11–12.

Edwards, J. E. and Hindle, B. 1991. 'The transportation system of medieval England and Wales', *Journal of Historical Geography* 17, 2, 123–134.

Edwards, J. E. and Hindle, B. 1993. 'Comment: inland water transportation in medieval England', *Journal of Historical Geography* 19, 1, 12–14.

Edwards, N. 1996. *The Archaeology of Early Christian Ireland*, Batsford: London.

Edwards, N. (ed.) 1997. *Landscape and Settlement in Medieval Wales*, Oxbow Books: Oxford.

Edwards, N. and Lane, A. (eds) 1988. *Early Medieval Settlements in Wales AD 400–1100*, University College: Bangor.

Edwards, N. and Lane, A. (eds) 1992. *The Early Church in Wales and the West*, Oxbow Books: Oxbow.

Ellis, P. 2000. *Ludgershall Castle, Wiltshire: A Report on the Excavations by Peter Addyman, 1964–1972*, Wiltshire Archaeological and Natural History Society: Devizes.

Elstobb, W. 1793. *An Historical Account of the Great Level of the Fens Called Bedford Level*, Whittingham: London.

Emery, A. 1996–2006. *Greater Medieval Houses of England and Wales. 3 Volumes*, Cambridge University Press: Cambridge.

Emery, A. 2007. 'Dartington Hall: a mirror of the nobility in late medieval Devon', *Archaeological Journal* 164, 227–248.

English, B. and Miller, K. 1991. 'The deserted village of Eske, East Yorkshire', *Landscape History* 13, 5–32.

English, J. 1997. 'A possible early Wealden settlement type', *Medieval Settlement Research Group Annual Report* 12, 5–6.

English Heritage 2007. *Understanding the Archaeology of Landscape: A Guide to Good Recording Practice*, English Heritage: London.

ESF-COST 2010. 'Landscape in a changing world: bridging divides, integrating disciplines, serving society', *Science Policy Briefing*, 41.

Evans, D.H. and Jarrett, M.G. 1987. 'The deserted village of West Whelpington, Northumberland: third report, part one', *Archaeologia Aeliana* 5th Series, 15, 199–308.

Evans, D.H., Jarrett, M.G. and Wrathmell, S. 1988. 'The deserted village of West Whelpington, Northumberland: third report, part two', *Archaeologia Aeliana* 5th Series, 16, 139–192.

Evans, E.E. 1945. 'Field archaeology in the Ballycastle District' *Ulster Journal of Archaeology* 3rd Series, 8: 14–32.

Evans, N. 2003. 'The Llanerchaeron Estate', National Trust interim report.

Everitt, A. 1977. 'River and wold: reflections on the origin of regions and pays', *Journal of Historical Geography* 3, 1–19.

Everitt, A. 1986. *Continuity and Colonization: The Evolution of Kentish Settlement*, Leicester University Press: Leicester.

Everson, P. 1986. 'Occupation du sol au moyen âge et à l'époque moderne dans le nord du Lincolnshire', in A. Ferdière and E. Zadora-Rio (eds), *La prospection archéologique: paysage et peuplement*, Documents d'Archéologie Française 3, 29–37.

Everson, P. 1988. 'What's in a name? "Goltho", Goltho and Bullington', *Lincolnshire History and Archaeology* 23, 93–99.

Everson, P. 1990. 'The problem of Goltho', *Medieval Settlement Research Group Annual Report* 5, 9–14.

Everson, P. 1995. 'The earthworks at Shenley Brook End', in Ivens, Busby and Shepherd, 79–84.

Everson, P. 2000. 'Dispersed settlement in England in the National Mapping Programme', *Ruralia* 3, Památky Archeologické – Supplementum 14, ed. J. Klápště, Prague, 233–239.

Everson, P. and Brown, G. 2010. 'Dr Hoskins I presume! Field visits in the footsteps of a pioneer', in Dyer and Jones (eds), 46–63.

Everson, P. and Stocker, D. 1999. *Corpus of Anglo-Saxon Stone Sculpture in England, Volume 5: Lincolnshire*, Oxford University Press: Oxford.

Everson, P. and Stocker, D. 2006. 'The Common Steeple? Church, liturgy, and settlement in early medieval Lincolnshire', *Anglo-Norman Studies* 28, 103–123.

Everson, P. and Wilson-North, W. R. 1993. 'Fieldwork and finds at Egerton, Wheathill', *Shropshire Archaeology and History* 68, 65–71.

Everson, P., Richards, J., Richardson, J., Stocker, D. and Wrathmell, S. (forthcoming) 'Wharram and its neighbours in the Middle Saxon Period: a debate and some conclusions', in Wrathmell (ed.)

Everson, P., Taylor, C. C. and Dunn, C. 1991. *Change and Continuity: Rural Settlement in North-West Lincolnshire*, HMSO: London.

Ewan, E. 1990. *Townlife in Fourteenth-Century Scotland*, Edinburgh University Press: Edinburgh.

Fairbrother, J. 1990. *Faccombe Netherton: Excavations of a Late Saxon and Medieval Manorial Complex*, British Museum: London.

Fairclough, G. (ed.) 1999. *Historic Landscape Characterisation, 'The State of the Art'*, English Heritage: London.

Fairclough, G. 2006. 'Our place in the landscape? An archaeologist's ideology of landscape perception and management', in T. Meier (ed.), *Landscape Ideologies*, Archaeolingua Alapitvany: Budapest, 177–197.

Fairhurst, H. 1960. 'Scottish clachans', *Scottish Geographical Magazine* 76, 67–76.

Fairhurst, H. 1968. 'Rosal: a deserted township in Strath Naver, Sutherland', *Proceedings of the Society of Antiquaries of Scotland* 100, 135–169.

Fairhurst, H. 1969. 'The deserted settlement at Lix, West Perthshire', *Proceedings of the Society of Antiquaries of Scotland* 101, 160–199.

Faith, R. 1997. *The English Peasantry and the Growth of Lordship*, Leicester University Press: London.

Faith, R. 2004. 'Cola's *tun*: rural social structure in late Anglo-Saxon Devon', in R. Evans (ed.), *Lordship and Learning. Studies in Memory of Trevor Aston*, Boydell: Woodbridge, 63–78.

Faith, R. forthcoming. 'Some Devon farms before the Norman Conquest', in Turner and Silvester (eds).

Fasham, P. J. 1987. 'The medieval settlement at Popham, excavation 1975 and 1983', *Proceedings of the Hampshire Field Club and Archaeological Society* 43, 83–124.

Fasham, P. J. and Keevill, G. (with Coe, D.) 1995. *Brighton Hill South (Hatch Warren): An Iron Age Farmstead and Deserted Medieval Village in Hampshire*, Trust for Wessex Archaeology Report 7, Salisbury.

Fasham, P. J. and Whinney, R. J. B. 1991. 'The Abbots Worthy Anglo-Saxon settlement, Itchen Valley parish', in P. Fasham and R. J. B. Whinney, *Archaeology and the M3*, Hampshire Field Club and Archaeological Society Monograph 7. Winchester.

Fasham, P. J., Farwell, D. E. and Whinney, R. J. B. 1989. *The Archaeological Site at Easton Lane, Winchester*, Hampshire Field Club and Archaeological Society Monograph 6. Winchester.

Faull, M. and Moorhouse, S. (eds), *West Yorkshire: An Archaeological Survey to AD 1500*, West Yorkshire Metropolitan County Council: Wakefield.

Fedden, R. 1968. *The Continuing Purpose: A History of the National Trust, its Aims and Work*, Longman: London.

Fenwick, C. 2001. *The Poll Taxes of 1377, 1379 and 1381*, pt 2 *Lincolnshire – Westmorland*, British Academy Records of Social and Economic History, n.s., 29. Oxford University Press: Oxford.

Finberg, H. P. R. 1949. 'The open field in Devonshire', *Antiquity* 23, 180–187.

Finberg, H. P. R. 1951. *Tavistock Abbey. A Study in the Social and Economic History of Devon*, Cambridge University Press: Cambridge.

Finberg, H. P. R. 1953. *The Early Charters of Devon and Cornwall*, University College of Leicester: Leicester.

Finberg, H. P. R. 1957. *Roman and Saxon Withington: A Study in Continuity*, Leicester Department of English Local History, Occasional Papers, 1st Series 8. Leicester.

FitzPatrick, E. 2004. *Royal Inauguration in Gaelic Ireland c. 1100–1600: A Cultural Landscape Study*, Studies in Celtic History, number 22. Boydell Press: Woodbridge & Rochester, N.Y.

FitzPatrick, E. 2009. 'Native enclosed settlement and the problem of the Irish "ring-fort"', *Medieval Archaeology* 53, 271–307.

Fitzsimmons, F. 2001. 'Fosterage and gossiprid in late Medieval Ireland: some new evidence,' in Duffy *et al.* (eds), 138–152.

Flatrès, P. 1949. 'La structure agraire ancienne du Devon et du Cornwall et les enclôtures des XIIIe et XIVe siècles', *Annales de Bretagne* 56, 126–134.

Fleming, A. and Barker, L. 2008. 'Monks and local communities: the late-medieval landscape of Troed y Rhiw, Caron Uwch Clawdd, Ceredigion', *Medieval Archaeology* 52, 261–290.

Fleming, A. and Ralph, N. 1982. 'Medieval settlement and land use on Holne Moor, Dartmoor: the landscape evidence', *Medieval Archaeology* 26, 101–137.

Foard, G. 1978. 'Systematic fieldwalking and the investigation of Saxon settlement in Northamptonshire', *World Archaeology* 9, 357–374.

Foard, G., Hall, D. and Partida, T. 2009. *Rockingham Forest: An Atlas of the Medieval and Early-Modern Landscape*, Northamptonshire Record Society, 44. Northampton.

Ford, W. 1976. 'Some settlement patterns in the central region of the Warwickshire Avon', in Sawyer (ed.), 274–294.

Foster, C. W. and Longley, T. 1924. *The Lincolnshire Domesday and the Lindsey Survey*, Lincolnshire Record Society 19. Lincoln.

Foster, I., Mighall, T., Wotton, C., Owens, P. and Walling, D. 2000. 'Evidence for mediaeval soil erosion in the South Hams region of Devon, UK', *The Holocene* 10, 2, 261–271.

Foster, S. 2004. *Picts, Gaels and Scots: Early Historic Scotland* (2nd edn), Batsford: London.

Fowler, G. 1931–32. 'Fenland waterways, past and present. South Level District. Part 1', *Proceedings of the Cambridge Antiquarian Society* 33, 108–128.

Fowler, G. 1932–33. 'Fenland waterways, past and present. South Level District. Part II', *Proceedings of the Cambridge Antiquarian Society* 34, 17–33.

Fowler, G. 1934. 'The extinct waterways of the Fens', *Geographical Journal* 83, 30–36.

Fowler, P. J. 2002. *Farming in the First Millennium: British Farming between Julius Caesar and William the Conqueror*, Cambridge University Press: Cambridge.

Fowler, P. J. 2006. *Land Plotted and Pieced: Landscape History and Local Archaeology in Fyfield and Overton, West Wiltshire*, Society of Antiquaries of London Research Report 64. London.

Fowler, P. J. and Blackwell, I. 1998. *The Land of Lettice Sweetapple. An English Countryside Explored*, Tempus: Stroud.

Fowler, P. J. and Thomas, C. 1962. 'Arable fields of the pre-Norman period at Gwithian', *Cornish Archaeology* 1, 61–84.

Fox, A. 1937. 'Dinas Noddfa, Gelligaer Common, Glamorgan: Excavations in 1936', *Archaeologia Cambrensis* 92, 247–268.

Fox, A. 1939. 'Early Welsh homesteads on Gelligaer Common, Glamorgan: excavations in 1938', *Archaeologia Cambrensis* 94, 163–199.

Fox, A. 1953. 'A monastic homestead on Dean Moor, S. Devon', *Medieval Archaeology* 2, 141–157.

Fox, C. 1932. *The Personality of Britain: Its Influence on Inhabitant and Invader in Prehistoric and Early Historic Times*, National Museum of Wales: Cardiff.

Fox, C. 1939. 'A settlement of platform houses at Dyrysgol, St Harmon, Radnorshire', *Archaeologia Cambrensis* 94, 220–223.

Fox, C. and Lord Raglan. 1951–54. *Monmouthshire Houses. A Study of Building Techniques and Smaller House-plans in the Fifteenth to Seventeenth Centuries*, 3 vols., National Museum of Wales: Cardiff.

Fox, H. S. A. 1972. 'Field systems of east and south Devon. Part 1: east Devon', *Transactions of the Devonshire Association* 104, 81–135.

Fox, H. S. A. 1973. 'Outfield cultivation in Devon and Cornwall: a reinterpretation', in M. Havinden (ed.), *Husbandry and Marketing in the South West, 1500–1800*, Exeter Papers in Economic History 8. Exeter, 19–38.

Fox, H. S. A. 1975. 'The chronology of enclosure and economic development in medieval Devon', *Economic History Review* (n.s.) 28, 2, 181–202.

Fox, H. S. A. 1983a. 'Contraction: desertion and dwindling of dispersed settlement in a Devon parish', *Medieval Village Research Group Annual Report* 31, 40–42.

Fox, H. S. A. (ed.) 1983b. 'Dispersed settlement', *Medieval Village Research Group Annual Report* 31, 39–45.

Fox, H. S. A. 1989a. 'Peasant farmers, patterns of settlement and *pays*: transformations in the landscapes of Devon and Cornwall during the later middle ages', in Higham (ed.), 41–73.

Fox, H. S. A. 1989b. 'The people of the wolds in English settlement history', in Aston, Austin and Dyer (eds), 77–101.

Fox, H. S. A. 1991a. 'The occupation of the land. J. Devon and Cornwall', in Miller (ed.), 152–174.

Fox, H. S. A. 1991b. 'Farming practice and techniques. J. Devon and Cornwall', in Miller (ed.), 303–323.

Fox, H. S. A. 1991c. 'Tenant farming and farmers. J. Devon and Cornwall', in Miller (ed.), 722–743.

Fox, H. S. A. 1994. 'Medieval Dartmoor as seen through its account rolls', *Devon Archaeological Society Proceedings* 52, 141–179.

Fox, H. S. A. (ed.) 1996. *Seasonal Settlement*, University of Leicester Department of English Local History: Leicester.

Fox, H. S. A. 1999. 'Medieval urban development', in Kain and Ravenhill (eds), 424–431.

Fox, H. S. A. 2000. 'The wolds before *c.* 1500', in Thirsk (ed.), 50–61.

Fox, H. S. A. 2001. *The Evolution of the Fishing Village: Landscape and Society along the South Devon Coast, 1086–1550*, Leopard's Head Press: Oxford.

Fox, H. S. A. 2003. 'Taxation and settlement in medieval Devon', in M. Prestwich, R. Britnell and R. Frame (eds),

Thirteenth Century England X. *Proceedings of the Durham Conference 2003*, Boydell: Woodbridge, 167–185.

Fox, H. S. A. 2006. 'Fragmented manors and the customs of the Anglo-Saxons', in S. Keynes and A. Smith (eds), *Anglo-Saxons: Studies Presented to Cyril Roy Hart*, Four Courts Press: Dublin, 78–97.

Fox, H. S. A. forthcoming. *Alluring Uplands: Transhumance and Pastoral Management on Dartmoor, 950–1550*, University of Exeter Press: Exeter.

Fox, H. S. A. and Padel, O. 1998. *Cornish Lands of the Arundells of Lanherne, Fourteenth to Sixteenth Centuries*, Devon and Cornwall Record Society (n.s.) 41. D&CRS: Exeter.

Fradley, M. 2005. 'Warrenhall and other moated sites in north-east Shropshire', *Medieval Settlement Research Group Annual Report* 20, 17–18.

Francovich, R. 2008. 'The beginnings of hilltop villages in Early Medieval Tuscany', in J. R. David and M. McCormick (eds), *The Long Morning of Medieval Europe. New Directions in Early Medieval Studies*, Ashgate: Aldershot, 55–82.

Frazer, W. 2009. 'A medieval farmstead at Killegland, Ashbourne, Co. Meath', in Corlett and Potterton (eds), 109–124.

Friel, I. 1995. *The Good Ship*, British Museum Press: London.

Fyfe, R. 2006. 'Palaeoenvironmental perspectives on medieval landscape development', in Turner (ed.), 10–23.

Fyfe, R., Brown, A. and Rippon, S. 2003. 'Mid- to late-Holocene vegetation history of Greater Exmoor, UK: estimating the spatial extent of human-induced vegetation change,' *Vegetation History and Archaeobotany* 12, 215–232.

Fyfe, R., Brown, A. and Rippon, S. 2004. 'Characterising the late prehistoric, "Romano-British" and medieval landscape, and dating the emergence of a regionally distinct agricultural system in South West Britain', *Journal of Archaeological Science* 31, 1699–1714.

Gaddis, J. L. 2004. *The Landscape of History*, Oxford University Press: Oxford.

Gage, J. 1838. *History and Antiquities of Thingoe*, London.

Galloway, J. A. 2009. 'Storm flooding, coastal defence and land use around the Thames estuary and tidal river *c*. 1250–1450', *Journal of Medieval History* 35, 171–188.

Galloway, J. A. and Potts, J.S. 2007. 'Marine flooding in the Thames estuary and tidal river *c*. 1250–1450: impact and response', *Area* 39, 370–379.

Gardiner, M. F. 1994. 'Old Romney: the examination for the evidence for a lost Anglo-Saxon port', *Archaeologia Cantiana* 114, 329–345.

Gardiner, M. F. 1995. *Medieval Settlement and Society in the Eastern Sussex Weald before 1420*, unpublished PhD thesis, University of London.

Gardiner, M. F. 1996. 'The geography and peasant rural economy of the eastern Sussex High Weald, 1300–1420', *Sussex Archaeological Collections* 134, 123–139.

Gardiner, M. F. 1997a. 'Trade, rural industry and the origins of villages: some evidence from south-east England', in G. de Boe and F. Verhaeghe (eds), *Rural Settlements in Medieval Europe, Papers of the Medieval Europe Brugge 1997: Conference 6*, Instituut voor het Archeologisch Patrimonium: Zellik, 63–73.

Gardiner, M. F. 1997b. 'The colonisation of the Weald of south-east England', *Medieval Settlement Research Group Annual Report* 12, 6–8.

Gardiner, M. F. 1998. 'Settlement change on Walland Marsh, 1400–1550', in Eddison *et al.* (eds), 129–145.

Gardiner, M. F. 2000a. 'Shipping and trade between England and the Continent during the eleventh century', *Anglo-Norman Studies* 22, 71–93.

Gardiner, M. F. 2000b. 'Vernacular buildings and the development of the later medieval domestic plan in England' *Medieval Archaeology* 44, 159–179.

Gardiner, M. F. 2004. 'Timber buildings without earth-fast footings in Viking-age Britain', in Hines *et al.* (eds), 345–358.

Gardiner, M. F. 2006a. 'Review of medieval settlement research, 1996–2006', *Medieval Settlement Research Group Annual Report* 21, 22–28.

Gardiner, M. F. 2006b. 'The transformation of marshlands in Anglo-Norman England', *Anglo-Norman Studies* 29, 35–50.

Gardiner, M. F. 2006c. 'Implements and utensils in *Gerefa* and the organization of seigneurial farmsteads in the high Middle Ages', *Medieval Archaeology* 50, 260–267.

Gardiner, M. F. 2007a. 'Hythes, small ports and other landing places in later medieval England', in Blair (ed.), 85–109.

Gardiner, M. F. 2007b. 'The origins and persistence of manor houses in England', in Gardiner and Rippon (eds), 170–182.

Gardiner, M. F. 2010a. 'Excavations of a late medieval or early modern house at Gortin, Ardclinis, Co. Antrim', Belfast: Data Structure Report, Queen's University Belfast.

Gardiner, M. F. 2010b. 'A preliminary list of booley huts in the Mourne Mountains, County Down', *Ulster Journal of Archaeology* (3rd Series) 67, 142–152.

Gardiner, M. F. 2011. 'Late Saxon settlements', in

H. Hamerow, S. Crawford and D. Hinton (eds), *A Handbook of Anglo-Saxon Archaeology*, Oxford University Press: Oxford, 198–217.

Gardiner, M. F. and Rippon, S. (eds) 2007. *Medieval Landscapes*, Landscape History after Hoskins 2. Windgather Press: Oxford.

Gardiner, M. F., Jones, G. and Martin, D. 1991. 'The excavation of a medieval aisled hall at Park Farm, Salehurst, East Sussex', *Sussex Archaeological Collections* 129, 81–97.

Gardiner, M. F, Cross, R., Macpherson-Grant, N. and Riddler, I. 2001. 'Continental trade and non-urban ports in Mid-Anglo-Saxon England: Excavations at *Sandtun*, West Hythe, Kent', *Archaeological Journal* 158, 161–290.

Garrow, D., Lucy, S. and Gibson, D. 2006. *Excavations at Kilverstone, Norfolk, 2000–02*, East Anglian Archaeology 113. Cambridge.

Gates, L. A. 1996. 'Widows, property, and remarriage: lessons from Glastonbury's Deverill manors', *Albion* 28, 19–35.

Gauthiez, B. 1998. 'The planning of the town of Bury St Edmunds: a probable Norman origin', in Gransden (ed.), 69–97.

Gawne, E. 1970. 'Field patterns in Widecombe parish and the forest of Dartmoor', *Transactions of the Devonshire Association* 102, 49–69.

Gaydon, A. and Rowley, R. T. 1964. 'Deserted villages in Shropshire', *Deserted Medieval Village Research Group Annual Report* 12, Appendix E.

Geary, B., West, S. and Charman, D. 1997. 'The landscape context of medieval settlement on the South-Western moors of England. Recent palaeoenvironmental evidence from Bodmin Moor and Dartmoor', *Medieval Archaeology* 41, 195–209.

Gelling, M. 1974. 'Some notes on Warwickshire place-names', *Transactions of the Birmingham and Warwickshire Archaeological Society* 86, 59–79.

Gelling, M. 1978. *Signposts to the Past. Place-names and the History of England*, Dent: London.

Gelling, M. 1984. *Place-Names in the Landscape*, Dent: London.

Gelling, M. 1990–2006. *The Place-Names of Shropshire*, 5 vols, English Place-Name Society: London.

Gelling, M. 1992. *The West Midlands in the Early Middle Ages*, Leicester University Press: Leicester.

Gelling, M. and Cole, A. 2000. *The Landscape of Place-names*, Shaun Tyas: Stamford.

Gent, T. 2007. 'The re-excavation of a deserted medieval longhouse at Hutholes, Widecombe in the Moor, Dartmoor', *Devon Archaeological Society Proceedings* 65, 47–82.

Gerrard, C. 1997. 'Misplaced faith? Medieval pottery and fieldwalking', *Medieval Ceramics* 21, 61–72.

Gerrard, C. 2003. *Medieval Archaeology: Understanding Traditions and Contemporary Approaches*, Routledge: London.

Gerrard, C. 2009. 'The study of the deserted medieval village: Caldecote in context', in Beresford, 2009, 1–19.

Gerrard, C. and Aston, M. 2007. *Shapwick Project Somerset: A Rural Landscape Explored*, Society for Medieval Archaeology Monograph 25. Maney: Leeds

Gerrard, C. and Rippon, S. 2007. 'Artefacts, sites and landscapes: archaeology and medieval studies', in A. Deyermond (ed.), *A Century of British Medieval Studies*, Oxford University Press for the British Academy: Oxford, 526–555.

Gerrard, S. 1994. 'The Dartmoor tin industry: an archaeological perspective', *Devon Archaeological Society Proceedings* 52, 173–198.

Gerrard, S. 1997. *Dartmoor*, English Heritage: London.

Gilchrist, R. 2008. 'Magic for the Dead? The archaeology of magic in later medieval burials', *Medieval Archaeology* 52, 119–160.

Gilchrist, R. and Reynolds, A. (eds) 2009. *Reflections: 50 Years of Medieval Archaeology, 1957–2007*, Society for Medieval Archaeology Monograph 30. Maney: Leeds.

Gilchrist, R. and Sloane, B. 2005. *Requiem. The Medieval Monastic Cemetery in Britain*, London: Museum of London Archaeology Service.

Giles, K. 2005. 'Public space in town and village', in Giles and Dyer (eds), 293–311.

Giles, K. and C. Dyer (eds) 2005. *Town and Country in the Middle Ages: Contrasts, Contacts and Interconnections 1100–1500*, Society for Medieval Archaeology Monograph 22. Maney: Leeds.

Gillard, M. 2002. *The Medieval Landscape of the Exmoor Region: Enclosure and Settlement in an Upland Fringe*, unpublished PhD thesis, University of Exeter.

Glass, H. J. 1999. 'Archaeology of the Channel Tunnel Rail Link', *Archaeologia Cantiana* 119, 189–220.

Glasscock, R. E. 1976. 'England circa 1334', in H. C. Darby (ed.), *A New Historical Geography of England before 1600*, Cambridge University Press: Cambridge.

Glasscock, R. E. 2009. 'Maurice Warwick Beresford 1920–2005', *Proceedings of the British Academy* 161 (Biographical Memoirs of Fellows, VIII), 19–38.

Goddard, S. 2000. 'The importance of illustration in archaeology and the exemplary work of Robert Gurd', *Sussex Archaeological Collections* 138, 7–13.

Gonner, E. C. K. 1912. *Common Lands and Enclosure*, Macmillan: London.

Good, G. L., Jones R. H. and Ponsford, M. (eds) 1991.

Waterfront Archaeology Research Report 74, Council for British Archaeology: York.

Goodburn, D. 1991. 'New light on early ship and boatbuilding in the London area', in Good *et al.*, 105–115.

Gosden, C. 2004. *Archaeology and Colonialism: Cultural Contact from 5000 BC to the Present,* Cambridge University Press: Cambridge.

Gossip, J. and Jones, A. M. 2007. *Archaeological Investigations of a Later Prehistoric and a Romano-British Landscape at Tremough, Penryn, Cornwall*, British Archaeological Reports British Series 443. Oxford.

Gould, I. Chalkley 1905. *Homestead Moats of Essex*, unpublished manuscript Essex Record Office.

Govan, S. (ed.) 2003. *Medieval or Later Rural Settlement in Scotland: 10 Years On*, Historic Scotland: Edinburgh.

Gover, J. 1948. *The Place-Names of Cornwall*, unpublished typescript, Royal Institution of Cornwall Courtney Library.

Gover, J. E. B., Mawer, A. and Stenton, F. 1931–32. *The Place-Names of Devon*, English Place-Name Society, 8–9, English Place-Name Society: Nottingham.

Gover, J. E. B., Mawer, A. and Stenton, F. M. 1975. *The Place-Names of Northamptonshire*, English Place-Name Society, 10. London.

Graham, A. H. 1986. 'The Old Malthouse, Abbotsbury, Dorset: the medieval watermill of the Benedictine Abbey', *Proceedings of the Dorset Natural History and Archaeological Society* 108, 103–125.

Graham, A. H. and Davies, S. M. 1993. *Excavations in Trowbridge, Wiltshire, 1977 and 1986–1988. The Prehistoric, Saxon and Saxo-Norman Settlements and the Anarchy Period Castle*, Wessex Archaeology: Salisbury.

Graham, B. J. 1988. 'Timber and earthwork fortifications in western Ireland', *Medieval Archaeology* 32, 110–129.

Graham, D. and Graham, A. 2000. 'The moated site at South Park Farm, Grayswood', *Surrey Archaeological Collections* 87, 127–145.

Graham, D., Graham, A. and Taylor, D. 2005. 'Trial trenching on a probable moated site at Downside Farm, Cobham', *Surrey Archaeological Collections* 92, 217–229.

Graham, J. 1954. *Transhumance in Ireland*, unpublished PhD thesis, University Belfast, Department of Geography.

Graham-Campbell, J. and Batey, C. 1998. *Vikings in Scotland: An Archaeological Survey*, Edinburgh University Press: Edinburgh.

Graham-Campbell, J. A., Hall, R., Jesch, J. and Parsons, D. N. (eds) 2001. *Vikings and the Danelaw: Papers from the Proceedings of the Thirteenth Viking Congress,* *Nottingham and York, 21st–30th August 1997*, Oxbow Books: Oxford.

Gransden, A. (ed.) 1998. *Bury St Edmunds. Medieval Art, Architecture, Archaeology and Economy*, British Archaeological Association, Conference Transactions 20. London.

Gras, N. and Gras, E. 1930. *The Economic and Social History of an English Village (Crawley, Hampshire) AD 909–1928*, Harvard University Press: Cambridge, Mass.

Gray, H. L. 1915. *English Field Systems*, Harvard University Press: Cambridge, Mass.

Green, H. S. 1954. 'Medieval platform sites in the Neath uplands', *Transactions of the Cardiff Naturalists' Society* 83, 9–17.

Greenhill, B. and Morrison, J. 1995. *The Archaeology of Boats and Ships*, Conway Maritime Press: London.

Grenville, J. 1997. *Medieval Housing*, Leicester University Press: London.

Gresham, C. A. 1954. 'Platform houses in north-west Wales', *Archaeologia Cambrensis* 103, 18–53.

Gresham, C. A. 1963. 'The interpretation of settlement patterns in north-west Wales', in I. Ll. Foster and L. Alcock (eds), *Culture and Environment. Essays in Honour of Sir Cyril Fox*, Routledge and Kegan Paul: London, 263–279.

Gresham, C. A., Hemp, W. J. and Thompson, F. H. 1959. 'Hen Ddinbych', *Archaeologia Cambrensis* 108, 72–80.

Griffith, F. 1988. *Devon's Past: An Aerial View*, Devon Books: Exeter.

Griffiths, D. 2004. 'Settlement and acculturation in the Irish Sea Region', in Hines *et al.* (eds), 125–138.

Griffiths, D. Philpott, R. A. and Egan, G. 2007. *Meols: The Archaeology of the North Wirral Coast*, Oxford School of Archaeology Monograph 68. Oxford.

Griffiths, N., Jenner, A. and Wilson, C. 1990. *Drawing Archaeological Finds – A Handbook*, Archetype: London.

Griffiths, W. E. 1954. 'Excavations on Penmaenmawr, 1950', *Archaeologia Cambrensis* 103, 66–84.

Groube, L. M. and Bowden, M. C. B. 1982. *The Archaeology of Rural Dorset: Past, Present and Future*, Dorset Natural History and Archaeological Society Monograph 4. Dorchester.

Grundy, G. B. 1926. 'The Saxon land charters of Hampshire with notes on place and field names', *Archaeological Journal* 33, 91–253.

Gulley, J. L. M. 1961. *The Wealden Landscape in the Early Seventeenth Century and its Antecedents*, unpublished PhD thesis, University of London.

Hadley, D. M. 2006. *The Vikings in England: Settlement,*

Society and Culture, Manchester University Press: Manchester.

Hadley, D. M. 2007. 'The garden gives up its secrets: the developing relationship between rural settlements and cemeteries, c. 750–1100', *Anglo-Saxon Studies in Archaeology and History* 14, 195–203.

Hadley, D. M. and Richards, J. D. (eds) 2000. *Cultures in Contact: Scandinavian Settlement in England in the Ninth and Tenth Centuries*, Brepols: Turnhout.

Hair, N., Newman, R., Howard-Davis, C. and Newman, C. 1999. 'Excavation of medieval settlement remains at Crosedale in Howgill', *Transactions of the Cumberland and Westmorland Antiquarian and Archaeological Society* 99, 139–158.

Hall, D. 1987. *The Fenland Project, Number 2: Fenland Landscapes and Settlement between Peterborough and March*, East Anglian Archaeology 35. Cambridge.

Hall, D. 1992. *The Fenland Project, Number 6: The South-Western Cambridgeshire Fenlands*, East Anglian Archaeology 56. Cambridge.

Hall, D. 1995. *The Open Fields of Northamptonshire*, Northamptonshire Record Society Publications 38. Northampton.

Hall, D. 1996. *The Fenland Project, Number 10: Cambridgeshire Survey, Isle of Ely and Wisbech*, East Anglian Archaeology 79. Cambridge.

Hall, D. 2001a. 'The woodland landscapes of southern Northamptonshire', *Northamptonshire Past and Present* 54, 33–46.

Hall, D. 2001b. *Turning the Plough. Midlands Open Fields: Landscape Character and Proposals for Management*, English Heritage/ Northamptonshire County Council: Northampton.

Hall, D. 2006. *Scottish Monastic Landscapes*, Tempus: Stroud.

Hall, D. and Martin, P. 1979. 'Brixworth, Northamptonshire: an intensive field survey', *Journal of the British Archaeological Association* 132, 1–6.

Hall, M. 2001. 'An ivory knife handle from the High Street, Perth, Scotland: consuming ritual in a medieval burgh', *Medieval Archaeology* 45, 169–188.

Hall, R. A. 2007. *Exploring the World of the Vikings*, Thames and Hudson: London.

Hall, T. 2007. 'Keeping the Faith: the physical expression of differing church customs in early medieval Britain', in Costen (ed.), 53–60.

Hall, V. A. and Bunting, L. 2001. 'Tephra-dated pollen studies of medieval landscapes in the north of Ireland', in Duffy *et al.* (eds), 207–223.

Hallam, H. (ed.) 1988. *The Agrarian History of England and Wales, Vol. 2*, Cambridge University Press: Cambridge.

Halliday, S. 2003. 'Rig-and-furrow in Scotland', in Govan (ed.), 69–81.

Hall-Torrance, M. and Weaver, S. D. G. 2003. 'The excavation of a Saxon settlement at Riverdene, Basingstoke, Hampshire', *Proceedings of the Hampshire Field Club and Archaeological Society* 58, 63–105.

Hamerow, H. 1991. 'Settlement mobility and the "middle Saxon shift": rural settlements and settlement patterns in Anglo-Saxon England', *Anglo-Saxon England* 20, 1–17.

Hamerow, H. 1993. *Excavations at Mucking. Volume 2: The Anglo-Saxon settlement*, English Heritage: London.

Hamerow, H. 2002. *Early Medieval Settlements: The Archaeology of Rural Communities in North-West Europe 400–900*, Oxford University Press: Oxford.

Hamerow, H. 2006. 'Special deposits in Anglo-Saxon settlements', *Medieval Archaeology* 50, 1–30.

Hamerow, H. 2010. 'The development of Anglo-Saxon rural settlement forms', *Landscape History* 31, 5–22.

Hamilton, J. R. C. 1956. *Excavations at Jarlshof, Shetland*, Ministry of Works Archaeological Reports 1, HMSO: Edinburgh.

Hansson, M. 2006. *Aristocratic Landscape: The Spatial Ideology of the Medieval Aristocracy*, Lund Studies in Historical Archaeology: Lund.

Hanworth, R. and Tomalin, R. J. 1977. *Brooklands, Weybridge: The Excavation of an Iron Age and Medieval Site, 1964–5 and 1970–1*, Surrey Archaeological Society: Guildford.

Harding, C., Marlow-Mann, E. and Wrathmell, S. (eds) 2010. [Wharram XII] *The Post-medieval Farm and Vicarage Sites. Wharram. A Study of Settlement on the Yorkshire Wolds, XII*, York University Archaeological Publications, 14. York.

Hardy, A., Charles, B. and Williams, R. J. 2007. *Death and Taxes: The Archaeology of a Middle Saxon Estate Centre at Higham Ferrers, Northamptonshire*, Oxford Archaeology Monograph No. 4. Oxford.

Hardy, J. and Healy, F. 2007. *A Neolithic and Bronze Age Landscape in Northamptonshire: The Raunds Area Project*, Oxbow Books: Oxford.

Hardy, M. and Martin, E. 1987. 'South Elmham All Saints and St Nicholas' and 'South Elmham St Margaret', *Proceedings of the Suffolk Institute of Archaeology and History* 36:3, 232–235.

Hardy, M. and Martin, E. 1988. 'South Elmham St Michael and St Peter', *Proceedings of the Suffolk Institute of Archaeology and History* 36:4, 315–317.

Hardy, M. and Martin, E. 1989. 'Flixton', *Proceedings of the Suffolk Institute of Archaeology and History* 37:1, 66–69.

Hare, J. 1994a. 'Agriculture and rural settlement in the

chalklands of Wiltshire and Hampshire', in Aston and Lewis (eds), 159–170.

Hare, J. 1994b. 'Northington, near Overton, and the deserted villages of Hampshire', *Hampshire Field Club and Archaeological Society Newsletter* 21, 26.

Hare, M. 1979. 'The Anglo-Saxon church and sundial at Hannington', *Proceedings of the Hampshire Field Club and Archaeological Society* 36, 193–202.

Harrison, B. 1990. 'New settlements in the North York Moors', in Vyner (ed.), 19–31.

Harrison, B. and Hutton, B. 1984. *Vernacular Houses in North Yorkshire and Cleveland*, John Donald: Edinburgh.

Hart, C. R. 1966. *The Early Charters of Eastern England*, Leicester University Press: Leicester.

Hart, S. 2000. *Flint Architecture of East Anglia*, Giles de la Mere: London.

Hartley, R. F. 1984. *The Mediaeval Earthworks of North West Leicestershire*, Leicester Museums: Leicester.

Hartley, R. F. 1987. *The Mediaeval Earthworks of North East Leicestershire*, Leicester Museums: Leicester.

Hartley, R. F. 1989. *The Mediaeval Earthworks of Central Leicestershire*, Leicester Museums: Leicester.

Hartley, R. F. 2008. *The Medieval Earthworks of South West Leicestershire*, Leicester Museums: Leicester.

Harvey, B. 1977. *Westminster Abbey and its Estates in the Middle Ages*, Oxford University Press: Oxford.

Harvey, M. 1982. 'Regular open-field systems on the Yorkshire Wolds', *Landscape History* 4, 29–39.

Harvey, P. D. A. 1989. 'Initiative and authority in settlement change', in Aston, Austin and Dyer (eds), 31–43.

Hatcher, J. 1988a. 'Farming techniques: F. South-Western England', in Hallam (ed.), 383–398.

Hatcher, J. 1988b. 'Social structure: F. South-Western England', in Hallam (ed.), 675–685.

Hauser, K. 2008. *Bloody Old Britain. O. G. S. Crawford and the Archaeology of Modern Life*, Granta Books: London.

Havis, R. and Brooks, H. 2004. *Excavations at Stansted Airport, 1986–91, Volume 2 Saxon, Medieval and Post-Medieval*, East Anglian Archaeology 107. Chelmsford.

Hayes, P. P. and Lane, T. W. 1992. *The Fenland Project, Number 5: Lincolnshire Survey, the South-West Fens*, East Anglian Archaeology 55. Sleaford.

Hayes, R. H. 1983. *Levisham Moor: archaeological investigations 1957–78*, North York Moors National Park: Helmsley.

Hayfield, C. 1984. 'Wawne, East Riding of Yorkshire: a case study in settlement morphology', *Landscape History* 6, 41–67.

Hayfield, C. 1987. [Wharram V] *An Archaeological Survey of the Parish of Wharram Percy, East Yorkshire. 1. The Evolution of the Roman Landscape*, British Archaeological Reports British Series 172. Oxford.

Hayfield, C. 1988. 'Cowlam deserted village: a case study of post-medieval desertion' *Post-medieval Archaeology*, 22, 21–109.

Healey, H. 1977. Moated sites in south Lincolnshire. *South Lincolnshire Archaeology* 1, 28–29.

Health and Safety Executive 2006. Essentials of Health and Safety at Work (4th edn), HSE Books: London.

Hedeager, L. 1992. *Iron Age Societies. From Tribe to State in Northern Europe, 500 BC to AD 700*, Blackwell: Oxford.

Hedges, J. 1978. 'Essex moats', in Aberg (ed.), 63–70.

Henderson, C. and Weddell, P. 1994. 'Medieval settlements on Dartmoor and in west Devon: the evidence from excavations', *Devon Archaeological Society Proceedings* 52, 119–140.

Herring, P. 1986. *An exercise in landscape history. Pre-Norman and medieval Brown Willy and Bodmin Moor, Cornwall*, unpublished MPhil thesis, 3 vols, University of Sheffield.

Herring, P. 1996. 'Transhumance in medieval Cornwall', in Fox (ed.), 35–44.

Herring, P. 1998. *Cornwall's Historic Landscape: Presenting a Method of Historic Landscape Character Assessment*, Cornwall Archaeological Unit: Truro.

Herring, P. 2006a. 'Medieval fields at Brown Willy, Bodmin Moor', in Turner (ed.), 78–103.

Herring, P. 2006b. 'Cornish strip fields', in Turner (ed.), 44–77.

Herring, P. and Berry, E. 1997. 'Stonaford', *Cornish Archaeology* 36, 151–175.

Herring, P. and Hooke, D. 1993. 'Interrogating Anglo-Saxons in St Dennis', *Cornish Archaeology* 32, 67–75.

Herring, P. forthcoming. 'Shadows of ghosts: early medieval transhumants in Cornwall', in Turner and Silvester (eds).

Hervey, F. (ed.) 1925. *The Pinchbeck Register*, Brighton.

Heslop, D. and Aberg, A. 1990. 'Excavations at Tollesby, Cleveland, 1972 and 1974', in Vyner (ed.), 77–106.

Hey, G. 2004. *Yarnton: Saxon and Medieval Settlement and Landscape. Results of Excavations 1990–96*, Oxford Archaeology Thames Valley Landscapes Monograph 20. Oxford.

Hickling, R. 1971–72. 'Deserted medieval villages', *Transactions of the Woolhope Naturalists' Field Club* 40, 172–176.

Higham, N. J. 1979. 'An aerial survey of the upper Lune valley', in N. J. Higham (ed.), *The Changing Past. Some Recent Work in the Archaeology of Northern England*, University of Manchester, Department of Extra-Mural Studies: Manchester, 31–38.

Higham, N. J. 1998–99. 'The Tatton Park project, part 2. The medieval estates, settlements and halls', *Journal of the Chester Archaeological Society* 75, 61–133.

Higham, N. J. 2004. *A Frontier Landscape: The North West in the Middle Ages*, Windgather Press: Oxford.

Higham, N. J. and Ryan, M. J. (eds) 2010. *The Landscape Archaeology of Anglo-Saxon England*, Boydell Press: Woodbridge.

Higham, R. A. (ed.) 1989. *Landscape and Townscape in the South West*, Exeter University Press: Exeter.

Higham, R. A. 2008. *Making Anglo-Saxon Devon*, The Mint Press: Exeter.

Higham, R. A. and Barker, P. 1992. *Timber Castles*, Batsford: London.

Higham, R. A. and Barker, P. 2000. *Hen Domen, Montgomery: A Timber Castle on the English-Welsh Border*, Exeter University Press: Exeter.

Hillaby, J. 1983. *The Journeys of Celia Fiennes*, MacDonald and Co.: London and Sydney.

Hilton, R. H. 1957. 'A study in the prehistory of English enclosure in the fifteenth century', in *Studi in Onore di Armando Sapori*, Milan, 673–685.

Hilton, R. H. 1966. *A Medieval Society. The West Midlands at the End of the Thirteenth Century*, Weidenfeld: London.

Hilton, R. H. 1980. 'Individualism and the English peasantry', *New Left Review* 120, 109–111.

Hilton, R. H. 1982. 'Towns in English feudal society', *Urban History Yearbook for 1982*, 7–13.

Hilton, R. H. and Rahtz, P. A. 1966: 'Upton, Gloucestershire, 1959–1964', *Transactions of the Bristol and Gloucestershire Archaeological Society* 85, 70–146.

Hindmarch, E. 2006. 'Archerfield Estate', *Discovery and Excavation in Scotland* (n.s.) 7, 59.

Hines, J. 2004. 'Sūþre-gē – the foundations of Surrey', in Cotton *et al.* (eds), 91–102.

Hines, J., Lane, A. and M. Redknap (eds) 2004. *Land, Sea and Home. Settlement in the Viking Period, Proceedings of a Conference on Viking-period Settlement at Cardiff, July 2001*, Society for Medieval Archaeology Monograph 20. Maney: Leeds

Hingley, R. (ed.) 1993. *Medieval and Later Rural Settlement in Scotland. Management and Preservation*, Historic Scotland Occasional Publication 1. Edinburgh.

Hinton, D. A. 1994. 'Some Anglo-Saxon charters and estates in south-east Dorset', *Proceedings of the Dorset Natural History and Archaeological Society* 116, 11–20.

Hinton, D. A. 1997. 'The "Scole-Dickleburgh system" examined', *Landscape History* 19, 5–12.

Hinton, D. A. 2002a. 'A "marginal economy"? The Isle of Purbeck from the Norman Conquest to the Black Death', in Hinton (ed.), 84–117.

Hinton, D. A. 2002b. 'Debate: south Hampshire, "East Wessex", and the *Atlas of Rural Settlement in England*', *Landscape History* 27, 71–76.

Hinton, D. A. (ed.) 2002c. *Purbeck Papers*, Department of Archaeology University of Southampton Monograph 4, Oxbow Books: Oxford.

Hinton, D. A. 2005. *Gold and Gilt, Pots and Pins: Possessions and People in Medieval Britain*. Oxford University Press: Oxford.

Hinton, D. A. 2010. 'Deserted medieval villages and the objects from them', in Dyer and Jones (eds), 85–108.

Hinton, D. A. and Trapp, H. 2002. 'The Worth Matravers strip fields in the eighteenth century', in Hinton (ed.), 139–144.

Hobbs, R., Honeycombe, C. and Watkins, S. 2002. Conservation for Metal Detectorists, Stroud: Tempus.

Hobhouse, H. 1987. 'Ninety years of the Survey of London', *Transactions of the Ancient Monuments Society*, 31, 25–47.

Hodgson, J. 1827. *A History of Northumberland, Part II, Vol. I*, Newcastle upon Tyne.

Hoek, C. 1981. 'Moated sites in the county of Holland', in Aberg and Brown (eds), 173–196.

Hogg, A. H. A. 1934. 'Earthworks in Joyden's Wood, Bexley, Kent', *Archaeologia Cantiana* 54, 10–27.

Holden, E. W. 1963. 'Excavations at the deserted medieval village of Hangleton. Part I', *Sussex Archaeological Collections* 101, 54–181.

Holden, E. W. 1980. 'Excavations at Old Erringham, Shoreham, West Sussex: Part II. The 'chapel' and ringwork', *Sussex Archaeological Collections* 118, 257–297.

Holden, E. W. and Hudson, T. P. 1981. 'Salt-making in the Adur valley, Sussex', *Sussex Archaeological Collections* 119, 117–148.

Holderness, B. A. 1984. 'East Anglia, The Home Counties and South-East England', in J. Thirsk (ed.), *The Agrarian History of England and Wales, Vol. 5, 1640–1750, I. Regional Farming Systems*: Cambridge University Press: Cambridge, 197–338.

Holdsworth, P. 1987. *Excavations in the Medieval Burgh of Perth, 1979–81*, Society of Antiquaries of Scotland Monograph Series 5. Edinburgh.

Hollobone, T. 2002. 'Six medieval moated sites near Arlington, East Sussex', *Medieval Settlement Research Group Annual Report* 17, 31–38.

Hollowell, S. 2000. *Enclosure Records for Historians*, Phillimore: Chichester.

Holt, R. and Rosser, G. 1990. *The Medieval Town 1200–1540*, Longman: London.

Homans, G. 1941. *English Villagers of the 13th Century*, Harvard University Press: Cambridge, Mass.

Hooke, D. (ed.) 1985a. *Medieval Villages: A Review of Current Work*, Oxford University Committee for Archaeology Monograph 5. Oxford.

Hooke, D. 1985b. *The Anglo-Saxon Landscape. The Kingdom of the Hwicce*, Manchester University Press: Manchester.

Hooke, D. 1985c. 'Village development in the west midlands', in D. Hooke (ed.), 125–154.

Hooke, D. 1987. 'Anglo-Saxon estates in the Vale of the White Horse', *Oxoniensia* 52, 129–143.

Hooke, D. 1990. *Worcestershire Anglo-Saxon Charter-Bounds*, Boydell Press: Woodbridge.

Hooke, D. 1994a. *Pre-Conquest Charter-Bounds of Devon and Cornwall*, Boydell Press: Woodbridge.

Hooke, D. 1994b. 'The administrative and settlement framework of early medieval Wessex', in Aston and Lewis (eds), 83–95.

Hooke, D. 1998. *The Landscape of Anglo-Saxon England*, Leicester University Press: London.

Hooke, D. 1999. 'Saxon conquest and settlement', in Kain and Ravenhill (eds), 95–104.

Hooke, D. (ed.) 2000. *Landscape. The Richest Historical Record*, Society for Landscape Studies, Supplementary Series 1. Birmingham.

Hooke, D. 2006. *The West Midlands*, English Heritage: London.

Hooke, D. 2007. 'Uses of waterways in Anglo-Saxon England', in Blair (ed.), 37–54.

Hooke, D. 2010. *Trees in Anglo-Saxon England, Literature, Lore and Landscape*, Boydell Press: Woodbridge.

Hooke, D. and Burnell, S. (eds) 1995. *Landscape and Settlement in Britain AD 400–1066*, University of Exeter Press: Exeter.

Hopkins, R. Thurston 1935. *Moated Houses of England*, Country Life: London.

Horning, A. 2002. 'A re-evaluation of the archaeology of transhumance in the north of Ireland', Paper presented at the second annual conference of the Irish Post-Medieval Archaeology Group, Trinity College, Dublin.

Horning, A. 2004. 'Archaeological explorations of cultural identity and rural economy in the North of Ireland: Goodland, Co. Antrim', *International Journal of Historical Archaeology* 8:3, 199–215.

Horning, A. and Brannon, N. 2004. 'Rediscovering Goodland: Neolithic settlement, booley site, or lost Scottish village?', *Archaeology Ireland* 18:3, 28–31.

Horning, A. and Brannon, N. 2007. 'Summary report on excavations at Goodland, Co. Antrim, April 2007', report submitted to the Environment and Heritage Service, Belfast.

Horning, A. and Palmer, M. (eds), *Crossing Paths or Sharing Tracks? Future Directions in the Archaeological Study of post-1550 Britain and Ireland*, Boydell Press: Woodbridge.

Horsey, I. 1973. *The Moated Homesteads of Essex*, unpublished BA thesis, University of Nottingham.

Horstman, C. (ed.) 1887. '*Mappula Angliae*', *Englische Studien* 10, 1–34.

Hoskins, W. G. 1950. *Essays in Leicestershire History*, Liverpool University Press: Liverpool.

Hoskins, W. G. 1954. *Devon*, Collins: London.

Hoskins, W. G. 1956. 'Seven deserted village sites in Leicestershire', *Transactions of the Leicestershire Archaeological and Historical Society* 32, 36–51.

Hoskins, W. G. and Stamp, L. D. 1963. *The Common Lands of England and Wales*, Collins: London.

Howe, G. M. and Thomas, P. 1968. *Welsh Landforms and Scenery*, Macmillan: London.

Howell, C. 1983. *Land, Family and Inheritance in Transition: Kibworth Harcourt 1280–1700,* Cambridge University Press: Cambridge.

Howell, R. 2004. 'The decayed medieval town of Trelech', *Medieval Settlement Research Group Annual Report* 19, 22–23.

Howell, R. 2006. 'Excavation in Trelech 2005–6', *Medieval Settlement Research Group Annual Report* 21, 49–52.

Hughes, H. H. and North, H. L. 1908. *The Old Cottages of Snowdonia*, Jarvis and Foster: Bangor.

Hughes, M. J. 1984. 'Rural settlement and landscape in late Saxon Hampshire', in M. L. Faull (ed.), *Studies in Late Anglo-Saxon Settlement*, Oxford University Department for External Studies: Oxford, 65–79.

Hughes, M. J. 1989. 'Hampshire castles and the landscape: 1066–1216', *Landscape History* 11, 27–60.

Hughes, M. J. 1994. 'Towns and villages in medieval Hampshire', in Aston and Lewis (eds), 195–212.

Hunter, J. 1999. *The Essex Landscape. A Study of its Form and History*, Essex Record Office: Chelmsford.

Hunter, J. 2003. *Field Systems in Essex*, Essex Society of Archaeology and History Occasional Papers, (n.s.) 1. Colchester.

Hurst, D. G. and Hurst J. G. 1969. 'Excavations at the medieval village of Wythemail, Northamptonshire', *Medieval Archaeology* 13, 167–203.

Hurst, J. G. 1956a. 'Deserted medieval villages and the excavations at Wharram Percy, Yorkshire', in R. L. S. Bruce-Mitford (ed.), *Recent Archaeological Excavations in Britain*, Routledge: London, 251–273.

Hurst, J. G. 1956b. 'Saxo-Norman pottery in East Anglia. Part I. General discussion and St Neots Ware', *Proceedings of the Cambridge Antiquarian Society* 49, 43–70.

Hurst, J. G. 1965. 'The medieval peasant house', in A.

Small (ed.), *Fourth Viking Congress 1961*, Aberdeen, 190–196.

Hurst, J. G. 1971. 'A review of archaeological research (to 1968)', in M.W. Beresford and J.G. Hurst (eds), *Deserted Medieval Villages*, Lutterworth Press: London, 76–144.

Hurst, J. G. 1979. [Wharram I] *Wharram Percy: Domestic Settlement I: Areas 10 and 6*, Society for Medieval Archaeology Monograph 8. London.

Hurst, J. G. 1986. 'The work of the Medieval Village Research Group 1952–1986', *Medieval Settlement Research Group Annual Report* 1, 8–13.

Hurst, J. G. and Hurst, D. G. 1964. 'Excavations at the deserted medieval village of Hangleton, Part II', *Sussex Archaeological Collections* 102, 94–142.

Hurst, J. G. and Hurst, D. G. 1967. 'Excavation of two moated sites at Milton, Hampshire and Ashwell, Hertfordshire', *Journal of the British Archaeological Association* (3rd Series) 30, 48–86.

Hurst, J. G. and West, S. E. 1957. 'Saxo-Norman Pottery in East Anglia. Part II. Thetford Ware with an account of Middle Saxon Ipswich Ware', *Proceedings of the Cambridge Antiquarian Society* 50, 29–60.

Hutcheson, A. and Andrews, P. 2009. 'A late Bronze Age, Anglo-Saxon and medieval settlement site at Manston Road, Ramsgate', in P. Andrews, K. Egging Dinwiddy, C. Ellis, A. Hutcheson, X. Phillpotts, A. B. Powell and J. Schuster, *Kentish Sites and Sites of Kent: A Miscellany of Four Archaeological Excavations*, Wessex Archaeology: Salisbury, 199–248.

Ingle, C. and Saunders, H. 2011. *Aerial Archaeology in Essex: The Role of the National Mapping Programme in Interpreting the Landscape*, East Anglian Archaeology 136. Essex County Council: Chelmsford.

Ivens, R. J., Busby, P. and Shepherd, N. J. 1995. *Tattenhoe and Westbury: Two Deserted Medieval Settlements in Milton Keynes*, Buckinghamshire Archaeological Society Monograph Series 8. Buckingham.

James, H., Swan, D. and Francoz, C. 2007. 'Laigh Newton', *Discovery and Excavation in Scotland* (n.s.) 8, 67.

James, T. B. and Gerrard, C. 2007. *Clarendon: Landscape of Kings*, Windgather: Oxford.

Jarrett, M. G. and Wrathmell, S. 1977. 'Sixteenth- and seventeenth-century farmsteads: West Whelpington, Northumberland', *Agricultural History Review* 25, 108–119.

Jennings, S. 1981. *Eighteen Centuries of Pottery from Norwich*, East Anglian Archaeology 13. Norwich.

Johnson, A. M. 1995. 'Wellstream medieval site at Bird's Corner, Emneth', *Norfolk Archaeology* 42:2, 200–205.

Johnson, M. 1993. *Housing Culture. Traditional Architecture in an English Landscape*, UCL Press: London.

Johnson, M. 2002. *Behind the Castle Gate: From Medieval to Renaissance*, Routledge: London.

Johnson, M. 2006. 'The tide reversed: prospects and potentials for a postcolonial archaeology of Europe', in M. Hall and S. W. Silliman (eds), *Historical Archaeology*, Blackwell: Oxford, 313–331.

Johnson, M. 2007. *Ideas of Landscape*, Blackwell: Oxford.

Johnson, M. 2010. *English Houses 1300–1800: Vernacular Architecture, Social Life*, Longman: Harlow.

Johnson, N. and Rose, P. 1994. *Bodmin Moor: An Archaeological Survey. Vol. 1, The Human Landscape to c.1800*, English Heritage Archaeological Report 24/ RCHME Supplementary Series 11, London.

Johnson, R. 2004. *Viking Age Dublin*, Town House: Dublin.

Johnstone, N. 2000. '*Llys* and *maerdref*: the royal courts of the Princes of Gwynedd', *Studia Celtica* 34, 167–210.

Joliffe, J. 1923. *Pre-Feudal England: The Jutes*, Oxford University Press: Oxford.

Jones, A. M. 2000–01. 'The excavation of a multi-period site at Stencoose, Cornwall', *Cornish Archaeology* 39/40, 45–94.

Jones, E. T. 2000. 'River navigation in medieval England', *Journal of Historical Geography* 26, 1, 60–82.

Jones, G. and Jones, T. 1948. *The Mabinogion*, London: Golden Cockerel Press.

Jones, G. R. J. 1969. 'The defences of Gwynedd in the thirteenth century', *Transactions of the Caernarvon Historical Society* 30, 29–43.

Jones, G. R. J. 1973. 'Field systems of north Wales', in Baker and Butlin (eds), 430–479.

Jones, G. R. J. 1976. 'Multiple estates and early settlement', in Sawyer (ed.), 15–40.

Jones, G. R. J. 1985. 'Forms and patterns of medieval settlement in Welsh Wales', in D. Hooke (ed.), 155–169.

Jones, G. R. J. 1989. 'The Dark Ages', in Owen (ed.), 177–198.

Jones, G. R. J. 1994. '"Tir Telych", the gwestfau of Cynwyl Gaeo and Cwmwd Caeo', *Studia Celtica* 28, 81–95.

Jones, G. R. J. 1996. 'The gwely as a tenurial institution', *Studia Celtica* 30, 167–188.

Jones, R. 2003. 'Hastings to Herstmonceux: the castles of Sussex', in D. R. Rudling (ed.), *The Archaeology of Sussex to AD 2000*, Heritage Publications. King's Lynn, 171–178.

Jones, R. 2004. 'Signatures in the soil: the use of ceramic manure scatters in the identification of medieval arable farming regimes', *Archaeological Journal* 161, 159–188.

Jones, R. 2010a. 'Contrasting patterns of village and hamlet desertion in England', in Dyer and Jones (eds), 8–27.

Jones, R. 2010b. 'The village and the butterfly: nucleation out of chaos and complexity', *Landscapes* 11.1, 25–46.

Jones, R. and Page, M. 2003. 'Characterizing rural settlement and landscape: Whittlewood Forest in the middle ages', *Medieval Archaeology* 47, 53–83.

Jones, R. and Page, M. 2006. *Medieval Villages in an English Landscape: Beginnings and Ends*, Windgather Press: Oxford.

Jope, E. and Threlfall, R. 1956. 'A late dark-ages site at Gunwalloe', *Proceedings of the West Cornwall Field Club* 1, 4, 136–140.

Jope, M. and Threlfall, R. 1958. 'Excavation of a medieval settlement at Beere, North Tawton, Devon', *Medieval Archaeology* 2, 112–140.

Kain, R. (ed.) 2006. *England's Landscape: The South West*, Collins: London.

Kain, R. and Prince, H. 2000. *Tithe Surveys for Historians*, Phillimore: Chichester.

Kain, R. and Ravenhill, W. (eds) 2000. *Historical Atlas of South-West England*, University of Exeter Press: Exeter.

Kain, R. J. P. and Oliver, R. R. 2006. *Historic Parishes of England and Wales: An Electronic Map of Boundaries before 1850 with a Gazetteer and Metadata*, Arts and Humanities Data Services: Colchester.

Keen, J. A. 1967. 'Chapel Wood, Hartley', *Archaeologia Cantiana* 82, 285–287.

Keen, L. 1984. 'The towns of Dorset', in J. Haslam (ed.), *Anglo-Saxon Towns in Southern England*, Phillimore: Chichester, 203–248.

Kelly, R. S. 1982a. 'The excavation of a medieval farmstead at Cefn Graeanog, Clynnog, Gwynedd', *Bulletin Board Celtic Studies* 29, 859–908.

Kelly, R. S. 1982b. 'The Ardudwy Survey: fieldwork in western Merioneth, 1971–81', *Journal of the Merioneth Historical Record Society* 9.2, 121–162.

Kenyon, J. R. 2008. *Castles, Town Defences and Artillery Fortifications. A Bibliography 1945–2006*, Shaun Tyas: Donington.

Kerr, T.R. 2007. *Early Christian Settlement in North-west Ulster*, British Archaeological Reports British Series 430. Oxford.

Kerridge, E. 1955. 'The returns of the Inquisitions of Depopulation', *English Historical Review* 70, 212–228.

Kershaw, J. 2009. 'Culture and gender in the Danelaw: Scandinavian and Anglo-Scandinavian brooches', *Viking and Medieval Scandinavia* 5, 295–325.

Ketteringham, L. L. 1984. 'Excavations at Lagham manor, South Godstone, Surrey (TQ 364481)', *Surrey Archaeological Collections* 75, 235–249.

Kidd, C. 1993. *Subverting Scotland's Past*, Cambridge University Press: Cambridge.

King, A. 1978. 'Gauber High Pasture, Ribblehead – an interim report', in R. A. Hall (ed.), *Viking Age York and the North*, CBA Research Report 27. London, 21–25.

King, A. 2004. 'Post-Roman upland architecture in the Craven Dales and the dating evidence', in Hines *et al.* (eds), 335–344.

Kinsella, J. 2010. 'A new Irish early medieval site type? Exploring the "recent" archaeological evidence for non-circular enclosed settlement and burial sites', Proceedings of the Royal Irish Academy 110C, 89–132.

Kissock, J. A. 1993. 'Some examples of co-axial fields systems in Pembrokeshire', *Bulletin Board Celtic Studies* 40, 190–197.

Kissock, J. A. 1997. '"God Made Nature and Men Made Towns": post-Conquest and pre-Conquest villages in Pembrokeshire', in Edwards (ed.), 123–137.

Kissock, J. A. 2000. 'Farmsteads of a presumed medieval date on Cefn Drum, Gower: an interim review', *Studia Celtica* 34, 223–248.

Kissock, J. A. 2001. 'The upland dimension: further conjectures on early medieval settlement in Gower', *Morgannwg* 45, 55–68.

Kissock, J. A. 2008. 'Settlement and society', in R.A. Griffiths, T. Hopkins and R. Howell (eds), *The Gwent County History. Volume 2. The Age of the Marcher Lords, c.1070–1536*, University of Wales Press: Cardiff, 70–88.

Kissock, J. A. and Anthony, M. D. 2009. 'The early landscapes of Llandewi and Henllys, Gower', *Medieval Settlement Research* 24, 70–77.

Kissock, J. A. and Johnston, R. 2007. 'Sheephouses and sheepcotes – a study of the post-medieval landscape of Cefn Drum, Gower', *Studia Celtica* 41, 1–23.

Klápště, J. (ed.) 2002. *The Rural House: From the Migration Period to the Oldest Standing Buildings* (Ruralia IV, 8–13 September 2001, Bad Bederkesa, Lower Saxony, Germany), Institute of Archaeology, Academy of Sciences of the Czech Republic: Prague.

Klein, B. 2001. *Maps and the Writing of Space in Early Modern Ireland*, Palgrave Macmillan: Basingstoke.

Knowles, D. and Hadcock, R. 1971. *Medieval Religious Houses. England and Wales*, Longman: London.

Kowaleski, M. 1995. *Local Markets and Regional Trade in Medieval Exeter*, Cambridge University Press: Cambridge.

Ladurie, E. le Roy, 1978. *Montaillou*, Scolar Press: London.

Laing, L. 2006. *The Archaeology of Celtic Britain and Ireland* c. *AD 400–1200*, Cambridge University Press: Cambridge.

Landsberg, S. 1996. *The Medieval Garden*, British Museum Press: London.

Lane, A. and Campbell, E. 2000. *Dunadd: An Early Dalriadic Capital*, Oxbow Books: Oxford.

Langdon, J. 1993. 'Inland water transport in medieval England', *Journal of Historical Geography* 19:1, 1–11.

Langdon, J. 2000. 'Inland water transport in medieval England – the view from the mills: a response to Jones', *Journal of Historical Geography* 26, 85–82.

Langdon, J. 2004. *Mills in the Medieval Economy: England, 1300–1540*, Oxford University Press: Oxford.

Langdon, J. 2007. 'The efficiency of inland water transport in medieval England', in Blair (ed.), 110–132.

Langdon, J. and Masschaele, J. 2006. 'Commercial activity and population growth in medieval England', *Past and Present* 190, 35–81.

Langdon J., Walker, J. and Falconer, J. R. 2003. 'Boom and bust: building investment on the bishop of Winchester's estate in the early fourteenth century', in R. H. Britnell (ed.), *The Winchester Pipe Rolls and Medieval English Society*, Boydell: Woodbridge, 139–155.

Laughton, J. 2008. *Life in a Late Medieval City. Chester 1275–1520*, Windgather Press: Oxford.

Laughton, J., Jones, E. and Dyer, C. 2001. 'The urban hierarchy in the later middle ages: a study of the east midlands', *Urban History* 28, 331–357.

Lawson, A. 1983. *The Archaeology of Witton, near North Walsham, Norfolk*, East Anglian Archaeology 18. Gressenhall.

Lawson, T. and Killingray, D. 2004. *An Historical Atlas of Kent*, Phillimore: Chichester.

Le Patourel, H. E. J. 1973. *The Moated Sites of Yorkshire*, Society for Medieval Archaeology Monograph 5. London.

Le Patourel, H. E. J. 1978. 'The excavation of moated sites', in Aberg (ed.), 36–45.

Le Patourel, H. E. J. 1986. 'The Moated Sites Research Group: 1971–1986', *Medieval Settlement Research Group Annual Report* 1, 15–17.

Le Patourel, H. E. J. and Roberts, B. K. 1978. 'The significance of moats', in Aberg (ed.), 46–55.

Leah, M. 1994. *The Late Saxon and Medieval Pottery Industry of Grimston, Norfolk: Excavations 1962–92*, East Anglian Archaeology 64. Gressenhall.

Leask, H. G. 1941. *Irish Castles and Castellated Houses* (2nd edn 1951), Dandalgan: Dundalk.

Lees, D. J. and Sell, S. H. 1984. 'Excavations of a medieval dwelling at Pennard', *Journal of the Gower Society* 34, 44–52.

Leighton, D. K. 1997. *Mynydd Du and Fforest Fawr. The Evolution of an Upland Landscape in South Wales*, RCAHMW: Aberystwyth.

Lelong, O. 2003. 'Finding medieval (or later) settlement in the Highlands and Islands: the case for optimism', in Govan (ed.), 7–16.

Lennon, B. 2009. '*Lēah* names in the Anglo-Saxon charters of Wiltshire', *Wiltshire Archaeological and Natural History Magazine* 102, 175–187.

Leslie, K. and Short, B. 1999. *An Historical Atlas of Sussex: An Atlas of the History of the Counties of East and West Sussex*, Phillimore: Chichester.

Letters, S. 2003. *Online Gazetteer of Markets and Fairs in England and Wales to 1516*. Institute for Historical Research: London. http://www.history.ac.uk/cmh/gaz/gazweb2.html: Cambridgeshire. Accessed August 2008.

Letts, J., Moir, J., Smith, D. and de Moulins, D. 2000. *Smoke Blackened Thatch: A Unique Source of Late Medieval Plant Remains from Southern England*, English Heritage: London.

Lewis, C. 1994. 'Patterns and processes in the medieval settlement of Wiltshire', in Aston and Lewis (eds), 171–194.

Lewis, C. 2000. 'Medieval settlement in Hampshire and the Isle of Wight', in Atkinson, Banks and MacGregor (eds), 78–89.

Lewis, C. (ed.) 2006. 'Beyond region and place', *Medieval Settlement Research Group Annual Report* 21, 7–21.

Lewis, C. 2007. 'New avenues for the investigation of currently-occupied rural settlement: preliminary observations from the Higher Education Field Academy', *Medieval Archaeology* 51, 133–163.

Lewis, C. 2010. 'Exploring black holes: recent investigations in currently occupied rural settlements in Eastern England', in Higham and Ryan (eds), 83–106.

Lewis, C. and Mitchell-Fox, P. 1993. 'The Leverhulme medieval settlements and landscapes project: report on site selection for future fieldwork in the east Midlands', *Medieval Settlement Research Group Annual Report* 8, 27–35.

Lewis, C. and Mitchell-Fox, P. 1995. 'Settlement in Hampshire and the Isle of Wight', *Medieval Settlement Research Group Annual Report* 10, 7–12.

Lewis, C., Mitchell-Fox, P. and Dyer, C. 1997. *Village, Hamlet and Field. Changing Medieval Settlements in Central England*, Manchester University Press: Manchester (2nd edn 2001, Windgather Press: Oxford).

Liddiard, R. 2000. *'Landscapes of Lordship': Norman Castles and the Countryside in Medieval Norfolk, 1066–1200*, British Archaeological Reports British Series 309. Oxford.

Liddiard, R. 2005. *Castles in Context: Power, Symbolism and Landscape, 1066 to 1500*, Windgather Press: Oxford.

Liddiard, R. (ed.) 2007. *The Medieval Park: New Perspectives*, Windgather Press: Oxford.

Liddiard, R. and Williamson, T. 2008. 'There by design? Some reflections on medieval elite landscapes', *Archaeological Journal* 165:1, 520–535.

Liddle, P. 1994. 'The Medbourne Area Survey', in M. Parker Pearson and R. T. Shadla-Hall (eds), *Looking at the Land. Archaeological Landscapes in Eastern England: Recent Work and Future Directions*, Leicestershire Museums, Arts and Records Service, 34–36.

Light, A., Schofield, A. J. and Shennan, S. 1995. 'The Middle Avon Survey: a study in settlement history', *Proceedings of the Hampshire Field Club and Archaeological Society* 50, 43–102.

Lilley, K. 1993–94. 'A Warwickshire medieval borough: Brinklow and the contribution of town plan analysis', *Transactions of the Birmingham and Warwickshire Archaeological Society* 98, 51–60.

Lilley, K. 1996. *The Norman Town in Dyfed*, University of Birmingham, Urban Morphology Research Monograph 1. Birmingham.

Lilley, K. 1998. 'Trading places: monastic initiative and the development of high-medieval Coventry', in T. Slater and G. Rosser (eds), *The Church in the Medieval Town*, Ashgate: Aldershot, 177–208.

Lilley, K. 2000. '*Non urbe, non vico, non castris*: territorial control and the colonisation and urbanisation of Wales and Ireland under Anglo-Norman lordship', *Journal of Historical Geography* 26, 517–531.

Lilley, K., Lloyd, C. and Trick, S. 2005. *Mapping the Medieval Townscape: A Digital Atlas of the New Towns of Edward I*, York Archaeological Data Service, accessible online at http://ads.ahds.ac.uk/catalogue/specColl/atlas/ahrb/2005/.

Lilley, K., Lloyd, C. and Trick, S. 2007. 'Designs and designers of medieval "new towns" in Wales', *Antiquity* 81, 279–293.

Linehan, C. 1965. 'Deserted sites on Dartmoor', *Transactions of the Devonshire Association* 97, 171–178.

Linehan, C. 1966. 'Deserted sites and rabbit warrens on Dartmoor, Devon', *Medieval Archaeology* 10, 113–144.

Lobb, S., Mees, G. and Mepham, L. 1986–90. 'Meales Farm, Sulhampstead', *Berkshire Archaeological Journal* 73, 54–65.

Locock, M. 2006. 'Deserted rural settlements in south-east Wales', in Roberts (ed.), 41–60.

Loeber, R. 2001. 'An architectural history of Gaelic castles and settlements, 1370–1600', in Duffy *et al.* (eds), 271–314.

Long, A., Hipkin, S. and Clarke, H. (eds) 2002. *Romney Marsh: Coastal and Landscape Change through the Ages*, Oxford University School of Archaeology: Oxford.

Longley, D. 1991. 'The excavation of Castell, Porth Trefadog, a coastal promontory fort in north Wales', *Medieval Archaeology* 35, 64–85.

Longley, D. 1997. 'The royal courts of the Welsh princes of Gwynedd', in Edwards (ed.), 41–54.

Longley, D. 2001. 'Medieval settlement and landscape change', *Landscape History* 23, 39–59.

Longley, D. 2004. 'Status and lordship in the Early Middle Ages', in M. Aldhouse-Green and R. Howell (eds), *Gwent County History Volume 1. Gwent in Prehistory and Early History*, University of Wales Press: Cardiff, 287–316.

Longley, D. 2006. 'Deserted rural settlements in north-west Wales', in Roberts (ed.), 61–82.

Longley, D. 2010. 'Gwynedd before and after the Conquest', in D. Williams and J. Kenyon (eds), *The Impact of the Edwardian Castle in Wales*, Oxbow: Oxford, 16–26.

Losco-Bradley, S. and Kinsley, G. 2002. *Catholme: An Anglo-Saxon Settlement on the Trent Gravels in Staffordshire*, Nottingham Studies in Archaeology 3. Nottingham.

Loveluck, C. P. 2001. 'Wealth, waste and conspicuous consumption: Flixborough and its importance for middle and late Saxon rural settlement studies', in H. Hamerow and A. MacGregor (eds), *Image and Power in the Archaeology of Early Medieval Britain: Essays in Honour of Rosemary Cramp*, Oxbow Books: Oxford, 78–130.

Loveluck, C. P. (ed.) 2007. *Rural Settlement, Lifestyles and Social Change in the Late First Millennium AD: Anglo-Saxon Flixborough in its Wider Context*, Excavations at Flixborough 4, Oxbow Books: Oxford.

Lowe, C. 2008. *Inchmarnock: An Early Historic Island Monastery and its Archaeological Landscape*, Society of the Antiquaries of Scotland: Edinburgh.

Lowerre, A. 2005. *Placing Castles in the Conquest: Landscape, Lordship and Local Politics in the South-Eastern Midlands, 1066–1100*, British Archaeological Reports British Series 385. Oxford.

Lowther, A. W. G. 1983. 'Pachenesham, Leatherhead. The excavation of the medieval moated site known as "The Mounts"', *Surrey Archaeological Collections* 74, 1–45.

Lucy, S., Tipper, J. and Dickens, A. 2009. *The Anglo-Saxon Settlement at Bloodmoor Hill, Carlton Colville, Suffolk*, East Anglian Archaeology 131. Cambridge.

Lynn, C. J. 1991. 'Early medieval houses', in M. Ryan (ed.), *The Illustrated Archaeology of Ireland*. Country House: Dublin, 126–131.

Lynn, C. J. 1994. 'Houses in rural Ireland, AD 500–1000', *Ulster Journal of Archaeology* 57, 81–94.

McCarthy, M. and Brooks, C. 1988. *Medieval Pottery*

in Britain AD 900–1600, Leicester University Press: London.

McClure, P. 1979. 'Patterns of migration in the late middle ages: the evidence of English place-name surnames', *Economic History Review* (2nd Series) 32, 167–182.

McCormick, F. 2008. 'The decline of the cow: agriculture and settlement change in early medieval Ireland', *Peritia* 20, 209–224.

McCormick, F. and Murray, E. 2007. *Excavations at Knowth 3: Knowth and the Zooarchaeology of Early Christian Ireland*, Royal Irish Academy: Dublin.

McCullough, C. and Crawford, W. 2007. *Irish Historic Towns Atlas No. 18 Armagh*, Royal Irish Academy: Dublin.

McDonagh, B. 2003. 'Church/manor/settlement relationships in the Yorkshire Wolds', *Medieval Settlement Research Group Annual Report* 18, 16–26.

McDonald, R. A. 1997. *The Kingdom of the Isles: Scotland's Western Seaboard, c. 1100–c. 1336*, Tuckwell Press: East Linton.

McDonald, T. 1992. *Achill: 5000 BC to 1900 AD Archaeology History Folklore*, I. A. S. Publications: Tullamore.

McDonald, T. 2009. Booleying in Achill, Achill Beg, and Corraun. http://www.nuigalway.ie/archaeology/Graduate_Program/Current_Postgraduate_Research_Pages/McDonald_Theresa_Postgraduate_Research/mcdonald_theresa_index.html

McDonnell, K. G. T. 1978. *Medieval London Suburbs*, Phillimore: Chichester.

McErlean, T. 1983. 'The Irish townland system of landscape organisation,' in T. Reeves-Smyth and F. Hamond (eds), *Landscape Archaeology in Ireland*, British Archaeological Reports British Series 116. Tempus Reparatum: Oxford, 315–339.

Macfarlane, A. 1978. *The Origins of English Individualism: The Family, Property and Social Transition*, Blackwell: Oxford.

McNeill, T. 1997. *Castles in Ireland: Feudal Power in a Gaelic World*, Routledge: London.

McNeill, T. 2001. 'The archaeology of Gaelic lordship east and west of the Foyle', in Duffy *et al.* (eds), 346–356.

McNicholl, K. 1972. *Gaelic and Gaelicised Ireland in the Middle Ages*, Gill and Macmillan: Dublin.

McOmish, D. 2002. 'Report on the survey of the strip lynchets at Worth Matravers, Dorset', in Hinton (ed.), 132–137.

McOmish, D., Field, D. and Brown G. 2002. *The Field Archaeology of the Salisbury Plain Training Area*, English Heritage: Swindon.

MacSparron, C. 2002. 'A note on the discovery of two probable booley houses at Ballyutoag, County Antrim', *Ulster Journal of Archaeology* 61, 154–155.

MacSparron, C. 2007. *The Medieval Coarse Pottery of Ulster* unpublished MPhil dissertation, School of Geography, Archaeology and Palaeoecology, Queens University Belfast.

Maitland, F. 1897. *Domesday Book and Beyond*, Cambridge University Press: Cambridge.

Mallory, J. P. and McNeill, T. 1991. *The Archaeology of Ulster: From Colonization to Plantation,* Institute of Irish Studies, Queens University Belfast: Belfast.

Margham, J. 2003. 'Charters, landscapes and hides on the Isle of Wight', *Landscape History* 25, 17–44.

Marshall, K. and Ward, J. C. 1972. *Excavation at Old Thornton Hall 1957–59*, Essex Record Office Pub. No. 61. Chelmsford.

Martin, C. and Oram, R. 2007. 'Medieval Roxburgh: a preliminary assessment of the burgh and its locality', *Proceedings of the Society of Antiquaries of Scotland* 137, 357–404.

Martin, D. 1989. 'Three moated sites in north-east Sussex, Part 1: Glottenham', *Sussex Archaeological Collections* 127, 89–122.

Martin, D. 1990. 'Three moated sites in north-east Sussex, Part 2: Hawksden and Bodiam', *Sussex Archaeological Collections* 128, 89–116.

Martin, E. 1976. 'The excavation of a moat at Exning', *East Anglian Archaeology* 1, Ipswich, 24–38.

Martin, E. 1978. 'St Botolph and Hadstock: a reply', *Antiquaries Journal* 58, 1, 153–159.

Martin, E. 1989. 'Medieval moats in Suffolk', *Medieval Settlement Research Group Annual Report* 4, 14.

Martin, E. 1995. 'Greens, commons and tyes in Suffolk', in A. Longcroft and R. Joby (eds), *East Anglian Studies, Essays Presented to J C Barringer*, Marwood Publishing: Norwich, 167–178.

Martin, E. 1998. 'Shelley Hall and church: the buildings of Sir Philip Tilney (d. 1533)', *Proceedings of the Suffolk Institute of Archaeology and History* 39, 2, 257–264.

Martin, E. 1999a. 'Suffolk in the Iron Age', in J. Davies and T. Williamson (eds), *Land of the Iceni: The Iron Age in Northern East Anglia*, Centre for East Anglian Studies: Norwich, 44–99.

Martin, E. 1999b. 'Medieval moats', 'Greens, commons and tyes' and 'Deserted, dispersed and small settlements', in Dymond and Martin (eds), 60–63, 88–89.

Martin, E. 2002. 'Little Wenham Hall, Suffolk: the reinterpretation of "one of the incunabula of English domestic architecture"', in D. Pitte and B. Ayers (eds), *La Maison Medievale en Normandie et en Angleterre. Actes des tables rondes de Rouen et de Norwich (1998–1999)*, Société Libre d'Emulation de la Seine-Maritime: Rouen, 157–166.

Martin, E. 2004. 'East Anglian field systems: patterns and

origins', *Medieval Settlement Research Group Annual Report* 19, 6–7.

Martin, E. 2007. 'Wheare most Inclosures be: the making of the East Anglian landscape', in Gardiner and Rippon (eds), 122–136.

Martin, E. 2008. 'Not so common fields: the making of the East Anglian Landscape', in A. M. Chadwick (ed.), *Recent Approaches to the Archaeology of Land Allotment*, British Archaeological Reports International Series 1875. Oxford, 342–371.

Martin, E. and Satchell, M. 2008. *Wheare most Inclosures be. East Anglian Fields: History, Morphology and Management*, East Anglian Archaeology 124. Ipswich.

Martin, E., Plouviez, J. and Feldman, H. 1986. 'Archaeology in Suffolk 1985', *Proceedings of the Suffolk Institute of Archaeology and History* 36:2, 139–156.

Martin, E., Pendleton, C. and Plouviez, J. 1991. 'Archaeology in Suffolk 1990', *Proceedings of the Suffolk Institute of Archaeology and History* 37:3, 255–279.

Martin, E., Easton, T. and Aitkens, P. 1993. 'More moats in the landscape: Columbyne Hall and Crow's Hall', *Proceedings of the Suffolk Institute of Archaeology and History* 38:1, 107–111.

Martin, E., Pendleton, C. and Plouviez, J. 1994. 'Archaeology in Suffolk 1993', *Proceedings of the Suffolk Institute of Archaeology and History* 38, 2, 335–362.

Masschaele, J. 1993. 'Transport costs in medieval England', *Economic History Review* 46, 2, 266–279.

Masschaele, J. 1997. *Peasants, Merchants and Markets. Inland Trade in Medieval England, 1150–1350*, St Martin's Press: New York.

Mate, M. E. 1984. 'Investment by Canterbury Cathedral Priory 1250–1400', *Journal of British Studies* 23, 1–21.

Mate, M. E. 1987. 'Pastoral farming in south-east England in the fifteenth century', *Economic History Review*, 2nd Series, 40, 523–536.

Mate, M. E. 1991. 'The occupation of land: Kent and Sussex', in Miller (ed.), 119–135.

Matless, D. 1998. *Landscape and Englishness*, Reaktion Books: London.

Matless, D. 2002. 'Nikolaus Pevsner and the buildings of England', *History Workshop Journal*, 54, 73–99.

Mawer, A. and Stenton, F. M. 1926. *The Place-Names of Bedfordshire and Huntingdonshire*, English Place-Name Society, III. Cambridge University Press: Cambridge.

Mayfield, P. 2003. 'T. D. Whitaker, 1759–1821: historian of Yorkshire and Lancashire', *Yorkshire Archaeological Journal* 75, 165–180.

Mays, S., Harding, C. and Heighway, C. 2007. [Wharram XI] *The Churchyard*, York University Archaeological Publications 13. York.

Medlycott, M. 1996. 'A medieval farm and its landscape: excavations at Stebbingford Farm, Felsted 1993', *Essex Archaeology and History* 27, 102–181.

Mein, A. G. 1994. 'Trostrey. The early medieval houses', *Archaeology in Wales* 34, 71.

Mellor, M. 1994. *Medieval Ceramic Studies: A Review for English Heritage*, English Heritage: London.

Metcalf, M. 2003. 'Variations in the composition of the currency at different places in England', in Pestell and Ulmschneider (eds), 37–48.

Mew, K. 2001. 'The dynamics of lordship and landscape as revealed in a Domesday study of the *Nova Foresta*', *Anglo-Norman Studies* 23, 155–166.

Mileson, S.A. 2009. *Parks in Medieval England*, Oxford University Press: Oxford.

Miller, E. 1951. *The Abbey and Bishopric of Ely*, Cambridge University Press: Cambridge.

Miller, E. (ed.) 1991a. *The Agrarian History of England and Wales, Vol. III, 1348–1500*, Cambridge University Press: Cambridge.

Miller, E. 1991b. 'The southern counties', in Miller (ed.), 136–151.

Millett, M. (with James, S.) 1983. 'Excavations at Cowdery's Down, Basingstoke, Hampshire, 1978–81', *The Archaeological Journal* 140, 151–279.

Mills, A. D. (ed.) 1971. *The Dorset Lay Subsidy Roll of 1332*, Dorset Record Society: Dorchester.

Milne, G. and Goodburn, D. 1990. 'The early medieval port of London AD 700–1200', *Antiquity* 64, 629–636.

Milne, G. and Richards, J. 1992. [Wharram VII] *Two Anglo-Saxon Buildings and Associated Finds*, York University Archaeological Publications 9. York.

Moore, H., Pine, J. and Taylor, A. 2008. 'Prehistoric and Saxon features and medieval land allotment at Lower Farm, Pennington, Hampshire', *Proceedings of the Hampshire Field Club and Archaeological Society* 63, 88–100.

Moorhouse, S. 1986. 'Non-dating uses of medieval pottery', *Medieval Ceramics* 10, 85–123.

Moorhouse, S. 1989. 'Monastic estates: their composition and development', in R. Gilchrist and H. Mytum (eds), *The Archaeology of Rural Monasteries*, British Archaeological Reports British Series 203. Oxford, 29–82.

Moorhouse, S. 2003. 'Anatomy of the Yorkshire Dales: decoding the medieval landscape', in T. G. Manby, S. Moorhouse and P. Ottaway (eds), *The Archaeology of Yorkshire. An Assessment at the Beginning of the 21st Century*, Yorkshire Archaeological Society: Leeds, 293–362.

Morris, B. 1954. 'Medieval platform sites in east Gower', *Gower* 7, 40–42.

Morris, C. D. 1996. 'From Birsay to Tintagel: a personal view', in B. E. Crawford (ed.), *Scotland in Dark Age Britain*, Committee for Dark Age Studies: St Andrews, 37–78.

Morris, C. D. 1998. 'Raiders, traders and settlers: the Early Viking Age in Scotland', in H. B. Clarke, M. Ní Mhaonaigh and R. Ó Floinn (eds), *Ireland and Scandinavia in the Early Viking Age*, Four Courts Press: Dublin, 73–103.

Morris, R. K. 1989. *Churches in the Landscape*, Dent: London.

Mortimer, R. 2000. 'Village development and ceramic sequence: the middle to late Saxon village at Lordship Lane, Cottenham, Cambridgeshire', *Proceedings of the Cambridgeshire Antiquarian Society* 89, 5–33.

Mortimer, R., Regan, R. and Lucy, S. 2005. *The Saxon and Medieval Settlement at West Fen Road, Ely: The Ashwell Site*, East Anglian Archaeology, 110. Cambridge.

MSRG 1996. *Medieval Rural Settlement. A Policy on Research, Conservation and Excavation.*

MSRG 2007. *Medieval Settlement Research Group. Medieval Rural Settlement. A Revised Policy on Research, Conservation and Excavation.*

Mudd, A. 2007. *Bronze Age, Roman and Later Occupation at Chieveley, West Berkshire*, British Archaeological Reports British Series 433. Oxford.

Muir, R. 2007. *How to Read a Village*, Random House: London.

Munby, J. 1985. 'Portchester and its region', in B. Cunliffe and J. Munby, *Excavations at Portchester Castle, Volume IV: Medieval, the Inner Bailey*, Report of the Research Committee of the Society of Antiquaries of London 43. London, 270–295.

Murphy, M. and O'Conor, K. 2006. 'Castles and deerparks in Anglo-Norman Ireland', *Eolas* 1, 53–70.

Murphy, M. and Potterton, M. 2010. *The Dublin Region in the Middle Ages: Settlement, Land-Use and Economy*, Four Courts Press: Dublin.

Murphy, P. 2010. 'The landscape and economy of the Anglo-Saxon coast: new archaeological evidence', in Higham and Ryan (eds), 211–221.

Murray, H. K. and Murray, J. C. 1993. 'Excavations at Rattray, Aberdeenshire. A Scottish deserted burgh', *Medieval Archaeology* 37, 109–218.

Musson, R. 1955. 'A thirteenth-century dwelling at Bramble Bottom, Eastbourne', *Sussex Archaeological Collections* 93, 157–170.

Musty, J. and Algar, D. 1986. 'Excavations at the deserted medieval village of Gomeldon, near Salisbury', *Wiltshire Archaeological and Natural History Society Magazine*, 80, 127–169.

Mynard, D. C. 1994. *Medieval Sites in Milton Keynes*, Buckinghamshire Archaeological Society Monograph Series 6. Buckingham.

Mynard, D. C., Zeepvat, R. and Williams, R. 1991. *Excavations at Great Linford, 1974–80*, Buckinghamshire Archaeological Society Monograph Series 3. Buckingham.

Myzelev, A. 2009. 'Craft revival in Haslemere: she, who weaves …', *Women's History Review* 18, 597–618.

Nash, G. 2006. *Looking Beyond the Walls: The Weobley Castle Project*, British Archaeological Reports British Series 415. Oxford.

Nash-Williams, V. E. 1933. 'An early Iron Age hill-fort at Llanmelin, near Caerwent, Monmouthshire', *Archaeologia Cambrensis* 88, 237–346.

Nash-Williams, V. E. 1939. 'An early Iron Age coastal camp at Sudbrook, near the Severn Tunnel, Monmouthshire', *Archaeologia Cambrensis* 94, 42–79.

Naylor, J. and Geake, H. (eds) 2010. 'Portable Antiquities Scheme 2009', *Medieval Archaeology* 54, 382–400.

Naylor, J. D. and Richards, J. D. 2006. 'Viking and Anglo-Saxon Landscape and Economy Project', in *Medieval Archaeology* 50, 275–278.

Neal, D. S. 1989. 'The Stanwick Villa, Northants: An Interim Report on the Excavations of 1984–88', *Britannia* 20, 149–168.

Neave, D. 2010. 'The late 17th- to early 19th-century farmhouse and vicarage house, and the vernacular building tradition of the northern Wolds', in Harding *et al.* (eds), 355–361.

Neilson, N. (ed.) 1920. 'A terrier of Fleet, Lincolnshire', *British Academy Records* 4, 1–214.

Newall, F. 1960. *Excavations at Walls Hill, Renfrewshire*, Paisley Museum and Art Galleries: Paisley.

Newall, F. 1965. *Excavations of Prehistoric and Medieval Homesteads at Knapps, Renfrewshire*, Paisley Museum and Art Galleries: Paisley.

Newman, J. 1989. 'East Anglian Kingdom Survey – final interim report on the South East Suffolk pilot field survey', *Bulletin of the Sutton Hoo Research Committee* 6, 17–20.

Newman, J. 1992. 'The Late Roman and Anglo-Saxon settlement pattern in the Sandlings of Suffolk', in M. O. H. Carver (ed.), *The Age of Sutton Hoo. The Seventh Century in North-Western Europe,* Boydell: Woodbridge, 25–38.

Newman, J. 1993. 'The Anglo-Saxon Cemetery at Boss Hall, Ipswich', *Sutton Hoo Research Committee Bulletin* 8, 32–35.

Newman, P. 2006. 'Tin-working and the landscape of medieval Devon *c.* 1150–1700', in Turner (ed.), 123–143.

Newman, R. and Parkhouse, J. 1983. 'Excavations at

Cosmeston, South Glamorgan', *Glamorgan-Gwent Archaeological Trust Annual Report for 1982–1983*, 1–13.

Newman, R. and Parkhouse, J. 1985. 'Cosmeston excavations, 1983–84', *Glamorgan-Gwent Archaeological Trust Annual Report for 1983–4*, 31–51.

Newton, M. 2009. *Warriors of the Word: The World of the Scottish Highlanders*, Birlinn: Edinburgh.

Nicholls, K. 2001. 'Woodland cover in pre-modern Ireland,' in Duffy *et al.* (eds), 181–206.

Nightingale, P. 1996. 'The growth of London in the medieval English economy', in R. Britnell and J. Hatcher (eds), *Progress and Problems in Medieval England: Essays in Honour of Edward Miller*, Cambridge University Press: Cambridge, 89–106.

Nowakowski, J., Quinnell, H., Sturgess, J., Thomas, C. and Thorpe, C. 2007. 'Return to Gwithian: shifting the sands of time', *Cornish Archaeology* 46, 13–76.

Ó Carragáin, T. 2010. 'Cemetery settlements and local churches in pre-Viking Ireland in light of comparisons with England and Wales', in J. Graham-Campbell and M. Ryan (eds), *Anglo-Saxon/Irish Relations before the Vikings*, Proceedings of the British Academy Vol. 157. London, 239–261.

O'Connor, P. 1987. *Exploring Limerick's Past*, Oireacht na Mumhan Books, Newcastle West, Co. Limerick.

O'Conor, K. D. 1998. *The Archaeology of Medieval Rural Settlement in Ireland*, Discovery Programme Monograph 3. Dublin.

O'Conor, K. D. 2000. 'The ethnicity of Irish moated sites', *Ruralia* 3, 92–102.

O'Conor, K. D. 2002. 'Housing in later medieval Gaelic Ireland', *Ruralia* 4, 201–210.

O'Conor, K. D. 2005. 'Gaelic lordly settlement in 13th and 14th century Ireland', in I. Holm, S. Innselet and I. Oye (eds), *Utmark: The Outfield as Industry and Ideology in the Iron Age and the Middle Ages,* University of Bergen Archaeological Series 1. Bergen, 209–221.

O'Conor, K. D. 2008. 'Castle studies in Ireland: the way forward', *Château Gaillard* 23, 329–339.

O'Donovan, E. 2008. 'The Irish, the Vikings and the English: new archaeological evidence from excavations at Golden Lane, Dublin', *Medieval Dublin VIII*, Four Courts Press: Dublin, 36–130.

O'Keeffe, T. 2000. *Medieval Ireland: An Archaeology*, Tempus: Stroud.

O'Keeffe, T. 2004a. *The Gaelic Peoples and their Archaeological Identities, AD 1000–1650*, Quiggin Pamphlets on the Sources of Medieval Gaelic History, 7. Cambridge University Press: Cambridge.

O'Keeffe, T. 2004b. 'Were there designed landscapes in medieval Ireland?', *Landscapes* 5.2, 52–68.

O'Neil, B. H. St J. 1948. 'War and archaeology in Britain', *Antiquaries Journal* 28, 20–44.

O'Néill, J. 2006. 'Excavation of pre-Norman structures on the site of an enclosed early Christian cemetery at Cherrywood, county Dublin', in S. Duffy (ed.), *Medieval Dublin VII*, Four Courts Press: Dublin, 66–88.

Oosthuizen, S. 1993. 'Isleham: a medieval inland port', *Landscape History* 15, 29–35.

Oosthuizen, S. 1994. 'Saxon commons in South Cambridgeshire', *Proceedings of the Cambridge Antiquarian Society* 82, 93–100.

Oosthuizen, S. 1997. 'Medieval settlement relocation in west Cambridgeshire: three case studies', *Landscape History* 19, 43–55.

Oosthuizen, S. 1998. 'The origins of Cambridgeshire', *Antiquaries Journal* 78, 85–109.

Oosthuizen, S. 2000. 'The Cambridgeshire Lodes', in A. Kirby and S. Oosthuizen (eds), *An Atlas of Cambridgeshire and Huntingdonshire History*, Centre for Regional Studies: Cambridge, 32.

Oosthuizen, S. 2002. 'Ancient greens in "midland" landscapes: Barrington, Cambridgeshire', *Medieval Archaeology* 46, 110–115.

Oosthuizen, S. 2010. 'Medieval field systems and settlement nucleation: common or separate origins?', in Higham and Ryan (eds), 107–132.

Oosthuizen, S. in prep. 'Managing pastoral husbandry in the peat fen: evidence from Rampton, Cambridgeshire, 1251–1834'.

Oram, R. D. 2008. 'Royal and lordly residence in Scotland *c.* 1050 to *c.* 1250: an historiographical review and critical revision', *Antiquaries Journal* 88, 165–189.

Oram, R. D. and Stell, G. (eds) 2005. *Lordship and Architecture in Medieval and Renaissance Scotland*, John Donald: Edinburgh.

O'Rourke, D. 2006. 'Archaeology and roads: an historic opportunity', in O'Sullivan and Stanley (eds), 1–6.

Orpen, G. 1911–20. *Ireland under the Normans*, Oxford University Press: Oxford.

Orser, C. 2009. 'The dialectics of scale in the historical archaeology of the modern world', in Horning and Palmer (eds), 7–18.

Orton, C., Tyers, P. and Vince, A. 1993. *Pottery in Archaeology*, Cambridge University Press: Cambridge.

Orwin, C. and Orwin, C. 1938. *The Open Fields*, Clarendon Press, Oxford.

Osterhammel, J. 1997. *Colonialism: A Theoretical Overview*, Marcus Wiener: Princeton.

O'Sullivan, A. 2008. 'Early medieval houses in Ireland: social identity and dwelling spaces', *Peritia* 20, 225–256.

O'Sullivan, J. and Stanley, M. (eds) 2006. *Settlement, Industry and Ritual: Proceedings of a Public Seminar on Archaeological Discoveries on Road Schemes, September 2005*, National Roads Authority: Dublin.

Oswin, J. 2009. *A Field Guide to Geophysics in Archaeology*, Praxis: Chichester.

Otway-Ruthven, A. J. 1980. *A History of Medieval Ireland*, Palgrave Macmillan: London.

Owen, D. H. (ed.) 1989a. *Settlement and Society in Wales*, University of Wales Press: Cardiff.

Owen, D. H. 1989b. 'The Middle Ages', in Owen (ed.), 199–224.

Owen, D. M. 1984. *The Making of King's Lynn*, British Academy and Oxford University Press: London.

Owles, E. J. 1968. 'A medieval moated farmstead at Debenham', *Proceedings of the Suffolk Institute of Archaeology and History* 31, 160–171.

Padel, O. 1985. *Cornish Place-Name Elements*, English Place-Name Society, 56–57. Nottingham.

Padel, O. 1988. *A Popular Dictionary of Cornish Place-Name Elements*, Alison Hodge: Penzance.

Padel, O. 1999. 'Place-names', in Kain and Ravenhill (eds), 88–94.

Page, F. M. 1934. *The Estates of Crowland Abbey*, Cambridge University Press: Cambridge.

Page, M. 1998. 'A note on the manor of Limerstone, Isle of Wight', *Hampshire Field Club and Archaeological Society Newsletter* 29, 25–26.

Page, M. 2009. 'Studying medieval settlement in Hampshire', *Hampshire Field Club and Archaeological Society Newsletter* 52, 20–22.

Page, M. and Jones, R. 2007. 'Stability and instability in medieval village plans: case-studies in Whittlewood', in Gardiner and Rippon (eds), 139–152.

Page, P., Atherton, K. and Hardy, A. 2005. *Barentin's Manor: Excavations of the Moated Site at Harding's Field, Chalgrove, Oxfordshire 1976–9*, Oxford Archaeology: Oxford.

Paine, C. R. 1969. *Moated Sites in West Suffolk*, unpublished manuscript, Suffolk Record Office, Bury St Edmunds.

Pallister, A. 2007. *Middleton St George. Windows on the Evolution of a Tees Valley Parish*, The History of Education Project: Durham.

Pallister, A. and Wrathmell, S. 1990. 'The deserted village of West Hartburn, third report: excavation of Site D and discussion', in Vyner (ed.), 59–75.

Palmer, B. 2003. 'The hinterlands of three southern English emporia: some common themes', in Pestell and Ulmschneider (eds), 48–60.

Pantin, W. 1962–63. 'Medieval English town-house plans', *Medieval Archaeology*, 6–7, 202–239.

Papazian, C. 1991. 'Excavations at Athenry Castle, Co. Galway', *Journal of the Galway Archaeological and Historical Society* 43, 1–45.

Parker Pearson, M. 2006. 'The origins of Old Norse ritual and religion in European perspective', in A. Andrén, K. Jennbert and C. Raudvere (eds), *Old Norse Religion in Long-Term Perspectives*, Nordic Academic Press: Lund, 86–91.

Parker Pearson, M., Smith H., Mulville, J. and Brennand, M. 2004a. 'Cille Pheadair: the life and times of a Norse-period farmstead c. 1000–1300', in Hines *et al.* (eds), 235–254.

Parker Pearson, M., Sharples, N. and Symonds, J. 2004b. *South Uist: Archaeology and History of a Hebridean Island*, Tempus: Stroud.

Parry, S. J. 2006. *Raunds Area Survey: An Archaeological Study of the Landscape of Raunds, Northamptonshire, 1985–94*, Oxbow Books: Oxford.

Parsons, D. and Styles, T. 2000. *The Vocabulary of English Place-Names (Brace–Cæster)*, Centre for English Name-Studies: Nottingham.

Partner, N. (ed.) 1995. *Writing Medieval History*, Hodder Arnold: London.

Patterson, N. 1994. *Cattle, Lords and Clansmen: The Social Structure of Early Ireland* (2nd edn), Notre Dame Press: Notre Dame and London.

Pattison, P. 1999. 'Challacombe revisited', in P. Pattison, D. Field and S. Ainsworth (eds), *Patterns of the Past: Essays in Landscape Archaeology for Christopher Taylor*, Oxbow Books: Oxford, 61–70.

Pearce, J. E., Vince, A. G. and White, R. 1982. 'A dated type-series of London medieval pottery part 1: Mill Green ware', *Transactions of the London and Middlesex Archaeological Society* 33, 266–298.

Pearson, S. 1994. *The Medieval Houses of Kent: An Historical Analysis*, HMSO: London.

Pearson, S. 2005. 'Rural and urban houses 1100–1500: "urban adaptation" reconsidered', in Giles and Dyer (eds), 43–63.

Peate, I. C. 1946. *The Welsh House*, Brython Press: Liverpool.

Pelham, R. A. 1928. 'The distribution of sheep in Sussex in the early fourteenth century', *Sussex Archaeological Collections* 69, 128–135.

Pelham, R. A. 1934. 'Timber exports from the Weald during the fourteenth century', *Sussex Archaeological Collections* 75, 170–182.

Pestell, T. 2004. *Landscapes of Monastic Foundation. The Establishment of Religious Houses in East Anglia, c. 650–1200*, Boydell: Woodbridge.

Pestell, T. and Ulmschneider, K. (eds) 2003. *Markets in Early Medieval Europe: Trading and 'Productive Sites'*

650–850, Windgather: Oxford.

Peterson, J. W. M. 1990. 'Why did co-axial systems last so long?', *Antiquity* 64, 584–591.

Pettit, P. A. J. 1968. *The Royal Forests of Northamptonshire: A Study in their Economy, 1558–1714*, Northamptonshire Record Society, 23. Northampton.

Petts, D. and Gerrard, C. (eds) 2006. *Shared Visions: The North East Regional Research Framework for the Historic Environment*, Durham County Council: Durham.

Phillips, N. 2006. *Earthwork Castles of Gwent and Ergyng AD 1050–1250*, British Archaeological Reports British Series 420. Oxford.

Phillpotts, C. 1999. 'Landscape into townscape: an historical and archaeological investigation of the Limehouse area, east London', *Landscape History* 21, 59–76.

Philp, B. 1973. *Excavations in West Kent 1960–1970*, West Kent Border Archaeological Group: Dover.

Philp, B. 2006. 'The medieval site at Well Wood, Aylesford', *Archaeologia Cantiana* 126, 27–48.

Phythian-Adams, C. 1979. *Desolation of a City. Coventry and the Urban Crisis of the Late Middle Ages*, Cambridge University Press: Cambridge.

Phythian-Adams, C. 1996. *Societies, Cultures and Kinship, 1580–1850*, Leicester University Press: Leicester and London.

Pierce, T. J. 1972. *Medieval Welsh Society*, University of Wales Press: Cardiff.

Pile, J. 1989. 'Aspects of the Forest of Bere from the late Iron Age to the Middle Ages', *Proceedings of the Hampshire Field Club and Archaeological Society* 45, 113–119.

Pine, J. 2001. 'The excavation of a Saxon settlement at Cadley Road, Collingbourne Ducis, Wiltshire', *Wiltshire Archaeological and Natural History Society Magazine* 94, 88–117.

Pirenne, H. 1925. *Medieval Cities*, Princeton University Press: Princeton, N.J.

Platt, C. 1969. *The Monastic Grange in Medieval England*, Macmillan: London.

Platt, C. 1978. *Medieval England. A Social History and Archaeology from the Conquest to AD 1600*, Routledge: London.

Platt, C. 2007. 'Revisionism in castle studies: a caution', *Medieval Archaeology* 51, 83–102.

Pluskowski, A. and Patrick, P. 2003. 'How do you pray to God? Fragmentation and variety in Early Medieval Christianity', in M. O. H. Carver (ed.), *The Cross Goes North: Processes of Conversion in Northern Europe, AD 300–1300*, Medieval Press: York, 29–50.

Poos, L. R. 1991. *A Rural Society after the Black Death. Essex 1350–1525*, Cambridge University Press: Cambridge.

Porter, Rev. T. 1857. 'Tullahog', *Ulster Journal of Archaeology* (Series 1) 235–242.

Postan, M. 1937. 'The chronology of labour services', *Transactions of the Royal Historical Society*, 4th Series, 20, 169–193.

Postan, M. 1972. *The Medieval Economy and Society*, Weidenfeld: London.

Postgate, M. R. 1962. 'The field systems of Breckland', *Agricultural Historical Review* 10, 80–101.

Postgate, M. R. 1973. 'Field systems in East Anglia', in Baker and Butlin (eds), 281–324.

Poulton, R. 1998. *The Lost Manor of Hextalls, Little Pickle, Bletchingley*, Surrey County Archaeological Unit: Woking.

Pounds, N. J. G. 1990. *The Medieval Castle in England and Wales: A Social and Political History*, Cambridge University Press: Cambridge.

Powlesland, D. 1995. 'The West Heslerton Assessment', *Internet Archaeology* 5.

Powlesland, D. 2003. *25 Years of Archaeological Research on the Sands and Gravels of Heslerton*, English Heritage: Yedingham.

Preston-Jones, A. and Rose, P. 1986. 'Medieval Cornwall', *Cornish Archaeology* 25, 135–185.

Proudfoot, W. F. 1978. 'The manor and chantry of Scotgrove', *Archaeologia Cantiana* 94, 7–26.

Quiney, A. 1994. 'Medieval and post-medieval vernacular architecture', in B. Vyner (ed.), *Building on the Past: Papers Celebrating 150 Years of the Royal Archaeological Institute*, Royal Archaeological Institute: London, 228–243.

Quinnell, H. 2004. *Excavations at Trethurgy Round, St Austell: Community and Status in Roman and Post-Roman Cornwall*, Cornwall County Council Archaeological Unit: Truro.

Quinnell, H. and Blockley, M. R. 1994. *Excavations at Rhuddlan, Clwyd: 1969–73. Medieval to Mesolithic*, Council for British Archaeology: York.

Rackham, O. 1976. *Trees and Woodland in the British Landscape*, Dent: London.

Rackham, O. 1986. *The History of the Countryside*, Dent: London.

Raftis, J. A. 1957. *The Estates of Ramsey Abbey*, Pontifical Institute of Medieval Studies: Toronto.

Rahtz, P. A. 1959. 'Holworth, medieval village excavation 1958', *Proceedings of the Dorset Natural History and Archaeological Society* 81, 127–147.

Rahtz, P. A. 1969a. *Excavations at King John's Hunting Lodge, Writtle, Essex, 1955–57*, Society for Medieval Archaeology Monograph 3. Leeds.

Rahtz, P. A. 1969b. 'Upton, Gloucestershire, 1964–1968', *Transactions of the Bristol and Gloucestershire Archaeological Society* 88, 74–126.

Rahtz, P. A. 1976, 'Buildings and rural settlement', in D.

Wilson (ed.), *The Archaeology of Anglo-Saxon England*, Cambridge University Press: Cambridge, 49–98.

Rahtz, P. A. 2001. *Living Archaeology*, Tempus: Stroud.

Rahtz, P. A. and Watts, L. 1983. [Wharram II] *Wharram Percy: The Memorial Stones of the Churchyard*, York University Archaeological Publications 1. York.

Rahtz, P. A. and Watts, L. 1984. 'Upton, deserted medieval village, Blockley, Gloucestershire, 1973', *Transactions of the Bristol and Gloucestershire Archaeological Society* 102, 141–154.

Rahtz, P. A. and Watts, L. 2004. [Wharram IX] *Wharram: A Study of Settlement on the Yorkshire Wolds. Vol. 9, The North Manor Area and North-West Enclosure,* University of York: York.

Rahtz, P. A., Hayfield, C. and Bateman, J. 1986. [Wharram IV] *Two Roman Villas at Wharram Percy*, York University Archaeological Publications 2. York.

Rahtz, S. and Rowley, T. 1984. *Middleton Stoney: Excavation and Survey in a North Oxfordshire Parish 1970–1982*, Oxford University Department for External Studies: Oxford.

Raistrick, A. 1976. *Buildings in the Yorkshire Dales,* Dalesman Books: Clapham.

Raistrick, A. and Holmes, P. F. 1962. *Archaeology of Malham Moor*, printed in advance for *Field Studies*, 1, 4 (with altered pagination).

Ramm, H. G., McDowall, R. W. and Mercer, E. 1970. *Shielings and Bastles*, Royal Commission on Historical Monuments (England), HMSO: London.

Ramsay, N. 2001. 'Introduction', in Blair and Ramsey (eds), xv–xxxiv.

Ratcliffe-Densham, H. B. A. and Ratcliffe-Densham, M. M. 1961. 'An anomalous earthwork on the late Bronze Age, on Cock Hill, Sussex', *Sussex Archaeological Collections* 99, 78–101.

Rathbone, S. 2009. 'Booley houses, hafods, and shielings: a comparative study of transhumant settlements from around the Northern basin of the Irish Sea', in A. Horning and N. Brannon (eds), *Ireland and Britain in the Atlantic World*, Wordwell: Dublin, 111–130.

Ravensdale, J. R. 1974. *Liable to Floods: Village Landscape on the Edge of the Fens, AD 450–1850*, Cambridge University Press: Cambridge.

Ravensdale, J. R. 1986. *The Domesday Inheritance*, Souvenir Press: London.

Rawson, R. 1953. 'The open field in Flintshire, Devonshire and Cornwall', *Economic History Review* 6, 51–54.

Raynbird, W. and H. 1849. *On the Agriculture of Suffolk*, Longman: London.

RCAHMS 1990. *North-east Perth: An Archaeological Landscape*, HMSO: Edinburgh.

RCAHMS 2002. *But the Walls Remained: A Survey of Unroofed Rural Settlement Depicted on the First Edition of the Ordnance Survey 6–inch Map of Scotland*, Historic Scotland: Edinburgh.

RCAHMS 2007. *In the Shadow of Bennachie: A Field Archaeology of Donside, Aberdeenshire*, RCAHMS and Society of Antiquaries of Scotland: Edinburgh.

RCAHMW 1913. *An Inventory of the Ancient Monuments in Wales and Monmouthshire. III County of Radnor*, RCAHMW: London.

RCAHMW 1956. *An Inventory of the Ancient Monuments in Caernarvonshire*, Vol. I, HMSO: London.

RCAHMW 1982. *An Inventory of the Ancient Monuments in Glamorgan. Volume III: Medieval Secular Monuments. Part II: Non-defensive*, HMSO: London.

RCAHMW 1988. *An Inventory of the Ancient Monuments in Glamorgan. Volume IV: Domestic Architecture from the Reformation to the Industrial Revolution*, HMSO: London.

RCHME 1911. *An Inventory of the Historical Monuments in Hertfordshire*, Royal Commission on the Historical Monuments of England, HMSO: London.

RCHME 1968. *West Cambridgeshire*, HMSO: London.

RCHME 1972. *North-East Cambridgeshire*, HMSO: London.

RCHME 1975. *An Inventory of Archaeological Sites in North-east Northamptonshire*, I, HMSO: London.

RCHME 1979. *An Inventory of Archaeological Sites in Central Northamptonshire*, II, HMSO: London.

RCHME 1981. *An Inventory of Archaeological Sites in North-west Northamptonshire*, III, HMSO: London.

RCHME 1982. *An Inventory of the Historical Monuments in the County of Northamptonshire*, IV, *South-West Northamptonshire*, HMSO: London.

Reaney, P. H. 1935. *The Place-Names of Essex,* English Place-Name Society 12. Cambridge University Press: Cambridge.

Reaney, P. H. 1943. *Place-Names of Cambridgeshire and the Isle of Ely*, Cambridge University Press: Cambridge.

Redknap, M. 2000. *The Vikings in Wales: An Archaeological Enquiry*, National Museums and Galleries of Wales: Cardiff.

Redknap, M. 2004. 'Viking-Age settlement in Wales and the evidence from Llanbedrgoch', in Hines *et al.* (eds), 139–175.

Redknap, M. and Lane, A. 1994. 'The early medieval crannog at Llangorse, Powys: an interim statement on the 1989–1993 seasons', *International Journal of Nautical Archaeology* 23, 3, 189–205.

Redknap, M. and Lane, A. 1999. 'The archaeological importance of Llangorse Lake: an environmental perspective', *Aquatic Conservation: Marine and Freshwater Ecosystems* 9, 377–390.

Reed, S., Juleff, G. and Bayer, O. 2006. 'Three late Saxon iron-smelting furnaces at Burlescombe, Devon', *Devon Archaeological Society Proceedings* 64, 71–122.

Reynolds, A. 1999. *Later Anglo-Saxon England. Life and Landscape*, Tempus: Stroud.

Reynolds, A. 2003. 'Boundaries and settlements in later sixth- to eleventh-century England', in D. Griffiths, A. Reynolds and S. Semple (eds), *Boundaries in Early Medieval Britain*, Anglo-Saxon Studies in Archaeology and History 12. Oxford, 98–139.

Reynolds, A. 2005. 'On farmers, traders and kings: archaeological reflections of social complexity in early medieval north-western Europe', *Early Medieval Europe* 13, 1, 97–118.

Reynolds, A. 2009. 'Meaningful landscapes: an early medieval perspective', in R. Gilchrist and A. Reynolds (eds), *Reflections: 50 Years of Medieval Archaeology 1957–2007*, Society for Medieval Archaeology Monograph 30. Maney: Leeds, 409–434.

Reynolds, S. 1977. *An Introduction to the History of English Medieval Towns*, Clarendon Press: Oxford.

Richards, J. D. 2000. 'Identifying Anglo-Scandinavian settlements', in Hadley and Richards (eds), 295–310.

Richardson, G. G. S. 1979. 'King's Stables – an early shieling on Black Lyne Common, Bewcastle', *Trans Cumberland and Westmorland Antiquarian and Archaeological Society* 79, 19–27.

Richardson, J. 1974. *The Local Historian's Encyclopedia*, Hampton Press: New Barnet.

Richardson, J. 2005. 'The animal remains', in Treen and Atkin (eds).

Riden, P. 1987. *Record Sources for Local History*, Batsford: London.

Ridgard, J. 1983. *The Local History of Worlingworth to c. 1400 AD*, unpublished PhD thesis, University of Leicester.

Rigold, S. E. 1982. 'Medieval archaeology in Kent', in P.E. Leach (ed.), *Archaeology in Kent to AD 1500*, Council for British Archaeology: London, 84–86.

Riley, D. N. 1996. *Aerial Archaeology in Britain*, Shire Archaeology: Princes Risborough.

Riley, H. 2006. *The Historic Landscape of the Quantock Hills*, English Heritage: Swindon.

Riley, H. and Wilson-North, R. 2001. *The Field Archaeology of Exmoor*, English Heritage: Swindon.

Rippon, S. 1991. 'Early planned landscapes in South-East Essex', *Essex Archaeology and History* 22, 46–60.

Rippon, S. 1996a. 'Essex c. 700–1066', in O. Bedwin (ed.), *The Archaeology of Essex. Proceedings of the Writtle Conference*, Essex County Council: Chelmsford, 117–128.

Rippon, S. 1996b. *Gwent Levels: The Evolution of a Wetland Landscape*, Council for British Archaeology: York.

Rippon, S. 2004. *Historic Landscape Analysis: Deciphering the Countryside*, Council for British Archaeology Practical Handbook 16. York.

Rippon, S. 2006. *Landscape Community and Colonisation: the North Somerset Levels during the 1st to 2nd Millennia AD*, Council for British Archaeology Research Report 152. York.

Rippon, S. 2007. 'Emerging regional variation in historic landscape character: the possible significance of the "Long Eighth Century"', in Gardiner and Rippon (eds), 105–121.

Rippon, S. 2008. *Beyond the Medieval Village. The Diversification of Landscape Character in Southern Britain*, Oxford University Press: Oxford.

Rippon, S. 2010. 'Landscape change during the "Long Eighth Century" in southern England', in Higham and Ryan (eds), 39–64.

Rippon, S., Jackson, A. and Martin, M. 2001. 'The use of soil analysis in the interpretation of an early historic landscape at Puxton in Somerset', *Landscape History* 23, 27–38.

Ritchie, A. 1976–77. 'Excavation of Pictish and Viking-Age farmsteads at Buckquoy, Orkney', *Proceedings of the Society of the Antiquaries of Scotland* 108, 174–227.

Ritchie, A. 2003. 'Great sites: Jarlshof', *British Archaeology* 69 (March), 20–23.

Rivers, T. J. 1977. *Laws of the Alamans and Bavarians*, University of Pennsylvania Press: Pennsylvania.

Roberts, B. K. 1968. 'A study of medieval colonisation in the Forest of Arden, Warwickshire', *Agricultural History Review* 16, 101–113.

Roberts, B. K. 1972. 'Village plans in county Durham: a preliminary statement', *Medieval Archaeology* 16, 33–56.

Roberts, B. K. 1977. *Rural Settlement in Britain*, Dawson: Folkestone.

Roberts, B. K. 1982a. 'Village forms in Warwickshire: a preliminary discussion', in T. R. Slater and P. J. Jarvis (eds), *Field and Forest: An Historical Geography of Warwickshire and Worcestershire*, Geo Books: Norwich, 125–146.

Roberts, B. K. 1982b. *Village Plans*, Shire Books: Aylesbury.

Roberts, B. K. 1987. *The Making of the English Village*, Longman: Harlow.

Roberts, B. K. 1989–90. 'Late -*by* names in the Eden valley, Cumberland', *Nomina* 13, 25–40.

Roberts, B. K. 1990. *The Field Study of Village Plans: A Short Handbook for Historical Geographers, Local Historians and Archaeologists*, Occasional Publications of University of Durham Department of Geography: Durham.

Roberts, B. K. 1993. 'Some relict landscapes in Westmorland: a reconsideration', *Archaeological Journal*, 150, 433–455.

Roberts, B. K. 1996. *Landscapes of Settlement: Prehistory to the Present*, Routledge: London.

Roberts, B. K. 2008. *Landscapes, Documents and Maps: Villages in Northern England and Beyond AD 900–1250*, Oxbow Books: Oxford.

Roberts, B. K. and Wrathmell, S. 1995. *Terrain and Settlement Mapping: The Methodology and Preliminary Results*, Durham Department of Geography for English Heritage.

Roberts, B. K. and Wrathmell, S. 2000. *An Atlas of Rural Settlement in England*, English Heritage: London.

Roberts, B. K. and Wrathmell, S. 2002. *Region and Place. A Study of English Rural Settlement*, English Heritage: London.

Roberts, B. K., Stocker, D. and Wrathmell, S. 1993. 'Medieval rural settlements and the Monuments Protection Programme', *Medieval Settlement Research Group Annual Report* 8, 15.

Roberts, E. 1986. 'The Bishop of Winchester's deer parks in Hampshire, 1200–1400', *Proceedings of the Hampshire Field Club and Archaeological Society* 44, 67–86.

Roberts, E. 1996. 'Overton Court farm and the late medieval farmhouses of demesne lessees in Hampshire', *Proceedings of the Hampshire Field Club and Archaeological Society* 51, 89–106.

Roberts, E. 2008. 'Dendrochronology of Hampshire buildings 2003–2008, Part 1', *Hampshire Field Club and Archaeological Society Newsletter* 50, 6–8.

Roberts, J. 1997. *Royal Landscape: The Gardens and Parks of Windsor*, Yale University Press: London.

Roberts, K. (ed.) 2006a. *Lost Farmsteads: Deserted Rural Settlements in Wales*, Council for British Archaeology Research Report 148. York.

Roberts, K. 2006b. 'The deserted rural settlement project: a summing up', in Roberts (ed.), 171–186.

Robinson, D. M. 1982. 'Medieval vernacular buildings below the ground: a review and corpus for south-east Wales', *Glamorgan-Gwent Archaeological Trust Annual Report 1981–2*, 94–123.

Robinson, P. 1984. *The Plantation of Ulster*, Gill and Macmillan: Dublin.

Rodwell, W. 1978. 'Relict landscapes in Essex', in H. C. Bowen and P. J. Fowler (eds), *Early Land Allotment in the British Isles*, British Archaeological Reports British Series 48. Oxford, 89–98.

Rodwell, W. 1993. *The Origins and Early Development of Witham, Essex, A Study in Settlement and Fortification, Prehistoric to Medieval*, Oxbow Monograph 26. Oxford.

Roffe, D. 2000. 'The early history of Wharram Percy', in

P. A. Stamper and R. A. Croft, *The South Manor Area. Wharram. A Study of Settlement on the Yorkshire Wolds, VIII*, York University Archaeological Publications 10. York, 1–16.

Rogers, T. 1979. 'Excavations at Hen Caerwys, Clwyd, 1962', *Bulletin Board Celtic Studies*, 28, 3, 528–533.

Rogerson, A. 1996. 'Rural settlement *c.* 400–200', in S. Margeson, B. Ayers and S. Heywood (eds), *A Festival of Norfolk Archaeology*, Hunstanton, 58–64.

Rogerson, A. 2000. *Fransham: An Archaeological and Historical Study of a Parish on the Norfolk Boulder Clay*, unpublished PhD thesis, University of East Anglia.

Rogerson, A. 2005. 'Moated sites', in Ashwin and Davison (eds), 68–69.

Rogerson, A. and Adams, N. 1978. 'A moated site at Hempstead near Holt', *East Anglian Archaeology* 8. Gressenhall, 33–44.

Rogerson, A. and Dallas, C. 1984. *Excavations in Thetford 1948–59 and 1973–80*, East Anglian Archaeology 22. Gressenhall.

Rogerson, A., Davison, A., Pritchard, D. and Silvester, R. 1997. *Barton Bendish and Caldecote: Fieldwork in Southwest Norfolk*, East Anglian Archaeology 80. Gressenhall.

Rose, P. and Preston-Jones, A. 1995. 'Changes in the Cornish countryside, AD 400–1100', in Hooke and Burnell (eds), 51–68.

Ross, M. S. 1985. 'Kington Magna: a parish survey', *Proceedings of the Dorset Natural History and Archaeological Society* 107, 23–46.

Rowe, A. 2009. *Medieval Parks of Hertfordshire*, University of Hertfordshire Press: Hatfield.

Rowlands, M. B. 1987. *The West Midlands from AD 1000*, Longman: London.

Rowley, T. 1978. *Villages in the Landscape*, Dent: London.

Rowley, T. 1981. *Origins of Open Field Agriculture*, Croom Helm: London.

Rowley, T. and Wood, J. 1982. *Deserted Villages*, Shire Archaeology: Princes Risborough.

Roycroft, N. 2005. 'Around the bay on the Great North Road: the archaeology of the M1 Dundalk Western Bypass', in J. O'Sullivan and M. Stanley (eds), *Recent Archaeological Discoveries on National Road Schemes 2004*, National Roads Authority: Dublin, 65–83.

Rushton, N. S. 1999. 'Parochialization and patterns of patronage in 11th-century Sussex', *Sussex Archaeological Collections* 137, 133–152.

Rushton, N. S. 2002. 'Some pre-Black Death surveys and extents of Purbeck', in Hinton (ed.), 118–125.

Russel, A. D. 1985. 'Foxcotte: the archaeology and history of a Hampshire hamlet', *Proceedings of the Hampshire*

Field Club and Archaeological Society 41, 149–224.

Ryan, P. 1996. *Brick in Essex from the Roman Conquest to the Reformation*, Pat Ryan: Chelmsford.

Saltmarsh, J. 1941. 'Plague and economic decline in England in the Later Middle Ages', *Cambridge Historical Journal* 7, 23–41.

Sambrook, P. 2006. 'Deserted rural settlements in south-west Wales', in Roberts (ed.), 83–109.

Sanderson, R. P. 1891. *Survey of the Debateable and Border Lands… taken AD 1604*, Alnwick.

Saunders, T. 2000. 'Class, space and "feudal" identities in early medieval England', in W. Frazer and A. Tyrrell (eds), *Social Identity in Early Medieval Britain*, Leicester University Press: Leicester, 209–232.

Savery, E., Smith, A. and Martin, E. 1994. 'Ixworth Thorpe', *Proceedings of the Suffolk Institute of Archaeology and History* 38:2, 205–207.

Savory, H. N. 1954–55. 'The excavation of an Early Iron Age fortified settlement on Mynydd Bychan, Llysworney (Glam), 1949–50', *Archaeologia Cambrensis* 103, 85–108.

Sawyer, P. H. 1968. *Anglo-Saxon Charters. An Annotated List and Bibliography*, Offices of the Royal Historical Society: London.

Sawyer, P. H. (ed.) 1976. *Medieval Settlement: Continuity and Change*, Edward Arnold: London.

Scarfe, N. 1972. *The Suffolk Landscape*, Hodder and Stoughton: London.

Schlesinger, A. and Walls, C. 1996. 'An early church and farmstead site at Llanelen, Gower', *Archaeological Journal* 153, 104–147.

Schofield, R. and Vince, A. 1994. *Medieval Towns*, Leicester University Press: London.

Schumer, B. 1984. *The Evolution of Wychwood to 1400: Pioneers, Frontiers and Forests*, Department of English Local History, Occasional Papers (3rd Series) 6. Leicester.

Schumer, B. 1999. *Wychwood. The Evolution of a Wooded Landscape*, Wychwood Press: Charlbury.

Scull, C. (ed.) 2009. *Early Medieval (Late 5th–Early 8th Centuries AD) Cemeteries at Boss Hall and Buttermarket, Ipswich, Suffolk*, Society for Medieval Archaeology Monograph 27. Maney: Leeds.

Searle, E. 1974. *Lordship and Community: Battle Abbey and its Banlieu 1066–1538*, Pontifical Institute of Medieval Studies: Toronto.

Seaver, M. 2006. 'Through the mill – excavation of an early medieval settlement at Raystown, County Meath', in O'Sullivan and Stanley (eds), 73–88.

Seaver, M. 2010. 'Against the grain; early medieval settlement and burial on the Blackhill. Excavations at Raystown, Co. Meath', in M. Potterton, and C. Corlett

(eds), *Death and Burial in Early Medieval Ireland in the Light of Recent Archaeological Excavations*, Wordwell: Bray, 261–280.

Seebohm, F. 1883. *The English Village Community* (repr. 1915), Longmans, Green: London.

Selkirk, A. and Boulter, S. 2003. 'Flixton Park Quarry, a royal estate of the first Anglo-Saxon kings?', *Current Archaeology* 187, 280–285.

Sell S. H. 1982. 'Excavations at Cosmeston, near Sully, South Glamorgan', *Glamorgan-Gwent Archaeological Trust Annual Report for 1981–1982*, 32–36.

Senecal, C. 2001. 'Keeping up with the Godwinsons: in pursuit of aristocratic status in late Anglo-Saxon England', *Anglo-Norman Studies* 23, 251–266.

Service, M. 2010. 'The home estates, granges and smaller properties of Waverley abbey', *Surrey Archaeological Collections* 95, 211–257.

Sharland, R. 2010. 'The king's parks in Hampshire', unpublished undergraduate dissertation, University of Southampton Department of Archaeology.

Sharples, N. (ed.) 2005. *A Norse Farmstead in the Outer Hebrides Excavations at Mound 3, Bornais, South Uist*, Oxbow Books: Oxford.

Sharples, N. and Parker Pearson, M. 1999. 'Norse settlement in the Outer Hebrides', *Norwegian Archaeological Review* 32:1, 41–62.

Shaw, M. 1993. 'The discovery of Saxon sites below fieldwalking scatters: settlement evidence at Brixworth and Upton, Northamptonshire', *Northamptonshire Archaeology* 25, 77–92.

Sheehan, J. 2008. 'The Longphort in Viking Age Ireland', *Acta Archaeologica* 79, 1, 282–295.

Shelley, A. 2003. *A moated rectory at Wimbotsham, Norfolk*, East Anglian Archaeology Occasional Papers 12. Gressenhall.

Shennan, S. 1985. *Experiments in the Collection and Analysis of Archaeological Survey Data: The East Hampshire Survey*, Department of Archaeology and Prehistory, University of Sheffield: Sheffield.

Sheppard, J. 1974. 'Metrological analysis of regular village plans in Yorkshire', *Agricultural History Review* 22, 118–135.

Sherlock, R. 2006. 'Cross-cultural occurrence of mutations in tower house architecture: evidence for cultural homogeneity in late medieval Ireland?', *Journal of Irish Archaeology* 15, 73–91.

Shopland, N. 2006. *A Finds Manual: Excavating, Processing and Storing*, Tempus: Stroud.

Silvester, R. J. 1988. *The Fenland Project, Number 3: Norfolk Survey, Marshland and Nar Valley*, East Anglian Archaeology 45. Gressenhall.

Silvester, R. J. 1991. *The Fenland Project, Number 4: The*

Wissey Embayment and Fen Causeway, Norfolk, East Anglian Archaeology 52. Gressenhall.

Silvester, R. J. 1993. '"The addition of more-or-less undifferentiated dots to a distribution map"? The Fenland Project in retrospect', in J. Gardiner (ed.), *Flatlands and Wetlands: Current Themes in East Anglian Archaeology*, East Anglian Archaeology 50. Gressenhall, 24–39.

Silvester, R. J. 1997a. 'Historic settlement surveys in Clwyd and Powys', in Edwards (ed.), 113–121.

Silvester, R. J. 1997b. 'The Llanwddyn Hospitium', *Montgomeryshire Collections* 85, 63–76.

Silvester, R. J. 2000. 'Medieval upland cultivation on the Berwyns in north Wales', *Landscape History* 22, 47–60.

Silvester, R. J. 2001. 'Tŷ Mawr and the landscape of Trefnant township', in Britnell (ed.), 147–162.

Silvester, R. J. 2005. 'Open-field agriculture in the central Welsh borderland', in M. Meek (ed.), *The Modern Traveller to our Past. Festschrift in Honour of Ann Hamlin*, DPK: Belfast, 252–258.

Silvester, R. J. 2006. 'Deserted rural settlements in central and north-east Wales', in Roberts (ed.), 13–39.

Silvester, R. J. 2010. 'Abandoning the uplands: depopulation amongst dispersed settlements in western Britain', in Dyer and Jones (eds), 140–161.

Simms, A. and Fagan, P. 1992. 'Villages in Co. Dublin: their origins and inheritance', in F. H. Aalen and K. Whelan (eds), *Dublin City and County: From Prehistory to Present*, Four Courts Press: Dublin, 79–119.

Simms, A. and Simms, K. 1990. *Irish Historic Towns Atlas No. 4. Kells*, Royal Irish Academy: Dublin.

Simpson, L. 2005. 'Viking warrior burials in Dublin: is this the *longphort*?', in S. Duffy (ed.), *Medieval Dublin VI*, Four Courts Press: Dublin, 12–62.

Skelton, R. and Harvey, P. (eds) 1986. *Local Maps and Plans from Medieval England*, Clarendon Press: Oxford.

Slater, T. 2000. 'Understanding the landscape of towns', in Hooke (ed.), 97–108.

Smith, A. H. 1956. *English Place-Name Elements*, English Place-Name Society, vols 25 and 26, Cambridge University Press: Cambridge.

Smith, C. T. 1964. 'Settlement and agriculture in Eastern England', in J. A. Steers (ed.), *Field Studies in the British Isles*, Nelson: London, 120–137.

Smith, G. and Thompson, D. 2006. 'Results of the project excavations', in Roberts (ed.), 113–132.

Smith, N. 1999. 'The earthwork remains of enclosure in the New Forest', *Proceedings of the Hampshire Field Club and Archaeological Society* 54, 373–398.

Smith, N. 2005. 'Medieval and later sheep farming on the Marlborough Downs', in G. Brown, D. Field and D.

McOrmish (eds), *The Avebury Landscape: Aspects of the Field Archaeology of the Marlborough Downs*, Oxbow Books: Oxford, 191–201.

Smith, P. 1988. *Houses of the Welsh Countryside: A Study in Historical Geography*, HMSO: London.

Smith, P. 1989. 'Houses and building styles', in Owen (ed.), 95–150.

Smith, P. 2001. 'Houses *c.* 1415–1642', in J. B. Smith and L. B. Smith (eds), *History of Merioneth. Volume II. The Middle Ages*, Merioneth Historical and Record Society and University of Wales Press: Cardiff, 422–506.

Smith, R. A. L. 1943. *Canterbury Cathedral Priory: A Study in Monastic Administration*, Cambridge University Press: Cambridge.

Smith, S. V. 2009. 'Towards a social archaeology of the medieval English peasantry: power and resistance at Wharram Percy', *Journal of Social Archaeology*, 391–416.

Smith, S. V. 2010. 'Houses and communities: archaeological evidence variation in medieval peasant experience', in Dyer and Jones (eds), 64–84.

Smout, T. C. (ed.) 2003. *People and Woods in Scotland: A History*, Edinburgh University Press: Edinburgh.

Soane, J. 1987. 'The decline of feudalism: 1347–1521', in L. Keen and A. Carrick (eds), *Historic Landscape of Weld: The Weld Estate*, Lulworth Heritage: East Lulworth, 32–38.

Spearman, R. 1988. 'Workshops, material and debris – evidence of early industry', in M. Lynch, G. Stell and R. Spearman (eds), *The Scottish Medieval Town*, Edinburgh University Press: Edinburgh.

Spoerry, P. 2008. *Ely Wares*, East Anglian Archaeology 122. Bar Hill.

Spoerry, P., Atkins, R., Macaulay, S. and Popescu, E. 2008. 'Ramsey Abbey, Cambridgeshire: excavations at the site of a fenland monastery', *Medieval Archaeology* 52, 171–210.

Spufford, M. 1974. *Contrasting Communities*, Cambridge University Press, Cambridge.

Spurgeon, C. J. 1981. 'Moated sites in Wales', in F. A. Aberg and A. E. Brown (eds), *Medieval Moated Sites in North-West Europe*, British Archaeological Reports International Series 121. Oxford, 19–70.

Spurgeon, C. J. 1991. 'Mottes and moated sites' in J. Manley, S. Grenter and F. Gale (eds), *The Archaeology of Clwyd*, Clwyd County Council: Mold, 157–172.

Stacy, N. E. (ed.) 2006. *Charters and Custumals of Shaftesbury Abbey 1089–1216*, Oxford University Press: Oxford.

Stafford, P. 1985. *The East Midlands in the Early Middle Ages*, Leicester University Press: Leicester.

Stamper, P. A. 1996. 'Markets and fairs existing by *c.* 1360',

50–51, in D. A. Hinton, '*Hamtunscire*: a review of the history and archaeology of medieval Hampshire', in D. A. Hinton and M. Hughes (eds), *Archaeology in Hampshire: A Framework for the Future*, Hampshire County Council: Winchester, 40–54.

Stamper, P. A. and Croft, R. A. 2000. [Wharram VIII] *Wharram: A Study of Settlement on the Yorkshire Wolds. Vol. 8, The South Manor Area,* University of York: York.

Steane, J. and Bryant, G. 1975. 'Excavations at the deserted medieval settlement at Lyveden, 4th report', *Journal of Northampton Museums and Art Gallery* 12, 2–160.

Stedman, M. 2005. 'Shavards Farm, Meonstoke', *Proceedings of the Hampshire Field Club and Archaeological Society* 60, 136–153.

Stenning, D. F. and Andrews, D. D. (eds) 1998. *Regional Variation in Timber-framed Building in England and Wales down to 1550. Proceedings of the 1994 Cressing Conference*, Essex County Council: Chelmsford.

Stocker, D. 2006. *The East Midlands*, English Heritage: London.

Stocker, D. and Everson, P. 2006. *Summoning St Michael. Early Romanesque Towers in Lincolnshire*, Oxbow Books: Oxford.

Stone, P. 2005. *Decision-Making in Medieval Agriculture*, Oxford University Press: Oxford.

Stoppard, A. 1909. *The Making of Ireland and its Undoing*, Macmillan: London.

Stout, M. 1991. 'Ringforts in the south-west midlands of Ireland', *Proceedings of the Royal Irish Academy* 91C, 201–243.

Stout, M. 1997. *The Irish Ringfort*, Four Courts Press: Dublin.

Stronach, S. 2004. 'The evolution of a medieval Scottish manor at Perceton, near Irvine, North Ayrshire', *Medieval Archaeology* 68, 143–166.

Suggett, R. 2003. 'Dendrochronology: progress and prospects', in C.S. Briggs (ed.), *Towards a Research Agenda for Welsh Archaeology*, British Archaeological Reports British Series 343. Oxford, 153–169.

Suggett, R. 2004. 'The interpretation of late medieval houses in Wales', in R. R. Davies and G. H. Jenkins (eds), *From Medieval to Modern Wales. Historical Essays in Honour of Kenneth O. Morgan and Ralph A. Griffiths*, University of Wales Press: Cardiff, 81–103.

Suggett, R. 2005. *Houses and History in the March of Wales. Radnorshire 1400–1800*, RCAHMW: Aberystwyth.

Sullivan, A. O., Sands R. and Kelly E. P. 2007. *Coolure Demesne Crannog, Lough Derravaragh*, Wordwell: Bray.

Summers, D. 1973. *The Great Ouse*, David and Charles: Newton Abbot.

Sussams, K. 1996. *The Breckland Archaeological Survey. A Characterisation of the Archaeology and Historic Landscape of the Breckland Environmentally Sensitive Area*, Suffolk County Council: Bury St Edmunds.

Sutton, A. F. 1989. 'The early linen and worsted industry of Norfolk and the evolution of the London Mercers' Company', *Norfolk Archaeology* 40, 3, 201–225.

Svensson, O. 1987. *Saxon Place-Names in East Cornwall*, Lund Studies in English 77. Lund University Press: Lund.

Sykes, N. J. 2005. 'The dynamics of status symbols: wildfowl exploitation in England AD 410–1550', *Archaeological Journal* 161, 82–105.

Sykes, N. J. 2007. *The Norman Conquest: A Zooarchaeological Perspective*, British Archaeological Reports International Series 1656. Oxford.

Sylvester, D. 1949. 'Rural settlement in Cheshire', *Transactions of the Historical Society of Lancashire and Cheshire* 101, 1–37.

Sylvester, D. 1956. 'The open fields of Cheshire', *Transactions of the Historical Society of Lancashire and Cheshire* 108, 1–33.

Sylvester, D. 1969. *The Rural Landscape of the Welsh Borderland*, Macmillan: London.

Tait, J. 1936. *The Medieval English Borough*, Manchester University Press: Manchester.

Tatton-Brown, T. 1984. 'The towns of Kent', in J. Haslam (ed.), *Anglo-Saxon Towns in Southern England*, Phillimore: Chichester, 1–36.

Taylor, C. C. 1967. 'Whiteparish: a study of the development of a forest-edge parish', *Wiltshire Archaeological and Natural History Magazine* 62, 79–102.

Taylor, C. C. 1970. *Dorset*, The Making of the English Landscape [series], Hodder and Stoughton: London (repr. 2004, Dovecote Press: Wimborne).

Taylor, C. C. 1971. *Domesday to Dormitory: The History of the Landscape of Great Shelford*, Workers' Educational Association: Cambridge.

Taylor, C. C. 1974a. *The Cambridgeshire Landscape*, Hodder and Stoughton: London.

Taylor, C. C. 1974b. *Fieldwork in Medieval Archaeology*, Batsford: London.

Taylor, C. C. 1974c. 'Total archaeology or studies in the history of the landscape', in A. Rogers and R. T. Rowley (eds), *Landscapes and Documents*. National Council of Social Service for the Standing Conference on Local History: London, 15–26.

Taylor, C. C. 1977. 'Polyfocal settlement and the English village', *Medieval Archaeology* 21, 189–193. London.

Taylor, C. C. 1978. 'Aspects of village mobility in medieval and later times', in S. Limbrey and J. G. Evans (eds), *The Effects of Man on the Landscape: The Lowland Zone*, Council for British Archaeology Research Report 21, 126–134.

Taylor, C. C. 1981. 'The role of fieldwork in medieval settlement studies', *Medieval Village Research Group Annual Report* 29, 29–31.

Taylor, C. C. 1982. 'Medieval market grants and village morphology', *Landscape History* 4, 21–28.

Taylor, C. C. 1983. *Village and Farmstead. A History of Rural Settlement in England*, George Philip: London.

Taylor, C. C. 1989. 'Whittlesford: the study of a river-edge village', in Aston, Austin and Dyer (eds), 207–227.

Taylor, C. C. 1992. 'Medieval rural settlement: changing perceptions', *Landscape History* 14, 5–17.

Taylor, C. C. 1994. 'The regular village plan: Dorset revisited and revised', in Aston and Lewis (eds), 213–218.

Taylor, C. C. 1995a. 'Dispersed settlement in nucleated areas', *Landscape History* 17, 27–34.

Taylor, C. C. 1995b. 'Reach, Cambridgeshire: a medieval fen-edge port and market', in A. Longcroft and R. Joby (eds), *East Anglian Studies*, University of East Anglia: Norwich, 267–277.

Taylor, C. C. 2000. 'Medieval ornamental landscapes', *Landscapes* 1.1, 38–55.

Taylor, C. C. 2002. 'Nucleated settlement: a view from the frontier', *Landscape History* 24, 53–71.

Taylor, C. C. 2005. 'The *Making of the English Landscape* and beyond: inspiration and dissemination', *Landscapes* 6, 96–104.

Taylor, C. C. 2010. 'The origins and development of deserted village studies', in Dyer and Jones (eds), 1–7.

Taylor, I. 2003. 'Roman and Iron Age finds at the medieval village of Boxworth, Cambridgeshire', *Medieval Settlement Research Group Annual Report* 18, 48–52.

Tebbutt, C. F. 1981. 'A deserted medieval farm settlement at Faulkner's Farm, Hartfield', *Sussex Archaeological Collections* 119, 107–116.

Tebbutt, C. F. 1982. 'A Middle Saxon iron smelting site at Millbrook, Ashdown Forest, Sussex', *Sussex Archaeological Collections* 120, 19–35.

Tester, P. J. 1980. 'A re-assessment of some features of the medieval house in the Joyden's Wood Square earthwork', *Archaeologia Cantiana* 95, 289–290.

Tester, P. J. and Caiger, J. E. L. 1958. 'Medieval buildings in the Joyden's Wood square earthworks', *Archaeologia Cantiana* 72, 18–40.

Thirsk, J. 1987. *Agricultural Regions and Agrarian History in England, 1500–1750*, Macmillan Education: Basingstoke.

Thirsk, J. (ed.) 2000. *Rural England: An Illustrated History of the Landscape*, Oxford University Press: Oxford.

Thirsk, J. and Imray, J. (eds) 1958. *Suffolk Farming in the Nineteenth Century*, Suffolk Records Society I. Ipswich.

Thomas, C. 1958. *Gwithian: Ten Years' Work*, West Cornwall Field Club: Camborne.

Thomas, C. 1963. 'Unpublished material from Cornish museums: 2 Gunwalloe pottery, Helston Museum', *Cornish Archaeology* 2, 60–64.

Thomas, C. 2001. 'Rural society, settlement, economy and landscape', in J. Beverley Smith and L. Beverley Smith (eds), *History of Merioneth. Volume II, The Middle Ages*, University of Wales Press: Cardiff, 168–224.

Thomas, G. 2000. 'Anglo-Scandinavian metalwork in the Danelaw: reconstructing social interaction and regional identities', in Richards and Hadley (eds), 237–255.

Thomas, G. 2008. 'The symbolic lives of Late Anglo-Saxon settlements: a cellared structure and iron hoard from Bishopstone, East Sussex', *Archaeological Journal* 165, 334–398.

Thomas, G. 2010a. 'Bringing a lost Anglo-Saxon monastery to life', *Medieval Archaeology* 54, 409–414.

Thomas, G. 2010b. *The Later Anglo-Saxon Settlement at Bishopstone: A Downland Manor in the Making*. Council for British Archaeology Research Report No. 163. York.

Thomas, H. J. 1966. 'Uchelolau (Highlight) deserted medieval village', *Morgannwg* 10, 63–66.

Thomas, H. J. 1967. 'Uchelolau (Highlight) deserted medieval village', *Morgannwg* 11, 314–315.

Thomas, H. J. 1970. 'Uchelolau (Highlight) deserted medieval village', *Morgannwg* 14, 88–92.

Thomas, H. J. and Davies, G. 1970–72. 'A medieval house site at Barry, Glamorgan', *Transactions of the Cardiff Naturalists' Society* 96, 4–22.

Thomas, H. J. and Dowdell, G. 1987. 'A shrunken medieval village at Barry, Glamorgan', *Archaeologia Cambrensis* 136, 94–137.

Thompson, F. H. 1960. 'The deserted medieval village of Riseholme, near Lincoln', *Medieval Archaeology* 4, 95–108.

Thorn, C. and Thorn, F. (eds) 1985. *Domesday Book. 9: Devon*, 2 vols, Phillimore: Chichester.

Thorpe, H. 1962. 'The lord and the landscape, illustrated through the changing fortunes of a Warwickshire parish, Wormleighton', *Transactions of the Birmingham Archaeological Society* 80, 38–77.

Thorpe, H. 1965. 'The green village in its European setting', in A. Small (ed.), *Fourth Viking Congress*, Oliver and Boyd: Edinburgh and London, 85–111.

Thorpe, H. 1975. 'Air, ground, document', in D. R. Wilson (ed.), *Aerial Reconnaissance for Archaeology*, Council for British Archaeology Research Report 12. London, 141–153.

Thrupp, S. L. 1948. *The Merchant Class of Medieval London*. Cambridge University Press: London.

Tierney, A. 2004. 'The Gothic and the Gaelic: exploring the place of castles in Ireland's Celtic Revival', *International Journal of Historical Archaeology* 8.3, 185–198.

Timby, J., Brown, R., Biddulph, E., Hardy, A. and Powell, A. 2007. *A Slice of Rural Essex. Archaeological discoveries from the A120 between Stansted Airport and Braintree*, Oxford Wessex Archaeology: Oxford and Salisbury.

Tipper, J. 2004. *The Grubenhaus in Anglo-Saxon England: An Analysis and Interpretation of the Evidence from a Most Distinctive Building Type*, Landscape Research Centre Archaeological Monograph Series 2 (1). Yedingham.

Titow, J. Z. 1969. *English Rural Society 1200–1350*, Allen and Unwin: London.

Tittensor, R. M. 1980. 'Ecological history of yew Taxus baccata L. in southern England', *Biological Conservation* 17, 243–265.

Toms, H. S. 1913. 'A record of the valley-side entrenchment in Bramble Bottom, Eastdean', *Transactions and Journal of the Eastbourne Natural History Society* 5, 58–62.

Toms, H. S. 1917. 'A record of the Mill Fields valley entrenchment and covered way, Willingdon Hill', *Transactions and Journal of the Eastbourne Natural History Society* 7, 45–53.

Toms, H. S. 1922. 'Long barrows in Sussex', *Sussex Archaeological Collections* 63, 157–165.

Toms, H. S. 1924. 'Valley entrenchments west of the Ditchling Road', *Brighton and Hove Archaeologist* 2, 57–72.

Toms, H. S. 1926. 'Valley entrenchments east of the Ditchling Road', *Brighton and Hove Archaeologist* 3, 42–61.

Toulmin Smith, L. 1910. *The Itinerary of John Leland in or about the Years 1535–1543*, 5 vols., Bell and Sons: London (repr. 1964, Centaur Press: London).

Travers, C. 2004. *Moated Sites in South and South-East Wales*, unpublished PhD thesis, University of Wales, Newport.

Treen, C. and Atkin, M. 2005. [Wharram X] *Water Resources and their Management*, York University Archaeological Publications 12. York.

Trick, S. and McHugh, R. 2006. 'Tullahogue Fort, Co. Tyrone: a geophysical survey carried out on behalf of Cookstown District Council', Centre for Archaeological Fieldwork, Queen's University Belfast: Belfast.

Tristram, W. Outram 1910: *Moated Houses*, Methuen: London.

Trump, D. H. 1961. 'Blunt's Hall, Witham', *Transactions of Essex Archaeological Society* (3rd Series) 1, 37–40.

Turner, D. J. 1966. 'A moated site near Burstow Rectory', *Surrey Archaeological Collections* 63, 51–64.

Turner, D. J. 1977. 'Moated site near Moat Farm, Hookwood, Charlwood', *Surrey Archaeological*

Collections, 71, 57–87.

Turner, D. J. 1987. 'Archaeology of Surrey, 1066–1540', in J. Bird and D. G. Bird (eds), *The Archaeology of Surrey to 1540*, Surrey Archaeological Society: Guildford, 223–261.

Turner, D. J. 2004. 'Manors and other settlements', in Cotton *et al.* (eds), 133–146.

Turner, S. 2006a. 'Historic Landscape Characterisation: a landscape archaeology for research, management and planning', *Landscape Research* 31, 4, 385–398.

Turner, S. 2006b. *Making a Christian Landscape: The Countryside in Early Medieval Cornwall, Devon and Wessex*, University of Exeter Press: Exeter.

Turner, S. (ed.) 2006c. *Medieval Devon and Cornwall. Shaping an Ancient Countryside*, Windgather Press: Oxford.

Turner, S. 2006d. 'The Christian landscape: churches, chapels and crosses', in Turner 2006c (ed.), 24–43.

Turner, S. 2006e. 'The medieval landscape of Devon and Cornwall', in Turner 2006c (ed.), 1–9.

Turner, S. 2007. *Ancient Country. The Historic Character of Rural Devon*, Devon Archaeological Society: Exeter.

Turner, S. and Silvester, R. J. (eds) forthcoming. *Life in Medieval Landscapes: People and Places in the Middle Ages. Papers in Memory of H. S. A. Fox*. Windgather: Oxford.

Tyers, I. 1999. *Tree-ring Analysis of Timbers from Tiptofts, near Wimbish, Essex*, Ancient Monuments Lab. Rep. 6/1999.

Ulmschneider, K. 2000. *Markets, Minsters and Metal-Detectors: The Archaeology of Middle Saxon Lincolnshire and Hampshire Compared*, British Archaeological Reports British Series 307. Oxford.

Understanding Historic Buildings 2006. *Understanding Historic Buildings. A Guide to Good Recording Practice*, English Heritage: Swindon.

Valante, M. 1998. 'Reassessing the Irish monastic town', *Irish Historical Studies* 31, 1–18.

Valenti, M. (ed.) 2008. *Miranduolo in Alta Val di Merse (Chiusdino – SI)*, Biblioteca del Dipartimento de Archeologia, Università di Siena, 17. All'Insegna del Giglio: Florence.

Van de Noort, R. 2004. *The Humber Wetlands: The Archaeology of a Dynamic Landscape*, Windgather: Oxford.

Victoria History of the County of Cambridge and the Isle of Ely, R. B. Pugh (ed.), 1953: Volume 4, Institute of Historical Research: London.

Victoria History of the County of Cambridge and the Isle of Ely, A. P. M. Wright and C. P. Lewis (eds), 1989. Volume 9. Institute of Historical Research: London.

Victoria History of the County of Cambridge and the Isle of

Ely, A. F. Wareham and A. P. M. Wright (eds), 2002. Volume 10. Institute of Historical Research: London.

Vyner, B. E. (ed.) 1990. *Medieval Rural Settlement in Northeast England*, Architectural and Archaeological Society of Durham and Northumberland: Durham.

Wacher, J. 1963–64. 'Excavations at Martinsthorpe, Rutland, 1960', *Transactions of the Leicestershire Archaeological Society* 39, 1–19.

Wacher, J. 1966. 'Excavations at Riplingham East Yorkshire 1956–7', *Yorkshire Archaeological Journal* 41, 164, 608–669.

Wade, K. 1997. 'Anglo-Saxon and medieval (rural)', in J. Glazebrook (ed.), *Research and Archaeology: A Framework for the Eastern Counties. 1. Resource Assessment*, East Anglian Archaeology Occasional Papers 3. Norwich, 47–58.

Wade-Martins, P. 1971. *The Development of the Landscape and Human Settlement in West Norfolk from 350–1650 AD with Particular Reference to the Launditch Hundred*, unpublished PhD thesis, University of Leicester.

Wade-Martins, P. 1975. 'The origins of rural settlement in East Anglia', in P. J. Fowler (ed.), *Recent Work in Rural Archaeology*, Moonraker Press: Bradford-on-Avon, 137–157.

Wade-Martins, P. 1980a. *Excavations at North Elmham Park 1967–1972*, East Anglian Archaeology, 9. Gressenhall.

Wade-Martins, P. 1980b. *Fieldwork and Excavation on Village Sites in Launditch Hundred, Norfolk*, East Anglian Archaeology, 10. Gressenhall.

Wade-Martins, P. 1983. *Two Post-medieval Earthenware Pottery Groups from Fulmodeston*, East Anglian Archaeology 19. Gressenhall.

Walker, J. 1999a. 'Fyfield Hall: a late twelfth-century aisled hall rebuilt *c*.1400 in the archaic style', *Archaeological Journal* 156, 112–142.

Walker, J. 1999b. 'Late 12th and early 13th century aisled buildings: a comparison', *Vernacular Architecture* 30, 21–53.

Wall, J. C. 1908. *Ancient Earthworks*, Talbot: London.

Wallace, P. 1992. *The Viking Age Buildings of Dublin*, Royal Irish Academy: Dublin

Ward, A. 1991. 'Transhumant or permanent settlement', in H. James (ed.), *Sir Gar. Studies in Carmarthenshire History*, Carmarthenshire Antiquarian Society: Carmarthen, 1–22.

Ward, A. 1997. 'Transhumance and settlement on the Welsh uplands: a view from the Black Mountain', in Edwards (ed.), 97–111.

Ward, J. C. and Marshall, K. 1972. *Excavation at Old Thorndon Hall 1957–59*, Essex Record Office Pub. No. 61. Chelmsford.

Warner, P. 1987. *Greens, Commons and Clayland Colonization: The Origins and Development of Greenside Settlement in East Suffolk*, Leicester University Department of Local History Occasional Paper, 4th Series, 2. Leicester.

Warner, P. 1996. *The Origins of Suffolk*, Manchester University Press: Manchester.

Warner, R. B. 1988. 'The archaeology of Early Historic Irish kinship', in Driscoll and Nieke (eds), 47–68.

Warwickshire County Council and the Countryside Commission, 1993. *Warwickshire Landscapes Guidelines*, 3 vols, Warwickshire County Council: Warwick.

Waterhouse, R. 2000. 'Keynedon Barton, Sherford, Kingsbridge', *Devon Archaeological Society Proceedings* 58, 127–200.

Watt, A. S. 1926. 'Yew communities of the South Downs', *Journal of Ecology* 14, 282–316.

Watteaux, M. 2009. 'Settlement and landscape in English historical studies: a French view', *Medieval Settlement Research* 24, 20–30.

Watts, D. G. 1982. 'Peasant discontent on the manors of Titchfield Abbey, 1245–1405', *Proceedings of the Hampshire Field Club and Archaeological Society* 39, 121–135.

Watts, V. 2004. *The Cambridge Dictionary of English Place-Names*, Cambridge University Press: Cambridge.

Webster, C. (ed.) 2008. *The Archaeology of South-West England*, Somerset County Council: Taunton.

Welch, M. G. 1983. *Early Anglo-Saxon Sussex*, British Archaeological Reports British Series 112. Oxford.

Welch, M. G. 1992. *Anglo-Saxon England,* English Heritage and Batsford: London.

Welch, M. G. 2007. 'Anglo-Saxon Kent to AD 800', in J. Williams (ed.), *The Archaeology of Kent to AD 800*, Boydell and Brewer: Woodbridge, 187–248.

West, S. E. 1970. 'Brome, Suffolk. The excavation of a moated site, 1967', *Journal of British Archaeological Association* (3rd Series) 33, 89–121.

West, S. E. 1985. *West Stow. The Anglo-Saxon Village. Volume 1: Text*, East Anglian Archaeology 24. Gressenhall.

West, S. E. 1988. 'Early Anglo-Saxon Suffolk', in D. Dymond and E. Martin (eds), *An Historical Atlas of Suffolk*, Suffolk County Council: Ipswich, 36–37.

West, S. E. and McLaughlin, A. 1998. *Towards a Landscape History of Walsham le Willows*, East Anglian Archaeology, 85. Gressenhall.

Wharram I, *see* Hurst 1979.

Wharram II, *see* Rahtz and Watts 1983.

Wharram III, *see* Bell and Beresford 1987.

Wharram IV, *see* Rahtz, Hayfield and Bateman 1986.

Wharram V, *see* Hayfield 1987.

Wharram VI, *see* Wrathmell 1989.

Wharram VII, *see* Milne and Richards 1992.

Wharram VIII, *see* Stamper and Croft 2000.

Wharram IX, *see* Rahtz and Watts 2004.

Wharram X, *see* Treen and Atkin 2005.

Wharram XI, *see* Mays, Harding and Heighway 2007.

Wharram XII, *see* Harding, Marlow-Mann and Wrathmell 2010.

Wharram XIII, *see* Wrathmell (ed.) forthcoming.

Whitaker, T. D. 1812. *The History and Antiquities of the Deanery of Craven in the County of York. Second Edition*, London.

White, S. D. and Vann, R. T. 1983. 'The invention of English individualism: Alan Macfarlane and the modernization of pre-modern England', *Social History* 8, 345–363.

Whitelock, D. 1930. *Anglo-Saxon Wills*, Cambridge University Press: Cambridge.

Whitelock, D. 1955. *English Historical Documents Volume 1: AD c.500–1042*, Eyre and Spottiswoode: London (2nd edn 1979, Eyre Methuen: London).

Whittaker, E. 2011. 'Self-conscious regionalism: Dan Gibson and the Arts and Crafts House in the Lake District', in P. Guillery (ed.), *Built from Below: British Architecture and the Vernacular*, Routledge: London, 99–122.

Wickham, C. J. 2005. *Framing the Early Middle Ages*, Oxford University Press: Oxford.

Wiliam, E. 1992. *Welsh Long-houses. Four Centuries of Farming at Cilewent*, National Museum of Wales: Cardiff.

Wilkinson, T. J. 1988. *Archaeology and Environment in South Essex: Rescue Archaeology along the Grays By-pass, 1979–80*, East Anglian Archaeology 42. Chelmsford.

Williams, A. 1992. 'A bell-house and a burh-geat: lordly residences in England before the Norman Conquest', in C. Harper-Bill and R. Harvey (eds), *Medieval Knighthood, IV. Papers from the Fifth Strawberry Hill Conference 1990*, Boydell: Woodbridge, 221–240.

Williams, B. B. 1984. 'Excavations at Ballyutoag, County Antrim', *Ulster Journal of Archaeology* 47, 37–49.

Williams, B. B. 1988. 'A late medieval rural settlement at Craigs, County Antrim', *Ulster Journal of Archaeology* 51, 91–102.

Williams, B. B. and Robinson, P. 1983. 'The excavation of Bronze Age cists and a medieval booley house at Glenmakeeran, County Antrim, and a discussion of booleying in North Antrim', *Ulster Journal of Archaeology* 46, 29–40.

Williams, G. and Muckle, I. 1992. *An Archaeological Survey of the Groes Fawr Valley, Caron-is-Clawdd, Cardiganshire*, Dyfed Archaeological Trust: Carmarthen (unpubl.).

Williams, R. 1993. *Pennyland and Hartigans: Two Iron Age and Saxon Sites in Milton Keynes*, Buckinghamshire Archaeological Society Monograph Series 4. Aylesbury.

Williams-Jones, K. 1978. 'Caernarvon', in R. Griffiths (ed.), *Boroughs of Medieval Wales*, University of Wales Press: Cardiff, 73–101.

Williamson, T. 1986. 'The development of settlement in north west Essex: the results of a recent field survey', *Essex Archaeology and History* 17, 124–128.

Williamson, T. 1987. 'Early co-axial field systems on the East Anglian Boulder Clays', *Proceedings of the Prehistoric Society* 53, 419–432.

Williamson, T. 1993. *The Origins of Norfolk*, Manchester University Press: Manchester.

Williamson, T. 1998a. 'Explaining regional landscapes: woodland and champion in southern and eastern England', *Landscape History* 10, 5–14.

Williamson, T. 1998b. 'The "Scole-Dickleburgh field system" revisited', *Landscape History* 20, 19–28.

Williamson, T. 2003. *Shaping Medieval Landscapes: Settlement, Society, Environment*, Windgather Press: Oxford.

Williamson, T. 2006. *England's Landscape. East Anglia*, English Heritage and Collins: London.

Wilson, D. 1985. *Moated Sites*, Shire: Princes Risborough.

Wilson, D. 2008. *The Vikings in the Isle of Man*, Aarhus University Press: Aarhus.

Wilson, D. R. 2000. *Air Photo Interpretation for Archaeologists*, Tempus: Stroud.

Wilson, J. 1846. 'Antiquities found at Woodperry, Oxfordshire', *Archaeological Journal* 3, 116–128.

Winbolt, S. E. 1923. 'Alfoldean Roman station', *Sussex Archaeological Collections* 64, 81–104.

Winchester, A. J. L. 1987. *Landscape and Society in Medieval Cumbria*, John Donald: Edinburgh.

Winchester, A. J. L. 2000. *The Harvest of the Hills*, University Press: Edinburgh.

Withers, C. 1992. 'The historical creation of the Scottish Highlands', in I. Donnachie and C. Whatley (eds), *The Manufacture of Scottish History*, Polygon: Edinburgh, 143–156.

Witney, K. P. 1976. *The Jutish Forest: A Study of the Weald of Kent from 450 to 1380 AD*, Athlone Press: London.

Woodward, P. J., Davies, S. M. and Graham, A. H. 1993. *Excavations at the Old Methodist Chapel and Greyhound Yard, Dorchester, 1981–1984*, Dorset Natural History and Archaeological Society Monograph 12. Dorchester.

Wrathmell, S. 1984. 'The vernacular threshold of northern peasant houses', *Vernacular Architecture* 15, 29–33.

Wrathmell, S. 1989. [Wharram VI] *Domestic Settlement 2: Medieval Peasant Farmsteads,* York University Archaeological Publications: York.

Wrathmell, S. (ed.) forthcoming. [Wharram XIII] *A History of Wharram Percy and its Neighbours. Wharram. A Study of Settlement on the Yorkshire Wolds, XIII,* York University Archaeological Publications 15. York.

Wylie, J. 2007. *Landscape,* Routledge: London.

Wymer, J. and Brown, N. 1995. *North Shoebury: Settlement and Economy in South-East Essex 1500 BC–AD 1500,* East Anglian Archaeology 75. Chelmsford.

Yates, E. M. 1954. 'The settlement of north-west Sussex', *Sociological Review* 2, 209–227.

Yates, E. M. 1960. 'History in a map', *Geographical Journal* 126, 32–51.

Yates, E. M. 1961. 'A study of settlement patterns', *Field Studies* 1:3, 65–84.

Yaxley, D. 1977. *Portrait of Norfolk,* Robert Hale: London.

Yeoman, P. 1991. 'Medieval rural settlement: the invisible centuries', in W. S. Hanson and E. A. Slater (eds), *Scottish Archaeology: New Perceptions.* Aberdeen University Press: Aberdeen, 112–128.

Yeoman, P. 1995. *Medieval Scotland: An Archaeological Perspective,* Batsford and Historic Scotland: London.

Yeoman, P. 1998. 'Excavations at Castle of Wardhouse, Aberdeenshire', *Proceedings of the Society of Antiquaries of Scotland* 128, 581–618.

Young, A. 2006. 'The National Mapping Programme in Cornwall', *Cornish Archaeology* 45, 109–116.

Zadora-Rio, E. 2003. 'The making of churchyards and parish territories in the early-medieval landscape of France and England in the 7th–12th centuries: a reconsideration', *Medieval Archaeology* 47, 1–20.

Zeepvat, R. J., Roberts, J. S. and King, N. A. 1994. *Caldecotte, Milton Keynes. Excavation and Fieldwork 1966–91,* Buckinghamshire Archaeological Society Monograph Series 9. Buckingham.

Index

Bold numbers indicate pages with figures